THE COLOR OF MONEY

THE COLOR OF MONEY

Black Banks and the Racial Wealth Gap

Mehrsa Baradaran

THE BELKNAP PRESS OF HARVARD UNIVERSITY PRESS

Cambridge, Massachusetts

London, England

First Harvard University Press paperback edition, 2019
Tenth printing

Library of Congress Cataloging-in-Publication Data
Names: Baradaran, Mehrsa, 1978– author.
Title: The color of money : black banks and the racial wealth gap / Mehrsa Baradaran.
Description: Cambridge, Massachusetts : The Belknap Press of Harvard
   University Press, 2017. | Includes bibliographical references and index.
Identifiers: LCCN 2017011011 | ISBN 9780674970953 (cloth) |
ISBN 9780674237476 (pbk.)
Subjects: LCSH: African Americans—Economic conditions. | African American
   banks—History. | Discrimination in banking—United States—History. | African
   Americans—Finance. | Wealth—United States—History.
Classification: LCC E185.8 .B24 2017 | DDC 330.9/008996073—dc23
   LC record available at https://lccn.loc.gov/2017011011

To be a poor man is hard, but to be a poor race in a land of dollars is the very bottom of hardships.
—W. E. B. Du Bois

CONTENTS

THE COLOR OF MONEY

Introduction

"All too often when there is mass unemployment in the black community, it's referred to as a social problem, and when there is mass unemployment in the white community, it's referred to as a depression," said Martin Luther King in 1968. "But there is no basic difference. The fact is, that the Negro faces a literal depression all over the U.S."[1] Today, across every socioeconomic level, blacks have significantly less wealth than whites.[2] Over a third of black families have either negative wealth or no assets at all.[3] The 2008 financial crisis devoured more than half the wealth of the black community, proving once again the adage that "when Wall Street catches a cold, Harlem gets pneumonia." To the extent that media and politicians focus on the racial divide, it is through its most urgent and salient features such as police shootings, burning cities, white supremacists, crime, and violence. Underneath it all is a deep and growing financial fault line between black and white. Though hard to detect, it is nonetheless *the* defining feature of America's racial divide because it is intimately linked to so many other problems. The wealth gap is where historic injustice breeds present suffering.

This book tells the story of how the wealth gap was created, maintained, and perpetuated. To tell the story, this book lifts the hood on the engines that the black community has used to fight this gap for generations—black banks. Banks are the drivers of wealth creation for any society, and banking policy is integrally tied up with politics and power—and yet scholars have all but ignored the black banking industry's unique role in black wealth development. What this history reveals is that black and white Americans have had a separate and unequal system of banking and credit. However, for over a century, black communities have been urged by black and white leaders to rely on these segregated black banks in order to reach individual and community prosperity. What comes into stark focus as we study these banks over time is the tangible barrier to prosperity presented by segregation, racism, and government credit policy. The effects of these forces on black banks demonstrate that successful banking and wealth accumulation would remain perpetually elusive in a segregated economy. Housing segregation, racism, and Jim Crow credit policies create an inescapable economic trap for black communities and their banks. Black banking has been an anemic response to racial inequality that has yielded virtually nothing in closing the wealth gap.

Despite these grim economic realities, each of the following leaders has championed black banking: Frederick Douglass, Booker T. Washington, President Lincoln, W. E. B. Du Bois, Marcus Garvey, Carter Woodson, Martin Luther King, Malcolm X, Jesse Jackson, the Black Panthers, President Johnson, President Nixon, Alan Greenspan, President Carter, President Reagan, President Clinton, and President Obama among others. On issues of race, there is likely little else that these leaders would have agreed on. Black-owned banks represented something different to each of them, but to all they held the promise that a successful black bank would lead to prosperity for blacks regardless of external circumstances.

Pushed outside the main arteries of American commerce, the black community turned inward and created its own institutions. The first black banks were formed less than a decade after slavery ended, in the hostile climate of racism and Jim Crow segregation. Most blacks could not save or borrow at white-owned banks, so they established their own. The creation of the black ghettos led to a surge in black banks in northern cities. As black bankers rose to the challenges of banking in a segregated economy, the community celebrated each hard-won success.

These banks were created to respond to racial hostility, but in spite of and because of this, they came to signify racial pride, black unity, and protest. For Booker T. Washington, black banking was salvation itself; he said it was by owning a home and "bank account" that the black man would eventually "find his way to the enjoyment of all his rights."[4] To Washington, money had no color and it was the only path toward racial equality.

Likewise, black banks galvanized the black community during the civil rights struggle. In 1968, Martin Luther King exhorted the black community to "take your money out of the banks downtown and deposit your money in [a black-owned bank]. We want a 'bank-in' movement."[5] To black nationalists, black banking was a necessary step toward asserting independence from white society. "Why should white people be running the banks of our community?" asked Malcolm X. Black banking became a symbol of resistance, black power, defiant self-determination, and active resistance to white racism.[6]

Black economic power and autonomy had a natural appeal in the face of segregation and racism, but also constitute a political diversion and a proxy for more meaningful reform. President Nixon threw his weight behind black banking so that he could oppose controversial desegregation programs and woo white moderates and conservatives unwilling to push any further on racial reforms. Presidential candidate Nixon's civil rights platform was centered on "black capitalism." He urged "more black ownership, black pride . . . and yes, black power."[7] The deceptively vague formula of black capitalism was a neutralizing racial détente amid an unprecedented and violent black insurgency and a hostile white backlash. Nixon co-opted the rhetoric of the radical black power movement to create a path through a political quagmire that would disarm black radicals and the white base on which his southern strategy relied. But what he meant by black capitalism was a cheap knockoff of white capitalism.

So politically successful was the promise of black capitalism that every administration since President Nixon has adopted it in one form or another. Presidents Carter, Reagan, Clinton, Bush, and Obama disagreed about many things, but they each sought to promote black banks and businesses through programs called "community capitalism," "enterprise zones," or "minority enterprise." President Reagan called black business and black banking the "key to black economic progress."[8] Bill Clinton even created robust legislation to promote "community empowerment" through banking—an infrastructure that Presidents Bush and Obama bolstered and maintained. President Trump has made promises along similar lines. Instead of meaningful financial support, the urban ghetto would get bankers.

The idea of community self-help, valuable as it was when there was no other choice, has been deployed cynically at several pivotal historical moments to thwart other, more direct answers to the racial wealth gap. The Freedmen's Bureau, for example, initially proposed to give freed slaves an allotment of the land their labor had enriched. Instead, they got a bank. Northern industrialists came out in support of Booker T. Washington's plan for a segregated black economy even as other black leaders were pushing for full integration. The New Deal programs that would have sent aid to build housing in the urban ghetto were instead used to create white suburbs that reinforced and perpetuated racial segregation for the rest of the century. And as soon as the civil rights coalition began to demand some form of wealth redistribution or poverty aid, President Nixon embraced black capitalism. Support for black banking and black capitalism have been consistent policy band-aid solutions, a decoy response to the fundamental challenge of overcoming America's legacy of slavery.

The theory of black banking is rooted in a foundational tenet of American banking policy. Thomas Jefferson believed that banks should be small and local as opposed to Alexander Hamilton's vision of large and national banks. Jefferson's ideal was a locally controlled economy, agrarian in nature, with decentralized monetary policy, but he was on the wrong side of history—it is Hamilton's centralized, national, and large banking sector that became essential to a vibrant American economy. Yet, when it comes to banking policy for poor and marginalized communities, it is Jefferson's outdated vision that is still dominant. Small community banking has always held a special appeal when applied to poor and marginalized pockets of the economy. The promise is that a beleaguered community, having been left out of the dominant banking industry, could pool its resources and collectively lift itself out of poverty.

Black banks promised to control the black dollar and grow it. If the color of the ghetto was black, so too would be the money flowing within. Blacks must "control the economy of our community," said Malcolm X. President Reagan believed that black enterprises "are especially important in neighborhood economies where the dollars . . . spent have a beneficial multiplier effect."[9] But could a ghetto, born from racism and segregation, overcome those forces through banking? Or was James Baldwin right when he wrote that "a ghetto can be improved in one way only: out of existence."[10]

Despite consistent bipartisan support and a few publicized success stories, there was never any evidence that the design would work. The very circumstances that created the need for these banks—discrimination and segregation—permanently limited their effectiveness and would ultimately cause their demise. The catch-22 of black banking is that the very institutions needed to help communities escape deep poverty inevitably become victims of that same poverty. Blacks were poor and, due to segregated housing, their homes were worth less. What this meant for black banks was that their deposits were costlier and their loans were less stable, which created a combustible situation over time. Housing segregation prevented the growth of black wealth and presented black bankers with an industry-crushing challenge. Not only were these banks more vulnerable to failure, but even in flush times, they were unable to perform the money-multiplying alchemy of banking. Pushed out of the mainstream, blacks needed to create their own economic engines, but their marginalization and exclusion from practically all aspects of American economic life made their engines weak and incapable of the economic growth bank financing is typically able to produce.

The truth was that segregated communities could not segregate their money. In fact, black banks, which were created to control the black dollar, became the very mechanism through which black money flowed out of the black community and into the mainstream white economy. The ghetto economy was weak, extractive, and costly. And the color of capital, commerce, property, trade, and money was white.

White, too, was the color of government credit. In America, each rung on the ladder toward prosperity consisted of bank credit—even more so in the twentieth century when homeownership became synonymous with both mortgage credit and prosperity. For blacks, the path toward wealth was closed by segregation, government policies, and economic reality. As the overall American economy grew by leaps and bounds, the urban black economy became locked in a state of perpetual depression.

The ghettos that initially trapped America's other immigrant groups did eventually improve themselves out of existence, once they were no longer segregated from the mainstream economy. In fact, the dilemma faced by black banks is highlighted when contrasted with the viable banks created by Italian, Jewish, German, Irish, and Asian immigrants. Each of these immigrant groups faced discrimination and exclusion like the black population, but the key difference was that none of them was systematically, uniformly, and legally segregated to the extent and for the length of time the black community was. Many immigrants eventually left their overcrowded ghettos and settled in suburbs where, through violence, zoning restrictions, and racial covenants, blacks were barred. This divergent path is illustrated by the fates of the home loans and banks established by these various immigrant groups. One instructive example is the Bank of Italy, which formed in San Francisco to serve Italian immigrants who could not get loans from the mainstream banks. Eventually, the Bank of Italy grew and merged into the mainstream U.S. banking system—just as Italian immigrants assimilated into American society. What was formerly the Bank of Italy is now the Bank of America—the largest and one of the most profitable banks in the country.[11]

The success of immigrant banks should not be misinterpreted. It was not self-help and community support that allowed them to finance themselves out of the ghetto. They left the ghetto first. And they did so only after being accepted as "white"; not through segregating their money. The bootstraps they were given were government-guaranteed mortgage loans, from which black people were excluded. Doubtless, many immigrants worked hard to achieve the American dream of homeownership, but so too did blacks.

The black ghetto and the white suburb were created by heavy state intervention. A government credit infrastructure propelled the growth of the American economy and relegated the ghetto economy to a permanently inferior position. The government-created credit apparatus did not cross the red lines that policymakers drew around the ghetto, and within the color line a separate and unequal economy took root. If free-market capitalism is understood as allowing the laws of supply and demand to operate without state intervention, then the black ghetto was certainly engaged in capitalism, but at a time when white America was not. Black capitalism, as it turned out, meant capitalism *only* for blacks.

There has always been an attempt at justifying and explaining wealth inequality in the United States. The economic oppression of slavery was justified in the eighteenth century by a corrupted version of Christian dogma that held that the white race had a divine right to subject the black one. Then science was conscripted to do the dirty work of white supremacy as social Darwinism held that race hierarchy was nature's will. Evolutionary theory and a sham science of eugenics and phrenology justified the wealth gap in the nineteenth century. In the twentieth century, economic theory was used

to justify the wealth gap. Market fundamentalists such as Barry Goldwater, Milton Friedman, and Alan Greenspan held that the wealth
gap was a natural result of market forces and that any government
remedy was an inefficient market intervention. Black capitalism and
its subsequent iterations became the modern era's justification for
wealth inequality. The theory held that the invisible hand had set
the price of black credit, the value of black homes, and the cost of
black labor. This book is a challenge to that premise and it lays bare
the fact that the hand that drives black poverty is not a natural and
invisible one, but rather the coercive hand of the state that has
consistently excluded blacks from full participation in American
capitalism.

This is not just a story about the harsh realities of American
racism—the violence and the repeated injustices—though these
forces are an essential background to the narrative. This story peers
inside the black community and studies its counterattack. But it is
not a story celebrating the heroic struggles of individual black
bankers who were triumphant despite the odds. There are certainly
stories of inspiration to be found, but the overemphasis on Horatio
Alger tales of success can lead to distraction. This is not a simple tale
of bad guys or good guys—the exploiters and exploited. In fact,
sometimes the exploited are the exploiters too. The story is larger
than the players within.

This is a story of economics, politics, and laws that sowed the
seeds of injustice into the soil of the American economy. The weeds
that grew from it did not need to be fed with racism. It used the materials available—commerce, credit, money, and segregation—to re-
generate inequality. It is too simplistic to blame the racists or the
loan sharks for the wealth gap. We need to identify the subterranean
forces that barely make a visible ripple on the surface as they perpetuate injustice over time. To examine the history and function of
black banks is to shine a spotlight directly onto the fault line of economic inequality.

In 2016, in conjunction with the Black Lives Matter movement,
activists renewed a focus on black banking. Yet, the industry is in
distress. In June 2015, Mechanics and Farmers Bank of Durham,
North Carolina, announced that it was shifting focus from specifically serving the black community to being just a standard community bank. It hired its first nonblack director, changed its name

to the more modern "M&F," and announced that it would start going after a broader customer base.[12] To most banking industry observers, this change was not newsworthy; in fact, hardly anyone noticed. But the move might reflect the last gasp of a dying industry. Mechanics and Farmers Bank was the oldest and strongest black-owned bank in the country. Since 1907, it has been financing black churches, black homes, and black businesses. It survived the Great Depression, saving several other black-owned banks in the process. And for almost a century, its insurance affiliate, the North Carolina Mutual Life Insurance Company, was the largest black-controlled business institution in the world.[13]

While the demise of black banks across the country may have been a foregone conclusion, their loss is significant because these institutions represented something more than their vulnerable balance sheets. These are the institutions the black community has repeatedly relied on to achieve prosperity amid forceful economic headwinds. Their loss is a tragedy not because it is surprising, but because no other institution is in a better position to illuminate the complex and persistent obstacles to creating black wealth.

Black banks are the engines of promised prosperity in the black community and it is by inspecting them that we can know most about the self-reinforcing nature of black poverty. In fact, poverty is the sand destroying these engines. Noting the "striking" trend of black bank failures, a recent study linked the epidemic to the "deep poverty" of the black community.[14] In other words, the very poverty that these banks have been trying to fight for generations is the main obstacle to their survival. But the poverty rut is perpetuated when communities lose access to banks. As a group, blacks are more unbanked than any other race—60 percent of the black population is unbanked or underbanked, while only 20 percent of whites are in the same category.[15] What this means is that blacks disproportionately rely on fringe banks, leading to a debt trap. Blacks pay higher interest on mortgages and small loans. They pay more fees on basic services than similarly situated whites and they are taken to court disproportionately by creditors for very small debts.[16]

All of this is both due to and contributes to the wealth gap. Without a cushion of wealth, black families pay more for credit and financial services and fall harder when they hit a bump. Wealth provides a layer of financial security, and this shock absorber is missing for many black families. Especially for families on the bottom rung, owning a home provides a substantial buffer against the harshest edges of poverty, a stable foundation that can be passed down to the next generation. It can determine whether your neighborhood has decent or failing schools, whether you will be able to go to college, whether you will face eviction, or whether you can meet unexpected costs without having to resort to a payday loan. A store of wealth is self-reinforcing, as is its absence. As Billie Holiday sang, "Them that's got shall get. Them that's not shall lose."[17]

Historian Manning Marable has lamented that "the most striking fact about American economic history and politics is the brutal and systemic underdevelopment of black people."[18] When the Emancipation Proclamation was signed in 1863, the black community owned a total of 0.5 percent of the total wealth in the United States. This number is not surprising; slaves were forbidden to own anything, and the few freed blacks living in the North had few opportunities to accumulate wealth. What is staggering is that more than 150 years later, that number has barely budged—blacks still own only about 1 percent of the wealth in the United States.[19] When Martin Luther King stood on the steps of the Lincoln Memorial in 1963, he said that "America has given the Negro people a bad check, a check which has come back marked 'insufficient funds.' "[20]

This bad check was, in large part, the consistent faith in and promotion of segregated black banking. The promise of black banking is that the color of money does not matter and that black banks can control and multiply black money in the same way that white banks multiply white wealth. Yet despite a century of honest toil, the check has continued to be marked "insufficient funds." Whether the next century yields a different result will depend, in part, on understanding the nature of the failures of the last.

1

Forty Acres or a Savings Bank

Slavery, "America's original sin," according to James Madison, created the foundation of modern American capitalism.[1] It was slavery and the "blood drawn with the lash" that opened the arteries of capital and commerce that led to U.S. economic dominance worldwide.[2] The effects of the institution of slavery on American commerce were monumental—3.2 million slaves were worth $1.3 billion in market value, almost equal to the entire gross national product.[3] Slaves were also a valuable store of capital because they were liquid assets that could be exchanged on markets more easily than other forms of property. Slavery's unparalleled bounty is what caused many Americans to tolerate such a barbarous institution. Growing international demand for cotton fueled the growth of slavery, and the legal and political arms of the state maintained and protected it. More cotton led to more profits, which led to more demand for slaves, which led to more legislation supporting slavery, and then even crueler methods of oppression to extract more work from slaves.

The institution of slavery was so at odds with the liberal notions of equality avowed in America's founding documents that a theory of racial hierarchy was used to explain away the dissonance. Blacks had to be seen as subhuman so that they could be treated as chattel. In the antebellum era, Christian religious principles were exploited to provide the rationale for racial subjugation.[4] Not only were slavery and white supremacy condoned by God, but it was seen as God's will that white men exploit the labor of the black race. In *The Christian Doctrine of Slavery,* a Presbyterian minister concluded, "It may be that *Christian slavery* is God's solution of the problem [of labor] about which the wisest statesmen of Europe confess themselves 'at fault.' "[5]

The stark wealth distortion caused by slavery and the longevity of its effects cannot be overestimated. Blacks were "articles of commerce," as illustrated by the Constitution's three-fifths rule. Slave bodies were assets, credit, debt, currency—forms of capital and wealth. Between 1820 and the Civil War, banks across the South issued notes with images of slaves printed on the money.[6] The currency of the South was the slave. Slaves were not just the labor in the cotton production process; they were the collateral used to finance the operations. Slavery modernized credit markets, creating complex new forms of financial instruments and trade networks through which slaves could be mortgaged, exchanged, and used as leverage to purchase more slaves. In highly profitable, speculation-based markets, many white men built fortunes trading in slave-backed securities.[7] As is true of property ownership in any era, those who held slaves had the ability to grow exponentially richer because they could use their property to create more wealth.

For all the economic gains created by slavery, the slaves themselves could never profit. During the 246 years of institutionalized slavery in America, enslaved individuals could not participate in the economy as buyers and sellers. In order for slavery to function, the slaves needed to serve as cogs in the machine and not its drivers. They were therefore not permitted to own assets or offer their labor for pay in any form. These prohibitions, which included ownership of land and trade of any kind, were often cemented in law and enforced through violence.[8]

And since slavery was premised on white supremacy in a racial hierarchy, an ideology avowed across the country and not just in the slaveholding South, even freed blacks were restricted from full participation in commerce. Small numbers of blacks in the North and small populations of free southern blacks did manage to participate in the economy, but they were tightly constrained. In virtually every aspect of northern life, blacks were segregated from whites. Jim Crow laws mandating segregation in practically all spheres of life began in the North and West well before the Civil War.[9] Alexis de Tocqueville, who came to marvel at America's democracy, was shocked at the level of racial prejudice he observed in the North. "The prejudice of race," he wrote, "appears to be stronger in the states that have abolished slavery than in those where it still exists; and nowhere is it so intolerant as in those states where servitude has never been known."[10]

Many states legally prohibited free blacks from owning property, testifying in courts, or practicing professions or trades above menial labor.[11] Black businessmen typically could not sue white debtors in courts and were often restricted from engaging in finance.[12] Similarly, an 1852 Maryland statute excluded blacks from membership in thrift or building and loan institutions.[13] Where there were no legal barriers, there were social forces that blocked blacks from organizing banks and businesses. "A mere legal grant of a thing," explained a black businessman, "does not mean that it will be immediately enjoyed. Public opinion is often more binding than law."[14] And public opinion relegated blacks to the lowest economic stratum.

During this era of exclusion, free black businessmen relied on their own race for capital and credit. Black banking began as a private affair.[15] There were several black men of means who lent their own money to other blacks, but the group was so small that their names could be recounted by historians writing about them half a century later.[16] To the extent that there were any formal banking structures, they operated through philanthropic societies and churches. The center of the free black community in the North was the city of Philadelphia, and as early as 1788, prominent black clergy and business owners had organized "mutual aid societies."[17] Mutual aid societies usually orbited the black church, the central pillar of the black community. The most prominent and long lasting of these was the African Methodist Episcopal Church (AME Church) in Philadelphia, founded by Richard Allen and Rev. Absalom Jones in 1787 with the governing slogan "To Seek for Ourselves." It did just that. Between 1847 and 1904, the church gave over one million dollars to educational programs for blacks, and by 1907 it had supported twenty-two schools. The collective power the black community harnessed through church membership also made black churches a target for racial hostility and social control. After Nat Turner's slave revolt in 1831, southern legislators passed laws forbidding blacks from preaching or congregating in their own churches. South Carolina even prohibited groups of black individuals from meeting together "for the purpose of mental instruction or religious worship."[18]

By the mid to late 1800s, free blacks began to press against trade restrictions by forming a financial sphere of their own. In 1851, leading black businessmen and ministers gathered in New York City "for the purpose of making plans for improving the Negroes' economic status." They decided that blacks needed their own banks if they were going to succeed in business.[19] The group resolved that "a mutual savings bank be established by Negroes" in order to "encourage savings and thrift and . . . assist Negroes who wished to enter business."[20] A constant preoccupation among free northern blacks trying to operate businesses or buy property was their inability to secure any type of credit. Abram Harris, a prominent black economist in the 1930s, listed the barriers to black enterprise before the Civil War in the following order: "(1) The Difficulty of Obtaining Capital and Credit; (2) Low Wages, Competition for Jobs, and Immigration; (3) Mob Violence; (4) Occupational Restrictions; (5) Prohibitions against Owning Certain Types of Property; (6) Denial of the Right to Sue; (7) Restrictions against Settlement in the West; and (8) Civic and Educational Handicaps." Harris emphasized that "the greatest handicap was, without a doubt, the difficulty of obtaining capital and credit."[21] Thus, on the eve of the Civil War, there was a vibrant ongoing discussion among free blacks in the North on how they might establish credit and banking associations.

The bank envisioned by this group of business leaders would be organized as a cooperative society and would rely on black investors in New York who, it was hoped, would invest their total accumulated wealth in the bank to be used as starting capital. It was crucial that the bank have access to the entire black community's resources—it was said that northern blacks held between $40,000 and $50,000 in Wall Street banks—so that it could lend to black entrepreneurs and would-be property owners. This was the first of many attempts by black leaders and businessmen to convince blacks to harness the collective power of black capital in support of black banking. The bank ultimately failed to attract enough capital and was never formed.[22]

The black community knew that it needed banks if blacks were ever going to advance economically. Alexander Hamilton, the first treasury secretary and the father of American banking system, explained that it was banks that could create the "augmentation of the active or productive capital of a country." Gold and silver, he said, "acquire life" and only through the operation of a bank. "Banks in good credit can circulate a far greater sum than the actual quantum of their capital in Gold & Silver." Explaining bank lending and the money-multiplying magic of banking, Hamilton explained that bank "credit keeps circulating, performing in every stage the office of money."[23] In other words, it was through banking that American wealth would be created.

Bank credit creates wealth, which is why the isolated free black community kept trying to create its own segregated banking system. Bank credit was needed to "augment" capital, but could a bank be created without capital? Could bank lending lead to wealth creation, or did banking only work to multiply already accumulated wealth? In a circular economic rut that would be repeated throughout history, there was too little available capital to create a bank that could extend credit so that more capital could be produced. And blacks' access to capital was limited because they did not have any political power.

Hamilton had emphasized that successful banking required a strong partnership with the federal government. He told Congress in 1790 that a bank is "not a mere matter of private property, but a political machine of the greatest importance to the state."[24] A healthy government needed a bank to survive, and strong banks relied on government support. In order to thrive, banks needed government charters, free and open access to enforcement of contract laws, and the orderly maintenance of capital and credit markets. Though government intervention in the economy was limited in the antebellum era, government's hand was most apparent in banking and currency markets, and it kept blacks out of both. If Hamilton was right in saying that only successful banking could multiply wealth and that strong central government support was needed for a healthy banking system, could a people on the margins of the economy ever create wealth through banking? Black banks would try to answer this question for two centuries.

Black leaders continued to discuss the bank even as the slavery question was being hotly contested on the national stage.[25] These were interdependent questions, for freedom would be severely restricted without the ability to fully participate in the economy. Black leaders stressed that emancipation would have to be followed by the accumulation of wealth if the black community was ever to achieve meaningful political equality. Frederick Douglass remarked that "the history of civilization shows that no people can well rise to a high degree of mental or even moral excellence without wealth. A people uniformly poor and compelled to struggle for barely a physical existence will be dependent and despised by their neighbors and will finally despise themselves."[26] The debate over a black bank became moot, however, when free blacks lost their political status as a result of the 1857 *Dred Scott* case, which held that no black individual, free or enslaved, could claim American citizenship. The case was the last gasp of the South, which was increasingly under pressure to release its grip on its profitable and abusive institution of slavery. The Industrial Revolution significantly changed the nature of the economy and unleashed forces that would eventually lead to southern secession, the Civil War, and ultimately emancipation.[27]

Even though the Civil War decimated the South, the ill-gotten spoils of slavery remained and grew in the former cotton empires in America and Europe for generations. The theories of racial superiority spun to justify centuries of enslavement stuck around too. These theories, so infused in American culture, could not be shed easily, and their long-lasting effects would lead to economic distortions that constantly impeded those formerly enslaved from participating in the white-dominated economy.

The freed slaves had to make the transition from being capital to becoming capitalists—from being chattel to owning it. They had to do this having "neither money, property nor friends," as Frederick Douglass explained.[28] The road to wealth presented severe obstacles during the terrible confusion and upheaval in the Reconstruction-era southern economy.

The victorious Union army granted the slaves their emancipation, and for a transitory moment the Union came close to giving them a share of the land. After his famous march from Atlanta to the sea, General William T. Sherman remained in Savannah as the war wound down. There, he consulted with several black leaders who told him that the ex-slaves, worried about lingering racial animosity, preferred to take care of themselves on their own land.[29] Black minister Garrison Frazier explained that the "way we can best take care of ourselves is to have land and turn it and till it by our own labor."[30] Blacks had already begun to establish self-governing communities in several places in the South.[31] After emancipation, black communities formed hundreds of mutual aid societies to work toward economic self-sufficiency. They set up charities to take care of the poor and sick and to educate each other. "We have progressed a Century in a year," said one freedman.[32] During the first year of freedom in 1866, a "Negro convention" held in Greene County, North Carolina, suggested that blacks could raise their economic status by creating joint stock companies and patronizing black businesses.[33]

The black community's main objective, which it sought through political means, was acquiring land. Emancipated slaves and their northern Republican supporters believed that land ownership was the only way to achieve a free market in the South. Without land, they would be at the mercy of their previous owners.[34] Sherman signed Field Order 15 in March 1865, which set aside 400,000 acres of confiscated land for freed slaves.[35] Sherman's plan was to create a territory exclusively for ex-slaves where they could live free of white control and manage their own economic and political affairs.[36] In justifying this action, Sherman borrowed from Thomas Jefferson's populist view of land as usufruct. The basic idea was that landholders owned property only due to the benevolence of the federal government, in which all land rights resided. The southern Confederates' traitorous act of secession forfeited their land rights.[37]

Two months after the Sherman order, Congress created the Freedmen's Bureau and tasked it with transitioning former slaves to their new lives; part of the plan was to dole out the seized land. The Freedmen's Bureau Act of 1865 formalized Sherman's field order into a law "providing that each negro might have forty acres at a low price on long credit."[38] The order came directly from President Lincoln, who wished to give freed slaves "an interest in the soil."[39] The price of land was to be fixed at $1.25 per acre, 40 percent of which was due up front. The land was to be protected by the military until Congress could act to formalize land titles. Some families even received leftover army mules.[40] It seemed that the government was about to create a black landowning class. In fact, during the Reconstruction era, racial equality was even contemplated. Black lawmakers and radical Republican allies like Thaddeus Stevens, Charles Sumner actively pursued full integration and equality.

Confiscating and breaking up the land meant destroying the slaveholder oligarchies that had controlled the Confederacy. The backlash was extreme and ruinous. Having contemplated a complete reordering of the South, and perhaps exactly because the stakes were so high, the Reconstruction revolution was violently overthrown. Ex-Confederates won back through violence, fraud, and coercion what they could not achieve through military victory or political process.[41] The Ku Klux Klan became a para-military force in the South whose purpose was the overthrow of Republican government, black politicians, and any other activists not fully in line with the established antebellum order. According to Reconstruction historian Eric Foner, "the largest number of violent acts stemmed from disputes arising from black efforts to assert their freedom from control by their former masters." Especially vulnerable were blacks who tried to purchase land.[42] Reformists were assassinated, and black voters were harassed. As W. E. B. Du Bois explained, "Guerrilla raiding, the ever-present flickering after-flame of war, was spending its forces against the Negroes, and all the Southern land was awakening as from some wild dream to poverty and social revolution."[43]

A postwar struggle was being waged over economic control of the South. The Freedmen's Bureau could not survive the violence and chaos that followed Appomattox and thus promises of land and equality vanished.[44] As Du Bois said of Reconstruction, "the slave went free; stood a brief moment in the sun; then moved back again toward slavery."[45]

President Andrew Johnson, the accidental president who assumed office after Lincoln's assassination, joined the white southern backlash and rolled back Lincoln's promises. He thoroughly undermined the Freedmen's Bureau bill, including the land grant, and fought the black rights movements, asserting that America would remain a "white man's government."[46] Though the southern rebels had expected to be hanged for their treason, Johnson welcomed them back into the fold, pardoned them, and restored their confiscated land. The land General Sherman had given to freed slaves in Georgia was returned to the original owners before a full harvest season had elapsed.[47] The effects were devastating for blacks. Had whites made good on this promise to blacks, claimed Du Bois, it "would have made a basis of real democracy in the United States."[48] Instead, the agents of the Freedmen's Bureau went south to "tell the weeping freedmen, after their years of toil, that their land was not theirs, that there was a mistake—somewhere."[49]

Union General Oliver Otis Howard, who had the unpleasant task of taking the land back from the freedmen after he had helped administer the order, nevertheless reasoned that the "freedmen should have land, but they . . . must pay for their land."[50] President Johnson said that the Freedmen's bill was advantaging blacks over whites and that it was time for blacks to fend for themselves. "It is earnestly hoped that instead of wasting away, they will, by their own efforts, establish for themselves a condition of respectability and prosperity." Johnson claimed that the laws of capitalism and free trade would allow the freedmen to accumulate land without any special help from the state. He was confident that freed slaves would be able to choose their "own employment and their own places of abode" and insist on and receive "proper remuneration" for their work and further that the "laws that regulate supply and demand will maintain their force, and the wages of the laborer will be regulated thereby."[51]

It is important to pause and note that during this time the government was in the process of confiscating and distributing millions of acres of land for railroad expansion—a heavy government subsidy to a private enterprise. Banks were also being supported by public taxes in order to induce them to extend credit to the South.[52] The Homestead Acts gave out millions of acres of government land to white settlers for years. The sheer scale of the land redistribution and its exclusion of blacks from the bounty was not the laissez-faire free market Johnson was describing.[53] Blacks were denied land, not because the government was beholden to market rules, but because the government was controlled by political factions favoring the southern white elite, and giving blacks land was politically unpopular.

The myth that free-market principles were guiding political choices was further exposed as hypocrisy because blacks could not even pay "market prices" for land. White southerners simply refused to sell land to blacks. Land was sometimes sold at half the price to white buyers compared to what black buyers were offering just to avoid selling their land to blacks. Even when white landowners did not have sufficient resources to cultivate the land themselves, they still spurned black buyers.[54] Southern states even passed laws that forbade white sellers to sell land to blacks.[55] The abstract laws of supply and demand could not work when actual state laws excluded blacks from free markets.

The southern economy was anything but a free market. Prominent southern lawyers, legislators, and judges drafted laws that governed all aspects of black life and spurred racial bias across the South. These "black codes" prohibited blacks from property ownership, trade, testifying in courts, and voting. Blacks could not engage in commercial trades other than what they were conscripted to do. An 1865 South Carolina law declared that "no person of color shall pursue or practice the art, trade, or business of an artisan mechanic or shopkeeper, or any other trade, employment or business . . . on his own account and for his own benefit until he shall have obtained a license which shall be good for one year only."[56] One black veteran remarked of these laws, "If you call this Freedom, what do you call Slavery?"[57]

By the end of the Reconstruction era, most freedmen were left landless, voteless, and with practically every profession blocked to them—their only choice was to grow cotton. Of course, that was the point. The world cotton market, headquartered in Great Britain, was heavily dependent on cheap and abundant cotton from the United States. The global web of cotton merchants that connected capital and trade through Liverpool, New York, Chicago, Paris, and Georgia had been closely following the turmoil of the Civil War. The moment the war ended, nervous cotton interests worked in local, state, and national courthouses and legislatures to restore a cotton-growing system as quickly as possible and as close to slavery as permissible. Across the globe, cotton traders and capitalists agreed that blacks needed to grow cotton. As Union general Frank C. Barlow put it in 1865 about his purchase of a southern plantation, "Making money there is a simple question of being able to make the darkies work."[58] Some northerners had opposed the land redistribution efforts for the same reason. New York Democrat John W. Chandler argued that the land bill "leaves the culture of cotton, which is one of the main sources of national wealth, without security and without any certain prospect of improvement."[59]

For blacks, freedom had meant that they would be in control of their own economic destiny. For white capitalists, black freedom meant that blacks would be paid wages for growing cotton. These two interests and definitions of freedom were directly at odds. In order to make blacks continue to work at growing cotton, it was crucial that the freed slaves not be permitted to engage in subsistence farming. In other words, America could not go the way of Haiti. After Haitians led a successful slave revolt against the French, the former slaves refused to grow sugar and output halted.[60] They grew crops they could eat instead. Subsistence farming meant that a family would grow what they could live on, diversifying their crops, with some portion going for sale and some going for consumption. There was every reason to believe that American blacks would also go this route. After the war, in the fleeting moment of freedom, freed slaves had created societies of communal landownership and grew subsistence crops. In Edisto, South Carolina, for example, an independent society of freedmen consisting of 5,440 people cultivating 3,230 acres of land grew 33 percent cotton, 54 percent corn, and the rest in garden vegetables. The land was owned cooperatively and the profits from the harvest were shared.[61] One South Carolina Bureau agent called the freed people's land use "contrary to the laws of Nature and Civilization as I understand them." He was appalled that they would be planting vegetables in the most productive cotton soil in the world.[62] Some blacks rejected growing cotton because it was a "slave crop," permanently associated with "the overseer, the driver and the lash."[63]

The southern plantation economy could not function without cotton, and the cotton machine could not hum as it had before the war without exploiting black labor. A South Carolina planter said "the negro [is] the proper, legitimate and divinely ordained laborer of the South . . . [who] has become wild in the exuberance of his freedom . . . and will be trained to work as a free man. He cannot be permitted to become what he is in St. Domingo [Haiti]."[64]

Denying blacks landownership took care of the threat of subsistence farming, but black labor also had to be "induced" back to the cotton plantations. The South worked quickly to turn freedom into a legal technicality as opposed to an experienced economic reality. The black codes and compulsory work contracts took care of that by mandating constant and unrelenting work and punishing resisters through vagrancy laws.[65] Work contracts forced blacks to stay on the plantation, and a contract breach, usually enforced through monetary damages, was punishable by violence, imprisonment, and loss of life.[66] So coercive was this system of enforced labor that freedmen were prohibited in many states from hunting or fishing, which prevented them even from exploiting natural resources for survival.[67]

The criminal and legal system of the South was used to prevent the free movement of blacks in the market. Besides unrelenting cotton production, there were other forms of exploitation. The South's burgeoning mining economy needed cheap labor, and southern entrepreneurs used the criminal justice system to re-enslave thousands of black men and work them, usually to death, in abhorrent labor camps.[68] Having relied on unpaid black labor for so long, southern entrepreneurs designed the new system of convict leasing and continued to extract it. Blacks would be arrested under "vagrancy violations," which could be used to arrest any free black man in the course of doing any activity at all except working for a white landlord. Once arrested, these men would have a speedy trial, and within an average of seventy-two hours after arrest, be sold to a southern industrial mill to work in deplorable conditions for twelve hours a day mining coal or iron. Half of all labor prisoners died within the year they were arrested. Often, good laborers nearing the end of their term in the mines would be rearrested while still convicts, found guilty of taking too much food or clothing that belonged to a mine owner, and re-enslaved in the mine.[69]

Ostensibly, labor contracts were built on consent and free labor. But in reality, the black workers had no choice and could not, as Johnson had promised, determine their own employment and wages. Laws prohibited other employers from reaching out to blacks under contract and punished contract breach with physical violence. Wages were capped by law and by cabal between the employers. They were never much above subsistence, which further bound blacks to their employer.[70] Black economic freedom was simply anathema to the profitable maintenance of the cotton market.

Freedmen wanted to control capital and have economic independence, but their former masters required them to work the fields. They could not be plantation labor if they had capital, which meant that they were prevented from accruing capital. Had they had land, they could not have been so easily conscripted back into cotton labor. Thus it was that in a few short years, most former slaves lived on the same plantations where they had been enslaved and went back to work, often with the same overseers, toiling the same hours on the same fields. James Baldwin called Reconstruction "a bargain between the North and South to this effect: We've liberated them from the land—and delivered them to the bosses."[71] The only difference was that now blacks too were entangled in the cotton–debt empire just as the plantation owners had been. The economic order had remained virtually unchanged, and so too the lives of the freedmen.[72]

Moderate northern Republicans began to pivot away from the fight for racial equality and began to see equal citizenship as an end goal to be attained by blacks gradually over time through increased education, work, and the accumulation of property. Republicans began losing elections because of their support for black rights. They shed the liability and shifted toward pushing for sound money, lower taxes, and free-market capitalism. As they backed away from specific economic aid and land grants for blacks, Reconstruction collapsed. But even as reformers abandoned land and economic reform, they fought for civil rights for blacks in form if not in function. According to Du Bois, "the Freedmen's Bureau died, and its child was the Fifteenth Amendment."[73] However, because freedom was contained only in constitutional law and not experienced in the southern economy, these rights were hollow and vulnerable. The legal right to participate in democracy could not overcome the legal prohibition against engaging in the free market or the gaping gap in wealth.[74]

As Martin Luther King Jr. echoed a century later, "the Emancipation Proclamation freed the slave, a legal entity, but it failed to free the Negro, a person."[75] This pattern would be repeated. This was just the first of several pivotal points in U.S. history when government reformers would choose to grant political rights instead of achieving real justice by addressing economic inequality. Indeed, it would happen to Dr. King's own movement a century later.

Instead of land, freed slaves got rights that they could not use due to their economic and political status at the bottom rung of society. They also got a savings bank, which was another form of diversion that would be repeated in the next century. In fact, the most tangible and long-lasting, but historically overlooked aspects of the Freedmen's Bureau was the bank it created. Even President Johnson, who voted to repeal the Freedmen's Bureau and opposed every aid measure directed at blacks, including schools and job training, left the bank alone and never uttered a word of protest over it.[76]

The Freedmen's Savings and Trust Company, also known as the Freedmen's Savings Bank, was the first and only savings bank created by the federal government. Blacks had not asked for the bank, but land grants having been foreclosed by violence and southern retrenchment, the bank was a stand-in. The reformers promised the black community that the bank was the preferred and proper means by which they would achieve landownership on their own.[77] The bank's founder, John Alvord, said that the freedmen "have a passion for land," and the bank would provide the way. "Their notion of having land given to them by government is passing away, and we hear them saying, 'We will work and save and buy for ourselves.' "[78] Saving their wages in the bank was offered not only as the only way to buy land, but as the respectable and proper way of doing so.

Frederick Douglass celebrated the bank, stating that the "mission of the Freedmen's Bank is to show our people the road to a share of the wealth and well-being of the world."[79] What the bank eventually did, according to Du Bois, was "not only ruine[d] thousands of colored men, but taught to thousands more a lesson of distrust which it will take them years to unlearn."[80]

The genesis of the bank was in small military banks created during the Civil War to hold black soldiers' wages. In Massachusetts, state authorities developed an "allotment system" already in use for white soldiers to place black soldiers' funds into an account to be distributed to family members. In 1864, General N. P. Banks established the first bank for black soldiers in New Orleans, called the Free Labor Bank. One regiment, called the "Rost Host Colony," deposited around $20,000 into the bank. Soon after, other military banks for blacks opened. These banks, located in New Orleans, South Carolina, and Virginia, were among the first banks organized for blacks, and were immediately trusted by their depositors because of their alliance with the military.[81]

After the war, there was about $200,000 of unclaimed funds in these banks, deposits from black soldiers who had died during the war. John W. Alvord, an abolitionist minister and army chaplain, encouraged Congress to use these funds to incorporate a bank for freed blacks in conjunction with the Freedmen's Bureau.[82] The Freedmen's Savings Bank and Trust Company was approved by Congress and signed into law by President Lincoln on March 3, 1865—the same day the Freedmen's Bureau was created. The bill passed without opposition and was championed by reformers like Sumner and Alvord, neither of whom had any experience with finance or banking. With the exception of the First and Second Banks of the United States, which were no longer in operation by 1865, the Freedmen's Bank was the only bank ever to have been chartered by Congress.

"This bank is just what the freedmen need," said President Lincoln when he signed the Act.[83] Pamphlets promoted the bank as "Abraham Lincoln's Gift to the Colored People. . . . He gave Emancipation, and then this Savings Bank."[84] The bank was based on a popular new philanthropic banking model, savings banks for the poor, that had recently proliferated in the Northeast. These banks differed from commercial banks of the time because commercial banks made loans and speculative investments. The purpose of a savings bank was to hold money instead of growing it through lending. The charter of the Freedmen's Bank was almost a copy of New York City's Savings Bank charter. These banks were usually charitable institutions meant to teach "working men" the lessons of "thrift," "industry," and "care for the future." Congress described it as a teaching institution—to instruct freed slaves about American values, or "to instill into the minds of the untutored Africans lessons of sobriety, wisdom, and economy," values that were integral to "the economic and industrial development of a people."[85]

Though a savings bank was useful in that it would ostensibly keep money secure until the freedmen had saved enough to buy property, the bank would do nothing to grow the wealth in the community. The Freedmen's Bank was not a lending institution. The deposits were to be invested in safe government securities. The bank was a magnificently constructed, highly regarded, and heavily advertised piggy bank.

The bank appeared to be backed by the full faith and credit of the federal government, and indeed, many freed slaves were "induced to believe that the bank was a government institution or that at least the government was responsible for their funds."[86] Massachusetts Senator Henry Wilson bragged that the depositors' money "was just as safe there as if it were in the Treasury of the United States."[87] Having been created the same day as the Freedmen's Bureau, it seemed obvious that the bank would be backed by the government. A U.S. Senate hearing described the federal imprimatur as follows: "The pass book issued to the depositors in the Freedmen's Bank bore on its cover the likeness of President Lincoln, General Grant, also General Howard and others whom the freedmen had learned to revere as the special benefactors of their race. The flag of the United States was draped over the buildings, and designed to assure them that the United States would protect their interest."[88] How else could a bank run by whites convince newly freed blacks to trust them with their hard-earned savings?

The bank was also seen as trustworthy because of its prominent white leaders. John W. Alvord, the superintendent of the

Freedmen's Bureau department of education, was the driving force behind the bank's creation and became an original trustee. Alvord convinced Congress to create a board of trustees with fifty prominent citizens, including William A. Booth, Peter Cooper, John Murray Forbes, George Whipple, Thomas Webster, and John Jay. Many of these trustees lent their reputation to the bank, but were never involved in managing the bank.[89] The charter of the bank also made clear that its purpose was to safeguard deposits and invest them in low-risk treasury notes and other U.S. securities.[90] The bank's charter stated that "the general business and object of the corporation hereby created shall be to receive on deposit such sums of money as may from time to time be offered, therefore by or on behalf of persons heretofore held in slavery in the United States or their descendants and to invest the same in stocks, bonds, treasury notes and other securities of the United States."[91] However, Section 6 of the charter provided a small opening for future changes by stating that a third of the deposits, called "available funds," could be invested anywhere. The section was vague and open to abuse, and perhaps because of its benevolent mission, the trustees were vested with broad discretionary powers with little oversight.[92]

The response to the bank was remarkable. Within ten years, it handled more than $75 million of deposits made by more than 75,000 depositors, an amount that would be approximately $1.5 billion today.[93] This number is even more impressive considering the poverty that pervaded the black community. It was immediately apparent that blacks not only trusted the institution, but also had faith in the promise that small savings would lead to landowner-ship.[94] Most of these deposits were being saved to buy land and other productive goods such as tools or agricultural supplies. In the South, bank deposits were usually made by young men trying to save for land.[95] Freedmen were using the savings bank in the way that they had been told to use it—to climb up the economic ladder, turning wages into landownership. Bank managers declared that the deposits were "irrefutable evidence of the colored man's ability and intention not only to care for himself, but also to provide for the necessities of the future."[96] The average account was less than $50, and parents opened accounts for their children of just a few pennies.[97] Recently freed slaves, entire regiments of army veterans, black mutual aid societies, black churches, and some black entrepreneurs all opened accounts.

Because the bank appeared to be a benevolent gift from President Lincoln, was connected to the federal government, and was run by the country's most prominent citizens—but also because the bank promised safekeeping and growing wealth—the freed slaves trusted the bank and deposited their money.[98] It was a façade. Most of the philanthropists who accepted their nominations immediately distanced themselves from the bank's management, leaving a small minority of the acting trustees in control.[99]

The bank started its operations as a simple savings bank, and in 1865, the first year of operation, the bank opened eleven branches across the Southeast. The headquarters were on Wall Street, but from 1865 to 1867, the deposits sat idle in the bank and paid very little interest.[100] The trustees decided to move its headquarters from New York City to an affluent neighborhood in Washington, DC, in 1867. The personnel turned over with the move. Alvord asked Henry Cooke to become the new finance chairman because of the prestige of his brother, Jay Cooke's investment bank, the First National Bank in Washington. Henry did not have Jay's business talent, but knew more about banking than Alvord and the other reformers. Jay Cooke was a friend of Treasury Secretary Salmon Chase and had made a fortune selling war bonds, but Henry was a careless spendthrift.

The change from safe banking to speculation was slow and imperceptible, and most of the depositors and trustees were never aware that the bank had changed. But slowly and surely, the piggy bank was raided. Flush with depositor funds, the bank quickly became a large private investment bank. Henry began to hold meetings at First National Bank and the Freedmen's Bank deposits were used to finance First National Bank's speculation.[101]

The whole point of banking is to collect money and to put it into productive use through lending. Yet the Freedmen's Bank was purposefully set up as a savings bank, a teaching institution, rooted in a paternalistic and condescending mission of instructing blacks in the ways of thrift and capitalism. But the bank left out the most important part of capitalism—the part where capital is able to grow and multiply through credit. By not lending to depositors, the Freedmen's Bank was counterfeit capitalism from its inception. It created a stagnant pool of money instead of a turbine like the one Alexander Hamilton had described. So much capital sitting idle was too much of a temptation for any banker to resist—especially one with loose morals and a speculative venture in need of funds like Henry Cooke.

The bank changed from a savings bank into a highly leveraged investment bank. In fact, Henry Cooke was using the funds to invest in the riskiest of all investments—railroad finance. As war bonds were no longer profitable, Jay Cooke turned toward financing the railroad, and in 1869 the Cookes used the Freedmen's Bank's deposits to bet on the railroads' westward expansion. Without their knowledge or consent, the freedmen's deposits were being used to finance what was essentially the first postwar asset bubble. Meanwhile, the well-meaning Freedmen's Bureau and bank officials were providing "financial education" to freedman on the importance of thrift and of avoiding all gambling and speculation. Indeed, John Alvord, who was by all accounts clueless about Cooke's speculation, chided freedmen for wasting money on lottery tickets and warned them of the terrible habit of gambling with their money.[102]

So successful were the returns on speculation after 1867 that the bank initiated a propaganda campaign to draw out more deposits. In 1868 the bank published its own monthly newspaper called the *National Savings Bank*, which it circulated to the freedmen. The advertisements were all about land—the man who saved "would buy his piece of land and become a thriving farmer!" "Let every man strive to become the owner of land—ever so small a tract even." The bank promised that land would mean "being your own master" and providing for your family.[103] The advertisements also promised that "There is no speculation" and "no risk in this Bank"[104]

By 1871, the bank was operating thirty-five branches, spanning the entire Southeast.[105] Thirty-two of the branches were in southern states, though the biggest branches and the bank's management were in New York and Washington.[106] Henry Cooke used reserve funds to purchase the extravagant Washington, DC, building, which cost the bank $260,000, about $4.5 million today.[107] The magnificence of the newly constructed headquarters was enough to convince even the most cautious depositors of the bank's stability and its managers' acumen. The building sat on the corner of Pennsylvania Avenue and Madison Place, and its graceful adornments were meant to reflect the future prosperity of the race.[108]

Though there was no federal oversight of banks during this time, with such supervision left to state banking regulators, this bank was chartered by Congress, and was officially under its auspices. But Congress was not a bank regulator, so it left the bank alone. The bank's managers lobbied Congress to amend and deregulate its charter, which it did on May 6, 1870. Alvord, still believing that the bank was being run in the interests of freedmen, joined Henry Cooke in asking Congress to deregulate the bank so that they could use the money to buy more railroad bonds. Sumner, also unaware of what this meant, backed the charter revision and Congress granted the change without much protest. There was one voice of dissent—Lincoln's former secretary of war Simon Cameron. Though he was "an especially corrupt politician in an era of stiff competition," according to Jonathan Levy, he had a significant background in banking and knew what Cooke was up to. He objected to the charter amendment on the grounds that it was immoral to speculate with the savings of freedmen.[109] The charter revision passed and the Freedmen's Bank turned into an investment bank.

This amendment lifted the original restrictions on permissible investments and authorized the trustees to invest deposits "to the extent of one-half in bonds or notes, secured by mortgage[s] on real estate in double the value of the loan."[110] Even with the expanded charter, there was no enforcement of this rule, and bank cashiers did a notoriously poor job organizing and maintaining the bank's books.[111] The bank managers began speculating in real estate and then, quite simply, a close ring of managers with unfettered discretion plundered the savings of the freedmen.[112] There were no black managers in this inner circle (even though virtually all of the bank's depositors were black), though the bank's management did use black tellers as a front in certain speculations. For example, a black cashier named Daddy Wilson was used often by the white management as a figurehead and a buffer in some of their speculative lending schemes.[113]

Soon the self-dealing and fraud became endemic.[114] Bank managers formed a "Washington Cabal," later dubbed "the Freedmen's

Bureau ring," who used their connection to the bank to extract favorable loans.[115] By 1871, "there was hardly an officer . . . who was not connected with some outside interest that borrowed from the bank."[116] As one white observer explained, the white managers, entrusted with guarding the meager savings of the freed slaves, "looted the bank."[117]

First National Bank even moved the worst of its liabilities onto the Freedmen's Bank's books and used the bank's deposits to purchase worthless paper. Jay Cooke was using the Freedmen's Bank's deposits to finance a losing venture. As the railroad's losses mounted, Cooke & Co. bled the freedmen for more deposits through increased advertisements. Again, they used land as bait.[118]

These vulnerabilities evaded detection by bank trustees, either because they were ignorant of the bank's actual condition or because they did not care about its fate.[119] The scheme began to unravel following the Panic of 1873, when railroad investments failed. The bank experienced several runs at the height of the panic. The panic would not have affected the bank if it had been a savings bank. But by 1866, the business of the bank had become, according to one observer, "reckless speculation, overcapitalization, stock manipulation, intrigue and bribery, and downright plundering."[120] Cooke's speculation on his brother's venture led to a loss of $2 million in deposits in eighteen months.[121]

In a last-ditch effort to save the bank, the trustees appointed Frederick Douglass as bank president in March of 1874. Douglass did not ask to be nominated, and the bank board knew that Douglass had no experience in banking, but they felt that his reputation and popularity would restore confidence to fleeing depositors.[122] Once in office, Douglass set out to determine the bank's viability.[123] Based solely on the bank's books and representations from managers, the bank appeared to be well situated to survive the panic. This perceived stability motivated Douglass to lend the bank $10,000 of his own money to cover the bank's illiquid assets.[124] Rather than validating his confidence, however, this loan tipped Douglass off that something was awry. Douglass quickly discovered that the bank was "full of dead men's bones, rottenness, and corruption."[125]

As soon as Douglass realized that the bank was headed toward certain failure, he imposed drastic spending cuts to limit depositors' losses. He then relayed this information to Congress, underscoring the bank's insolvency and declaring that he "could no longer ask [his] people to deposit their money in it."[126] Despite the other trustees' attempts to convince Congress otherwise, Congress sided with Douglass, and on June 20, 1874, Congress amended the charter to authorize the trustees to end operations. Within a few weeks' time, the bank's doors were shut for good on June 29, 1874, leaving 61,131 depositors without access to nearly $3 million in deposits.[127] More than half of accumulated black wealth disappeared through the mismanagement of the Freedmen's Savings Bank.[128]

"And what is most lamentable," noted prominent banker Arnett Lindsay decades later, "is the fact that only a few of those who embezzled and defrauded the one time liquid assets of this bank were ever prosecuted."[129] It proved difficult to secure any convictions for wrongdoing in court. Congress did appoint a commission, led by John A. J. Creswell, to look into the failure and to attempt to recover as much of the deposits as possible. In 1880, Henry Cooke testified about the bank's failure and said that the bank's depositors were "victims of a widespread, universal, sweeping financial disaster."[130] In other words, it was the market's fault, not his.

The misdeeds of the bank's management never came to light. Perhaps "because the bank was identified with the endeavors of the newly-freed Negro," wrote historians Kinzer and Sagarin, "anyone who dared to raise a cry against the mismanagement was charged with being anti-Negro; inasmuch as the enemies of the Negro were not interested in the bank, and the friends were effectively silenced with the anti-Negro charge, there was no exposure of the condition of the bank."[131] The belief that the failures of black institutions could not be accurately studied because of the sensitivity of "the race issue," whether accurate or not, would be a recurring theme through history.

Because the bank had represented much more than just a place to store money, its failure cost the black population more than just their deposits. It cost them trust in the federal government, which ultimately bore responsibility for the bank's misdeeds.[132] Many blacks were convinced that they had been "deliberately swindled by the United States government."[133]

Not only did blacks lose confidence in the United States government; they lost faith in banks in general. A prominent black banker in the 1920s said of the Freedmen's Bank, "this attempt at a bank had been so monstrous and so widespread that few, if any, private groups attempted an organization from 1864 to 1874. More than a decade passed after the closing of this bank before confidence was even partly restored."[134] For many black leaders, the trauma lasted much longer. The bank caused financial ruin for many blacks who had been diligently saving their money to purchase a home, and those that were not ruined internalized a warning about banking. In summarizing a report on the state of black banking in the United States fifty years after the failure, Arnett Lindsay wrote that one conclusion he drew from the history of black efforts at banking was that "the so-called governmental aid which was given in establishing the Freedmen's Bank proved to be an almost insurmountable obstacle for the Negroes who later attempted to organize banks of their own."[135] This is because a solid banking system is built on trust and the rule of law, and the Freedmen's Bank violated both of those pillars. In fact, even into the 1970s, commenters acknowledged that the black banking industry had yet to shake "the unfortunate image" created by this colossal failure.[136]

W. E. B. Du Bois went so far as to claim that that "not even ten additional years of slavery could have done so much to throttle the thrift of the freedmen as the mismanagement and bankruptcy of the series of savings banks chartered by the Nation for their special aid."[137] If the government and the philanthropists' purpose was to teach the freed slaves thrift and responsibility, the lesson they actually learned was to distrust the government and philanthropists.

Though the bank's failure sowed distrust of banking, some black leaders also claimed that the bank planted the seeds for a century of obsession with establishing successful black banking. Although few blacks were part of the management of the bank, many had become employed as clerks, tellers, and bookkeepers in the bank's many branches. Economist Abram Harris claims that this training "built up a nucleus of business talent which in less than a decade and a half after the failure of the Freedmen's Bank asserted its leadership in the organization of fraternal insurance societies and banks owned and managed by Negroes."[138] Du Bois noted a different reason the bank led blacks into private banking: "Of all disgraceful swindles perpetrated on a struggling people, the Freedmen's Bank was among the worst, and the Negro did well not to wait for justice, but went to banking himself as soon as his ignorance and poverty allowed."[139] That the bank was the only tangible outcome of the Freedmen's Bureau made banking a focal point of black progress, or, as E. Franklin Frazier put it, it implanted "bourgeois ideals" in the freed slaves. Frazier claimed that the Freedmen's Bank's heavy propaganda campaign sparked the black community's "obsession" with banking. Pamphlets and booklets containing pictures, poems, and stories taught blacks that thrift would lead to wealth.[140]

This was not all. The bank offered the freed slaves a feeling of racial pride and dignity. Years later, Frederick Douglass recounted his overwhelming wonder upon seeing the black bank employees at the Washington office:

> In passing it on the street I often peeped into its spacious windows, and looked down the row of its gentlemanly and elegantly dressed colored clerks, with their pens behind their ears and button-hole bouquets in their coat-fronts, and felt my very eyes enriched. It was a sight I had never expected to see. I was amazed with the facility with which they counted the money. They threw off the thousands with the dexterity, if not the accuracy of old fashioned clerks. The whole thing was beautiful. I had read of this bank when I lived in Rochester, and had indeed been solicited to become one of its trustees, and had reluctantly consented to do so; but when I came to Washington and saw its magnificent brown stone front, its towering height, its perfect appointments and the fine display it made in the transaction of its business, I felt like the Queen of Sheba when she saw the riches of Solomon, that "the half had not been told me."[141]

Indeed, it was a sight that Douglas, born into slavery, must have viewed as a miracle of progress. Douglass remembered one morning when he "found [him]self seated in a comfortable arm chair, with gold spectacles on [his] nose" and heard himself referred to as "President of the Freedmen's Bank." It made him reflect on "the contrast between Frederick the slave boy, running about at [his master's home] with only a tow linen shirt to cover him, and Frederick—President of a bank—counting its assets by [the] millions."[142] For the new bank president and the depositors, the bank held a promise of the independence, respect, and power that was not yet within their grasp.

Such was the allure of counterfeit capitalism—it had such a convincing semblance to the real thing that it was able to conceal the fact that blacks were still being consumed by capitalism as opposed to fully participating in capital production. The reality of Reconstruction was that the southern plantation economy still exploited black labor, and through the Freedmen's Bank, the northern capitalist economy also exploited black capital. The bank was an effective decoy, but blacks were not in control of their economic destiny.

The credit arrangements of the South also had the veneer of self-determination and freedom, but this turned out to be yet another form of bondage. Without wealth or land, the majority of black southerners turned toward sharecropping arrangement to make a living.[143] Legally, the sharecroppers were freedmen and the white plantation owners were their landlords; in reality, the arrangement was fraught with many of the tensions and inequalities of their former relationship. "The strong economic chain between master and slave had not been broken by the stroke of Lincoln's pen," said an observer at the turn of the century.[144] Physical bondage was replaced by debt bondage.

Sharecroppers paid for the land, supplies, and tools using credit, and they paid back their debts with their crop yields, typically with nothing left to spare. Usually the landlord did the calculations himself, and the illiterate debtor would have to trust that he had made no surplus year after year.[145] Each plantation became its own system of banking and debt collection as blacks lost access to the democratically accountable justice systems of the state. Moses Burge, whose father was a sharecropper in Georgia, explained, "We went barefooted. My feet been frostbitten lots of times. My dad couldn't afford to buy no shoes. He'd get in debt and he'd figure every year he going to get out . . . [then] they'd tell you, 'You bought so and so.'

They get through figuring it up you lacking $100 of coming clear. What the hell could you do? You living on his place, you couldn't walk off."[146] Nor could he dispute the debt for fear of violence or worse.

W. E. B. Du Bois, who conducted extensive interviews and data collection on sharecropping arrangements, called it "a system of peonage that kept [blacks] in debt virtually from cradle to grave."[147] Sharecroppers paid exorbitant interest for their supplies, and all "wages" or "payments" were in the form of "store credit" to be redeemed at the local store, where money rarely changed hands and account keeping was loose. These merchants were "a curious institution,—part banker, part landlord" or "part banker, and part despot."[148] Even black landowners were at the mercy of their creditors, on whom they relied for their supplies. Any unwelcomed behavior, like voting Republican or speaking out in any way, could imperil one's access to a loan.[149]

High debt made sharecroppers plant more cotton, which was the only crop they could sell for money to pay down their debt, which meant that they had less land and resources to grow crops that could feed their families. The cotton traders could not have been happier with the outcome.[150] Not only did the United States retain its position as the world's top cotton exporter, but the new system produced even more cotton than before the war.[151] But for sharecroppers, the credit cycle ensured both perpetual debt and perpetual poverty and a singular focus on cotton production.[152] To be sure, white yeomen farmers were also sucked into the cotton / debt cycle.

The hardships caused by cotton and debt almost erupted into a revolution during the depression of the 1880s and 1890s. The downturn stirred the simmering angst relentless debt had created and almost upset the hard-won economic and social ordering of the South once again. Indeed, for a moment, a window opened where it seemed possible that poor whites and blacks would join together to overthrow the cotton oligarchy. Southern historian William Garrott Brown called the upheaval a "revolution," explaining, "I would use a stronger term if there were one; for no other political movement—not that of 1776, nor that of 1860–1861—ever altered Southern life so profoundly."[153]

The southern Populists led the political revolution. They railed against credit shortages, debt peonage, and powerful northern bankers and industrialists whose tight monetary policies they blamed for the South's poverty. They demanded looser credit through expansion of the money supply. Specifically, they rejected the gold standard, which they believed favored Northeast bankers and constricted credit flow to the farmers of the South and West. Williams Jennings Bryan most famously articulated their cause in 1896, telling bankers that they could not crucify humanity, or southern farmers, on their "cross of gold."[154] A variety of populist coalitions including the Grangers, the Farmers Alliance, the Knights of Labor, the free silverites, and greenbackers demanded silver currency, labor reform, breaking up of banking monopolies—in short, an end to their debt trap.[155] On a smaller scale, these groups joined together to form small cooperative banks like credit unions and building and loans. These "people's banks" sought to counter the power of big Wall Street and London banks with local control by small farmers. In the American South and West, populism was about credit, or the lack thereof.[156]

Poor black and white farmers were natural allies in this fight, and the Populist Party in the South attempted to forge this alliance. "They are in the ditch just like we are," said a Texas Populist leader.[157] Thomas Watson, leader of the southern Populist Party, explained that white supremacy was a deception that blinded the poor and pitted them against each other in order to perpetuate "a monetary system which beggars you both." The Populists urged "color tenants" to stand with white tenants and promised that the People's Party would "wipe out the color line and put every man on his citizenship irrespective of color."[158] The Populists went further than all the other parties, including the Republican Party, with respect to racial equality. "I am in favor of giving the colored man full representation," said the president of the Populist convention in Texas. "He is a citizen just as much as we are, and the party that acts on that fact will gain the colored vote of the south."[159] In the 1890s the Knights of Labor attempted to build the first biracial populist organization, claiming that 15 percent of their 600,000 members were black.[160] Frederick Douglass had suggested just such an alliance between yeomen and freedmen in 1866—"a party . . . among the poor."[161]

Just as the Reconstruction reformers had failed to break the cotton oligarchy and achieve black equality, so too did the Populists. They failed because the established political parties of the North and South had already understood that sowing animosity between poor whites and poor blacks was the easiest way to maintain the status quo and to reject the costly and disruptive demands of a coalition of the poor. In the end, a racial hierarchy was preferable to class revolt. Once again, the revolution was stifled by violence. Public lynching, cross burnings, and the Klan vented rage and resentment at the black underclass. The war-ravaged and economically depressed South created a breeding ground ripe for racial hostility. If aggression is the result of frustration, said historian C. Vann Woodward, "then the South toward the end of the [1890s] was the perfect cultural seedbed for aggression against the minority race. Economic, political, and social frustrations had pyramided to a climax of social tensions."[162]

Southern planters and northern industrialists joined forces in maintaining a racial hierarchy that benefited both by preserving the status quo. Northern liberals left the divisive "Negro issue" alone and even enabled the South's racial hierarchy for the sake of peace and unity. The most powerful and effective formula for "redeeming the South" was the "magical formula of white supremacy," which the South used unapologetically.[163] Judges, politicians, and newspapers all obliged—preferring to save the union that survived the Civil War by sacrificing the rights of blacks. It became common during the 1890s to hear northern liberals profess the strength of the union and accept the South's need to keep black labor under the fist of the state.[164]

In order to maintain absolute control of the levers of state power and enforce a permanent racial hierarchy, southerners worked tirelessly to keep blacks from the polls. Having to contend with the Fifteenth Amendment, innovative southern politicians created literacy tests, property ownership requirements, and poll taxes, making sure to create loopholes for poor whites through "grandfathering" clauses.[165] Disenfranchisement was swift and total. Slowly and then suddenly, all the rights written into the Thirteenth, Fourteenth, and Fifteenth Amendments were nullified by southern legislatures, courts, and the paramilitary-style violence of the Klan.[166]

Economic and political necessity required the continued exploitation and disenfranchisement of blacks. Although white supremacy accrued justifications based on religious texts, or on moral and ethical grounds, its true intent was economic subjugation.[167] As Hannah Arendt observed, "the tremendous power of persuasion inherent in [the ideology of race thinking] is not accidental. Persuasion is not possible without appeal to either experiences or desires, in other words to immediate political needs." She called race thinking a "political weapon," and so it was in the South.[168]

The inhuman institution of slavery required the dehumanization of black slaves, and so too did the South's post-Reconstruction economy. U.S. congressman David A. DeArmond of Missouri described blacks as "almost too ignorant to eat, scarcely wise enough to breathe, mere existing human machines."[169] Senator James K. Vardaman of Mississippi, justifying the disenfranchisement of the black vote, explained, "I am just as much opposed to Booker Washington as a voter, with all his Anglo-Saxon re-enforcements, as I am to the coconut-headed, chocolate-colored, typical little coon, Andy Dotson, who blacks my shoes every morning. Neither is fit to exercise the supreme function of citizenship."[170] Senator Benjamin Tillman of South Carolina bragged in a public lecture that he did not know how many black men he had killed himself, and even advocated the extermination of the 30,000 blacks in his state.[171]

The South was not alone in enforcing the racial and economic order. The U.S. Supreme Court also fell in line, though instead of inflammatory language, they used sophisticated constitutional interpretation to deprive blacks of their rights. In 1883, the Supreme Court declared the Civil Rights Act of 1875—a law that would have fined businesses for racial discrimination—unconstitutional. The Court held that the law was an infringement on freedom and was unnecessary since slavery had already been over for twenty years. It was time for blacks to stand on their own two feet without the help of the state. Justice Joseph Bradley wrote in the majority opinion, "When a man has emerged from slavery, and, by the aid of beneficent legislation, has shaken off the inseparable concomitants of that state, there must be some stage in the progress of his elevation when he takes the rank of a mere citizen and ceases to be *the special favorite of the laws*, and when his rights as a citizen or a man are to be protected in the ordinary modes by which other men's rights are protected."[172] Since 2,000 blacks would be lynched over the next several years for alleged crimes without any due process, it was premature to declare that their rights were being protected by ordinary modes of justice.[173]

In a series of decisions between 1873 and 1898, including the *Slaughterhouse Cases, United States v. Reese,* and *United States v.*

Cruikshank, the Supreme Court weakened the rights of black citizens and their ability to contest racism. The Supreme Court was not just reconciling the North and the South, but navigating federal and state tensions that had simmered to a boiling point during the Civil War. Each of these cases gave states power over the treatment of their citizens and weakened federal oversight. In two 1890 cases, *Louisville, New Orleans, and Texas Railroad v. Mississippi,* the Court ruled that states were permitted to segregate their carriers.[174] In *Williams v. Mississippi,* the Court cleared the way for southern states to disenfranchise black voters. And then in 1896, *Plessy v. Ferguson* dealt the most devastating and long-lasting blow by blessing the doctrine of "separate but equal," which legitimatized Jim Crow laws and segregation for half a century.[175] By the time the Supreme Court was finished, the Equal Protection Clause of the Fourteenth Amendment was deprived of all meaning. In fact, for the next century, it came up more to defend corporations against state overreach than it did black men and women against the hostile arm of the state. These cases moved the law toward protection of property as the primary objective as opposed to protection of blacks from violence.[176] According to one historian, by 1900, "the slave law of the South may have been dead, but it ruled us from its grave."[177]

Jim Crow laws, virtually absent during Reconstruction, now proliferated and governed all social interaction between the races. Doors and walls were painted with "white only" signs and different entrances were created at public venues, worksites, and common spaces. A typical code was the South Carolina law that prohibited textile workers from working in the same room or using the same entrances, exits, pay windows, doorways, stairways, or windows at the same time as black workers. White bathrooms, drinking fountains, glasses, and buckets were not to be used by blacks at any time.[178] These laws, both written and unwritten, effectively cut blacks out of public life. Jim Crow was the dead and heavy hand of slavery pushing down a new generation of blacks born free. It was the defining feature of southern life after Reconstruction, and each citizen was implicated in its enforcement.[179]

Once the Supreme Court deprived blacks of their rights to due process, southern courts and police became tools of oppression and the maintenance of the new social and economic order. The legislatures made Jim Crow the rule of law, police enforced it, and courts punished violators. Blacks lived in a police state in the South with the tacit approval of the Supreme Court.[180] Added to that were the constant, random, and vicious acts of terrorism—the "Southern trees that began to bear strange fruit, Blood on the leaves and blood at the root."[181] All of which was condoned, enforced, and perpetuated by state power.

Capitalism without Capital

Because race was used as a political weapon to marginalize and exploit blacks, race also created a vibrant community. As modern writer Ta-Nehisi Coates put it, "They made us into a race. We made ourselves into a people."[1] Blocked from the political process by law and violence, black communities formed their own institutions. There were charities to care for the poor and insurance funds to protect against risk. There were fraternal societies for social and cultural events and travel agencies that facilitated excursions to celebrate a variety of black holidays and celebrations such as Juneteeth and Freedom Day. All of these institutions were created because Jim Crow pushed blacks out of white society, but they all became focal points of racial pride and solidarity.[2]

Post-Reconstruction, the first wave of black institutions were mutual aid societies or fraternal societies, which provided a variety of essential services. Churches were usually the central pillars that hosted an array of ancillary social and economic institutions.[3] By the turn of the century, practically every black church was linked with at least one or more "benevolent societies." In the 1880s, churches began creating insurance-like funds, but their administration was unsophisticated. They were not based on actuarial models that took account of risk probabilities. They often took on people who were sick and elderly and did not charge enough in premiums to stay solvent. These early insurance funds looked more like charities than businesses, and most quickly ran out of funds.[4] By the turn of the century, however, these funds separated from the church and became more sophisticated and profitable.[5]

The early black banks grew to support these insurance funds and the other functions of the mutual aid society. They were usually structured as savings banks, used primarily to safeguard the church's or the society's accounts. However, there were a few that were more ambitious and began to engage in fairly limited commercial lending. The most advanced black financial organizations after the Civil War were in the former capital of the Confederacy: Richmond, Virginia.

The Grand United Order of True Reformers was the first organization to offer a formal insurance policy. In 1888, the True Reformers Bank became the first of the fraternal banks to obtain a formal state banking charter.[6]

The founding of the True Reformers Bank exemplifies the climate in which these institutions were founded and the problems they were created to address. The bank founders explained that before their bank, when the mutual aid society had a large sum of money collected from new members, it was usually deposited with a white storeowner. But this shopkeeper could not be trusted and was reportedly "envious, bitter, and jealous of the progress made by the Negroes of this town." When a white mob lynched a black man, this shopkeeper "informed the white people of the large amount of money entrusted to his care and of the danger of allowing Negroes to organize in that community." The Order decided they needed to create their own bank, stating, "If we had a bank of our own, the white people would not have any information about our activities."[7]

All of the Order's funds were deposited in its bank, and it operated conservatively. Five years after its founding, it was among only a few banks in Richmond able to pay out each of its depositors during the Panic of 1893, a feat that was celebrated across the black community as a source of pride. A black commentator wrote of the bank's survival: "Amid the crash of banks, the hush of manufacturers' hammers, their wheels, cogs, and belts, your Savings Bank moves gloriously on, while none dare molest her or make her afraid. She has paid every check presented to her, while others have dropped their heads, drooped their wings and failed, having their very life choked out of them." The *Richmond Times* confirmed the bank's success through the panic: "The Savings Bank, Grand Fountain of True Reformers, the only colored banking institution in this city, has made a record during the recent financial difficulties. It is the only bank which honored all checks and did not stop paying full value in the currency." For this and its longevity, the bank was dubbed the "Gibraltar of Negro Business."[8]

Still, not even the Gibraltar could survive an expansion into full-scale commercial lending. After the 1893 panic, the bank began offering loans to community leaders and to finance the Order's own ventures, which included real estate, a home for the elderly, a chain of grocery stores, and other commercial ventures. After several of these businesses suffered heavy losses, the bank folded in 1910.[9]

There were certain advantages to these "affiliated banks," or banks that worked in support of a church or fraternal society. These banks had a steady and reliable source of deposits coming from the monthly fees members paid to the societies. This relationship and the conservative use of these deposits made these banks the most durable of the black banks during a turbulent era for banking. However, these banks also faced specific challenges. When they began to offer loans, there was often a dangerous conflict of interest. Successful banking relies on good underwriting, or the ability to choose between a profitable loan and a losing loan or a creditworthy borrower and one who is likely to default. This is not an exact science, and banks are often famously wrong, but this sorting of borrowers is a bedrock of sound banking. Because these affiliated banks were created to serve the needs of a society, church, or community, they often made loan decisions based on factors having less to do with good underwriting and more to do with community need or pressure from well-intentioned leaders or clergy, who were often unaware of bank operations. Because these banks were usually part of a religious organization, their operations were also infused with religious meaning, which complicated their lending decisions.

Customers of these banks expected to receive services and terms, according to one black banker, "on the basis of friendship rather than according to strict up-to-date [business] methods." In describing the failure of the Wage Earners Savings Bank, established in 1900 in Savannah, Georgia, black banker Arnett Lindsay observed that the bank's "failure was quickened . . . by the inability of the bank to collect many of the commercial loans which were not made on the sound financial condition of businesses requesting credit but on friendship." Lindsay added that "a large number of Negro business enterprises have been developed because they have had the support of churches and lodges," so that patrons of these organizations would often expect special treatment "because of their long connections with fraternal and religious establishments." And banks that did not provide favorable treatment to members of an affiliated group would "lose their support and invite their antagonism."[10]

The affiliation between the black bank and the black church was therefore a double-edged sword, bolstering support for the banks but raising expectations that these institutions would treat clients as "friends" and not as customers, or, even more unsettlingly, as "debtors." This conflict was not limited to affiliated banks. Black bankers often complained that black customers expected black banks to give them more favorable deposit rates or lending terms than white institutions offered.[11] The touchy relationship between these banks and the communities they served was inevitable given the paradoxical pursuit of these banks. These banks represented uplift and progress, but they were businesses, which meant that there would always be a conflict between the black banker's dual roles as lender and community leader.

The other noteworthy fraternal society bank was Maggie Walker's bank. Walker was the first black woman to own a bank and the second woman of any race to do so in the United States.[12] She was born in 1864 in Richmond, Virginia. Her mother was a former slave and her biological father was an Irish Confederate soldier. Maggie and her mother lived in abject poverty after Maggie's stepfather was murdered when she was young. Her mother made a living by washing laundry for the area's wealthy whites. Maggie was a brilliant student, and after she finished high school at age nineteen, she became a teacher, but was forced to quit when she married (it was illegal for married women to teach).[13]

Maggie Walker was a member of the Order of St. Luke's mutual aid society, which was in jeopardy due to a dwindling membership. She quickly got to work and turned the dying organization into a thriving one. Based on the needs she observed in her community, she established a newspaper, a printing press, an insurance company, and a college education fund. In 1903, she started St. Luke Penny Savings Bank with $9,400 collected from small deposits of the group members.[14] She organized the bank as a cooperative and sold shares to the Order's members, who became joint owners. She convinced the Order's members that a savings bank could take their "hard-earned nickels and turn them into dollars." She created little cardboard banks for the kids who came into her bank with their mothers and taught them how to save their money. Walker believed that these savings accounts would help her kin achieve self-sufficiency and equality.

By running a safe bank, Walker was working for her community, race, and gender. "God knows I love this race of mine, especially the women. . . ." She dedicated the bank to helping black women achieve financial independence.[15] "The great all absorbing interest, the thing which has driven sleep from my eyes and fatigue from my body, is the love I bear women, our Negro women, hemmed in, circumscribed with every imaginable obstacle in our way, blocked and held down by the fears and prejudices of the whites—ridiculed and sneered at by the intelligent blacks."[16] But Walker was not just an idealist—she was one of the most successful black bankers of her time. Her notoriety as a female bank executive only grew when she became the first black banker to be extended membership in the Virginia Bankers Association. She accepted the invitation and remarked, "I shall hope to conduct myself so as to reflect credit upon my race and people."[17] The governor of Virginia said of Walker in 1924, "If the State of Virginia had done no more, in fifty years, with the funds spent on the education of the Negroes than to educate Mrs. Walker, the State would have been amply repaid for its outlays and efforts."[18]

By 1920, the bank had reportedly helped its customers buy 600 homes, a remarkable feat during a time when mortgage loans were rare.[19] During the Great Depression, Walker managed a merger that consolidated her bank with two other black-owned banks, saving all the banks in the process. Walker was appointed chairman of the board in 1931, but she died a few years later in 1934 at the age of seventy of diabetic gangrene. Maggie Walker's bank endured the Great Depression and two world wars, but it could not survive the 2008 financial crisis.[20]

There was another cohort of black-owned banks formed between 1888 and 1900 that were not directly linked to fraternal societies or churches. Some of these pioneering private black banks, about thirty in total, attempted full-scale commercial lending, but most were short-lived and unsuccessful. "Pioneers under such conditions often become martyrs," said one black businessman. Many of these banks fell, just like their white counterparts, under the stress of the Panic of 1893. The first private black-owned bank was the Capitol Savings Bank, which was organized in October 17, 1888, by a group of prominent black community members in Washington, DC.[21] The former headquarters of the Freedmen's Bank, dubbed "the mecca of Negro finance and education," was a fitting home to the first black commercial bank. The bank survived the 1893 panic, but failed quickly after severe loan losses in 1904.[22] This period marked the most turbulent time for the nation's banks, both white and black. Many banks lived short and rocky lives and bank failure was the norm, with almost yearly bank panics between 1880 and the culminating banking catastrophe of the Great Depression. The average lifespan of a bank during this era was about five years.[23]

In 1890, the Alabama Penny Savings and Loan Company was organized in Birmingham, Alabama.[24] The bank was founded by a schoolteacher and a Baptist clergyman with the help of ten thousand community members who deposited over $200,000 into the bank. The bank thrived in Birmingham as a commercial bank. Booker T. Washington visited the bank in 1900 and congratulated it for "the excellent and far reaching work that has been done in Birmingham and vicinity."[25] To Washington, this bank was an exemplar for the entire race. "Few organizations of any description in this country among our people have helped us more, not only in cultivating the habit of saving, but in bringing to us the confidence and respect of the white race."[26] Washington believed wholeheartedly in black banking and said that it was black savers who would be "the ones who are going to control the destinies of the country."[27] The bank lent money to Birmingham's black churches and professionals. In 1913, the bank helped construct a six-story church building called the Pythian Temple, using the black-owned company Windham Construction. But in 1915, the overextended Penny Savings bank failed due to a run.

If their affiliations within the black community were a source of weakness for these banks, so was their lack of association with any of the white banks in the area. To survive a run, a bank can either find liquidity from another bank or sell off its loans to another bank in a "fire sale" so that it can meet depositor demands and live to open its doors another day. Both of these solutions proved very difficult in a Jim Crow economy, as seen in the case of the Penny Bank's failure. The bank first sought liquidity help through a short-term loan from a local bank, the Steiner Brothers, but that larger bank chose instead to help another struggling white bank, the First National Bank.[28] This could have been due to racism or to the Penny Bank's weaker loan portfolio, possibly both. Safe banking would have required affiliations across racial lines, which proved difficult in the Jim Crow South. The segregated economy also prevented the other route to survival—selling off bank assets. Because their assets were long-term loans to black churches and based on black real estate, they were considered risky, and other banks were not willing to buy them. These loans were essentially "frozen" on their balance sheets and could not be sold in an emergency. This would be a recurring theme for black banking before the Great Depression and was a direct result of Jim Crow banking.

When the bank closed, one of the bank's founders, N. B. Young Sr., observed, "It was an honest effort to establish a bank in the very heart of the South."[29] All its depositors lost their savings when the bank failed. One such depositor was A. G. Gaston, who would go on to open his own savings and loan in Alabama in 1957—the only black-owned bank in Birmingham after the Penny Bank's failure.[30] The shock and devastation of the 1915 failure was still alive in the community half a century later, and Gaston had to assure the community that their deposits were safe in his bank. For black communities living on so little, the loss of their savings was surely a devastating financial setback. To lose your money at the hands of a black institution that was an integral part of your core community created a stark dilemma for depositors and the bankers responsible for safeguarding their life savings.

Hemmed in by the walls of Jim Crow, black communities had to create their own financial institutions, but the injustice of segregation that created these banks also made them weak. In other words, the same forces of racism and segregation that created black banks would continually work against their success. James Baldwin explained the dilemma with regard to black leadership, which he defined as a "nicely refined torture [of] having been created and defeated by the same circumstances." Baldwin explained that black leaders were created by "the American scene, which thereafter works against them at every point; and the best that they can hope for is ultimately to work themselves out of their jobs."[31]

Yet several leaders emerged with national influence and far-reaching visions about how blacks would overcome their circumstance. The prominent black leaders of the early twentieth century, Booker T. Washington and W. E. B. Du Bois, urged contrasting paths toward progress, with Washington focusing on building a segregated black community and Du Bois demanding full integration and equal rights. Washington and Du Bois, however, were surprisingly in sync in their support for black banking as a critical feature of the economic road map through and out of a milieu of adverse conditions.

Washington, a conservative southerner who had been born into slavery, was labeled "the great accommodator" because he accepted segregation and black political disenfranchisement and stressed the significance of industrial education.[32] Washington gained national prominence after his 1895 Atlanta speech, later dubbed "The Atlanta Compromise," in which he seemingly endorsed segregation, telling a majority-white audience that "in all things that are purely social we can be as separate as the fingers, yet one as the hand in all things essential to mutual progress."[33] Though Washington's most controversial stances were his political capitulation, or perhaps "capture" by the white elite, his forceful advocacy of black business has been less controversial. Black nationalists and radicals during the civil rights era adopted his stance toward a segregated economy even while denouncing him as an Uncle Tom.[34] Washington believed black business was a means of achieving prosperity from the ground up.[35] He promised that if they cultivated "industry, thrift, intelligence and property," blacks would eventually be accepted by white society.[36]

Washington's program of building a segregated black business economy was exactly the agenda favored by the white Republican political establishment and northern industrialists. Washington's critics even accused him of being a leader *created by* white industrialists because he delivered them a subdued population of industrious laborers whom they could continue to exploit for profit.[37] All Washington asked of whites was philanthropic support of his non-profit educational institutions, and they delivered. Andrew Carnegie contributed $2,700 yearly to finance Washington's institutions and organizations, calling him the "combined Moses and Jehovah of his people" because he promoted "good moral character and industrial efficiency, resulting in ownership of property." He also liked the fact that Washington was pursuing the "wise policy" of not pushing for "the free and unrestricted vote immediately."[38] One white booster admitted as much, praising Washington's conciliatory agenda because he believed Washington "shall not threaten the Anglo-American supremacy."[39]

It wasn't just his submissive stance that appealed to wealthy capitalists like Carnegie and Rockefeller, but also his complete faith in their "gospel of prosperity," which held that free-market capitalism, property ownership, and bootstrap entrepreneurship was the one and only path toward equality, prosperity, and personal virtue. Washington believed that this gospel espoused by white capitalists would apply equally to black entrepreneurs; that despite segregation, discrimination, and trade restrictions, blacks had equal access to the free market and could build wealth through hard work. He also believed, along with his white capitalist boosters, that once blacks accrued enough wealth through hard work, the wealth itself would eventually defeat Jim Crow. A bank account and ownership of property became articles of faith for black progress.[40]

Washington believed that wealth would bring self-respect ("A man never begins to have self-respect until he owns a home"),[41] respect from whites ("whether he will or not, a white man respects a negro who owns a two-story house"), power ("a black man can get a mortgage on a white man's house that he can foreclose at will"), and even the restoration of the vote, because "a white man on whose house the mortgage rests will not try to prevent that negro from voting when he goes to the polls."[42] Washington believed that if a black man had enough wealth, even Jim Crow would not apply to him. "Do you suppose that, when [a wealthy] black man takes his family aboard the train, they are going to put him in a Jim Crow car and run the risk of losing that $10,000 a year? No, they will put on a Pullman palace car for him."[43] This hope was tragically naïve. Washington did not consider that instead of respect, a white man would resent the black man's $10,000 and the two-story house. And did he suppose that a white man would willingly submit to any black man who threatened foreclosure on his home rather than opt for violence?

Southern white supremacist Thomas Dixon was enraged that Washington would even suggest that blacks should become financially independent. Dixon was angry that Washington was not training "servants," but instead was "training them all to be masters of men, to be independent, to own and operate their own industries, plant their own fields, buy and sell their own goods." This was unacceptable since, to Dixon and the southern ideology he represented, "the Negro remains on this continent for one reason only," and that reason was that "the Southern white man has needed his labor."[44] So it was likely dubious for Washington to claim that blacks with economic power would gain respect, because it was unlikely that Dixon and his Klan would allow any "uppity" black men to gain that power in the first place. Washington was also overly optimistic when he wrote in *Up from Slavery* (1901) of "the great change that has taken place since the days of the 'Ku Klux'" in the South. He predicted that the Klan had died and that "public sentiment" in the South was solidly against it.[45] In fact, the Klan was headed toward a violent resurgence. The peak in Klan membership and activity was yet to come.

Washington was, however, very realistic in his assessment of the South's mood. It is unlikely a more radical or demanding leader would have succeeded, let alone survived, in the South for as long as Washington did. And history has redeemed Washington's dim prospects for full integration—it has yet to happen. However, Washington's unflinching faith in black capitalism may have stood in the way of or diverted other avenues toward reform because it occupied such a central position in the black community. As the black community's most prominent post-Reconstruction leader, Washington set the tone and the agenda for generations of black and white leaders and businessmen. Although Washington's faith-inspiring advocacy for black business may have set a misguided course, more meaningful avenues for reform would have required help from the white power structure, and that help was not forthcoming.

W. E. B. Du Bois, a Harvard Ph.D. born free in the North, had no patience for Washington's moderation; he wanted blacks to fight for integration and full legal rights, without which equality would never be achieved. Du Bois cofounded the National Association for the Advancement of Colored People (NAACP) in 1909 to dismantle Jim Crow and to confront the South's racial violence. Du Bois urged blacks to mobilize and act against their continued oppression, rejecting the idea that southern whites would ever grant blacks equal rights without continued political and legal pressure.[46]

Though Du Bois is remembered as a critic of capitalism, he was an enthusiastic supporter of black business enterprise. He was clear, however, that black business and black wealth were not the panacea against racial inequality that Washington believed them to be. He denounced the black community's belief in "wealth as a remedy for every social ill," advocating instead for black cooperative enterprise with a focus on community building as opposed to profit maximizing.[47] Nevertheless, with no apparent hesitation, Du Bois promoted black enterprise. He was the first black scholar to conduct a comprehensive study of black business. In his seminal 1899 study *The Negro in Business*, Du Bois remarked, "It is hardly possible to place too great stress on the deep significance of business ventures among American Negroes." He remarked that economic emancipation had yet to be achieved for a "Negro then to go into business means a great deal. It is, indeed, a step in social progress worth measuring."[48]

When two black businesses, a bank and a life insurance company, went bankrupt, Du Bois urged readers of *The Crisis* not to lose confidence but to continue to support them. In fact, he urged blacks to patronize only black businesses. He also proposed the idea of a National Negro Business League, which was formally founded by Washington. Du Bois suggested in an Atlanta conference of black leaders in 1899 "the organization in every town and hamlet where colored people dwell . . . [of] Negro Business Men's Leagues."[49]

One could hardly be a leader of the black community and not endorse the only avenue the community had toward self-determination. To do otherwise would be to admit defeat or to ask the black population to suffer until more adequate reforms, such as integration or land grants or a new economic order, made them equal participants in the economy. John Hope, president of Atlanta University, made this point forcefully, stating, "the policy of avoiding entrance in the world's business would be suicide to the Negro."[50] Living in a land of wealth and capitalism, "is it not obvious that we cannot escape its most powerful motive and survive?"[51] The black community had to live their lives, find credit, invest their wages, and make a living. And in the segregated society blacks inhabited, they could not receive credit from a white bank, insurance from a white broker, or purchase a home from a white realtor.[52] Economic theorist Max Weber, in *The Protestant Ethic and the Spirit of Capitalism*, pointed out that when groups face national oppression, they react by organizing entrepreneurial ventures.[53] Blacks certainly did, and their leaders threw their full support behind them.

Black leaders hoped that successful black enterprise would move blacks upward from the lowest rung of the economic ladder. Blacks had thus far only provided labor, which turned into someone else's capital. According to Hope, black business was an attempt to "take in some, if not all, of the wages, turn it into capital, hold it, increase it."[54] But to obtain meaningful capital creation, black businesses had to expand beyond their current state, which Hope described as "pebbles on the shore of business enterprise."[55] The black community needed large and powerful black enterprises to grow viable banks. For "without these factories, railroads and banks," blacks would never be able to fully participate in capitalism.[56] Hope was right. Without large businesses, the black community would not have access to large enough stores of capital to serve as a basis for an economy.

And indeed it did not. The absence of factories, railroads, and black enterprise on a large scale hindered black banks. Black business would remain pebbles on the shore, but there would be many pebbles. Between 1867 and 1917, 4,000 black-owned businesses grew to 50,000.[57] By 1930, the number of black businesses had grown to 70,000.[58] Many businesses arose as a direct response to segregation, producing goods and services for blacks in the self-help economy. Du Bois's survey of almost 2,000 businesses with over $500 in capital found that most had evolved from occupations dictated by slavery.[59] "House servants became barbers, restaurant keepers, and caterers; field hands became gardeners, grocers, florists, and mill owners. Those who had been plantation craftsmen used their talents to become builders and contractors, brick masons, painters, and blacksmiths."[60] These businesses were almost always individually owned; few had corporate charters, and they often died with their founder. This was a weak infrastructure in the black community for the accumulation and generation of capital.

At the turn of the century, black leaders converged on a plan to grow black enterprise that included urging young people in churches and black societies to go into business, creating black business leagues, and harnessing all of the resources of the black community in support of black business.[61] Booker T. Washington founded the National Negro Business League (NNBL) in 1900 to help promote and develop black business.[62] In his inaugural address at the conference, Washington repeated his unverifiable and likely untrue promise that wherever he had "seen a black man who was succeeding in business . . . that individual was treated with the highest respect by members of the white race."[63] Washington continually urged blacks to create more banks to provide financing for black businesses. He celebrated each bank opening and dreamed of a day when the South could support more than forty black banks.[64] The NNBL even proposed its own financing corporation to provide credit to black business, but it was never able to get enough capital together.[65]

The NNBL gained membership over the next five years, with 300 local business leagues organized. In 1907 Washington wrote *The Negro in Business,* as a follow-up to Du Bois's *Negro in Business* written in 1899. Unlike Du Bois's statistically heavy treatise, Washington's book contained a series of inspirational success stories aimed at highlighting the "undoubted business awakening among the Negro people of the United States." One story was of a minister who started a bank, which to Washington demonstrated "how closely the moral and spiritual interests of our people are interwoven with their material and economic welfare."[66]

Not only was black business infused with religious meaning, but religious meetings were also infused with the spirit of black business. Respected black pastors often urged their congregants to support a black bank, support that instilled the institution with the community trust that it needed to operate. Of the Citizens Trust Bank, founded in Atlanta in 1921, a local Reverend remarked, "the preachers made Citizens Trust Bank. They put in deposits that Monday morning. Around 11:00 o'clock the lobby would be full of nothing but preachers. And the people, seeing their preacher deposit God's money from the churches in Citizens Trust, put their money into it and helped to put it over, in a great way."[67]

Washington saw black business itself as a Christian principle. During his 1910 annual address at the NNBL convention, he delivered a "Business Sermon," in which he used the biblical precept "to him that hath shall be given" as an analogy to black business, explaining, "these lines spoken by the Master strike the keynote for individual success and equally for racial success." He wanted the attendees to go out and proselytize the message of the business gospel, claiming that "each individual shall be a missionary in his community—a missionary in teaching the masses to get property, to be more thrifty, more economical, and resolve to establish an industrial enterprise wherever a possibility presents itself."[68] Created out of economic necessity, black businesses became steeped in religious meaning. According to E. Franklin Frazier, "faith in business enterprise was mingled with the Negro's religious faith."[69]

Though Washington painted a rosy picture of black business success, many black businessmen and leaders spoke of the tremendous challenges they faced. The main financial challenge was that black businesses relied exclusively on black clientele. Jim Crow segregation prevented black businesses from branching out to white customers. In *The Negro as a Business Man*, a report compiled in 1929, black historians and business leaders lamented that "German and Irish immigration into this country drove the Negroes even out of menial services in many Northern cities."[70] White riots led by immigrant groups, who saw black businesses as competition, "often broke up Negro businesses which had been prosperous for years."[71] This was not the respect Washington had promised would greet successful black business establishments.[72]

Black businesses had to find customers for whatever they were selling from within their own race, but the prohibitions did not work in reverse. White businesses often sold goods to blacks, which meant that black businesses had to compete not only with other black businesses but with any white businesses serving black customers as well. Prominent insurance executive Merah Stuart explained the bind of black businesses in these terms: "the American Negro has been driven into an awkward, selfish corner, attempting to operate racial business to rear a stepchild economy." Stuart explained that this was an "economic detour" that no other immigrant group had to pass through, as these groups were allowed passage to the "economic Broadway of America." By contrast, blacks, despite "centuries of unrequited toil . . . must turn to a *detour that leads he knows not where*."[73]

The economic detour made it difficult for black businesses to grow and expand or to take advantage of economies of scale, which usually meant that their operation was usually more costly.[74] This presented black customers with a conundrum.[75] Black leaders had each exhorted the black community to patronize only black business because black business survival depended on patronage from the black community. "We must cooperate or we are lost," said John Hope. "The mass of the Negroes must learn to patronize business enterprises conducted by their own race, *even at some slight disadvantage.*"[76] But black customers were indeed suffering a disadvantage by "buying black." They were usually paying more for an inferior product because of the inherent weakness of black businesses operating in the distorted Jim Crow economy. This was the surcharge of collective self-help and racial pride—piling another unfair disadvantage on the heap.

In this "stepchild economy" or "economic detour," it is no wonder that the few black businesses that experienced sustained and profitable growth were providing services for which there was large demand that white businesses were unwilling or incapable of meeting.[77]

The first black entrepreneur in the United States to become a self-made millionaire was Madame C. J. Walker, born Sarah Breedlove in 1867. Walker made her fortune in 1910 selling hair products to black women. Many black women were suffering from severe hair loss because of malnutrition and constant labor. Walker herself suffered from the scalp condition, which led her to create an elixir from sulfur and capsicum that ameliorated the effect. She later labeled the formula "Wonderful Hair Grower" and enlisted a sales force of black women, called Walker Agents, to sell the product to friends and acquaintances in their communities. She expanded her market even further by adding a hot comb and other hair-straightening products, calling the entire process the Walker System. She would sell millions of products to black women who wanted "symmetrical, deep and lasting waves" in their hair.[78]

It is telling that one of the few African Americans who could achieve financial success in the early twentieth century did so by selling a product that gained its value directly from the hardship and racism experienced by blacks. This was not yet a market that white businesses were interested in pursuing. And because segregation facilitated marketing and distribution by making her customer base more geographically concentrated, Madame Walker could grow her business greatly.

Another open marketplace for blacks was for undertakers and funeral homes, a thriving niche created because whites either refused to handle black bodies or treated them differently than white ones.[79] A. G. Gaston, one of the wealthiest black entrepreneurs in the country, made his fortune in the death business.[80] If Booker T. Washington's vision could have lived in human form, it would have been through Gaston. In fact, Gaston said that *Up from Slavery* was his primary source of inspiration—especially the wisdom that acquiring wealth would lead to equality. Gaston began his business career while working in the Alabama coal mines of the Tennessee Coal and Iron Company with convict laborers. He knew that he would die quickly if he remained a miner, so he decided instead to become a small entrepreneur. First, he sold the miners lunches cooked by his mother, and with that small pool of profits, he became a lender. He lent small sums of money to the miners at 25 percent interest. In another financing venture, Gaston bought the state-issued scrip that black teachers were being paid their salaries with in exchange for cash. He bought the scrip at a 50 percent discount and sold it at full value, taking half the teachers' salary for the service.[81] With practices like these, it is no wonder that critics would blame black businessmen for exploiting their own race.

Gaston saw an opportunity in insuring the burial costs of the miners, a high-demand service because the miners lived short lives and because funeral costs ranked among the biggest financial burdens of black families.[82] Gaston first created the Booker T. Washington Burial Society and then the Booker T. Washington Insurance Company, and he went door to door collecting premiums. Gaston's insurance company would soon be the basis of a large business empire, which included a bank, funeral homes, and a motel in Birmingham, Alabama, that would be central to the civil rights struggle.

The largest industry to fill a market void was black insurance companies. These companies were first created to provide a cushion against the risks of life on the margins, but the industry thrived because of the racist practices of white insurers. Insurance was an interpersonal exchange at the time, requiring trust between the salesperson and the customer. A customer needed to believe that insurance contracts would be enforced when payouts were due after years of paying premiums. A relationship of trust and respect between an insurance salesman and his customer was a business imperative. Reports indicate that white agents visiting black clients not only failed to show "common courtesy," but they "frequently abused the property of their clients."[83] One scholar of the period noted that "nothing has more greatly aided Negro agents in meeting the competition of their more experienced competitors than the abundance of examples of insults to and abuses of Negro policy holders at the hands of white agents which could nearly always be pointed out in every community."[84] After a white insurance agent participated in the lynching of a black man in Mississippi in the late 1800s, black customers flocked to black insurers. In a market based on mutual trust, white insurers for the most part failed to attract black customers.

Many proactive white insurers refused to insure blacks altogether based on their actuarial models and "scientific data." Frederick L. Hoffman's 1896 book *Race Traits and Tendencies of the American Negro* convinced insurers that black lives should not be insured, because blacks were destined for extinction. Hoffman claimed that the rampant disease and premature death in the black community was a feature of their race and had nothing to do with their circumstances. "It is not the *conditions of life* but in *the race traits and tendencies* that we find the causes of the excessive mortality."[85] He concluded that "a combination of these traits and tendencies must in the end cause the extinction of the race."[86] Hoffman based his conclusion on scientific data collected from chest measurements said to show that blacks had a deteriorated physique, which he attributed not to overwork or malnutrition but to racial inferiority.[87] Hoffman was a statistician for the Prudential Insurance Company of America, and his argument was that the company should not insure blacks. Based on his widely read study, insurance providers concluded that it would be "unwise to insure Negroes." Black insurance companies stepped into the breach, and a few of them eventually grew to become the most profitable of all black-owned businesses.[88]

The most successful was the North Carolina Mutual and Provident Association, later called the North Carolina Mutual Life Insurance Company. It was affiliated with the Mechanics and Farmers Bank. From the 1920s until the 1970s, the North Carolina Mutual Life Insurance Company was "the largest black-controlled business institution in the world."[89] Charles Spaulding, the founder of the insurance company and its affiliated bank, grew both organizations in Durham.

If black leaders envisioned a self-sustaining black economy, it came close in only two places: Durham, North Carolina, and Tulsa, Oklahoma. The fate of these two black business sectors reveals the environment in which black business operated. Tulsa held the

most successful enclave of black business, banking, and insurance—
it was called the "Negro Wall Street." The black district in Durham
was called "Hayti" and was created as an independent black community just after the Civil War. Businesses grew immediately to support the black population, and they named the black business core
after Haiti, the first independent black republic. At the center of Durham's Hayti stood two prominent black churches, St. Joseph's AME
and the White Rock Baptist Church, a black college, the North Carolina Central University, and the Mechanics and Farmers bank and
insurance company.[90]

In 1928, a Richmond newspaper writer urged black businessmen
in need of inspiration to skip Europe and to go to Durham instead.
"Go to Durham and see the industrious Negro at his best. Go to
Durham and see the cooperative spirit among Negroes at its best.
Go to Durham and see Negro business with an aggregate capital of
millions. Go to Durham and see twenty-two Negro men whose
honesty and business sagacity are making modern history." When
Booker T. Washington, on a tour of North Carolina, expressed enthusiasm for business development, the black leaders escorting him
reportedly responded, "You haven't seen anything yet. Wait 'til you
get to Durham." Du Bois noted enthusiastically after visiting the city,
"there is in this city a group of five thousand or more colored people
whose social and economic development is perhaps more striking
than that of any similar group in the nation." The city had less of the
creative life or flair of Harlem or South Chicago, but its business
leaders were presented as men who "have mastered the technique
of modern business and acquired the spirit of modern enterprise."[91]

Founded in 1907, the Mechanics and Farmers Bank was a pillar institution in Durham. Its founders were nine prominent businessmen
who intended to start a small building and loan with $10,000 of cap-
ital, but ultimately created a bank that would operate for a century as
one of the most successful black banks in the country.[92] The bank
served as the only source of financing for more than 500 black farmers
and small borrowers during the 1920s, providing $200,000 in loans.
The bank's policy stated its conservative lending philosophy: "no
large loans . . . to a few profiteers, but rather conservative sums to
needy farmers and laborers."[93] The Mechanics and Farmers Bank
even had a second branch in Raleigh, North Carolina, making it the
only black bank to have two branches. Only 119 banks nationwide,

or less than 1 percent of all banks at the time, had a branch operation.[94] Having a second branch likely contributed to the bank's
stability over time. In 1929, robbers held up the Raleigh branch of the
bank and stole a considerable amount of the bank's money.[95] The
bank's president, Charles Spaulding, immediately transferred thousands of dollars in cash from the Durham branch to ward off a run
induced by the crime. After Franklin Roosevelt's mandated "bank
holiday" in 1933, Mechanics and Farmers opened without any restrictions and met all of its obligations.

Black business success in Durham owed much to the general
prosperity of the city. Durham became known as "the Bright Tobacco Belt," and flourished due to its thriving tobacco enterprises.
There were twelve companies manufacturing tobacco there by
1872, and these businesses, such as the Duke factory, began to hire
black workers at the turn of the century. Textile factories also developed in Durham, and they too hired black workers. In short, widespread prosperity engendered a culture of inclusion; after all, there
was plenty of work for all capable citizens of the town. The 1930
census revealed that 10,000 blacks had gainful employment in
Durham (18,000 blacks lived in the city)—a remarkable number
given the large-scale devastation that spread across the South
during the Great Depression.[96] Historian William K. Boyd noted
that in Durham, "live and let live has characterized the attitude of
the leading white men toward the colored race."[97] A Durham newspaper, the *Morning Herald,* spoke of the city's "hands-off" policy in
criticizing the governor's hostility to black businesses in the state:
"If the Negro is going down, for God's sake let it be because of his
own fault, and not because of our pushing him."[98] From the headquarters of the Mechanics and Farmers Bank, the mayor of Durham
addressed a group of black bankers, saying: "You visitors go back
home and tell your people that the whites and the blacks here are
working shoulder to shoulder."[99]

The well-being of a community and the economic health of its
banks are usually correlated, and Durham's black financial sector reflected general business health. Indeed, Du Bois noted that Durham
differed from other black enclaves in that blacks had developed
"five manufacturing establishments which turned out mattresses,
hosiery, brick, iron articles, and dressed lumber. Beyond this, the colored people have a building and loan association, a real estate com-

pany, a bank, and three industrial insurance companies."[100] These industries were successful in large part because they could and did attract a white clientele. Thus, black businesses in Durham did not have to take an "economic detour," but could compete in a larger market. A black hosiery mill, the Durham Textile Mill, even hired white agents. This firm became "the first large-scale black enterprise to hire whites, and the first firm owned by Afro-Americans where whites earned most of their income." As one commentator said of the firm's products, "so far as I have heard, there has been no man to raise the color question when he put on a pair of socks made by Negroes."[101] Local black businesses continued to flourish alongside the insurance company and the bank, lending support to a growing black middle class. Though certainly some of these accounts of racial harmony are exaggerated, there was widespread agreement that relations between white and black businesses in Durham were much better than anywhere else in the country, especially considering how strong the black business sector was allowed to get. Durham continued to be a vibrant business center until 1958, when the state of North Carolina built a freeway through the heart of Hayti, bifurcating the area.

If the successful parallel black economy in Durham stood as a beacon for the black community, what happened in Tulsa sounded an ominous warning. After the land that now makes up Tulsa was acquired through the Louisiana Purchase of 1803, Tulsa's first black settlers arrived as slaves of white and Native American homesteaders. More free blacks migrated there after the Civil War. By 1900, there were 18,719 black residents in the state of Oklahoma, and Tulsa with its post office and railroad became the business hub of the state. Business did not take off in Tulsa until oil was discovered nearby in 1905, but then it boomed. By 1910, blacks made up 10 percent of the population in Tulsa, and in the face of racial hostility, they developed their own financial district in the Greenwood section of the city. Soon black businesses were flourishing and black Tulsans began to accumulate wealth. When one of Booker T. Washington's National Negro Business League agents visited Tulsa, he called it "a regular Monte Carlo." Others in the state dubbed it another "Negro Wall Street."[102]

By 1921, there were some 860 stores and homes in Greenwood. The black community included a number of men who had acquired considerable wealth due to oil speculation. It may have been this wealth in the hands of prominent black citizens that precipitated the calamitous events of May 1921, or—as historian Scott Ellsworth put it, "death in a promised land."[103] It has been a difficult endeavor to piece together the events and circumstances that led to the riotous destruction of the Greenwood district because of a paucity of press coverage at the time and the likely desire of some participants to cover up the details. Though racial hostility was on a low simmer in the town due to perceived inequalities of oil windfalls, the spark that lit the violence was the claim by a young woman that a black man had attacked her in an elevator. The man denied any culpability, but he was arrested and held in a town prison to await trial.[104]

After a white lynch mob gathered outside of the prison, the black community in Tulsa responded with a show of force. The black citizens of Tulsa, having aligned with Du Bois and established an NAACP branch in 1917, were not passive with respect to race relations. A group of thirty armed black men came to defend the prisoner, which caused the white mob to swell to more than 2,000. Apparently, a white man tried to disarm a black war veteran who would not let go of his weapon and fired a shot into the air around 9:30 P.M. Then a few more shots rang out, and the blacks retreated into the Greenwood district. Throughout the night, whites began to loot the stores in Greenwood. The police were called and a race riot erupted. According to a leading account, the white mob began to "invade" Greenwood in order to "burn the nigger out." The white mob set the city ablaze. By the time the destruction was over, 18,000 homes had been burned, 304 homes had been looted, 300 people—mostly black—had died with many more injured, and $2 to $3 million in property damage had occurred, including the lavishly built Mount Zion church, the heart of black Greenwood.[105]

The National Guard arrived the next day and set up temporary camps to house the more than 6,000 displaced black residents. Two days after the riot, martial law was declared and the troops marched the displaced blacks through town with their hands above their heads. At the camps, they were given identification tags that they were forced to display prominently while moving through the city. The tags had a place where their white employers had to sign so that the blacks could return to work. Many black Tulsans fled to other parts of the country as a result of the riot. An NAACP office in New

York explained that "refugees have come to this office in New York City . . . possessing little or nothing except the clothes they were wearing."[106]

Upon reviewing the available evidence, the Tulsa grand jury blamed the riot on the unfortunate elevator encounter, although they also noted "that there existed indirect causes more vital to the public interest than the direct cause. Among them were . . . agitation among the negroes of social equality and the laxity of law enforcement."[107]

Historians place the blame on white resentment at the success of black businesses in Tulsa. When blacks in Tulsa explained the riot, they did not focus on the elevator incident or the alleged assault. Instead, they claimed that they had been warned through printed cards placed in their homes months earlier to leave the state—a warning that many blacks interpreted as being linked to their economic success. A white newspaper in a neighboring town even published a similar warning. In a 1921 editorial, entitled "Blood and Oil," the writer linked the violence directly to economic pressures faced by whites and their use of black success as a scapegoat: "Every increase in the price of oil made the strife more bitter. With the depression of the labor market, white employers of labor at last thought they had the whip hand and ordered Negro employees to sell out or quit. Even housewives refused to continue to keep colored women in their employ. Petty persecutions, the refugees say, were common, though there had been no physical violence during the last few years."[108]

By the time of the alleged elevator incident, racial tensions had reached the boiling point as blacks refused to heed threats that they should leave. Sometimes the hostility was directly apparent, as explained by one account from Tulsa in 1921:

> [T]he Negro in Oklahoma has shared in the sudden prosperity that has come to many of his white brothers, and there are some colored men there who are wealthy. This fact has caused a bitter resentment on the part of the lower order of whites, who feel that these colored men, members of an "inferior race," are exceedingly presumptuous in achieving greater economic prosperity than they who are members of a divinely ordered superior race. . . . In one case where a colored man owned and operated a printing plant with $25,000 worth of printing machinery

in it, the leader of the mob that set fire to and destroyed the plant was a Linotype operator employed for years by the colored owner at $48 per week.[109]

Throughout American history, there have been several examples of majority groups reacting violently when their economic power has been threatened—a theory of host group dominance that holds that the host group, or majority group, should benefit most if any money is to be made. Those groups that are not dominant "host groups" must occupy positions that the dominant group neglects so as not to compete with them for major business profits. Lower-status groups can compete for scraps or for middle positions, but must not occupy the most profitable rungs of the business sector. For example, the state of California passed laws against Japanese businessmen after they became economically successful. Land rights held by blacks during Reconstruction were another example. Native Americans were likewise expelled from their land when oil was discovered on it. What happened in Tulsa was a vivid example of the theory of host group dominance—the black business district was simply too successful to survive.[110]

Tulsa was not the only black district targeted by organized violence. In Wilmington, North Carolina, according to Leon Prather, white business classes came to resent the "black entrepreneurs, located conspicuously downtown [that] deprived white businessmen of legitimate sources of income to which they thought they were entitled." Wilmington was also destroyed by a riot, and "immediately after the massacres, white businesses moved in and filled the economic gaps left by the flight of the blacks." The violence permanently derailed black business efforts and hard-won racial progress. According to Prather, "when the turbulence receded the integrated neighborhoods had disappeared."[111] The violence in Tulsa also had a lasting effect, including the end of the Greenwood business district, the black Wall Street.[112]

It is unclear why Durham escaped the fate of Tulsa, Wilmington, and other cities that became targets of white resentment.[113] Most likely, it was because of the overall prosperity of the city and the complacency of the "host race," whose members did not feel threatened by black advancement. The black leaders of Durham were also careful to mute their wealth. For example, the North Carolina Mutual Company, when constructing its high-rise building, made sure it was not as tall as any building in the white community.[114] The black community in Tulsa did not show such caution. In Tulsa, blacks took the center of town for their enterprise, owned guns, and built large, ornate churches and mansions. Coupled with inequalities caused by a fluctuating oil market, the result was a violent backlash that destroyed a thriving black community and likely sent a message to other such aspirants.[115]

At the turn of the century, it was increasingly clear that blacks would have to rely on their own communities to advance economically. It was also clear that racial hostility would meet their efforts at self-determination every step of the way. On the national stage, even Republicans had stepped away from pursuing racial equality or fighting segregation for fear that they would not be reelected with such a platform because of the South's adamant opposition. President Theodore Roosevelt learned firsthand the racial animosity of the South when he invited Booker T. Washington to dine at the White House in 1901. The southern reaction was severe, immediate, and ugly. Senator Tillman of South Carolina quipped, "Now that Roosevelt has eaten with that nigger Washington, we shall have to kill a thousand niggers to get them back to their places." A Memphis newspaper called the dinner invitation "the most damnable outrage which has been perpetrated by any citizen of the United States." Governor Mc-Sweeney of South Carolina revealed the fear at the root of the South's problem with the visit: "It is simply a question of whether those who are invited to dine are fit to marry the sisters and daughters of their hosts." Southern lawmakers quipped that the inevitable next step was that Washington's daughter would marry Roosevelt's son. Mississippi politician James K. Vardaman said that the White House was "so saturated with the odor of nigger that the rats have taken refuge in the stable."[116]

In 1903, President Roosevelt addressed a crowd of former black Union soldiers at the Lincoln Memorial and exclaimed, "A man who is good enough to shed his blood for his country is good enough to be given a square deal afterward."[117] His words and his vague promise of a "square deal" created such an intense backlash that the president never followed up on his promise. Roosevelt could not have been more wrong when he declared in 1901, "I am confident the South is changing."[118]

What was changing in the South was their appraisal of the past. The Civil War was no longer an embarrassing defeat over slavery, but an honorable and patriotic war fought by the South for their right to autonomy and freedom. General Robert E. Lee was canonized and the Southern rebel became a national hero. The institution of slavery was whitewashed, as the slave plantation took on a romantic hue as an idyllic place where master and slave lived together in harmony. Slavery's cruel history was muted in the name of national unity, and the victims, the black population, had to be recast in the national psyche in order to achieve peace about the past. For northern and southern whites to reunite, they had to suppress the "race issue" that had previously divided them.

Race hierarchy was still necessary as a political weapon to justify economic subjugation. This time, instead of the Bible, white supremacists turned to Darwin. Social Darwinist theories of "survival of the fittest" created a more virulent and hostile strand of racism than had existed under slavery. Evolution-based theories cast the racial hierarchy as an inevitable by-product of natural selection. Once it infected the academy, national policy, and popular thought, it would take generations to cure. In *The Evolution of the Race Problem*, Du Bois lamented that Darwin's "splendid scientific work" was being misused in America as a "justification of disfranchisement, the personal humiliation of Jim-Crowism, a curtailed and purposely limited system of education and a virtual acknowledgment of the inevitable and universal inferiority of black men." He called this perversion of science to prop up oppression "the most cowardly dilemma that a strong people ever thrust upon the weak."[119]

Phrenology, the sham science of skull measurement, attempted to demonstrate the biological hierarchy of race. Formal-looking charts and graphs showed whites as the most advanced race and blacks as close to the apes. Generally, scientists found that whites, or more accurately those descended from certain regions in Europe such as Germany, were the pinnacle of racial advancement.[120] Below them were others including the Irish, Italians, and Eastern Europeans. Much further down were Mongols (Middle Easterners and Asians) and the indigenous tribes of the Americas. At the bottom of every racial chart was the "African," who was portrayed as a step above the common ape. This racial ordering coincidentally mapped exactly onto the socioeconomic order created by slavery and European imperialism. A democratic society cannot accept such sharp divisions of fortune without a theory of racial inferiority to rationalize the gap. Evolutionary theory was corrupted to deal with this cognitive dissonance. Americans could now see blacks not as victims of racial oppression, violence, and exploitation, but as a naturally inferior race who were a burden on the nation, just as Europe cast its colonial peoples as the "white man's burden."

Blacks were popularly portrayed as unevolved primates, or gorillas dressed as humans. The dominant stereotype of blacks was as "subhuman or a beast."[121] Columbia University professor Howard Odum concluded that blacks were "as destitute of morals as any of the lower animals."[122] Doctor E. C. Ferguson explained to the Medical Association of Georgia that the "negro is monkey-like; has no sympathy for his fellow-man; has no regard for the truth, and when the truth would answer his purpose the best, he will lie. He is without gratitude or appreciation of anything done to him; is a natural born thief,—will steal anything, no matter how worthless. He has no morals."[123] Once blacks were relegated to being subhuman, it became justifiable to subjugate them economically.

The darkest chapter of white supremacy soon metastasized to envelop not just the South but the entire nation. Notions of race hierarchy seeped northward through fiction and art. Most popular were the novels of Thomas Dixon, who took his racism on tour across the country. Dixon's play *The Clansmen* was revived by D.W. Griffith into the blockbuster movie, *Birth of a Nation,* which played to sold-out theaters in 1915. Dixon and other revisionists retold the history of Reconstruction not as a subversion of the democratic process through white violence and animosity, but as the unleashed brutality of black men having to be tamed by the Klan. The takeaway, according to Dixon, was that "God ordained the southern white man to teach the lessons of Aryan supremacy."[124] In the movie's climactic scene, the black villain tries to woo a white woman to marry him by promising to make her a queen in his "black empire." The Klan fights a black militia, saves the white woman, and restores social order by lynching the black criminal. The movie closes with Jesus and his angels smiling approvingly.

The resurgent Klan reached its peak year in 1920, with a membership of 4 million members nationwide. In 1925, 40,000 hooded members of KKK marched in front of the White House.[125]

President Woodrow Wilson, an acknowledged racist and a college classmate of Dixon's, aired the film at the White House, the first movie shown there. The audience marveled at the new technology and soaked in the film's racist dogma. Wilson founded his candidacy on both southern progressivism and white supremacy. According to Wilson, "Negro rule under unscrupulous adventurers has been finally put an end to in the South and the natural, inevitable ascendancy of the whites, the responsible class has been established."[126] Wilson purged the federal bureaucracy of any blacks who had managed to secure a government job. He prohibited the hiring of any black employees and fired those his predecessor had hired. The South had determined that it would not move forward without total separation of the races, and they wanted the rest of the country to follow suit. One of Wilson's cabinet members explained that "the South would never feel secure until the North and West had adopted the whole Southern policy of political proscription and social segregation of the Negro." "There is no room for [the Negroes] here," wrote a Charleston newspaper.[127]

There was also no room for the Negro in Wilson's progressive reforms, all of which were made possible by his southern cabinet and congressional leaders. The South had not only been embraced back into the national fold, but their legislators now held the key levers of national power. Southern legislators maintained control of the Senate through an unrivaled unity of purpose and organized their own ranks to maintain the racial hierarchy on which their economy was based. The continued exploitation of black labor was a preoccupation of southern legislators, and they brought it to pass by blocking any reforms that threatened it. Yet these Democratic southerners were progressives when it came to the government's role in the economy. The South, built on agriculture and an outdated plantation system, resisted free markets and laissez-faire credit reform. They understood that capital was not interested in financing southern ventures and farms, but rather in Wall Street and the industrial north. So the southern legislators fought laissez-faire markets and sought to impose trade restrictions, break up banks, ease credit to farmers, and resist the excesses of capitalism. They did so while maintaining their racial caste system, which assured that whites would sit atop the economic hierarchy. Southern interests dominated the Wilson administration, but this mix of progressive credit and traditional racial ordering would be even more formative in shaping the American economy when the two strains converged again in creating the New Deal.

Wilson carried forward the populist ideas related to the democratization of banking and credit that had percolated in the South. While he did not go as far as the Populists or William Jennings Bryan would have liked, he instituted reforms to help poor whites gain access to easier credit and fought the monopoly power of northern banks. Wilson's newly established Federal Reserve was a hybrid structure of populist reforms and private interests. "Our system of credit is privately concentrated," said Wilson. "The growth of the nation, therefore, and all our activities are in the hands of a few men." The prospect of fixing credit shortages, especially for rural farmers, was the reason President Wilson was able to convince Congress to create the Federal Reserve.[128] The offices of the Federal Reserve were spread across the country in order to prevent centralization of power and money in the North.

After creating the Federal Reserve, President Wilson and the 64th Congress passed the Federal Farm Loan Act of 1916 for the express purpose of increasing credit to rural family farmers. The act established the Federal Farm Loan Board to administer the loans, twelve Federal Farm Loan Banks, and National Farm Loan Associations (established groups of ten or more mortgage-holding farmers).[129] The bill reduced interest rates on farm loans across the South and made credit much more accessible. This bill was the first federal government loan program, and thanks to southern senators, it left black farmers out.[130] The legislators created loopholes and provisions to exclude blacks and left the program to be administered in local offices in the South, with significant discretion given to local bureaucrats in lending, which effectively meant that blacks would not be given loans.[131]

Wilson was a progressive hero and champion of a mixed economy, with government working with business to advance the interests of the majority of American citizens. Wilson was the first president to use the state apparatus to make the market work for the benefit of all the people. The Federal Trade Commission, Federal Reserve, and loan programs were a combination of private incentives and public projects that continue to be used in one form or another. These progressive acts were a harbinger of the New Deal. Both Wilson and

Franklin Roosevelt relied on southern participation to pass their programs in Congress. The South controlled the Senate, a body which acted, in the words of Robert Caro, as "the stronghold of the status quo, the dam against which the waves of social reform dashed themselves in vain."[132] Thus the Senate and the president worked in tandem to democratize credit, check excessive corporate power, and empower the people over the wealthy few. But the "people" did not include blacks. Because the black community's autonomy and full participation in the market was in direct conflict with the South's economic needs, it was continually subverted at all levels of government. The justification used to enforce this order was not economic. Rather, racial Darwinism convinced Americans that blacks were less-evolved humans, and so they could be put to work for the profitable use of white men and their institutions. The black southern experience at the turn of the century was one of economic exploitation backed by state-sanctioned violence. And so it was that many blacks decided to flee the only home they knew.

3

The Rise of Black Banking

The Great Migration, which lasted roughly from 1910 until 1970, radically transformed the country.[1] During this seismic shift, approximately six million blacks left the south. In 1900, ninety percent of black Americans lived in the rural areas of Southern states. By 1970, 80 percent of black Americans lived in urban areas and nearly half outside the South. Blacks left the South because of racial injustice and the general decline of economic conditions below the Mason-Dixon line. They were pulled to the North by the promise of better jobs, better pay, and more opportunities for advancement.[2]

Great northern cities swelled with black migrants and put them to work. The poet of the Harlem Renaissance, Langston Hughes, articulated the appeal of the northward migration:

> The lazy, laughing South
> With blood on its mouth.
> The sunny-faced South,
>   . . .
> And I, who am black, would love her
> But she spits in my face.
> And I, who am black,
> Would give her many rare gifts
> But she turns her back upon me.
> So now I seek the North—
> The cold-faced North,
> For she, they say,
> Is a kinder mistress,
> And in her house my children
> May escape the spell of the South.[3]

It was easy to escape the South into the North's booming economy and vibrant city life. Yet it was the "kinder mistress" that imposed systematic segregation and created the black ghetto. The North welcomed these migrants, but then quickly told them to proceed to

Harlem and stay put. It was the kinder mistress's ghettos that came to be called the "cities of destruction."[4]

The concept and terminology of a racial ghetto derives from the forced segregation of Jews in Europe—first in enclaves in the seventeenth century and then with barbed wire during the Nazi regime.[5] There was no barbed wire in America's black ghettos, but even more effective modes of containment through racial covenants and government credit and zoning policies that maintained the boundaries of the ghetto. Often referred to as black enclaves, black neighborhoods, or other racially neutral descriptions, the word ghetto is a much more accurate descriptor because it captures the involuntary nature of segregation. The ghetto was created by white racism, which in turn generated a complex web of interrelated social, political and economic challenges. Blacks were forced into a parallel and inferior economy simply because whites in the north would not accept them as neighbors. This had profound effects on African American economic advancement for the next century. Black racial segregation was so complete and so entrenched, that it is the defining characteristic of racial inequality in the twentieth-century and the major roadblock to economic progress.[6]

The first wave of the Great Migration from 1910 to 1930 coincided with the height of discriminatory segregation and the golden era of black banking. These developments were correlated in important ways: the surge of migrants entering cities of the north triggered racial animosity and housing segregation, which in turn created a separate and parallel economy and in time, a thriving black banking sector. From 1900 until 1934, some 130 black banks came into being, 88 of which were formed between 1900 and 1928.[7] This did not include approximately 50 savings and loans and credit unions formed by blacks during this time.[8] The resources of these institutions grew steadily, but the most robust expansion of black banking came from 1918 to 1929. The peak year of black banking came in 1926, when total assets held by these institutions reached roughly $13 million (this was still only 0.2 percent of all U.S. bank assets).[9]

Wherever African American populations could be found, black banks flourished to meet both the opportunities and challenges of a segregated economy.[10] Concentrated populations of black wage workers proved to be a bounty for the black banks. But that same concentration also created special vulnerabilities. These banks were created by the same forces that worked against them at every turn—a segregated economy held the seeds of its own destruction. There would be many bank failures in due time, but not before some of these institutions had cemented their place in history as the pioneering giants of black finance. The 1920s roared for black banks too, but these machines were never able to perform the magic of banking that is the multiplication of capital through fractional reserve lending. As well, the bust following the boom would last much longer for black commercial institutions and their customers.

Chicago's black belt, the most segregated black ghetto, was also the center of black banking in the North. Philadelphia, Washington D.C., and Boston were homes to several black-owned banks, but these institutions were far smaller than the banks of Chicago.[11] The "titans of black finance" in the north were both located in Chicago: The Binga State Bank and the Douglass National Bank. At their peak in 1928, they controlled almost one-third of the combined resources of all black banks in the country.[12] Most observers viewed these two banks as the best managed and strongest of all the black banks and as models for successful commercial banking in the black economy.[13]

Jesse Binga was born in Detroit in 1865. His father was a barber and his mother, who was Binga's inspiration throughout his life, created a food shipping business while dabbling in real estate development. Binga was one of ten children and the family lived on limited means. He briefly practiced law, but would make his mark as a businessman.[14] He moved to Chicago's black belt district and opened a real estate business in 1896. The Chicago real estate market was in a state of rapid change as blacks migrated in to the city and whites moved out. The industrious Binga found a way to profit from segregation and neighborhood turnover by buying houses at below-market rates from whites desperate to sell, fixing them up and selling them to black buyers. Binga ran an advertisement in the Tribune in 1905: "WANTED—OWNERS, SOUTH SIDE—QUICK returns; if you desire to sell to reliable colored people submit your property for sale."[15]

Binga was viewed by his community as a fair and beloved businessman, setting him apart from the droves of exploitative contract sellers and loan sharks that would dominate the real estate market in Chicago in the next epoch. Binga quickly became Chicago's top black real estate broker because he did the buying and selling as well as the fixing up. "I could do the repair work myself. I could do everything from digging a posthole to topping a chimney." He explained that his greatest asset in business was exploiting the discrimination of white businessmen. "It was partly the disposition of the average white man to underestimate my knowledge of real estate values. They wouldn't believe that a colored man could take almost any old building and whip it into shape."[16]

Just as discrimination and white flight led to his real estate success, he turned the white banks' refusal to lend to his real estate clients into another source of profit. When the white-owned McCarthy Bank on 35th and State failed in 1907, Binga purchased the building and chartered "Binga State Bank." In 1911, the *Defender* called Binga "Our Only Banker" and lauded his accomplishments, stating, "He was the pioneer in securing good houses and flats for the race and the beginning of his remarkable business along that line has been one of the main factors in the wonderful growth of the citizens of color in Chicago." Another black business leader called Binga's Bank "one of the leading banks owned and operated by Negroes anywhere."[17]

Binga's bank deposits grew from $300,000 to over $1.1 million between 1921 and 1924. During that same time period, Binga bought a prominent home in a white neighborhood near Washington Park. His purchase drew ire and triggered violence. During the race riots of 1919, his house was bombed seven times.[18] Each time, the bomber left a note demanding that Binga leave the property and sell it to a white buyer. Binga was resolute. "I will not run. The race is at stake and not myself. If they can make me move they will have accomplished much of their aim because they can say, 'We made Jesse Binga move; certainly you'll have to move' to all the rest. If they can make the leaders move, what show will the small buyers have?"[19] Binga claimed that it was his right as a proud American to defend his home, life, and liberty.[20]

Binga's bank was consistently more capitalized than what was required by the Illinois State Charter and his bank was held out by black and white contemporaries as a model of sound banking.[21] Binga also bought a membership into the Chicago Clearinghouse, through which top banks paid into a fund used to rescue the member banks when they needed emergency liquidity during a run or a downturn.[22] Before the Federal Reserve was founded in 1913 to offer similar protection, top bankers joined such funds, paying dues that would be set aside to help them in a liquidity crisis.[23] The Chicago fund saved many banks from failure, and Binga's bank was the only black bank granted membership. As Binga would later find out, however, fair dealing with this elite group was not reciprocated.

In 1926, Binga's bank, located in the center of the black belt, was the most expensive property in the district, valued at $120,000. He owned over $500,000 in other real estate as well. On the eve of the Great Depression, Jesse Binga, sixty-four years old and at the height of his success, began collecting capital to start a second bank. Binga's unparalleled success made him a storied leader in the black community, and so the funds flowed in. The 1929 stock market crash, however, shattered his plans. By the end of the year, Binga's bank became the "canary in the coal mine" for bank failure in Chicago.[24] His bank was the first in Chicago to fail during the Great Depression.[25]

Binga used all means available to him to save his bank and his customers' deposits, including lending the bank his own money. The balance sheets of Binga's bank from 1929 and 1930 reveal that the bank held $800,000 of home loans in default.[26] He reached out to the Chicago Clearinghouse for a short-term loan from the fund he had helped build, but the board rejected his request. One member of the clearinghouse later explained that during one meeting, the chairman had referred to Binga's bank as "a little nigger bank that does not mean anything."[27] It was the first closure of a member bank of the Chicago Clearinghouse in twenty years. All the other banks that belonged to this clearinghouse were given aid and survived the Great Depression.[28] W. E. B. Du Bois noted that the bankers' association "could have saved the bank and saved it easily without loss or prospect of loss. Yet the Binga Bank was allowed to fail because owners and masters of the credit facilities of the nation did not care to save it. Binga was not the kind of man they wanted to succeed."[29] On July 31, 1930, Illinois bank auditors closed Binga's bank, and his depositors lost most of their savings.[30]

The bank's failure erased the wealth of many members of Chicago's black elite. Dempsey Travis, who went on to run his own mortgage company and who held Binga as a personal hero, describes a successful uncle who saved all of his money at Binga's bank and who "became destitute with the turn of the examiner's key in the front door of the bank." He died just a few years later, "broke and broken-hearted."[31] No doubt the same fate befell many others in Chicago. Some black residents were angry at Binga and called him a "crook," while others were more forgiving and thought he was a "creative businessman who ended up taking too many risks." Still others claimed that he was "a victim of circumstances brought down by the white system, and that his mistake had been in overextending the bank by making too many first mortgages to blacks desperate to buy homes."[32] If black bankers' success had been celebrated as a source and symbol of racial pride and progress, their failures were felt as a failure of the entire community—a source of shame and shaken morale.

The bank's failure bankrupted Binga too, but that was the least of his problems. His wife filed for divorce and Binga was indicted for embezzlement of funds. The charge was that he had deposited the $39,000 that he had raised for his second bank into a personal account. Binga defended himself against the charge by explaining that state laws did not allow capital funds for a national bank to be held in a state bank. After a jury heard testimony from eighty witnesses, they could not reach a verdict. The state's attorney immediately prepared for a second trial and this time won a conviction in November 1933. Binga was sent to prison. According to recorded history, this made Binga the only banker in the entire country who was sent to prison for financial crime during the Great Depression.[33]

At his parole hearing eleven months later, the nation's most famous attorney, Clarence Darrow, came to Binga's defense. Darrow did so because "I have known Binga for thirty years and he is a man of fine character. He lost a fortune trying to keep his bank open." Even Darrow, however, could not secure Binga's release, and he remained in prison. In 1938, 10,000 Chicago residents, including many who lost their deposits at Binga's bank, signed a petition in support of his parole and he was finally released. In 1941, Governor Dwight Green issued a pardon. By then, Binga was sick and broke. He died in 1950. His bank remained closed until 1943 and was reopened as the Phoenix National Bank—no longer a black-owned bank.

The Binga Bank was not without a rival in Chicago. The black belt district was so densely populated and so thoroughly segregated that its financial needs supported two of the most successful banks in the country. Anthony Overton founded the Douglass National Bank, named after the first black bank president, Frederick Douglass. The bank capital came from the profits of the successful Overton Hygienic Company. Anthony Overton, much like Madam C. J. Walker, earned his wealth by creating cosmetics and hair products for black women and then built on his success to start the Victory Life Insurance Company, the *Chicago Bee* newspaper, the *Half Century* magazine, and the bank.[34] By 1920, Overton's Hygienic Company was worth over a million dollars and sold more than 250 products.[35]

Before the Great Depression, his bank had $2 million in assets, which made it the largest of any black-owned bank in the nation. It was also the only black bank that was chartered as a national bank and that became a member of the Federal Reserve after it was formed in 1913. In order to affiliate with the Federal Reserve, the bank had to meet certain capital requirements and undergo additional regulation, but membership came with added prestige and privileges.[36] One white scholar wrote in 1926 that the Douglass bank "surrounded itself with the best possible safe-guards which American banking science has been able to evolve, and by so doing, has instilled ambition, courage and confidence in the hearts of countless Negroes throughout America."[37] The Douglass bank failed along with Binga's bank in 1930.[38]

Remarkably, New York City had no black-owned banks during the entire golden era of black banking.[39] The black population in New York was around 150,000 in 1920, slightly larger than Chicago's 110,000 blacks, and it was the nation's unrivaled capital of finance.[40] If anything, New York's Harlem was a more vibrant center of business activity than Chicago's black belt.

Why was New York, with its large, segregated, income-earning black population, less hospitable to black-owned banks than Chicago, Washington, or the cities of the South? It was not for lack of trying. In 1916, the *New York Age* lamented, "One of the urgent business needs of Harlem is a Negro bank. Several attempts have been made at the formation of one, but so far to no avail. In the meantime the financial affairs of the district are provided for by the Harlem branch of the Chelsea Exchange Bank."[41] In 1920, the *Sun and New York Herald* reported that "the Wage Earners Bank, a rich corporation of Savannah, Ga., purchased a large plot of ground at the southwest corner of 135th Street and Seventh Avenue, where it will erect a large bank building," but the bank never formed.[42] Then in 1921, Charles H. Anderson attempted to start a bank in Harlem at 135th Street and Lenox Avenue, across the street from the large, white-owned Chelsea Bank.[43] However, Anderson, who was treasurer of the National Negro Business League and owner of the largest fish and oyster business in Jacksonville, was nevertheless unable to open a bank.[44]

There were profits to be made in taking deposits from the citizens of Harlem, and several white banks established branches there.[45] It is possible that these white banks were adequately serving the black population and there was thus no market demand for a black bank. This is unlikely, however, as the black press continually trumpeted the need for black-owned banks and lamented the lack of credit in Harlem. In fact, the white-owned banks with branches in Harlem focused on deposit-taking as opposed to lending.[46] The lack of bank credit for blacks in Harlem led many of its residents, especially new Caribbean immigrants, to form informal credit circles to lend to each other to facilitate businesses and home purchases.[47] There was certainly a dire need for bank credit in Harlem.

Another possible explanation for the dearth of black banks is that New York's chartering laws were more stringent than those of other states. Prominent black banker Arnett Lindsay posited in 1926 that although would-be black banks made attempts to enter the Harlem market over the years, "the rigid bank requirements of New York State were never met by the many promoters who essayed this role."[48] There is, however, much reason to doubt this theory. A review of the bank chartering codes for New York, Illinois, and Massachusetts during the years between 1910 and 1930 reveals that they imposed very similar capital and bonding requirements, but the state left it to the banking superintendent's discretion to approve the banks and their boards. This discretion was more robust in New York and Illinois than in Massachusetts, meaning that the bank superintendent could for any reason deny a banking charter if he was not satisfied with the character of bank managers.[49] On their face, the New York chartering laws were not more rigid, but the discretion held by the banking superintendent could have led to disparate enforcement.

The most likely explanation of the paucity of black banks in Harlem is the one put forth by the black press at the time: the white banks already established in the area prevented black banks from getting charters. The *New York Age* reported in 1923 that the Chelsea Bank had used the discretionary bank chartering laws and its influence on New York's banking regulators to prevent black bankers from obtaining a charter.[50] The bank, fearing a loss of black depositors, allegedly persuaded the New York State Banking Commission to deny Charles Anderson's charter request in 1921.[51] Facing community backlash after these charges appeared in the press, the Chelsea Bank sought to placate depositors by hiring two black tellers.[52]

The Chelsea Exchange Bank likely did not want to give up their near monopoly on black depositors in Harlem. The Chelsea Bank had opened its first branch in Harlem at 135th Street and Seventh Avenue in 1912, and the community welcomed its services. At the time, the *New York Age* reported with pride, "[q]uite a number of the leading Negro business men [of Harlem] are customers of this bank, and the ample facilities of the institution are always courteously and freely placed at their disposal by the capable manager."[53] The paper reported that the bank treated African American depositors respectfully and courted both small and large depositors. The branch had many large depositors—businessmen with average monthly deposits of $75,000 to $100,000. "Running over the list of Negroes who are customers of this bank is like calling the roll of 'Who's Who' in the business and professional ranks of our people in Harlem."[54] By 1916, 85 percent of the bank's depositors were individuals, and 14 percent were businesses.[55] The Chelsea Exchange Bank of Harlem retained its monopoly on deposits well into the mid-1920s. "The nearest financial institution is at least ten blocks away, at 125th Street, and so the Chelsea Bank has the opportunity to control almost entirely the banking clientele of a community in which one race group alone numbers approximately 170,000 people."[56] In 1924, the *New York Age* reported that the Chelsea Exchange Bank "serves more small depositors and small business establishments than any similar institution" in Harlem.[57] Chelsea's deposit base was almost entirely Harlem residents, but they had no black board members, just the two black tellers.[58]

Although Chelsea Exchange Bank took all of Harlem's deposits, it did not make loans to Harlem. One white bank manager observed that black customer accounts were "based on straight cash deposits."[59] By 1920, there were complaints of prejudice and objections to the bank's refusal to extend credit to black customers:

It has also been alleged that business men of the race
have found it extremely difficult, if not impossible, to
secure from the bank's officials any credit consideration.
Temporary loans, secured by the endorsement of reputable and financially responsible people, have been
refused in many instances, it is reported, under circumstances which pointed strongly toward the color of the
would-be borrower and endorsers as the bar to credit at
this bank.[60]

The Chelsea bank manager responded that the bank's refusal to
extend credit to African Americans was not due to prejudice, but rather
to the bank's strictly conservative policies.[61] The bank said they did
not advance loans to anyone "unless the applicant can show a sat-
isfactory balance and business statement and has a generally good
character." Of course, with so much discretion as to an applicant's
character, how could racism not be a factor in the loan denials?

A white teller of the Chelsea Exchange Bank who went on to write
a dissertation on black-owned banks in the 1930s explained that his
bank received a "tremendous amount" of money from black customers. He also observed without apology that, "*All of this money is
transferred downtown* to the home office where it is *loaned to white
customers.*"[62] He defended this practice as one that was properly followed by most banks because they wanted to ensure their loans
were "one hundred per cent sound." According to him, safe loans
could be made much more easily to their white customers because
"the Negro is entirely untutored in the business world; he is historically not a business man."[63] This idea that blacks were not ready for
business or incapable of it due to lack of training or that, unlike immigrants, blacks were "not from an entrepreneurial culture" has had
a long life despite much evidence to the contrary.[64] George Bernard
Shaw revealed the backward logic: "the haughty American nation . . .
makes the Negro clean its boots, and then proves the moral and
physical inferiority of the Negro by the fact that he is a shoeblack."[65]

Not only were blacks unworthy of loans, but the white clerk also
blamed fickle depositors for the instability of black banks, lamenting
that if only these black depositors would allow their deposits to grow,
the banks would not be so burdened. He reasoned that the wage
earners would often take out their deposits during the Christmas

season, moralizing that this was because they lacked proper perspective and self-control.[66] While his institution was diverting the scant resources of Harlem downtown, he was blaming the "unlearned" and "emotional negro" for his own poverty and lack of resources. This moral indictment of the poor by institutions complicit in their poverty is a recurring theme. In fact, privileged observers often cast the rational behavior of the economically disenfranchised as a sign of moral inferiority that explains their poverty and simultaneously justifies apathy toward them.

The Chelsea Bank's most prominent competitor in Harlem was the Dunbar National Bank.[67] Dunbar Bank was established in 1928 by John D. Rockefeller Jr. and was described at its opening by *Time* magazine as a significant addition to "the long list of gifts which [its founder] has made toward the betterment of Negroes."[68] The Dunbar Bank was organized along the same lines as the Freedmen's Bank— it was basically a large depository created by white philanthropists for the purpose of teaching blacks about "thrift."[69] The managing director of the Dunbar National Bank stated in 1932 that the bank provided savings accounts to "help the Negro help himself." The bank would not be lending on real estate, but would take deposits and invest them in government securities, a promise which they kept. Rockefeller still expected that it would be "a profitable venture."[70] Black banker Arnett Lindsay remarked that, although blacks were the "chief beneficiar[ies]" of the bank, "the promoters of the bank are receiving their due compensation, a fair return on their investments."[71]

The community embraced the bank. On the day of its opening, September 17, 1928, the *New York Age* reported that "more than 5,000 persons including a number of the most prominent Negro business men of the country" visited the bank.[72] Other black banks and businesses, including Mechanics and Farmers Bank of Durham, the Victory Life Insurance Company of Chicago, and the Citizens and Southern Bank of Philadelphia, deposited funds into the Dunbar Bank.[73] Dunbar's management explained that they were not organized as "a colored or white bank, but to serve all the people of Harlem."[74] By 1932, the *New York Age* reported, "depositors are made up of both races, the employees are both white and colored."[75]

With its white management and black staff, the Dunbar National Bank was reported to be the "only interracial banking operation in the United States."[76] *The Crisis* noted that the bank employed "Negroes as tellers, bookkeepers and clerks."[77] In other words, *not* as management. The community protested and asked the bank to consider hiring black managers. Dunbar responded by hiring one black director, Roscoe C. Bruce.[78] The Harlem newspaper *Amsterdam News* was not impressed, complaining that "The desire on the part of prominent and capable Negro businessmen of Harlem to have serving the community a bank with a white and colored board of directors has not been realized." A Dunbar Bank representative countered, condescendingly, "The Dunbar Bank is an experiment and we must move slowly in deciding upon our policies, and until we see the response of the representative Negro businessmen of Harlem to this effort to be of assistance to them, we have to delay consideration of appointing any of them as directors of the institution." The Harlem business community was at first promised a 50 percent stake in the available stock, but once the bank opened, Rockefeller retained 75 percent of the stock and refused to sell the remaining 25 percent to the community until he was "sure the bank would succeed." Even when the bank did succeed, Rockefeller never sold stock in the bank to the black community.[79] Harlem felt betrayed by this decision, which sowed a suspicion that would resurface thirty years later when Jackie Robinson tried to convince Harlem to invest in his bank. The community suspected that Robinson's bank was a front for another Rockefeller venture.

Having avoided real estate lending, the Dunbar Bank sailed through the Great Depression and became one of the first banks to open after President Roosevelt's 1933 bank holiday.[80] The bank was affiliated with the Rockefeller-financed Dunbar Apartments, which—according to the New York City Landmarks Commission—was the first large cooperative residence built for blacks.[81] The structure, constructed in 1926, was designed to provide blacks with a path toward property ownership through a cooperative. During the height of the Harlem Renaissance the apartments housed several famous black luminaries, including W. E. B. and Nina Du Bois. In 1936, Rockefeller foreclosed on the cooperatively owned building due to defaults in payments in the wake of the Great Depression.[82] The Dunbar National Bank was liquidated in 1938 when Rockefeller decided, according to *The Afro-American* newspaper, that it was no longer profitable and "convenient for him to continue it."[83]

It is notable that Harlem did not have a thriving black bank sector, or at least one similar to that enjoyed by other major cities—not only because Harlem was located just a few miles from the heart of American capitalism on Wall Street, but more significantly because Harlem at the time was the focal point of a new and powerful strand of black nationalism championed by Marcus Garvey.[84] Garvey was not as prominent a national leader as Du Bois or Washington, but he was undoubtedly the most influential voice emanating from the northern ghetto—a voice that would echo throughout the twentieth century. Unlike Du Bois and Washington, Garvey was not interested in the South's problems, nor did he care to speak to the black middle class or whites. His primary concern was for the "poor black masses" living in northern ghettos. His answer for them was to embrace segregation and to build an independent community. If Du Bois had sought to tear down the walls of segregation and Washington had wanted to build a respectable community within the walls and wait for the white community to take them down eventually, Garvey wanted to build the walls even higher and establish guards on top lest the whites try to exert any control within the black center.

Blacks, whom Garvey called "a mighty race," would never be accepted by white America, so they were better off developing an independent nation. This meant either going "back to Africa" or building a sovereign nation in America from reparations he demanded as recompense for slavery. Garvey, a Jamaican immigrant, likened the black ghetto to a domestic colony. This framing resonated with blacks living in densely segregated northern ghettos. The proper response to colonialization was to demand self-determination. "Where is the black man's government?" demanded Garvey. "Where is his president, his country, and his ambassadors, his army, his navy, and his men of big affairs? I could not find them, and I declared, 'I will help make them!' "[85] He was called "the Black Moses," and his movement attracted millions of "Garveyites" out of a nucleus of acolytes in Harlem.

The language and insignia of his movement—military apparel—made him the most incendiary of the early leaders. He founded the Universal Negro Improvement Association (UNIA) in 1914 as a step toward establishing "a country and absolute government of their own."[86] In August 1920, the UNIA had four million members and held an international convention at Madison Square Garden before a crowd of 25,000 people. Ironically, Garvey's commitment to absolute segregation and rejection of any help from whites aligned him with staunch white supremacists. He even met with the Grand Wizard of the Ku Klux Klan to oppose integration.[87] The meeting infuriated other black leaders and drew harsh criticism from black labor organizer and fellow Harlemite A. Philip Randolph, who launched a "Marcus must go" campaign. Du Bois called Garvey "the most dangerous enemy of the Negro race in America."[88] Garvey, in turn, condemned Du Bois for acting like an agent for the white elite.

Although Garvey irritated prominent black leaders, his economic road map bore a striking resemblance to Washington's own rhetoric—Garvey was inspired by Washington's philosophy, and the two had corresponded and intended to meet before Garvey immigrated to America, but Washington died before they could meet. Garvey enthusiastically embraced capitalism and preached a gospel of success that included self-mastery, hard work, and self-sufficiency, all of which he promised would result in black wealth and power. He echoed Andrew Carnegie when he admonished black Harlem: "Be not deceived, wealth is strength, wealth is power, wealth is influence, wealth is justice, is liberty, is real human rights."[89] Blacks needed to own "more stores, more banks, and bigger enterprises," said Garvey. So long as blacks had "no banks of our own," they could not survive and prosper as a race.[90]

Garvey even began his own business empire, including a grocery store chain, restaurants, and laundries in Harlem in 1919. He incorporated the Negro Factories Corporation to manage a variety of subsidiary businesses—all of which relied on de facto segregation. Garvey's Harlem newspaper, *The Negro World*, published the first voices of the Harlem Renaissance. His most ambitious venture was a shipping company, the Black Star Line, built to enable trade and commerce between the Caribbean, Central and South America, and the United States. The Black Star Line faltered and then failed. Garvey himself was arrested for mail fraud and subsequently deported to Jamaica in 1927.

For many in the black community at the time and thereafter, Garvey's movement was anything but a failure. According to one contemporary, "it was an economic failure . . . but a psychological success . . . [and] created a spirit that has yet to be paralleled in any other black movement." Earl and Louise Little were loyal Garveyites in Chicago who rejected black integration and the "Uncle Tom-ism" of the black middle class. Their son, Malcolm X, would resurrect Garvey's vision years later, as would the Black Panthers, the Nation of Islam, Rastafarianism, and other black radical groups.[91]

Black nationalism was a distinctly political philosophy and a direct result of racism and segregation. It was in the heavily concentrated ghettos of the North that such a response was most appealing. The ghetto was predominantly black, and its business establishments were all white-owned. It felt like exploitation akin to colonization. The black nationalist solution was to create a parallel economy with rival black institutions in the ghetto. The end result, however, was not just the black institutions but complete autonomy—not Washington's "social separation," but a revolutionary political break from the American polity. This would have required military violence and would certainly have failed, which is likely the reason the nationalists focused on creating economic institutions first. But the premise was that ownership of black institutions meant *control* of the black ghetto economy.

Black bankers were not political nationalists, but they were operating under the same foundational principle that black banks would lead to black economic power and independence. Richard R. Wright Sr., founder of the National Negro Bankers Association (NNBA), articulated the goal of black banking. Wright believed that black banking would provide "a tangible start toward real financial emancipation."[92] "[M]ost of the Negroes' money is not now organized for the Negro, but actually organized against us. Millions of dollars that colored people have put in banks (probably 12 million in this city alone) are used to build up businesses for people who discriminate against Negroes. Do you think it's about time to help organize the finances of our people?"[93] Wright was born a slave in Georgia and worked to help the family survive after slavery. He told a story of giving his paycheck to his mother one day and being struck when she responded, "I'm going to take this money and put it in the bank and live off the interest." Her words surprised her son and the message stayed with him. When he walked past the bank, he told the banker, "I'm going to have money in your bank."[94] Wright eventually became a college president, and in 1921, at the age of sixty-seven, he founded the Philadelphia's Citizens and Southern Bank and Trust Company.

He founded the NNBA in 1927 and urged all prominent black leaders to create their own banks. "We must unite all the Negro banks in the country," said Wright, "to restore confidence in our business. No bank can stand alone."[95] The organization, according to its own history, was "born in hostile times."[96] The mission of the league was:

> to promote the general welfare, and the usefulness of banks and banking institutions, and to secure uniformity of action, together with the practical benefits to be derived from personal acquaintance and from the discussion of subjects of importance to the banking and commercial interests of the country, and especially in order to secure the proper consideration of questions regarding the financial and commercial usages, [and of] customs and laws which [a]ffect the banking interest of the country.[97]

In 1927, the NNBA convened in Durham, and Mechanics and Farmers President C. C. Spaulding delivered the keynote address to the group. He pressed a message he would sound many times, urging black bankers to "pull together" and cooperate in order to survive. Between 1927 and the onset of the Great Depression, the most pressing topics during meetings were cooperation among black banks, eliciting the support of the black community, countering discrimination by whites, and overcoming negative stereotypes. To help address the latter point, the NNBA invited the black press to their 1927 meeting and asked them for assistance in portraying a positive image of the industry to the public.[98]

The bankers invited editors from the *Pittsburgh Courier, Norfolk Journal and Guide,* and the *Philadelphia Tribune,* and asked for their help convincing an often reluctant black population that black banks were just as trustworthy as white ones. Wright complained about the unequal treatment black banks received from their newspapers. "The news of a single failure of a Negro bank goes about like wildfire," he complained. "Everyone knows it and everyone talks about it. The announcement of a Negro bank failure forms glaring headlines in red letters across the pages of every Negro newspaper." Wright implored his colleagues to "change this by making our bank successes interesting news."[99]

If the association's goal was to mobilize black money into black banks, they needed the black community to trust banks—in other words, trust that they would not fail—for what banks were asking their community was no small favor. They were asking blacks to entrust black bankers with their hard-earned savings in the days before deposit insurance, when a bank failure meant that the deposits were gone. Bankers had to convince their customers that they were honest, smart, and prudent, but the pervasive racism of the era worked to demonstrate just the opposite. Many black bankers and industry observers noted that black banks were weakened by perceived racial inferiority even in their own communities. As one white banker observed, "[As to] practically every Negro bank in the country: when it opens its doors for business, only a comparatively small number of people deal with it."[100] Banking was impossible without this confidence.[101] But the bankers knew that if the population trusted them with their savings, they could be of service to their customers by providing them with loans that no other banks were giving them. Trust would beget stability, which would beget sound lending, which would beget more trust. Black bankers wanted to spark this virtuous circle. This is why Wright and the other bankers pleaded with the black press to help "to dignify our banking, to organize our banks for bigger and better business and for mutual protection."[102]

The press obliged. In 1927, the *Norfolk Journal and Guide* wrote, "If Negro banks, selected with due regard for safety and service, were made the depositories of one half of [the black community's] money, its circulation through the arteries of Negro trade and commerce would add wonderful strength to our economic structure."[103] The editor of the *Washington Bee* claimed that the black banking industry meant "more to the present and future of the Negro race in America than possibly all of the other agencies concerned with the progress and welfare of our group combined." Pointing to the banking industry as the ship captain of black economic progress, he called on the entire black population to amass their money and support these institutions:

> With most of our business enterprises just emerging
> from their swaddling clothes, to rival and battle against
> long established and experienced competition; with the

enterprising home-owners and home builders being im-
periled by lack of capital, impossibility of securing or
renewing loans; . . . with industrial and economic barriers
being erected against the Negro every day in all parts of
the country; with the facts of his forced isolation from
other groups and the realization that he must work out
his own problems and overcome and conquer his hazards
himself, the Negro needs a strong, trained arm at the
wheel to pilot him safely into the port of his dreams.[104]

To help with the public relations challenge, the NNBA kicked off
Negro Bankers Week on February 10, 1929, with scheduled mass
meetings and education campaigns. The League called on President
Coolidge to support thrift among blacks as part of his ongoing Thrift
Week celebrations.[105] While Coolidge did not offer any specific support for black banks, he did create the first government agency to
support black businesses, the Commerce Department's Division of
Negro Affairs, in 1927. James A. "Billboard" Jackson was its first director. Jackson earned his nickname when he became the first black
editor of *Billboard* magazine in 1920, and in his position at the Commerce Department his duties were to collect and disseminate information about black businesses. Besides Jackson's periodic reports
on the state of black businesses, however, the agency did little else.[106]

The NNBA was gearing up just as the Great Depression decimated
the industry. In fact, the 1928 meeting had been scheduled for Savannah, Georgia, but the two black-owned banks in the city—the
Wage Earners Savings Bank and the Savannah Savings Bank—closed
before the meeting could take place. The group reconvened in
Louisville, Kentucky. The focus of the 1929 meeting was making it
through the crisis by cooperation, and a few banks were proving just
that principle. When Citizens Trust, the pillar of the Atlanta community, was suffering a liquidity shortage, Mechanics and Farmers'
C. C. Spaulding gave the bank a loan that enabled its survival.[107]
Citizens Trust reopened triumphantly after the bank holiday of
March 6, 1933, having paid out every claim.[108] Maggie Walker also
arranged a merger that saved her bank along with two others.

Most were not so lucky. The Great Depression brought down both
the titans of black finance and the budding shoots of smaller black
banks. After the Dust Bowl trauma settled, only eight black-owned

banks survived: Citizens and Southern Bank and Trust Company of Philadelphia (Wright's bank), Citizens Savings Bank and Trust Company of Nashville, Citizens Trust Company of Atlanta, Consolidated Bank and Trust Company of Richmond (Maggie Walker's bank), Crown Savings Bank of Newport News, Danville (Virginia) Savings Bank and Trust Company, Mechanics and Farmers Bank of Durham, and Charleston (South Carolina) Mutual and Savings Bank. These surviving banks were affiliated with either another commercial entity, a church, or a fraternal organization.[109]

Black commercial banks in the North failed due to runs and heavy loan losses. As the saying goes, when Wall Street gets a cold, Harlem gets pneumonia. Black ghetto properties quickly lost value, creating severe loan losses for black banks holding these loans.[110] When the NNBA met in 1930, Maggie Walker was the featured speaker, and she tried to restore confidence in the industry. She reminded the press and the public that bank failures were universal and that "a thousand times more Negro money is lost year after year in other banks than is lost in Negro banks."[111]

This was true, but the trauma-inducing insolvency of black banks during the Great Depression could not mask their more fundamental weakness. After having visited "practically every large city where a Negro bank is operating," studying their financial statements, and speaking with management, prominent banker Arnett Lindsay concluded in 1929, months before the Great Depression, "that there are not more than half a dozen banks owned and operated by Negroes, which are actually making even ordinary bank profits by specializing in commercial loans." He added that although these banks served "a useful purpose in promoting thrift and homeownership, "this is not commercial banking in the true sense of the word."[112] The truth was that even before the Great Depression, these banks could not have grown wealth for the black community insofar as they operated in a segregated economy.

In the parlance of the later battles for school integration, not only was it impossible for black banking to be separate and equal, they could not even be separate and profitable. Three specific features of the black condition impeded even the strongest black banks in the pre-Depression era from their central aim of wealth accumulation: poverty, housing segregation, and the centripetal pull of the money multiplier to the dominant banking sector.

The first source of weakness was the black banks' liabilities. When a customer deposits money into a bank, she creates a loan to the bank, but a loan that the customer can demand back at any time—this is why it is called a "demand deposit." For a bank customer or a business, a deposit is an asset; but for a bank, customer deposits are liabilities. Banks, therefore, fund their business through liabilities that can best be described as short-term, unpredictable loans. Commercial banks rely on the probability that not all of their customers will demand their money at one time, and therefore they do not hold these deposits at the bank—they only hold a fraction at any one time. This is called "fractional reserve banking," which means banks hold a small amount at the bank called "reserves" and lend out the rest. Banks make money on the spread between what they pay to their depositors and how much they charge on their loans. Bank profits are made by taking these deposits and turning them into loans—called maturity transformation.

This process is risky. If bank customers suddenly demand more money than the bank has in reserve, there is trouble for the bank—especially before the creation of federal deposit insurance. Customers knew that that the bank could not pay all depositors at once, so they would "run" the bank—sometimes literally running to the bank—to demand their deposits before there was nothing left to claim. Fractional reserve banking meant that there were only enough reserves to pay out a fraction of the depositors—the "runners" needed to make sure they got to the bank first. A run usually meant certain failure unless the bank could find enough liquidity (cash) to satisfy enough depositors so that they would leave their deposits in the bank.

Black bank deposits differed from those in white banks—they were smaller and were more frequently withdrawn, which made them more risky.[113] Most black depositors had no stores of wealth to invest in the bank and were just depositing money from their wages, keeping small amounts to live on. They put their sums into black banks for safekeeping, but also looked to those deposits as rainy-day funds during frequent stormy weather. Deposits so small and volatile are a costly liability for banks. Banks spend the same amount of money in overhead and servicing costs for a deposit of $1,000 as for one of $1.50, but the larger deposit can yield more profit when it is lent out. In other words, a bank receiving three large deposits amounting to $500,000 from three big businesses spends less money and makes more profit off those deposits than a bank that receives $500,000 dollars of deposits from 5,000 people. Black banks had much higher operating costs than white banks because they spent more and earned less from their poor customers.[114]

A customer base that deposits little and withdraws often creates another less obvious financial bind for banks.[115] Because of the volatility of their deposits, black banks had to keep more cash on hand as reserves or invest in other more liquid assets such as government securities, which were safer than loans. They did so because they needed to make sure they always had enough cash at the bank to pay out to depositors. They also held very high capital ratios to offset this risk.[116] In 1920, the mean capital ratio for white banks was 18 percent; black banks had an average capital ratio of 32.9 percent.[117] This meant that the bank owners invested more of their own money and earnings in the bank to keep it secure, but this severely restricted their profitability and lending capacity.

In order to minimize the risks presented by their small and fickle deposits, bank managers held more capital, cash reserves, and liquid assets. All of this meant that they could make fewer loans and thus were not able to fully enjoy the benefits of fractional reserve lending.[118] Fewer loans meant less revenue for the banks, less credit for the community, and less wealth creation overall. A profitable bank tries to hold as few reserves as possible, have as low a capital ratio as allowed by law, and make as many loans as possible in order to maximize profits.[119] Black banks were trying to stay safe, but their weak deposit structure put them in a bind. Black banks were lending with one hand tied behind their back. What weakened these banks is the paltry wealth of the communities they served, which was also the reason they were created—to provide financial services to a poor population.

Another source of vulnerability for black banks was their assets, or loan portfolios. The fate of black banks was tied up with the fate of black businesses, and the precarious state of the latter meant that black banks lacked the healthy diversity required for sound banking. Most thriving banks prefer to hold a mix of commercial and real estate loans, because a diversified portfolio is safer and more profitable. But black banks made loans almost exclusively on residential real estate because the vast majority of black businesses were "pebbles on the seashore," small service operations with no need of bank financing.[120]

The black banking market was thus created to meet one key credit demand: home loans. It was widely acknowledged that white banks did not lend to blacks for home buying, and if they did, they charged much higher interest rates.[121] The portfolios of black banks were dominated by home loans, which were the balance sheet equivalent of a ticking time bomb. Home loans were inherently risky, but the key problem for black banks was not the proportion of these loans they held, but their nature.[122] The problem was that the collateral for these assets—properties owned by blacks in locations where blacks could buy—diminished in value as soon as the loan was made. To understand this phenomenon, which reveals the core problem of black wealth creation and bank viability, it is important to understand how thoroughly enforced segregation was in the North and how it affected housing prices.

The North maintained strict racial segregation through a series of tools used consecutively and simultaneously, including violence, zoning laws, and racial covenants—much of which was organized by neighborhood associations and realtors.[123] The color line—the place where the black ghetto met the white community—was a highly contested space and the scene of much of the race rioting and violence.[124] As the swelling ghetto pushed against the white community, the white community pushed back forcefully.[125] The black middle class were usually the early settlers forging into the racial frontier by buying homes in new territory. With a 50 percent down payment required for a home purchase at the time, the only buyers of black property were the black upper class—only 2 percent of the black population in the North in the 1920s.[126]

These professional-class pioneers were often the primary victims of bombings and mob violence. A famous case was that of Doctor Ossian Sweet and his wife Gladys, who bought a home outside Detroit's Black Bottom slums in 1925. The Sweets bought their home for $18,500, which was $6,000 more than its market value. The home was shortly besieged by a white mob that surrounded the home for several days hoping to pressure the Sweets to abandon their property. When the mob began to break windows, Sweet fought back. He and several friends fired into the crowd and killed a member of the mob. Sweet was charged with murder and was defended by Clarence Darrow and Walter White, president of the NAACP. This case was an outlier, not just because Sweet was acquitted of a murder charge by an all-white jury, but because he fought back in the first place. Most black professionals were not willing to wage a violent defense of their home.[127]

The reason white neighbors would threaten a black doctor was not necessarily that they did not want him in their neighborhood, but because it signaled a racial breach. Members of the black middle class moving into a neighborhood were seen as harbingers of a neighborhood being swallowed by the ghetto.[128] These fears turned into self-fulfilling prophesies, because once a neighborhood "tipped" and was seen as a "black neighborhood," whites fled and the neighborhood declined and was swallowed up by the ghetto. In 1930, a realtor turned University of Chicago economist, Homer Hoyt, created an economic model based on extensive real estate data that revealed that real estate in a neighborhood declined as soon as a few blacks purchased property there. The lower market values were a result, he explained, "due entirely to racial prejudice, which may have no reasonable basis."[129] This declining property value did not affect the home prices of most immigrant groups—only blacks and Mexicans.

This is why whites were so vigilant in keeping blacks out of their neighborhoods. They were motivated not only by outright prejudice, but also by fears of asset depreciation (which was, of course, a correlated result of racism). Otherwise, why go through the trouble of organizing associations, making contracts, and planting bombs? Whites on the edges of the black community were protecting their financial investments by keeping blacks out. This racial cartel not only reinforced white advantage; it created a negative feedback loop for black wealth creation. Because black homes were not increasing in value, black homeowners were excluded from the clearest path to wealth creation available to the middle class. On the flip side, through racial violence, whites retained the racial purity of their neighborhoods, and their home values increased precisely because they were not in black neighborhoods. The ability to retain property value—even through violence—was a uniquely white privilege.

Data also revealed what was already obvious to the black middle class: that the first blacks to own a home in a formerly white neighborhood paid a premium to buy the home to break the color barrier. So values rose slightly, and then, as more blacks entered the neighborhood, home values suffered a drastic decline.[130] In other words, blacks paid much more for properties, which came to be worth much less the second they were purchased by blacks. This sluggish real estate market contrasted sharply with the inflated rental market within the ghetto. In the densely packed black ghetto, the low supply of tenant housing coupled with high demand meant that rents skyrocketed by 50 percent or more in comparison to rental properties outside the ghetto.[131] Tenants were paying very high prices for increasingly dilapidated housing, and black home-owners paid too much for homes that then lost value. Both sides of the black income scale lost wealth due to segregation. This situation seemingly defies the economic laws of supply and demand, but those laws have never been fully able to account for the intensity of white racism. It is difficult to overestimate the damaging effects of housing segregation on the creation of black wealth or the viability of black banking.

For banks, these mortgages created severe balance sheet prob-lems, because loans often went "underwater" as soon as they were issued.[132] Not only were black banks losing the value of their own in-vestments as their mortgaged properties declined in value, but these loans also created a liquidity bind for black banks because they could not sell them quickly. Black banks had highly illiquid assets, which were essentially stuck on their balance sheets—there was no ready market for black mortgages.[133] When Binga needed liquidity, he selected his best mortgages on "choice pieces of real estate" and offered them for sale to a few white banks in Chicago. The banks re-fused to purchase even these loans because they were "unable to market mortgages on Southside properties."[134] This was likely due to the twin forces of direct racism and the plummeting house values that racism had indirectly wrought. When the Binga Bank failed, it held $800,000 in mortgages in Southside properties.[135]

The raison d'être of these banks—making loans on black property—was also a principal cause of their failure. The rigid lines of segregation had created a robust black banking sector, but the same forces of segregation infected their balance sheets, making it impossible for them to lend at a profit. Black banks might have been able to survive the low incomes of their customers and their focus on home loans—after all, credit unions and building and loans were flourishing during this era by pooling the resources of their low-income customers to buy real estate. The crucial difference, one that would perpetually prove insurmountable, was that black banks' assets, loans on black properties, were not appreciating in value. And this was not a problem the credit unions or building and loans had to deal with, for once the building and loan or credit union helped a member buy a home, that property either retained or increased its value.

Though minutes from NNBL meetings reveal that the black bankers understood their balance sheets to be more vulnerable and risky than their counterparts', there is no evidence that the bankers suspected that these loans would perpetually diminish in value. Even Arnett Lindsay, who observed firsthand that these banks were not profitable, did not think residential loans were a problem and focused his lament on the lack of business loans. The bankers seemed to believe that these loans, if they could be held long enough, would eventually increase in value for the banks and the homeowners.[136]

The hopeful premise on which the entire enterprise was based was that either black communities would eventually acquire enough wealth and buy enough properties to stabilize their prices—or that perhaps whites would stop fleeing black middle-class homeowners. Neither hope has yet to fully materialize. In fact, after the Great Depression, segregation continued to undermine black property values and wealth accumulation. In some ways, it became even harder in the coming decades. Yet to realistically confront and prepare for the obstacles these bankers were facing would have required too bleak a vision—that the U.S. economy would sink into a dramatic decline, that segregation would increase in resiliency, and that racism would continue unabated.

The most crucial structural problem black banks faced was their inability to multiply money due to segregation. Banks create money and wealth through fractional reserve lending. By lending customer deposits, banks create new money; they "multiply" existing money in a process called "the money multiplier effect." A bank customer, Alice, deposits her money in Bank A. Her bank holds a fraction of that money as "reserves" at the bank and lends out the majority of it to another customer, Betty. Betty uses that money to buy a home from

Celia, who deposits that money into her own bank, Bank C. That is new money created from the loan. Alice's bank deposit slip shows that she still has her money at Bank A, but now Celia also has a deposit at Bank C—money that was not there before. In this process, if Alice's initial deposit was $100 and it was lent out ten times, with each bank holding 10 percent for reserves, it would have created $900 of new money.[137] The money supply increases from $100 to $1,000. This is the "magic" of fractional reserve lending. Every time a loan is made, a deposit is *created*. To repeat, banks create money, or bank deposits, by making new loans. This money multiplier effect is what makes banks the engines at the center of the economy— the new money is "created literally out of thin air."[138] This is what Alexander Hamilton meant when he said that banks allow capital to "acquire life" and become productive—banks increase the overall wealth of a community by simply taking deposits and lending them out.

The catch is that they can only do so insofar as the creditors and debtors are operating in the same system. Now let's see what happens when a black bank attempts fractional reserve lending. Anton deposits his money at black-owned Bank A. Bank A makes a loan to Bella, who is black. Bella uses that money to buy a home. For the money multiplier to work in a segregated economy, Bella's money must be recycled in the black economy. Theoretically, black banks would circulate and multiply this money and hum along with white banks doing the same thing—both multiplying money in their own segregated economies. However, this was not possible. During this era, practically without exception, the sellers of the real estate were white and the buyers were black, placing them in separate banking systems. The sale proceeds usually landed in a white bank, while the loan was held at the black bank. Because blacks did not own property, their banks would constantly be stuck in an inferior position and their loans would be swallowed into the white system.

As soon as the black bank loan was deposited into the seller's bank, it had already escaped the black community and would continue to multiply in the white community. Even assuming that the first seller was black, she would have had to deposit her proceeds from the sale back into the black banking sector. Only if both the buyer and seller were black and each deposited their money at black banks could the money multiplier work. Every seller down the line would have to do that for the black banking system to be able to "control the black dollar" and multiply money in the black community. In reality, there would eventually be a white seller in the chain and the money would escape the black community. In the days of strict segregation, when white banks did not lend to blacks and white customers did not deposit money into black banks, the resulting "new" money always went into the white banking sector.[139] Money could not be multiplied in two different segregated banking systems when one did not have much capital to begin with. In other words, the banks themselves could not help the black community hold and multiply capital without changing the structure of property ownership first.

White banks had the advantage of circulating and growing money, and black bank loans just fed into that circulatory system. Not only were black banks not multiplying money in the black community, they were multiplying money in the dominant (white) banking system. Put another way, not only were the white banks multiplying white money, they were multiplying black money as well. If the whole point of black banking was to control the black dollar and put it to work in the black community, black banks simply could not do this.

Not only could black banks not "control the money of the community"; they actually acted like a sieve through which money drained into the mainstream white banks and the mainstream, exclusionary economy. Instead of multiplying money, black banking effected a slow trickle-up of wealth into the white banking system. The profits were being skimmed off the top by the robust mainstream economy, leaving the ghetto economy with the scraps. Eventually, government credit markets would replace the simple apparatus of the money multiplier by providing new sources of loans. But even then, black money continued to leak out of the black economy. Because the dominant economy was taking place outside of the ghetto, its pull could not be resisted. Once in the banking system, money flows toward more money.

Just as the money multiplier circulated white advantage, the ghetto money trap also circulated disadvantage. Because blacks were not home sellers, black banks did not have access to the large deposits received in home sales. This led back to the problem on the liability side, which is that the small deposits in black banks were too costly and had to be offset by fewer loans, which ultimately meant lower profits.

The money multiplier was not broken just for small black banks, but also for large banks like Binga's and the Douglass National Bank.[140] This meant that no matter how much money black leaders, bankers, and the press could convince blacks to put into black-owned banks, the "power of the black dollar" would not push forward the black economy in a significant way. The truth was that segregated communities could not segregate their money. The irony is that black banks, which were created to control the black dollar, *were the very mechanism through which black money flowed out of the community.* Through deposit-taking and lending, black money would always end up in the white banking industry despite the best efforts and highest skills of black bankers. Black banks could not participate in the wealth-producing process around which the entire banking industry is built, precisely because black banks operated on the fringes of a white banking system.

This is not to say that a truly segregated black economy like the one Garvey imagined was not possible. If blacks could have accumulated all black resources into an all-black economy with control of large businesses and ownership of property, their money would not have easily escaped the borders. Blacks would need to be completely independent of whites and buy from, lend to, and employ only blacks. Though some whites and some blacks would have welcomed this outcome, such a world was out of reach because the black community did not accumulate enough property to sustain itself. The underlying problem for blacks was that whites started with all the property and blacks with none of it. This basic economic reality created a positive feedback loop for whites and a negative one for blacks, cycles that continue to have profound effects to the present day. Black banks' segregated assets, volatile liabilities, and broken money-multiplying apparatus were causing a slow bleed of money and resources in the sector even before the Great Depression dealt the fatal blow.

The Depression only ratcheted up the hardships faced by the black community because Jim Crow segregation concentrated and intensified poverty.[141] Starvation and disease were rampant, and infant mortality and premature death were much higher in the black community.[142] In 1935, W. E. B. Du Bois said, "No more critical situation ever faced the Negroes of America than that of today."[143] Gunnar Myrdal called the economic situation of blacks "pathological" in his momentous 1944 study of the state of the black population, *The American Dilemma*. He concluded that, "except for a small minority enjoying upper or middle class status, the masses of American Negroes, in the rural South and in the segregated slum quarters in Southern and Northern cities, are destitute. They own little property, even their household goods are mostly inadequate and dilapidated. Their incomes are not only low but irregular. They thus live from day to day and have scant security of the future." Myrdal concluded that America's professed creed of equality and freedom did not match the unjust and immoral treatment of its black citizens—this was the American Dilemma.[144]

The initial optimism of the Great Migration and the promise of the "kinder mistress" of the North went unfulfilled as the black migrants faced the hardening walls of segregation. Meanwhile, many blacks in the South lost their land, which led to more migrants flooding the northern ghettos. Racial hostility in the South had not abated. Black children were being denied education in the South and black men were still being lynched without even the fiction of legal process. It was clear that Booker T. Washington's hope that whites would come to respect blacks after seeing their industriousness was only a pipe dream. Du Bois quipped, "The colored people of America are coming to face the fact quite calmly that most white Americans do not like them."[145]

Having lost hope that whites would eventually yield to black integration, Du Bois doubled down on black business, arguing again that the only path forward for blacks was to build a separate economy. Du Bois warned blacks that to "await the salvation of a white God is idiotic."[146] This was no time for black leaders to retreat into a resigned despair over their lack of economic progress. He urged the black community to deploy their "political power, their power as consumers, and their brainpower" to bolster their segregated communities without waiting for white help. He promised that by "voluntary and increased segregation" and "by careful autonomy and planned economic organization," blacks could build a strong community.[147] He sounded a lot like his foe Washington with this advice, but lest one overemphasize the similarities, Du Bois displayed a characteristic distrust of black capitalists and the profit motive. In a 1942 newspaper column, he described black entrepreneurs as a group without ethics or concern for their people. "What American Negro businessmen have got to remember is that a new economic morality is facing the world, and the emancipation from unfair private profit is going to be as great a crusade in the future as emancipation from Negro slavery was in the past."[148] While he still championed black business, he urged black businessmen to seek the economic interests of the entire race instead of their own profits.

Not only were black bankers stuck in a perpetual money pit, but they were often cast as the villains when things went wrong. That their loans went primarily to the black middle class and were out of reach of the majority of blacks sometimes made black banks the targets of criticism.[149] Abram Harris was one of these critics. Harris was the first nationally renowned black economist and the first to do a comprehensive study of black banks, called *The Negro as Capitalist* (1936). Harris headed the Howard economics department from 1936 to 1945, when he became the first black economist at the University of Chicago. He was recruited there by Frank Knight, a founder of the famed Chicago School of Economics who fostered the likes of Milton Friedman and George Stigler. Harris had held Marxist sympathies while at Howard, but with his move to Chicago, his economic philosophy became more traditional. Harris was close friends with sociologist E. Franklin Frazier and was one of the handful of black "insiders" who helped shape Gunnar Myrdal's formative study.

Harris claimed that the bankers' success was made possible by the "skillful exploitation of the Negro masses."[150] His argument was that because black banks were run on the deposit base of the masses of low-income savers and their loans were real estate loans to black elites, they were enriching the elite and themselves on the backs of the poor. Put another way, the losses of these banks were primarily borne by the small depositors and the gains rarely benefited them, particularly because bank loans did not address the problem of the "appalling housing needs" of lower-class black citizens.[151] However, Harris's criticism overstated the gains made by middle-class blacks and black banks. The poor certainly lost their hard-earned savings, but the bankers lost their banks as well. Apart from his claims of exploitation, Harris's study was also the first to challenge the notion that a segregated black banking system could work. As a trained economist and without the burden of being a black political leader, Harris was able to confront and challenge one of the central tenets of black self-help—that black banks were a good idea. Harris had understood the trap of segregated banking and had tried to explain the flawed assumptions underlying the enterprise.

Carter Woodson rejected Harris's blasphemy. Woodson, a prominent scholar and historian, believed that community self-help in the form of supporting black business and black banking was the only path forward. In *The Mis-Education of the Negro,* Woodson criticized the skeptics of black banking and business, explaining that "the 'highly educated' Negroes who have studied economics at Harvard, Yale, Columbia, and Chicago will say that the Negro cannot succeed in business because their professors who have never had a moment's experience in this sphere have written accordingly."[152] According to Woodson, those who argued that blacks could not operate a separate financial system had been misinformed by white hegemony and "miseducated" to hate themselves.[153] He did not name Harris specifically, but he hardly had to because Harris was alone among the "highly educated" critics of black banks.

Woodson had his own explanation for why black banks had failed. "Negro banks, as a rule, have failed because the people, taught that their own pioneers in business cannot function in this sphere, withdrew their deposits. An individual cannot live after you extract the blood from his veins. The strongest bank in the United States will last only so long as the people will have sufficient confidence in it to keep their *money* there. In fact, confidence of the people is worth more than money."[154] Blacks had avoided black enterprise because they believed whites would serve them better—a complaint lodged by many other black leaders and bankers.[155] He recounted a few stories about blacks frequenting a white restaurant that would only serve them through the back door, when they could have received much better service by several black restaurants in the same area.[156] To Woodson, black businessmen had "made mistakes," but "the weak link in the chain is that they are not properly supported and do not always grow strong enough to pass through a crisis."

Commerce Department official Billboard Jackson also blamed the black community for their lack of support of their banks. After a survey of the black banking and business landscape, Jackson noted with dismay that the average deposit in black banks was only $70, compared with $365 in white banks, and said "in the larger cities, especially, much of that larger figure is the money of the Negroes which ought to be made available for their businessmen."[157] He did not consider that perhaps smaller deposits were the norm because the black population had less money to save.

Despite the failure of the industry and despite the only thorough economic research showing the fundamental problems with black banking, most prominent black leaders continued to urge the community to support black banks and businesses. As long as Jim Crow dominated the South and segregation the North, what choice did they have? "If the whites are to continue for some time in doing drudgery to the exclusion of Negroes, the latter must find another way out." Woodson explained "that under the present system of capitalism the Negro has no chance to toil upward in the economic sphere" except by building their own economy.[158] Moreover, economic self-sufficiency provided a way to resist the powerlessness of living in a racist society and to maintain a glimmer of hope, or, as Du Bois explained, "a hope not hopeless but unhopeful."[159] This is not to say that black leaders were not fighting for civil or political rights—that fight had never ceased. But it had yet to yield meaningful fruit. While equality, integration, and acceptance into white society were not forthcoming, what else was there to do but rely on your own community and hope for a radical change? In fact, just such a change was coming.

4

The New Deal for White America

The New Deal changed America's legal and political landscape in myriad ways, but perhaps nothing changed more radically than the nation's banking and credit markets. Unfortunately, most of the significant New Deal policies were administered in such a way as to maintain the South's racial hierarchy, which meant an almost categorical exclusion of blacks from government subsidies. The bulk of the New Deal reforms can accurately be described as "white affirmative action" because state resources were used to provide direct financial advantages to white Americans at the expense of other racial groups.[1]

And this outcome was no accident. The only way Roosevelt could enact his progressive platform was with the backing of the Senate's southern Democrats. And this strong, influential, and coherent political wing of the party was adamant that their economic structure and racial hierarchy be protected. Though southern legislators were a minority, their unified bloc gave them outsized influence in their own party and allowed them to hold most of the senior committee positions in Congress—nothing could get done without the blessing of the southern wing. Roosevelt had to make a difficult choice: equal treatment of the races or large-scale historic social reforms. He chose the latter, and the choice had long-lasting effects.[2]

Without explicit racial exclusions, the laws were crafted in such a way as to exclude most blacks from the social welfare programs. For example, most blacks in the South were farmworkers and domestic workers. In devising legislation that regulated work hours, enabled unions, set minimum wages, and established Social Security, the southern bloc excluded both groups, and thus the majority of black southerners, from the protective legislation. The purpose of these exclusions, as expressed by southern legislators, was to maintain the inferior status of black laborers in the southern economy.[3] Speaking in opposition to setting a minimum for farm wages, Florida Representative James Mark Wilcox explained, "[T]here is another matter of great importance in the South and that is the problem of our Negro labor. There has always been a difference in the wage scale of white and colored labor . . . [fixing wages] might work on some sections of the United States but those of us who know the true situation know that it just will not work in the South. You cannot put the Negro and the white man on the same basis and get away with it."[4] Most often, southern senators did not even have to speak against the legislation. They used their seniority positions on Senate committees to make sure bills were drafted in such a way as to exclude blacks; otherwise, a bill would never reach the floor for a vote.[5] According to the NAACP, the legislation aimed at protecting workers against hostile labor conditions was "like a sieve with holes just big enough for the majority of Negroes to fall through."[6]

Where blacks could not be left out, the southern bloc ensured that the laws would be administered locally, where officials would allocate benefits in accordance with the racial order. One administrator of the Federal Emergency Relief Administration (FERA) said that "he had to tailor relief . . . to accommodate the demands of southern plantation owners for cheap farm labor by curtailing [the level of] relief payments to agricultural laborers and sharecroppers."[7] This was done across the New Deal programs to exclude the large majority of blacks from relief measures and the newly created social safety net, a result characterized as "a form of policy apartheid."[8]

One pivotal outcome of these labor-protecting exclusions, and specifically regarding the right to collective action, was that they left black workers powerless to organize and demand better working conditions. The result not only hurt black workers; it gave white workers a leg up as the union movement achieved monumental improvements in workers' rights for their members. Through collective action, white workers gained a voice and a seat at the bargaining table, while black workers were effectively silenced.

These exclusions drove a wedge between black and white working classes as black workers became a point of contention between labor and employers. Often, when a union and an employer were in a labor dispute, black workers were recruited to cross the picket line to fill the whites' places. Black workers thus came to represent strikebreakers who posed a threat to union negotiations, which resulted in acts of open hostility and violence by union members toward the black workers. As a measure of goodwill to boost labor relations, it was customary for companies to charter trains to ship blacks back south. As more blacks left the boll weevil–infested cotton fields of the South for the promise of work in northern industry, they faced factories infested with racial animosity. Where they could have joined together and drawn more strength from numbers, blacks were scapegoated in industrial labor struggles because they were left out of union membership.[9]

Even as the South's grip on Congress ensured that the New Deal would be passed along racial lines, southern progressivism and populism assured that the New Deal was a rejection of unrestrained capital markets. The New Deal was a radically progressive reordering of American business regulation. Its centrally controlled economic planning, Keynesian stimulus programs, and foundational social welfare infrastructure made it the closest Americans came to democratic socialism.[10] That too was led by the South. The South had long fought the northern "money trusts" and advocated more government intervention in breaking up monopolies, loosening credit, and regulating financial markets. The New Deal achieved all of these aims by restructuring financial markets to achieve specific policy goals.[11]

This combination of progressive banking reform and a regressive racial hierarchy meant that postwar American prosperity was propelled through a mortgage and consumer credit apparatus that was exclusionary. The modern credit system created by New Deal reforms segregated access to loans based on race. The alphabet soup of new credit and banking agencies, the Home Owners Loan Corporation (HOLC), the Federal Home Loan Banks (FHLB), the Federal National Mortgage Association (FNMA or Fannie Mae), the Federal Housing Administration (FHA), and the Federal Deposit Insurance Corporation (FDIC), were all geared toward the rapid and effective dissemination of low-cost credit to new homeowners. These agencies coupled with postwar economic growth created a robust homeowning, capital-creating, and predominantly white middle class. They also made the black ghetto a permanent feature of the twentieth century.

This result was not inevitable. There was another route available to the Roosevelt administration, which would not have resulted in such stark inequality. During the era of big government spending programs, Roosevelt could have used public funds to build low-income housing and a much-needed infrastructure for the urban poor. He almost did just that. One of the most robust New Deal programs was the Public Works Administration (PWA), which was run by Secretary of the Interior Harold Ickes, a committed civil rights advocate and former president of the Chicago NAACP. The PWA was the federal government's largest construction effort to date, with a $6 billion budget used to build thousands of bridges and roads that put millions of Americans to work. But the initial plan of the PWA's housing division was to use funds to build homes and infrastructure in poverty-stricken areas, including inner-city ghettos. The motivation was not the housing per se; rather, as with many New Deal programs, the point was to provide a job-creating economic stimulus while offering a benefit to the public.

Ickes believed that the financial stimulus should be used to address America's economic and social problems, including urban poverty. He warned that if the slums were not rehabilitated, they would continue to perpetuate poverty and inhibit economic recovery in America's cities.[12] No less than "the future financial stability of many of our urban centers" depended on "the prompt reclamation of their slum areas," said Ickes. By 1933, Ickes had set aside $485 million to build low-cost apartment buildings across the country. This plan was fiercely opposed by critics who said that it was not the responsibility of the federal government to deal with inner-city housing problems.[13] The opposition believed that the goal of the PWA should be to get private investors on board by offering them a share of the profits. Investors were not interested in rebuilding the slums, so the plan was scuttled.[14]

However, investors were interested in revamping the single-family mortgage market, so this was the route the reforms followed. Not only did this choice not help the ghetto, it would work directly against it in both predictable and unexpected ways. For example, many PWA grants in major cities like New York and Chicago were used to route roads and bridges over and through the ghetto, a decision that favored suburban car commuters, left public transportation in a state of neglect and disrepair for decades, and bifurcated neighborhoods in long-established communities.[15] On the other side of the color line, government-fueled mortgage markets offered the white middle class an escape from the cities even as it trapped the black poor within them. Consequently, race became the primary determinant of homeownership for the next century.

Before banks pumped mortgage credit into America's suburbs, the Home Owners Loan Corporation fatefully mapped out America's racial geography. The HOLC permanently changed mortgage lending in the United States by simplifying and streamlining the home mortgage. Part of the streamlining process was the creation of standardized home appraisals. HOLC appraisers used census data and elaborate questionnaires to predict the likelihood of property appreciation in neighborhoods across the country. The HOLC then used this data to create meticulous maps giving each metropolitan region and neighborhood across the country a value. These maps had four color categories based on perceived risk: A (green), B (blue), C (yellow), and D (red), green being the most desirable and red being the least.

In making judgments about a home's potential to appreciate, HOLC mapmakers, like individual appraisers before them, used the race of residents as a proxy for desirability. Green neighborhoods were homogeneous and white. At the other end of the scale, the red neighborhoods were predominantly black. In fact, race was a greater factor in a neighborhood's predicted decline than other structural characteristics such as the age of homes, proximity to city centers, creditworthiness of residents, transportation opportunities, public parks, or any other features.[16] Obviously, these designations became a self-fulfilling prophesy. This process of "redlining" eventually created a dual credit market based on race. W. E. B. Du Bois was vindicated in his 1903 prophecy that "the problem of the Twentieth Century is the problem of the color line," but perhaps in a way that even the wary Du Bois could not have imagined.[17]

The HOLC appraisers did not create the ghetto, and they were no more racist than the broader American public. Nor were they wrong when they labeled black neighborhoods undesirable—whites simply did not want to live near blacks. But they did institutionalize racial segregation in housing and made it a formal feature of the mortgage credit markets. This not only meant that blacks could not buy homes and build capital in the "undesirable" inner city; it also meant that they were trapped in neighborhoods in rapid decline, having been defined as such by the self-reinforcing judgments of government bureaucrats. The reason these maps lingered for so long was that private banks used them as models when creating their own "residential security maps" and deciding where to lend. Even this discriminatory practice might have abated with time had the Federal Housing Administration and the Veterans Administration (VA) not used them for their more consequential mortgage program.

The FHA did more to shape American life than any other government agency created during the New Deal. It is also unparalleled in the injustice its policies wrought on the black population. The FHA was created by the National Housing Act of 1934 and was supplemented and expanded through the 1944 Servicemen's Readjustment Act (the GI Bill), administered by the VA. Between 1934 and 1968, the FHA and VA programs operated to open a spigot of mortgage lending that flowed through the banking system.[18] The FHA did not lend money itself, but it created a large insurance fund backed by the U.S. Treasury that would guarantee all approved mortgage loans, which shifted the bulk of the risk of loan default from banks to the government.[19] By creating a buffer to absorb default risks, this new government infrastructure opened the floodgates for an unprecedented amount of private capital to flood mortgage markets. Virtually overnight, mortgage loans became easy, risk free, and abundant.

This transformation was aided by the 1938 creation of the Federal National Mortgage Association (FNMA or Fannie Mae), which created a network in which buyers and sellers could exchange mortgage loans. Private and institutional investors in one part of the country could invest in mortgages in another, ensuring that capital would always find yield. Because capital was so richly rewarded, it increased, as did bank profits.[20] What the government was doing was creating a network and a platform that drew in capital from all corners and multiplied it. The FHA, together with Fannie Mae, were blowing on the embers of the lending market until it became a full flame. The fuel was provided by private capital and the profits would go to those private investors. (However, as became clear decades later, catastrophic losses in this credit market would not be borne by the private sector alone.)

Banks increasingly relied on the protocol and standards provided by the government agencies that were insuring the mortgages and managing their resale. Interest rates and terms converged, as did the types of borrowers. Banks were much less likely to take risks on borrowers who did not fit the gold standard, which was white, middle class, and male. Yet to call those who qualified for these loans "the middle class" is an evasive and circular description. Many were blue-collar wage workers, but it was precisely through these mortgages that they became the much-heralded American middle class. These borrowers would not have been able to buy homes before these reforms; over half of mortgage borrowers earned less than $2,500 per year, or the equivalent of $40,000 in 2017.[21] After these programs, mortgage loans became far more accessible than they had ever been, as banks significantly reduced down payment requirements, lengthened loan terms, and slashed interest rates.[22] In the transformed mortgage market, borrowers could pay less in mortgage payments than they had been paying in rent. A borrower who moved from renting a small apartment in the city to owning a large home in the suburbs was actually saving money. Typical was the former New York City resident who said of his new home in suburban New Jersey, "We had been paying $50 per month rent, and here we come up and live for $29.00 a month." If you could save a few thousand dollars, you could buy a house, build wealth, and become middle class.[23]

Millions of mortgage loans on mass-produced homes created ready-made communities across the country, fundamentally changing American culture. Pop-up suburbs came prepackaged with parks, restaurants, bowling alleys, and movie theaters to provide the setting that would define middle-class life. The Norman Rockwell vision of America, of community, family, and hard work, was born during this era and mythologized thereafter. Many traditionalists wistfully remember this golden era of American life when things were "simple" and "wholesome" and there was optimism, prosperity, and growth as far as the eye could see. Yet this was a manufactured prosperity that left blacks out. It was achieved at their expense.

The prosperity fueled by the abundant flow of mortgage credit stopped firmly at the red lines around the black ghettos. The protocols and standards of the FHA pushed whites up and out of the slums into the suburbs, but they held blacks in. The discriminatory policies of the FHA were even more explicit than the HOLC mapmaking. The bureaucracy was now actually enforcing segregation. The FHA's 1939 *Underwriting Manual* explicitly prohibited lending in neighborhoods that were changing in racial composition.[24] In a 1941 memo, the FHA unapologetically explained that "the rapidly rising Negro population has produced a problem in the maintenance of real estate values."[25] A good neighborhood, according to the FHA, was one that prevented "inharmonious racial groups," which meant that the only groups that did not threaten property values were white families.

Once the FHA made its preferences clear, the natural operations of the credit market created racially pure white suburbs. Enforcing racial purity, or a "harmonious racial mix," became a vested interest for homeowners, realtors, and banks—all of whom held a financial stake in the mortgages. "If a neighborhood is to retain stability," said the FHA manual, "it is necessary that properties shall continue to be occupied by the same social and racial classes." The FHA even offered suggestions for the best way of achieving this result, which they said was through "[race-based] subdivision regulations and suitable restrictive covenants."[26] So neighborhood groups vigilantly enforced racial covenants. Racial covenants were promises made by homeowners that they would never sell, rent, or lease their homes to nonwhites, guaranteeing that a neighborhood association could sue any white homeowner who stepped out of line by selling to blacks. The FHA only stopped recommending racial covenants in February 1950, two years after the Supreme Court found such covenants unenforceable in the landmark 1948 case *Shelly v. Kramer*.[27]

The FHA policies resulted in some outrageous acts of segregation. Kenneth Jackson describes how, when a white neighborhood in Detroit came too close to the borders of the black neighborhood, the homes were denied mortgage approvals. The solution? A white developer built a concrete wall between the two neighborhoods. It worked, and the white mortgages were approved.[28] Such strong enforcement of the color line unsurprisingly led to an uptick of violence against black homeowners.[29] But in the end, the policies achieved their desired outcome. Between 1934 and 1968, 98 percent of FHA loans went to white Americans.[30] In some cases, *whole cities* were ineligible for FHA funds.[31] Levittown, New York, the emblematic suburb, was typical of the racial divide. As late as 1960, "not a single one of the Long Island Levittown's 82,000 residents was black."[32] Even if whites preferred to buy homes in racially mixed neighborhoods, the FHA prevented them from doing so. The federal government was now enforcing credit discrimination with the full force of its monetary powers.

The FHA was not creating these preferences, but reflecting the reality that white Americans preferred to live in segregated communities. If "the market" punished home prices in mixed-race neighborhoods, the FHA manual was simply reflecting that market reality and protecting the agency's investments. But the only "market" that mattered to the FHA was the white majority, and the FHA was unwilling to use the strength of the government and its leverage in the credit market to challenge this racism. In his 1955 book *Forbidden Neighbors,* urban planner Charles Abrams said that the "FHA adopted a racial policy that could well have been culled from the Nuremberg laws. From its inception FHA set itself up as the protector of all white neighborhoods."[33] What resulted was a Jim Crow credit market.

The problem with suburbs full of homeowners and urban ghettos comprised of tenants was not just that it caused generational wealth inequality; it also affected the avenues of opportunity available to residents of these disparate communities. The disparity in community resources had to do, in part, with the operation of the American tax system, which gives local municipalities control of the bulk of their own tax dollars instead of distributing taxes nationwide or statewide. The creation of the white suburb meant that white communities had more tax revenues with which to build better schools, parks, and infrastructure, and the ghettos did not. Government credit led to a housing boom, a homeowning American middle class, and communities where future generation could be nurtured through well-funded public and private accommodations. Meanwhile, the cycle worked the other way in the ghetto—poverty led to institutional breakdown, which led to even more poverty.

As black neighborhoods became overpopulated, blight and crime rose. The largest wave of the Great Migration, spanning from 1940 to 1970, involved an exodus of several million blacks out of the South, which further concentrated the population of the ghetto.[34] Harlem, which had been in full bloom in the 1920s, had by the 1950s become dilapidated and rat-infested—so bad was the rat problem that specific coalitions were formed to address the problem, and it was a repeated topic of conversation in Congress.[35] Asthma, disease, drug addiction, and tuberculous were rampant. By 1952, nearly fifteen times as many African Americans in Harlem were dying of tuberculosis than among the all-white residents of Flushing, Queens.[36]

Such a stark disparity between the races led some observers to conclude that the black community was suffering as a result of some cultural failing such as family breakdown or lack of education.[37] It seemed incomprehensible to some Americans living amid postwar prosperity to believe that there were any economic or systemic barriers that might have been responsible for the divergent fates of the communities. A black businessman in Chicago lamented that the banks refused to lend to qualified black borrowers on the one hand, and then turned around and blamed the black community's credit problems on poor education or inferior culture.[38] The government credit programs had so fundamentally tilted the scale against poor blacks and toward the white middle class that using "culture" to explain away the difference was absurd and insulting. Yet these theories would only gain momentum over time.

As harmful as the government-produced segregation was, it is only half the story. Into the void created by the FHA's red lines came high-cost lenders and contract sellers. Deprivation is often linked with exploitation. Because blacks were deprived of the mortgage bounty created by government guarantees, they were ripe for exploitation by the sharks. Contract sellers took what little equity remained in the ghetto through an abusive innovation that looked a lot like a home mortgage. By the 1950s, 85 percent of the homes sold to blacks in Chicago were sold on contract with exploitative terms.[39] Speculators bought properties for a few thousand dollars with private capital and then "sold" the home to a black buyer through contract for three to four times the price they had paid.[40] But the sale was a ruse.[41] These were contractual arrangements and not mortgages, which made a world of difference. Practically speaking, the "buyer" was just a tenant with an option to own the home at some point in the future. Blacks were paying much more than anyone else in the country on a mortgage, and they were not even getting an actual mortgage.[42] As soon as they missed a payment, they lost everything—house, down payment, and all the work they had put into the property.

The same bankers who refused to lend to black buyers directly were profiting circuitously from such sham sales. Banks gave loans to the speculators who purchased the homes and then used them as "bait" to lure in black buyers.[43] The bankers and brokers defended their actions as a natural consequence of market pricing. "In a free economy a house is worth what anyone will pay for it," said one contract seller.[44]

Of course, mortgage lending at the time was not exactly a free market because interest rates and prices were being artificially lowered due to unprecedented government interventions in credit markets. It was exactly the lack of government mortgage guarantees in the ghetto that made black mortgages so costly. Zooming in solely on the ghetto, the laws of supply-and-demand market pricing seemed to justify these high prices. There was simply too much risk, and investors had to be adequately compensated for taking on the risk of default. But zooming back out to consider the entire nation, it became clear that the government was absorbing all mortgage market risk except for mortgages in the ghetto. So capitalism and the natural rules of the market were indeed responsible for the high price of the properties of the ghetto—it's just that those rules *only* applied to the ghetto. Everywhere else, there was an artificial buoy undergirding the natural markets. As Du Bois had said, "to be a poor man is hard, but to be a poor race in a land of dollars is the very bottom of hardships."[45] The ghetto housing market was poor in the land of credit.

Even blacks who managed to leave the ghetto were caught in the Jim Crow credit market. In a few racially mixed or black suburbs in Atlanta, Memphis, New Orleans, Long Island, and Philadelphia, the black middle class was able to buy homes and find a "good living," according to the *Chicago Defender*. Though these families could obtain mortgages, they were paying much more for them than their white neighbors even when they were buying the same amount of home. In fact, the data on these loans is clear: being black was directly correlated with paying high interest, more clearly than any other factor.[46] The FHA cared more about the race of the borrowers than their creditworthiness, so the black middle class was left to find mortgage loans in the private market. There were few institutional investors willing to provide capital for black mortgages, and black institutions did not have enough capital to provide for all such loans.[47]

After the original exclusion from the low-cost FHA loans, the debt cycle became self-reinforcing. While the small black middle class may have been earning incomes similar to the white middle class, their upward mobility carried much higher interest. Over 70 percent of suburban black families had to borrow just so they could purchase cars, appliances, furniture, and other life necessities. Because the black middle class had more debt, they were charged higher interest on each new loan. More debt begets higher interest and vice versa. The added debt burden and high interest was a direct result of the lack of wealth, and, looping around once again, the debt made it even harder to accumulate more wealth. The debt–wealth cycle fed on itself. Black middle-class families making the same income as the white middle class had much less wealth—a disparity that both created their need for debt and was *caused by* their costly debt. White families had twenty times more wealth than black families.[48] Even the lowest-income whites had average wealth greater than the highest-earning black families.[49]

This amount of spending on debt drew the ire of anticapitalists and black intellectuals like E. Franklin Frazier, who assailed the black middle class, or the "black bourgeois," for living on debt just to maintain their social status.[50] Others like Edwin Berry of the Young Urban League also chastised the group's indebtedness as irresponsible and showy.[51] Research reveals, however, that black families were not buying more than whites, they were just paying much more for the same amount of household goods.[52] Whites too were financing middle-class life through mortgage and consumer debt, but the black middle class was paying more for the same life.

It was not just mortgage credit that diverged along racial lines; the New Deal also transformed the consumer credit market. Consumer lending before the Great Depression was usually in the form of installment loans, a loan that is paid off in small amounts over a short period of time. The loan was provided by the same store that sold the merchandise—an arrangement that was risky for the lender and expensive for the borrower. The interest rates on these loans were usually high, and retailers often charged even more than what was allowed by law by simply marking up the price of the goods. Black families in the ghetto, with low wages and wealth, relied almost exclusively on installment loans to buy appliances and furniture.[53]

The FHA transformed the consumer credit market by lowering its risks and enabling banks, finance companies, and credit card companies to make profits on consumer loans for the first time. Once the

FHA guarantees fueled the creation of the robust consumer credit market, the guarantees were no longer needed, and the market tumbled forward on its own with capital from private finance companies and banks. The same mechanism of government guarantees and secondary market networks was used to propel the consumer credit industry, attract capital, reduce risk, and increase profits. Interest rates were also lower because the risk was being shared across the market instead of by an individual seller. If suburban life was created by FHA home loans, it was enhanced by consumer loans that bought life-enhancing luxuries like cars, appliances, and apparel. The consumer credit market shifted from the rigid and expensive installment lending model to the flexible and less expensive "revolving credit" enabled by the credit card. Credit card companies allowed borrowers to "revolve" their debt, or roll over their balances. Credit cards also gave borrowers flexibility and significantly expanded purchasing power because they could be used at any retailer.[54]

Most of these consumer loans went toward making purchases that made life easier and more enjoyable, but credit also provided a buffer to protect wealth and livelihood against the predictable tumults of life. Small loans gave families flexibility in dealing with unexpected costs or tragedies. For example, if wages fell short one month, a car broke down, or the breadwinner lost a job, a family could shift some expenses onto a revolving credit line and protect themselves from hardship or bankruptcy.

There were two groups that did not rely on consumer credit in postwar America: the very wealthy and the poor black population—the wealthy because they did not need it, and blacks who desperately did need it but were excluded from the credit card market. Credit card and finance companies avoided the ghetto due to both racism and its risk-prone economy. Blacks had to keep relying on expensive and extractive installment credit that assured instability and continued poverty.[55] This was another instance in which the New Deal credit reforms created an abundant and low-cost credit market for whites and an extractive and inescapable debt trap for blacks.[56]

The black community was neither ignorant of the effects of the exclusionary Jim Crow credit market nor passive in the face of it. However, the obvious solution—providing their own mortgage loans—proved extremely difficult, as revealed by the struggles of black bankers and mortgage lenders. Black banks were created to offer mortgages to the black community and to fill the void created by government credit policy, but their exclusion from the federally subsidized mortgage markets made their mission much more difficult than that of any other bank operating at the time. Their stories highlight this dilemma as well as the complicated relationship between the bankers and the growing resistance movement. Some saw their role as an integral part of the budding civil rights movement, and others were caught in a conflict between black banking success and the black struggle for equality.

In 1950s Chicago, Dempsey J. Travis tried to provide mortgages to the segregated black belt as Binga had done before him. In his book *An Autobiography of Black Chicago*, Travis explained that there was a lot of demand for mortgage loans by black families, but banks would not lend to them. He refused to get involved in contract selling, which he said had a "slaveship stench." "Exploiting an economically and culturally disadvantaged people in their efforts to seek basic shelter is vile." Instead, he "starved for months" in the business rather than becoming "a bird dog" for the speculators as they plundered the black community.[57]

Travis lamented that the majority of black savings were in white institutions and protested the injustice: "they can't just take Negro savings and not offer loan services in return."[58] He would testify to the U.S. Commission on Civil Rights in 1959 that out of 234 savings and loans institutions in Cook County (Chicago), only twenty-one were willing to make loans to blacks at all, and only *one* bank was willing to grant mortgages to black families buying in white neighborhoods. Commercial banks and life insurance companies were even worse.[59] Travis told a *Wall Street Journal* reporter that "Commercial banks, union pension funds and life insurance companies are scouting all over the country looking for sources of higher investment earnings, but they're almost completely overlooking a market that is screaming to be discovered—mortgage loans on Negro housing.[60]

Knowing he could not rely on any help from the government and "lily-white" mortgage companies, Travis was determined to create his own mortgage bank, and so formed the Sivart Mortgage Corporation ("Travis" spelled backward) in 1953. His ambitious aim was to raise "the 'cotton curtain' between the black community and the

FHA" and counteract the "mortgage bottleneck."[61] Travis explained that the magnitude of the discrimination and "the oppressive effect of the land contract on the black community" convinced him "that the only way a black man could survive in real estate and serve his people was by creating a source within the black community to use some of the community's own wealth." He hoped to harness the "85 percent" of black savings held in white institutions.[62]

Before he could make FHA-approved loans in Chicago, he had to be accredited by the FHA. His application was denied seven times before finally being approved in 1961. This was not uncommon. Edward Irons, founding dean of Howard University's business school suggested that part of the reason that so few black banks formed during this era was that regulators "systematically discouraged [black banks] from seeking charters."[63] Travis's next setback was immediately apparent: even with the FHA approval, banks would not provide him with capital for his business. He was humiliated when a bank executive at Exchange National offered him $15,000 after he had requested a $500,000 line of credit. Travis noted that these banks offered very generous loans to the white realtors in the area. But the bank must have felt that their small loan was an act of benevolence, writing to Travis, "May I also say that it is a pleasure to do business with people like yourself."[64] He rejected the loan and kept his self-respect. When he asked the Drexel National Bank, the bank that his family had used since 1900, he was refused once again. But he said that the rejection hurt less than "the condescending tone of [the chairman's] voice when he made the credit offer." He recounted that it "offended me so deeply that I stormed out of the bank empty-handed, never to return except to close all my accounts." These refusals were inexcusable to Travis because the loans would have been guaranteed through the FHA, which made them effectively risk free. "The cost of maintaining black pride and personal dignity," wrote Travis, "can be extremely high." Finally, through the intervention of a personal friend, Travis secured a $200,000 line of credit from a local immigrant Polish bank so he could start his mortgage business.[65]

Travis, like many other black businessmen, saw his role as both a businessman and a civil rights leader. "To this day, I cannot differentiate between economic problems and civil rights problems—they are irrevocably saddled with each other, more so in this country than anywhere else on planet earth." He believed that social and political rights would be achieved through business success, explaining, "black-controlled businesses could bring more and more blacks into mainstream America." Travis observed the rise and fall of Jesse Binga, Anthony Overton, and cosmetics magnate Charles Murray, and considered these men personal heroes. "My attitude toward material success would always be bound up with my feelings about the situation of blacks in America."[66]

Though Travis's outlook on business success was the modern embodiment of Booker T. Washington's vision, his source of inspiration was Marcus Garvey. He explained that his desire for success came from hearing his family members talking about Garvey's black power movement. He wanted to build a business that countered the white exploitation of the black community. The solution was to harness black capital and put it to use to build the community from within. He therefore opposed efforts to integrate the black community fully into the white one. He lamented that "the desire to integrate and to bury the black identity was very strong in the 1950s." He complained that the National Negro Business League considered deleting the word "Negro" from its title in 1954, and that the Chicago Negro Chamber of Commerce changed its name to the Cosmopolitan Chamber of Commerce.[67]

Travis was able to sustain his mortgage business, but he became convinced that without government help, blacks would never achieve equality. At the tail end of the civil rights era, Dempsey Travis proposed a plan he called "The 1970 Homestead Act," a new credit guarantee program targeted at black homeownership. When white Americans had been given land through the various Homestead Acts, blacks were left out, he reasoned. Nor had blacks been able to own land in America without fear of "being dispossessed by angry white individuals or mob[s]." He was speaking from personal experience as a realtor and longtime resident of Chicago.[68] The proposal went nowhere.

In Harlem, too, there was a movement to harness black money to build the community. The most prominent black-owned banks formed during this period, and the first in Harlem was the Carver Federal Savings Bank, founded in 1948. A group of fourteen community leaders and businessmen formed the bank in order to help servicemen returning from the war, as well as "black working people [who] were effectively barred elsewhere from home loan financing."[69]

The bank raised $225,000 in investment capital from hundreds of Harlem residents. The bank obtained a federal bank charter after the state denied it one. Carver Bank soon became the largest black-owned financial institution in the country, having amassed more than $24.4 million in assets by 1963.[70]

The Reverend Milton Moran Weston II, the bank's president, was born in Tarboro, North Carolina, in 1910, the son and grandson of Episcopal priests. He left the South for New York, stating, "I knew I'd never live to be a man in North Carolina, so I left."[71] In 1928, he enrolled in Columbia University and graduated as one of only five black graduates. Moran led one of Harlem's most prominent churches, St. Philip's Episcopal Church, which was created in 1818 when blacks were told they could not attend Trinity Church on Wall Street.

Weston believed that his experience as an Episcopal priest prepared him for banking. He told *Ebony* magazine in 1969 that "being in banking is consistent with the involvement of my parish in the life of my community. . . . A banker-priest is really no more strange than an educator-priest or a social worker-priest."[72] Before becoming pastor, Moran had worked as a real estate broker. He noticed that white banks refused to lend to blacks even when they held substantial deposits at that bank, and he came to believe that these "white bank officers hadn't understood that we were persons." Instead, they were relying on racist stereotypes in making lending decisions. "They had no understanding of the sense of responsibility of the hardworking [black] family that struggles to build itself, and grows up to acquire a piece of property."[73] The Carver Bank was created to correct this injustice and help hardworking black families get mortgages. It was a bold move. The *New York Times* noted that before Carver opened as a storefront, only one black person was working above the rank of janitor in a New York bank.[74]

Moran, like many other black leaders, held many different leadership roles and moved seamlessly from one to another. He was a preacher, a civil rights advocate, a labor organizer, and a banker. He was active in civil rights demonstrations against lynching in the South and whites-only clubs in New York. He organized large civil rights rallies in Madison Square Garden and wrote a column called "Labor Forum" in the black *Amsterdam News,* in which he advocated for labor rights and collective action. His activism was done mostly out of the limelight. He was a quiet intellectual and told the *New York*

Times in a 1986 interview, "I cause things to happen. If I have a gift, it is to encourage people that they can do the impossible."[75]

Moran was as significant a figure in the Harlem community as the more visible and outspoken Adam Clayton Powell Jr., who was pastor of the Abyssinian Baptist Church in Harlem before becoming a congressman. When Powell called for a boycott by schoolchildren to protest segregation, Moran publicly opposed him, arguing that they should prove their point by keeping children in the schools. Yet Powell and Moran worked together to promote Carver Bank. In 1955, Powell called for a boycott of the white Harlem savings banks that "practice 'Jim Crow-ism' and 'economic lynching'" and urged his Abyssinian Baptist Church's 15,000 congregants to withdraw their funds and place them either in the Carver bank or in the black-owned Tri-State bank in Memphis.[76]

Moran served the bank for nearly fifty years, finally retiring in 1997.[77] And when he did retire, Moran and the other founders tried to choose community leaders instead of "businesspeople or bankers" as their replacements. These nonbankers were extremely risk-averse. In 1979 its president stated, "We are conservative. . . . We are not flamboyant or spectacular."[78] But this meant that the bank was not providing loans. In fact, the *Times* reported that they "made almost no loans, except to churches. Instead, like many other minority-owned banks, they simply accepted deposits and invested them in money market funds and mortgage securities."[79] As a federally chartered savings and loan association, Carver was statutorily required to invest a certain percentage of its loans in family dwellings, but it did so very cautiously.

In Birmingham, Alabama, A. G. Gaston opened the Citizens Federal Savings and Loan Association (CFS Bancshares) in 1957—the second black bank in Birmingham after the Penny Savings Bank had failed.[80] Gaston's sizable fortune had been built on a vertically integrated empire consisting of insurance, a funeral home, a hotel, and a black business college. He observed that black families were being denied residential mortgages, and he opened his bank so that he could fill that market need. He explained that it was very difficult to gain the trust of the black community as they were still reeling from the failure of the Penny Savings Bank in 1915, but he was able to use his reputation and support from the town clergy to boost the bank's status.[81]

Martin Luther King deposited money in the bank and served on its advisory council. King was the most iconic, but certainly not the only black preacher who was also a civil rights leader and black bank booster. Supporting black enterprise had been one of King's consistent messages, repeated in over a decade of leadership. Coretta Scott King had worked as a teller at Atlanta's black-owned Citizens Trust bank, and King had formed a relationship with the bank early on. After the breakthrough success of the 1956 Montgomery bus boycott, King was launched onto the national stage. He immediately wrote a formative article outlining his goals and a road map for the movement called "We Are Still Walking." King expressed his ambitious agenda, which he said extended "far beyond the desegregation of the buses," but was "a long-range constructive program." He listed six of the group's top goals for the future, and the top two were to organize banks:

1. To establish the first bank in Montgomery to be owned and operated by Negroes. We have found that in the present situation many Negroes who are active in the protest have been unable to secure loans from the existing banks.
2. To organize a credit union. As a result of the protest, there is a strong desire among the Negroes to pool their money for great cooperative economic programs. We are anxious to demonstrate that cooperation rather than competition is the way to meet problems.[82]

His third goal had to do with voting. In 1958, in a monthly advice column in *Ebony*, King said that every black community should have black-owned credit unions, savings and loan associations, and finance companies, and he urged blacks to "pool their economic resources." Doing so would "lift the economic level of the Negro which would in turn give him greater purchasing power."[83]

Though the civil rights leader was an unhesitant supporter of black banks, the black bankers did not always see their interests as being aligned with the movement. When Birmingham became the site of the civil rights movement's most monumental battles, Gaston the banker was at cross purposes with King the activist. Gaston, with Booker T. Washington's picture hanging in a frame in his office, was

called the "accommodator" (many called him an Uncle Tom) for opposing what he saw as the King coalition's inflammatory tactics. He
urged cooperation with the white leaders, as he had always done,
and negotiations to achieve their aims. He spoke out harshly against
the use of schoolchildren in the nonviolent campaign, which some
believe led to the movement's most significant public victory. In his
"Letter from Birmingham Jail," King was likely addressing Gaston
when he answered his critics urging negotiations instead of sit-
ins.[84] He responded that this was exactly the aim of the civil rights
movement.

According to his biographer, Gaston was committed to civil rights,
but believed that the movement should focus on economic issues
and poverty alleviation instead of pushing for rights.[85] Gaston himself had been following Booker T. Washington's "cast down your
bucket" philosophy and had built his empire in Birmingham instead
of moving north. He and his wife were actively involved in the
Tuskegee Institute. Gaston's own autobiography, which was inspired
by *Up from Slavery,* was called *Green Power,* and in it he advocated
hard work and wealth-building as the only means toward equal
rights. Had the promise that "green power" would lead to equality
come to pass for Gaston? Andrew Young recounted watching the millionaire getting lunch at a Birmingham establishment and having
to get it at the back door like all the other black customers.[86]

Though Gaston was uncomfortable with King's methods, he also
provided financial aid to King's coalition and offered a suite of his
motel as the headquarters for King and the SCLC. The A. G. Gaston
Motel was bombed in retaliation. Gaston also bailed Dr. King and
Ralph Abernathy out of jail when the county set the bail at the unreasonable rate of $2,500 each. King did not want anyone to pay for
his bail because he believed that remaining in jail would be better
for the movement's long-term aims. President Kennedy sought a
de-escalation of the conflict and dispatched Robert Kennedy to
persuade Gaston to pay for bail against the civil rights leaders'
wishes. Gaston did so, perhaps because he too was eager to avoid
provoking the white community. King's coalition brought the race
conflict to a peak in Birmingham, and it threatened Gaston's business success, which relied on the blessing of the town's white leadership. As a businessman who had built an enterprise on Washington's philosophy and an uncritical embrace of the segregated

economy, his relationship to the civil rights movement was ambivalent. When Gaston's Birmingham home was bombed in 1963 and the perpetrator was not found, Gaston was torn between casting the blame on the Klan or on the black power movement.[87]

The conflict between the objectives of black bankers and civil rights leaders led socialist black intellectual E. Franklin Frazier to paint black businessmen as the villains in the cause of black progress. Frazier, a Baltimore native, was awarded Howard University's top scholarship and received his Ph.D. in sociology from the University of Chicago in 1931. Frazier taught at Fisk University from 1929 to 1934, and then at Howard from 1934 until his death in 1962.[88] In his 1957 book, *Black Bourgeoisie,* Frazier took aim at the striving black elites, whom he believed to have a "deep-seated inferiority complex" because they felt superior to the black masses while suffering from "the contempt of the white world." Frazier denounced Booker T. Washington for deluding the black community with the theory that business success would lead to acceptance and respectability, which he called "a world of make believe."[89] Black leaders and the black press were creating a misplaced faith in black businesses and exaggerating their success and influence, which he said was actually irrelevant to the American economy.[90] He also believed that since the propaganda campaign of the Freedmen's Bank, the black bourgeoisie had become obsessed with black banking as a symbol of business success, and that "it was mainly in the field of banking that the new spirit of business enterprise manifested itself."[91]

Frazer condemned whites who, on the one hand, promoted black business while, on the other hand, they refused to admit black businessmen into the corridors of power.[92] Yet his harshest judgment was reserved for the black bankers and businessmen, who he believed were exploiting "the Negro masses . . . as ruthlessly as have whites."[93] Frazier compared black business leaders and the black bourgeoisie to the "house slaves" who he claimed benefited from the exploitation of the "field slaves." This class division between the house slaves, the Uncle Toms, and the black bourgeois versus the field slaves, the black masses, and the exploited became a common theme picked up by Malcolm X and the Black Panthers. After World War II, there emerged a tense divide between the black elite who enjoyed a modicum of upward mobility and the masses who had been left to languish in the ghetto, but the divergence was not as clear-cut as Frazier portrayed. Black bankers were not making exorbitant profits off the backs of the black masses. In fact, they were hardly making profits at all—as they were all suffering from the same Jim Crow credit market.

Critics of black businesses often tended to inflate their success. According to the U.S. Department of Commerce, there were a total of fourteen black banks in 1951, most of which were survivors from the previous era.[94] Given the obstacles to making mortgage loans, which is the mainstay of banking, it is unsurprising that only a handful of black banks were formed between 1940 and 1965.[95] What is jarring, however, is the paucity of the black banking sector in the context of the broader banking landscape. This was the unparalleled heyday of American banking. Never have banks been so numerous, nor the banking sector in America so profitable and safe. For example, between 1934 and 1980, there were 23,564 new charters for credit unions.[96] Total commercial bank branches grew from around 3,000 in 1935 to 40,000 in 1980. There were 11,000 S&Ls created in the 1930s, and many more were added over the years.[97] This makes the anemic scale of black banking a glaring anomaly.

The black banking industry essentially lay dormant for the decades spanning from the New Deal reforms and postwar era prosperity until the civil rights era. This was a direct consequence of the exclusionary federal mortgage bounty. The golden era of American banking, especially the surge in credit union and S&L charters, was also a direct result of New Deal credit and banking reforms. Though the S&L and credit union movements were rooted in progressive and populist ideals of cooperative ownership, self-help, and grassroots community building, it was only after they were plugged into the robust government-backed credit markets that these small marginal institutions became growth industries. These banks boomed because of and only because of FHA loans. Without them, these community-based enterprises would have withered on the vine, which is where they were headed before the New Deal.[98] It was so easy to run a profitable bank, thrift, or a credit union during this era that the adage was that bankers followed a 3-6-3 rule—3 percent interest on deposits, 6 percent interest on loans, and be on the golf course at 3 P.M.[99]

So monumental were the New Deal reforms that banking history can be divided into the Before New Deal and After New Deal eras.

Before, banking law was primarily governed state by state, and each state determined which banks would be granted charters. The New Deal banking reforms imposed federal governance, including new restrictions, rules, and chartering requirements. In return, banks got access to federal networks of deposit insurance, loan guarantees, and other buffers and protections. Most significant was federal deposit insurance, which effectively ended runs on bank deposits. FHA insurance on loans created a torrent of investor capital. Deposit insurance had the same effect on customer deposits. Confident savers entrusted their money to the banking system to be deployed in the great lending markets.

Once the federal deposit insurance scheme was established, it was impossible for a bank to operate without it. In order for a bank to be viable, it had to be sanctioned by the FDIC and had to follow a standard set of federal rules and norms. It had to hold a minimum amount of capital, avoid certain activities, and submit to routine examination by regulators. Certainly, under the state-by-state chartering regime, black banks had been denied charters as a result of discrimination, but under the new regime black banks rarely had enough capital to obtain charters. Black banks were almost categorically too weak to be granted FDIC insurance.

There were other shifts, more substantial but harder to notice, that would affect black banking. Specifically, the New Deal reforms tilted the scales toward small, community banking as opposed to large, nationwide bank conglomerates. The debate in the banking industry between large and small banks mirrored the North–South divide as it put industrial interests and agricultural interests on opposite sides. The North, home to J.P. Morgan, Chase National Bank, and Wall Street, wanted more permissive banking laws that allowed larger banks to operate across several regions. Bankers in the South and West feared that large and powerful conglomerates would attract capital from across the country, increase their market share, and drive them out of business. This was a legitimate fear and would soon become a reality, but Roosevelt sided with the South and protected small banking through anti-competitive banking laws.[100] The South pushed for FDIC insurance, which made small banking possible. They also demanded provisions in the Glass-Steagall Act of 1933 and the Banking Act of 1935 that prohibited bank conglomeration, mergers, or even bank branching across state lines.[101]

These laws went against natural market forces and favored the small and the weak against the banking market's natural winners, the large and the well-capitalized.

The rationale of community banking is that capital stays put within a region. The peril of this arrangement before the New Deal was that the fate of a community's banks was linked to the community's prosperity or decline. Small community banks were inherently more vulnerable to runs and less stable than larger conglomerates, which could diversify their risks and count on liquidity and capital from robust financial markets. Federal deposit insurance fixed this problem by providing a federal subsidy that enabled these weaker community banks to compete. This is why the small bankers fought for it. With deposit insurance, they could make profit from their control over a community's resources while being protected from the constant failure and runs that had besieged their industry up until that point.

The New Deal banking reforms favored these small community banks not only because they protected the banks from runs, but also because they shielded the banks from competition from banking conglomerates. They had a monopoly on a region's deposits and loans, but thanks to a nationwide insurance fund, they were protected from the downside risk of the community banking model. So regional banks, especially in the South and West, thrived after the New Deal to an extent that they had not been able to previously. The FHA guaranteed their loans, FDIC insurance prevented runs, and federal reserve liquidity protection saved them from a regional credit crunch. "Community banking" worked because of federal government support.

The decision to favor small community banks over larger bank networks was not racially motivated, but it did negatively affect the prospects for black banking. The unanticipated effect was that the black community, with little stored wealth and little access to credit, could not thrive in a system that tied all its deposits and loans only to those within its community borders. Black communities, now thoroughly segregated and relegated to living outside the systems of credit, were paralyzed by this structure. They did not have the federal government mortgage support and yet had to rely on their own community's meager resources to operate.

Before the New Deal reforms had taken shape, Abram Harris had suggested that the best hope for black banks going forward was for them to become a branch of a large national bank, or in other words, to cease being stand-alone black banks. The arrangement would benefit white banks, which could profit from black customers without having to integrate their bank branches. As a subsidiary of a large holding company, black banks could dock into the mainstream banking network and benefit from the large capital base they could not access on their own. The bank holding company ownership structure would at least enable credit to flow down occasionally instead of always up and out. Though Harris, like the New Deal progressives, was wary of the "un-slackening growth in the size and power of white financial and industrial organizations," he recognized that this was the only way black banks could overcome their impoverished and segregated communities.[102] It was better to join forces with a powerful bank, even a Wall Street "money trust" powerhouse, than to go it alone. He knew that black banks would lose their autonomy and independence, but Harris was skeptical that they could ever operate successfully as stand-alone entities. But riding on the wave of backlash against big banking, the New Deal reforms cut off this potential structure in its prohibition against conglomerates.[103]

The frustrating dilemma of black banks is highlighted when contrasted with banks created by Italian, Jewish, German, and Irish immigrants that they are often compared to. Though these immigrants were never segregated to the extent that the black community was before the Great Depression, they were discriminated against by the white banking sector and had been forced to create their own banks.[104] "No Italians" and "No Irish" signs were prevalent during the era when racial dogma deemed these groups inferior and unworthy races. The plight of these other marginalized immigrant groups parted ways significantly from blacks only after the New Deal reforms and the end of the world wars. These immigrants would eventually leave their overcrowded ghettos and settle in white suburbs where blacks were still barred entry.

Their banks reflected these immigrants' own integration. For example, the Bank of Italy was formed in San Francisco to serve Italian immigrants who could not get loans from white banks. The bank was founded in 1904 by Italian immigrant Amadeo Giannini for the same purpose that black banks were created—to serve a population that was being discriminated against by the mainstream banks.[105]

Giannini's bank would have a drastically different trajectory than Binga's, and the divergence would mirror the disparities between the assimilation of America's immigrants and its native blacks: eventually, the Bank of Italy grew and merged into the mainstream U.S. banking system—just as Italian immigrants assimilated into American society. What was formerly the Bank of Italy is now the Bank of America—the largest and one of the most profitable banks in the country.[106]

The Bank of Italy's transformation into the Bank of America was directly financed by the FHA. Bank of America was able to expand its consumer lending market to take advantage of the FHA consumer credit guarantees. FHA loan guarantees allowed Bank of America to increase profits by 40 percent from 1935 to 1936 and establish branches across the state of California. In May of 1937, Giannini told the *Los Angeles Times* that these new loans had "trebled and quadrupled activity in our branches."[107] Before the New Deal, Bank of Italy was a bank for Italians, and after the New Deal it became a bank of Americans because Italians too became American.

Italian, Irish, Polish, and other European immigrants who had each been deemed inferior races decades earlier came to be accepted as white Americans. Italians for the most part could not attend college before the war, but most gained entry afterward through the GI Bill.[108] Black GIs were not given similar access. Education was still highly segregated, and there were not enough black-only colleges to accommodate them.[109] Education led to economic mobility, which led to more social and political power and control.[110] The immigrant groups were able to move "up and out" of the ghetto with the help of federal government programs. Certainly, discrimination remained, but legal segregation of the immigrant groups was erased by the end of World War II, and their full integration was a direct result of FHA and VA credit policies for them.

There is a pervasive myth that immigrant success was based purely on individual work ethic.[111] Certainly there was a lot of hard work and perseverance, but left out of this popular narrative was the significance of the FHA–GI Bill combination, the government subsidy that bolstered the work and turned it into capital-producing assets. Hollywood legend Frank Capra's family, for example, immigrated to America in 1903 and landed in "the sleazy Sicilian ghetto of Los Angeles."[112] Capra enlisted in the army, was naturalized, and, with a boost from the GI Bill and the FHA, moved out of the slums and into the American middle class. He went on to make films that defined America, and in his 1946 *It's a Wonderful Life*, Capra immortalized the myth of self-help community banking through George Bailey's fictional Building and Loan. The fiction that poor communities can pool their resources and bank themselves into prosperity like the upstanding and tireless George Bailey was thereafter cemented in American culture and policy. In reality, most immigrants' bootstraps had been provided by the government. Indeed, blacks were working hard too, but their wages were going to exploitative contract sellers, landlords, or much more expensive mortgages, instead of helping them build wealth. The black population was left out of the capital-building and prosperous decades of the 1940s to the 1960s.[113]

However, change was coming. Seeds of the national civil rights movement were beginning to take root as the black community began pursuing various strands of protest during this era. There was no coordinated national struggle yet, but each fight paved the way for future coalitions as well as future divisions. The movement that most resembled King's own occurred in 1941 when A. Philip Randolph organized what was to be the first large-scale act of civil disobedience aimed at getting the attention of the federal government. He proposed a march on Washington to protest discrimination in government defense contracts. The prospect of the expected 100,000 demonstrators alarmed the White House enough that it led to a preemptive executive order. Roosevelt signed Executive Order 8802, which forbade government military contractors to discriminate "because of race, creed, color or origin."[114] Black leaders were elated and described it as the "gateway to the millennium for millions of blacks."[115] Randolph compared the Order to the Emancipation Proclamation and the black-owned *Amsterdam News* declared it "epochal to say the least. . . . If President Lincoln's proclamation was designed to end physical slavery, it would seem that the recent order of President Roosevelt is designed to end, or at least, curb, economic slavery."[116] Although the order was never sufficiently enforced by the administration, it was fateful, for it became the legal framework on which civil rights laws were founded. Randolph was instrumental in organizing the

1963 March on Washington, during which he spoke next to Dr. King twenty years later. This strand of the movement, which would be the successful one, was focused on coordinated and peaceful protests meant to result in federal legislation focused on equal rights and nondiscrimination.

Meanwhile, in another precursor to what was coming, the first urban riot led by blacks against white businesses occurred in Harlem in 1935. The spark was lit when a teenage shoplifter was beaten by a store owner. Over several nights of violence, rioters destroyed white business establishments in Harlem—while sparing black-owned businesses.[117] Though resorting to violence was still rare in this era, collective action was beginning to coalesce around specific economic demands in northern ghettos. These protesters were not demanding national legislation, but were objecting to their perceived exploitation by white shop owners operating at high markups in the ghetto. The Harlem protests were focused on economic justice at the local level.[118]

One side of the protests focused on encouraging more black businesses and called for "Bigger and Better Negro Business."[119] This movement was being waged by local black organizations that spanned the political spectrum from radical black nationalists to the conservative National Business League. There was a widespread perception that white businesses were extracting profits from the ghetto and a frustration that, after a century of effort, black businesses were still hardly in a position to compete. The latter was certainly true. When the first study of black business was conducted in 1898, it found that the average capital investment in the average black business was $4,600.[120] By 1944, that capital investment had actually decreased to $3,260. The vast majority of these businesses (90 percent) were divided equally between small retail stores and small service establishments.[121] Many ghetto businesses were small mom-and-pop shops that were barely profitable—still pebbles on the seashore.[122]

Another strand of collective action was aimed not at rejecting the white business establishments, but demanding that if they were going to make money in the ghetto, they should at least share the wealth with the black community by hiring black employees. Black communities began using organized boycotts. The Harlem Labor

Union, made up of former Garveyites, picketed white stores that refused to hire blacks in the 1932 "Don't Buy Where You Can't Work" movement. Soon black leaders across the country began talking about leveraging the purchasing power of the black dollar to fight discrimination.[123] Adam Clayton Powell emerged as the most vocal leader of the boycott movement, and several years later he formed the Greater New York Coordinating Committee for Employment, which aimed at securing jobs through nonviolent protest.[124]

In 1935, several white merchants challenged a black boycott of their Baltimore businesses in the Maryland Court of Appeals.[125] The court ruled in favor of the black boycotters, stating that so long as violence, intimidation, and threats were not used, blacks had "an unquestionable right" to present their cause "in a peaceable way."[126] The judge even seemed to be encouraging black groups to boycott in order to "persuade white employers to engage colored employees," and to protest discrimination "by organization, public meetings, propaganda and by personal solicitation." However, the court seemed to put the onus on the black community to achieve their demands, stating, "whether they succeed or fail will depend on the cooperation of their people." The unstated subtext was that it was the responsibility of the black population to work to end racism. The ruling set the stage for the civil rights movement's early strategy of leveraging black market power and using organized boycotts against Jim Crow buses in Montgomery, Alabama.

As another harbinger of what was to come, movements demanding more black control of the ghetto came to be embraced by whites who championed a segregated economy—for the benefit of blacks, of course. An illustrative example was an editorial written by a white supporter of the black community who urged Harlem to follow Chicago's lead and establish segregated black banks and businesses. The cleverly named article, "If Negro Quarters for Negroes— Negro Dollars for Negroes, Too" was published in the *New York Daily Mirror* in 1935 and urged Harlem's black population to do as blacks in Chicago had done and work toward a "conscious and a kind of prideful segregation—a segregation which was WON, not imposed." Indeed, the author believed that Chicago's black belt was "an achievement rather than imposition," which had given blacks the power to control their own dollars.[127]

The writer said that Harlem was being "bled white" and urged the black community to drive out the white exploiters and fight for a black economy. "It is for the 'Black dollar' that Harlem fights now, because it has to." In other words, the "fight" was to maintain a segregated Harlem for Harlem was being overtaken by "white exploiters" after blacks had first claimed the land. "Block by block, store by store, house by house, white profit seekers here infiltrated back into the district which became black by *common consent* in the decade after the war." The story being told was that blacks had chosen segregation and now these infiltrators were ruining the mutually beneficial arrangement. Once the white "infiltrators" were eradicated, Harlem could *win back* its total segregation.

Not only had Harlem not wanted its segregation, there was also an anti-Semitic subtext to the tale because the "infiltrators" of the black ghetto were understood to be Jewish shop owners. The tension between Jewish shop owners and black residents had led to some incidents of violence even as black leaders rejected the scapegoating of Jewish merchants. Abram Harris and Adam Clayton Powell pushed back against anti-Semitism when these claims arose among black protestors. They warned that anti-Semitism was the same as the racism they were fighting and cautioned blacks not to "do Hitler's work here at home.[128]

Indeed, the end of the war heralded a monumental shift in race relations. Despite integration of the U.S. armed forces in 1948, a segregated home front, continued racial hostility, and limited economic opportunity greeted black war veterans upon their return. Just as black Union soldiers had returned to the South after the Civil War to demand equality, so too did black veterans of World War II agitate for better treatment from the country they had risked their lives for. James Baldwin recounted that the "treatment accorded the Negro during the Second World War [marked] a turning point in the Negro's relation to America. . . . A certain hope died."[129] Hitler's outrageous acts of racial cleansing disgusted Americans and highlighted the racial hypocrisy at home. How was it that the good guys abroad maintained their own brand of racial violence at home?

During the 1948 Democratic National Convention, Senator Hubert Humphrey forcefully denounced Congress's intransigence on civil rights. "There's no room for double standards in American politics," he said. "Our demands for democratic practices in other lands will be no more effective than the guarantee of those practices in our own country." He demurred, "to those who say that we are rushing this issue of civil rights, I say to them we are 172 years late. To those who say that [civil rights] is an infringement on states' rights, I say this: The time has arrived in America for the Democratic Party to get out of the shadow of states' rights and to walk forthrightly into the bright sunshine of human rights."[130]

Congress began to see more antilynching laws, though ultimately none made it past the southern bloc. However, the federal government finally recognized and formally ended the cruel practice of convict leasing in southern prisons after the war. As explained by Douglas Blackmon, "It was a strange irony that after seventy-four years of hollow emancipation, the final delivery of African Americans from overt slavery and from the quiet complicity of the federal government in their servitude was precipitated only in response to the horrors perpetrated by an enemy country against its own despised minorities."[131] In 1946, Truman created the Commission on Higher Education, with the aim of repealing segregation. He also created a Committee on Civil Rights, which called for the "elimination of segregation, based on race, color, creed, or national origin, from American life." Truman eventually lost the votes of four southern states because he enacted laws outlawing poll taxes, lynching, segregation in interstate transportation, and discrimination in federal employment and the armed services.[132] Though these gains were modest, there was forward momentum.

As the world wars shifted to the Cold War, communist regimes abroad began to highlight stories of U.S. racism in their propaganda. Black soldiers being lynched in their military uniforms, Klan violence, rampant black poverty, and the everyday injustices of Jim Crow segregation were being advertised by enemies of the state. A 1952 brief written by the Democratic attorney general exhorted the federal government to enact antidiscrimination laws as a matter of foreign policy. "It is in the context of the present world struggle between freedom and tyranny that the problem of racial discrimination must be viewed. . . . Racial discrimination furnishes grist for the Communist propaganda mills, and it raises doubt even among friendly nations as to the intensity of our devotion to the democratic faith. . . . Other peoples cannot understand how such a practice [of school segregation] can exist in a country which professes to be a staunch supporter of freedom, justice, and democracy."[133] After the Supreme Court in *Brown v. Board of Education* ruled against segregation in schools, Voice of America broadcast the praiseworthy decision to the world in thirty-five different languages.

To defeat communism, America needed to tell the world a story of American racial progress. It was decided to focus on telling the story of the black elite. As part of a public relations blitz on race, the U.S. Information Service (USIS) released a promotional pamphlet called *The Negro in American Life* in 1950. The story the pamphlet portrayed was one of redemption: America had made a tragic mistake by sanctioning slavery, but since then, American democracy had been a long march toward racial progress.

In reality, the injustice was ongoing. From the New Deal and through the Cold War era, unparalleled U.S. prosperity bypassed blacks through purposeful exclusion. The grand-scale economic and political injustices operating in this era were created and sustained by an invisible Jim Crow credit market. The pushback had already begun and the economic frustration of the impoverished black community in the segregated ghettos would erupt soon enough. However, in communicating progress on race to the communist nations, the State Department chose to measure racial progress through the success of the black middle class. "Some Negroes are large land-holders; some are wealthy businessmen. . . . Negroes work in banks, public utilities, insurance companies, and retail stories. They are physicists, chemists, psychologists, doctors, metallurgists." Although the report conceded that "much remains to be done," this measurement of racial progress became ubiquitous.[134]

In need of more inspirational stories of black rights to broadcast, the State Department called on the Division of Negro Affairs in 1951. Voice of America wanted to broadcast biographical information of successful black entrepreneurs across the world to be used as an ideological weapon—the story of black capitalists was a strong counterpoint to communist charges that American capitalism relied on racial exploitation. As the State Department noted in a letter to Archie A. Alexander, a successful black contractor, they wanted to share his story in order to "improve its prestige with the darker races of people in the Asiatic countries."[135]

Besides compiling reports, this was the most notable action the Division of Negro Affairs had accomplished thus far, and it would not survive much longer. In 1953, President Eisenhower terminated the office in order to cut waste, though it is likely racial discrimination also played a part in the decision—Roy Wilkins famously quipped that if Eisenhower "had fought World War II the way he fought for civil rights, we would all be speaking German now."[136] However, the idea of using black business as a political tool did take root in President Eisenhower's vice president, Richard Nixon. Nixon would build his own division of black capitalism in the Commerce Department, but with a much wider scope. He too would use black entrepreneurship as a weapon in a war, but not a foreign one.

Civil Rights Dreams,
Economic Nightmares

There was a brief window between 1963 and 1965 when it seemed inevitable that the arc of the moral universe would actually bend toward justice quickly and without detour. At the centennial commemoration of the Emancipation Proclamation in September 1962, President Kennedy stood on the steps of the Lincoln Memorial and acknowledged that blacks were "not yet freed from bonds of injustice." He promised to "complete the work begun by Abraham Lincoln," to "eradicate the vestiges of discrimination and segregation." A year later at that same memorial, Dr. Martin Luther King led the March on Washington and asked the country to honor its founding principles of equality. When the King coalition's disciplined nonviolence was met with the South's unruly backlash against federal law, cameras captured the clash and made the case for the petitioners. "We will soon wear you down by our capacity to suffer," said Dr. King.

For a brief moment, King's powerful message of peace and optimism united the complex and varied voices of the black community. The American public embraced the message that it was time to turn the page from racism toward progress. For the first time since Reconstruction, there was harmony among all three branches of government—this time, the Supreme Court, the executive branch, and Congress all pushed toward racial equality. The Court, the same institution that had sanctioned Jim Crow segregation in the South during the first Reconstruction, began to tear it down in case after case with masterful assistance from the NAACP's Thurgood Marshall.[1]

President Kennedy urged Congress to pass a sweeping civil rights bill in 1963, "not merely for reasons of economic efficiency, world diplomacy and domestic tranquility—but above all because it is right." Kennedy also envisioned broader reforms aimed at addressing the conditions of poverty. "There is little value in a Negro's obtaining the right to be admitted to hotels and restaurants if he has no cash in his pocket and no job." He remained committed to the bill until his life was cut short in November 1963.

It took a "master of the senate" to finally break the South's stranglehold on Congress and pass the Civil Rights Act.[2] President Lyndon Johnson knew how to breach the southern legislative gamesmanship that had successfully blocked every attempt at civil rights legislation since the New Deal because he had practiced the hold-up game himself. First as junior Texas senator and then during his six years as majority leader, he practically controlled the southern bloc, and by extension the entire Senate. But now he pushed vigorously for reform; after all, he quipped, "what the hell's presidency for?" Upon his sudden inauguration, Johnson met with the leaders of the civil rights coalition: King of the Southern Christian Leadership Council (SCLC), Roy Wilkins of the NAACP, Whitney Young of the National Urban League, James Farmer of the Congress of Racial Equality (CORE), and A. Philip Randolph of the Brotherhood of Sleeping Car Porters.[3] Young told reporters after the meeting that "a magnolia accent doesn't always mean bigotry."[4] When Andrew Johnson had taken office after President Lincoln's assassination in 1865, he halted Reconstruction reforms and set the black community back for generations. With this second accidental President Johnson, things went very differently. Lyndon Johnson made the civil rights cause his own. Together, LBJ and MLK were at the helm of the most monumental forward movement in race relations in American history. Their partnership was neither natural nor comfortable, but the timing was right and a large part of the public was with them— at least for a little while.

Johnson pushed Kennedy's original civil rights bill in Congress and made clear that he wanted "nothing less than the full assimilation of more than twenty million Negroes into American life." The Civil Rights Act was passed in July of 1964, banning racial discrimination in employment and in all public accommodations.[5] Jim Crow was dead. In August of 1965, Congress passed the Voting Rights Act, which guaranteed blacks the vote. These acts were not empty gestures. Both laws were immediately enforced by the administration and the Supreme Court. Blacks achieved more rights in a few short years than they had in the previous two hundred.

While the reforms of 1965 were in fact the beginning of historic changes that continue today, they were also the high water mark of the civil rights movement. Soon there would be backlash, divisions, and retrenchment. Even President Johnson wavered. Johnson has been described as "the last president to offer committed leadership that challenged racial injustice," but even he stepped back from the civil rights struggle as the United States became mired in Vietnam. Civil rights historian Taylor Branch explains that it was Kennedy's assassination that fully launched the civil rights era— and it would be Martin Luther King's assassination five years later that would bring it to a halt.[6]

Yet even before the civil rights momentum ground to a halt with the war in Vietnam and King's coalition broken, the movement's scope had been too limited to address the full problem of racial inequality. The assumption of too many Americans was that once discrimination was purged from the law, the effects of discrimination would disappear. American racism was mistakenly seen as an issue of bigoted white-hooded Klansmen, but that was just the ugliest symptom of a broader problem, the visible tumor of a cancer that went far deeper. Blacks living in the urban North were not being told to sit at the back of the bus because most did not have access to public buses in the first place. The financial isolation of the urban black population was a result of years of racism, but there were no ready villains, no Bull Connor or whites-only water fountains. "The segregated practices in the South are kind of public butchery," noted Saul Alinsky. "It's visible. There's bleeding all over the place. Up here [in the North] we use a stiletto, it's internal bleeding, it's not visible, but it's just as deadly."[7] The violence of northern segregation had been sown years before and was continually bearing another sort of strange fruit—economic exploitation. Black northerners applauded the gains of the civil rights movement, but they demanded change for their communities. Intractable poverty and inequality were just as oppressive as the South's brute hostility, but a far more complex problem to address. And as a stunned North would soon find out, the unrest was far closer to home than Selma, Alabama.

Yet when the black movement shifted to address the problem of black poverty, it became constrained by its own rhetorical demands. The movement's song, most masterfully harmonized by King, Marshall, Kennedy, and Johnson, was legal *equality*. The tune had a familiar ring because its force came from America's founding documents—"all men are created equal" and "equal protection under the law." Though Dr. King's message was much broader than is commonly portrayed, what captivated and chastened many was how closely his message hewed to these common American ideals. King recited the Constitution's promise and summoned the nation to bring its deeds in line with its democratic aspirations. "The home that all too many Americans left was solidly structured idealistically. Its pillars were soundly grounded in the insights of our Judeo-Christian heritage: . . . all men are created equal. . . . What a marvelous foundation for any home!" King was calling Americans home. And home was the classic liberal notion of equality. According to liberal principles, individuals must be free to pursue their own aims using their own talents. No group trait, like race or ancestry, should be used to exclude someone from free participation in markets and society. A country built on liberalism could not tolerate discrimination because it punished a person based on a group attribute instead of the content of their character. The civil rights movement was founded on aligning America's liberal democratic ideal with its hypocritical racial hierarchy—on reconciling the "American Dilemma." The 1964 Civil Rights Act and the Voting Rights Act of 1965 aimed to fix the bug in the system by erasing the dissonance between word and deed.

But what was to be done about the centuries that America had been explicitly violating its own foundational myths? As soon as the acts were passed, it was apparent that the victory had been a hollow one. Blacks were still unemployed at twice the rate of whites, they occupied low-wage jobs, had little wealth, and these momentous laws provided no conceivable path out of poverty.[8] Abolishing racist laws was not the same thing as achieving equality. Ending segregation was not the same thing as integration. Ending job discrimination was not the same thing as having jobs. Ending credit discrimination was not the same thing as providing credit. A legal right to equality was meaningless to the destitute and marginalized unless it could open a path to actual equality. The movement shifted toward "achieving the fact of equality," as Bayard Rustin wrote in 1965, rather than merely "removing the barriers to full opportunity." If it was true, according to Rustin, that "freedom must be conceived in economic categories," the civil rights movement turned its focus to achieving justice as an economic matter.[9] But economic demands faced a major roadblock: equality.

The sweet-sounding tune of equality soon became a noose around the movement as leaders began to seek the "fact of equality" and not just its scent. In the beginning of the civil rights era, equal rights had meant giving blacks the rights they had always been entitled to—the same rights whites enjoyed. The only people who objected to this were those who believed blacks to be unworthy of these rights, the incorrigible southern racists, who were a shrinking minority. But intractable economic problems required stronger weapons than just equality before the law—it meant that whites had to allow blacks to move into their neighborhoods and that centuries of exclusion needed redress. It meant providing public funds or specific privileges to blacks to even the playing field. In 1963, Dr. King said "just as we granted a GI Bill of Rights to war veterans," we should "launch a broad-based and gigantic Bill of Rights for the Disadvantaged." "For it is obvious," stated King, "that if a man is entering the starting line in a race three hundred years after another man, the first would have to perform some impossible feat in order to catch up with his fellow runner." Whitney Young, executive director of the Urban League, stated, "Many of these [white] people are now middle-class, their rise made possible by a host of federal programs—the GI Bill, home loan insurance, road-building, and economic and employment policies."[10] Maybe it was time to provide the same boost to blacks.

The mood suddenly turned. By the end of the decade, whites were lambasting the government for depriving whites of *their* rights to equality.[11] Once the message of equality and nondiscrimination was heeded, it was clung to. "The way to stop discrimination on the basis of race," said Chief Justice John Roberts in 2007, "is to stop discriminating on the basis of race." This sentiment was already beginning to form at the tail end of the civil rights movement and would only grow over time. This late-term egalitarianism could not erase, overnight, the wealth gap caused by centuries of racism, yet many proclaimed that it already had.

The other edge of the sword of equality was used to cut down any claims for special privileges. If blacks demanded that they not be judged based on their race, using the same logic, whites demanded that blacks not be given any special favors based on their race. A U.S.

senator who wished to remain anonymous explained that his white voters were angry—"I'm getting mail from white people saying 'Wait a minute, we've got some rights too.'"[12] Whites felt threatened, believing that black gains were coming at the expense of whites. By 1966, a poll found that 85 percent of whites believed that "the pace of civil rights progress was too fast."[13] The more the Johnson administration pushed for programs that would benefit blacks, the more whites began to demand equality. The irony, of course, was that Congress needed to enforce color-blind civil rights legislation because the nation had never actually been color-blind.

Almost before the decade was over, a rewriting of the history and the purpose of the civil rights movement had already begun. Dr. Martin Luther King's modern legacy has been boiled down to his historic "I Have a Dream" speech. More accurately, his dream was reduced to just a few sentences of that pivotal 1963 speech: "I have a dream that my four little children will one day live in a nation where they will not be judged by the color of their skin but by the content of their character." In its distilled form, King's dream was interpreted as a color-blind utopia, the liberal ideal of individual equality. This is unfortunate because in the same speech, there was a forceful indignation in the face of past injustice. He was asking the nation for redress of past wrongs—specifically in economic terms:

> In a sense we've come to our nation's capital to cash a check. When the architects of our republic wrote the magnificent words of the Constitution and the Declaration of Independence, they were signing a promissory note to which every American was to fall heir. This note was a promise that all men, yes, black men as well as white men, would be guaranteed the "unalienable Rights" of "Life, Liberty and the pursuit of Happiness." It is obvious today that America has defaulted on this promissory note, insofar as her citizens of color are concerned. Instead of honoring this sacred obligation, America has given the Negro people a bad check, a check which has come back marked "insufficient funds." But we refuse to believe that the bank of justice is bankrupt. We refuse to believe that there are insufficient funds in the great vaults of opportunity of this nation. And so, we've come

to cash this check, a check that will give us upon demand the riches of freedom and the security of justice.[14]

King, who chose his words carefully, was asking for a financial reckoning. Inspired by Mahatma Gandhi, King was genuinely and passionately committed to nonviolent protest, but like Gandhi, he was aware of systemic economic exploitation. He was as committed to changing structures and systems as he was to changing hearts and minds. Segregation was not wrong because it judged people by the color of their skin, but because it was exploitative. King believed that "the underlying purpose of segregation was to oppress and exploit the segregated, not simply to keep them apart . . . the basic purpose of segregation was to perpetuate injustice and inequality."[15]

King knew that talk of love and unity would only go so far without cold economic realism. "When all is finally entered into the annals of sociology; when philosophers, politicians, and preachers have all had their say, we must return to the fact that a person participates in this society primarily as an economic entity. At rock bottom we are neither poets, athletes, nor artists; our existence is centered in the fact that we are consumers, because we first must eat and have shelter to live."[16] He understood that blacks had been excluded from full economic participation, and he maintained that any strides toward civil rights had to be linked with antipoverty programs to be effective because "the inseparable twin of racial justice was economic justice."[17] Yet King acknowledged that the latter was a more difficult battle because it would require radical change.[18]

Just one year after the historic Civil Rights Act and two years after the March on Washington, King was frustrated by the lack of progress and by political retrenchment. In a 1965 sermon called "The American Dream," he offered a more realistic sequel to the famous Dream speech. He revisited his dream metaphor at Ebenezer Baptist Church, but this time with much less publicity and fanfare. And the dream had changed.

> About two years ago now . . . I tried to tell the nation about a dream I had. I must confess to you this morning that since that sweltering August afternoon in 1963, my dream has often turned into a nightmare; I've seen it

shattered. . . . I continue to see it shattered as I walk through the Harlems of our nation and see sometimes ten and fifteen Negroes trying to live in one or two rooms. I've been down to the Delta of Mississippi since then, and I've seen my dream shattered as I met hundreds of people who didn't earn more than six or seven hundred dollars a week. I've seen my dream shattered as I've walked the streets of Chicago and seen Negroes, young men and women, with a sense of utter hopelessness because they can't find any jobs. And they see life as a long and desolate corridor with no exit signs.[19]

By the 1960s, black poverty was deeply entrenched, but more importantly, it was marked by its stark contrast to the white middle class's prosperity.[20] Not only had the majority of blacks not ridden the postwar economic boom; conditions in the ghetto had actually worsened.[21] Almost half of black children lived in poverty in contrast with only 9 percent of white children.[22] Black families had less than one-fifth the wealth of white families.[23] A Federal Reserve study concluded that the source of the wealth gap was historic inequalities in income and opportunities, "a legacy of past economic deprivation," which would not be fixed even if the income gap were eliminated. The study held that it could only be closed by a reversal of past privileges.[24] The wealth and opportunity gap would continue unabated without direct government action—in other words, something more than just stopping racial discrimination.

Laws set in motion a century earlier had created a black ghetto economy that was uniquely ruinous. Black poverty, having been created by economic exclusion and segregation, was distinct from white poverty. The urban ghettos were zones with fewer public resources such as quality schools, roads, hospitals, universities, and infrastructure. In fact, even the urban renewal programs that upgraded and revived America's cities in the 1960s did so at the expense of the black population. James Baldwin referred to "urban renewal" programs as "negro removal," for the effect was that highways and roads built through ghettos pushed and packed black residents into increasingly overcrowded and under-resourced neighborhoods.[25] The segregated ghetto contained too little capital, and its main export, labor, was struggling to find work as industries abandoned America's cities for the less costly suburbs before eventually moving offshore.[26]

These trends were self-reinforcing. Urban decline pushed businesses out of the ghetto, which led to further urban decline. As businesses moved to the suburbs where land was cheaper and business costs lower, the ghetto suffered from both high prices and general deterioration. In the economic trap of the ghetto, small retailers sold inferior products at higher prices because they had lower sales volumes, lower profits, and higher costs. Because suburban retailers had an economically diverse set of customers and higher sales volume, their costs were lower. The economy of the black inner city was a unique vortex of negative forces that further compounded poverty. In 1965, Kenneth Clark described the "dark ghettoes" as "social, political, educational, and—above all—economic colonies."[27]

The situation was explosive.[28] Sixteen days after the Civil Rights Act of 1964 was passed, Harlem erupted in violence. Five days after the Voting Rights Act was signed into law, the Watts district in Los Angeles exploded in a deadly riot that killed and injured many and destroyed millions of dollars worth of property. One in three people in Watts was unemployed, all but a single industrial plant had abandoned the Los Angeles district, and Watts had been thoroughly segregated over the preceding decades, making poverty concentrated and extreme.[29] Watts was a tinderbox. Against this backdrop, a mundane incident of police aggression lit a fuse that exploded into days of violent rioting and looting. About 30,000 people participated in the riots. White property was a common target as rioters turned their anger toward their perceived exploiters—white absentee property owners, pawn shops, and grocery stores. In Chicago's West Side, rioters claimed that they wanted to "drive white 'exploiters' out of the ghetto."[30] Black communities were demanding attention to their economic plight in ways that the white public could no longer avoid.

This new phase of the black movement was not calling America to honor its founding message of equality, they were venting pentup rage at their economic state and demanding more opportunity. With no unifying leader or clear agenda, the rage that exploded in the streets fractured the civil rights coalition, creating a confounding national crisis on the heels of radical reforms. Dr. King noted that these rioters were "so fed up with . . . powerlessness" that they would "rather be dead than ignored."[31] King urged the nation to focus on the causes of rioting and the "daily violence" that society imposed on blacks due to unemployment, poverty, and segregation.[32] He also tried to persuade the rioters that violence was not effective, that it would lead to a white backlash, and crucially that they stood no chance against a well-armed majority.[33]

But King was not their leader. He and the other heads of the civil rights movement were powerless against this new form of resistance. When Bayard Rustin tried to quell a crowd in Harlem, they shouted him down as an "Uncle Tom!"[34] Having led hundreds of thousands of people in the March on Washington, Rustin could no longer command a few hundred people.

To many, it felt like a domestic war—especially when the National Guard was sent in with military equipment to deal with the insurgency.[35] Doug McAdam's study of the civil rights movement after 1965 explained, "It would not seem an overstatement to argue that the level of open defiance of the established economic and political order was as great during this period as during any other in the country's history, save the Civil War."[36] A CBS TV broadcast announced, "This was not a riot. It was an insurrection against all authority."[37] One official report on the violence was titled *Violence in the City— An End or a Beginning?* The answer was, unfortunately—and unequivocally—just a beginning.

Though rioting and looting in some places looked like random destruction of imprecise orientation, many observers noted that there were usually specific targets. Black rioters destroyed white business establishments, but even more specifically, according to press accounts and government research, the pent-up anger was directed at the ghetto lenders.[38] The *Washington Post* reported that the stores that sold on credit were the "most popular victims of the riots."[39] A congressional hearing determined that rioters engaged in "selective burning and looting" of the stores they felt "had treated them unfairly," and that these rioters went to the lenders "not to loot, but to destroy the credit records of the stores they burned. This was their final solution to oppressive debt."[40] During a riot in Chicago, an elderly black man watched as a grocery store burned and chanted, "Burn, burn, burn. White man ain't milking me no more."[41] Looters destroyed the leather-bound books on which their debts were recorded before they destroyed anything else. Onlookers reportedly yelled, "Burn the damn records"; a mother told looters at a grocery store, "Don't grab the groceries, grab the book."[42] Just as King's coalition had protested Jim Crow buses in Birmingham, in Harlem and Chicago and other black ghettos across the country, residents were protesting Jim Crow Credit markets.

As credit became a ubiquitous feature of American life, neither credit cards nor mortgage credit had crossed the color line. Almost every large purchase was paid for with high-cost installment credit, and even some small ones like groceries, doctor visits, and encyclopedias.[43] Black families across all income levels had more installment debt than whites.[44] Installment credit added high debt loads to those living on the economic margins, and thus it was debt that turned the ghetto into a pressure cooker.

The money-pit economy of the ghetto meant that black consumers paid much more for everything than those living just across the color line. In the 1963 study *The Poor Pay More,* Columbia professor David Caplovitz described the debt market in the ghetto as a "deviant one in which exploitation and fraud are the norm rather than the exception."[45] Specifically, he found that residents of New York ghettos paid much higher prices—"unbelievably" high, according to the author—for goods than anywhere else. These customers were not buying more goods than the average consumer or even relying more on credit, but obtained "considerably less value for their dollar."[46] Another 1968 study conducted by the Federal Trade Commission (FTC) reported that 93 percent of sales in the ghetto were on installment, compared with only 27 percent in white suburbia. The FTC's study, which was also titled "The Poor Pay More," calculated that for $100 of goods, the poor paid $300 compared to $150 paid by those buying from general retailers outside the ghetto.[47] The report also found costs to be higher for housing, food, and services across the board.[48] The FTC called these results "disturbing."[49]

The disturbing price of credit had to do with the economic trap of the ghetto, which led to a constrained credit market. Due to the triple forces of racism, poverty, and segregation, ghetto residents were not offered credit cards or consumer loans from banks. Large retailers did not operate within the ghetto, so most purchases were financed at the store that sold the goods through informal debt contracts.[50] Because these consumers were a "captive market," there was no price competition among these retailers. Lenders courted customers through advertising, promises of easy credit, and peddling from door to door to solicit sales.[51] Borrowers fell into a relationship of continuous debt with these merchants, a situation appropriately described as an "urban sharecropping system."[52]

Loan default was common, and had to do in part with the financial instability created by poverty and wage irregularities. But it also had to do with resentment. Ghetto retailers were selling shoddy merchandise at high prices. Furniture advertised as new was usually not.[53] When the furniture inevitably fell apart, the borrower stopped paying. As explained by Senator William Proxmire at a Senate hearing, this felt like exploitation, "so many of them stop making payments."[54] This obviously meant that their credit would be further restricted in the future and they would have to pay more, but noncomplicity in this debt cycle seemed to be a matter of dignity. But even a dignified default came with a world of trouble.

These informal neighborhood transactions often entailed repossession, wage garnishments, court judgments, and even shakedowns by lenders, all of which were unimaginable in the suburbs. The loss of a job could lead to default on a furniture loan, but a missed payment could also lead to loss of a job, because it was common for an employer to fire an employee whose wages were garnished in order to avoid the hassle.[55] There were many more court judgments in the ghetto than in the suburbs, which meant that law enforcement and the court system were a part of the credit system for blacks.[56] Repo men, courts, lawyers, police, bankruptcy—all from buying a refrigerator and a television set. These lenders were the very face of exploitation, humiliation, shame, and injustice. So it is not surprising that they were the first targets of the violence.

But they were the wrong targets. In fact, these lenders were not even making high profits on the backs of the poor. The poor paid more and the sellers made less. To repeat, the poor paid more, but it was not because someone was profiting from their exploitation. Poverty, segregation, and exclusion from robust credit markets meant high costs, low profits, and higher risks for everyone. The vortex of these forces created the money-pit economy of the ghetto—prices were high, quality was low, and profits were deceptively scarce. This is not to say that merchants were not taking advantage of the poor. They were. There was predatory behavior, misleading advertisements, misrepresentation of prices, bait-and-switch advertising and sales, and fraud to be sure, but everyone was affected by the ghetto's destructive economic undertow.[57]

Because their customers had too little wealth, these lenders had higher loan losses and collection costs, including hiring repo men and taking their customers to court. These collection tactics and the "unbelievably" high prices these lenders charged for their merchandise caused much suffering for borrowers, but they also cut into the lenders' margins. They had to hire more staff, lost more money on default, and paid more to finance their own businesses—all costs that were borne by their customers. Historian Louis Hyman found that "between bad debt losses, lawyers' collection fees, higher insurance premiums, more accounting staff, and higher sales commissions, the higher costs of ghetto retailers accounted for 94 percent of the difference in the gross margins."[58]

Situating these lenders in the broader framework makes the disparity even more striking. Because of the high defaults and loan losses of ghetto lenders, they could not participate in the robust credit markets that were driving down credit prices in the suburbs. These lenders paid more for capital because they could not sell their loans into the secondary market. They could not sell these loans to a secondary market because they were too risky. They were too risky because they did not have access to the network that lowered risks, and on and on. They were stuck in an ancient debt market while the rest of the country had taken off into the modern world of risk sharing, secondary markets, and large finance companies that all worked to lower the risks and the costs of debt. Lower-cost debt meant a lower burden for customers outside the ghetto, which also meant lower default rates. A virtuous cycle of credit had taken hold in American suburbs (at least until it was no longer sustainable for the country as a whole). The network did not work without all of the pieces in place. The black ghetto was not part of this infrastructure, so they were on their own. Americans lived in two different worlds of credit—*separate and unequal.* But the civil rights laws had not been designed to address the Jim Crow credit market.

In the aftermath of the riots, the Banking and Currency Committee in the Senate held two separate hearings to discuss the problem of the poor paying more and what could be done about it. The hearings were led by Senator Proxmire, a Democrat from Wisconsin who did more to shape the legislative response to credit inequality than any other senator. His moral zealotry earned the senator a reputation as a maverick lawmaker and a righteous crusader against excess government spending. He won Joseph McCarthy's seat in 1957 when the infamous senator died, and he called his predecessor a "disgrace to Wisconsin, to the Senate, and to America." Proxmire famously created the "Golden Fleece Award," a dubious honor he presented monthly to projects he viewed as self-serving and wasteful of taxpayer dollars.[59] He spent only $200 on his Senate campaigns as a protest against corrupt political spending and never missed a roll call vote in over twenty years of service in the Senate, setting a record that has yet to be broken.[60] Proxmire was an incorruptible reformer who was as committed a policymaker in the cause of fixing inequalities as any other.

Proxmire expressed "outrage" at the injustices faced by consumers in the ghetto, and he believed that the government needed to play a role in alleviating the suffering.[61] Proxmire and the other members of his committee expressed genuine puzzlement that market competition had not brought down prices in the ghetto. But many witnesses testified that these lenders were not making money, even though they were charging exorbitant prices. The legislators seemed to understand that the ghetto lending economy created a vicious cycle of high prices and lack of competition. They understood that the cycle had to be broken somehow and that the "economic illness of the ghetto" needed a strong cure. Yet when they began discussing the antidote, they homed in on getting more black banks, credit unions, and lenders in the ghetto.[62]

During the hearings, the senators converged on a diagnosis of the problem as one of white institutions exploiting the black ghetto. While "white-owned stores were burned and looted," said New York Republican Senator Jacob Javits, " 'soul brother' establishments were spared."[63] Indeed, this was the case. Many black businesses had even put signs up in their windows during riots positively identifying themselves as "soul brother" establishments.[64] And certainly, many rioters felt that they were protesting white exploiters. Based on this framing, the solution to the ghetto money pit was to throw more black businesses into it, which is exactly what was proposed. But what was causing the misery was not necessarily the race of the installment lenders, but their interest rates. The misreading of the problem as a lack of enough black lenders would lead to decades of misguided policy. But at first, these programs were meant to work alongside other antipoverty measures.[65]

Javits put forward a plan to spur black-owned small business, but he emphasized that only a robust federal intervention aimed specifically at the ghetto could reverse the trend of decline because "no conceivable increase in the gross national product would stir these backwaters" without targeted assistance.[66] President Johnson's Small Business Administration director, Howard J. Samuels, said that the "inner cities of this country will be dead economically" and would remain "forever ghettos" unless blacks became "owners of American businesses."[67] The SBA's response was a small business lending program called Project OWN, which ran alongside a larger War on Poverty program. Samuels promoted a program of "compensatory capitalism" aimed at the "economic emancipation" of the black population.[68] John Jacob of the Washington Urban League believed that credit card issuers were discriminating against blacks and suggested instead a "credit card for the poor—extended by a black credit card company in the black community."[69]

Proxmire himself, an avid believer in small business, put his faith in credit unions.[70] Following the hearings, he introduced a bill that he said was "designed to help the poor break out of this vicious cycle" by "authorizing a strong federal program to encourage the formation of credit unions and consumer counseling programs for the poor."[71] The bill was a continuation of Project Moneywise, which had created 218 credit unions in poverty-stricken areas with the help of "indigenous leaders."[72] The director of the program said that the goal was for these credit unions to use consumer education and rely on the "latent savings in the community" to build wealth.[73] Of course, there were few savings, and such a plan had been tried for a hundred years without any results.

By 1968, most of these credit unions were struggling to remain viable, and the program was nearing its end, but Proxmire still believed. As he told the credit union industry representative, "we really count on credit unions heavily to solve a large part of this problem." After all, he said, "this is one of the purposes for which credit unions were initially established, in order that people with modest incomes could establish credit and be able to operate in this free enterprise economy."[74] The myth of the credit union was that through local control of money, a marginalized community could eventually gather enough capital to join the economy. But this was not actually how credit unions had created the middle class—they had done it through federally subsidized mortgage loans. However, so strong was the allure of this banking model as an answer to poverty that even the learned chair of the Senate Banking Committee, an honest reformer who understood the forces of this deviant ghetto market, could not break the spell of the credit union as the answer to poverty. He knew that these ghetto lenders were not making money, a fact he repeated many times during the hearings. He also understood that the heart of the problem was concentrated poverty and not the profitable exploitation of a few mischievous lenders. Yet he believed that locally owned credit unions would break the "vicious cycle." Perhaps it was because any other solution was politically impractical or cost too much, or perhaps he believed that credit unions could overcome these obstacles through their commitment to the community. To Proxmire's credit, this was only his first proposal, with many more to follow in the years to come.

Just a few years later, Proxmire would home in on eliminating credit discrimination and would push for passage of the 1970 Fair Credit Reporting Act (FCRA) and the 1974 Equal Opportunity Act (ECOA). It was the advocacy of feminist groups that ushered in equal credit laws, which eliminated race and gender identification from loan applications and forced lenders to use credit scores based purely on financial information and data. Before their passage, even affluent women could not get a credit card. These antidiscrimination provisions also applied to minorities, but women and other minorities were not similarly situated. Creditors were indeed discriminating against creditworthy women and blacks based solely on negative stereotypes. But for blacks, discrimination had created a plethora of other conditions that actually affected their default risk.

This was not a straightforward matter of racism that could be fixed by the same laws that effectively mandated the removal of "whites only" signs. Racism was the root cause of the problem, but it was the segregated and undercapitalized ghetto that was responsible for much of the disparity. Unable or unwilling to eliminate the ghetto credit market in its entirety, legislators focused exclusively on discrimination in credit applications. But mandating nondiscrimination would not change the fundamental ghetto economy. Lenders soon found another fairly obvious way to avoid lending to blacks after these laws were imposed—they used zip codes as a proxy for race. Zip codes were perfect indicators of a community's racial and economic makeup because segregation had almost perfectly correlated geography and race.[75]

Misunderstanding the problem entirely, the FTC admonished lawmakers to create "financial education" programs so that blacks would not enter into exploitative contracts. However, their own study found that the poor knew they were paying too much for credit, but that they had no other options.[76] Caplovitz ended his study with a proposal for financial education, suggesting that ghetto consumers should be taught to avoid buying in the ghetto and should try to shop at outside retailers.[77] Ultimately, Caplovitz conceded, however, that all these suggestions are limited and futile "until poverty itself is eradicated."[78] Financial education is useful insofar as consumers are making bad choices as a result of their ignorance of better options. However, high-cost borrowing is usually a result of a lack of better choices. In a survey of ghetto consumers, only 15 percent thought it was a "good idea" to buy on credit. The rest said it was only a good idea in certain circumstances, or a bad idea. When asked why, more than half of those surveyed said "it costs too much" or "you pay too much in carrying charges." Though these consumers seemed to understand the exact nature of their problem, they admitted that this was "the only way poor people can buy."[79] What more could financial education have taught them?

In reality, all these solutions were incomplete and short-sighted. The only way to eliminate the drastic credit disparity was to eliminate the wide disparity in wealth. One path toward equality was to integrate the credit market. By concentrating the poor in income and the poor in assets in the ghetto, segregation had cordoned off the riskiest borrowers. Large national chains could avoid this area entirely, and thus avoid the higher costs of underwriting, servicing, and collection. That is what they were doing. But not all of these borrowers were poor credit risks. In fact, most of them were not—if they could have been given lower-cost credit. The more they paid for loans, the greater the debt burden, and the greater the likelihood that it would break them and they would default, which cost the lender more. If these borrowers could be integrated into the general market and large retailers allowed to do individual credit evaluations, the borrowers could have paid less for credit. This would have allowed lenders to diversify their risks, thus driving down prices for everyone. Increased diversity would even have been preferable for the large finance companies as most lenders prefer some borrowers who pay off their balance and many who roll over their balances and pay interest. But integrating the credit market would have been difficult to do without physical integration, which was simply not politically feasible.

The other alternative was to break the poverty cycle directly by giving black residents an infusion of capital to jump-start wealth creation. The racial wealth gap had been created by state law and policy, and so a reversal of the wealth gap through a program of reparations would have been justifiable. But while forced integration would have been unfeasible and unlikely, subsidizing black communities was inconceivable. If giving blacks land the year after their emancipation from slavery proved unenforceable, one hundred years later, financial grants didn't stand a chance. Moreover, such a race-based redistribution of wealth had to contend with the bedrock principle of the civil rights movement: color-blind equality. Yet such a reckoning had recently happened in Europe. In 1952, West Germany agreed to pay the new nation of Israel three billion marks over the next fourteen years as reparations for the atrocities of the Holocaust. But the United States, at least under Johnson's administration, never conceptualized the remedy for past wrongs in this way.

Johnson did understand that poverty was the root cause of racial inequality. In his 1964 State of the Union address, President Johnson declared an "unconditional war on poverty." Johnson's Great Society and War on Poverty programs, contained in the Economic Opportunity Act of 1964 (EOA), were the largest federal government economic measures since the New Deal. The Office of Economic Opportunity (OEO) would launch job-training programs, food and income assistance, and the early childhood program Head Start. However, from the start, these programs were geared toward charity and education as opposed to control, power, or building capital.[80] Congress was clear on this point: "These are not programs to bring about major structural change in the economy or to generate large numbers of additional jobs."[81]

Though Johnson framed his poverty program as an heir to the New Deal, and the two programs now stand as bookends to an age of American progressivism in action, Johnson's Great Society fell far short of the ambitious economic restructuring of the New Deal. Although there were job-*training* programs, there were no job-*creating* programs—no public works projects or wealth-creating credit markets. Cyril deGrasse Tyson, who founded an antipoverty organization in Newark, New Jersey, lamented that the War on Poverty had no *wealth-building* functions, no "multiplier effect."[82] Johnson's program was also much less popular than the New Deal. During the New Deal era, poverty was seen as a systemic problem. Change the system and poverty goes away, and so do its symptoms. Not so in the 1960s, when poverty came to be seen as a moral failure. What changed? According to economic research, race has been the single most important predictor of support for American welfare programs. In other words, black poverty has been viewed as a moral failing, whereas white poverty had been viewed as a systemic problem. Therefore, once welfare came to be associated with black poverty, it was delegitimized.[83]

The War on Poverty eventually ran up against a torrent of protest and accusations of favorable treatment, and its "handouts" quickly became a target of conservative scorn. Not only did these programs not actually alleviate black poverty, but they have since been maligned by conservatives as the *cause* of black poverty. But they could hardly have caused anything, as they were largely abandoned shortly after they began. The money, energy, and political capital that Johnson was to use in the proverbial War on Poverty were quickly diverted into the actual war in Vietnam. By 1968, all of the programs were mere shells of the robust 1964 promises, as the administration's budget, resources, energy, and all of their political capital were pulled toward Southeast Asia. In 1967, King lamented that the War on Poverty had been "broken and eviscerated as if it were some idle political plaything of a society gone mad on war," and that he watched as "Vietnam continued to draw men and skills and money like some demonic destructive suction tube."[84]

President Johnson himself was conflicted about the underlying rationale for the War on Poverty and came close to acknowledging that there needed to be a leveling of the playing field after centuries of white advantage. In a 1965 speech that still stands as the closest any U.S. president has come to reckoning with the history of racial injustice, Johnson told a black audience at Howard University that America had "failed the Negro" and that "freedom was not enough." He even seemed to be rejecting the late-term egalitarianism that assumed that ending discrimination could erase a legacy of past injustice. "You do not take a person who, for years, has been hobbled by chains and liberate him, bring him up to the starting line of a race and then say, 'you are free to compete with all the others,' and still justly believe that you have been completely fair."[85] He further acknowledged that blacks were trapped in "inherited, gateless poverty," which stemmed from a "devastating heritage of long years of slavery; and a century of oppression, hatred, and injustice." Crucially, he understood that black poverty was not like white poverty, and that "there are differences—deep, corrosive, obstinate differences," and that the differences were not attributable to race, but were a "consequence of ancient brutality, past injustice, and present prejudice."[86]

Johnson's speech was bold and unprecedented, and he immediately faced an angry reaction from conservatives, who felt that Johnson had gone too far—anger that held the first inklings of the political mayhem that was to follow.[87] Yet Johnson's own words reflected an uneasy clash between two theories of black poverty, and Johnson seemed torn between the two, veering first one way and then another. Although he explicitly linked present poverty to past injustice, he also seemed to be saying that poverty was a result of a moral failing and that it was the responsibility of the black community to straighten up and deal with it. He claimed that it was a black "cultural tradition" and "the breakdown of the Negro family structure" that were causing poverty and that blacks would have to "rely mostly upon his own efforts" to escape poverty. The speech thus held the seeds of a new dogma about black poverty. In fact, the principal author of the cultural theory of poverty, Daniel Patrick Moynihan, was also the principal author of Johnson's speech. In the end, Johnson exhorted his audience to change their own circumstances stating that "nothing is more freighted with meaning for our own destiny than the revolution of the Negro American." Indeed, a revolution was happening, but not the one Johnson was hoping for.

What started in Watts in 1965 had spread like wildfire across the country, as urban ghettos in the north and west exploded into over

150 full-scale riots over four years. Johnson was initially bewildered, "How is it possible after all we've accomplished? How could it be? Is the world topsy-turvy?" Then he surmised that the problem was "We're not getting our story over." Johnson expressed sympathy for the protesters. "He's still nowhere. He knows it. And that's why he's out on the streets. Hell, I'd be there too."[88] But by 1967, Johnson began to change his tune of sympathy for protesters to a forceful denunciation of the violence. "We will not tolerate lawlessness. We will not endure violence."[89] Between 1967 and 1968, 70,000 federal troops were called out to suppress the urban black revolution, which had resulted in forty-six deaths, 2,600 serious injuries, and $100 million in property loss, all leading to 22,000 arrests.[90]

As the government bureaucracy tried to make sense of the surge of violence, they turned to Assistant Secretary of Labor Daniel Patrick Moynihan's 1965 report, *The Negro Family: The Case for National Action* (referred to as the Moynihan Report), distributed among policy circles in Washington as an explanation for the uprisings.[91] The report revealed that the wealth and employment gap between black and white families had been widening instead of closing, a phenomenon referred to as "Moynihan's scissors." Moynihan acknowledged that American racism was the original sin responsible for the gap in economic opportunity.[92] Having diagnosed the problem as being rooted in historic harm, he proposed that the way to fix it was to address black culture, which he called a "tangle of pathology." Specifically, the Moynihan Report blamed the prevalence of single mothers for "the deterioration of the Negro family," which was "the principal source of most of the aberrant, inadequate, or anti-social behavior that . . . serves to perpetuate the cycle of poverty and deprivation."[93]

The logical policy outcome was that any other intervention was futile; "the cycle can be broken only if these [cultural] distortions are set right." This was the idea that determined public policy going forward. Moynihan concluded the report bluntly by stating, "how this group of Americans chooses to run its affairs, take advantage of its opportunities, or fail to do so, is none of the nation's business."[94] The Moynihan Report, or the ways in which it has been interpreted and misinterpreted, formed the narrative of black poverty. The breakdown of the black family has been the lens through which many policymakers and Americans have viewed black poverty.

Decades later, in 2014, a congressional budget report on poverty listed as the number one cause of poverty, "The Family," and cited Moynihan's report as primary evidence. The second cause was "work participation," followed by "lack of education," and the fourth cause of poverty, ironically, was the programs of the War on Poverty itself.[95]

The tide had turned for white moderates and conservatives, who demanded a retreat from any more legislation, programs, or aid. In fact, some said civil rights legislation was only making the situation worse. Protesters were pushing too hard, too fast, and being ungrateful and disruptive.[96] Some argued that civil rights reforms were being "repaid with crime-ridden slums and black discontent." The *Wall Street Journal* editorialized that the more civil rights laws were passed, the more violence ensued.[97]

If there was no way to fix poverty, the best that could be done was to contain it. Quickly, the War on Poverty morphed into the War on Crime.[98] So fast was the transformation that the tools, bureaucracies, and funds allocated to the poverty war were instead used by police stations across the country to fight crime. Police departments began to fill the spaces meant for the War on Poverty. It was police who delivered food and toys to needy black families. Law enforcement would be the front line of the War on Poverty, and would thereby increase its presence in and surveillance of the black communities. This criminalization of black life would increase over the next several decades, but its seeds and structure were planted during the Johnson administration.[99] The War on Crime would take a heavy toll on the black population, leading to the mass incarceration of black men and the further devastation of the black ghetto, and it began ironically as a response to the violent protests of an already desperate and impoverished community.

Once Jim Crow was destroyed and equality before the law established, a new strand of colorblind racism emerged. As Ibram Kendi explained, there have always been "two historical forces at work: a dual and dueling history of racial progress and the simultaneous progression of racism."[100] "Law and order" became the language of the former white supremacists, who were now engaged on the front lines of the War on Crime.[101] George Wallace, Strom Thurmond, and the last defenders of Jim Crow, once defeated, shifted their rhetoric to push for stronger criminal enforcement.[102] But it wasn't just the southern segregationists. Ronald Reagan's gubernatorial campaign ran ads with footage of riots and a warning that "Every day the jungle draws a little closer."[103] This new story of the ghetto focused on the violence, erasing the poverty beneath.

By 1968, President Johnson was mired between black-led violence in the ghetto and a growing conservative backlash. According to a White House advisor, what could he do but "set up a commission and say a prayer." The Kerner Commission, which relied on hundreds of researchers who collected testimonies and statistics, was the first thorough governmental exploration of black economic disparity. The first draft of the report was titled *The Harvest of American Racism,* and it was a forceful denunciation of the failure of Great Society programs, which the report dismissed as "tokenism that did not tamper enough with the 'white power structure' to have an impact." The administration was so angry about the first draft that it fired all 120 social scientists who had worked on it. The final report was less damaging to Johnson's reputation, though no less blunt.[104]

The final report determined that the riots stemmed from poverty, racism, inequality, and other social ills, but that the underlying cause was segregation. "Segregation and poverty have created in the racial ghetto a destructive environment totally unknown to most white Americans," the report said. "What white Americans have never fully understood—but what the Negro can never forget—is that white society is deeply implicated in the ghetto. White institutions created it, white institutions maintain it, and white society condones it."[105] The report was an unapologetic excoriation of white society, which the commission deemed guilty not just of racism, but of apathy toward black poverty.

This report drew a clear line from past discrimination to present poverty and violence, without a detour through cultural inferiority. It also dispensed with the color-blind language of equal opportunity, but insisted that only race-based economic policy could repair the damage created by racism.

The commission ultimately warned, "Our Nation is moving toward two societies, one black, one white—separate and unequal." The report offered three future scenarios: The first was maintaining the status quo, which the commission warned would have "ominous consequences" and would lead to more violence, retaliation, and eventually a garrison state. The second path was to promote separatism, or the "enrichment" of segregated ghettos, but this path would also result in a "permanently divided country" in which equality would not be achievable. According to the commission, the only way to end the divide was to push for complete integration. Only full integration would produce a "single society, in which every citizen will be free to live and work according to his capabilities and desires, not his color." This would require a large-scale federal involvement, much like the New Deal. As it turned out, Americans would pick a watered-down version of the second option and the commission's dire predictions of intractable inequality would come to pass.

The Kerner Report was the closest the United States ever came to a public admission of wrongdoing or "truth and reconciliation." Ultimately, the report was more truth than reconciliation. Johnson all but ignored its findings and later explained that it was a matter of funding. "That was the problem—money. At the moment I received the report I was having one of the toughest fights of my life, trying to persuade Congress to pass the 10 percent tax surcharge without imposing deep cuts in our most critical Great Society programs. I will never understand how the commission expected me to get this same Congress to turn 180 degrees overnight and appropriate an additional $30 billion for the same programs that it was demanding I cut by $6 billion. This would have required a miracle."[106]

By 1968, Johnson was an unpopular president deeply enmeshed in a failing war. The report came out on February 29, 1968. On March 31, Johnson stunned the nation by revealing that he would not seek reelection. Republicans made significant gains in the 1968 election, which was widely seen as a renunciation of Johnson, his Great Society, and the civil rights movement. Johnson, looking back on the loss, lamented, "I don't think I lost that election. I think the Negroes lost it."[107] Even though Johnson was involved in the country's most unpopular war, the administration believed that the nastiest public backlash they faced was on the race issue.[108]

Toward the end of his life, King also came to the realization that achieving racial equality would require radical measures of integration and poverty alleviation that the government would not pursue. What is often left out of the popular narrative of Dr. King's movement is his bout of clinical depression as the nation seemed to be backtracking after unleashing so much hope with the groundbreaking

Civil Rights and Voting Rights Acts. Though he had earned the Nobel Peace Prize for his optimism and unflagging commitment to nonviolence, King's most forthright admonitions were ignored by the public. Militant black groups denigrated his nonviolence as weak, and President Johnson sidelined him after his vocal antiwar pronouncements. A 1967 Gallup poll revealed that for the first time in a decade, King was not on the list of the ten most admired Americans.

Perhaps this fall from grace was because King's demands and rhetoric became much more damning as he began connecting America's racism, militarism, and economic exploitation.[109] King came to believe that to address poverty, "a major structural reform of the American economy was needed."[110] Despite years of violence, "not a single basic cause of riots has been corrected," lamented King. King began calling for a "Poor People's Movement" to address not just black, but also white poverty. King called his last planned project before his death "the most important meeting [the SCLC] ever convened." The plan was to conduct another march on Washington, DC, in the spring of 1968 to address economic inequality.

Using the only tool he believed to be effective, a massive nonviolent demonstration, he sought to organize a multiracial movement to stir the nation's leaders to address poverty. He knew that white policymakers had stopped paying attention both to him and to civil rights in general, and so he sought to make an eye-catching and dramatic public spectacle.[111] He called on demonstrators to come to Washington on mules and buggy trains from the rural South as well as the urban North to show vividly how little economic progress blacks had made in a generation.[112] As Gerald McKnight explains, "King was proposing nothing less than a radical transformation of the Civil Rights Movement into a populist crusade calling for redistribution of economic and political power."[113]

While pushing for large-scale reform, King was also admonishing blacks to harness their own economic power. In his last speech, "I've Been to the Mountaintop," he pleaded, "we've got to strengthen black institutions. I call upon you to take your money out of the banks downtown and deposit your money in Tri-State Bank. We want a 'bank-in' movement in Memphis. Go by the savings and loan association. . . . We are telling you to follow what we [the SCLC] are doing. Put your money there. You have six or seven black insurance companies here in the city of Memphis. Take out your insurance there. We want to have an 'insurance-in.' "

King advocated black banking as a key weapon in his arsenal of nonviolent resistance. He believed his most successful northern project was Operation Breadbasket, which proclaimed, "If you respect my dollar, you must respect my person." This was an extension of the "Don't Buy Where You Can't Work" Harlem boycotts. "We will no longer spend our money where we cannot get substantial jobs."[114] King describes the philosophy of Operation Breadbasket as "the belief that many retail business and consumer goods industries depleted the ghetto by selling to Negroes without returning to the community any of the profits through fair hiring practices."[115] Operation Breadbasket was not just about jobs, King insisted; it was about "the development of financial institutions which were controlled by Negroes and which were sensitive to problems of economic deprivation of the Negro community." One of the operation's projects in Chicago was to convince a large grocery store chain, Hi-Lo, to make deposits in the two black banks in Chicago. Operation Breadbasket had "demanded" that the black community "put money in the Negro savings and loan," and then requested that businesses with stores in the ghetto deposit funds in black-owned banks. The Poor People's Movement and Operation Breadbasket ended abruptly when Dr. King was killed in April 1968.

After King's assassination in 1968, the civil rights coalition he helped build began to unravel. King's last book was appropriately titled *Where Do We Go from Here?* James Farmer explained that the movement was "reeling," and the major groups "didn't know where they were going or what to do at that point." Without King, it seemed that there was not a single black leader that white Americans would listen to. But as it turned out, neither the White House nor the black movement was in the mood to talk anyway.

The black movement's tone, demands, and orientation had changed. Stokely Carmichael famously initiated this shift with his pivotal 1966 speech. "Everybody owns our own neighborhoods except us," he said. "We want Black Power." The new leaders held that the civil rights reforms had been meaningless in the face of poverty, a position King himself would have agreed with. Carmichael was not seeking to reform the American political system, but rejected it outright because it had always exploited blacks.[116] "Ultimately," he said "the economic foundations of this country must be shaken if black people are to control their lives." In inflammatory language that made the black activist notorious, he said he wanted a black power movement "that will smash everything Western civilization has created."[117] James Forman was even more blunt: "If we can't sit at the table, let's knock the fucking legs off!"[118]

This was not just a rejection of King's nonviolence, but also of Booker T. Washington's ideal of racial equality through hard work and thrift. In fact, Washington's name became an insult synonymous with Uncle Tom.[119] "We are told," said Carmichael, "'If you work hard, you'll succeed'—but if that were true, black people would own this country. We are oppressed because we are black—not because we are lazy, not because we're stupid (and got good rhythm), but because we're black."[120] James Baldwin articulated the changing mood in *The Fire Next Time:* "God gave Noah the rainbow sign / No more water but fire next time." Baldwin warned of what was coming. "Crime became real, for example—for the first time—not as *a* possibility but as *the* possibility. One would never defeat one's circumstances by working and saving one's pennies; one would never, by working, acquire that many pennies, and, besides, the social treatment accorded even the most successful Negroes proved that one needed, in order to be free, something more than a bank account. One needed a handle, a lever, a means of inspiring fear."[121]

If King had been the leader of the early civil rights movement, Malcolm X, though he had been dead since 1965, became the voice and spirit of what ensued.[122] Malcolm was the de facto leader of the urban ghetto, having experienced poverty, crime, unemployment, and prison himself.[123] Malcolm picked up where Marcus Garvey had left off and considered himself a leader of the black masses. He was not interested in speaking to whites or even wealthy blacks, who he blamed for exploiting the poor. Like Garvey, he rejected integration, saying that the white man would never allow blacks to enter "his house" anyway.[124]

To Malcolm, the ghetto was a colony, and the only solution to achieve black economic prosperity was to demand control of all the levers of economic and political power within the black community. Malcolm was not asking white Americans to provide equal rights to blacks. "I don't even consider myself an American," he said. Blacks needed to defend themselves against American exploitation because "the [U.S.] government has proven itself either unwilling or unable to defend the lives and the property of Negroes." Malcolm was uninterested in antidiscrimination laws; he wanted an uprising. Malcolm urged the black movement to reconsider their failed strategies of nonviolence. "Revolution is bloody, revolution is hostile, revolution knows no compromise, revolution overturns and destroys everything that gets in the way. . . . You don't do any singing [in a revolution]; you're too busy swinging. *It's based on land.* A revolutionary wants land so he can set up his own nation, an independent nation." His radical call to arms terrified the public. J. Edgar Hoover's FBI spied on him for most of his life.[125]

Malcolm's black nationalism required black control of the economic infrastructure of the ghetto. In a defining speech called "The Ballot or the Bullet," Malcolm asked, "Why should white people be running the banks of our community?" Echoing Carter Woodson, he explained that blacks needed to be "re-educated" with regard to economics. "Our people have to be made to see that any time you take your dollar out of your community and spend it in a community where you don't live, the community where you live will get poorer and poorer, and the community where you spend your money will get richer and richer."[126] The ghettos existed, he explained, because blacks did not know how to control their money. Every dollar spent at a white-owned institution was a dollar lost to the ghetto. Malcolm wanted blacks to own stores, banks, and industry within the ghetto so they wouldn't have to "picket and boycott and beg some cracker downtown for a job in his business."[127] His economic plan was strikingly similar to King's, but Malcolm's rhetoric was more inflammatory and was sometimes laced with a threat of violence.

If James Baldwin had warned of the "fire next time" and Malcolm alluded to the bullet, it was Huey Newton who picked up the gun and loaded it. Newton created the Black Panthers to organize the ghetto as King had organized the South. The Panthers were where many of the principals in King's coalition went after his death, but the Panther leadership was more eclectic, with several leaders embedded in criminal networks.[128] The Panthers' mission was to coordinate random violence into a coherent movement, or more accurately, a revolution. The point of the Panthers' revolution was to overcome poverty and oppression through violent resistance. The movement has had no rival in American history. It did not recognize

U.S. sovereignty over the black nation and intended to ultimately fight it.[129]

Newton published the Black Panthers' "Ten Point Program," which underscored the disillusionment with the earlier civil rights movement. "We have listened to the riot producing words 'these things take time' for 400 years." The Panthers, claiming to speak for the entire black community, made a list of what black people wanted and what black people believed. The list of wants could be summarized in the tenth, all-encompassing point: "we want land, bread, housing, education, clothing, justice and peace." As to beliefs, they believed in a right to self-defense, self-determination, fair trials, and a reversal of centuries of racist policies. Most provocatively, they declared that "whenever any form of government becomes destructive of these ends, it is the right of people to alter or to abolish it, and to institute new government, laying its foundations on such principles and organizing its powers in such form as to them shall seem more likely to effect their safety and happiness." The Panthers' mission, in sum, was "to throw off" any despotic regime, which in this particular case was the United States government.[130]

Everything had changed in just the few short years spanning 1965 to 1968. When reflecting on the civil rights movement, most Americans focus on the Montgomery bus boycott, King's "I Have a Dream" speech, the Civil Rights and Voting Rights Acts, Rosa Parks, and *Brown vs. Board of Education*. But all these events happened before 1965.

By 1969, the leaders of the movement, Malcolm X, King, John F. Kennedy, and Robert Kennedy, had all been killed, and Johnson was out of office. The consensus of the black community toward the civil rights movement, if there was one, was that it had failed, or at least that it was incomplete. Black leaders knew that the progressive momentum had halted. Yes, the "whites only" signs were now gone and employers could no longer legally discriminate based on race, but many still suffered from unemployment, dilapidated housing, and intractable poverty.

The civil rights movement held America to its democratic promise and undoubtedly opened opportunities for the black community, but these initial successes produced significant obstacles to future progress. The initial face of the movement cemented the country's focus on legal and political rights rather than economic equality, even though the black community and white leaders knew that the former would be meaningless without the latter. The rhetoric of color-blind equality entrapped reformers who could not and did not conceive of reforms that included recompense for past wrong. Moreover, many white Americans saw legislative and Supreme Court victories as a fait accompli and excused policymakers from pressing for more meaningful and necessary reforms. And finally, the uprisings, which sprang from a mix of hope and despair, created a public and policy backlash that spawned a new system of control through the criminal justice system. The war against poverty was subsumed by the new war against crime before the former had ever been fully waged.

Most of the civil rights reforms were embattled or weakened within a few years. And some of the demands were skirted altogether. The historic 1963 March on Washington was officially called the March for Jobs and Freedom. Though Johnson worked on freedom, the jobs were not forthcoming. And the next group of black power activists no longer wanted jobs. They demanded land.

The Decoy of Black Capitalism

As the radical black movement gained momentum, it was met with a strong white backlash, which President Nixon rode into office. Faced with a political quagmire, the politically savvy Nixon was able to neutralize black resistance without sacrificing the Republican coalition built on the "southern strategy."[1] Not only did Nixon find his way through the race minefield; he forged a path that many politicians after him would follow. The strategy included opposing all forms of legal race discrimination while rejecting any government effort at integration. The black militants would be met with "law and order," and antipoverty efforts were curtailed on the grounds that they were costly and created dependence on the state.[2]

Most importantly, in a nimble political move that has gone largely unnoticed, Nixon co-opted the black power movement's rhetoric of economic self-determination to push for a segregated black economy, thereby justifying his neglect of other proposals for meaningful reform. Capitalism, specifically "black capitalism," became yet another rhetorical weapon used to rationalize economic inequality.

Johnson may have been the master of the Senate, but Nixon was the master of political sleight of hand. Not only would the promise of black capitalism curb the stronger demands of black separatists; it would appeal to white voters across the political spectrum, especially because the very loosely conceived plan was open to multiple interpretations. To blacks, it was a grant of power. Nixon said, "people in the ghetto have to have more than an equal chance. They should be given a dividend."[3] To suburban whites, it would cure violence. After the riots in Chicago in 1968, he reasoned, "People who own their own homes don't burn their neighborhoods."[4] To middle-class voters who held to the American values of community and upward mobility, any program using the words "capitalism," "entrepreneurship," and "self-help" struck a chord. To fiscal hawks, it would cost nothing. Upon accepting the Republican presidential nomination, Nixon declared at the August 1968 convention, "Instead of government jobs, and government housing, and government welfare, let government use its tax and credit policies to enlist in this battle the greatest engine of progress ever developed in the history of man— American private enterprise." To the business community, it was to be market-driven: "we can get a bigger social return on a given level of investment and get some of the jobs done through the market system."[5]

Nixon's was not the first administration to promote minority banks and businesses, but unlike his predecessor, this was Nixon's chief focus.[6] Black business would not only lead to black prosperity, it would also lead to integration by "build[ing] bridges to human dignity across that gulf that separates black America from white America."[7] The fine print was that the bridge-building would be the sole responsibility of the black community. It placed the "black problem" in the hands of black entrepreneurs to fix with a little federal aid.

Black capitalism was disguised as a program catering to the black community's own demands, but what black leaders had been asking for was control of the infrastructure and institutions of local power in order to grow capital. Roy Innis, an initial proponent of black capitalism, had conceived of a "transfer of institutions within the black community to the management and control of the people themselves." He said that "Nixon should support the concept of community control of schools, welfare, sanitation, fire, police, hospitals, and all other institutions operating in the so-called 'ghettos.' "[8] But Nixon never intended to give blacks control of their community institutions, but rather, ownership of the problem of poverty. Black capitalism delegated the responsibility to solve the racial wealth gap to the black community without the help of the white political establishment who had always held power and the purse strings, and who continued to do so.

Nixon was a pragmatist and an astute politician, so his actions were geared toward leveraging the most votes with the fewest possible actions. The biggest appeal of black capitalism was that it cost very little—financially and especially politically. Nixon had already calculated that he had "nothing to gain" by cooperating with black civil rights leaders, and he had made clear during his first State of the Union Address that he was through meeting the demands of black activists: "it is time for those who make massive demands on society to make minimal demands on themselves."[9] Daniel Patrick Moynihan, who was head of Nixon's urban affairs office, proposed that "the time may have come when the issue of race could benefit from a period of 'benign neglect.'"[10] Nixon put it bluntly when he promised southern Republicans that he would retreat on civil rights and "lay off pro-Negro crap" if elected president.[11]

Not only would he not push forward, but he would claw back some of the progress already made. Nixon diluted the Voting Rights Act and refused to spend money on many of Johnson's Great Society programs. The NAACP said of the Nixon administration that it was "the first time since 1920 that the national administration has made it a matter of calculated policy to work against the needs and aspirations of the largest minority of its citizens."[12] Black capitalism allowed Nixon to accomplish a great deal with very little: he neutralized black militants, gained business support, lost none of his political base, and spent virtually nothing.

In order to understand this tactical political diversion, it is important to understand the context surrounding the decision and the other paths not taken. Particularly relevant are failed integration efforts and demands by black leaders for reparation—both of which were being actively pursued in 1968. By 1970, the administration had scuttled each of these plans without fanfare.

The most crucial path not taken was on integration, and on this issue Nixon was adamant. This was truly unfortunate because a window for reform had opened in 1968, and if followed, could have potentially ended the ghetto economic trap. Johnson had tried to fight housing segregation as early as 1966, but this effort had been defeated in Congress at least partly by the forceful lobbying of bankers and realtors, who had labeled nondiscrimination laws in housing as "anti-market"—the subtext of the argument being that the market, presumably meaning white home buyers, was opposed to integration.[13] The national appetite for civil rights reform had shifted so much by 1966 that White House aid Harry McPherson quipped that "it would have been hard to pass the Emancipation Proclamation in the atmosphere prevailing now."[14]

Johnson was relentless, and finally found an opening. On April 11, 1968, just a week after Martin Luther King was killed, Johnson pushed for action on Article VIII of the 1968 Civil Rights Act, commonly known as the Fair Housing Act (FHA, but not to be confused with the

Federal Housing Administration). Johnson found and exploited the only window available to push through Congress the last and most crucial part of his civil rights agenda even as the shocked nation mourned the civil rights leader. Johnson was elated. "We have passed many civil rights pieces of legislation," he said when he signed the bill. "But none is more important than this." The law banned racial discrimination in housing, including steering blacks toward segregated neighborhoods, and any intimidation and coercion of black home buyers, a common tactic of northern segregationists. In order to pass the congressional gauntlet, the bill's enforcement provisions were weak, but the law, to be administered by the Department of Housing and Urban Development (HUD), required government officials to do everything possible to "affirmatively further" fair housing, which was understood to mean housing integration.[15]

Nixon had to contend not only with this recent mandate, but also with George Romney, his HUD director. Romney took the charge to affirmatively further fair housing as seriously as any HUD director before or since. He was the perpetual thorn in Nixon's side, and in many respects Romney was Nixon's foil—he was a moral crusader in a highly politicized administration. Romney had refused to endorse Barry Goldwater and the GOP's right-wing extremists in 1964, explaining that he was on a "crusade" for moderate Republican principles.[16] Nixon, by contrast, had stumped for Goldwater, and his political opportunism earned him the GOP nomination in 1968. Romney denounced the southern strategy, befriended King, and urged Republicans to take up the civil rights cause. In his 1963 State of the State address as governor of Michigan, he had pronounced that the state's "most urgent human rights problem is racial discrimination—in housing, public accommodations, education, administration of justice, and employment."[17]

Romney was the only member of Nixon's cabinet interested in pushing forward on civil rights instead of pulling back. After Nixon announced his cabinet, one commentator quipped in the *New York Times*, "the Cabinet [is] George Romney and eleven fellows named Clyde."[18] Nixon's director of the Office of Economic Opportunity (OEO), the agency in charge of advancing the War on Poverty (or in Nixon's case of retreating from it) was Donald Rumsfeld. Rumsfeld began to dismantle the OEO's mission immediately. In charge of the office dealing with urban affairs was his token "liberal," Daniel

Patrick Moynihan. The entire cabinet was white. Black commentators derisively referred to Nixon's White House as "Uncle Strom's Cabin."[19]

Though Nixon and Romney had been rivals, Nixon still appointed Romney as his HUD secretary, a decision he would soon regret. Romney was convinced that poverty led to crime, drugs, and violence, and that the principal source of poverty was segregation. Romney believed that "Force alone will not eliminate riots. . . . We must eliminate the problems from which they stem," and he rejected the idea that integration would occur naturally without state intervention.[20] So Romney fought for integration with messianic zeal, but within a hostile administration. He was opposed by the president every step of the way.

Romney ordered HUD to reject any applications for water, sewer, or road projects from any state or municipality that fostered segregated housing. Romney did not clear his strategy with the White House, and as loud complaints rolled in about HUD grant rejections, they went directly to the president's desk. Nixon was livid and put an end to it immediately. "I am absolutely opposed to this. Knock it in the head now."[21]

Romney turned his attention to an even more ambitious plan, called "open communities," which he defined as communities "in which choices are available, doors are unlocked, opportunities exist for those who have felt walled within the ghetto."[22] The basic plan was to integrate a few neighborhoods by building public housing in white suburbs and by offering loans to aspiring black homeowners. In other words, he wanted to move blacks from the cities into the suburbs. He believed that the only way to fix the ghetto was to break it down.[23]

Romney chose a few suburbs across the country to test his open communities plan, including one in his home state. Warren, Michigan, was a white working-class suburb of Detroit and was a racial tinderbox, having broken out in rioting when a black family moved to a white neighborhood in 1967. Just three years later, Romney chose Warren as a pilot for his program in spite of, or perhaps because of, this history. Romney told the population of Warren that he was withholding $3 million in federal funds from the city until they accepted low-income housing.[24] The backlash was extreme. According to Nixon, "George Romney found out in Warren, that there's as much racism in the North as in the South."[25] In the weeks after the Warren encounter, Strom Thurmond and other southern congressmen began referring to Nixon as "Mister Integrator."[26] Romney forged ahead.

Romney knew these initiatives would face political and public backlash, but he fervently believed that it was simply the right thing to do. He explained to his task force that the question for him was not "*whether* we should work toward open communities," but rather "how explicit we should be in announcing our goals."[27] Knowing he was alone in his commitment, he decided to do it in secret. Without the president's backing, Romney pushed an ambitious bill in Congress that would have developed open communities and restricted discriminatory zoning laws. He also drafted legislation that would have allowed the federal government to override any local zoning laws that restricted public housing. Romney's rationale was that if the government was footing the bill on community betterment projects, the communities in question could not be permitted to actively thwart the goals of the Fair Housing Act.

When Nixon heard about Romney's plan through an internal memo, he scrawled a three-word response to his aide John Ehrlichman: "Stop this one." But he didn't have to. The Republican-dominated House Banking Committee quickly shut down the bill.[28] In another internal memo, Nixon explained his reasoning: "I am convinced that while legal segregation is totally wrong that forced integration of housing or education is just as wrong." And he understood what this meant. "I realize," he continued, "that this position will lead us to a situation in which blacks will continue to live for the most part in black neighborhoods and where there will be predominately black schools and predominately white schools."[29]

Romney, who admitted that he was not as astute a politician as Nixon, had underestimated white suburbanites' fear and racism. Nixon had understood it—the government "can't force blacks into housing," explained Nixon, "or we'll have a war." Nixon was so sure that integration was a losing issue that he urged his staff "to nail every Democratic senator and congressmen to the cause of 'compulsory integrated housing.'" Integration was "political poison."[30]

Nixon tried the poison on Romney, labeling him an integrationist in order to force him to quit in 1970. Romney didn't flinch. Then Nixon tried to send Romney to Mexico as an ambassador. In refusing the post, Romney tried to explain his position to the president, probably believing that if Nixon could be convinced of the merits of the issue, he would understand. Romney wrote, "It is becoming increasingly clear that the lower, middle income and the poor, white, black and brown family, cannot continue to be isolated in the deteriorating core cities without broad scale revolution." He underlined this sentence. But it was Romney who did not understand that Nixon was not interested in the merits of racial integration, having perfectly understood its politics. Nixon responded by shutting Romney out of the administration until Romney finally resigned in 1972. In his resignation letter, Romney wrote the president, "I want to thank you for the privilege of serving the nation under your great leadership. The experience has been a rewarding and invaluable one that, among other things, has deepened my understanding of our country's political processes." It is hard not to detect a hint of sarcasm.[31]

Once Romney left, no other administration would pursue active integration again.[32] Instead, they would follow Nixon's strategy of enforcing the FHA through litigating cases of outright discrimination. In choosing only to enforce cases of demonstrated bias, the administration made it clear that it would only concern itself with racial and not economic discrimination.[33] In other words, a community could refuse all low-income housing even if that meant maintaining an all-white community. There was no plan to deal with systemic segregation or the effects of past discrimination. Roy Wilkins called the distinction between economic and racial discrimination "hogwash," but in 1971 the Supreme Court upheld the distinction in *James v. Valtierra*, holding that a California town had the right to prevent public housing within its borders. Even though the town's vote to exclude housing for the poor meant that they were effectively excluding minorities, it was not unconstitutional discrimination because they were not explicitly discriminating against black residents. The brief representing the town's position stated, "If the poor want the affluent to provide them with housing, it would seem only reasonable that they should expect and be willing to accept the willing consent of a simple majority of those persons who are expected to help pay."[34]

Dempsey Travis remarked that "[i]n the 1960s, John Fitzgerald Kennedy turned on the light at the end of the housing corridor for black Americans. Lyndon Johnson kept it burning but Richard Milhous Nixon turned it off in the 1970s."[35] Nixon did not turn off the light unilaterally, however; he did it with the willing consent of the majority of the public who were unwilling to pay any price for integration. De facto segregation would continue, which meant that the ghetto economic trap would too.

Having seen the handwriting on the wall, black leaders had already stopped pushing for integration. "Integration is as dead as a doornail," said CORE director Roy Innis. "If a man is broke and hungry," said Floyd McKissick, "he needs bread and money, not [to] sit down beside a white man." Stokely Carmichael explained the problem with integration: "We should begin with the basic fact that black Americans have two problems: they are poor and they are black. But integration speaks not at all to the problem of poverty, only to the problem of blackness."[36] However, poverty and segregation were indeed linked, and integration could have addressed the poverty by working to break down the ghetto money trap. But it hardly mattered because white society rejected integration in any case.

There were still two separate and unequal economies, but instead of trying to merge the two, black leaders demanded economic control, self-determination, and some form of start-up capital to build up the economy of the ghetto. "If we are to proceed toward liberation, we must cut ourselves off from the white people," said a Student Nonviolent Coordinating Committee (SNCC) manifesto. "We must form our own institutions, credit unions, co-ops, political parties, write our own histories."[37]

If there was any platform that nationalists, militants, integrationists, and moderates could agree on in the late 1960s, it was the imperative of wealth, property ownership, and community economic strength.[38] No doubt the shift was in part a result of the emptiness of the civil rights reforms. F. Naylor Fitzhugh, vice president of Pepsi-Cola, explained, "Ten years ago when the militants criticized the system, they were talking about the political system. Today when they are talking about the system, they are talking about the economic system. They have seen the controls that the economic system exerts over the political."[39] Urban violence had drawn national attention to economic issues instead of legal rights. "Teenagers with jobs don't throw Molotov cocktails," explained A. Philip Randolph. "Bad conditions make for violence," Floyd McKissick wrote in the *New York Times*. Black leaders were not asking for charity or government aid; they were demanding power and control.[40] "Ownership," said McKissick, was "the only answer to keeping Black people from becoming a totally dependent population." "We had full employment of the hard core under slavery," quipped Berkeley G. Burrell, National Business League director. "Today we want a piece of the action in the mainstream business system."[41]

On the first anniversary of King's death, April 25, 1969, the Interreligious Foundation for Community Organization called a National Black Economic Development Conference to discuss plans for black economic advancement. If the transformation of the civil rights movement could be distilled into a single moment, it might be when James Forman stepped to the podium to offer his "Black Manifesto." Forman himself embodied the changing tone, message, and ideology of the cause. In 1961, Forman was a leader in SNCC. By 1969, he had become a leading member of the Black Panthers. He went from marching alongside King, asking for peaceful integration, to proclaiming that "only an armed, well-disciplined, black controlled government can insure the stamping out of racism in this country."[42]

His speech was called "Total Control as the Only Solution for the Economic Needs of Black People." In it, he put forth his manifesto, which was a demand for reparations for slavery. "We, the black people . . . are fully aware that we have been forced to come together because racist white America has exploited our resources, our minds, our bodies, our labor." Forman demanded $500 million—or "$15 per nigger"—to be paid by Christian churches and Jewish synagogues whose members were complicit in capitalism's exploitation of black labor.[43]

Demands for reparations were not just provocations by the Black Panthers and other radical groups; they usually took the form of realistic proposals with concrete details. In 1968, two hundred black separatists met in Detroit to plan a "Republic of New Africa," which was to be a separate sovereign nation built in the South through reparations, with its own government and elected officials, "forever free and independent of the jurisdiction of the United States."[44] Economist Richard F. America Jr. proposed that 10 percent of Fortune 500 companies should be turned over to black control. He wanted the government to use its antitrust powers to confiscate businesses and transfer ownership to black businessmen. He envisioned that eight companies would be transferred to black control each year for fifteen years, at which point "Blacks will have achieved economic parity roughly equivalent to their proportion of the population."[45]

With these radical demands as a backdrop, other black scholars, leaders, and businessmen offered more politically practical plans for economic development. In 1969, there was Dunbar S. McLaurin's Ghetto Economic Development and Industrialization Plan (called the "Ghediplan"), which was akin to a domestic Marshall Plan. Outside funds would help the ghetto develop itself into a thriving community. McLaurin had a significant banking background and believed that the obstacles black entrepreneurs faced were much bigger than just capital and training. The ghetto resembled an "underdeveloped country," and its businesses were cut off from the outside economy, he said.[46] Central to the plan was a provision to spur black banking in the ghetto. "If we accept the premise that no business community can achieve its full business potential without adequate banking facilities, it is easily seen that the Negro business community is suffering from this situation."[47] The Ghediplan asked New York City to allocate $200 million to a fund that would guarantee financing for businesses in the ghetto, with the fund to be administered by banks within the ghetto.[48]

The CORE plan for community development stood out from the rest because, in an unlikely turn of events, a watered-down version of the proposal made its way to the Senate in 1968. Roy Innis called the plan "separatist economics"; it was based on black liberation through control of institutions inside the black community. Innis viewed the proposal as both compensation for past wrongs and a new contract with black America for the future. "The constitution of the United States of America, which is a national contract for this nation, was never meant for Black people. . . . The obvious solution then is a new social contract (constitution). This contract will redefine the relationship between Blacks and Whites."[49] He said that blacks could achieve liberation only through total control of their own institutions.[50] The authors of the plan, Innis and Floyd McKissick, had not started out as separatists. In fact, CORE was a leading integrationist organization in the early part of the decade; but like other leaders, they had moved on. In one sense, they were admitting defeat. "We are past the stage," wrote Innis, "where we can talk seriously of whites acting toward blacks out of moral imperatives. It doesn't work." The idea of supporting a separatist economy appealed to several Republicans, who brought the bill to Congress.

The Community Self-Determination Bill proposed creating a Community Development Corporation (CDC), which would act like a conglomerate corporate and charitable foundation in urban ghettos.[51] Each adult individual in the community would be able to buy shares in the CDC, which in turn would own controlling shares in other companies within the community. The Community Development Bank (CDB) would be a wholly owned subsidiary of the CDC modeled after the Federal Home Loan Banks; it would offer loan guarantees on mortgage and business loans. The CDB would be funded like the World Bank or the Import-Export Bank—the Treasury would sell $400 million in bonds on the market at 6 percent interest. The government would provide the initial credit for the bank, but without the use of any taxpayer funds. The government's stock would earn dividends for the Treasury, which would offset any interest or principal payments on the bonds. The bank would thus be self-financing with a kick-start credit boost from Treasury.[52]

The bill, co-drafted by CORE, was a foreshadowing of the political alliances that would converge on Nixon's black capitalism initiatives: the bill's sponsors included liberal Republican Jacob Javits of New York and conservative Republican John Tower of Texas. Many legislators spoke in favor of the bill, including Republican Senator Charles Percy from Illinois, who quoted one of his constituents with approval: "Away with Black Power. Away with Soul Power. What we need to make it in this atomic age is borrowing power. The difference between Black Power and White Power is—White Power has more green in it."[53] In fact, then presidential candidate Nixon met with Innis and McKissick to discuss the plan, after which the black leaders endorsed the candidate.[54] In return, Nixon endorsed their bill in July of 1968, calling it "an imaginative proposal" for economic development in the ghetto "for building pride and independence, for enlisting the energies of private enterprise and creating new institutions by which private capital can be made available for ghetto investment." He also liked the fact that it was under Republican sponsorship.

There was opposition to the bill. The AFL-CIO called the bill "apartheid antidemocratic nonsense." Surprisingly, and revealing the complex relationship inherent in the black business community, the bill's most vocal opposition came from black business representatives. The National Business League came to Congress to oppose the bill because they saw it as a threat to already established black businesses. One of the most vocal opponents was William Hudgins, president of black-owned Freedom National Bank of Harlem, who said that he opposed the bill because it would undercut existing black banks. The president of the National Bankers Association, Edward Irons, also opposed the bill.[55]

These objections to a plan that was ostensibly good for the ghetto vindicated Frazier, Malcolm X, Abram Harris, and all those who had long felt that black businessmen were no better than the white exploiters. The most recent critic of the black business class was psychologist Kenneth Clark, who in his 1965 book *Dark Ghetto* described them as "insecure" in their power and wealth and "estranged from black society." Unsure of his social standing, the black businessman was "conservative and careful of his wealth," and reluctant to "share it with the ghetto community at large." Clark blamed the ghetto economy itself for creating this "ghetto pathology," which he defined as "an unwillingness to make any voluntary sacrifice" for the community because the ghetto itself "demanded so many involuntary ones."[56]

Perhaps it was insecurity and selfishness that caused a few black business representatives to oppose the bill. Perhaps black businesses opposed the bill for other reasons, for instance, because they had not been asked to help design it. This was the charge leveled by the Reverend Franklin Florence of the FIGHT Corporation of Rochester, whose organization was one of the models on which the bill was based. He protested loudly during the hearings: "If this is to be a community self-determination bill," he quipped, "then we better start by letting the black community determine what should be in the bill."[57]

When the senators realized that the bill did not have the support of the entire black community, they backed away from it.[58] But the bill's failure was probably due to more than just the opposition from a few black leaders. One of the labor lobbyists said of the failure, "You know, if there had been some evidence that Nixon was really interested in any of this, none of those blacks would have jumped on it like they did. They would have tried to work something out beforehand. I think it's a sideshow, and everybody senses it."[59] The bill had been the only plan sponsored by black separatists to have any political traction at all. After this failure, further plans would come from within the administration without any community input, and none would resemble anything as broad in scope as the plans proposed by the CORE leaders—though they would certainly use the same language: black and white leaders alike were using words like "economic self-help," "minority entrepreneurship," "community economic development," and "ghetto self-determination." If there was a common denominator among these groups, it was that it was more realistic to shore up ghetto businesses than to improve it out of existence, to paraphrase James Baldwin.

During the 1968 election, each candidate had a platform plank related to black economic self-determination. Before his assassination, Robert Kennedy had been the frontrunner in the Democratic primary. His community development program was the most robust and holistic of the lot; it included tax incentives for businesses, Community Development Corporations, job training programs, and government funding for antipoverty programs. The eventual 1968 Democratic candidate, Hubert Humphrey, called his proposal "Black Entrepreneurship: Need and Opportunity for Government Help," which put forth a number of plans geared to "enhance black pride and quell black insurgency." His plan included more funding for businesses through Small Business Administration (SBA) programs initiated by the Johnson administration, and called for the creation of an "urban development bank" to fund businesses in the ghetto.[60] For Humphrey, black capitalism was a part of his reform package, which included a continuation of War on Poverty programs. In the presidential race, Humphrey jabbed at Nixon's black capitalism plan, calling it "double talk." When Nixon promised voters that the program would cost little, Humphrey retorted, "Of course it will take money. Talking about black capitalism without capital is just kiting political checks."[61]

The check may have had insufficient funds, but Nixon's double talk on black capitalism paid political dividends. Nixon's "southern strategy" was effective because he used race as a wedge issue without actually talking about race. For example, by associating crime with blackness and promising "law and order," he could signal allegiance to white voters fearful of blacks without sounding like a racist.[62] Black capitalism was another side of the strategy. By associating blacks with welfare dependency and embracing "black enterprise," he was able to cut economic aid to the ghetto and oppose integration in the guise of promoting black power. By using the unobjectionable and racially neutral rhetoric of free-market capitalism, Nixon undermined black demands for economic redress and reparations.

He unveiled this strategy in a series of campaign ads and speeches. In one ad, called "The Wrong Road," across images of poverty-stricken, mostly brown and black faces, and a sign saying "Government Checks Cashed Here," Nixon's voice explained, "For the past five years we've been deluged by programs for the unemployed—programs for the cities—programs for the poor. And we have reaped from these programs an ugly harvest of frustration, violence and failure across the land." This was a subtle subversion of the Kerner Commission's language, which called violence the harvest of racism. Now violence was a result of government aid—never mind that the violence preceded the poverty programs. Then the music became more upbeat, and the camera panned across images of construction sites, a factory line, a shipyard, and the candidate intoned, "We should enlist private enterprise to solve the problems of America."[63]

In a follow-up ad called "Black Capitalism," candidate Nixon promised to rescue the ghetto with a "hand up" and not a "handout." Specifically, he promised "to get private enterprise into the ghetto and the ghetto into private enterprise." He said that more black ownership of land, businesses, and homes would create a "multiplier of pride that will end our racial strife."[64] "Integration must come," he said, "but in order for it to come on a sound and equal basis the black community has to build from within." Presumably he meant that blacks would have to work toward integration themselves, as though segregation had been an act of nature and not a system imposed and enforced by racism and state power.[65]

Nixon believed that government's "overpromising and underproducing" had caused the rioting, and he vowed "not to overpromise now." He was clear that the "federal government does not have the funds at this time to appropriate billions of dollars for our cities."[66] He believed that it was time to think not about what the government could do, but what "private enterprise and individuals" can do to "provide hope" and "reconciliation."

In a speech called "Human Dignity," he said that the country needed to "go beyond civil rights." Actually, in the initial draft in Nixon's presidential files, the speech said "Forget civil rights," and Nixon highlighted the word "forget" and replaced it with "go beyond." The message was the same. "We cannot meet the needs of the late sixties with the solutions of the early sixties." He wanted to put an end to "more laws" and "more money," because they would only lead to "more of the same frustration," "more of the same rioting," and "more of the same despair." He said that "civil rights is no longer an issue," Jim Crow and segregation were over, and that it was time to focus on self-determination and "dignity." By using the word *dignity*, Nixon was communicating that blacks needed to stand on their own feet and that asking the government for help was depriving them of their dignity. "At long last, the Negro has his bill of rights—but he cannot pay the bill."[67]

In a radio program in April 1968, Nixon took his case directly to blacks. He said that black Americans "do not want more government programs which perpetuate dependency. They don't want to be a colony in a nation. They want the pride, and the self-respect, and the dignity that can only come if they have an equal chance to own their own homes, to own their own businesses, to be managers and executives as well as workers, to have a piece of the action in the exciting ventures of private enterprise."[68] Nixon sold his program as a companion to the black power movement—his plan was in sync with the true spirit of black nationalism, he assured them. "Black extremists are guaranteed headlines when they shout 'burn' or 'get a gun,' but much of the black militant talk these days is actually in terms far closer to the doctrines of free enterprise than to those of the welfarist 30s."[69] Nixon promised "more black ownership, black pride, black jobs, black opportunity, and yes, black power, in the best, the constructive sense of that often misapplied term."[70] Nixon was practically repeating Malcolm X, who had said that the "black man should be focusing his every effort toward building his *own* business, and decent homes for himself," although Nixon left out the part where Malcolm had said, "show me a capitalist, I'll show you a bloodsucker."[71] He also ignored the point of the black power platform that included a demand for land, reparations, and political sovereignty. The part Nixon embraced enthusiastically was voluntary segregation, self-reliance, and private enterprise.

Nixon and his advisors intended black capitalism to be a total replacement for Johnson's antipoverty programs. According to a Nixon biographer, he "presented black capitalism as both a panacea and a *fait accompli*."[72] Nixon's speechwriter Raymond K. Price explained that the path forward was to replace "the Negro habit of dependence" with "one of independence" and "personal responsibility."

But had the black community not been trying to "help themselves" for generations while being repeatedly blocked by law and thwarted by policy? As Nixon seemed to portray it, the history of the black community was a perpetual state of dependency on government largesse. This explanation was inconceivably shortsighted. Never mind that the meager "handouts" had only begun a few years earlier, or that the ghetto was the only pocket in the entire American landscape that had not been the recipient of generous postwar government subsidies. In fact, the ghetto was created due to the complete and utter lack of any handouts. It had only ever had an economic system of unchecked, unmitigated, and absolute capitalism. Yet now that the deferred dream had erupted into violence, policymakers proposed that blacks learn how to be capitalists.

Black capitalism was a commercial success, winning Nixon the Republican nomination and the White House. It all sounded great to the press. The *Wall Street Journal* and *Time* magazine embraced Nixon's black capitalism rhetoric, calling it "thoughtful" and "promising."[73] Even the Democratic-leaning *New York Times,* which usually showed the same disdain for the president that the president showed for it, endorsed black capitalism. The paper's associate editor Tom Wicker wrote, "Richard Nixon's radio speech on the need for the development of black capitalism and ownership in the ghetto could prove to be more constructive than anything yet said by other presidential candidates on the crisis of the cities." Max Ways, the editor of *Fortune* magazine, wrote that "business is the one important segment of society Negroes today do not regard with bitter suspicion."[74] This likely had much less to do with the black community's trust in business than their distrust of the government. The black *Chicago Defender* was more cautious. Though the paper endorsed black capitalism, it expressed some suspicion over the candidate's motives, noting that without actual capital, "black power takes on the insignificant aspect of a paper tiger."[75]

Republicans embraced black capitalism wholeheartedly. Nelson Rockefeller's strategist called the concept "a stroke of political genius," and Rockefeller himself supported the idea.[76] *National Review* editor William Buckley praised the "spirit" of "militant black leaders who have been preaching black initiative, black capitalism, and yes, black power." Buckley aligned black capitalism with a libertarian small-government philosophy, stating that the black power movement was allied with conservatives in their fight against "that huge monster on the banks of the Potomac."[77] Buckley proposed that the still-undefined program need not involve the entire black populace, because "scattered success can give universal hope." This was the key objective. The government would not need to underwrite black businesses, just the community's *hope* in black businesses.

Black capitalism was a win-win, according to the administration. Nixon's top aide, John Ehrlichman, explained that "with a relatively small budget impact this is one program which can put the Administration in good light with the Blacks without carrying a severe negative impact on the majority community, as is often the case with civil rights issues."[78] The budget was small, as was the impact. In fact, there was more emphasis on black capitalism in Nixon's advertising and press response than there ever was in White House policymaking.[79]

In 1969 President Nixon signed Executive Order 11458, establishing the Office of Minority Business Enterprise (OMBE) within the Department of Commerce. The OMBE was not allocated any direct funds, but was instructed to seek private business contributions and help from other federal agencies. What this meant in real political terms was that the "OMBE was given responsibility for 'advising,' 'encouraging,' 'mobilizing,' 'evaluating,' 'collecting,' information and 'coordinating' activities," but beyond this vague mission it did not have a mandate or a budget with which to make unilateral decisions or to make any loans or grants. Any money it got its hands on came from the OEO's antipoverty budget.[80] Even so, the House Select Committee on Small Business immediately opposed it, calling the agency "discrimination in reverse."[81]

Nixon asked Secretary of Commerce Maurice Stans, a longtime Republican stalwart and an accountant by profession, to manage the black capitalism program in 1969. After this, Nixon expressed no interest whatsoever in black capitalism. Stans selected Tom Roeser, a conservative business executive at Quaker Oats Company, to head the OMBE. He was charged with assembling an advisory committee on minority enterprise, and managed to create a committee of respectable conservative businessmen from a variety of Fortune 500 firms and banks.[82] The sixty-three-member board was predominantly white and comprised of philanthropists and successful businessmen, eerily reminiscent of the Freedmen's Bank Board. Like Nixon, the council was not particularly engaged in the management of the program. Rumsfeld and Moynihan also expressed indifference to the OMBE.[83]

There were some within the administration who did not see black capitalism as a political ploy and were genuinely committed to it. Among them were Roeser and his deputy, Abe Venable, who became the highest-ranking black director at OMBE. Another true believer in black capitalism was Theodore Cross, a white entrepreneur and philanthropist who served as a key Nixon advisor on black capitalism. In fact, it was his 1969 book, *Black Capitalism*, that laid out the policy framework for building the ghetto economy. Instead of providing blacks with an exit from the ghetto through jobs, Cross believed that the government should focus on enriching the ghetto through significant government investment.[84]

Cross understood that black businesses were stuck outside of the systems of power, prohibited from entry by its white gatekeepers, who were the ones "in possession of jobs, housing, and capital." Blacks needed to gain power simply because those with power had used it against those without it and had no incentive to share their wealth. Cross explained that the problem with black banking in particular was not lack of supply, but lack of demand. To make his point, Cross used black athletes as an example. He explained that there had always been a strong supply of black boxers because there had long been a demand for them. Yet until 1945, there had been rampant discrimination in other sports like baseball and football, and thus there was no market demand for black players in those sports, which produced no black athletes until the 1960s. Once there was a demand, black athletes came to dominate those sports in much greater numbers than their proportion of the population. "This did not come about because black people are stronger or more agile than whites. Certainly it did not occur because we suddenly instituted training programs for black athletes. That was not necessary. When the demand opened up, the supply grew."[85]

There had never been a market demand for black businessmen—just the opposite. During the century that the United States had allowed blacks to respond to market forces rather than forced labor, the demand for black labor had been for domestic labor, factory work, railroad work, farm work, or other menial jobs. Moreover, there had been a "solid aversion" to and "discouragement" of blacks in high-powered commercial roles.[86] To put it bluntly, the dearth of black bankers and entrepreneurs was an "assured economic result of the sustained and collective preference of white people not to trade or exchange commercial promises with black people."[87] Black businessmen did not need education or training. After all, most of the best entrepreneurs had no formal training at all. There just needed to be market demand. And that would not come from the business community's sense of altruism. "Enterprise capitalists, big or small, are designed to share these turfs with no one—even if he is black, sports a new loan from the Freedom National Bank, and holds a fresh degree from a leading business college."[88] Cross never held an administrative position and his ideas were ignored. And as it turned out, the program came to rely exclusively on white businesses to open their doors and their coffers to blacks based purely on altruism.

At first, there was a sincere effort from within the OMBE to create a real boost to black businesses. Venable proposed an ambitious plan called the "National Strategy," which he distributed internally in 1969. He called for "nothing less than full equality of access to business opportunities and resources"; he recognized that even a robust national program was not enough because it would take many years of effort to achieve "the demise of the economic colonialism of our minority communities." The plan promised to invest $8.6 billion and to create 400,000 new minority businesses in ten years, using the FHA loan guarantee program as a model.[89]

As soon as Stans heard of the plan, he shut it down. Stans was not interested in anything so broad and costly, even if the plan was to be built on private money and was designed to be profitable for investors. The OMBE had misjudged its mission and the political basis of black capitalism. Stans informed Roeser that the most important objective was to create success *stories*, which would "create pride among the minority which, in turn, creates aspirations of those down the line." In other words, the program was to be symbolic. "What the black people, the minority people, need more than anything else today is a modern Horatio Alger," said Stans. "This is the way we will build the pride of these people, and this is the way we will convince the young fellows coming up that they have a chance to do the same thing." There would be no financial support from the administration for black capitalism. It was clear that for Stans and Nixon, black capitalism was no more than a public relations strategy.[90]

Roeser resigned from his post at OMBE in 1970, and Stans took over control of the OMBE after an initial public kerfuffle. With its reputation on the line, the OMBE launched the Minority Enterprise Small Business Investment Company (MESBIC), an idea conceived by Menlo Park executive Robert Dehlenford. The MESBIC initiative was based on the idea that what black businesses needed was credit, "technical assistance," and "mentorship."[91] The credit would be provided on a fifteen-to-one leverage ratio—for every dollar invested by a black company, the program promised to attract fifteen more from investors. The *Chicago Tribune* introduced the program with the headline "MESBIC Multiplies Money for Minorities."[92] The plan was for a hundred black MESBIC companies to put up a minimum of $150,000 of capital, which would be used as a down payment to be "multiplied" by private credit.[93]

A year later, the program was a failure. Of the fifty minority businesses in the program, twenty-five had already failed by 1970 and sixteen more were in trouble. The fund was bankrupt.[94] The flaw in the program, as pointed out by economists Richard Rosenbloom and John Shank in a *Harvard Business Review* article, was that it required these companies to operate with an extremely large debt burden—the companies were being 100 percent financed by debt. The only equity came from the companies themselves. "No matter what color the owner, successful businesses just do not get started with debt financing alone," said the economists, because the interest payments would be "an oppressive cash flow problem for a new business." Operating without capital in a high-crime, economically depressed, and resource-poor ghetto meant that shocks would be high and unavoidable, and there would be virtually no buffer or cushion of equity to absorb them. Even more disturbing was the Government Accounting Office (GAO) finding that the volunteer white firms that were providing technical assistance were charging unreasonably high rates, some taking almost 30 percent of the small black business profits as management fees.[95]

By 1970, the country was in a recession. Jobless numbers were so bad by 1971 that the Nixon administration decided to stop reporting them. The new aspiring entrepreneurs in the ghetto suffered most acutely as inflation soared and banks closed the credit pipeline. A black accounting firm in New York summed up the situation facing new black enterprises, noting that "the people least likely to succeed in business were trying to make it at a time when seasoned businessmen were having trouble."[96]

Small businesses were the most vulnerable and least likely to succeed, yet all these programs were geared toward creating more small businesses. This focus was in part due to the lack of funds to support large businesses, as well as the fact that the program was more about business myth-making and platitudes of racial pride than it was an outcome-oriented effort to help the black community accumulate business power. Small businesses were supposedly the lifeblood of entrepreneurship, and this may have been true at some point in time; but small business was no way to grow wealth in the 1970s. Large multinational firms were making more profits and using economies of scale to reduce costs, and they were already squeezing out small businesses, a trend that was only just beginning. As Walmart was building its profitable empire, blacks were being told that to prosper, they should focus small and local. Black businesses, which were already swimming upstream due to the deviant ghetto market, were facing an even stronger economic current, pushing businesses to grow larger and more efficient.

Yet the focus remained relentlessly on small business. In 1969, Section 8(a) of the Small Business Act authorized the SBA to manage a program to coordinate government agencies in allocating a certain number of contracts to minority small businesses—referred to as procurements or contract "set-asides." Moynihan helped shape the program.[97] By 1971, the SBA had allocated $66 million in federal contracts to minority firms, making it the most robust federal aid to minority businesses. Still, the total contracts given to minority firms amounted to only one-tenth of 1 percent of the $76 billion in total federal government contracts that year.[98] The program was not without controversy. The minority set-asides immediately faced backlash from blue-collar workers, white construction firms, and conservatives, who called it "preferential treatment" for minorities. Moreover, multiple studies revealed that 20 percent of these set-

asides had gone to white-owned firms, which led to a 1973 amendment that stated specifically that the businesses had to be owned by
minorities. Unsurprisingly, it was also revealed that Nixon had used
these set-asides to bestow political favors. A frustrated SBA employee
resigned, claiming that the agency's "main purpose was political."[99]
The charge was accurate and could extend to cover the entire black
capitalism framework.

The least controversial and most durable black capitalism program was the 1969 Minority Bank Deposit Program (MBDP). Ever
since Washington policymakers had linked ghetto rioting with credit
exploitation, multiple programs had been proposed to fix credit inequalities. They ranged from creating new banking institutions to
providing loan guarantees, capital infusions, or Marshall Plans for
the ghetto. Rejecting all of these proposals, the Nixon administration's program simply asked government agencies to deposit their
accounts in black banks. In 1968, when William Proxmire's Senate
Banking Committee had discussed whether agency deposits might
help bolster black banks, a representative black banker remarked
that these agency deposits would not provide a good basis for financing banks in the ghetto because they were too unstable.[100] No
matter. The program cost nothing. The initial goal was to encourage
federal agencies to deposit $100 million of their accounts in black
banks; the actual yield was about $35 million by 1971.

The first agency to volunteer was the Post Office, which announced that it would be depositing $75 million in black banks. It
would actually deposit only about $150,000. And even this small sum
was rotated through several different banks. One businessman
quipped, "It was like me saying I'll lend you $365,000 for the next
year and then lending you a dollar every morning and taking it back
every night."[101] These were not the deposits that black banks
needed—they were the same type that had been crippling them for
years. The president of Unity Bank in Roxbury, Massachusetts, complained that the Post Office refused even to bring the money to the
bank. "They expected us to hire a security service to collect deposits
that we couldn't even make any money on."[102] After complaints
about the added cost burden of the postal deposits, the program
promised the banks that they would send them more valuable deposits from other agencies. While this did happen, all the government
deposits ended up costing banks more than they were worth.

Another piece of the Nixon administration's black capitalism program was affirmative action, which was initiated by the Equal Employment Opportunity Office (EEOC) with the aim of encouraging companies to hire more black employees.[103] The 1969 Philadelphia Plan required construction companies that had federal contracts to set numerical goals for hiring blacks. The word "quotas" brought a quick backlash from employers and blue-collar unions, so Nixon withdrew the demand and asked businesses to set voluntary hiring goals.[104] Striking a political compromise, the EEOC began measuring and keeping track of these "voluntary goals." It did this across a variety of businesses that had government contracts, and it encouraged other businesses to prioritize hiring minorities.

In supporting affirmative action, Nixon claimed that "jobs are more important to the Negroes than anything else." This was obviously not true, but while asking businesses to provide jobs was not politically popular, it was an acceptable compromise in a politically fraught climate. Nobody lobbied for affirmative action, and no one had demanded it. It was a weak compromise position meant to throw a bone to the black middle class and deal with black militants without spending too much politically or financially.[105] According to historian John David Skrentny, "Affirmative action was legitimated very quickly, in a matter of a few years, in a very turbulent time, and by a variety of people pursuing very different goals."[106] Affirmative action would be fiercely attacked by Nixon's own Republican Party until it was almost fully dismantled. It was more vulnerable than black capitalism because it cost whites more, and it would become the epicenter of a white backlash that claimed it was "reverse discrimination."

All the black capitalism programs, including affirmative action, relied primarily on the voluntary participation of private firms and government agencies. But these companies and agencies had no experience with this type of social activism. Even the philanthropic involvement of U.S. businesses had not been directed at addressing ghetto poverty. Congressman Wright Patman quipped in 1968 that "while our cities fell into decay and Negro youths rioted in our streets [the Mellon Foundation] sent thousands of dollars abroad to uncover the dust of centuries and study Roman and Etruscan town plans."[107] The Nixon administration sought to change this orientation and to direct the attention and good will of American firms toward the inner city.

The administration asked large companies and banks to help alleviate ghetto poverty by increasing minority franchise opportunities, investing in minority businesses, and lending to minority businesses. With weak incentives, few complied. These efforts were to be coordinated through the National Center for Voluntary Action. Even the conservative *Wall Street Journal* reported in 1970 on the "stillborn" business volunteer program. According to the *Journal,* the volunteer committee's administrator conceded in a "masterful understatement" that they "have not been able to treat very many of the nation's social problems up to now."[108]

In 1970 the *Harvard Business Review* surveyed the top 500 industrial corporations and business leaders about their participation in the black capitalism programs; it found that only a handful of business executives had made any financial contribution to black businesses. The executives believed that there was not enough financial incentive to participate. Most revealing in the survey was the report's finding that "Whatever may be said in public, it is clear from many private conversations that most of the existing efforts by white corporate executives to assist black business came about as a result of fear engendered by the ghetto riots, threats, and pressures from militants, and to some extent pressure of influence from government officials." With only fear as a motivation to help, the researchers concluded that "we cannot leave the promotion of corporate involvement in developing minority business solely to the conscience and moral views of corporate executives."[109]

Though few businesses volunteered, that is not the impression the public received. Several corporations, including AT&T and Coors, took out a series of long-form advertisements to promote all the ways in which they were helping black business. General Motors President James Roche served on Nixon's advisory council and publicly promoted black capitalism initiatives, stating that it was the responsibility of businessmen "who have worked within and gained from the free enterprise system, to help others share in it. It is us, who must cherish the freedom in free enterprise, to assure that it is freely open to everyone."[110] (General Motors had indeed gained from free enterprise, but they had also gained from $4 billion in federal defense contracts over the prior ten years.) Despite such advertisements, most of these companies put up little or no money at all. Perhaps this was because of the slow economy. According to

Undersecretary of Commerce Rocco C. Siciliano, "It's hard to imbue businessmen with social consciousness when business is bad."[111] Or perhaps Theodore Cross was right when he said that white businesses would never give up power voluntarily.

In 1970, Whitney Young lamented, "I remember listening to the head of a major corporation brag about all his firm was doing. After some close questioning, I found the sum total of these grand efforts added up to less than two dozen summer jobs for black youths in only three of the sixty cities in which that company operates."[112] In 1969, Young had proposed a National Economic Development Bank that would look like a cross between the Federal Reserve and the World Bank, with regional offices across the country to help black communities finance community self-help projects.[113] He was a committed advocate of black self-sufficiency until he met his untimely death in 1971 in Lagos, Nigeria. His last printed words appeared in the *New York Times* three days after his death. They were words of disappointment. He called corporate America's engagement with black capitalism the "great copout." He blasted the business community for being dilettantes, first flirting with civil rights and then quickly moving on to other "causes." He said that "the period of corporate activism in social concerns [1967–1969] coincided with two phenomena of great importance—a booming economy and the spread of urban rioting." Young said of the corporate executives, "when he's trying to help solve social problems four hundred years in the making, created by the racialist attitudes of companies and unions like his own, he suddenly expects fast returns and instant successes."[114]

If there were no fast returns for corporations or for the black community, Nixon did reap a fast and instant result from black capitalism. The biggest win for his administration was that black capitalism turned out to be a very effective antidote to militant black uprisings. Nixon and his FBI had targeted the Black Panthers as enemies of the state. "The Black Panther party, without question, represents the greatest threat to the internal security of this country," said J. Edgar Hoover. Hoover had sent FBI agents to infiltrate the Panthers' ranks and subvert their organization. Panthers were imprisoned, harassed, and even killed by the administration in showdown after showdown. Party leaders like Huey Newton and Eldridge Cleaver led the movement at its height from prison and from exile in Cuba, respectively. However, the Panthers were killed not by force, but by a slow drying up of funds and supporters due both to a change in the environment and to a subtle subversion of their cause by President Nixon.[115] First, the Vietnam war abated and the draft diminished, so they lost support from white student protesters who no longer had a shared colonizer to fight. The other base of their support was a large part of the black community—the moderates. This group was neutralized by superficial concessions from the administration. The concessions were black capitalism and affirmative action.

Nixon masterfully adopted and co-opted the black radicals' demand for power and then used it against them by turning it into a vague yet beguiling promise of black capitalism. The movement's leaders themselves were divided over the lure of black capitalism. A 1972 *Washington Post* article titled "The Transformation of the Panthers" featured two cartoons side by side—on the left was Huey Newton holding a gun with a bandolier across his chest, and on the right was Newton holding a bag of golf clubs. As it turned out, Newton and Bobby Seale were now manufacturing golf bags in Oakland, California. The venture was a means of funding Panther activities, but it sometimes looked like a racketeering operation.[116] In the early 1970s, the Black Panther newsletter urged blacks to "Support the businesses that support our community."[117] A revolution having been thwarted, the Panthers put aside talk about "capitalist bloodsuckers" and moved toward a more "pragmatic" approach of small black businesses. According to noted black sociologist Robert Staples, "one of the most curious turnabouts was the Panthers' embrace of Black Capitalism."[118]

Exiled Black Panther Eldridge Cleaver split with Newton and Seale and maintained an anticapitalist stance. He wrote Stokely Carmichael, who had recently stepped down from Panther leadership, an open letter in 1969 calling him out for providing the administration with a potent weapon against the black community. Black capitalism was just a continuation of black exploitation, according to Cleaver.[119] He said that Carmichael had surrendered "black power" to the Nixon administration to be corrupted into "black capitalism," thereby rendering the term and the movement powerless. "It has been precisely your nebulous enunciation of Black Power," he scolded Carmichael, "that has provided the power structure with its new weapon against our people." Cleaver believed that by letting Nixon use the terminology of black power, the activists had surrendered the force and potential of the revolutionary idea to be corrupted by the administration who would "cash in" on the slogan and use it to "ease the black bourgeoisie into the power structure."[120]

Cleaver had hit on a tension in the black power philosophy—was it possible to derive black power as a concession from the white power structure, or could the movement's aims only be achieved through complete political sovereignty brought about by revolution against that power structure? The genesis of the black power ethos was a natural enough response to white oppression, a rebuttal to white power, but would white power have to be defeated to achieve black power, or would half measures do? For the Panthers, the objective had always been political independence, but at least part of the movement was persuaded that black power could be achieved through economic success. This is what black capitalism was proposing.

The theory behind developing a separate black economy had been that economic power would lead to political power, but perhaps they had it backward. If the rollout of the black capitalism program had demonstrated anything, it was that economic power could not be achieved without government help. American businesses, banks, and homeowners had all benefited from being inside the power structure and receiving its bounty. Blacks had been on the outside, and their lack of political control translated into a lack of economic power. Until black people could access the levers of political power, they could not unleash government or business support, both of which were essential for economic success. In fact, the only reason government or business had contributed anything at all to growing black businesses had been as a reaction to the threat of violence that the Panthers and militants had created. The initial Black Panther movement had held a modicum of power, even if it was a weak and artificial power derived from fear. But this fear was the reason the business community and the federal government had focused on black ownership in the first place. The black capitalism program and its reliance on the white power structure removed this source of power.

It also deprived the black community of another important source of power derived from collective action. By dividing the community between the entrepreneurs and the masses of consumers, the black community was placed at cross purposes. By linking large white corporations with aspiring black businessmen, the race cohesion—that rage the Panthers had channeled and amplified—was dissipated. This, in turn, removed the incentive for businesses to participate in black capitalism. Black capitalism also cannibalized the budget of the War on Poverty—the OEO budget was successively cut and siphoned off to OMBE programs. The War on Poverty, which was designed to help the poor of all races, was instead being diverted to help aspiring black entrepreneurs, isolating the black community from yet another source of strength—the interracial collective action of the poor.

An expert in political détente, Nixon used black capitalism to let out just enough steam from the pent-up pressure cooker of rage in the poverty-stricken ghetto to squelch the brewing revolution.[121] Ultimately, black capitalism was anemic and utterly unresponsive to the needs of the black community. But it was vague enough to offer just the hope needed to cool the boiling anger just as it was about to spill over. With this one move, Nixon took the sting out of the black radicals' demand for black power, jettisoned Johnson's anti-poverty programs, maintained his opposition to integration, and even won the support of many black leaders. Checkmate.

The harvest of black capitalism was the retreat of the black radical groups from center stage and the emergence of a more pragmatic, moderate, and "business-oriented" black leadership. A black leader who embodied this change was Jesse Jackson, who went from a forthright denunciation of black capitalism in 1969 to becoming its champion just a year later. In 1969, he called black capitalism a divisive force in the black community, which should be seeking "total economic development of the Black community" instead of "a few additional entrepreneurs." He had said that attaching "the name 'Black' to capitalism is not a description, but a diversion." By 1970, he advertised his "Black Expo" as "an annual trade fair for black business, both local and national, as well as a general celebration of black capitalism."[122] He sounded Nixonian when he said in 1970 that blacks "would rather own A&P [grocery store] than burn it."[123] He urged blacks to focus less on fiery speeches *on* the corner of 125th and 7th Avenue and try to *own* the corner instead.

Jackson became a champion of black businesses and celebrated them without hesitation. "Our banks grooved," explained Jackson, "[be]cause we fed the 40 stores in the black community and put our money in our banks, that all future stores in our community be built by us." He praised the Harlem Freedom National Bank and said that its financial strength was "[not a] manifestation of goodness, but power." Jackson urged blacks to harness the influence of the black dollar and invest in black enterprise. Jackson's operation PUSH (People United to Save Humanity) asked the black community to buy insurance from black insurers and deposit money in black banks.[124] Several other black groups and institutions, including the National Urban League, the NAACP, and Howard University, launched programs focused on promoting black businesses after the program launched.[125] Even the Nation of Islam, black nationalists who had a long-standing policy of staying out of politics, endorsed Nixon's black capitalism program in the April 1970 issue of *Muhammad Speaks*.[126]

The celebratory focus on black business success, spurred by Nixon's public rhetoric, led to a renewed social and cultural emphasis on black business within the black community. In 1970, *Black Enterprise* launched as a new magazine primarily focused on highlighting black business success. In 1973, the magazine debuted a list of the top one hundred black-owned businesses, which prompted Nixon's praise as "clear evidence that the government, in active partnership with the private sector, can create the kind of climate of opportunity in which those with energy and drive can share more equitably in the rewards of the world's most productive economic system."[127] Established black periodicals like *Ebony* and *Jet* began to feature a black business section highlighting black business success stories.[128] One of the most popular 1970s television shows, *The Jeffersons*, featured George Jefferson's successes and struggles as a dry-cleaning tycoon in Harlem and opened with the theme song "We're Moving on Up."

And many in the black community were "moving on up." If Nixon's stated aim was to increase the black middle class, he could have deemed the program a success. Between 1960 and 1980, the proportion of black workers in professional and technical positions jumped from 11 to 21 percent.[129] But while wealthy blacks were heralded as heroes of progress, the black poor continued to stagnate. "In the economic sphere," remarked historian John Hope Franklin, "obviously the black middle class is increasing. But the black under-class is increasing too."[130]

This vast disparity, coupled with the emphasis on black capitalism, stoked class tensions already present in the black community. On the one hand, the black community lauded its successful entrepreneurs as symbols of racial progress and as a counternarrative to claims of black inferiority. On the other hand, black intellectuals and activists continued to blame black businessmen for making profits out of a segregated economy that kept a majority of blacks impoverished.[131] Socialist scholar Robert L. Allen derided black capitalism as "bourgeois nationalism" that would "line the pockets" of the black middle class and do nothing for the black masses.[132] Dr. Ralph Abernathy, the new president of Southern Christian Leadership Council, said that he was not interested in making black people rich, but in lifting up the poor through community programs, public aid, and the nonprofit sector. "I do not believe in Black Capitalism," he said. "I believe in Black socialism."[133] Another prominent socialist scholar, Manning Marable, called black business "snake oil" and black businessmen "the linchpin of underdevelopment and capital accumulation within the Black community." He denounced black leaders, Jesse Jackson in particular, for convincing the black community to "move from Civil Rights to Silver Rights and from aid to trade." Earl Ofari also denounced black businessmen for making profits off the backs of the poor in his book *The Myth of Black Capitalism*. However, these critics often overestimated the size, numbers, and profits of black businesses.[134]

And just what was the state of black business profits in the late 1960s? Paltry. After hundreds of years, over 90 percent of black businesses had yet to expand out of the same personal service category they had always occupied—beauty parlors, mortuaries, tailor shops, and so on.[135] The institutions regarded as the most successful were the black banks, according to surveys.[136] The OMBE ended up measuring its success by emphasizing how many small businesses it had helped, but the businesses they were celebrating were tiny mom-and-pop service establishments.[137] Abraham S. Venable, the highest-ranking black OMBE official, lamented that "many Negro businesses are a symbol of frustration and hopelessness rather than an example of achievement, success, and leadership."[138]

To the extent there was a large and profitable business sector in the ghetto, it was criminal enterprise. Though difficult to measure, a 1967 presidential commission reported that annual intakes from gambling alone were anywhere from $7 to $50 billion.[139] These numbers dwarfed legitimate business enterprises. Most of this business sector was Mafia-controlled, which made the Mafia the largest employer of blacks in the ghetto. Black Congressman William Clay described the black entrepreneur as a "hustler" forced to live on the margins of society, but doing so with white society's consent. "Blacks have developed a network of crime completely acceptable to the white majority. That system of survival is clearly outside the law, clearly in violation of the law, but certainly with the tacit approval of the decision makers."[140] Because white banks were not lending to blacks, black businessmen turned to the Mafia for venture capital funding. One estimate held that 25 percent of black business was financed by the Mafia.[141]

Perhaps this was because despite the prodding by the administration, banks were still avoiding the ghetto. A survey of over 4,000 commercial banks revealed that their total investments in minority business in 1967 was less than $8,000 per bank—or one-twentieth of 1 percent of total bank assets. Less than a handful of white banks had made any significant investment in black business.[142] Frustrated by the banking community's pathetic record of lending to blacks, Federal Reserve Governor Sherman Maisel admonished bankers during a 1971 conference that by refusing to offer loans to businesses and individuals in the ghetto, the banking community had "helped create major social and economic problems of crime, decay, and segregation."[143] Banking was a cautious and conservative industry at the time, and almost as a rule, bankers avoided lending in the ghetto because they perceived greater risks in such loans. Even when bank management expressed a commitment to lending to minorities, it was difficult to change bank culture because middle management and lower-ranking loan officers had discretion on individual loan decisions. Often these loan officers understood that their promotion and success depended on "keeping his desk neat and keeping his default rate as low as possible."[144]

Banks were also one of the last industries to integrate their staff.[145] Business Professor Armand Thieblot Jr. conducted a national survey of bank hiring in 1970, which showed that to the extent banks were employing blacks, it was as guards, messengers, or porters.[146] Most banks admitted that they had not hired even black tellers because of "fears that Negro employees would be unacceptable to customers."[147]

The fact that blacks weren't being employed at banks speaks volumes about the availability of banking services to black customers.[148] But what did it say about the banking industry? It was not the case that the banking sector was dominated by groups that tended to be more discriminatory, like southerners or less-educated whites. The EEOC's guess as to why banks dragged their feet longer than other industries was that "discrimination becomes more virulent as the jobs involved become more prestigious; that although some whites are now willing to help Negroes onto the economic ladder, they are willing to help them only onto the bottom rung."[149] The other reason, hinted at by Thieblot's study, is that banks were more risk-averse than other industries and less likely to engage in experimental or radical policies, which apparently included hiring black tellers. Indeed, "only a very daring and adventurous personnel officer would have considered undertaking the risk of making his bank the only one in town to have Negro tellers."[150] And bankers were not the daring sort.

An alternative explanation is that banking is an enterprise built on trust, making it a business imperative for banks to portray sophistication, prudence, and acumen. The image of soundness, stability, and sophistication plays a greater role in banking than any other enterprise. Banks might have wanted to avoid placing blacks in prominent positions because of the prevalence of implicit and explicit bias. Even the most open-minded Americans would have preferred a white teller counting their deposits. If implicit racism meant that whites viewed blacks as having inferior skills and morals, it also meant that they did not trust them enough to be their bankers. This is perhaps why a New York City bank "was running what was obviously a 'Jim Crow' operation, using its Negro employees almost exclusively in its black branches in Harlem and Washington Park." The disheartening fact was that this was the only black bank manager in Thieblot's survey.[151] Even in Baltimore's heavily concentrated black community, "Baltimore's banks had no Negro officers."[152]

This was especially unfortunate, because even though racial covenants were now unenforceable and the FHA was guaranteeing loans in black areas, bankers made most lending decisions based on "relational lending," meaning that they met with potential borrowers and made lending decisions based on personal interactions. Even though blacks were no longer being formally discriminated against in the lending market, most lending decisions were being made informally, which meant that discrimination was likely happening during one-on-one meetings, making it impossible to detect. The community bankers who were the key decision makers were integrated into their communities and often made deals on the golf course or at the country club. The most successful bankers were those at the center of a community's social structure—who had relationships with businesses and potential lenders. Black businessmen were at an obvious disadvantage when banking was conducted through "gentlemen's agreements."

If white banks were still discriminating in lending and hiring, the obvious solution would be to have more black banks. And many were created during this era. The National Business League said that the number of black banks increased from twenty-four to seventy between 1969 and 1974 alone.[153] Despite the boom, it was still a tiny industry—with total assets of $259 million and deposits of $230 million, which represented 0.049 percent of total bank assets and 0.053 percent of total deposits.[154] The NBL credited the OMBE with playing an "important role" in this increase, but the surge in black banks likely had as much to do with the general environment of racial resistance coupled with the emphasis on black business as with the OMBE's deposit program. Economist Courtney Blackman noted in 1971 that the surge in black banks was a result of "the heightened sense of humiliation among blacks in recent years" and "is directly traceable to this emotional upheaval."[155] Black banks were created as another manifestation of the protest against "white exploiters" that had led to the ghetto uprisings. Many of the black banks created during this time were formed by groups of community activists or individuals motivated to respond to the civil rights struggle.

The two largest banks created in the 1960s demonstrated the motivation for "freedom" and "unity" prevailing during this era, and they were so named. In 1964, baseball legend Jackie Robinson led a group of black and white investors to form the Freedom National Bank (FNB) in Harlem, which would become one of the largest black-owned banks of the era.[156] After he left baseball, Jackie Robinson became convinced that "there were two keys to the advancement of blacks in America—the ballot and the buck."[157] He became involved in both the civil rights movement and the Republican Party—that is, until Nixon was elected and he became convinced that "the GOP didn't give a damn about my vote or the votes—or welfare—of my people."[158] For Robinson, the first breach had been the selection of Goldwater in 1964, which he believed was an embrace of the racist southern wing of the party. Robinson had hoped that Nelson Rockefeller would get the nomination in 1968 and endorsed him at the convention, but he was dismayed when the Republican Party chose Nixon and his southern strategy.

Freedom Bank sold shares to the entire Harlem community, and Robinson emphasized that the bank's mission was to build the community and not just to make profits. Harlem's churches and small businesses invested in the bank, "not with the idea that they'd reap any benefit," according to a bank spokesman, "but rather that Freedom would be a financial resource for people in the minority community to get loans." Robinson recounted hearing about a white banker who said that "he had never known a Negro in whom he had confidence for more than a $300 loan." Yet blacks kept faithfully depositing their money in white banks despite the mistreatment. CORE leader Clarence Funnye explained, "Before Freedom National, you went into a white bank with the distinct impression you went with what you had in your hand, begging the powers that be and generally you were turned down. With Freedom the community looks less like a colony, less of an area of exploitation."[159] Harlem embraced the bank and called it "our bank."

Robinson explained that blacks in Harlem had had negative experiences with banks since John D. Rockefeller's Dunbar Bank, which was ostensibly biracial, but in reality had only hired a few token black clerks and maintained a white management. Because of Robinson's political support of Governor Nelson Rockefeller, a rumor started in Harlem that the bank was actually Nelson Rockefeller's bank and that he was up to the same sort of bait-and-switch as Dunbar's founder. Robinson explained, "Maybe I should have wished that was true. It wasn't."[160] The bank struggled to remain profitable in its first years of operation. By 1971, FNB had a loan portfolio consisting of 57 percent in real estate loans, with 30 percent of those loans in default. The bank posted losses of $704,530.[161]

Running the bank was not a proud or happy experience for Robinson. In fact, in his autobiography he expressed "mixed emotions" about the bank, which he said was "approaching the brink of disaster" due to its loan losses. Robinson was very worried about the large amount of money they were writing off as bad loans. Robinson even tried to engage with the bank regulators, who he believed were handling his bank with "kid gloves." He knew they were writing down thousands of dollars of loans, yet they kept telling him everything was fine. Robinson said the "Comptroller's office was patting us on the back when they should have been hitting us over the head with a club," and he told them that he thought his bank was not "being judged by the same standards that would have applied if ours were a white bank." Robinson said he had many sleepless nights over the bank's failing books and even suffered "a very serious health crisis" on account of the stress.[162] In fact, Robinson died of a heart attack in 1972, at the age of fifty-three, shortly after the bank's most serious troubles and before the bank was able to turn a profit.

In his autobiography, which he finished just weeks before his death, he wrote honestly about the struggles of being a black banker, an experience which he said was "painful to relate." This was a man who served in a segregated military, single-handedly integrated Major League Baseball, and was a civil rights activist within the GOP, and he believed his most challenging struggle was running a black bank. Robinson said that black banks were in a "delicate position" because, on the one hand, the white banking community "coddled them" and "patted them on the back" instead of dealing with them like any other business. "Our doors could have closed because of this kind of paternalism," he said. He believed that until they could grow and mature on their own, they would always be "subservient" to the white industry. But on the other hand, black bankers faced pressure from the black community. There too, "we had to be different because we were a black bank." He said that they had to be "a lot less rigid than white banks," but without being too "loose in policies."[163] In other words, because Harlem saw Freedom as "our bank," Harlem did not treat it like any other business. This conflict was as old as black banking, but Robinson was very troubled by his position.

Robinson sought the help of businessman Robert B. Boyd to help make the bank profitable, and after Robinson's death Boyd would continue to run the bank. According to Boyd, the bank's problems resulted from the previous management being overly concerned with the bank's social and altruistic mission. "The focus before was social. Now it's on profit. I'm completely comfortable with social motivation, but monies allotted for social purposes can only come after a profit. Then it is a business decision." To that end, Boyd restricted residential real estate investments and emphasized commercial loans. He aimed to develop a small-business infrastructure in Harlem by guiding small business loan applicants through the loan process. The bank teetered on the edge of profitability and, as the *Times* reported in 1974, its constant struggle was to find a way "to balance fiscal prudence and profitability against its founders' goal of helping small businesses and home-buyers in black neighborhoods by offering low-cost loans."[164] They would continue to struggle until they failed in 1990.

Similarly motivated by a social mission was the Unity Bank and Trust Company, the second biracial bank, which was founded in 1968 to serve the black population of Roxbury, a black district in Boston. Donald E. Sneed, the bank's first president, described the bank as a demonstration of "constructive black power." "The Bank with a Purpose," as the founders called it, operated longer hours and offered free financial counseling services and community education programs to their low-income customers. Like FNB, the founders saw their goal not just as supporting existing black businesses, but helping to create black business from the ground up. The bank was also trying to fight lending discrimination. "Slum residents are eliminated [from the lending market] solely on the basis of where they live," said Vice President Bernard Fulp. "This drives those who can least afford it to finance companies and loan sharks who charge unreasonable interest."[165]

Unity was trying to break the ghetto debt cycle by offering lower-interest loans and opening its doors to marginalized black borrowers. The bank's ambitious mission included providing student loans, "so the kids in this community can go to college, home improvement loans to make the houses here livable, and business loans so small businesses can be bought by black people." The bank was off to a solid start as many in the community helped with its start-up capital. The Commonwealth of Massachusetts even deposited $360,000 in the bank, becoming its single largest depositor.

Other foundations, including the United Front Foundation, Brandeis University, Andover Theological School, Northeastern University, and Boston College, all maintained deposit accounts and MIT was a stockholder. Still, 65 percent of the 40,000 accounts were from the inner-city Roxbury and Dorchester neighborhoods.

Even with the entire community's support, Unity struggled to remain profitable. The bank leaders approached this struggle as a point of pride. "There are factions of both the black and white community that are watching to see whether we are going to pass the supreme test of survival." The bank's Vice President Fulp struck a zealous tone: "we intend to remain here with a quasi-crusading role." Fulp admitted that "black institutions historically have had inferiority complexes," but he cautioned, "this complex can't be allowed to immobilize us." "Every time someone comes in here I can't think 'We mustn't take this risk because we are a new black bank.' " But the risks were real. The same forces of discrimination and poverty that had led to the creation of these banks would continue to be their main obstacle.

There were other banks created in this pivotal era with the same ethos as the Unity and Freedom banks. The civil rights movement, the black capitalism program, and the increasing cultural emphasis on black business fueled this second historic boom in black banking. This time, white leaders joined the chorus to herald the enterprise as a self-help solution to poverty. For the first time, whites were paying attention to and celebrating black banks. The potential and promise that stronger black banks meant stronger black communities without requiring change or sacrifice from the broader community was too seductive to be scrutinized. But there were a few dissenters—they were those focusing on the numbers instead of the politics.

Andrew Brimmer provided the sharpest critique of black capitalism and black banking. Brimmer was born to a family of sharecroppers in Louisiana, received his Ph.D. in economics from Harvard, and was appointed by President Johnson as the first black governor of the Federal Reserve in 1966. As Federal Reserve governor, he presented a number of ideas that have been vindicated over time. For example, he suggested in 1970 that financial institutions engaged in risky activities should be forced to hold more money as reserves than typical commercial banks. The Federal Reserve chairman, Arthur Burns, rejected the idea because he believed that markets would know how to deal with the overly risky investment banks and that the Fed should not be involved. After the 2008 financial crisis, this prescient warning was resurrected and is now being seriously considered.[166]

Brimmer forcefully denounced black capitalism, maintaining that "the only really promising path to equal opportunity for Negroes in business as in other aspects of economic activity lies in full participation in an integrated, national economy. It cannot be found in a backwater of separation and segregation."[167] He called black capitalism a "cruel hoax" and "one of the worst digressions that has attracted attention and pulled substantial numbers of people off course."[168] In 1971, Brimmer testified before the House Committee on Small Business in opposition to black capitalism, explaining that black families, who were meant to be the cornerstone of the black business market, simply did not have enough wealth or income to support a viable industry.

He even took his argument directly to the black community in an *Ebony* essay in 1970, in which he denounced the "mirage" of the black community operating as a separate nation.[169] He noted that blacks were 11 percent of the population, but held less than 2 percent of the nation's assets—the black community did not have the economic strength to go it alone. As another economist, Robert S. Browne, explained, "there is no question of 'pulling ourselves up by the bootstraps.' We have no bootstraps."[170] Brimmer played the wet blanket role that Abram Harris had played before him, standing apart from virtually every other black leader and activist. And, like Harris before him, his words of caution were drowned out by the optimistic champions of black business.

Like Harris, Brimmer reserved his most thorough and specific criticism for black banking. He had nothing against black banks or bankers—unlike Harris, this was not the sort of criticism that labeled black bankers as exploiters or "house slaves." Black bankers, said Brimmer, "should not be encouraged in the belief that they can make a major contribution to the financing of economic development in the black community." Brimmer emphasized that the objective of these banks, of fostering economic growth in black communities, was critically important. He just did not believe that black-owned banks were up to the task. He dismissed the banks as merely "ornaments," suitable only as "a mark of distinction or a badge of honor which provides a symbol of accomplishment." They might be "a source of racial pride," but they would never "become vital instruments of economic development."[171]

Research on black banks and available public data on banking in this era validate Brimmer's position. Balance sheet analyses reveal that the specific financial hurdles these banks faced were caused by the same factors that had remained stubbornly unchanged over time, but with a few new and unexpected obstacles.

The typical black bank was one-third the size of an average commercial bank, as measured by assets, and they were one-quarter to one-third as profitable.[172] Black banks still had much higher operating costs than white banks; these costs absorbed 93 percent of operating income at black banks, compared to 78 percent at white banks. High operating costs were a result of small and volatile deposit accounts from their mostly poor clientele. Their high operating costs and low profits meant that black banks paid lower interest to their customers for their deposits than did white banks. Commercial banks paid an average interest on deposits of 4.4 percent in 1969; black banks only paid 3.1 percent. So black customers depositing at black blacks were losing an extra 1–2 percent in interest on their deposits. The banks also had to charge higher service fees to make up for their expenses, an additional cost borne by their customers. Loyal customers not driven away by this surcharge were making a financial sacrifice to support the black banks.[173]

One of the most surprising reasons that black banks' deposits were of such low value was the federal government's deposit program. By 1971, black banks had received $44.9 million in government deposits, which made up 18 percent of their total deposit balances. In contrast, government deposits in white-owned banks were about 2 percent of their total deposits. The point of the deposits was that they would strengthen the banks and create more community-building loans. As it turned out, these deposits ended up harming black banks because they were the wrong kind of deposits—unstable accounts from government agencies. Their volatility meant that they required higher servicing costs. One study even found that such deposits were actually more costly to black banks than their regular customers' deposits.[174]

Even more problematic in their effects on operating costs was their effect on the asset side of the banks' balance sheet. Black banks were required by law to pledge government securities for any government deposits they held over $100,000.[175] An FDIC study explained that the black banks formed after 1963 invested a staggering 40 percent of their assets in government securities.[176] This meant that they could make fewer loans and therefore take fewer profits, which meant that their investors made less money on their investments. In a seemingly endless cycle of problems, this meant that black banks could attract fewer capital investments, making them even weaker.[177]

Adding even greater insult to injury was that government deposits, instead of bringing money *into* the black community, were diverting black deposits *out* of the community. Instead of using deposits to invest in the community through local lending, black banks were overinvested in government securities on the asset side, which, according to one economist, turned black banks into "a conduit by which local deposit funds are exported to other markets through sales of federal funds and purchases of securities."[178] The black banks were taking deposits from the community and channeling them to investments in government securities that were being used to finance mortgages in other communities. "It appears," said Brimmer, "that black banks may be in the anomalous position of campaigning for U.S. government funds which they then use to finance a disproportionate share of the Federal debt."[179] This was not a matter of simple racial discrimination or even an effect that was obvious, but money that was supposed to stay in the community for loans was actually being funneled outside of the community through a program meant to bolster black community enterprise.

On the asset side, not only did black banks make fewer loans than white banks; the loans they did make suffered higher losses because the ghetto had always been a risky place to do business. Brimmer explained that there was an "inherent risk of doing business in the urban ghetto"; specifically, "the high unemployment rates, low family incomes, the high failure rates among small businesses (compounded by high crime) make the ghetto an extremely risky place for small banks to lend money." Cut off from the rest of the community, ghetto businesses could not take advantage of economies of scale or the robust infrastructure of the outside community. And the few profitable industries in low-income markets were captured by nonblack banks outside the ghetto.[180]

Thus, black bank loans, concentrated in the ghetto, lost more money due to default than those of white banks. Their losses were so heavy that the black banks' net income was less than one-half what it could have been without the defaults. Moreover, because of the high risk and high default rate of their loans, the banks held on to more cash and other liquid assets, which meant that more of their money sat dormant at the bank instead of yielding profits through fractional reserve lending. The average set-aside for loan losses at white banks was 11.4 percent of income. The difference was striking for black banks, which set aside an astounding 137 percent of their income to cover loan losses.[181] Not only did they hold on to more cash, but they hedged against the risk of high loan defaults by over-investing in government securities, furthering the slow leak of funds out of the ghetto. These securities may have offered predictable and solid returns, but it was no way to grow a bank or a community. It was evidence, however, that these banks were making every effort to operate as safely as possible.

In trying to protect themselves against the hazards of lending in the ghetto, black bankers were inadvertently using the incomes of their customers to undercut the ghetto economy by investing in the outside community.[182] In other words, black banks were not able to use fractional reserve lending to multiply or even to keep the black dollar within the ghetto. For the most part, they either held the black dollar dormant in a bank vault or they invested it in a white community through government securities. In any case, they were not able to control the black dollar or multiply it in the ghetto, which was their raison d'être and the reason they were supported and celebrated by both white and black leaders as the key to growing a separate economy.

Despite the stark economic reality of these banks, there still were more cheerleaders for black capitalism than naysayers. Edward Irons, the founding dean of the Howard Business School and executive director of the NBA, conducted a study of black banks. He conceded that they were performing poorly and stuck in a trap, but he remained optimistic about the prospects of black enterprise.[183] He encouraged federal, state, and local governments to place deposits in black banks, but urged major corporations to follow suit as well. Irons underscored the idea that black banks were an important source of racial pride and community building.

This benefit was enough for some. Economist Rawle Farley extolled black banks, calling them "one of the key determinants of the course and character of black economic development." To Farley, "the psychological impact of their emergence cannot be ignored in that they make the seemingly impossible a practical and attainable area of reality." He explained that to the black community, banking had always seemed an impossibility and, just as Jesse Owens had broken barriers in track and field, black bankers' success in the field of banking could serve as important role models. Black banks were thus closing the racial gap, even if only psychologically. They offered an "ethnic psychic pleasure" for the black community who kept account of the "economic achievements of their brothers," and this pleasure would spur further development.

More than racial pride however, many observers believed that there was no other choice. Farley himself joined with other black scholars in viewing the ghetto as a permanently separate economic environment and an isolated economy. In this framework, black entrepreneurship was necessary and unavoidable, because mainstream banks would never lend there. Farley believed that American businessmen avoiding taking risks in the ghetto was akin to "nonnative" corporations avoiding investing in the unknown jungles of Brazil. Black banks had to take risks that were "greater than the traditional risks" because they were acting as development banks. Economist William K. Tabb, a specialist in globalization and international development, believed that "the economic relations of the ghetto to white America closely parallel those between third world nations and the industrially advanced countries."[184]

Black nationalists had also envisioned the ghetto as a colony and had fought for decolonization and full sovereignty. With full sovereignty, control of land and resources, including the ability to block "foreign" competition in the ghetto, black banking could have been viable. Segregation and discrimination had operated like a tariff wall between the black and white economies, raising the price of goods and services crossing the barrier and creating two different economies—one subservient to the other. This situation, which economist Lester Thurow called "the monopoly power of whites," could be overcome through full sovereignty in the ghetto, which meant monopoly power over its resources.[185] But the majority of the black population did not want this; nor would white policy-makers ever consider such a proposal. Yet black banking continued to be supported and endorsed with the unfounded belief that control of banks was akin to control of capital and resources. Banking does not beget control and power; rather, control and power beget sound banking.

In order to have a healthy banking system with the ability to increase wealth, the choice was either full sovereignty or complete integration. Black banks would be unnecessary with full integration, but would be essential in an independent black territory. But the banks themselves could not create either condition. Black capitalism and black banking constituted a frustratingly futile halfway position.

It was clear that Nixon did not understand the segregation trap for black banks when he promised that black capitalism would "[open] the full range of business opportunity to all by removing the inherited and institutional barriers to entry."[186] But the intellectual founder of black capitalism, Theodore Cross, understood that black banking had become a diversion. He wrote in 1971 that black banks were still just "toy banks" or "specks of gold dust in the $1 trillion private capital and credit markets of America." Yet they had become magnets for government money and press, for, as he explained, "when the heat is on the temptations are great to build a few monuments to black affluence."[187] Shining a spotlight on a few successful black banks obscured the true problems of the wealth gap and the ghetto economic trap. At best, black capitalism was being used as state paternalism, but at heart it was deployed as a decoy instead of an honest account of a systemic problem.

Blacks had been excluded from full participation in American capitalism. Just as the civil rights laws were finally aligning the American creed with its deeds, black capitalism could be seen as a late-term remedy for systemic exclusion. The American economy was built on the theory of free-market capitalism, which meant open markets for all participants, with no government intervention, only the invisible hand of the market. In *The Wealth of Nations*, Adam Smith had explained that excluding any group from free market participation was antithetical to capitalism.[188] The foundational premise of capitalism was that it did not discriminate; rather, it provided equal opportunity to trade and prosper based on one's skill and ability to produce marketable goods. Smith railed against any artificial exclusions to entry into a profession or trade. In *The Philosophy of Money,* Georg Simmel claimed that money was a "democratic leveling social form that excludes any specific individual relationships."[189] For a market economy to thrive, any person's money should be as good as any other's. Even Karl Marx recognized that capitalism would do away with "ancient and venerable prejudices" because it left "no other nexus between man and man than naked self-interest, than callous 'cash payment.' "[190]

Yet blacks had been excluded from the main avenues of free trade and forced into an economic detour. Their property was not protected by law. They were banned from occupations, schools, neighborhoods, and trades. Not only that, but government intrusions into free markets had favored whites at their expense. The mixed economy of the progressive reforms that began in earnest with the Wilson administration, and had been the guiding principle through the Johnson administration, had almost completely excluded blacks from governmental infusions of credit and wealth into housing markets.[191] The result was a situation in which blacks paid more for everything—where their money was not as good as any other's. The black community was demanding that it either be allowed full entry into the system or be given monopoly state power over their own separate economy.

However, this demand for economic redress by the black movement came at the same moment that capitalism itself seemed to be under siege by revolutionary communist regimes abroad. In the fog of domestic and foreign war and an existential Cold War, it was hard to draw lines. Identifying enemies at home turned out to be just as confusing as finding them in the jungles of Vietnam. The Panthers, the Vietcong, the Russians, student protesters, domestic terrorists— all challenged the status quo and led to paralyzing fear. Nixon's gift to the American public was his ability to draw crisp lines between "real Americans" and ne'er-do-wells; hippies, draft dodgers, and black activists were the latter. Black protesters were often labeled communists, including Martin Luther King, who was wiretapped and blackmailed by Hoover's FBI as a domestic enemy.[192] King felt compelled to respond: "You don't have to go to Karl Marx to learn how to be a revolutionary. I didn't get my inspiration from Karl Marx; I got it from a man named Jesus."[193]

King was not a communist, but many principals of the black power movement were communist or communist sympathizers who associated with Cuba, China, and other revolutionary regimes. The ninety-three-year-old W. E. B. Du Bois, living in Ghana, joined the Communist Party in the 1960s before his death, lamenting that capitalism could not save itself.[194] In a 1967 speech in Havana, Cuba, Stokely Carmichael explained his opposition to the U.S. political and economic system: "The 'civil rights movement' did not actively involve the masses, because it did not speak to the needs of the masses. . . . [Civil rights] laws did not speak to our problems. Our problems were an inherent part of the capitalist system and therefore could not be alleviated within that system."[195]

Aside from the radical margins, the majority of black activists were essentially claiming that they had been left out of capitalism, or that it had not worked for them. Black nationalist Reverend Albert Cleague explained his aversion to capitalism as being about exclusion: "as far as the black community is concerned, the capitalistic economy doesn't work for us because we don't have any stake in it. It just happens that when we got to a place where we were able to do something, we were outside and the concentration of wealth in the white capitalistic set up is so complete now that you can't break into that . . . we are frozen outside of it."[196] Black separatist Harold Cruse remarked that blacks had been "prevented" from participation in American capitalism: "It is not that the Negro suffers so much from capitalism in America, but from a *lack of capitalistic development.*"[197] This sentiment was a common theme among black leaders. Daniel Watts, editor of the most prominent black militant publication, *The Liberator,* posed the question in 1968 "whether black people [should] accept capitalism." His answer was realistic: "whether you like it or not, the basic fact of life is that the capitalistic system in America does produce. There is no question about it, the system works, it produces." He urged blacks to adopt capitalist principles and make it work for them.[198] Many of the black nationalist and radical movements' demands centered around meaningful inclusion in capitalism. The demand for reparations was a demand for capital in order to remedy past exclusion that had left the community bereft of that capital.

Paradoxically, the most potent weapon against a demand for reparations was *capitalism*. Free-market fundamentalists said that reparations or compensatory capital was anticapitalist. Shortly after the civil rights community had asked that the equal opportunity myth be made a reality, a white majoritarian backlash demanded that the law treat everyone equally based on race and bestow no special race-based favors. And when the black community began rejecting the deviant ghetto market and demanding a share of American capitalism, the response it received was pure capitalism with a hard-core libertarian edge. Equality and capitalism were used as weapons against black demands for inclusion. Just as equality had become a noose around the first wave of civil rights demands, capitalism was used to strangle the second wave of economic demands.

Alan Greenspan, who served as Nixon's economic advisor, discussed demands for reparations in a personal memo titled "The Urban Riots of the 1960s" in 1967. He wrote that capitalism itself was under attack by demands made by black militants and that "ghetto riots have become a rallying cry for an attack upon America's system of free enterprise and individual rights." Greenspan outlined his reasoning: "The critical question is, of course, whether the Negroes are correct in claiming that they have been exploited and that their violent reaction is the rational response. There can be little doubt that discrimination has been rampant. However, the charge of exploitation in the sense of value being extracted from the Negroes without their consent for the profit of the whites is clearly false." In other words, because white businesses had not profited directly from black misery, reparations should be rejected. He claimed that black activists had misunderstood capitalism and the natural market of the ghetto, and had erroneously and unfairly blamed whites for exploitation. "This distinction between discrimination and exploitation is all the difference in the world," said Greenspan.[199]

But the difference was not quite as stark as Greenspan portrayed it to be—especially for those trapped in the ghetto market who had no choice but to pay the high price of discrimination. He was correct when he said that "profit rates in slum areas are doubtless distressingly low considering the risks," but he erred when he con-

cluded based on that observation that the white community was
not gaining any "advantage and profit," and that therefore cries of
"injustice" were "erroneous." Perhaps it was unfair to blame just
the ghetto lenders for exploitation because of their limited profits,
but only because they were a small part of a larger system—a
symptom rather than the disease itself. He could not see that the
same system that discriminated against blacks had brought benefits to whites—this was why the ghetto was created and redlined in
the first place. Whites had not wanted to live near blacks and thus
they were benefitting from segregation. Nor did he acknowledge
that, for blacks who were being crushed by the ghetto debt trap, it
could still feel like an "injustice" even if the lenders were not
making direct profits. Discrimination had led to the deviant market
and it felt like exploitation. It's just that the mechanism of exploitation and the individual exploiters were hard to detect. The benefits had not accrued only to the ghetto lenders, but to all of white
society.

Greenspan underscored in the memo his belief that any capitulation to demands for federal spending in the ghetto was a threat to
free enterprise. He believed that the cries of exploitation were not
only misguided, but had destroyed the status of the "more moderate old-line Negro civil rights leaders" and turned the black middle
class anti-capitalist. He rejected the liberal notion that "the Negro
ghetto must be elevated to the level of affluence of middle class
America" because "this can only be done by massive governmental
expenditures." Instead, he advised Nixon to pursue programs to
"help Negroes help themselves."

Capitalist theory was even used to fight basic antidiscrimination
laws in Milton Friedman's foundational 1962 book *Capitalism and
Freedom*. The intellectual father of neoliberalism opposed civil rights
laws as a violation free-market capitalism. He decried discrimination as a matter of bad taste, but said that antidiscrimination laws
were an "interference with the freedom of individuals to enter into
voluntary contracts with one another."[200] He compared laws *prohib-
iting* discrimination to laws *requiring* discrimination, such as the
infamous Nuremberg laws—it was all unjustified government intervention. Friedman believed that markets would themselves root
out discrimination because it was costly and inefficient. Friedman
claimed that anyone who opposed buying goods from black busi-

nessmen or employing black employees was expressing an inefficient preference and would therefore pay a higher price for that preference. Theoretically this was true, but historically it was not. Because the ghetto had cordoned off a segment of risky borrowers, whites actually paid significantly less for goods, credit, and housing. Racial discrimination had not cost whites, but had actually brought many advantages in the form of all-white suburbs, lower competition for lucrative jobs, and labor protections that benefited whites at the expense of blacks.[201]

Friedman, Greenspan, and other market capitalists grounded their arguments in economic theory. They were chasing a libertarian, laissez-faire vision of the economy, but what they were describing was a hypothetical future that bore no relationship to the actual lived experience of American history. This was a common trope of the Chicago school economists, one that relied on models that often assumed perfect information and rational behavior and did not account for the decision-making flaws of average humans.[202] The historical American reality was that blacks had never fully participated in free-market capitalism and that whites had benefited from heavy government interventions that had worked to the direct disadvantage of blacks. The arteries of trade and commerce had not flowed freely through the ghetto, at least not in the realm of credit and banking. The credit markets lay atop a federal government apparatus including guarantees, secondary markets, deposit insurance, and Federal Reserve support. The only place where those forces were not intervening was inside the ghetto. The ghetto itself had been an unnatural creation of antimarket impositions of racist policies. Indeed, discrimination was incredibly costly, but only to blacks.

The neoliberal faith in capitalism and market efficiency was rooted in an ideal much like the egalitarian principles of the founding documents. They were aspirational faiths, but they were not accurate descriptions of the real world. In theory, it was costly to refuse to buy products from blacks if they were offering the same or lower prices. In reality, whites often refused to associate with blacks at any cost. Besides, even if discrimination did suddenly disappear, the broken markets of the ghetto would not. Discrimination had created macro market forces that were now operating on their own. Yet neoliberal dogma and market fundamentalism demanded adherence to market theory, which meant an aversion to any and all "government intervention" aimed at black poverty.

Barry Goldwater's failed presidential run in 1964 was the watershed moment for libertarian market principles on the national political stage, and created a movement that only grew stronger over time.[203] Goldwater demanded less government involvement and spending in all spheres. Without spewing the racial animus of the George Wallace wing of American politics, he opposed civil rights laws, integration, and any government program meant to address poverty—all in the name of free-market capitalism. There is no reason to doubt that Goldwater was a true believer in market fundamentalism, but Goldwater won back the South for the Republican Party not on a promise of small government, but based purely on his opposition to integration and civil rights laws. He used the principles of libertarianism as a weapon against racial equality, and he did so to court the votes of the white supremacist wing of the party.[204]

Since any redress for past economic exclusion required heavy federal government action, an immediate libertarian backlash began to delegitimize all government action. Conservatives began to demand a bill of rights that guaranteed the right to free use of property, including the right to segregated neighborhoods. The movement could hardly be seen as anything but a direct response to the economic demands of the black movement and the government antipoverty program.[205] Nixon was not a libertarian—he expanded the federal bureaucracy and created more government agencies than any other modern president—but he still opposed government interference of any kind when it came to integration or antipoverty measures. Republican strategist Lee Atwater gave away the playbook in a 1981 interview: "You start out in 1954 saying nig***, nig***, nig***. By 1968, you can't say nig***—that hurts you, backfires. So you say stuff like, uh, forced busing, states' rights, and all that stuff, and you're getting so abstract. Now, you're talking about cutting taxes, and all these things you're talking about are totally economic things and a byproduct of them is, blacks get hurt more than whites."[206]

Free-market capitalism and its faithful defenders were no doubt responding to the political threat of communism. But they were also specifically and forcefully using free-market dogma to fight the economic demands of the black power movement. This dogma would only be emboldened and perfected under President Reagan, but it began in the 1960s with Friedman, Goldwater, Buckley, and Greenspan. The economic theory that James Kwak has called "Economism" began to be adhered to like a religious dogma and was used to fight each and every government intervention to remedy past sins.[207]

Economism even provided a new justification for stark wealth inequality and exploitation. Inequality along racial lines has been a constant on the American scene, but different eras have justified it with different myths. Christianity was corrupted to prove that white men had a divine right—even a duty—to subjugate and enslave blacks. When religious theory fell out of favor, social Darwinism and skull measurements held that blacks were an inferior species that had lost the evolutionary race, and thus their subjugation was nature's will. Now economic theory established that "market forces" decreed that blacks should hold the bottom rung because, for example, the law of supply and demand caused blacks to pay more for credit and the market determined how much their labor was worth, and that integration was antimarket. Any effort to change these "market laws" was delegitimized and labeled as harmful government interference with, in the words of President Reagan, "the magic of the marketplace."[208] And just as God's will was difficult to challenge in the 1800s, so too was free-market economic theory after the neoliberal revolution of the late 1960s, lest one be labeled a heretic or a communist.

For the ascendant libertarians who were taking hold of American politics, the only acceptable remedy for a history of exclusion was black capitalism. But what these white policymakers surely meant by black capitalism was capitalism for blacks only. Government intervention in markets had been the norm, as were government-imposed Jim Crow laws. Capitalism had not created the ghetto and black poverty—racist laws and state intervention in the markets had created both. There had never been free-market capitalism for blacks. After years of exclusion, Jim Crow, segregation, and the deviant markets these state interventions had created, the Nixon administration was actually proposing that maintaining the segregated market was the remedy—that somehow attaching the word "black" to "capitalism" would fix past wrongs.

The irony of the politics of libertarianism is that it ran comfortably alongside a draconian criminal justice system, which was the antithesis of liberty. Both Nixon and Goldwater strongly supported federal intervention in the form of a stronger police state.[209] For Gold-water, even Martin Luther King's nonviolent mass demonstrations consisted of "bullies and marauders" running rampant. He called for Stokely Carmichael to be charged with high treason, a crime punishable by death.[210] Goldwater ran his campaign on promises of law and order, with the ominous warning, "Choose the way of [the Johnson] Administration and you have the way of mobs in the street."[211] Nixon followed suit by releasing fear-stoking radio ads featuring violence, with a promise that "we shall have order in the United States." As John Ehrlichman, special counsel to Nixon, admitted, "that subliminal appeal to the anti-black voter was always present in Nixon's statements and speeches." By 1969, over 80 percent of Americans felt that "law and order had broken down in this country," and a majority blamed "Negroes who start riots" and "communists."[212] So began the slow deprivation of the rights and livelihoods of generations of black men in the ghetto.

Advocates of libertarianism and neoliberalism claimed to want more liberty for individuals and a smaller government, but in reality they only wanted less government for the wealthy and the white. The War on Crime had increased surveillance on the black community, overregulated the informal black economy, and imposed excessive sentences for crimes—all of which cost many poor black men their liberty. Not only was the civil rights upheaval co-opted by the carceral state, but a lesser-known diversion took place during this pivotal era. In a pattern that resembled what happened during Reconstruction, exactly at the point of inflection when the black community began to demand economic integration and a transfer of wealth and land, a libertarian free-market backlash couched in "black capitalist" rhetoric headed off their demands.

The Free Market Confronts
Black Poverty

No sooner had the complicated, overdue, and incomplete racial turmoil of the civil rights era subsided than a rewriting of its history began. The story was that the civil rights laws had permanently altered race relations in America, dividing history into a racist past and a color-blind present. Civil rights was a fait accompli, justice had finally been achieved, and America's institutions were at last only concerned with the "content of one's character." Even Dr. King's complicated legacy was recast. King was now seen as a singular American hero who sought and ushered forth racial harmony, finally reconciling America's stated ideals of equality with its dissonant history. This retelling not only erased the long history of injustice and its effects, which in fact had not abated in the least; it also pushed the burden of economic disparity squarely onto the black population.

On the campaign trail and as president, Jimmy Carter portrayed the country as postracial. He chastised his Democratic primary opponent, Jesse Jackson, for overemphasizing racial problems, which he referred to as "an issue that's already divided the people," yet he enthusiastically embraced the once-divisive leader of the previous era, stating "I see an America in which Martin Luther King's dream is our national dream."[1] President Ronald Reagan also harshly denounced racism and embraced King's dream. When Reagan made King's birthday a national holiday in 1983, he announced, "We've made historic strides since Rosa Parks refused to go to the back of the bus. As a democratic people, we can take pride in the knowledge that we Americans recognized a grave injustice and took action to correct it."[2] Yet he had consistently maintained opposition to civil rights laws because he believed them to be unnecessary government intrusions into private markets.[3]

Black poverty came to be seen as a direct result of a culture that lacked responsibility, work ethic, and "family values." Having achieved racial equality, what else could explain the wide wealth gap? Government interventions and the welfare state had allegedly created perverse incentives for blacks to avoid employment and have children out of wedlock.[4] President Reagan attacked welfare spending, characterizing it as tax dollars being spent on "welfare queens" feasting on T-bone steak while hardworking Americans "were standing in the checkout line with [their] package of hamburgers." In railing against welfare, Reagan used the example of a particular black female fraudster who had snatched unearned privileges by exploiting the welfare system at the expense of honest taxpayers. This was an inaccurate picture of welfare, as whites received the large majority of welfare benefits and welfare fraud was rare. However, the depiction of the black population as riddled with crime and drugs, unwilling to work, and living comfortably off government largesse had remarkable durability.[5]

It is worth distilling this message in order to fully appreciate the irony. The story was that after decades of New Deal–era federal subsidies had created a white middle class, reinforced a segregated black underclass, and created cyclic poverty that made it difficult for many to find shelter and food without government aid, it was *black people* who were being unjustly enriched by the overly generous hand of the state.

According to this story, the only state intervention required in the ghetto was "law and order." By the time Ronald Reagan took office, the groundwork for the war on crime had been laid, but the Reagan administration turned up the heat. Part of President Reagan's appeal, according to one political insider, was derived from "the emotional distress of those who fear or resent the Negro, and who expect Reagan somehow to keep him 'in his place' or at least echo their own anger and frustration."[6] In 1982, Reagan initiated the War on Drugs, even though drugs had not yet registered as a perceived public problem.[7] Even the staunchest advocates of the drug war now admit that it was unfairly skewed to impose the harshest prison sentences on black drug criminals rather than white ones, and it resulted in a generational devastation of the lives of young black men.[8] In just a few years, federal funding for antidrug law enforcement skyrocketed (while funding for treatment or prevention programs plummeted). Anyone selling or possessing crack cocaine could face a lifetime in prison. A media offensive sensationalized a crack "epidemic" in the inner city, one that didn't really exist yet. But it would.

The ghettos were an open sore and "crack blew through [them] like the Four Horsemen of the Apocalypse," leaving behind disease, suffering, and acute poverty.[9] By 1986, *Newsweek* declared crack to be a bigger story than the Vietnam war or Watergate.[10] Once the nation focused on crack abuse, it was hard to pay attention to the larger, less sensational problem of structural poverty. As Adam Walinsky, President Kennedy's speechwriter, exclaimed: "If we blame crime on crack, our politicians are off the hook. Forgotten are the failed schools, the maligned welfare programs, the desolate neighborhoods, the wasted years. Only crack is to blame. One is tempted to think that if crack did not exist, someone somewhere would have received a Federal grant to develop it."[11]

Crime, drugs, and gang violence eventually enveloped the ghetto. Segregation, poverty, and a distrust of police led to increased crime, which led to further marginalization, poverty, and even more policing. According to Jill Leovy's study of black crime, *Ghettoside*, high rates of murder among black men are a by-product of poverty, a history of distrust of the white justice system, and especially of segregation. "Indices of segregation are strong homicide predictors. Homicide thrives on intimacy, communal interactions, barter, and a shared sense of private rules."[12] Max Weber defined a functioning state as one that "claims the monopoly of the legitimate use of physical force within a given territory." According to Leovy, "slavery, Jim Crow, and conditions across much of black America for generations after worked against the formation of such a monopoly where blacks are concerned." Because the law failed to "stand up for black people," brutal gang "laws" filled the void.[13] Black men viewed the American legal system with suspicion, and so extralegal violence filled the void and ordered the lives of young black men; it also took their lives. As crime increased, so did community trauma and isolation, which limited opportunity for young black men in the ghetto. With few ways out, crime became ubiquitous— or as James Baldwin explained, "not as *a* possibility, but as *the* possibility."[14]

Instead of dealing with the complex set of forces causing black crime, the state response was to contain it, lock it up, and demonize black criminals. American politics became a ratcheting up of "tough on crime" sound bites. President George H. W. Bush defeated Democrat Michael Dukakis in 1988 by infamously linking him to a convicted black felon, Willie Horton, who, while serving a life sentence in Massachusetts, was given a furlough from which he never returned and went on to commit a rape and robbery. This occurred while Dukakis was governor of the state, and Bush's chief strategist Lee Atwater bragged that he would make Willie Horton a household name. By repeatedly airing television ads featuring Horton, the Bush campaign stoked fear of black crime and pegged Dukakis as being too soft on crime. Bill Clinton heeded the lesson, and when he was running for office in 1992, he went to Arkansas to witness and tacitly encourage the execution of a mentally incapacitated black criminal, Ricky Ray Rector. He won the election on a tough-on-crime, antiwelfare platform.[15]

As president, Clinton escalated the War on Crime, and incarcerations steadily increased during his administration. The Clinton administration also slashed funding for welfare and public housing and initiated a "One Strike and You're Out" public housing policy that resulted in many evictions. By the year 2000, almost 800,000 black men were in prison, compared to 600,000 who were in college.[16] Thus, there were more black men in prison than had been held under slavery in 1850.[17] After serving time, ex-felons could not find jobs, and many lost their right to vote. King's legacy assumed an even more cynical meaning under President Clinton, who used King's words to admonish the black community. In 1993 Clinton told a congregation at the Masonic Temple in Memphis Tennessee, where King had delivered his "Mountaintop" speech:

> If [Martin Luther King] were to reappear by my side today and give us a report card on the last 25 years, what would he say? . . . You did a good job, he would say, letting people who have the ability to do so live wherever they want to live, go wherever they want in this great country. . . . But he would say, I did not live and die to see the American family destroyed . . . I did not fight for the right of black people to murder other black people with reckless abandon.[18]

It is more likely, however, that if Dr. King had been alive, he would have lamented the fact that blacks were still living in segregated and impoverished communities and suffering from the resulting crime that accompanied their situation. Clinton celebrated the fight against segregation as a "mission accomplished," but the reality was that while the War on Crime and the War on Drugs were heating up, the fight against housing segregation had long since halted.

During the 1976 election, candidates from both parties took Nixon's lead and opposed any measures pushing integration. Gerald Ford committed to making sure "all constitutional rights are fully protected," while refusing to impose integration on white neighborhoods, which he labeled an "ethnic treasure." Jimmy Carter said, "I see nothing wrong with ethnic purity [of neighborhoods] being maintained. I would not force racial integration of a neighborhood by government action." The rhetoric of "ethnicity" allowed policymakers to pretend that the racism and segregation that had created inner-city ghettos were akin to protecting "ethnic culture," as though the segregation had been voluntary. The clichéd "celebrating diversity" replaced the harsher accusation of "segregation" and could not be challenged as discriminatory.[19]

The Fair Housing Act mandate to "affirmatively further" fair housing came to be interpreted only as a mandate to oppose outright discrimination in housing. Active integration simply stopped being discussed, and even communities that were flagrantly segregating housing continued to receive block grants. Ultimately, the FHA was an empty promise. The act allowed the country to publicly denounce segregation while never actually pursuing integration.[20] In a testament to how permanent segregation had become, major U.S. cities responded to overcrowding and housing shortages in the ghetto by constructing large-scale public housing projects, which maintained and bolstered segregation patterns. By 1980, the isolation index for the black ghetto was the same as it was during the pre-Depression era of bombings and racial covenants, despite the passage of laws outlawing discrimination.[21]

Segregation, white flight, and declining home values continued to hamper black families' ability to grow wealth.[22] In 1984, black middle-class families had only twenty cents of wealth for every dollar of wealth held by white middle-class families.[23] Half of black children were growing up in poverty. Wherever poverty was concentrated, education was subpar, and crime replaced legitimate institutions.[24] While de jure racism was now illegal, economic forces set in motion by years of segregation and discrimination were still perpetuating black disadvantage. But as for targeted race-based economic programs—there were no new ideas.

The racial compromise struck during the Nixon era proved as durable as it was weak. When it came to the racial wealth gap, every administration after Nixon's focused on some variation of black capitalism. The OMBE was still the coordinating branch for black business initiatives, although, starting with the Ford administration, the program was no longer called "black capitalism." Now it was referred to as "minority enterprise." The OMBE's budget remained small and its mission continued to be vague. When the OMBE and SBA minority programs were evaluated by a Commerce Department report in 1975, it was found that most of their programs amounted to little more than "technical assistance to minority firms."[25]

One could not tell this from the way it was discussed. President Ford called the OMBE "undoubtedly the most popular and visible program started by a Republican administration geared specifically toward minorities" and "the single domestic program positively identified within minority communities as a Republican brainchild."[26] As part of the Railroad Revitalization and Regulatory Reform Act of 1976, Ford created a new agency called the Minority Business Resource Center within the Department of Transportation. The National Business League called the bill "the first original piece of legislation to recognize minority enterprise as a national objective."[27] President Ford reiterated the GOP mantra that black capitalism "is not a civil rights or jobs program." This was not an apology—it was a boast. Those programs had developed a negative association by then. "It is a business program," said Ford.[28]

President Carter appointed more African Americans to federal offices than any president before him, but he had no coherent or visible message on black poverty or civil rights.[29] He expressed a strong public commitment to black capitalism programs, stating in 1977 that "building strong minority business enterprise is in the national interest because they contribute to our efforts to reduce unemployment and to stimulate community development."[30] His administration doubled government purchases from black firms and deposited substantially more federal dollars in minority-owned banks.[31] In 1977, President Carter promoted the Minority Bank Deposit Program in a memorandum to all of his heads of departments and agencies, urging them to use minority banks. Carter boasted that the program had begun in 1970 with about $3.7 million of funds deposited in thirty-one participating banks, and that by 1977 there was $86.6 million in over eighty minority banks.[32]

The SBA's contract set-asides became a point of public controversy in 1978 when Mike Wallace of *60 Minutes* aired an exposé revealing several grant recipients as fronts for white construction firms.[33] The Carter administration studied the program in 1979 and found that it suffered from a "lack of focused leadership; lack of consensus on major goals and objectives; inadequate utilization of limited resources; and unrealistic business expectations."[34] The minority businesses getting grants were floundering, and the program, having no clear mandate, was riddled with inefficiencies.[35] After the report, the Carter administration in 1979 streamlined programs at the OMBE and renamed the agency the Minority Business Development Agency (MBDA). The change in name also marked a shift in philosophy. Now the agency focused exclusively on ensuring minority business success. It would try to pick among the most successful minority businesses and provide them with assistance.

If black capitalism had been launched as a response to the deviant ghetto economy, the connection was no longer apparent.[36] However, the politics were still appealing. Denouncing discrimination, avoiding systematic race-based economic reform, not pushing integration, and heralding black business—ensuing administrations pursued the political path Nixon had forged in addressing racial inequality. President Reagan perfected the rhetoric of the libertarian ideology that Goldwater had initiated, and he sharpened the weapon of "free-market capitalism" against government aid. While fighting both welfare and minimum wage hikes, he claimed he was waging a fight *for* the black community. "We are the party of real social progress," which meant moving toward an "opportunity society," not a welfare state. The way to deal with poverty in the black community was not government aid, but tax cuts. When President Reagan spoke to minority business owners in 1987, he explained that tax cuts "created opportunity for those who had before been economically disenfranchised: the poor and minorities."[37] In line with his "trickle-down" economics theories, Reagan equated his cost-cutting "Economic Bill of Rights" with fighting for civil rights. "Let's complete the civil rights movement by writing a guarantee of the American dream into the Constitution, a guarantee that America will always be, for our children and our children's children, the land of opportunity."[38]

While cutting antipoverty programs, Reagan enthusiastically supported black business. Speaking to the NAACP in 1981, he extolled black business leaders, saying that minority business development "is a key to black economic progress. Black-owned businesses are especially important in neighborhood economies where the dollars, as I said, spent have *a beneficial multiplier effect.*"[39] Here was Garvey and Malcolm's theory of control of the black dollar. Here was also Milton Friedman's theory of free enterprise as the bulwark against discrimination. "A free economy helps defeat discrimination by fostering opportunity for all," promised Reagan.[40] In a 1982 speech, President Reagan declared that for the rest of his administration, the first week of October would be Minority Enterprise Development Week.[41] In 1983, he issued an executive order requiring federal agencies to issue annual goals on increasing procurements from minority businesses.[42] The 1988 GOP platform promised "we will increase, strengthen, and reinvigorate minority business development efforts to afford socially and economically disadvantaged individuals the opportunity for full participation in our free enterprise system."[43]

As for the ghetto, Reagan promised that lower taxes and fewer regulations would revitalize the area and attract more small businesses. He began to call inner-city ghettos "enterprise zones." The 1984 GOP platform had called on Congress to pass legislation to help "enterprise zones, to draw a green line of prosperity around the redlined areas of our cities and to help create jobs and entrepreneurial opportunities."[44] Apart from tax cuts, Reagan did not offer any specific plans to create jobs or opportunities. The free market, it was believed, would take care of the rest.

While the theory and infrastructure of black capitalism continued unabated, its original purpose—as a remedy for the ghetto economy and a response to the black power movement—changed over time. For example, both Presidents Carter and Reagan put forth initiatives to include women in the SBA and MDBA grant programs.[45] Reagan's Women's Business Ownership Act of 1988 mandated that the SBA provide additional aid to female-owned enterprise.[46] Black capitalism initiatives and affirmative action had begun as a politically neutralizing response to one of the biggest racial uprisings in history, but now these programs encompassed business support for all minority groups, including women. The theory of black enterprise was no longer discussed as an antipoverty measure, and certainly not as a black power initiative. Rather, it came to be conceived of as providing positive role models for minority communities and "diversifying" white male–dominated fields. Nor were these programs about remedying past injustice, which, according to the Supreme Court, was now unconstitutional.

In the 1978 case *Regents of the University of California v. Bakke,* a plurality of the Court upheld race-based preferential treatment in university admissions, but rewrote the underlying premise of affirmative action in the process. Justice Lewis Powell held that the only "compelling state interest" that could justify affirmative action was increasing "diversity."[47] It was no longer a legitimate state interest to create programs meant to remedy past discrimination.

Understanding what this meant for the prospect of future reforms, Justice Thurgood Marshall wrote a forceful and plaintive dissent. Having personally waged a fight against centuries of unjust laws and having case by case "rethreaded parts of the Constitution itself, stitching the Negro, at long last, into the fabric of the nation," Marshall knew the stakes involved.[48] He explained to the Court that the "legacy of years of slavery and of years of second-class citizenship in the wake of emancipation could not be so easily eliminated." He could not believe that the Constitution stood as a barrier to remedying such a legacy, especially as it had only been a decade since the civil rights laws had banned racial discrimination, and too little had changed. "Measured by any benchmark of comfort or achievement, meaningful equality remains a distant dream for the Negro." Marshall explained that blacks were still economically disadvantaged, a position that was an "inevitable consequence of centuries of unequal treatment." Marshall pleaded that "bringing the Negro into the mainstream of American life should be a state interest of the highest order" and warned that a "[failure] to do so is to ensure that America will forever remain a divided society."[49]

Affirmative action for the sake of diversity survived, but the obvious theory that blacks had suffered past injustices that continued to cause present problems did not. Neither did the black capitalism set-aside program. In 1989, a white construction company sued Richmond's minority set-aside program, arguing that the program

violated the white company's constitutional right to equal protection under the law. In *City of Richmond v. Croson,* the Supreme Court
agreed and ended the program. The Court rejected Richmond's claim
that "past societal discrimination" could justify a racial preference.
Justice O'Connor even summoned Dr. King's rhetoric in order to reject any program that would favor blacks over whites, stating that
"the dream of a Nation of equal citizens in a society where race is
irrelevant to personal opportunity and achievement would be lost
in a mosaic of shifting preferences based on inherently unmeasur-
able claims of past wrongs."[50]

King's confused legacy was often wielded as a potent weapon in
opposition to affirmative action programs. When Attorney General
Edwin Meese tried to eliminate minority hiring goals in 1986, he
said that his plan was "very consistent with what Dr. King had in
mind." When Louisiana Governor Mike Foster signed an executive
order eliminating affirmative action in his state, he said, "King sort of
believed like I do. I can't find anywhere in his writings that he wanted
reverse discrimination."[51] That was not what King had believed. In
Where Do We Go from Here, King had said, "A society that has done
something special *against* the Negro for hundreds of years must
now do something special *for* him."[52]

While the judicial branch was dismantling the executive branch's
black capitalism program, the legislature was enshrining features of
it in the law. In 1989, Congress passed the Financial Institutions Reform, Recovery, and Enforcement Act (FIRREA) in response to the
savings and loan crisis. The act was primarily focused on regulating
the failed thrift sector, but it also included a much less discussed
provision on minority banks. Section 308 of FIRREA, entitled
"Preserving Minority Ownership of Minority Financial Institutions,"
contained the first legislative decree concerning minority banks.
Section 308 did not authorize any financial help to black banks, but
instructed the FDIC, Treasury, and the now-defunct Office of Thrift
Supervision to pay attention to the sector—specifically, to work
toward preserving "the present number" and "character" of minority
deposit institutions. For example, in the event a minority institution
was threatened with failure, the law said that bank regulators should
work to ensure that the bank's minority nature was preserved by, if
possible, merging it with another minority bank in the region. The
act also mandated federal regulators to provide "training, technical

assistance and education programs" to all minority banks as well as to work to "promote and encourage" new minority banks.[53]

This was the first time Congress had provided a legal definition for minority banks. The definition itself revealed just how muddled the issue of black banking had become and how far the concept of black capitalism had migrated from its initial purposes. During the era of Jim Crow and strict segregation, a legal definition for a black bank was unnecessary—a black bank was one that served black customers in a black community. When Nixon issued Executive Order 11458 establishing the OMBE and the black capitalism framework, he did not include a legal definition—it had been fairly obvious that he was talking about establishing black-owned institutions in the ghetto as a response to black riots and the black power movement.[54] However, after the initial crisis had passed, the Nixon administration began speaking more vaguely about "minority business enterprise." According to some observers, this was because Nixon had seen the political utility in courting the Mexican vote. In fact, his only minority appointment to his administration was conservative Mexican, Hilary Sandoval, to head the SBA.[55]

In 1971, Nixon revised the initial black capitalism program through Executive Order 11625, which for the first time defined the term "minority business enterprise" as a business that was "owned or controlled by one or more socially or economically disadvantaged persons. Such disadvantage may arise from cultural, racial, chronic economic circumstances or background or other similar cause. Such persons include, but are not limited to, Negroes, Puerto Ricans, Spanish-speaking Americans, American Indians, Eskimos, and Aleuts." It is fair to say that this vague and convoluted definition affords as much clarity as could be expected from a program that began as an ill-defined political response to an acute national crisis. The categories of disadvantage had been loosely expanded over time—for example, to include female-owned businesses.

The FIRREA legislation was now creating a specific regulatory program aimed at minority banks, and so it created a binding legal distinction. That definition was not just ambiguous; it also revealed the doublespeak at the heart of the federal policy framework around black capitalism. Section 308(b) defined a minority institution as a bank that is 51 percent owned by "one or more socially and economically disadvantaged individuals." For public banks, it required a majority of stockholders to be "socially and economically disadvantaged."[56] The statute did not go on to define what this meant or how it should be interpreted. To further the confusion, when the act defined minority "cooperatives" or "mutually owned minority banks" in the very next sentence of the section, it changed the definition of a minority bank to one that has a "majority of the Board of Directors, account holders, and the community which [the bank] services is predominantly minority." The act then defined "minority" as "any black American, Native American, Hispanic American, or Asian American."[57] In defining a minority institution simultaneously as one that serves economically disadvantaged individuals and one that serves a defined group of minorities, the act underscored the conflicting agendas that bred black capitalism.

In order to enforce Congress's mandate, the confused regulators simply created their own definition. "Given the ambiguous nature of the phrase 'socially and economically disadvantaged individuals,'" the FDIC regulators threw up their hands and said that they had determined that a minority deposit institution was one that is majority owned by U.S. citizens who are "Black American, Asian American, Hispanic American, or Native American." The OTS did the same.[58] The black capitalism program was a response—albeit a misguided one—to remedy past discrimination and to provide a boost to the economically disadvantaged ghetto. But the Supreme Court had put an end to any programs meant to remedy past discrimination, so the purpose of the program had shifted to focus instead on diversity and providing positive role models for marginalized groups. But this new program was utterly disconnected from dealing with economic disadvantage, which rendered the entire framework meaningless. In other words, the best way to describe the federal government's regulatory apparatus as it related to black banking was as a "tangle of pathology."

President Clinton brought some much-needed clarity to policy as he revitalized the black capitalism programs. He began to talk about black banks the way Nixon initially had, as a means of confronting black ghetto poverty. But in the new color-blind reality, he did so without mentioning race. President Clinton, calling himself a "New Democrat," proposed a "third way" politics situated in between traditional Republicans and Democrats. Clinton slashed welfare benefits, which he believed caused a "cycle of dependence."[59] He did expand the Earned Income Tax Credit, Head Start, and increased the minimum wage, which he said properly "emphasize[d] work and independence."[60] However, instead of resurrecting Johnson's soaring rhetoric and ambitious War on Poverty, Clinton tried to steer the party away from it. In fact, both Clinton's and Carter's rhetoric and actions on racial equality followed President Nixon's lead as opposed to their Democratic predecessors.

Clinton embedded his urban poverty programs firmly in libertarian market ideology, which held that private enterprise operating in free markets would be the answer to poverty. The country's racial ghettos, created by Jim Crow laws and policies, whose walls still remained intact, came to be referred to as enterprise zones, emerging markets, and niche industries. These were places that could surely yield a profit if creative entrepreneurs looked hard enough.

Clinton signed a series of laws that provided tax inducements to encourage private firms to invest in impoverished communities.[61] Clinton's policies provided an incentive-based boost to Nixon's black capitalism framework. Nixon had tried—with minimal effort—to induce large white-owned firms to *voluntarily* contribute to black businesses as a civic duty. And that is how the firms themselves had viewed their involvement. Clinton's program also relied on private businesses to pour money into the ghetto, but he did not appeal to philanthropic aims at all; he promised profits. Clinton's HUD secretary, Andrew Cuomo, told reporters that it "is not about charity. It's about investment."[62] Academics and progressive reformers agreed that ghetto poverty was just a result of misaligned market incentives and could only be addressed through private enterprise. Influential Harvard Professor Michael Porter wrote that instead of aid or social investments, the only way to build the economy of the ghetto was "through private, for-profit initiatives and investment based on economic self-interest and genuine advantage. . . . The cornerstone of such a model is to identify and exploit the competitive advantages of inner cities that will translate into truly profitable businesses."[63] Ghettos were labeled "emerging markets" and "untapped markets," which contained hidden opportunities that profit-oriented private enterprises could exploit, creating a win-win of profits for the entrepreneurs and poverty alleviation for the ghetto. Instead of working to break down the walls of segregation and the poverty trap they had created, the ghetto would be sent entrepreneurs.

Because of the color-blind delusion, now enforced by the Supreme Court, these programs had to be race neutral. Instead of black capitalism, it was "community capitalism." In 1997, a conference called the American Assembly brought together business and community leaders and academics to discuss poverty and community development. The final conference report urged policymakers to "energize community capitalism in distressed areas." Community capitalism was defined as a "for-profit, business-driven expansion of investment, job creation, and economic opportunities in distressed communities, with government and the community sectors playing key supportive roles."[64] Vice President Al Gore endorsed the report, stating, "The greatest untapped markets in the world are right here at home, in our distressed communities."[65]

Just like Nixon's black capitalism, Clinton's "community capitalism" was a bipartisan winner. Missouri Republican Representative James Talent heralded the proposed program as "not only the most comprehensive antipoverty package coming out of the federal government . . . in a generation, but it also . . . has assimilated the lessons that people on both sides of the aisle have learned over the last generations."[66] Jesse Jackson enthusiastically joined Clinton's community enterprise agenda with his 1998 "Close the Gaps. Leave No American Behind" campaign. Jackson proposed that the president create "vehicles to move capital" into disadvantaged areas. Clinton joined Jackson's 1999 "Wall Street Project" conference to promote community capitalism, during which the president told attendees that "the largest pool of untapped investment opportunities and new customers are not beyond our shores; they're in our back yard."[67]

Black leaders praised Clinton's $38 million boost to MBDA in 1994, as well as his order reinforcing Reagan's designation of Minority Development Enterprise Week. Clinton declared that the "growth and development in the minority business community are crucial to the social fabric, as well as to the overall economy, of this Nation."[68] Minority businesses, he said, would "prove that we can bring the benefits of free enterprise to every neighborhood in America." All free enterprise needed was a nudge from the tax code.[69]

Clinton's "community capitalism" program as applied to banks was embodied in the Riegle Community Development and Regulatory Improvement Act of 1994, commonly known as the Community Development Banking Act (CDBA).[70] The act provided tax incentives for banks, or Community Development Financial Institutions (CDFIs), that served underprivileged areas.[71] President Clinton said that the bill was inspired by a living bank that was putting the theory of community capitalism into practice. South Side Chicago's Shore-Bank was the country's most famous "black bank," even though it was not black-owned. As white flight accelerated in Chicago after the 1960s, the remaining South Side banks followed their white customers out.[72] ShoreBank was one of the few remaining banks, but only because their request to move was denied by its regulators. A group of civil rights activists—Ronald Grzywinski, Milton Davis, James Fletcher, and Mary Houghton—acquired the bank in 1973.[73]

ShoreBank's motto—"Let's Change the World"—was not an empty marketing pitch. The exemplar of community capitalism, the bank promoted a "triple bottom line: profitability, community development impact, and an environmental return."[74] ShoreBank's primary aim was to fight urban decline. At its peak, it had $4.1 billion invested in inner-city Chicago.[75] The bank's ambitious mission drew many admirers, including Grameen Bank founder Muhammad Yunus, who visited the bank before launching microcredit in Bangladesh and receiving a Nobel Peace Prize for his innovative approach to poverty.[76]

This is not to say that the bank didn't struggle against the same profitability trap that had ensnared black banks for nearly a century. For the first ten years, the bank lost money because its loans were risky, deposits were small, and operation costs were high.[77] In short, ShoreBank's founders came to the same realization that many had before them—that operating a profitable bank in a poor and segregated ghetto is a challenge. Still, ShoreBank enjoyed more outside "socially inclined" capital investment than most black-owned banks. They had private funders who "invested with the understanding that the primary purpose of their investment is to do development and not maximize return on capital."[78]

Bill Clinton had visited the bank in 1985 as Arkansas governor and called it "the most important bank in America."[79] In promoting the ShoreBank model, Clinton outlined his early vision for community empowerment:

> You have to enable people to take control of their own destiny. We need to create a small-business entrepreneurial economy in every underclass urban area and rural area in the country through the use of banks like the South Shore Bank, which played a major role in revitalizing the South Side of Chicago. To most people, "empowerment" sounds like a buzzword, but the truth is that America can't get very far with a dependent or helpless population. Trying to create an entrepreneurial economy around a different sort of banking system, investing in public-works jobs in the near term and giving people control over their living conditions and requiring them to take more responsibility for it—those are the kinds of things that I think would make a real difference.[80]

What he called a "different sort of banking system" was one in which a community's banks were "owned and operated by the people who live there." This had been the theory of black capitalism all along—the premise being that control of banking within a community would lead to "empowerment" and economic equality. This philosophy was not new, but Clinton would back up his vision of community capitalism with significant tax credits, unlike previous administrations, whose support of the idea was limited to rhetoric.

In 1992, Clinton made a campaign promise that he would establish one hundred banks modeled after ShoreBank across the country.[81] The result was the CDBA, which promised to "promote economic revitalization and community development through investment in and assistance to community development financial institutions." The law was race-neutral, but its clear mission was to propagate more banks in the ghetto just like ShoreBank. These banks, called CDFIs, were defined as institutions that (1) had "a primary mission of promoting community development"; (2) "[served] an investment area or targeted population"; and (3) "provide[d] development services in conjunction with equity investments or loans."[82]

This "third way" approach to black banking found proponents across the racial and political spectrum. African American Senator Carol Mosely-Braun remarked that the bill "suggests that the financial institutions can do well and do good simultaneously . . . that financial institutions can make money by expanding credit opportunities to underserved communities."[83] Republican Congressman Tom Ridge remarked that "communities without credit are very much like land without rain, nothing grows."[84] Democratic Senator Ted Kennedy said that "whole segments of our people in this country are unfairly denied access to credit, [it is our job] to make certain that financial institutions make credit available to all of those people who can afford to pay it back."[85] The issue at hand, according to one senator, was "not *whether* community development banks are a good idea . . . , but rather how do we establish them."[86]

The central theory behind the CDFI was that it would find heretofore hidden profits in the ghetto. Former Treasury Secretary Lawrence Summers envisioned "[a] successful CDFI [as] perhaps best compared to a niche venture capital firm that deploys its superior knowledge of an emerging market niche to invest and manage risk better than other investors."[87] Summers labeled these banks "market scouts" that would seek out profits in overlooked markets. Yet black-owned banks had long been using their "superior knowledge" to try to make profits in the ghetto, only to find that the stubborn financial ecosystem of the ghetto economy had always stood in the way, as CDFIs would soon learn. Like black-owned banks, CDFI's have struggled to remain profitable despite help from the tax code. CDFIs routinely show weaker financial performance across the board compared with their more conventional peers.[88] The lodestar, Shore-Bank itself, did not fare well, and its eventual demise would be as newsworthy as its rise.

The CDFI fund got a boost in 2000 with the New Market Tax Credit (NMTC), which was created to "direct new business capital to low-income communities, facilitate economic development in these communities, and encourage investment in high-risk areas." The NMTC was passed along with the New Markets Venture Capital (NMVC) initiatives, and Clinton called them "the most significant effort ever" to help distressed communities by leveraging private investment.[89] The bill provided that any project whose primary aim was to invest in low-income communities would get a tax break equaling 39 percent of its investment over time.[90] However, the design of the program carried certain distorting features that made it more likely that funds would flow toward projects or proposals that were more profitable, rather than those that were more effective at meeting the program's goals. One reason was that the Treasury, the fund's administrator, used geography to determine what areas were disadvantaged. This would not seem to be a problem as poverty was usually concentrated in geographically defined ghettos or rural areas, but the areas marked as eligible were too large and included affluent downtown business areas close to historically disadvantaged ghettos. For example, Wall Street was initially classified as an eligible low-income area.

Moreover, Treasury, whose institutional concern was to maintain the fund's profitability, consistently chose projects that promised more profits and had less risk. The majority of CDFI investments have gone to real estate developments in low-income communities, and the recipients have been larger, more established banks.[91] Minority banks have been essentially shut out of this program—since its inception, only between 2 and 6 percent of these funds have been awarded to minority banks.[92] Funds meant to revitalize the ghetto have instead gone to firms outside the ghetto that have financed development projects within it, a situation that only exacerbated the ghetto's profit leakage.[93] For a mission focused on extracting profits from enterprise zones, this is not surprising.

If the CDFI fund was rooted in the black capitalism model, the Community Reinvestment Act (CRA) was rooted in the original affirmative action model. Its justification was to remedy a history of discriminatory redlining, and its mission was to require mainstream banks to lend a fair portion of their loans to the ghetto. Although redlining had been based on explicit racial discrimination, the CRA had to be designed to be color-blind. Much like affirmative action, the act has been one of the most vilified of banking laws, even as it was criticized by civil rights groups as "toothless" in counteracting the legacy of past injustices such as redlining.[94]

The bill was sponsored by Senator William Proxmire in 1977 when he served as chair of the Senate Banking Committee. Proxmire had helped pass the Home Mortgage Disclosure Act (HMDA) in 1975, which had forced banks to divulge loan information based on race. Armed with HMDA data that revealed that banks were deliberately avoiding making loans in black communities, Proxmire crafted a legislative remedy. He reasoned that because banks had created the problem, they had a duty to remedy it. He also believed that banks had an "obligation to help meet the credit needs" of their local communities. He said that the CRA was based on the "widely shared assumption" that "a public charter conveys numerous economic benefits and in return it is legitimate for public policy and regulatory practice to require some public purpose. . . ." The senator claimed that banking was "a franchise to serve local convenience and needs," and therefore "it is fair for the public to ask something in return."[95] In other words, Proxmire acknowledged that banks benefited from a healthy amount of public support, which meant that they had to serve public needs, or at least not discriminate against disadvantaged members of the public. This perspective was out of sync with the prevailing neoliberal market philosophy that held that the only obligations banks had were to their shareholders.

Specifically, the bill required banks to prepare annual reports describing whether they were meeting the credit needs of low- to moderate-income residents. Bank regulators were to rate each bank from "Outstanding" to "Substantial Noncompliance" based on the quantity of loans they were issuing in low-income areas.[96] The bill did not force banks to lend or open branches in any particular community, but a negative CRA rating could be used by a bank regulator to deny a bank's application for merger or any other change that required regulatory approval.[97]

When it was introduced, the law was reviled by many bankers and their allies. Republican Senator Phil Gramm called the act "an evil like slavery in the pre–Civil War era."[98] "It's unbelievable," fumed one anonymous southern banker, "These people are trying to enforce a change in social policy over the back of the banking industry."[99] Other opponents claimed that the bill went against efficient market forces and required banks to make unprofitable loans. Indeed, if the loans were profitable, banks would not have needed regulatory nudges to make them.[100]

On the other side, community groups have argued that the CRA is more about process than actual reform.[101] For example, banks are rated by how many times they meet with a community group, as opposed to whether anything comes of those meetings. Loans are also measured by quantity as opposed to quality. The CRA does not ask whether the bank's practices are building the community or are likely to produce positive results in the long run; rather, it keeps a checklist of actions meant to prove that the bank is making an effort. The law also hurt black banks as they have struggled to comply with the CRA. This seems counterintuitive—black banks had been doing the very thing the law requires other banks to do. However, since the CRA has assessed compliance by measuring the quantity of loans granted, black banks consistently fall short because they offer fewer loans than average. Many black banks thus had noncompliant CRA ratings that then entail regulatory censure.[102]

The CRA still sits awkwardly between a group of people who believe it does not achieve nearly enough and another group that believe it requires too much.[103] As a result, the resemblance to affirmative action in college admission is striking. Much like affirmative action, there is a perceived feeling that institutions are being forced to hire lower-quality employees or make lower-quality loans to appease "PC culture," "social justice," "community activism," or some vague sense of social morality that is not meritocratic and poses unjustified social burdens on the bottom line. Schools should only select students based on academic merit, and banks should only lend based on profitability. Affirmative action and the CRA, their detractors claim, conflict with a natural meritocracy or an efficient market.

Affirmative action opponents claim that the pool of minority applicants perform worse than white applicants, and therefore when underperforming minority students are admitted, there is a "mismatch" of capacity that harms both the school and the applicant.[104] According to this widely cited "mismatch theory," whites should continue to dominate elite universities until blacks catch up naturally. Banks also claim that they should avoid lending in distressed areas, not because they are discriminating, but because those areas are not profitable and those loans are riskier. Residents of such areas have fewer resources and are more likely to default on a loan. Applying the mismatch model to banking, borrowers should work to earn those bank loans instead of being offered them before they are ready—a mismatch that can hurt the bank, society, and the borrower.

Such arguments are based on snapshots of surface-level problems and fail to explore why black students and black borrowers fall behind whites in the first place. A longer historical view reveals that the reason the ghetto does not yield profitable loans is due to a history of segregation—segregation that was enacted through lending discrimination perpetuated by the very firms now being asked to mend the gap. Once the Supreme Court decided that past injustice could not justify present benefits, it seemed to erase the nation's memory of the past injustice and allow for these types of short-sighted arguments in opposition to any program meant to address a historic wrong. The long debate over the CRA erupted after the financial crisis, with some even implausibly blaming the CRA for precipitating the financial crisis.

Though the CRA is still in effect, Proxmire's view of banks as public-serving community institutions soon became a historical relic. During the 1980s and 1990s, the very nature of U.S. finance and banking changed fundamentally, with profound and surprising repercussions for black wealth accumulation.

One of the most consequential financial innovations of the century was the mortgage-backed security (MBS), which fundamentally changed the secondary mortgage market. In 1938, Fannie Mae, the first government-sponsored enterprise (GSE), was created to facilitate the sale of mortgages in the secondary market. The 1968 Fair Housing Act privatized Fannie Mae and spun off a new entity, the Government National Mortgage Association (GNMA, or Ginnie Mae), which was to remain under government control. Fannie Mae mortgages would no longer be counted on the government's books. The third GSE, Freddie Mac, was created in 1970 to help expand the private secondary market for mortgage loans. Freddie Mac was never sponsored by the government, but it had the warm glow of government support because of its association with the other two giants.

In 1971 Freddie Mac issued a product called a participation certificate, which grouped mortgages together and allowed an investor to buy a slice of a bundle of mortgages and receive a proportion of dividends on the entire bundle. This innovation diminished investor risk by spreading out the losses from defaults onto multiple parties. Fannie Mae improved on the idea in 1981 with the mortgage-backed security, which was similar to the participation certificate, but was more easily tradable and accessible to investors. Lower risk of loss led to more investments, which led to more capital flowing through the mortgage market, which led to more mortgage lending. The MBS accelerated the mortgage market and became an attractive vehicle for large investors, including pension funds, foreign countries, and corporations. Banks could now originate a mortgage and immediately sell it on the secondary market, where it would be bought and traded by a variety of new MBS investors.

Mortgage-backed securities rescued the mortgage market from a severe capital shortage. By 1970, bank withdrawals had surpassed bank deposits at thrifts and banks around the country. According to Robert Pease of the Mortgage Bankers of America in a 1970 statement, "except for FNMA, there is almost no money available for residential housing. We are in a real honest-to-goodness housing crisis!"[105] Thanks to Fannie Mae's creation of the MBS, capital from around the world began pouring into American mortgage markets, and capital became plentiful once again. The transformed mortgage market was built on a chain of transactions that separated borrowers from investors across a coordinated world market. It resembled the eighteenth-century cotton market, where capital from abroad flooded U.S. markets and created financial innovations, new products, and new sources of profits.

Lending decisions were no longer made based on a relationship between lender and borrower, but through objective numerical formulas. Banks or other mortgage originators would make any loan the secondary market would buy. Because banks were not keeping these loans on their books, they worried less about whether the borrower could actually repay. Their main objective was to issue loans that conformed to the standards set by Fannie and Freddie, which made them tradable. Lending became standardized and hassle-free. Some believed that the new market was also risk-free. The secondary mortgage market soon developed an insatiable appetite for mortgage loans. Banks kept originating them. Investors kept buying. There were not enough loans to feed the beast, so ingenious bankers created products that were based on other products. For example, the collateralized debt obligation (CDO) was a complex bundle of tradable debt based on mortgage securities. These derivative products created new investments based on "tranches" of mortgage debt. Derivatives split and spliced mortgage loans that were so far removed from the actual mortgage loan that the whole system resembled a house of cards.[106]

Even with the bundling and splitting of tranches, Wall Street needed more mortgage borrowers, so it created the subprime market. These were loans to borrowers who did not meet the underwriting standards set forth by the GSEs, or "prime" loans. Subprime borrowers were riskier borrowers, either because they had fewer assets, lower credit score, or lower incomes. But in finance, higher risk is rewarded with higher yield, so mortgage brokers made even higher premiums from subprime loans.[107] So they went looking for a group of potential borrowers who had heretofore been deemed too risky. And they found them in black communities.

The flip side of deprivation has always been exploitation. After years of being a banking desert, as barren as Death Valley itself, the ghetto became a hub for casinos. The black population found itself courted by, or more accurately targeted by, subprime lenders. Just as contract sellers had exploited the credit-starved and redlined ghettos, once again, high-priced lenders filled the void. High-interest mortgages were made legal by Congress and the courts, who, guided by the ethos that fewer government regulations would produce a healthier banking industry, lifted caps on interest rates. The 1980 Depository Institutions Deregulation and Monetary Control Act (DIDMCA), the 1982 Garn-St. Germain Depository Institutions Act, and other deregulatory legislation paved the way for subprime loans, and the 1978 Supreme Court case *Marquette National Bank v. First of Omaha* made state usury laws practically ineffectual, leading to a steady rise in interest rates. Some of these mortgage interest rates—34 percent APR with fees and balloon payments—were in loan shark territory.[108]

As early as the 1980s, studies confirmed that another Jim Crow credit market had formed—this time in mortgages. Whites systematically received lower interest rates and longer repayment periods than blacks.[109] A 1991 study by the Federal Reserve of 6.4 million home mortgage applications found that there was widespread and institutionalized racial discrimination in the U.S. banking system.[110] Blacks who qualified for prime mortgages were being disproportionately sold subprime loans. A HUD study found that subprime loans were five times more likely in black neighborhoods than in white ones between 1993 and 1998. In other words, "high-cost subprime lending accounted for 51% of home loans" in black neighborhoods, versus only 9 percent in white ones. Moreover, "homeowners in *high income* black neighborhoods [were] twice as likely as homeowners in low income white neighborhoods to have subprime loans."[111]

Several of these studies identified race of the borrower as the
key predictor determining how much interest was paid on a
mortgage.

Massachusetts Congressman Joe Kennedy quipped that these results "portray an America where credit is a privilege of race and
wealth, not a function of ability to pay back a loan."[112] The reality was
probably far more complex than a simple matter of racial discrimination, however. There was certainly racism in lending—lenders
continued to view blacks as being less creditworthy regardless of
their financial statements, and they continued to offer blacks higher
rate loans. However, many blacks also had fewer assets and lower
incomes, which made them inherently riskier borrowers.[113] The
market had come looking for risky borrowers to exploit—and they
used race as a blunt proxy, such that wealthy and creditworthy
blacks were sold more expensive loans than they merited.

Consumer loans also came flooding into the ghetto. Where credit
card issuers had been avoiding the zip codes where blacks lived, by
the 1980s they joined the mortgage lenders and began looking for
them. Credit cards had previously been sold to the affluent—in fact,
having a credit card was considered a sign of wealth. But wealthy
customers were no longer profitable for credit card companies,
which were now flush with capital and looking for more yield.
Wealthy customers paid no interest or fees because they paid off
their balances each month—they were not "revolvers"—borrowers
who paid interest to carry their balance from one month to the next.
Credit card companies needed more revolvers if they wanted to
make more profits.[114] With the usury cap lifted and the general aversion to risk abated, lenders went looking for higher profits on high-
risk borrowers. They found their ideal customers in the credit- and
wealth-starved ghetto. And when they did, these revolvers, who paid
interest each month, began to subsidize the credit cards of the
wealthy. Academics who studied the mechanisms used by credit
card companies to find revolvers discovered that credit card companies were using race to find new customers. According to their
data, "the most profitable group to lend to, if a bank were maximizing
finance charges, would be black Americans," because blacks were
three times as likely as whites to revolve their debts.[115]

Credit issuers pulled on blacks to borrow so that they could profit
from the attendant fees and interest. At the same time, blacks were

being pushed to borrow by their low and volatile wages. Credit had become a necessity for both middle-class and low-income Americans of all races as wages and real economic growth had stagnated. Consumer debt exploded in the 1970s and kept expanding; and what was even more alarming was that the gap between what was being borrowed and what was being repaid was also growing exponentially larger.[116] The economy was running on fumes—wages were stagnant, prices were increasing, and debt was being used to bridge the gap. Americans borrowed because they had to, and credit card issuers lent because there were profits to be made. The two sides made a Faustian bargain, but it was the borrowers who paid for it dearly every month—in perpetuity, with interest.

The problem for black borrowers was no longer an inadequate *quantity* of mortgage credit, but the inferior *quality* of that credit. In other words, instead of refusing to lend in black neighborhoods, subprime lenders were focusing their efforts there. Senator Donald Riegle of Michigan called it "reverse redlining." One attorney claimed, "This is a system of segregation, really. We don't have separate water fountains, but we have separate lending institutions."[117] The "market scouts" or entrepreneurs became "incentivized" to make profits in the ghetto "enterprise zones." After years of being left out of the mortgage market, black subprime borrowers were exactly what Wall Street's hungry mortgage beast was looking for. The ultimate effect was a disproportionate wiping out of black wealth when these subprime loans blew up two decades later.

Alongside the massive changes in the credit market, and certainly spurred by it, the nature of American banks also changed. From the mid-1970s until the early 2000s, banks asked for and were granted wave after wave of deregulation that eroded the walls that the New Deal–era legislation like the Glass-Steagall Act had imposed around banks to keep them safe and simple. Banks wanted to compete in the fast-moving, highly profitable, globalized markets—even if that meant taking risks with other people's money.[118] Some of the prohibitions had indeed become outdated and overly restrictive, but after years of stability and profits, bankers had also regained their appetite for risk. Free-market ideology was deeply entrenched in Washington, and there were few dissenters when the bank lobbyists pushed on regulators to leave them alone and let the market's invisible hand regulate them. Policymakers and regulators believed, despite much historical evidence to the contrary, that banks could operate safely without any government interference. Most scholars agree that the 2008 financial crisis was caused, in part, by bank deregulation, but there is still ongoing disagreement and debate about the right balance of regulation.

What is not debated is the effect of the era of deregulation on the character of the banking sector. American banking went from an industry consisting of small community banks to one that was dominated by a few large bank holding companies operating extensive branch networks. As a result of the banking transformation enabled by deregulation, financial innovation, globalization, and new technology, the simple banking of the past half century—the 3-6-3 model of taking deposits, lending, and golf—became obsolete and unprofitable. No longer can a community bank survive by simply taking deposits and making FHA loans to the middle class. Today, a profitable bank holding company engages in deposit-taking and lending, but also trading in derivatives, stock market speculation, broker-dealer operations, insurance, and merchant banking. This increased size and complexity has led to a finance-dominated economy and unprecedented profits (and risks). It also led to cannibalization of weak banks by the strong.

Bank of America, formerly the Bank of Italy, was emblematic of the change. Hugh McColl, CEO of the conglomerate from 1983 until 2001, succinctly described the mantra of the age: "You're either growing or dying. So we grew."[119] By mergers and acquisitions, the bank created a vast financial empire. It was not alone. Citibank, Wells Fargo, and JPMorgan Chase were doing the same thing. As part of the transformation, these banks closed branches in less profitable locations and moved operations to higher-yield markets. Community banks now had to compete with larger and far more efficient mammoth banks. This was the centripetal force the small rural bankers had been trying to fight during the New Deal and that Thomas Jefferson had feared. Now that the New Deal barriers were gone, a massive migration and conglomeration of money toward Wall Street was only natural. In this atmosphere, community banks either merged or died. Many died.[120] More banks merged between 1980 and 1990 than in any preceding decade in U.S. history. In just ten years, from 1982 to 1992, 1,500 banks failed—three-quarters of all U.S. bank failures since the Great

Depression.[121] The least able to compete were banks in rural areas or inner-city ghettos.[122]

The largest black bank to fail was Jackie Robinson's Freedom National Bank of Harlem.[123] The bank's 1990 failure was a devastating blow to Harlem and sent a shock wave through the entire black banking industry, especially because there were cries of discrimination and a double standard by the federal regulators that administered its liquidation. The "kid gloves" that Jackie Robinson had complained about were off now in the new hypercompetitive banking world. Not only did the bank's regulator, the FDIC, not follow the FIRREA mandate to preserve the minority bank; it did not even use its standard protocol in liquidating the bank, causing more hardship than necessary to the banks' customers.

Typically, when a bank fails, the FDIC steps in as a "receiver" and has several options for closing a bank: it can sell the failed bank and all of its accounts to another bank; it can just transfer the deposits to another bank while liquidating the bank's assets; it can pay off insured depositors up to $100,000, the deposit insurance cap at the time; or it can manage the bank until it becomes profitable again. During the heavy merger era of the 1980s and 1990s, the FDIC almost always (90 percent of the time) chose the first route—selling the bank to another one, which assumed all the bank's obligations. In other words, for most bank failures, all the depositors were made whole when the bank failed, even customers who had deposits exceeding the $100,000 insurance cap.[124]

However, when Freedom National Bank of Harlem failed in 1990, the FDIC chose the unusual method of paying off insured depositors only up to the $100,000 maximum. In fact, the FDIC made the even more unusual decision to combine all accounts of a given depositor into one account and then applying the cap, which left many more depositors exposed to losses. Many depositors had purposefully opened several accounts in order to gain the protection of the FDIC, but the FDIC refused to insure those accounts, even though that had been their typical practice. This decision by the FDIC meant that the many churches and Harlem-based community groups that were Freedom Bank depositors lost their deposits.[125] The FDIC was heavily criticized for its handling of the matter. After a year of pushback from the borrowers, a special act of Congress was required to force the FDIC to restore most of these deposits.[126]

Observers saw discrimination in the bank's treatment. According to Harlem clergyman and former bank leader Wyatt T. Walker, "Had this been a white bank of comparable size and circumstance, the decision to shut its doors would not have been made so pre- cipitously."[127] In fact, at the same time regulators allowed the FNB to fail, Treasury funds were used to prop up another similarly situ- ated failing bank, the Bank of New England. Scholars reviewing the failure noted that the disparity in treatment was unjustified and likely hastened Freedom Bank's failure and caused more losses than it should have.[128]

Some also criticized the FDIC for not doing more to save the bank, especially because the FDIC had explicit legislative authority to make an extra effort in certain circumstances. Not only did FIRREA require the FDIC to try to maintain minority banks, but the FDIC's "essentiality doctrine" held that if a bank's services are found to be essential in a community, the FDIC had the authority to prevent the bank's failure.[129] The FDIC had invoked this standard in saving other community banks, and as one of the few community banks in Harlem, there was a very good argument to be made that Freedom's services were essential. However, columnist Murray Kempton sug- gested that the bank was likely too small to save. "Freedom National was enfeebled and small, and the regulators reserve their oxygen for the enfeebled and massive." This was a prescient statement consid- ering the "too big to fail" bank bailouts of 2008. Summing up the dilemma of just about every black-owned bank, Kempton lamented, "The tragedy is not that Freedom National had forgotten to do much for the community it was designed to serve but that it did more than any other bank. Poor thing though it was, there is now available nothing even as good." The managers had felt this as well. Former president Sharnia Buford explained, "We had to be businesslike and our credit criteria couldn't be different from banks downtown, but we also had a greater responsibility because we were chartered as a minority bank. We had to empathize with the customer."[130] Jackie Robinson had lost sleep over this same dilemma two decades earlier.

The *Times* reported the failure in November 1990 with the head- line, "Freedom Bank's Failure Hits Harlem Like a Death in the Family." By all accounts, the community's loss was more than financial—it was psychological. The bank's mission had been larger than just finance. Representative Charles B. Rangel, who was working with Mayor David Dinkins and a group of clergymen on a last-minute rescue effort for the bank, called the loss "devastating" to the community. "Symbolically, it's a terrible blow, because this was a black bank formed by Jackie Robinson that was more sensitive to the businesses and people in this community." Depositors, even those who recouped their entire investment, perceived the failure as a blow to the race. One depositor lamented that with the bank's failure, "I lose and Harlem loses." This mirrored the sentiment at the bank's opening, when the Harlem community had called it "our bank." Another customer reported to the *Times*, "It makes me feel helpless, like I've been robbed. . . . It's a step backward for the empowerment of black people." Referring to the FDIC notices on the windows, one depositor quipped, "Freedom Bank is now an enslaved bank." The truth was that the bank was just under FDIC receivership, a process that all failed banks enter.[131]

Black banks were not enslaved by their regulators, but even decades after the Civil Rights Acts, they were still stuck in the same economic trap. Across the board in the 1980s and 1990s, black banks continued to be fragile. Despite renewed focus on community capitalism and the minority banking provisions in legislation, economic studies of these banks continued to show that black banks made fewer loans, were undercapitalized, and had lower profits than other banks.[132] After the deregulatory wave, all small banks struggled to remain competitive against the large bank conglomerates, but black banks also had to contend with the particular circumstances that had always been a particular challenge for them—with a few modern updates. Black banks were still overinvested in less-profitable government securities and were making too few loans. They held 46.5 percent of their total assets in highly liquid securities as opposed to white banks, which only held 29.5 percent on average.[133] They overinvested in government securities because they had high loan losses and too much deposit volatility.[134]

Black banks also had a new capital problem. Capital is the amount of the bank that is owned by investors. Capital is therefore linked to bank profitability in a circular fashion. The more profitable a bank, the more investors it can attract. Black banks had higher costs and higher risks, and therefore lower profits. This meant that they could not attract enough capital investment. Moreover, the legislation aimed at helping them, Section 308 of FIRREA, had created a specific problem for these banks in trying to raise capital. According to Section 308, in order to remain a black-owned bank, the bank had to be owned by a majority of black investors.[135] In other words, they had to make sure that a majority of their shareholders were black. This limited their pool of potential investors and diminished their ability to attract capital. Those black investors who did support black banks were receiving lower profits on their investments—they were making a financial sacrifice in supporting black banks. Still, many did it as a matter of racial pride.

There was also the old and familiar problem of extreme deposit volatility. Economists Timothy Bates and William Bradford conducted a regression analysis on black bank portfolios and determined that their depositors withdrew their deposits at a much higher rate than white banks and in an unpredictable manner, meaning that the banks' inflow and outflow of cash could not be determined beforehand. These volatile deposits needed to be offset by safer assets than loans. Hence the overinvestment in government securities.[136]

Though their customer deposits were highly variable, the government deposits were still the main cause of the bank's deposit volatility, especially because of the regulatory requirement that government deposits exceeding the insured maximum of $100,000 had to be matched dollar for dollar with U.S. government securities. Every deposit dollar held in government securities was one less dollar available for community lending. Economist Lawrence Nash studied the effects of the deposit program on black banks in the 1990s and found that holding these government deposits, instead of aiding black firms, had instead resulted in reduced bank lending in minority communities.[137] The analysis showed a direct correlation: the more government deposits a bank held, the smaller their loan portfolio. These findings challenged allegations that black banks had been lending less because they were just too risk-averse. In fact, their portfolios showed that the banks were making maximum profits given their circumstances. They simply had more hurdles to jump than other banks. Some of these hurdles had been created by the very programs designed to help, like the government deposits and capital bind created by FIREA.

Black banks were still exporting funds from the ghetto. Their overinvestment in government securities meant that they were using their customer deposits to finance mortgages outside their communities. During the era of secondary mortgage markets, the outflow of deposit funds into other people's mortgages was accelerated by the mortgage-backed security. Now, banks anywhere were investing in mortgages everywhere. For black banks, this process was a newer and less obvious way for them to serve as financial sieves—dispersing funds from the ghetto to the broader economy.

The process whereby savings dollars from inner urban areas were being used to invest in assets in other regions was labeled "disinvestment" or "capital export" and was identified and measured in several cities. Economists Harriet Taggart and Kevin Smith measured disinvestment in Boston and found that the mortgage-to-deposit ratio (savings dollars deposited by residents of a neighborhood that are returned to that same neighborhood as mortgage dollars) in core urban areas ranged from 3 percent to 33 percent, but in the outermost suburbs, this ratio ranged from 108 percent to 543 percent.[138] Only a fraction of the deposits invested in urban banks were being used in those areas. They were being deployed instead to multiply capital investments in the suburbs. Another study found that only 10 percent of savings invested in banks in the Bronx were used in the Bronx, with 30 percent being used elsewhere in New York state and the remaining 60 percent used across the country.[140]

As one observer noted, "Given the chance, bankers would do for their business what they had already done for themselves—leave the city."[139] The same could be said of their deposits and capital. To paint a complete picture, deposits from the urban ghetto where prime mortgages were sparse were being used to lend on mortgages in new housing communities across the country. Meanwhile, subprime lenders were sucking away wealth by lending into the black community and exporting the profits to the financial conglomerates on Wall Street. Black banks could not control or multiply the money in the ghetto. Yet policymakers continued to promote the industry while allowing Wall Street–funded loan sharks to plunder the community's wealth.

Even as the Jim Crow credit market and the ghetto economic trap continued, policymakers insisted that race was no longer an issue, that Martin Luther King's dream had been realized, and an equal playing field had been established. Yet despite the rise of black stars in entertainment, sports, business, and the arts, multitudes of black

men and women were born without a chance of ever prying themselves loose from the crime, prison, and poverty trap of the ghetto.
With the firmly established myth that equality had finally been
achieved, black poverty and crime could only be explained as a sign
of moral failure, and the only acceptable response to the failure to
rise out of the ghetto was tough love and forceful containment. While
policymakers were celebrating the triumph of equality and capitalism, the invisible hand of the free market was actually pulling
apart and *increasing* the opportunity and wealth gap between black
and white.[141]

The Color of Money Matters

In 2004, the young senator from Illinois, Barack Obama, riveted the nation as he took center stage at the Democratic National Convention and promised, among other things, to bridge the racial divide. His message and his very identity seemed to be the end of the road—the capstone to two centuries of racial struggle, an outcome that could hardly have been dreamed of by Douglass, Washington, Du Bois, King, or Malcolm, a final rebuke to centuries of Jim Crow and outright hostility. "There's not a black America and white America and Latino America and Asian America," he said, "there's the United States of America." Here was the human bridge across the racial chasm. "Yes, we can," he promised, and the majority of the country fervently believed in Obama's hope.[1] And yet eight years could not uproot three centuries of racism that has sustained the social and economic segregation of African Americans.

By 2015 43 percent of Republicans believed the president was a Muslim.[2] Having entered politics by speculating that President Obama was actually a foreign-born African masquerading as an American and demanding that he produce his birth certificate, Donald Trump was elected president in 2016. Trump's electoral upset was due to many factors, but undeniably, part of Trump's appeal was rooted in a racist backlash to Obama's presidency.[3] After a long and painful recession, there were signs that blacks and other outsiders had once again become the scapegoats for the economic pressures affecting white Americans. White Americans expressed a feeling of having been betrayed by their government, believing that the government was helping blacks and other minorities at their expense. They blamed the "special status of blacks" as a "serious obstacle to their personal achievement."[4] By 2016 almost half of whites surveyed believed that discrimination against whites was just as bad or an even bigger problem than discrimination against blacks.[5] Once racial tribalism was used to justify political actions, it remained a potent political weapon.[6]

Donald Trump's campaign targeted this resentment in much the
same way that Nixon's campaign had done, using the same racial dog
whistles as his predecessors. In President Trump's first Black History
Month address, he began by praising Martin Luther King as an "incredible example [who] is unique in American history" and then
quickly shifted to his repeated campaign promise to strengthen law
and order by increasing the presence of law enforcement in black
communities.[7] On the campaign trail, he outlined his "New Deal
with Black America" at a Charlotte, North Carolina, rally. Trump recognized that black poverty had not abated due to years of failed
policies and promised that through his plan, "the cycle of poverty
can be broken."[8] He promised to do this by lowering taxes, providing
"tax holidays for inner-city investments," and rolling back financial
regulations in order to "make it easier for young African-Americans
to get credit to pursue their dreams in business and create jobs in
their communities." He said that he would pursue as a top priority
"helping African-American businesses get the credit they need" and
vowed to "encourage small-business creation by allowing social
welfare workers to convert poverty assistance into repayable but
forgiveable micro-loans." He also repeated his promise to increase
law enforcement in black communities.[9]

In fact, the tension between law enforcement and the black community had hit another boiling point. The city of Ferguson, Missouri, erupted after police killed Michael Brown, a black man, in
2014. This was one of the largest race riots the country had seen in
recent memory, and it marked the genesis of the Black Lives Matter
movement. Ferguson is a suburb of St. Louis, one of the most segregated cities in the United States.[10] It was defined as a "resegregated" city, created by the exodus of black residents from the
newly gentrified inner city of St. Louis.[11] Ferguson's population was
two-thirds black and predominantly low-income, with more than
one-fifth of the residents living below the poverty level.[12] The
subpar schools were almost completely segregated, and 26 percent
of blacks there were unemployed compared to 6 percent of whites.[13]
Rioters destroyed white-owned commercial property. The National
Guard was dispatched, and Americans watched as demonstrators
burned cars and buildings; police in military gear descended on the
city, imposed a curfew, and eventually quelled the protests. When
Fox News interviewed one looter, he explained that the message the

city had sent to its black residents was "we're gonna eat and you guys are gonna starve." He replied, "It's not gonna happen. Not in St. Louis.[14]

The following year Baltimore exploded. A Harvard study found that Baltimore was the nation's worst city with respect to childhood poverty and lack of economic opportunity.[15] It was also one of the most segregated cities in the country, and the financial crisis had created an acute foreclosure crisis there.[16] In 2015 Baltimore was the scene of another uprising after the funeral of Freddie Gray, who had died of spinal injuries while in police custody. What began as a peaceful protest turned violent when rioters looted a CVS and destroyed a police vehicle. Soon fires engulfed the downtown business area. "It's regrettable, what's happening now," the Reverend Jesse Jackson told the *Baltimore Sun*. "You're looking at the actions of cynicism and hopelessness."[17] Governor Larry Hogan declared a state of emergency, and about 5,000 state and national law enforcement officers descended on the city, quickly putting an end to the riots.

The financial crisis of 2008 disproportionately affected segregated black communities and turned the persistent racial wealth gap into a chasm. The financial crisis wiped out 53 percent of total black wealth.[18] As the head of the Congressional Black Caucus, Representative G. K. Butterfield, said in 2015, "Black America is in a state of emergency!"[19] Today, black families have an average net wealth of $11,000 compared to a white family's average of $141,900. Pew data reveals that white families have thirteen times more wealth than black families.[20] The wealth gap exists at every income and education level. On average, white families with college degrees have over $300,000 more wealth than black families with college degrees. A third of black families have no assets at all.[21] Moreover, studies reveal that the gap is accelerating—over the last thirty years, the average wealth of white families has grown at three times the rate for average black families.[22] This growing divide perpetuates injustices hard to capture behind the latest news of riots and protests.

The wealth gap is where the injustices sown in the past grow imperceptibly in the present.[23] The cumulative effects of discrimination, segregation, and the economic detour for black businesses have created self-perpetuating forces that continue to make black wealth accumulation difficult. The perpetuation of poverty is stunning—75 percent of black children who grow up in families in the bottom wealth category remain in that same category as adults.[24] A 2013 study found that for white families, every additional dollar they earn in income leads to $5.19 in wealth. For black families, each dollar creates only sixty-nine cents in total wealth.[25] This is why the wealth gap between blacks and whites can continue to grow even when de jure discrimination ended decades ago. Blacks are no longer prohibited from highly paid employment, and there are black stars in every field and almost every top office, including the highest political office, but the majority of black people are as poor as they have ever been and live in regions that offer them little hope for economic progress.

President Obama acknowledged in his first public speech in 2004 "that in no other country on earth is my story even possible." But if Obama's identity was uniquely American, he was also unique among black Americans. He started his 2004 speech by introducing his Kansan grandparents who helped raise him. He said that "after the war, they studied on the GI Bill, bought a house through FHA and later moved west, all the way to Hawaii, in search of opportunity."[26] Here was a black man who was able to enjoy a uniquely white privilege passed down through the postwar generation.

From one generation to the next, wealth can perpetuate and reinforce itself, not only as it is passed down literally, but because the attendants of wealth also ripple across generations. Many iterations of racial inequality, such as differences in educational attainment, income, and even incarceration, can be traced back to differences in generational wealth.[27] Nevertheless, because of the prevalent belief that the wealth gap is a natural result of market forces, many Americans continue to blame the poor for their own predicament, an idea described by Lawrence Bobo as "laissez faire racism."[28]

It is worth noting that a broad body of research reveals just how connected wealth is to a broad array of outcomes and how poverty perpetuates itself. For example, lower wealth is not caused by blacks refusing to work or get an education, as some have claimed.[29] In fact, it is more likely that a family's wealth determines a family member's ability to get an education or a high-paying job.[30] Those without wealth often live in resource-poor communities with subpar schools and restricted social networks.[31] More directly, a family's assets strongly predict whether and where a child can secure higher education.[32] Crime also grows where opportunities are few, and crime in turn tends to diminish opportunity. It is therefore unlikely that the education gap between blacks and whites was caused by inherent biological differences between the races, as Charles Murray and Richard Herrnstein explained in their much-discussed 1994 book, *The Bell Curve*.

It is also unlikely that black poverty is caused by a lack of "family values" or of broken families.[33] It is true that single-parent homes perpetuate the cycle of poverty and that poverty, in turn, creates more single-parent homes. But which came first, the "lack of fathers" or the lack of jobs for them? Economic hardship *causes* black families to extend their homes to encompass many extended family members who need support.[34] Poverty also causes stress, depression, and poor heath, all of which threaten family stability. Not surprisingly, the level of asset ownership is a much more significant determinant of stable marriages within the black, no less than the white, community.[35] Blacks are not choosing to be in single-parent households because they are gaming the welfare system. Poverty creates joblessness, crime, social decay, and family deterioration. To state that poverty is linked to these "cultural forces" is to state the obvious, but it is a gross oversimplification to say that culture *creates* poverty and stop there. Culture is as much a reflection of poverty as it is a cause.

Recent research has revealed even more profound psychological effects of poverty on behavior and outlook. Eviction, homelessness, and extended poverty are experienced as psychological trauma, especially for children. Children who grow up in an environment of scarcity, fear, or social disorder are exposed to stress that significantly hinders their social and academic capacity. It even affects their decision-making process.[36] The famous "marshmallow experiment" revealed that children who could practice self-control and delay gratification (wait for the second marshmallow) were more successful as adults across the board.[37] Yet the experiment has been misunderstood as it relates to poverty. One consistent result of the experiment, noted by its designer Walter Mischel and replicated by every subsequent experimenter, was that the poor consistently "failed" the marshmallow test. One might be tempted to believe that being poor was thus a result of a lack of self-control. However, as researchers like Melissa Sturge-Apple have homed in on the decision-making process, they have revealed a much more complex story. By measuring the heart rate and brain activity of the children during the test, the experimenters revealed that the poor children were making a careful and calm choice to enjoy the marshmallow immediately instead of waiting for an uncertain second marshmallow. "When resources are low and scarce, the rational decision is to take the immediate benefit and to discount future gain." Calmer decision making—or less impulsiveness—among wealthy children led them to wait for the additional treat, but that same measured and calm decision making led the poor children to decide not to wait. Poor children's rational decision making was misinterpreted as lack of self-control.[38] Today, one in three black children grows up in poverty compared to one out of ten white children. One out of five black children under the age of five grow up in extreme poverty.[39]

Poverty changes decision making for adults as well. Behavioral economists Sendhil Mullainathan and Eldar Shafir have demonstrated that poverty, or scarcity of any kind, creates a distinct mental state. A state of scarcity is such a heavy mental burden that it can lead to temporarily lower cognitive ability and shortsighted decision making. This does not mean that the poor have less capacity, but that their capacity is overburdened because living in scarcity takes up significant mental space and leaves less room for other mental processes. Those operating under the pressure of scarcity have been shown to eat poorly, parent poorly, make bad decisions, and even wash their hands less often.[40] Scarcity also creates tunneling, which is a hyperfocused mind-set that homes in on the resource in scarcity. Those who are hungry show extreme attention to food. Those who are lonely, to human interactions. Those who are poor focus intensely on money and little else. The poor are actually much more careful with their money than the wealthy. For example, customers leaving a grocery store were asked about the price of certain purchases. The majority of middle-class customers could not recall the amount they had just spent or how much they had spent on items such as toothpaste. The poor overwhelmingly got it right. This undercuts the premise that the poor need financial education so that they can pay attention to where they are spending their money.

Scarcity is not caused by having a low income. It is financial volatility and insecurity that create bandwidth overload. In other words, it is the lack of *wealth*. Wealth is a crucial pillar of stability and a bulwark against devastation, and many black families do not have it. Even a small buffer of savings can shield a person from the immense psychological toll of a scarcity mind-set. Can it be that what Moynihan called the "tangle of pathology" was just a natural response to financial insecurity and scarcity? Modern science has undercut the old dogmas of biological and cultural inferiority by making it clear that decision making is much more connected to surrounding circumstances than previously thought. Instead, policymakers continue to address poverty as though it were a result of individual decision making, which is why solutions like financial literacy or education have predictably yielded little fruit. "Somehow, people absurdly believe—and they have done do for much of our history," laments Eddie Glaude, "that black social misery is the result of hundreds of thousands of unrelated bad individual decisions by black people all across this country."[41]

When Treasury Secretary Jack Lew was asked by the president of *Black Enterprise* magazine in 2016 to address the racial wealth gap, he said that the Treasury Department was very concerned about the gap, and he acknowledged that the financial crisis had wiped out a significant portion of black wealth. He then went on to offer some advice on how to accumulate wealth. "A lot of people say they can't afford to save. I understand. Living on a paycheck to paycheck income is really challenging. I experienced it at the beginning of my career and I know how hard it is. By the same token, most people buy a cup of coffee without thinking about it. Most people buy an extra magazine or a video without thinking about it. . . . If you take the accumulated decisions people make lightly and in one of those occasions say, I am going to put money away for retirement, you'd see people start out with more. . . . I think financial education, financial literacy is about understanding that some people buying a home might not be a good idea."[42] This is all sound advice from the treasury secretary, but the entire black community could abstain from lattes indefinitely and yet the wealth gap would persist. In reality, blacks save an average of 11 percent of their annual income while whites save only 10 percent.[43] The idea of blacks spending frivolously while whites save their pennies is a meaningless, damaging, and sadly persistent stereotype.

While government officials urge blacks to save, government policies are perpetuating the wealth gap. The American tax code distributes wealth toward homeowners because the most significant tax deductions for the middle class are related to mortgage interest deductions. These tax benefits cost the government over $130 billion a year, and their benefits flow to the wealthiest 20 percent of Americans. This redistribution of wealth operates as a significant disadvantage to blacks, who have much lower rates of homeownership than whites. Over 70 percent of white families but only 40 percent of blacks own homes, according to the 2016 census.[44] Meanwhile, welfare, affordable housing subsidies, and other first-time homeowner initiatives have been gradually cut over the last decades.[45]

Even though segregation remains a primary driver of racial inequality, virtually no one is fighting it. Blacks are still the most segregated group in the country, and the poorest neighborhoods in America are still usually the blackest. Yet after George Romney's Open Communities program failed, there has not been a single federal effort to integrate America.[46] Walter Mondale, who helped pass the Fair Housing Act in 1968, lamented the total lack of progress on integration in a 2015 interview, calling the failure to integrate "one of the great moral failings of our country."[47] A disheartening result of housing segregation is the erosion of the *Brown vs. Board of Education* mandate.[48] The majority of American children today attend de facto segregated schools that have resegregated with the passage of time and the absence of court mandates.[49] Even the black middle class lives in neighborhoods that are more disadvantaged than the white middle class. For example, black families earning $75,000 a year typically live in poorer neighborhoods than white Americans earning $40,000.[50] As Ta-Nahisi Coates has explained, "As a rule, poor black people do not work their way out of the ghetto—and those who do often face the horror of watching their children and grandchildren tumble back."[51]

There was reason to hope that the Obama administration would enforce the Fair Housing Act more effectively. Obama selected affordable housing advocate Shaun Donovan as HUD secretary and civil rights advocate John Trasviña as head of the fair housing office within HUD. For the first time since the 1960s, racial segregation was being discussed by a federal policymaker. In several speeches, Donovan gave a forceful rationale for government action to fight segregation, explaining, "Far more often than not, segregation, isolation and poverty don't occur in spite of government. They happen because of government—by government dollars and government decisions made with government authority." Under Obama, HUD began by unearthing substantial noncompliance with the agency's own rules, a finding substantiated by the Government Accountability Office a year later. In fact, it became clear that HUD officials were not even trained to ensure compliance with fair housing requirements. A senior HUD official explained, "There's a car here and nobody knows how to drive it."[52] The Obama administration, like those before it, chose to focus on litigating housing discrimination.

President Trump has expressed hostility to HUD's mission, and as a real estate mogul, he was sued by the Justice Department for discriminating against black tenants in his apartment buildings.[53] Trump appointed neurosurgeon Ben Carson as HUD secretary. Dr. Carson, who once remarked that "poverty is really more of a choice than anything else," has opposed all government measures to oppose segregation, calling them "social engineering" and akin to communism.[54] The modern Republican Party opposes the very mission of HUD and the FHA mandate, and has pursued dismantling it. In 2012 integrationist crusader George Romney's son, Mitt, told a group in Florida that he would consider closing HUD permanently. "I'm going to take a lot of departments in Washington, and agencies, and combine them," he said. "Things like Housing and Urban Development, which my dad was head of, that might not be around later."[55]

Segregation is the reason the financial sting of the economic downturn most acutely affected blacks. Some called the catastrophic effect on black wealth "the largest drain of wealth" ever to befall the black community.[56] Former Congressman Brad Miller called the crisis and the resulting loss of wealth "an extinction event" for the black community.[57] More than 240,000 black families lost their homes. By 2009, 35 percent of black families had zero or negative wealth.[58] According to Eddie Glaude Jr., "by every relevant statistical measure (employment, wages, wealth, etc.) black America has experienced and is experiencing a depression. This is more like the symptoms of a national congenital disease than the flu."[59] It was subprime mortgage lending that swallowed much of this black wealth.

Even as blacks and other minorities were the hardest hit victims of the crisis, they were also blamed by some conservative hardliners for causing it. When the Financial Crisis Inquiry Commission released its definitive report, it determined that the crisis was caused essentially by banks taking too much risk in the pursuit of profit. Commission member Peter Wallison, a senior fellow at the conservative think tank the American Enterprise Institute, dissented from the group and blamed the financial crisis on government policies like the CRA that promoted lending to minorities.[60] The claim was that the CRA forced banks to lend to minority communities. The theory has since been parroted by politicians, pundits, and academics.[61] Republican congressmen blamed the CRA, stating that "for years Congress has been pushing banks to make risky subprime loans. . . . Congress passed laws that said we're going to fine you and we're going to file lawsuits against you lenders if you don't make risky loans."[62] Two of President Trump's economic advisers explained that the housing crisis was actually caused by the CRA and Bill Clinton, who pushed banks to lend unjustifiably into "credit-deprived areas."[63] A Fox News commentators remarked, "Look . . . you go all the way back to the Community Reinvestment Act, under Jimmy Carter, expanded under Bill and Hillary Clinton—they put the guns to the banks' heads, and said, 'You have got to do these subprime loans.' . . . That's what caused this mess."[64]

Blaming the CRA became code for lending to minorities, and many directed their moral outrage at the "reckless" subprime borrowers. Rick Santelli's infamous rant on the Chicago trading floor that supposedly started the Tea Party movement was a diatribe against the injustice of hardworking Americans who had to pay for irresponsible debtors who greedily bought homes they could not afford. Santelli shouted, "How many of you people want to pay for your neighbor's mortgage that has an extra bathroom and can't pay their bills?" and denounced those being foreclosed on as "losers." The resentment, bearing more than a hint of racial animosity, resonated with many. Research showed that the Tea Party movement itself, ostensibly about government overreach, was directly correlated with a racist backlash.[65] This is consistent with Goldwater's and Nixon's message associating government largesse with free-loading blacks.

The theory that the CRA or government mortgage policy in any way led to the financial crisis has been debunked by scholars as well as influential policymakers including the Federal Reserve chair and the treasury secretary.[66] Every serious analysis has concluded that the CRA did not cause the rise in subprime lending. How could it?

The act was passed in 1977, and subprime lending started heating up more than twenty years later. The majority of the crisis-causing subprime loans were not made by lenders with any CRA obligations—only 6 percent of subprime loans were even CRA loans.[67] Those who blame Fannie and Freddie also miss the mark, as most subprime loans were not standard GSE loans, and the timing of lowered underwriting standards did not match the heating up of the subprime market.[68] Yet pundits and politicians continue to blame the financial crisis on the one law that was aimed at increasing minority lending. It is likely that at least some part of the public still believes blacks and other minorities are undeserving of government benefits and that they take more than their share. Like President Reagan's "welfare queen" story, this narrative paints low-income subprime borrowers as exploiters of taxpayer money and government largesse.[69] It is a convenient fiction that protects banks from appropriate regulation and ignores a history of injustice.

Those who construct a story in which banks grudgingly give out loans in order to appease their powerful and high-minded regulators, or to ward off robust coalitions of inner-city poor activists, which is exactly the narrative many have espoused, do not understand the banking industry.[70] The banks wanted subprime loans because they were making unprecedented profits. Subprime lenders popped up in ghettos not because the government or community activists wanted them, but because that was where they could convince more people to take out subprime loans. In fact, many activist and consumer groups were trying to fight these subprime lenders.[71]

Subprime mortgage lending took over the market not because borrower demand increased, but because banker and investor demand did. It is a simple story of profits. Wall Street banks had previously stayed away from this market because there was no profit in it, but they became hungry for subprime loans once they became profitable. The story of the MBS and the transformation of the mortgage market has already been discussed in Chapter 7, but in the years preceding the crisis, the subprime market began overheating due to increased demand for investments by what economists have labeled a "savings glut." Foreign investors flooded U.S. markets with money. This oversupply of cheap cash lowered U.S. treasury note yields, and so the money flowed into the next safest investment—

asset-backed securities, or home mortgages. The financial sector met the demand by selling, bundling, insuring, and creating new "structured products," and then originating more mortgage loans. This demand created the subprime mortgage market—a new supply of loans that produced even higher yields for investors. The crisis was not created by poor minorities demanding housing loans, but by Wall Street demanding more loans and then lobbying for government policies that lowered underwriting standards.[72]

A small army of mortgage brokers went looking for new borrowers, knowing that as soon as they could get the papers drawn up, a Wall Street bank would buy the loan. These neighborhoods were open for the attack. Most ghetto residents had "thin file" credit scores, meaning they had very little meaningful credit history. They were risky borrowers because of their marginal economic standing, but they were a source of untapped profits in the house of cards being created by debt. For example, JPMorgan Chase marketed its "no doc" and "liar loans" (where the lender did not verify any of the information provided on the application), claiming to investors, "It's like money falling from the sky!"[73] The money was actually falling from the subprime borrowers.

So profitable was the subprime market in the years preceding the crisis that banks *chose* not to give prime loans (those insured by the GSEs) and focused instead on subprime loans. The *Wall Street Journal* reported that more than 50 percent of borrowers who were sold subprime loans could have qualified for prime loans. At the peak of the subprime market in 2006, 61 percent of borrowers were steered toward subprime, which meant that "a significant number of borrowers with top-notch credit signed up for expensive subprime loans."[74] Mortgage brokers made more money for convincing—duping—borrowers into taking out costlier subprime loans than the prime loans that they were eligible for and could more easily afford. The higher the interest paid by borrowers, the bigger the bonus received by the mortgage broker.[75]

And predictably, blacks were much more likely to be sold subprime loans. As economist Vivian Henderson argued decades ago, "racism put blacks in their economic place, but changes in the modern economy make the place in which they find themselves more and more precarious."[76] It was revealed after the crisis that banks were specifically targeting black borrowers for their worst loan products even when they qualified for prime loans.[77] The Center for Responsible Lending found that black borrowers were 150 percent more likely to get high-cost loans.[78] Data collected under the Home Mortgage Disclosure Act confirmed that blacks were being targeted for subprime loans even when they would have qualified for prime loans.[79] Mortgage originators like Countrywide opened branches in inner cities to peddle as many subprime loans as possible. Most of the areas that were targeted for subprime lending were formerly redlined districts—Chicago's black belt, for example, was the area with the most subprime loans between 2004 and 2006.[80] Subprime was just the new face of predatory lending, with some lenders even targeting elderly black homeowners to sell them sham reverse mortgages that resulted in their losing their homes.[81] Deprivation again led to exploitation.[82]

The Department of Justice sued Wells Fargo in 2010 for intentionally and systematically targeting minority borrowers and pushing them toward subprime loans. The DOJ claimed that Wells Fargo and Bank of America, two of the largest mortgage lenders, steered thousands of minority borrowers into costlier subprime loans when whites with a similar credit score were given prime loans.[83] The DOJ unearthed signs of explicit discrimination at Wells Fargo, with loan officers referring to black borrowers as "mud people" and to subprime loans as "ghetto loans."[84] "We just went right after them," Beth Jacobson, a former Wells Fargo loan officer, told the *Times.* "Wells Fargo mortgage had an emerging-markets unit that specifically targeted black churches because it figured church leaders had a lot of influence and could convince congregants to take out subprime loans."[85] Wells Fargo settled the case and avoided trial. Bank of America also settled their discrimination lawsuit, in which the DOJ accused its mortgage issuer, Countrywide, of racial discrimination in lending.[86]

This market was not created by poor minority borrowers, but those at the bottom are often the most likely to be exploited by new credit innovations. Just as exploitative credit arrangements like sharecropping were created because of demand from the worldwide cotton market, subprime lending was connected to a worldwide demand for mortgage loans. Global capital markets found yield in the cotton produced by sharecroppers and in the interest paid by subprime borrowers. That the black community was exploited in both situations speaks to their lack of wealth, political power, and their exclusion from the main channels of economic power. During Reconstruction, black borrowers had no other option for credit, so they entered sharecropping arrangements. A similar situation played out with contract selling when blacks were redlined out of the government loan market. Once again, during the subprime era, the market demanded more loans, and the black population was the most vulnerable population of borrowers—having had limited access to credit for generations. Without malice, capital looking for yield can lead to exploitation if there are structural inequalities. Capitalism itself cannot overcome those inequalities because capital only seeks to accumulate unto itself. Without structural changes, the urban ghetto would never be a lure for wealth-building capital, only a magnet for exploitation.

There are two banking systems in America. One is the regulated and heavily subsidized mainstream banking industry; the other is the unregulated, costly, and often predatory fringe industry. The black community has historically been under the latter system, having been left out of the former. This has come at great expense to that community. Richard Thaler and Cass Sunstein found that blacks pay on average of $425 more for loans than white customers.[87] Most black neighborhoods are "banking deserts," neighborhoods abandoned by mainstream banks.[88] The FDIC's surveys on the "unbanked and underbanked" reveal that 60 percent of blacks are either unbanked or underbanked.[89] In striking contrast, only 3 percent of whites do not have a bank account and 15 percent are underbanked. Those without bank accounts pay up to 10 percent of their income, or around $2,400 per year, just to use their money.[90] That is a meaningful amount of money for low-income Americans, and it is being sucked up by alternative financial services. This problem has been exacerbated since the crisis of 2008, when 93 percent of all bank closings occurred in low-income neighborhoods.[91]

When banks leave a neighborhood, the sharks usually fill the void. Banking deserts are left vulnerable to high-cost payday lenders, title lenders, and other fringe banks.[92] Once the subprime profits dried up as a result of the crisis, banks began avoiding the ghetto again. By 2016, an investigation of mortgage lending in St. Louis found that banks made fewer loans to borrowers in black neighborhoods than white ones. Mortgage applicants from minority zip codes were denied at significantly higher rates than applicants in white neighbor-hoods.[93] Unsurprisingly, it appears that contract selling has actually made a comeback in these areas abandoned by banks. This time, private equity firms are leading the charge.[94] Buyers are given loans that look like mortgages, but they are in fact more like rental agreements, under which the borrower can be evicted because of a missed payment. In one example, a private equity investor bought a foreclosed home for $8,000 and sold it on contract for $36,000.[95]

In banking deserts, blacks rely disproportionately on payday lenders—they are more than twice as likely as any other race to use payday loans.[96] With such costly credit options, it is no wonder that debt collectors extract as much as *five times more* judgments against black neighborhoods than white ones. Two studies conducted between 2015 and 2016 revealed that blacks were much more likely to be sued by debt collectors than any other racial group, even when differences in income were accounted for. One in four black residents in the studied communities was being sued by a debt collector. Most of these lawsuits were similar: large debt collectors suing for small amounts.[97] The study found that debt collectors were not intentionally discriminating, but that "white consumers are, in general, better able to resolve smaller debts."[98] Indeed, the study confirmed that black communities simply have less wealth than white ones and therefore enjoy less of a buffer against hardship.[99]

Unsurprisingly, black college graduates owe an average of $53,000 more than their white counterparts in student debt. Blacks have to borrow more for college and have to carry greater debt several years after graduation—usually from two to three times the amount of white graduates. Black students default on student debt at a rate five times higher than white or Asian graduates and because student loans cannot be discharged in bankruptcy, this debt is carried until it is paid off.[100]

The racial wealth gap not only means that black families have greater difficulty ascending the economic ladder; it also means that it is much easier for these families to fall. Because wealth provides a cushion against life's hard edges, those without it are exposed to devastating financial shocks like bankruptcy, eviction, and apparently lots of lawsuits. These lawsuits further ratchet up the financial pressure through wage garnishments, aggressive collection practices, and criminal prosecutions. These actions create what one black resident in the study called a "web of indebtedness."[101] A wage garnishment can feel like extortion, but increasingly, creditors are using actual extortion. Often the original credit, such as a municipality, sells its debts to an underworld of unregulated debt collectors who threaten debtors with criminal prosecution in order to intimidate them into paying their debts.[102] These threats are usually baseless and illegal, but that does not stop these unscrupulous bounty hunters from continually harassing debtors.

In 2015, a cell phone video showed a police officer shooting an unarmed man, Walter Scott, who was running away from the officer. The press coverage focused on the fact that the officer had allegedly lied about the shooting and appeared on video to be planting a weapon near Scott's body. Less attention was paid to the reason Scott was running away from the officer in the first place. It was revealed that he was likely running because he had unpaid debt and may have been worried about criminal retribution.[103] The wealth disparity leads cryptically and tragically to many seemingly unrelated injustices suffered by the black community.

The destructive economic and social forces created within the boundaries of a racially segregated ghetto are interrelated. The effects of the most recent loss of black wealth were not just in lost homes and bank accounts, but in the resulting loss of social and community capital. From 2003 to 2013, Detroit closed 150 public schools and Chicago closed fifty in 2013 alone, primarily in black and brown neighborhoods. Black unemployment reached a twenty-year high, and black and brown prisoners make up almost 60 percent of the prison population.[104] Many black communities are "opportunity deserts," lacking in paths toward upward mobility yet with an overabundance of pitfalls that result in incarceration or worse. Languishing in what Chimamanda Ngozi Adichie has called "the oppressive lethargy of choicelessness," many are born into and live their whole lives with the certainty that they will not be able to escape their circumstances. The National Urban League reported in 2015 that the state of black America was one of "crisis." The report followed up, in words reminiscent of the Kerner Commission, "America today is a tale of two nations."[105]

The Obama administration did make inroads into poverty alleviation; specifically, the Affordable Care Act was aimed at lowering health-care costs, which are a major source of financial distress for the low income.[106] President Obama, like his predecessors, did not specifically target the racial wealth gap, nor did he advocate a race-based economic agenda. The administration's efforts were a continuation of theories underlying black capitalism and the updated community capitalism of the Clinton administration. In several speeches, Obama heralded the importance of small businesses and minority businesses, including renewing Minority Business Enterprise Week and praising the importance of minority businesses in several small forums.[107] On the campaign trail, he had promised "to help bring businesses back to our inner-cities." He envisioned creating institutions akin to the World Bank to "spur economic development." He lamented that "less than one percent of the $250 billion in venture capital that's invested each year goes to minority businesses that are trying to breathe life into our cities. This has to change." He promised that he would make sure every community had "financial institutions that can help get them started" on the road to building wealth.[108]

These promises were not pursued, either because of the game-changing financial crisis, the antagonistic legislative environment, or perhaps due to the president's lack of conviction on black capitalism. When Obama was asked in 2012 to respond to criticism that his administration had not done enough to support black business—the premise being that helping black business was akin to addressing black poverty—he responded, "I'm not the president of black America. I'm the president of the United States of America."[109] The Treasury did announce in 2015 that it would name its newly created wing after the Freedmen's Bank. This would be the first time, of course, that the Treasury would actually be linked to the bank. (The last time, the link was purely speculative and the depositors paid the price.) The Treasury also decided to put Harriet Tubman on the $20 bill.

Banking agencies are still carrying out their FIRREA legislative mandate to support minority banks. The Minority Bank Deposit Program (MBDP) is still ongoing, which means that federal agencies and federal grant recipients are encouraged to deposit funds into banks owned or controlled by women or minorities.[110] Typical deposit funds are agency deposits of public money, cash advances to federal contractors and grantees, Postal Service funds, and other moneys held by the agencies.[111] The FDIC also runs its own minority bank deposit program, called the Minority Depository Institution

Program (MDIP).[112] The MBDA, the successor to the OMBE, is still active and advertises on its website that it is "the only federal agency created specifically to foster the establishment and growth of minority-owned business in America." Its most advertised feature is a website for minority entrepreneurs called the "Minority Business Internet Portal," which is described as "an e-commerce solution designed for the MBE [Minority Business Enterprise] community."[113]

In 2007, the House Committee on Financial Services held a hearing to assess whether regulatory agencies were meeting the FIRREA mandate of "preserving and expanding minority banks." Black bank representatives and top agency officials testified about the state of minority banks, with a focus on black-owned banks. The hearing was accompanied by an expansive GAO report. The FDIC testified that it was offering "technical assistance" and "training and educational programs" to minority banks.[114] As for the charge to preserve and promote minority banks, the agency explained that it did not have a process in place to do this, but made decisions on a case-by-case basis. The Office of the Comptroller explained that it had held conferences, offered technical assistance, and then after periodic bank examinations, the examiners contacted minority institutions to "make sure that the institution understands any issues or concerns that we have highlighted in the report. And we can help them."[115] The Office of Thrift Supervision (OTS) explained that its program consisted of technical assistance and education.

Education, guidance, training, and counseling—that was the theme of the support being given to black banks. Apparently, it was not just minority subprime borrowers who needed "education," but also minority banks. The regulators have essentially been playing the role of high school guidance counselor—available for advice or technical assistance with the occasional workshops for good measure. With Section 308's vague requirements and no clear mandates from either the president or Congress, what else were they supposed to do but offer regulatory hand-holding?

Unsurprisingly, the minority banks were not relying on their regulators for help. The GAO reported that only 30 percent of minority banks had used the technical assistance offered by regulators.[116] Moreover, no agency had ever assessed whether its "assistance" was actually helping these banks. The GAO revealed that the agencies had "not undertaken the more difficult and time-consuming, but ultimately much more important, task of truly understanding the unique challenges these institutions face" or of trying to tailor their "regulations, supervision and examinations" to help black banks to "survive and prosper."[117] Less than one-third thought the regulators were doing a "very good" or "good" job.[118] Robert Cooper, representing the National Bankers Association, the main trade group for black-owned banks, put it bluntly. "To be honest," said Cooper, "we have not seen much benefit from FIRREA Section 308." Regulators had not applied "any different rules or approaches to minority institutions than majority institutions." Regulators were doing the bare minimum required by law, which amounted to "technical assistance," and had "steadfastly refused" to make use of their available power to benefit minority banks.[119] The regulatory support was a façade, but then again, so was the premise underlying the entire framework.

Even before the financial crisis virtually wiped out the industry, several government studies showed that black banks were lagging *significantly* behind their peers in profitability. According to Standard & Poor's data, the average median return on equity in 2016 was 8.04 percent for the banking industry as a whole. For black-owned banks, the median was just 1.19 percent.[120] The reasons black banks remained unprofitable had not changed after almost a century of operation. Cooper told Congress that the biggest struggles black banks faced were (1) the economically depressed communities they operated in, (2) their need to keep high reserves for losses, (3) higher general expenses than other banks, and (4) higher transaction costs because they dealt with a higher proportion of retail customers on a face-to-face basis.[121] Black banks were still hamstrung by their reliance on small, high-activity deposits, and they made fewer and smaller loans than white banks, which reduced their profitability. They had lower non–interest-based income—19.5 percent compared to 42.7 percent for nonminority banks—because they sold fewer fee-based products to their less wealthy customers.[122] The CEO of Liberty Bank, one of the largest and most successful black-owned banks, described his bank's struggle: "my expenses are twice as much because I have to do more counseling to my borrower. I may have to have guard service because I am in a high crime area. My deposits are much smaller."[123]

While regulators were offering education and training programs to help black banks, it was clear that the black banks knew exactly what their problems were, and it was not a lack of technical knowledge. However, just as it is unfair to place the burden of the black wealth gap on black banks, it is unfair to blame bank regulators for not helping enough. The regulators' sole focus is to manage bank risks; they do not have the tools, mandate, or even the *education* to understand and fix the unique bind in which black banks find themselves.

Perhaps recognizing this limitation, black bank advocates did not ask for more help from regulators during the congressional hearing. What they wanted was meaningful regulatory and legislative action. Specifically, NBA President Cooper asked that banking regulators consider how their broad policies might affect minority banks, and consider changing them so as not to unduly burden the banks. For example, recent regulatory changes had added another obstacle for black banks in raising capital. Most banks in need of capital can issue "common stock," but minority banks cannot sell shares in their banks in this way because it threatens their minority status. In order to maintain minority ownership, they issue preferred stock. However, banking capital rules, specifically the Basel I guidelines put into effect in 2004, discounted preferred stock and favored common stock, which gave black banks a weaker capital profile than majority banks.[124]

Kim Saunders, president of Mechanics and Farmers, explained that black banks are "at a significant disadvantage regardless of our stature of profitability in our abilities to raise capital."[125] Saunders proposed that the existing CDFI fund, which offered tax breaks to banks in underserved communities, reserve some of those benefits for minority banks. According to Representative Maxine Waters, out of $16 billion in tax credits available through the New Markets Tax Credit program, only one black bank had received a grant.[126] Instead, large banks such as Capital One, Wachovia, Bank of America, and others had received tax credits for development projects in the inner city. According to Saunders, mainstream banks had recently and "suddenly found those unserved or underserved markets to be a worthwhile place for a bank branch," but according to Saunders, they were not there for the benefit of the community.[127] Black bankers had always seen their mission as being larger than profitability.

If the economic milieu in which black banks found themselves had not changed significantly in the preceding century, neither had their noneconomic appeal. NBA President Robert Cooper explained that "these institutions aren't just providers of financial products and services. They truly are beacons of hope for the community."[128] Maxine Waters admitted during the 2007 congressional hearings that she had investments in several of the black banks being discussed. In the black community, according to Waters, "the test of your commitment to economic expansion and development and support for business is whether or not you put your money where your mouth is . . . you will find that most black professionals belong to, participate with, their minority banks in their community. It is expected of us. We should do it. And it is a true test of our commitment."[129]

Before the legislators could resolve any of the issues presented at the hearing, the 2008 financial crisis rocked the country, especially the established banking regulatory framework. Congress responded with the 2010 Dodd-Frank Act. Dodd-Frank did contain specific provisions dealing with minority banks, but they were far from robust. The act ignored most of the recommendations that came up during the hearings. The only change to the regulatory framework consisted of Section 367(4)(A) of the act, which amended FIRREA Section 308 to apply to all the banking agencies instead of just the OTS and the FDIC, which was due in part to the act's termination of the OTS altogether.[130] Section 342 of Dodd-Frank also required each banking agency to establish an Office of Minority and Women Inclusion (OMWI), which is required to increase the diversity of agency staff and to offer assistance to minority- and women-controlled banks. Now all the agencies offer technical assistance, but still no tax breaks, no help with capital, and no structural reforms.

Yet regulators continue to celebrate black banks relying on myths that bear little resemblance to actual history. Comptroller of the Currency Tim Curry said at the National Bankers Association meeting in 2013, "As in the early years after the Civil War, when the Freedmen's Bank provided a secure place for savings and a source of credit to encourage economic growth, minority institutions today can be a catalyst to ensure the vitality of low-income communities."[131] In fact, the Freedmen's Bank was not a secure place for savings and it provided no credit. Likewise, minority institutions have been unable to "catalyze vitality."

The black banking industry has ebbed and flowed since the 1860s, with several peaks in the 1920s, 1960s, and 1980s that correlated with peaks in the economy, racial unrest, and sometimes increased segregation. By 2016 the industry was in a decade-long decline. Mechanics and Farmers of Durham, North Carolina, announced in June 2015 that it was "revamping its business model" to become a community bank and not a black-owned bank. The bank changed its name to M&F, and CEO James Sills explained that the bank will be trying to "reach new customers, to attract younger customers, and diversify [their] customer base."[132] This is a historic shift for the largest, oldest, and strongest of the black-owned banks, one of a handful that have withstood the Depression and every other recession since 1907. In the last decade, the black-owned banking industry has shrunk by more than half, from fifty-one banks in 2000 to twenty today.[133] The struggles of the largest black-owned banks reveal some of the ongoing tensions in this sector.

The poster child of community capitalism, ShoreBank, failed in 2010. The bank's failure was not due to anything remarkable or unusual—the bank failed because inner-city Chicago was financially devastated after the 2008 financial crisis. The bank had not made subprime loans, but it was still affected by the widespread fallout.[134] Some criticized the bank's overzealousness and wondered whether the bank failed because it was "too much into the social welfare thing."[135] Although the failure was unremarkable, what happened afterward was.

ShoreBank's application for $70 million in TARP bailout funds created a media firestorm and a rage disproportionate not only to the funds requested, but completely disconnected from the scale of the total bank bailout.[136] The unprecedented scrutiny and attention over ShoreBank's failure matched the hubbub over its founding—the press couldn't resist reporting on the demise of Clinton and Obama's favorite bank and calling out "political favoritism." Representative Judy Biggert (R-IL) demanded information from the White House, suggesting that "the government was rescuing a *politically connected* bank while letting hundreds of others fail."[137] President Obama had no connection to the bank except that they were both in Chicago at the same time. Even though the president played no role in allocating TARP funds, conservative conspiracy theories abounded about special treatment.[138] Glenn Beck used his famous chalkboard to weave a ludicrous conspiracy theory that connected ShoreBank to all of his favorite enemies, including President Obama, ACORN, Bill Ayers, and Hillary Clinton.[139]

The bank did not receive a bailout and failed, causing losses to inner-city Chicago residents and bank investors. After the failure, the bank's assets were taken over by Urban Partnership Bank, which was a consortium of top Wall Street banks and investors, including Goldman Sachs, American Express, Citigroup, Bank of America, JPMorgan Chase, GE Capital, Morgan Stanley, and Wells Fargo.[140] All of these *politically connected* banks had received not millions, but billions in TARP bailout funds. The bank is now a certified CDFI, and all of the investor banks receive CRA credit for their investment.[141]

Harlem's bank also failed, but with a slightly different result. After its main competitor, Freedom National Bank, failed in 1990, Carver remained as the only black-owned bank in New York and one of the largest in the country.[142] As is often the case, Harlem was hit especially hard during the financial crisis, and Carver suffered more than $60 million in loan losses. The bank held very few subprime loans (only 2 percent of its portfolio), but the domino effect of the financial crisis could not be avoided.[143] For a bank that had seen only $20 million in total earnings since it went public in 1994, the loss was substantial.[144] On the brink of collapse, the bank had to turn to the behemoths downtown for salvation. Carver received help from Treasury and a $55 million cash injection from a consortium of Wall Street banks, including Goldman Sachs, Morgan Stanley, Prudential Financial, and Citigroup. After the bailout, the U.S Treasury owned 25 percent of the bank, with the Wall Street consortium controlling another 73 percent.[145] Thus, the original shareholders were left with just 2 percent of the shares of their bank. The purchase helped Goldman secure an "outstanding" CRA rating after its purchase.[146]

The purchase saved the bank but wiped out its shareholders, many of whom were Harlem residents and longtime investors in the community institution. The bank is now listed as *black-controlled* instead of black-owned.[147] The country's largest black-owned bank had ceased to be owned by blacks, but is owned by the same few banks that own virtually every other bank in the country. In announcing the deal to shareholders, Carver CEO Deborah Wright announced, "I understand the optics, but there was no alternative. The amount of capital we needed wasn't available locally."[148]

The "optics" are indeed bad, especially when one considers what happened when Citigroup and Goldman Sachs, key actors responsible for the financial crisis, were exposed to severe losses during the 2008 financial crisis: the government bailout restored 100 percent of their shareholder value. Their shareholders lost nothing. The same Wall Street banks that were enriched by pushing black families into subprime loans now owned one of the few remaining black banks that were working to serve rather than exploit the community. And the reason they now owned the bank was that they survived the crisis they helped create through a taxpayer bailout, while Carver did not. Goldman was saved because it was deemed too big (in reality, too important) to fail. Carver was not.

The transformation of Carver from a struggling black bank to a Wall Street–owned bank mirrors exactly the transformation of the neighborhood it serves. Indeed, Harlem is experiencing something of a real estate renaissance, which looks more like a transformation. Instead of a smattering of small-scale businesses, Harlem now has large retail outlets, hotels, and businesses that have followed the wave of more prosperous residents. Many black residents are being priced out of Harlem as Manhattan's booming population begins to overflow uptown. Carver is also being priced out of the new Harlem. When the largest new residential property, a twenty-eight-story condominium, was built in Harlem, large banks downtown did all the financing. Carver sat out the monumental transformation of Harlem because it did not have enough capital to participate.

The bank's current management remains committed to helping the black community with their distinctive business needs. In 2015, Carver's CEO Michael Pugh, a Detroit native who worked as a bank teller in college and became a Capital One executive, outlined a plan for meeting Harlem's small business needs. Pugh proposed offering the community loans of $10,000 or less, which most banks consider too small to be worthwhile. Pugh explains, "If a person who's running a kiosk on 125th Street came looking for a loan, another bank might offer him a credit card—or nothing. We're going to provide something better." The bank is starting to turn a profit, but has a very small margin.[149] Carver is being told to carry on with a commitment to the community. In a recent meeting at Carver's headquarters, the head of the U.S. Small Business Administration, Maria Contreras-Sweet, praised the bank for its history of creating opportunities for the community. "We need more like you," she told the Carver management. "Thank you for being here. I know it hasn't been easy." Pugh responded, "No argument there."[150]

Another pillar of the black banking industry, OneUnited, has faced struggles of its own. OneUnited Bank is the new name for Unity bank, which formed in Boston in 1968 as the "bank with a purpose;" the purpose being to demonstrate "constructive black power." The bank has since grown into a nationwide operation and defines its mission today as helping the black community by focusing on "financial literacy" as well as "originating and purchasing mortgage loans—with a focus on urban and low-to-moderate income communities."[151]

The bank was on the brink of failure during the financial crisis when it was revived by bailout funds. The bank received $12 million out of the $700 billion TARP bailout as a result of a specific addendum sponsored by Barney Frank and Maxine Waters in December 2008.[152] The special provision was necessary because TARP bailout funds were reserved for healthy banks, and OneUnited would not have qualified. The bailout sparked outrage in the press, with the *Washington Post* calling it "special treatment" of a bank that was too weak to deserve a bailout. Waters was charged with ethics violations for her intervention—charges that have since been dropped.[153] The denunciations in some quarters were much more vitriolic for this $12 million bailout than they had been for the billions of bailout dollars that had been directed at Wall Street, demonstrating yet again the aversion to government funds being directed toward the black community. The *National Review* called Maxine Waters a corrupt "swamp queen," a "corporate-welfare fixer," and proclaimed that "Mad Maxine Waters's cronyism of color can't be whitewashed."[154]

The bailout also became a point of controversy within the black community, though through a different lens. OneUnited was caught in one of the oldest struggles facing black banks—the tension between their mission and their bottom line. The clash occurred publicly when St. Charles Street AME Church, a two-hundred-year-old church and Boston's most prominent black institution, defaulted on a loan.[155] The AME Church was founded in 1818 and was a hub for the early abolition movement, connected to leaders such as William Lloyd Garrison, Frederick Douglass, and Sojourner Truth. It had been a haven on the "freedom trail" and a leading voice against the 1850

Fugitive Slave Act. OneUnited had been the church's primary lender, and in 2006 it made a $3.6 million construction loan to the church to build the Roxbury Renaissance Center. The church fell on hard times during the financial crisis, and by 2012 it began to miss loan payments. The loan was backed by the church building, and OneUnited decided to foreclose on the property. The result was akin to an ugly public divorce—a heated and highly publicized clash between two of the pillars of the community. The auction was scheduled to occur on the steps of the church, a move the church's pastor, Rev. Gregory G. Groove, said was "as mean-spirited and as godless as you can get."[156]

Predictably, in the post-crisis environment, the bank lost the PR battle. Cheryl J. Sanders, professor of Christian ethics at the Howard University School of Divinity, called the foreclosure a "callous disregard for people's lives and livelihood." She urged the bank to have "compassion" and to "give people a break."[157] The press, public, and community leaders joined forces to decry the bank and to persuade it not to foreclose. Hundreds organized in rallies against the bank and urged a national boycott. "We are calling on all black people to withdraw every dime they have in OneUnited if they don't resolve this issue," said one minister. Mayor Thomas M. Menino said during a protest, "You've shown the whole country we're not going to stand for this corporate, greedy individual to take away one of the bedrocks of the city of Boston."[158]

In an interview with the *Washington Post,* another pastor analogized the predicament to the biblical parable of the ungrateful servant. The story concerns a servant whose debt is mercifully forgiven by his creditor, a powerful king. This servant, having just been forgiven, turns around and sends his own debtor to prison for not paying him. The king then severely punishes the servant for his ingratitude. In the analogy, OneUnited was the ungrateful servant who, having received bailout funds from the king (or here the more powerful Treasury Department), had turned around to cruelly foreclose on the nation's oldest black church. "We forgave the banks and bailed them out, and now they're coming after the little borrower," said Pastor Ryan Bell.[159] But the bailout was not quite a biblical wiping out of debt. The bank still had to pay back the federal government, and it was struggling to do so while facing heat for having received possibly "unethical" and certainly unearned "special treatment."[160]

The perception was that not only was the bank acting immorally, but it was going against its own mission. Black City Councilor Ayanna Pressley said in a statement, "I am shocked that OneUnited, which claims to be fulfilling the civil rights dream by investing in urban areas, would treat the foreclosure of one of Boston's most historic black churches as simply the cost of doing business." She called the bank's apparent unwillingness to restructure the loan "sadly ironic." Pressley quipped, "Apparently, OneUnited's commitment to urban communities only lasted until their $12 million check from the federal government cleared."[161]

What is sadly ironic is that the bank was being blamed for its very commitment to the community. If the bank had not been committed to "fulfilling the civil rights dream," it would not have lent money to the black church or drawn nearly as much criticism as it did when it decided to foreclose on the loan. The black community expected its black bank to save its black church. And because it couldn't or wouldn't, the bank, like many black banks and businesses before it, was seen as a traitor. Indeed, the *Boston Globe* asked pointedly, "What purpose can a minority institution serve when its own community is turning against it?"[162]

In fact, one of the purposes of black banks is to lend to black churches. Broadway Federal Bank, another of the pillars of the black banking sector, explained in its 2011 public disclosures that "[o]riginating loans secured by church properties is a market niche in which we have been active since our inception." Like most black-owned banks, roughly 25 percent of its loans went to black churches. "We believe that the importance of church organizations in the social and economic structure of the communities we serve makes church lending an important aspect of our community orientation."[163] Jim Willis of M&F explained that his bank had been lending to black churches for over 150 years, and that in 2016 the bank had over $175 million in church loans. In fact, 55 percent of all of the bank's loans were to black churches. But these loans present specific problems for black bankers.[164]

Broadway Federal suffered so much in losses on its church loans that in 2011 federal regulators labeled the bank as "troubled" and barred it from issuing any more church loans. The bank admitted that its loan losses "raise substantial doubt about the company's ability to continue as a going concern." The bank had seven church loans in default, but when it tried to foreclose on properties held as collateral, they faced a protest by a coalition of black churches.[165]

The unrelenting financial depression that hit the black community infected the churches too, linking the fates of the black church and the black bank together, sometimes uncomfortably. Often a preacher advises his parishioners to deposit funds at a black bank. Martin Luther King did this. Black churches in turn borrow money from black banks. These loans, which are meant to further the goals of each institution and of the community, can nevertheless put the bank and the church at cross purposes. The bank needs to foreclose on a loan if it is to remain profitable, and the church usually asks for mercy instead of the cold justice of debt collection that is one of the bank's core duties. Mercy can come in the form of a loan modification, which can save a church from bankruptcy, but that comes at a cost to the bank. The bank must sacrifice its own profits under a modification. Black banks that are already operating with a sliver of a profit margin may not be able to afford the mercy.[166]

In interviews, black bankers explained that they try to offer modifications to black churches whenever possible. Jim Sillis of M&F recounted that in 108 years of lending to black churches, the bank had seen only two failures because the bank always tried to work with the church first. Other mainstream banks are not so merciful. Bankruptcy law expert Pamela Foohey's research revealed that black churches made up around 75 percent of bankrupt congregations over the last decade. This number is astonishing because black churches represent only 21 percent of churches nationwide.[167] Foohey uncovered a stunning case of discrimination by creditors. Lenders not only charged black churches more for credit, but disproportionately denied their loan modification requests, pushing these churches toward bankruptcy. Foohey rejected other possibilities that might account for the disparity, such as type of denomination, location, financial resources, management structure, financial decisions, or views on bankruptcy. This finding corroborates empirical research showing that black borrowers are also steered toward more costly Chapter 13 bankruptcy than the more borrower-friendly Chapter 7.[168]

Indeed, the demise of black banks mirrors the fall of the other pillars of the black community, including the black press, historically black colleges and universities (HBCUs), and black churches. Five HBCUs have closed over the past twenty years. In the 1970s, HBCUs educated 75 to 85 percent of the black population; today only 9 percent of blacks attend them. Black newspapers have all but collapsed, whereas they were once the "primary means of group expression," and "the strongest, most influential institution among blacks was its crusading press."[169] On the one hand, this could be seen as a sign of racial progress because blacks are being included in historically white spaces. Black institutions are no longer needed, like black water fountains. On the other hand, the country remains racially divided, especially with regard to subterranean economic forces. While the black community is legally entitled to entry at any college, bank, or neighborhood, these institutions remain practically out of reach for many in the black community, who simply cannot afford to pay the entry fee.

Moreover, unlike other black institutions, black banks have held the additional promise of controlling and multiplying the black dollar. Policymakers have built an entire framework to support black banks based on this premise, and community groups continue to advocate for the industry. Yet after hundreds of years of trying to enrich their customers, black banks are still serving customers with low incomes and "very limited asset holdings," according to a Boston Federal Reserve study.[170] The areas served by black-owned banks still suffer from "deep poverty," meaning that the majority of residents live below the poverty line. Black banks are actively engaged in closing these gaps, or at least drawing attention to them. Black banks were created to bridge the wealth gap, but they are dying before the goal has been achieved, before the black community has gotten safely to the other side.

The industry is still not strong enough to be a source of strength for the community it serves. "They have survived everything, including world wars and Jim Crow, but this has been one of the most difficult periods of all," said NBA President Michael Grant. However, if the future is anything like the past, the black banking industry will likely bounce back from this seemingly inevitable doom. The industry, like the community it serves, has rebounded many times and continues to find hope against the odds. The NBA president remained resolute in 2016 despite widespread failure. "Doom and gloom? No, and hell no," he said. "It's resolve, it's 'we are more determined than ever to preserve these banks.' "[171] Black bankers and advocates claim that black banks are needed now more than ever because these are institutions of last resort.[172] Black banking advocate Michael Cunningham explained why black banks have become even more appealing after the financial crisis: "the conclusion I draw is that you can't rely on the financial system itself to protect your interests. Now that's a lesson that everybody learned, but it's especially relevant for African-Americans. Nobody's going to protect you but you. And that's justification, rationalization enough for the creation, maintenance, expansion of black-owned banks."[173] Black banks still promise and offer refuge from exploitation.

An interesting turn of events occurred in 2016. Lack of trust in the banking industry, coupled with an uptick in racial violence, led to a revival of black banking, or #BankBlack, as an expression of protest. Rapper Killer Mike was the most forthright advocate: "We don't have to burn our city down," he said. "But what we can do is go to your banks tomorrow. . . . And you can say 'Until you as a corporation start to speak on our behalf, I want all my money. And I'm taking all my money to Citizen's Trust.' . . . What we're gonna do is start to divert money away from the system. . . . I ain't saying march, hold hands, speech. . . . I'm saying take your money out of this dog's hands. Out of their paws. Take your money. . . . Don't allow a dollar of your money to leave your community again until these dogs that ask for your vote, ask for your money, come begging for you to get back into their economic system. Don't you spend a dollar for a dog who don't speak up for you."[174]

In February 2016, Killer Mike put his money in Citizens Trust Bank in Atlanta. He was joined by Usher and Jermaine Dupri, and the well-publicized event kicked off Black History Month and spurred a national movement. Other celebrities including Solange Knowles, Jesse Williams, Alicia Keys, and Queen Latifa all endorsed the #BankBlack movement.[175] The movement was dubbed Black Money Matters, in sync with the national Black Lives Matter movement. As the Black Lives Matter movement expanded beyond protests over police shootings, the organization led a renewed focus on black businesses with a newly formed coalition called Backing Black Business. Its website urged the black community to support black business, invoking the words of both Malcolm X and Martin Luther King.[176] *American Banker* reported that executives at the top black-owned banks in the country all reported a huge surge in deposits. Thomas McLaurin, chief operating officer of Industrial Bank, remarked, "I've been in banking since 1989 and I've never experienced anything like this."[177]

These deposits have breathed life into a dying industry. OneUnited had just announced plans to close two California branches when the Black Money Matters drive brought in $3 million in deposits in 2016. "We've seen a big influx of applications online, and the lines have been out the door," said the bank president Teri Williams. "We didn't see this coming." Carver also attracted $2.4 million in deposits after having reported a loss in 2015. A Carver representative explained, "We attribute this growth to the deep relationships we have built with our customers and community partners at a time when messages of social justice, community, and diversity have taken on renewed importance." This movement is in the spirit of Garvey, Carter Woodson, Malcolm X, Dr. King, and others. In the face of discrimination and powerlessness, these leaders, now joined by a new movement, have urged their community toward protest through control of their dollars. When the climate is hostile, what can a community do but resort to self-help and protest? But can black banks offer effective protest or self-help? If history is any guide, the answer is, unfortunately, no. Or at least, not yet.[178]

Epilogue

A history of racism institutionalized through slavery, sharecropping, Jim Crow, white affirmative action, redlining, job discrimination, and white flight created self-reinforcing cycles of segregation and poverty. These institutions were often violent, extractive, and openly condoned, but their lingering effects are quiet, subtle, and hard to detect. They are no less destructive for that. But because they operate under the surface and on complicated bank balance sheets, they have been misunderstood, and this misunderstanding has caused perverse social policies. Instead of recognizing that white-run institutions have been complicit in and even benefited from black America's poverty, the state has repeatedly placed the burden of closing the wealth gap on the black community itself.

Yet the history of black banking remains a story of struggle rather than triumph. The dilemma these banks face in the twenty-first century mirrors almost exactly what plagued them in the nineteenth century. Black banks are hamstrung by small and volatile deposits. Their loans are smaller and riskier than other banks'. Their assets are pulled out of the community, either through overinvestment in government securities or through national pools of mortgages. The magic of banking is that banks can create money by lending, but the money multiplier is broken for black banks because they have traditionally operated in a segregated economy.

The clear message that emerges from the history of black banks is that relying on these banks to do the work of achieving wealth equality without changing the economic environment in which they operate is unfair, cynical, and fruitless. Insofar as there is segregation and widespread poverty in the black community, banks that exclusively serve this community cannot be successful. The black community needs banks to grow and prosper, but the banks cannot achieve that growth and prosperity alone. Self-help microfinance cannot overcome macro inequality and systemic racism. Policymakers have been placing the weight and responsibility of centuries of wealth inequality on these tiny economic engines, and the results have been failure and frustration. Banks reflect the economic conditions of a community; they cannot change them. Yet we continue to rely on black banks to control the black dollar, to empower the community, to sow prosperity. This is a fundamental misunderstanding of what banks do.

Although black banks are unable to fulfill the promise of prosperity in the climate of poverty and segregation, they are the only institutions focused on the particular economic problems facing the black community and so their preservation is essential. They know what it takes to overcome financial obstacles, and they are the only institutions focused solely on closing the wealth gap. They are a place of refuge, banks of last resort, and institutions committed to the community. Unlike the contract sellers, payday lenders, and subprime mortgage brokers, they are not motivated purely by profits at all costs. The fact that they often lend at a loss means that they are lending to institutions and people who would otherwise not get loans, including black churches and other pillars of the black community. The banks' mixed mission of community-building and profitable lending has occasionally led to combustible situations, as demonstrated by the foreclosures on black church properties. Such conflicts have historically attracted the scorn of black socialist leaders who have derided black banks as exploiters of the black population. However, the *dual* mission of the black banks makes them at least *half* concerned about the community and sets them apart from the lenders whose sole mission has been profit-taking.

If policymakers are committed to closing the wealth gap, black bankers must be seated at the head of the table. The point is that they should not be the only ones in the room. Black bankers have a firsthand understanding of the headwinds affecting black prosperity. While black banks cannot close the wealth gap alone, their specialized focus and expertise must play a role in any plan to address this problem. The fact that black banks have not yet met their goal is not an indictment of them. Rather, it reflects an enduring ecosystem of economic forces that perpetuate black poverty and resist efforts to create black wealth.

A 2016 study glibly predicted that, based on the current racial wealth gap, it would take 228 years for blacks to have as much wealth as whites do today. The prediction is inaccurate on two dimensions.[1] If nothing changes, no amount of time will close the wealth gap because of the self-perpetuating cycles of poverty and lack of wealth. However, heretofore untried strategies might close the wealth gap very quickly. In 1894, a London newspaper predicted that "in 50 years, every street in London will be buried under nine feet of manure." This dire outcome did not consider that horses would not be the primary mode of transportation in fifty years and that the automobile, an invention that was right around the corner, would transform life. Once people are motivated to deal with the wealth gap, radical solutions may emerge. There is no reason to believe that the future is just more horse manure.

There have been major political and social roadblocks to dealing effectively with the wealth gap, and each of history's potential reformers has faced them. The biggest roadblock is inherent in majoritarian democracy itself. If reform is seen as zero-sum, the institutional structure of American government resists any wealth transfer viewed as a benefit to a minority of the population. However, there is a way to overcome the resistance by convincing the majority that reforms aimed at a segment of the population will benefit the entire population. For example, passage of civil rights laws was made easier when policymakers became aware that communists and other foreign enemies were exploiting Jim Crow and using it in propaganda against the United States. When civil rights came to be seen as a matter of critical foreign policy import, it was actively pursued. To point this out is not to cast doubt on the sincerity of the individuals or groups pursuing reforms or to throw an overly cynical taint on monumental changes, but it is to acknowledge the reality of human nature and democratic governance. Then, as now, the public must be convinced that their own interests are aligned with the advancement of racial minorities or that they will not suffer when others are promoted.

Indeed, greater wealth equality will benefit not just the poor, but the entire society. Drastic inequality is a drag on economic growth and has pernicious effects on society such as eroding trust, increasing illness, and leading to excessive consumption.[2] Chicago economist Richard McAdams found that "economic theory and empiricism suggests that material inequality increases crime, increases corruption, and, at some levels, decreases growth."[3] Lifting people out of poverty can have trickle-up economic effects and raise all boats.[4] Research conducted by prominent economists, including

Thomas Piketty, demonstrates that the postwar era may have been a unique time in terms of economic growth and that the modern era (post-1970s) is a period of stagnant economic growth and possibly of decline. This stagnant economy is at least in part caused by acute wealth inequality, which must be remedied in order to spur the economy toward growth and increased production.[5] In other words, to make America great again we should look at the redistributive government programs that made America great during the postwar era and emulate them in a more inclusive way.[6]

Proposals to address the wealth gap directly by providing some form of reparations will be met with powerful political resistance. A 2016 Marist / PBS poll found that 81 percent of white Americans opposed reparations (58 percent of blacks supported the idea).[7] Yet economic equality must proceed down a path that acknowledges past wrongs and provides compensatory damages.[8] An essential first step in dealing with the wealth gap is to acknowledge that it was created through racist public policy. Full justice demands a recognition of the historic breach of the social contract between America's constitutional democracy and black Americans. And contract breach requires a remedy. Without that recognition, the Constitution itself stands as a roadblock to redress because it demands that all individuals be neither harmed nor benefited based on group characteristics. But it is unfair to be held to a contract that has already been violated. Blacks have been harmed in direct contradiction to the Constitution's promise of equal treatment, yet they have still have to contend with its requirement for equal treatment in seeking a remedy. It is indeed time for a new social contract with black Americans that deals honestly with the past breach.

We must confront history directly, to recognize the breach, and provide compensation. There are a few examples of how such a reckoning might take place and what it could achieve. In 2016, Georgetown University admitted that it had purchased 272 slaves in 1838 and promised to give each descendant of these slaves preferred treatment in admissions.[9] The university is planning a "Mass Reconciliation" where it will recognize and apologize for its history. University President John DeGioia explained, "We cannot do our best work if we refuse to take ownership of such a critical part of our history."[10] Another example involves private companies that benefited financially from the convict labor system. The spoils of the system have enriched some of the largest southern companies, including the First Atlanta Bank, which held the fortune of one of the largest convict-slave holders in the South, James English. After Wachovia acquired First Atlanta, the bank decided to formally recognize its ill-gotten gains. In 2005 Wachovia issued a formal apology to "all Americans and especially to African Americans and people of African descent" and established a scholarship for minorities. Ken Thomas, former CEO and a white southerner, explained that he was "overwhelmed by the emotional impact our apology had . . . for African American employees." After the apology and internal group discussions with employees, "workers cried, held hands, embraced one another regardless of company rank, and, in an unprecedented way, began speaking to one another."[11] A formal apology and a scholarship fund do not erase the injustice of the past, but at Wachovia it represented tentative first steps to healing and harmony.

Beyond a formal apology, however, designing a compensation program would present significant practical and legal hurdles. The recently created myth of color-blindness is so doggedly defended by the courts and the American public that it would prove difficult to dismantle. Yet it is clearly worth the effort to try to untangle some of these complexities. As Al Brophy explains in *Reparations: Pro and Con,* "the cost of a meaningful program of reparations—and racial justice—will be colossal, though so will the benefits."[12]

The point of this book has not been to propose a particular proposal, but rather to demonstrate that past efforts of economic inclusion have fallen short and that any plan to bridge the wealth gap must include integration or a means to acquire capital. Based on these findings, there are many policy designs worth considering. A reparations program could take many forms from simple cash payments or baby bonds to more complex schemes such as subsidized college tuition, basic income, housing vouchers, or subsidized mortgage credit. Evaluating each of these programs is outside the scope of this book, but nonprofits, academics, and policymakers should be encouraged to propose creative proposals that garner full and meaningful financial inclusion that reverse the effects of historic exclusions from wealth creation.

One possibility is to just follow the redlines and focus on homeownership. Most of the neighborhoods that were initially redlined in 1934 have been perpetually denied credit and thus remain pockets of poverty. Racial ghettos, once created, have had remarkable staying power. Across the country, these ghettos are still the areas where the wealth and well-being gaps are most dramatically visible. These are the districts where poverty is still concentrated, schools are segregated, and properties continue to be devalued. By focusing a reparations program on geography as opposed to identity, policymakers can avoid the sacred cow of color-blindness and link reparations with combatting segregation. Moreover, a program focused on homeownership has the potential to lead to long-term intergenerational benefits as the home and land are passed down. A home can also be used as collateral for other life-enhancing loans, like consumer or student loans. Such a program might also be more palatable to policymakers and the public because there is sound historic precedent. Because land grants and mortgage subsidies were the instruments through which white Americans gained a wealth advantage over black Americans, it would be apt to use land grant or mortgage credit programs as the means to level the playing field.

To evaluate future reforms, we must absorb the lessons of the past and make sure we are not repeating the same mistakes. We might want to apply the following short litmus tests to any policy proposal: does the program require some collective sacrifice or does it place the burden of closing the wealth gap entirely on the black community? If the latter, this is a cop-out that refuses to acknowledge that the black community did not create the problem in the first place. Like black capitalism, such programs are trying to get something for nothing and not acknowledging that there was a benefit gained by the white majority as a byproduct of segregation and exclusion. Political expediency should not be the impetus for policymaking. Rather, policy design should proceed out of an honest accounting of the problem at hand and its history. The reality is that any program aimed at compensatory wealth creation will be unpopular. It will have problems and downsides and complications. And it will take time. But the alternative of allowing the wealth gap to continue to grow and perpetuate suffering is unacceptable and unjust.

In contemplating the possibility of change, it is crucial to keep in mind that social and political evolution is possible and has indeed been made already. Decidedly, we do not live in a postracial society, but it is important to step back and note the undeniable progress in social, scientific, and political thought. Take the case of interracial marriage. Fears of miscegenation were the backdrop to the Jim Crow framework and the fuel that fed much of the violence toward black men. In 1958, only 4 percent of Americans approved of interracial marriage. By 2013 a Gallup poll found that 87 percent of Americans approve.[13] Having mapped the human genome, modern science has now fully dispelled the myth that race is a meaningful genetic trait.[14] Racial division has never been a biological fact, but rather a political weapon, and our shared humanity will soon become an obvious fact, hopefully leading to more inclusive policymaking. Politically, Americans are much more tolerant and pluralistic than before, even when it seems as though things never change. The majority of the American public elected Barack Obama to office twice. Putting aside the ugly racist backlash engendered by his presidency, a black president would not have been possible in any previous era.

Racism is not only harmful to blacks; it is a corrosive influence on white culture. Frederick Douglass explained that he watched his white mistress change as she became a slave master. Her ownership of a human being warped and corrupted her previously decent character and turned her into hateful person.[15] C. Vann Woodward describes how the South lost its soul in its obsessive and pervasive enforcement of Jim Crow.[16] James Baldwin worried about "the death of the heart" that racism had wrought on American culture, for "whoever debases others is debasing himself."[17] Baldwin also understood that the "future of the Negro in this country is precisely as bright or as dark as the future of the country."[18] The sooner Americans recognize that the fate of black America is tied to the fate of white America, the faster it can achieve true democracy and shed the weight of historic injustice.

Americans must decide whether to keep embracing our history of racial tribalism or to shed these divisions and go forward as one people, indivisible. Can America's majoritarian democracy support a program intended solely to benefit the black minority? It certainly did not in 1870, 1930, or 1960. However, there is reason to hope that this is more likely now than ever. We are facing another pivot point. The racial détente of the 1960s has fallen apart. The myth of postracial America has been dispelled, and renewed tensions have erupted on the national stage as well as in segregated pockets of poverty in America.

Modernity will inevitably bring us closer together, which can lead to either greater resentment or greater cooperation. Perhaps more people will realize that what benefits a minority will also benefit the majority. Full racial integration will eventually remove pockets of blight, crime, and deprivation across the country. This will advance the entire American population. Integrated schools will improve education for all students, and increased equality will spur economic growth.[19] We must shed the destructive myths that separate can be equal, that a segregated economy will reach prosperity on its own, or that black banks can lead to black prosperity without fundamental economic changes. We cannot deflect the responsibility of economic equality onto black communities alone. W. E. B Du Bois declared in 1948 that the problem of American democracy was that "we have not tried it."[20] Perhaps it is time to try.

NOTES

ACKNOWLEDGMENTS

INDEX

NOTES

Introduction

1. Martin Luther King, "The Other America," Grosse Pointe High School, March 14, 1968.
2. "The typical Black household now possesses just 6 percent of the wealth owned by the typical white household." http://www.demos.org/publication/racial -wealth-gap-why-policy-matters.
3. Rakesh Kochhar, Richard Fry, and Paul Taylor, "Wealth Gaps Rise to Record Highs Between Whites, Blacks, Hispanics," Pew Research Center, September 26, 2011, 2, http://www.pewsocialtrends.org/2011/07/26/wealth-gaps-rise-to-record-highs -between-whites-blacks-hispanics/.
4. Booker T. Washington, "The Awakening of the Negro," *Atlantic Monthly*, September 1896.
5. Martin Luther King Jr., "I've Been to the Mountaintop," Speech, Memphis, TN, April 3, 1968; cited in *A Testament of Hope: The Essential Writings and Speeches of Martin Luther King, Jr.*, ed. James M. Washington (New York: HarperOne, 2003), 283.
6. Malcolm X, "The Ballot or the Bullet," Speech, Cleveland, OH, April 3, 1964.
7. "Nixon Urges 'Black Ownership' to Help Solve Racial Problems," *New York Times*, April 26, 1968, 27.
8. Ronald Reagan, "Remarks in Denver, Colorado, at the Annual Convention of the National Association for the Advancement of Colored People," Denver, CO, June 19, 1981, http://www.reagan.utexas.edu/archives/speeches/1981/62981a .htm.
9. Ibid.
10. James Baldwin, *Nobody Knows My Name: More Notes of a Native Son* (New York: Vintage International, 1993).
11. "The Humble Beginnings of a Large Bank," Office of the Comptroller of the Currency, http://www.occ.gov/about/what-we-do/history/giannini-bank-article -html-version.html.
12. Kristin Broughton, "Black-Owned Banks Must Revisit Their Business Models, M&F Chief Says," *American Banker*, June 9, 2015, https://secure.mfbonline.com /wp-content/uploads/2015/07/jimsills-news.pdf.
13. Christy Ford Chapin, "'Going Behind with That Fifteen Cent Policy': Black-Owned Insurance Companies and the State," *Journal of Policy History* 24(4) (2012): 644–674.
14. Russell D. Kashian, Richard McGregory, and Derrek G. McCrank, "Whom Do Black-Owned Banks Serve?," Federal Reserve Bank of Boston, *Communities & Banking*, Summer 2014, http://www.bostonfed.org/commdev/c&b/2014 /summer/whom-do-black-owned-banks-serve.htm.
15. Federal Deposit Insurance Corporation, *2013 FDIC National Survey of Unbanked and Underbanked Households*, October 2014, 16, https://www.fdic.gov /householdsurvey/2013report.pdf.
16. Paul Kiel and Annie Waldman, "The Color of Debt: How Collection Suits Squeeze Black Neighborhoods," *ProPublica*, October 8, 2015, https://www.propublica.org /article/debt-collection-lawsuits-squeeze-black-neighborhoods.
17. Billie Holiday, "God Bless the Child," Okeh, 1942.
18. Manning Marable, *How Capitalism Underdeveloped Black America* (Chicago: Haymarket Books, 2015), 1.

19. Dalton Conley, *Being Black, Living in the Red: Race, Wealth, and Social Policy in America* (Berkeley: University of California Press, 2010), 25.
20. Martin Luther King Jr., "I Have a Dream," Speech, Lincoln Memorial, Washington, DC, August 28, 1963.

Chapter 1 Forty Acres or a Savings Bank

1. Andrew Delbanco, *The Abolitionist Imagination* (Cambridge, MA: Harvard University Press, 2012), 68–69.
2. Abraham Lincoln, "Second Inaugural Address," Washington, DC, March 4, 1865, http://avalon.law.yale.edu/19th century/lincoln2.asp.
3. As Edward Baptist recounts, "3.2 million people enslaved in the United States had a market value of $1.3 billion in 1850." Edward E. Baptist, *The Half Has Never Been Told* (New York: Basic Books, 2014), 352.
4. Cotton Mather wrote that the Law of Christianity allows slavery. Cotton Mather, *Negro Christianized: An Essay to Excite and Assist That Good Work, the Instruction of Negro-Servants in Christianity* (1706), Second (North) Church, Boston.
5. George D. Armstrong, *The Christian Doctrine of Slavery* (New York: C. Scribner, 1851), 134.
6. John Jones, *Confederate Currency: The Color of Money, Images of Slavery in Confederate and Southern States Currency* (New York: New Directions, 2002). Images available at http://www.colorsofmoney.com/.
7. Baptist, *Half Has Never Been Told*, 244–248.
8. Historian Betty Wood explains, "economic self-interest dictated that all the fruits of a slave's labor should accrue to the owner. . . . Slaves were not allowed to hire out their own labor. Neither could they 'buy, sell, or exchange any goods, wares, provisions, grains, victuals or commodities of any sort or kind whatsoever' without first obtaining the permission of their owners." Betty Wood, "White Society and the 'Informal' Slave economies of Low-Country Georgia: 1763–1830," *Slavery and Abolition: A Journal of Comparative Studies* 11 (1990): 313.
9. According to historian Leon F. Litwack, the situation of blacks in the north during the 1800s was "at best deplorable" due to their restricted access to even menial employment. Moreover, "in virtually every phase of existence, Negroes found themselves systematically separated from whites" in the North. Leon F. Litwack, *North of Slavery: The Negro in the Free States, 1790–1860* (Chicago: University of Chicago Press, 1965), 97; see also Leon Litwack, "The Emancipation of the Negro Abolitionist," in *The Antislavery Vanguard,* ed. Martin B. Duberman (Princeton, NJ: Princeton University Press, 1965), 141–143. Historian Charles Wesley explains that in the 1850s in the North, though blacks were physically free, "they were enslaved and placed in degraded economic positions by the apathy of their friends and the hostile attitude of their fellow workers." Quoted in Charles L. Franklin, *The Negro Labor Unionist of New York* (New York: Columbia University Press, 1936), 21.
10. Alexis de Tocqueville, trans. Henry Reeve, *Democracy in America,* vol. 1 (Clark, NJ: Law Book Exchange, 2007), 339.
11. In 1805 Maryland prohibited free blacks from selling corn, wheat, or tobacco without a license. In North Carolina, any free black who wanted to trade or sell any goods needed a license, and these licenses were practically impossible to obtain. In 1844, Virginia revoked the license of a mulatto innkeeper without explanation. John Seder and Berkeley G. Burrell, *Getting It Together: Black Businessmen in America* (Boston: Houghton Mifflin Harcourt, 1971), 5.
12. Manning Marable, *How Capitalism Underdeveloped Black America,* 126.
13. Harris, *Negro as Capitalist,* 8.

14. John Henry Harmon Jr., Arnett G. Lindsay, and Carter G. Woodson, *The Negro as a Business Man* (College Park, MD: McGrath, 1969), 7.

15. The origin of black banking is described as "beginning with the pioneers who not only loaned their money but also the savings of their fellowmen, which were entrusted to their care." Harmon et al., *Negro as a Business Man*, 42.

16. Ibid. For example, there was John Stanley of North Carolina, who was a barber and a farmer and who sold tradable debt on the side. He was backed by white men in town who preferred not to get their hands dirty with the "social stigma attached to sharp [lending] practices," which included lending to blacks with interest. Thomy Lafon of New Orleans was a dry goods merchant who lent money out of his considerable wealth, valued at around $400,000. Harris, *Negro as Capitalist*, 21.

17. John Sibley Butler, *Entrepreneurship and Self-Help among Black Americans: A Reconsideration of Race and Economics* (Albany: State University of New York Press, 1991), 46–48, 106.

18. The South Carolina Act of 1800, *The Anti-Slavery Record*, vol. 3 (New York: The American Anti-Slavery Society, 1838).

19. Butler, *Entrepreneurship and Self-Help*, 133.

20. Joseph A. Pierce, *Negro Business and Business Education: Their Present and Prospective Development* (Westport, CT: Negro University Press, 1971), 9, 30.

21. Harris, *Negro as Capitalist*, 23–24. It should be noted that credit was also scarce for poor white farmers, but many of them had the option of going west and obtaining private sequestration of assets like gold, timber, and other natural resources.

22. Ibid., 24.

23. Alexander Hamilton, "Report on a National Bank," Communicated to the House of Representatives, December 14, 1790, quoted in *The Debates and Proceedings in the Congress of the United States*, ed. Joseph Gales (Washington, DC: Gales and Seaton, 1834), 2101.

24. Ibid.

25. According to a black leader at the turn of the century, their "discussions were indulged in at length notwithstanding the fact that the political rights of the Negroes—free men and slaves—were being questioned, debated, and bitterly fought over by the pro-slavery and anti-slavery factions." Harmon et al., *Negro as a Business Man*, 44.

26. Circular No. 1, issued by Frederick Douglass, U.S. Senate, 46th Congress, 2nd Session, Report No. 440.

27. *Dred Scott v. Sandford*, 60 U.S. 393 (1856).

28. Frederick Douglass, *The Life and Times of Frederick Douglass: From 1817–1882*, ed. John Lobb (London: Christian Age, 1882), 331.

29. "Newspaper Account of a Meeting between Black Religious Leaders and Union Military Authorities," Freedmen and Southern Society Project, January 1865, http://www.freedmen.umd.edu/savmtg.htm.

30. Douglas R. Egerton, *The Wars of Reconstruction: The Brief, Violent History of America's Most Progressive Era* (New York: Bloomsbury Press, 2014), 100.

31. Ibid., 109. "Disinclined to wait for a reconstituted state or distant president to restore order, blacks along the [South Carolina and Georgia] coast sensibly proceeded to govern themselves."

32. Eric Foner, *Reconstruction: America's Unfinished Revolution, 1863–1877* (New York: Harper, 1989), 102.

33. Ibid., 118.

34. Ibid., chap. 4.

35. The land was bounty from the Confiscation Acts, which declared that the Union could seize the property of Confederate supporters, or property that had been

"abandoned" by Confederate soldiers. The government's purported purpose for confiscation was to pay the expenses of the war, to punish the Confederates, and to provide for "Union loyalists" and freed slaves. Walter L. Fleming, "Forty Acres and a Mule," *North American Review* 182 (1906): 721, http://www.jstor.org/stable /25105565.

36. Henry Louis Gates Jr., "The Truth Behind '40 Acres and a Mule,'" PBS, http://www .pbs.org/wnet/african-americans-many-rivers-to-cross/history/the-truth-behind -40-acres-and-a-mule/.

37. Brooks D. Simpson and Jean V. Berlin, eds., *Sherman's Civil War: Selected Correspondence of William T. Sherman, 1860–1865* (Chapel Hill: University of North Carolina Press, 1999), 600.

38. Fleming, "Forty Acres and a Mule," 729

39. Egerton, *Wars of Reconstruction*, 99.

40. Ibid., 100.

41. "Revolutionary movements can be stopped by violence, provided enough politicians are assassinated, enough party registrars are eliminated, and enough voters are intimidated into remaining home on election day." The violent upheaval led by the Klan and other vigilante groups achieved a restoration of the pre-war social hierarchy through targeted attacks on black legislators and their Republican allies. The first targets were blacks in uniform. Egerton, *Wars of Reconstruction*, 287.

42. Foner, *Reconstruction*, 121

43. W. E. B. Du Bois, *The Souls of Black Folk* (New York: Dover, 1994). 17.

44. Ibid.

45. W. E. B. Du Bois, *Black Reconstruction in America* (London: Transaction Publishers, 2013), 26.

46. Andrew Johnson, *The Papers of Andrew Johnson,* vol. 10: *February–July 1866,* ed. Paul H. Bergeron (Knoxville: University of Tennessee Press, 1992), 174–175. Johnson faced backlash from his party, leading to his impeachment after two attempts, but not before he had successfully opposed Republican reformers. Thaddeus Stevens led the first impeachment effort. Carol Berkin, Christopher Miller, Robert Cherny, James Gormly, Douglas Egerton, and Kelly Woestman, *Making America: A History of the United States,* vol. 2: *Since 1865* (Boston: Wadsworth, 2014), 363.

47. Paul A. Cimbala, "The Freedmen's Bureau, the Freedmen, and Sherman's Grant in Reconstruction Georgia, 1865–1867," *Journal of Southern History* 55 (1989): 597–598.

48. Du Bois, *Black Reconstruction in America,* 602.

49. Du Bois, *Souls of Black Folk,* 20. E. Franklin Frazier echoed, "for a brief period, less than a decade in most Southern states, the Negro enjoyed the rights of a citizen. If the Second American Revolution had not been aborted it would have established a democracy in the South in which the poor whites and black freedmen would have shared power. Franklin Frazier, *Black Bourgeoisie* (New York: Free Press Paperbacks, 1997), 141.

50. Claude F. Oubre, *Forty Acres and a Mule: The Freedmen's Bureau and Black Land Ownership* (Baton Rouge: Louisiana State University Press, 1978).

51. Veto of the Freedmen's Bureau Bill, Andrew Johnson, February 19, 1866. Cited in Edward McPherson, *The Political History of the United States of America during the Period of Reconstruction: April 15, 1865–July 15, 1870* (Washington, DC: Solomon and Chapman, 1875), 71.

52. Foner, *Reconstruction*, 463–469.

53. Carol Anderson, *White Rage: The Unspoken Truth of Our Racial Divide* (New York: Bloomsbury, 2016), 16. The lack of systematic land grants to the freed slaves during this era contrasts sharply with the generosity and speed with which whites

were acquiring cheap land. Seventy-five percent of white farmers came to own their farms due to nineteenth-century federal land grant programs from which blacks were either legally or practically barred. Dalton Conley, *Being Black, Living in the Red* (Berkeley: University of California Press, 1999), 35. Christie Farnham Pope, "Southern Homesteads for Negroes," *Agricultural History* 44(2) (1970): 201–212, http://www.jstor.org/stable/3741673.

54. A white southerner, when asked if it would not have been better for both whites and blacks if blacks were given land, responded: "No, for it would have made the Negro 'uppity' . . . and the real reason . . . why it wouldn't do, is that we are having a hard time now keeping the nigger in his place, and if he were a landowner, he'd think he was a bigger man than old Grant, and there would be no living with him in the Black District. . . . Who'd work the land if the niggers had farms of their own?" Gunnar Myrdal, *An American Dilemma: The Negro Problem and Modern Democracy* (New Brunswick, NJ: Transaction, 1996), 227.

55. Alexander Tsesis, *The Thirteenth Amendment and American Freedom: A Legal History* (New York: New York University Press, 2004), 51.

56. McPherson, *Political History*, 36.

57. Claudine L. Ferrell, *Reconstruction* (Westport, CT: Greenwood Press, 2003), 65.

58. Sven Beckert, *Empire of Cotton: A Global History* (New York: Vintage Books, 2014), 281.

59. 2/3/1866: John W. Chandler- Democrat, New York re: Freedmen's Bureau. The Congressional Globe: Containing the Debates and Proceedings of the First Session of the Thirty-Ninth Congress, vol. 36, part 5, ed. F. and J. Rives (Washington, DC: Congressional Globe Office, 1866), 82.

60. Kenneth Pomeranz and Steven Topik, *The World That Trade Created: Society, Culture, and the World Economy, 1400 to the Present*, 2nd ed. (Armonk, NY: M. E. Sharpe, 2006), 82.

61. Foner, *Reconstruction*, 102–110.

62. 11/7/1865 A. J. Willard to George W. Hooker, quoted in Julie Saville, *The Work of Reconstruction: From Slave to Wage Laborer in South Carolina, 1860–1870* (New York: Cambridge University Press, 1996), 17; Levy, *Freaks of Fortune*, 122–123.

63. Foner, *Reconstruction*, 108.

64. Beckert, *Empire of Cotton*, 281.

65. Ibid., 284. At a New York meeting of the business community in 1865, a cotton trader expressed that the freed people's mobility "cannot be deemed anything more than a temporary state of affairs to be corrected by the joint influence of the vagrancy laws and the necessity of the vagrants."

66. Foner, *Reconstruction*, 55–56.

67. Ferrell, *Reconstruction*, 72–73

68. Douglas A. Blackmon, *Slavery by Another Name: The Re-Enslavement of Black Americans from the Civil War to World War II* (New York: Anchor Books, 2008), 335–337.

69. Ibid., 207.

70. Ibid., 128–140.

71. James Baldwin, *The Price of the Ticket: Collected Nonfiction, 1948–1985* (New York: St. Martin's, 1985), 329.

72. "In the backwoods of the Gulf States, for miles and miles," Du Bois observed, the black southerner "may not leave the plantation of his birth; in well-nigh the whole rural South the black farmers are peons, bound by law and custom to an economic slavery, from which the only escape is death or the penitentiary. . . . Before the courts, both in law and custom, they stand on a different and peculiar basis. Taxation without representation is the rule of their political life. . . . That is the large legacy of the Freedmen's Bureau, the work it did not do because it could not." Du Bois, *Souls of Black Folk*, 24.

73. Ibid., 39.

74. Lionel C. Bascom, *Voices of the African American Experience* (Westport, CT: Greenwood Press, 1978), 362.

75. Martin Luther King Jr., personal note, *Crisis in Black and White* by Charles E. Silberman (New York: Random House, 1964).

76. Andrew Johnson Presidential Papers, Freedmen Bureau Congressional Reports (Johnson opposed the Freedmen's Bureau and urged repeal its measures, but he did not seek repeal of the bank charter or vocally oppose it).

77. For a thorough history of the Freedmen's Bank, see Carl R. Osthaus, *Freedmen, Philanthropy, and Fraud: A History of the Freedmen's Savings Bank* (Urbana: University of Illinois Press, 1976); and Walter Fleming, *The Freedmen's Savings Bank: A Chapter in the Economic History of the Negro Race* (Chapel Hill: University of North Carolina Press, 1927).

78. John Alvord to Major General O. O. Howard, Commissioner of Bureau of Refugees, Freedmen, etc., United States Congressional Serial Set, vol. 1256 (Washington, DC: Government Printing Office, 1866), 348.

79. Douglass, *Life and Times*, 487. "The history of civilization shows that no people can well rise to a high degree of mental or even moral excellence without wealth. A people uniformly poor and compelled to struggle for barely a physical existence will be dependent and despised by their neighbors and will finally despise themselves. While it is impossible that every individual of any race shall be rich—and no man may be despised for merely being poor—yet no people can be respected which does not produce a wealthy class."

80. Sheldon Garon, *Beyond Our Means: Why America Spends While the World Saves* (Princeton, NJ: Princeton University Press, 2013), 104.

81. Harmon et al., *Negro as a Business Man*, 46.

82. These leftover funds served as the starting capital of the Freedmen's Savings Bank. Harris, *Negro as Capitalist*, 27.

83. President Abraham Lincoln, Speech at Signing of Freedmen's Bureau, March 3, 1865.

84. Quoted by Osthaus, *Freedmen, Philanthropy, and Fraud*, 55.

85. Harris, *Negro as Capitalist*, 26. U.S. Congress, Senate, Freedmen's Savings & Trust Co., Statement by Rev. James L. White relative to the Freedmen's Bureau and the Freedmen's Bank, later the Freedmen's Savings & Trust Co., and the balance due its depositors, together with the establishment of a national memorial home for colored people, June 4, 1912, 62d Congress, 2d session, S. Doc. 759, 192.

86. Harris, *Negro as Capitalist*, 28.

87. Henry Wilson, Speech, April 1865, in Egerton, *Wars of Reconstruction*, 128.

88. U.S. Senate, 62nd Congress, 2nd Session, S. Doc. 759, 4.

89. Harmon et al., *Negro as a Business Man*, 48. In fact, Douglass claimed that "some did not give their consent to the use of their names" in the founding documents. Instead, "[t]hey were thrust in for appearance' sake and to make the delusion attractive and complete." Report to Accompany Bills S. 711 and S. 1581, at II.

90. Congressional Series of United States Public Documents, vol. 2213, 54.

91. An Act to Incorporate the Freedmen's Savings and Trust Company, March 3, 1865; quoted in Frederick E. Hosen, *Federal Laws of the Reconstruction* (Jefferson, NC: McFarland, 2010), 23–24.

92. Section 6 of the charter required the trustees to invest "all sums received by them beyond an available fund not exceeding one third of the total amount of deposits with the corporation, at the discretion of the trustees" in stocks, bonds, treasury notes, or other U.S. securities. Harris, *Negro as Capitalist*, 31.

93. Whitelaw Reid, *After the War: A Tour of the Southern States* (Cincinnati, OH: Moore, Wilstach and Baldwin, 1866), 50.

94. Butler, *Entrepreneurship and Self-Help*, 135.

95. Jonathan Levy, *Freaks of Fortune: The Emerging World of Capitalism and Risk in America* (Cambridge, MA: Harvard University Press, 2012), 126. Orders issued by Commissioners and Assistant Commissioners of the Freedmen's Bureau, 4, 20.

96. Osthaus, *Freedmen, Philanthropy, and Fraud*, 131.

97. Egerton, *Wars of Reconstruction*, 129.

98. "The fact that men of unquestionable character and unusual ability were advertised as incorporators together with the report that the United States Government protected the savings which were deposited inspired confidence and made easy the successful organization of [the bank]." Harmon et al., *Negro as a Business Man*, 48.

99. It was not until 1874, when the bank was virtually bankrupt, that Congress amended the bank's charter to state that any officer of the bank caught embezzling funds or engaging in fraudulent activities would be charged with a misdemeanor. Osthaus, *Freedmen, Philanthropy, and Fraud*, 123.

100. Harris, *Negro as Capitalist*, 33. There were too few deposits—less than $100,000. Alvord believed that this was because the people had no confidence in the bank, but in fact it was because they had no wages to save during this time. In 1867, there was a proposal to close the bank for good, but it did not pass. Osthaus, *Freedmen, Philanthropy, and Fraud*, 136–142.

101. First National Bank was financing the federal debt, which was where the Freedmen's Bank's assets were primarily invested. Levy, *Freaks of Fortune*, 130.

102. Ibid., 134.

103. Ibid., 132.

104. Ibid., 133.

105. Report to Accompany Bills S. 711 and S. 1581, S. Rep. No. 46-440, app. 41. Monique Nelson, "The Freedmen's Savings Bank: A Historical Place in the Financial Empowerment of African Americans," Department of the Treasury, February 21, 2014, http://www.treasury.gov/connect/blog/Pages/Freedmans-Savings-Bank.aspx.

106. Harris, *Negro as Capitalist*, 28. Harmon et al., *Negro as a Business Man*, 49. Branches were established in Alexandria, LA; Atlanta, GA; Augusta, GA; Baltimore, MD; Beaufort, SC; Charleston, SC; Chattanooga, TN; Columbia, TN; Columbus, MS; Huntsville, AL; Jacksonville, FL; Lexington, KY; Little Rock, AR; Louisville, KY; Lynchburg, VA; Macon, GA; Memphis, TN; Mobile, AL; Montgomery, AL; Nashville, TN; Natchez, MS; New Bern, NC; New Orleans, LA; Norfolk, VA; Philadelphia, PA; Raleigh, NC; Richmond, VA; Savannah, GA; Shreveport, LA; St. Louis, MO; Tallahassee, FL; Vicksburg, MS; Washington, DC; and Wilmington, NC. I think the confusion is that Harmon et al. (p. 48) list the New York branch as one that was established during this time period, while Harris (p. 28) considers the New York branch to be headquarters and thus excluded as a "branch." See also Richard Zuczek, *Encyclopedia of Reconstruction Era: A–L* (Westport, CT: Greenwood Press, 2006), 268.

107. This $260,000 in 1870 would be worth approximately $4,565,000 today.

108. Egerton, *Wars of Reconstruction*, 128–129.

109. Levy, *Freaks of Fortune*, 140.

110. An Act to amend an act entitled "An act to incorporate the Freedmen's Savings and Trust Company" (Approved May 6, 1870) in United States Congressional Serial Set, vol. 1 (Washington, DC: Government Printing Office, 1875), 88. Specifically, the amendment stated:

[T]he fifth section of the act entitled "An act to incorporate the Freedmen's Savings and Trust Company" . . . is hereby amended, adding thereto, at the end thereof, the words following: "and to the extent of one-half in bonds or notes, secured by mortgage on real estate in double the value of the loan; and the corporation is also authorized hereby to hold and improve the real estate now owned by it in the city of Washington."

111. Harris, *Negro as Capitalist*, 35.
112. Ibid., 41.
113. Earl Louis Brown, "Negro Banks in the United States" (M.A. thesis, Boston University, 1930), 11, http://archive.org/stream/negrobanksinunit00brow/negro banksinunit00brow djvu.txt; Harmon et al., *Negro as a Business Man*, 51.
114. Upon reviewing the kinds of self-dealing loans made, Lindsay observed, "such banking practices are almost incredible, but authoritative sources record even grosser irregularities at the bank." Harmon et al., *Negro as a Business Man*.
115. Harris, *Negro as Capitalist*, 34. Fleming, *Freedmen's Savings Bank*, 39–40.
116. U.S. House of Representatives, Select Committee on the Freedmen's Bank, H.R. Rep. 44-502 (1876), VII.
117. Brown, "Negro Banks in the United States," 11.
118. Levy, *Freaks of Fortune*, 141–142.
119. Because there was no mechanism or process to resolve such conflicts of interest, and because the freedmen were unaware of the fraud and were politically powerless, these transactions went unnoticed. Report to Accompany Bills S. 711 and S. 1581, S. Rep. 46-440, III.
120. Harris, *Negro as Capitalist*, 33. As one observer put it, "there were, of course, many other causes [of failure] but the most obvious cause was the audaciously planned schemes of the officers to fill their own pockets, to feather the nests of their business associates and friends who had formed cliques, rings and other combines for selfish gains." Harmon et al., *Negro as Businessman*, 52.
121. Armand J. Thieblot, *The Negro in the Banking Industry* (Philadelphia: Wharton School of Finance and Commerce, 1970), 181.
122. Harris, *Negro as Capitalist*, 42.
123. Douglass, *Life and Times*, 355–356.
124. Ibid., 354.
125. U.S. House of Representatives, Select Committee on the Freedmen's Bank, H.R. Rep. 44-502 (1876), II.
126. Douglass, *Life and Times*, 355–356.
127. U.S. House of Representatives, Select Committee on the Freedmen's Bank, H.R. Rep. 44-502 (1876).
128. "[H]alf the depositors [in the Freedmen's Bank] received compensation—an average of $18.51 per person, or about three-fifths the value of their accounts." Foner, *Reconstruction*, 532.
129. Harmon et al., *Negro as a Business Man*, 52.
130. Report of the Select Committee to Investigate Freedmen's Savings & Trust Co., 52.
131. Robert H. Kinzer and Edward Sagarin, *The Negro in American Business: The Conflict Between Separatism and Integration* (New York: Greenburg, 1950), 63–64.
132. Harmon et al., *Negro as a Business Man*, 54.
133. Seder and Burrell, *Getting It Together*, 9.
134. Harmon et al., *Negro as a Business Man*, 54.
135. Ibid., 85.
136. Seder and Burrell, *Getting It Together*, 9.
137. Du Bois, *Souls of Black Folk*, 37.
138. Harris, *Negro as Capitalist*, 45.
139. W. E. B. Du Bois, *The Crisis* 22–24 (May 1921): 253.
140. Frazier, *Black Bourgeoisie*, 38. "The spirit of business enterprise which had been implanted among Negroes by the Freedmen's Savings Bank began to blossom forth within fifteen years after the failure of that institution. Beginning in 1888, Negroes organized at least 134 banks between that year and 1934."
141. Douglass, *Life and Times*, 292.
142. Ibid., 293.

143. By 1900 more than three-quarters of the former plantations were being culti-vated by sharecroppers. Beckert, *Empire of Cotton*, 285.

144. Harmon et al., *Negro as a Business Man*, 45.

145. Charles Lewis Nier III, "The Shadow of Credit: The Historical Origins of Racial Predatory Lending and Its Impact upon African American Wealth Accumulation," *University of Pennsylvania Journal of Law and Social Change* 11 (2007–2008): 131.

146. Conley, *Being Black*, 34.

147. Melvin L. Oliver and Thomas Shapiro, *Black Wealth / White Wealth: A New Perspective on Racial Inequality* (New York: Routledge, 1997), 50. Blackmon, *Slavery by Another Name*, 272–273.

148. A typical interest rate was 50–70 percent. Ferrell, *Reconstruction*, 175; Du Bois, *Souls of Black Folk*, 89.

149. Loren Schweninger, *Black Property Owners in the South, 1790–1915* (Chicago: University of Illinois Press, 1990), 146. See also Levy, *Freaks of Fortune*, 136.

150. According to Beckert, "Few observers in 1865 had expected such a spectacularly successful transition away from slavery and toward new systems of labor—a transition that filled with hope the hearts of imperial statesmen and metropol-itan cotton manufacturers the world over." Beckert, *Empire of Cotton*, 291.

151. Ibid., 292. "Reconstruction resulted in a rapid, vast, and permanent increase in the production of cotton for world markets . . . by 1870 their total production surpassed their previous high, set in 1860, and by 1880, the U.S. was exporting more than it had in 1860. By 1891, the U.S. was exporting twice as much cotton as any year pre-slavery."

152. Du Bois, *Souls of Black Folk*, 90–91. Du Bois, writing in 1906, explained that the "direct result of this system is an all-cotton scheme of agriculture and the con-tinued bankruptcy of the tenant. The currency of the Black Belt is cotton. . . . There is no use asking the black tenant, then, to diversify his crops—he cannot under this system."

153. William Garrott Brown, *The New Politics* (Boston: Houghton Mifflin Company, 1914), 248.

154. Richard F. Bensel, *Passion and Preferences: William Jennings Bryan and the 1896 Democratic Convention* (Cambridge: Cambridge University Press, 2008), 1–3.

155. *Encyclopedia of Populism in America: A Historical Encyclopedia*, ed. Alexandra Kindell and Elizabeth S. Demers (Santa Barbara, CA: ABC-CLIO, 2014), 521. The Republicans had always held the allegiance of blacks, though they had not fought for their economic interests. Frederick Douglass had articulated the political po-sition for a generation of blacks: "The Republican Party is the Ship. All else is the open sea." The southern Democrats were the party of the Confederacy and white supremacy. Frazier, *Black Bourgeoisie*, 107.

156. Marion Butler, a former member of the Farmers Alliance and senator from North Carolina from 1895 to 1901, left the Democratic Party to become the chairman of the Populist Party because of the Democratic Party's racism. Butler argued that "white race-baiting to sustain monopoly was a crime" and that people who stirred up racial tensions and deflected attention from greater economic reforms were the "most dangerous elements of society." He declared white supremacy "unpopulist" and was one of the foremost proponents of postal banking as a means to provide banking services to poor black and white southerners. James L. Hunt, *Marion Butler and American Populism* (Chapel Hill: University of North Carolina Press, 2003), 134.

157. C. Vann Woodward, *The Strange Career of Jim Crow* (Oxford: Oxford University Press, 1955), 61.

158. Ibid., 63 When a black Populist was threatened with lynching, Watson called on 2,000 armed men to remain on guard for two nights to protect the party member

from angry white mobs. The 1896 Georgia Populist Party platform denounced lynching.

159. Ibid., 63. H. S. P. Ashby, quoted in the *Dallas Morning News*, August 18, 1891.

160. Political economist Victor Perlo explained that this "represented a high point of an approach in industrial unionism and of black-white labor unity." Indeed, just decades later, the progressive labor coalition viewed black workers as the enemy. Marable, *How Capitalism Underdeveloped Black America*, 31.

161. Frederick Douglass, Statement to President Andrew Johnson, February 7, 1866.

162. Woodward, *Strange Career of Jim Crow*, 81.

163. Ibid., 82–83.

164. Beckert, *Empire of Cotton*, 287.

165. Larry J. Sabato and Howard R. Ernst, *Encyclopedia of American Political Parties and Elections* (New York: Facts on File, 2007), 483.

166. As Frederick Douglass lamented, "in most of the Southern States, the fourteenth and fifteenth amendments are virtually nullified. . . . The citizenship granted in the fourteenth amendment is practically a mockery, and the right to vote . . . is literally stamped out in face of government." Douglass, *Life and Times*, 611.

167. Frazier, *Black Bourgeoisie*, 142. Indeed, according to Frazier, a "studied campaign was carried on to prove that the Negro was subhuman, morally degenerate and incapable of being educated."

168. Hannah Arendt, *The Origins of Totalitarianism* (New York: Harcourt, 1951), 159.

169. Rayford W. Logan, *The Negro in American Life and Thought* (New York: Dial Press, 1925), 90.

170. William A. Sinclair, *The Aftermath of Slavery* (Boston: Small, Maynard and Company, 1905), 216.

171. Roy L. Brooks, *When Sorry Isn't Enough: The Controversy over Apologies and Reparations for Human Injustice* (New York: New York University Press, 1999), 403.

172. Emphasis added. *Civil Rights Cases*, 109 U.S. 3 (1883).

173. Eddie S. Glaude Jr., *Democracy in Black: How Race Still Enslaves the American Soul* (New York: Broadway Books, 2016), 41.

174. *Slaughterhouse Cases*, 83 U.S. 36 (1873); *United States v. Reese*, 92 U.S. 214 (1876); *United States v. Cruikshank*, 92 U.S. 542 (1875); *Louisville, New Orleans & Texas Ry. Co. v. Mississippi*, 133 U.S. 587 (1890).

175. *Williams v. Mississippi*, 170 U.S. 213 (1898); *Plessy v. Ferguson*, 163 US 537 (1896).

176. Foner, *Reconstruction*, 529–530.

177. Alexander Tsesis, *The Promise of Liberty: The History and Contemporary Relevance of the Thirteenth Amendment* (New York: Columbia University Press, 2010), 80.

178. Woodward, *Strange Career of Jim Crow*, 98, 118.

179. The Jim Crow South was "an all-absorbing autocracy of race, an animus of aggrandizement which makes, in the imagination of the white man, an absolute identification of the stronger race with the very being of the state." Edgar G. Murphy, *The Basis of Ascendancy: A Discussion of Certain Principles of Public Policy Involved in the Development of the Southern States* (New York: Longmans, Green, 1910), 30.

180. Du Bois explained that the South's "police system was arranged to deal with blacks alone, and tacitly assumed that every white man was ipso facto a member of that police." Du Bois, *Souls of Black Folk*, 107–108. The southern press played up the threat of black crime to justify swift and cruel punishment for any breach. E. Franklin Frazier claimed that a black person's "picture was never carried in the newspapers of the South . . . unless he had committed a crime." Frazier, *Black Bourgeoisie*, 144.

181. "Strange Fruit," Billie Holiday and Abel Meeropol, 1937, http://www.npr.org/2012/09/05/158933012/the-strange-story-of-the-man-behind-strange-fruit.

Chapter 2 Capitalism without Capital

1. Ta-Nehisi Coates, *Between the World and Me* (New York: Spiegel and Grau, 2015).
2. According to Carter Woodson, "the freedman practically monopolized the celebration of holidays throughout the South during the reconstruction period." John Henry Harmon Jr., Arnett G. Lindsay, and Carter G. Woodson, *The Negro as a Business Man* (College Park, MD: McGrath, 1969), 89–90. For early mutual aid societies, see John Sibley Butler, *Entrepreneurship and Self-Help among Black Americans: A Reconsideration of Race and Economics* (Albany: State University of New York Press, 1991), 47–48; Juliet E. K. Walker, *The History of Black Business in America: Capitalism, Race, Entrepreneurship* (Chapel Hill: University of North Carolina Press, 2009), 111–112.
3. Harmon et al., *Negro as a Business Man*, 87. Carter Woodson explains, "Wherever Negroes had their own churches benevolence developed as a handmaiden of religion."
4. Historian John Butler explained that "the promoters of these various companies had no experience whatever in insurance, and it never occurred to them that all successful insurance is based on some well-established mortality table. . . . The woods are full of the graves of these earlier companies which failed for the want of knowledge of business." Butler, *Entrepreneurship and Self-Help*, 118.
5. Christie Ford Chapin, " 'Going Behind with That Fifteen Cent Policy': Black-Owned Insurance Companies and the State," *Journal of Policy History* 24(4) (2012): 649.
6. The state of Virginia granted True Reformers a charter with permission to engage in typical banking activities, such as lending on personal and real property and exchanging notes and currency, as well as investing in securities, bonds, and other commercial paper. Its charter was clear that the purpose of the bank was to safeguard the deposits of the Order's members. "The object of this corporation is to provide a depository for the Grand and Subordinate Fountains of the United Order of True Reformers, a benevolent institution incorporated for such purposes by the Circuit Court of the State of Virginia." Harmon et al., *Negro as a Business Man*, 57–58.
7. Ibid., 58.
8. Ibid., 60–61; letter from W. H. Grant to W. W. Browne, date unknown.
9. Ibid., 95. Abram L. Harris, *The Negro as Capitalist: A Study of Banking and Business among American Negroes* (New York: Haskell House, 1936), 63, 73; E. Franklin Frazier, *Black Bourgeoisie* (New York: Free Press Paperbacks, 1997), 41n36.
10. Harmon et al., *Negro as a Business Man*, 39.
11. NNBL Minutes, 1926, 1927.
12. The first woman to own a bank in the United States was Anna Henriette Mebus Martin; Deborah S. Large, "Martin, Anna Henriette Mebus," http://www.tshaonline.org/handbook/online/articles/fmaax.
13. Museum Collections, National Park Service, Maggie L. Walker National Historic Site, Virginia, https://www.nps.gov/museum/exhibits/Maggie_Walker/index.html; Determined Spirit, https://www.nps.gov/mawa/index.htm; Gertrude Woodruff Marlowe, *A Right Worthy Grand Mission: Maggie Lena Walker and the Quest for Black Economic Empowerment* (Washington, DC: Howard University Press, 2003), 1–30.
14. After the failure of the other Richmond fraternal bank, True Reformers, the state of Virginia changed the rules that applied to banks linked with fraternal orders and forced a separation between fraternal societies and their banks as an effort to promote sound banking; Harmon et al., *Negro as a Business Man*, 63.
15. Marlowe, *Right Worthy Grand Mission*, 56.
16. Ibid.

17. National Park Service, Maggie L. Walker National Historic Site, Virginia, "The St. Luke Penny Savings Bank," https://www.nps.gov/mawa/the-st-luke-penny -savings-bank.htm. Marlowe, *Right Worthy Grand Mission*, 91.

18. Maggie L. Walker, *A Testimonial of Love Tendered Mrs. Maggie L. Walker: 25 Years of Service* (Richmond, VA: St. Luke Press, 1925).

19. National Park Service, "St. Luke Penny Savings Bank."

20. Consolidated was merged into Premier Bank in 2010 when it suffered severe losses, and is no longer considered a black-owned bank. Michael Schwartz, "Bank's Heritage Consolidated into the History Books," University of Richmond, September 2, 2010, http://www.richmondbizsense.com/2010/09/02/banks -heritage-consolidated-into-the-history-books/.

21. Arnett G. Lindsay, "The Negro in Banking," *Journal of Negro History* 14(2) (April, 1929): 179. The bank's directors were Robert H. Terrell, Whitfield McKinley, W. S. Montgomery, John A. Pierre, J. R. Wilder, and Henry Baker; they raised $6,000 of capital to start the bank. Harmon et al., *Negro as a Business Man*, 54, 64, 85.

22. Ibid., 85, 55. As described by Lindsay, the main reasons for the failure were: "Long time and unprofitable commercial loans, bringing about frozen assets; financing speculative schemes of officers." Earl Louis Brown "Negro Banks in the United States" (M.A. thesis, Boston University, 1930), 15, https://archive.org/stream /negrobanksinunit00brow/negrobanksinunit00brow_djvu.txt.https://archive .org/stream/negrobanksinunit00brow/negrobanksinunit00brow_djvu.txt.

23. Richard S. Grossman, *Unsettled Account: The Evolution of Banking in the Industrialized World since 1800* (Princeton, NJ: Princeton University Press, 2010).

24. Harris, *Negro as Capitalist*, 46. The same year, the Mutual Trust Company in Chattanooga, Tennessee, was formed. The Chattanooga bank was short-lived, failing in 1893. Harmon et al., *Negro as a Business Man*, 57; Butler, *Entrepreneurship and Self-Help*, 132–133, table 3.23.

25. Booker T. Washington, *The Booker T. Washington Papers*, vol. 5: *1899–1900*, ed. Louis R. Harlan, Raymond W. Smock, and Barbara S. Kraft (Champaign: University of Illinois Press, 1976), 393.

26. Washington, *Papers*, vol. 5, 393.

27. Jefferson County Historical Commission, *Birmingham and Jefferson County, Alabama* (Charleston, SC: Arcadia, 1998); Washington, *Papers*, vol. 5, 393.

28. Harmon et al., *Negro as a Business Man*, 56.

29. N. B. Young Sr., Interview, February 20, 1929.

30. Carol Jenkins and Elizabeth Gardner Hines, *Black Titan: A. G. Gaston and the Making of a Black American Millionaire* (New York: Random House, 2004).

31. James Baldwin, *Baldwin's Collected Essays: The Harlem Ghetto*, ed. Toni Morrison (New York: Library of America, 1998), 43.

32. W. E. B. Du Bois, *The Souls of Black Folk* (New York: Dover, 1994), 30.

33. Booker T. Washington, "Atlanta Compromise Speech," http://historymatters .gmu.edu/d/39/, as found in Washington, *Papers*, vol. 3, ed. Louis R. Harlan (Urbana: University of Illinois Press, 1974), 583–587.

34. His probusiness stance was not without criticism, but usually by Marxist thinkers before the civil rights movement, such as E. Franklin Frazier. Black radicals reviled Washington while themselves pushing for black business growth. For a modern debate on Washington's legacy, see Rebecca Carroll, *Uncle Tom or New Negro: African Americans Reflect on Booker T. Washington and* Up from Slavery *100 Years Later* (New York: Harlem Moon / Broadway Books), 107.

35. Washington's placatory message to blacks facing discrimination and hostility in the South was to befriend, not fight, the white community. To blacks itching to leave the South, he exhorted, "to those of my race who depend on bettering their condition in a foreign land," he pleaded, "cast down your bucket where you are.

Cast it down, making friends in every manly way of the people of all races, by whom you are surrounded." Washington, "Atlanta Compromise Speech."

36. In Washington's famous 1895 message to black leaders in Atlanta, he said of the two races, "In all things that are purely social we can be as separate as the fingers, yet one as the hand in all things essential to mutual progress." Booker T. Washington, *Up from Slavery* (New York: Doubleday and Company, 1901), 112.

37. Du Bois even accused Washington of being a leader created by northern Republicans and southern Whites because his message demanded nothing from either side. E. Franklin Frazier claimed that it was his acceptance of the subordination of blacks that caused "northern industrialists [to accept] Washington as the spokesman of Negroes and as the arbiter in the distribution of funds for Negro education." Frazier, *Black Bourgeoisie,* 67.

38. Andrew Carnegie, *The Negro in America: An Address Delivered before the Institute of Edinburgh* (Cheyney, PA: Committee of Twelve), 22, https://archive.org/stream/negroinamericaad00carn#page/22/mode/2up/search/free+and+unrestricted.

39. Quote from William Dean Howells "An Exemplary Citizen," *North American Review* 173 (1901): 287.

40. Booker T. Washington, *Black Belt Diamonds: Gems from the Speeches, Addresses, and Talks to Students of Booker T. Washington* (Charleston, SC: Nabu Press, 2011), 91–92; Frazier, *Black Bourgeoisie,* 76; Harris, *Negro as Capitalist,* 46.

41. Frazier, *Black Bourgeoisie,* 76; Washington, *Black Belt Diamonds,* 91–92.

42. Wealth and its attendant power would lead blacks toward "the enjoyment of all his rights." E. L. Thornbrough, ed., *Booker T. Washington* (Englewood Cliffs, NJ: Prentice-Hall, 1969), 44.

43. Louis R. Harlan, *Booker T. Washington: The Making of a Black Leader, 1865–1901* (New York: Oxford University Press, 1972), 269.

44. Thomas Dixon, *Saturday Evening Post,* August 19, 1905. Washington was not "training Negroes to take their place in any industrial system of the South in which the white man can direct or control him."

45. Washington, *Up from Slavery,* 40.

46. Du Bois, *Souls of Black Folk,* 41–60. W. E. B. Du Bois, *Dusk of Dawn: An Essay toward an Autobiography of a Race Concept* (Piscataway, NJ: Transaction, 2011), 67. David L. Lewis, *W. E. B. Du Bois: A Biography* (New York: Henry Holt, 2009), 222.

47. Du Bois, *Souls of Black Folk,* 49–50.

48. W. E. B. Du Bois, *The Negro in Business* (Atlanta: Atlanta University Press, 1899), 5.

49. Ibid.; Manning Marable, *How Capitalism Underdeveloped Black America* (Chicago: Haymarket Books, 2015), 131, 145.

50. Du Bois, *Negro in Business,* 59.

51. Ibid.

52. As historian August Meier explained, blacks faced "difficulties involved in obtaining credit from white banks, the discrimination practiced by white insurance companies and real estate firms, exclusion from white restaurants, hotels, and places of amusement." Thus, black business was a way for the black community to "solve their economic and other problems." August Meir, *Negro Thought in America, 1880–1915: Racial Ideologies in the Age of Booker T. Washington* (Ann Arbor: University of Michigan Press, 1988), 140–141.

53. Max Weber, *The Protestant Ethic and the Spirit of Capitalism* (Mineola, NY: Dover, 2003).

54. Du Bois, *Negro in Business,* 57.

55. Ibid., 59.

56. "The Negro's status has changed considerably since the Civil War, but he is today to a great extent what he has always been in this country—the laborer, the day hand, the man who works for wages. The great hiring class is the white people. . . .

[T]he white man has converted and reconverted the Negro's labor and the Negro's money into capital." Ibid., 56–57, citing Hope.

57. Melvin L. Oliver and Thomas M. Shapiro, *Black Wealth/White Wealth: A New Perspective on Racial Inequality* (New York: Routledge, 2006), 48.

58. Harris, *Negro as Capitalist*, 53.

59. Du Bois, *Negro in Business*, 7. Harmon et al., *Negro as a Business Man*, 12. The census of 1890 showed the following distribution of occupations: 17,000 barbers, 420 hotel keepers, and 2,000 restaurant keepers.

60. John Seder and Berkeley Burrell, *Getting It Together: Black Businessmen in America* (New York: Harcourt Brace Jovanovich, 1971), 10.

61. Du Bois, *Negro in Business*, 50.

62. The NNBL held their first convention in Boston in 1900 with 115 delegates, 80 percent of them from the South. National Negro Business League, *Proceedings of the National Negro Business League* (Boston: J. R. Hamm, 1901) 23, 24.

63. NNBL, *Proceedings*, 26, 129.

64. NNBL, Report of the Fifteenth Annual Convention of the National Negro Business League, Washington, DC, 83–84. During the same address, Washington claimed that before the establishment of the NNBL there was not a single black bank in Mississippi, but at that time—1910—there were eleven. In all of the United States, before the NNBL there were only four banks, and by 1910 there were fifty-six. During the 1914 convention in Oklahoma, Washington stated that "when the 2,000,000 Negroes in the Southwest have made the most of their opportunities . . . and brought up the riches contained in the earth they will be able to support . . . 40 more banks."

65. Seder and Burrell, *Getting It Together*, 12. NNLB, Report of the Thirteenth Annual Convention of the National Negro Business League, Washington, DC, 52.

66. Booker T. Washington, *The Negro in Business* (Coshocton, OH: Hertel, Jenkins, 1907), 136.

67. Clifford M. Kuhn, Harlon E. Joye, and E. Bernard West, *Living in Atlanta: An Oral History of the City, 1914–1948* (Athens: University of Georgia Press, 2005), 106. The bank's founders were commonly referred to as the "Fervent Five"—Herman E. Perry, James A. Robinson, Thomas J. Ferguson, W. H. King, and H. C. Dugas. The mission was articulated as: "promote financial stability and business development; to stress the principles of thrift; and to make home ownership possible to a larger number of people." Citizens Trust Bank, http://www.ncif.org/connect/ncif-network/network-banks/citizens-trust-bank-0#.WLXbsjsrLIU.

68. NNLB, Report of the Eleventh Annual Convention of the National Negro Business League, 79, Nashville, TN, AME Sunday School Union, 1911.

69. Frazier, *Black Bourgeoisie*, 40.

70. Harmon et al., *Negro as a Business Man*, 4.

71. Ibid.

72. Ibid.

73. Oliver and Shapiro, *Black Wealth/White Wealth*, 46–47, in part citing Merah Stuart.

74. "Restricted patronage does not permit the enterprises owned and operated by Negroes to capitalize on the recognized advantages of normal commercial expansion. It tends to stifle business ingenuity and imagination, because it limits the variety of needs and demands to those of one racial group—a race that is kept in a lower bracket of purchasing power largely because of this limitation." Joseph A. Pierce, *Negro Business and Business Education: Their Present and Prospective Development* (New York: Springer, 2013), 31.

75. As Pierce explained, "The practice of Negro business in catering almost exclusively to Negroes has contributed to the development of an attitude that the

Negro consumer is obligated, as a matter of racial loyalty, to trade with enterprises owned and operated by Negroes." Ibid.

76. John Hope, Speech at the Fourth Atlanta University Conference, 1898, in Harris, *Negro as Capitalist*, 53.

77. Oliver and Shapiro, *Black Wealth/White Wealth*, 46. John Butler observed that "throughout history, when Afro-American business enterprises developed a clientele outside of their community, they were more likely to be successful." Butler, *Entrepreneurship and Self-Help*, 77.

78. Henry Louis Gates Jr., "Madame Walker, the First Black American Woman to Be a Self-Made Millionaire," PBS, http://www.pbs.org/wnet/african-americans-many-rivers-to-cross/history/100-amazing-facts/madam-walker-the-first-black-american-woman-to-be-a-self-made-millionaire/.

79. "Most Negro wealth comes from businesses that white society did not wish to control or from services peculiarly personal—newspaper publishing of the segregated press; real estate and insurance, which grew out of Negro burial societies; and undertaking, which owes its Negro monopoly in the ghetto to the fact that white undertakers did not wish to handle Negro bodies." Kenneth Clark, *Dark Ghetto* (New York: Harper & Row, 1989), 189.

80. Jenkins and Hines, *Black Titan*.

81. Ibid., 108.

82. Ibid., 75–76.

83. Butler, *Entrepreneurship and Self-Help*, 110–111.

84. Merah Steven Stuart, *An Economic Detour: A History of Insurance in the Lives of American Negroes* (New York: Wendell Mallet, 1940), 36. Cited in Butler, *Entrepreneurship and Self-Help*, 118–119.

85. Frederick L. Hoffman, *Race Traits and Tendencies of the American Negro* (New York: Macmillan, 1896), 95; Robert William Fogel and Stanley L. Engerman, *Time on the Cross: The Economics of American Negro Slavery* (New York: W. W. Norton, 1995), 125.

86. Hoffman, *Race Traits and Tendencies*, 176.

87. Ibid., 310–311. Hoffman claimed that as whites were becoming stronger, blacks were becoming weaker and that "mulattos" were even weaker than pure blacks or whites: "The mixture of the African with the white race has been shown to have seriously affected the longevity of the former and left as a heritage to future generations the poison of scrofula, tuberculosis, and most of all, of syphilis."

88. Joseph A. Pierce, *Negro Business and Business Education* (New York: Plenum Press, 1995), 12.

89. Seder and Burrell, *Getting It Together*, 9; Chapin, "Fifteen Cent Policy," 647.

90. Butler, *Entrepreneurship and Self-Help*, 176, 180.

91. Clipping, *St. Luke Herald*, January 7, 1928; Walter B. Weare, *Black Business in the New South: A Social History of the North Carolina Mutual Life Insurance Company* (Chicago: University of Illinois Press, 1973), 4–5; William K. Boyd, *The Story of Durham: City of the New South* (Durham, NC: Duke University Press, 1925), 277; E. Franklin Frazier, "Durham: Capital of the Black Middle Class," in *The New Negro*, ed. Alaine Locke (New York: Simon & Schuster, 1997), 333.

92. M&F Bank, "Our History," https://www.mfbonline.com/our-history/.

93. The clientele of the bank is reflected in its name: "mechanics" refers to the legal term "mechanic's lien" which was a form of credit that the various service trades used to collect payments from their customers. Wiley J. Williams, "Mechanics and Farmers Bank," http://ncpedia.org/mechanics-and-farmers-bank.

94. Armand J. Thieblot Jr., *The Negro in the Banking Industry* (Philadelphia: University of Pennsylvania Press, 1970), 14.

95. A Durham newspaper at the time called the robbers' races "Unknown." https://www.newspapers.com/newspage/40788827/.

96. Butler, *Self-Help and Entrepreneurship*, 182.

97. Boyd, *Story of Durham*, 279.

98. Ibid., 278.

99. Butler, *Self-Help and Entrepreneurship*, 193, *Durham Morning Herald*, September 16, 1927. Quoted in Thomas H. Houck, *A Newspaper History of Race Relations in Durham, North Carolina, 1900–1940* (Durham, NC: Duke University Press, 1941), 81.

100. Butler, *Entrepreneurship and Self-Help*, 194.

101. Ibid., 191.

102. Ibid., 216.

103. Scott Ellsworth, *Death in a Promised Land* (Baton Rouge: Louisiana State University Press, 1982), 10–13.

104. In 2016, a lost eyewitness account of the massacre in Tulsa emerged to provide a new perspective on the horrific attacks by white mobs. See Allison Keyes, "A Long-Lost Manuscript Contains a Searing Eyewitness Account of the Tulsa Race Massacre of 1921," *Smithsonian*, May 27, 2016, http://www.smithsonianmag .com/smithsonian-institution/long-lost-manuscript-contains-searing -eyewitness-account-tulsa-race-massacre-1921-180959251/.

105. Ibid., 224.

106. W. E. B. Du Bois, *The Crisis* 21–22 (1920): 114.

107. Ellsworth, *Death in a Promised Land*, 95. *Tulsa World*, June 26, 1921; see also *Daily Oklahoman*, June 26, 1921. R. Halliburton Jr., "The Tulsa Race War of 1921," *Journal of Black Studies* 2(3) (1972): 333–357.

108. "Blood and Oil," *The Survey* 46 (June 11, 1921): 369.

109. Walter White, "The Eruption of Tulsa," *Nation*, June 29, 1921, 909.

110. Butler, *Entrepreneurship and Self-Help*, 229.

111. H. Leon Prather, *We Have Taken a City: The Wilmington Racial Massacre and Coup of 1898* (Madison: NJ: Fairleigh Dickinson University Press, 1984), cited in Oliver and Shapiro, *Black Wealth/White Wealth*, 49–50.

112. Ibid., 50.

113. Between the "red summer" of 1919 and 1923, race riots broke out in Chicago, IL; Washington, DC; Elaine, AR; Charleston, SC; Longview, TX; Omaha, NE; Knoxville, TN; and Rosewood, FL. During the "Rosewood Massacre" of January 1923, a white mob burned the entire Florida town to the ground. Jessie C. Smith and Linda T. Wynn, *Freedom, Facts, and Firsts: 400 Years of the African American Civil Rights Experience* (Canton, MI: Visible Ink Press, 2009), 64. Gregory Mixon and Clifford Kuhn, "Atlanta Race Riot of 1906," http://www.georgiaencyclopedia .org/articles/history-archaeology/atlanta-race-riot-1906; Tabitha C. Wang, "East St. Louis Race Riot: July 2, 1917," http://www.blackpast.org/aah/east-st -louis-race-riot-july-2-1917. For a list of race riots, see http://www.personal.utulsa .edu/~marc-carlson/riot/oldriots.html.

114. Walter B. Weare, *Black Business in the New South* (Durham, NC: Duke University Press, 1993), 116–119.

115. By the 1970s, when there was a renewed effort to revive the urban areas around the Greenwood district, "blacks as a group did not finance, nor did they own, the [center] of the old Greenwood section." Butler, *Entrepreneurship and Self-Help*, 234–236.

116. William Albert Sinclair, *The Aftermath of Slavery* (Boston: Small, Maynard and Company, 1905), 187–188; William B. Gatewood Jr., *Theodore Roosevelt and the Art of Controversy* (Baton Rouge: Louisiana State University Press, 1970), 36–37; Douglas A. Blackmon, *Slavery by Another Name: The Re-Enslavement of Black Americans from the Civil War to World War II* (New York: Anchor, 2008), 166–167. Vardaman was elected governor of Mississippi the next year. Nancy Isenberg,

White Trash: The 400-Year Untold History of Class in America (New York: Viking, 2016), 397.

117. Theodore Roosevelt, *A Square Deal* (Allendale, NJ: Allendale, 1906), 133.

118. Blackmon, *Slavery by Another Name,* 162.

119. W. E. B. Du Bois, "Evolution of the Race Problem," Atlanta University, 1909, http://www.webdubois.org/dbEvolOfRaceProb.html.

120. Nell Painter, *The History of White People* (New York: W. W. Norton, 2010).

121. Frazier, *Black Bourgeoisie,* 145.

122. Howard W. Odum, "Social and Mental Traits of the Negro: Research into the Conditions of the Negro Race in Southern Towns" (Ph.D. dissertation, Columbia University, 1910), 171.

123. William A. Sinclair, *The Aftermath of Slavery* (Boston: Small, Maynard, 1905), 221–222; The St. Louis World's Fair in 1904 featured a display of live pygmies taken from the Belgian Congo during King Leopold's brutally violent reign. After the fair, one of the men displayed, named Ota Benga, was taken to two other museums in New York and then placed in the Bronx Zoo in a cage with an orangutan. After several years of being displayed with a primate, he killed himself in 1916. This was America at the turn of the twentieth century. Blackmon, *Slavery by Another Name,* 240.

124. Ibid., 269

125. The Klan was not exclusively a southern phenomenon. According to a black observer, "many non-sheet-wearing whites supported the Klan ideology because whites were beginning to feel the economic pressure of black competition for living space and jobs in urban areas." Dempsey Travis, *An Autobiography of Black Chicago* (Evanston, IL: Agate), 38. Southern Poverty Law Center, "Ku Klux Klan," https://www.splcenter.org/fighting-hate/extremist-files/ideology/ku-klux-klan.

126. Woodrow Wilson, *Division and Reunion* (New York: Longmans, Green, and Co., 1893), 18.

127. News and Courier, 1906, cited in C. Vann Woodward, *The Strange Career of Jim Crow* (Oxford: Oxford University Press, 1955), 77, 81.

128. Roger Lowenstein, *America's Bank: The Epic Struggle to Create the Federal Reserve* (New York: Penguin), 199.

129. Stuart W. Shulman, "The Origin of the Federal Farm Loan Act: Issue Emergence and Agenda-Setting in the Progressive Era Print Press," in *Fighting for the Farm: Rural America Transformed,* ed. Jane Adams (Philadelphia: University of Pennsylvania Press, 2003), 113–128.

130. Ira Katznelson, *When Affirmative Action Was White: An Untold History of Racial Inequality in Twentieth-Century America* (New York: W. W. Norton, 2005), 20–22.

131. Farm Act of 1916, Public Law 64-158, 64th Congress, S. 2986, § 7. http://credo .library.umass.edu/view/full/mums312-b035-i254; Gerald Jaynes, ed., *Encyclopedia of African American Society* (Thousand Oaks, CA: Sage, 2005), 314.

132. Robert Caro, *Master of the Senate* (New York: Random House, 2002), 65.

Chapter 3 The Rise of Black Banking

1. Isabel Wilkerson, *The Warmth of Other Suns: The Epic Story of America's Great Migration* (New York: Random House, 2010), 9–10.

2. William Loren Katz, ed., *The American Negro: His History and Literature,* 141 vols. *The Negro in Chicago: A Study in Race Relations and a Race Riot in 1919* (New York: Arno Press and New York Times, 1968), 79–86.

3. Langston Hughes, *The Collected Poems of Langston Hughes,* ed. Arnold Rampersad (New York: Vintage Books, 1995), 26–27.

4. James Baldwin, *The Evidence of Things Not Seen* (New York: Henry Holt, 1985), 25.

5. The word "ghetto" originated in Italy in the early seventeenth century to describe the area of a city where Jewish residents were forced to live by law and then by economic and cultural pressure. Indeed, the northern American ghettos were also occupied by Jewish and other European immigrants before the black migrants arrived. Mitchell Duneier, *Ghetto: The Invention of a Place, the History of an Idea* (New York: Farrar, Straus and Giroux, 2016).

6. For a history of America's racial ghettos, see Douglas Massey and Nancy Denton, *American Apartheid: Segregation and the Making of the Underclass* (Cambridge, MA: Harvard University Press, 1993); Robert Samson, *Great American City: Chicago and the Enduring Neighborhood Effect* (Chicago: University of Chicago Press, 2013).

7. Abram L. Harris, *The Negro as Capitalist: A Study of Banking and Business among American Negroes* (Philadelphia: American Academy of Political and Social Science, 1936), 48. John Henry Harmon Jr., Arnett G. Lindsay, and Carter G. Woodson, *The Negro as a Business Man* (College Park, MD: McGrath, 1969), 65, citing *Directory of Negro Banks from 1900 to 1928* from the Tuskegee Institute. There were several banks that were not recognized as such by their chartering state. For example, the *Negro Year Book* for 1925 listed nine banks in Georgia, but the state of Georgia has never recognized more than four black-owned banks. Joseph A. Pierce, *Negro Business and Business Education: Their Present and Prospective Development* (New York: Springer, 1995), 151, 159. Total black bankers in 1900 were 2,105 and 6,405 in 1920. Harmon et al., *Negro as a Business Man*, 26. Between 1900 and 1920, black bankers exploded by more than 300 percent.

8. Pierce, *Negro Business and Business Education*, 159.

9. Harris, *Negro as Capitalist*, 49, app. 4. Total combined assets in all U.S. banks in 1926 was $65 billion. Thayer Watkins, "The Money Supply and the Banking System before and during the Great Depression," http://www.sjsu.edu/faculty/watkins/depmon.htm.

10. Harmon et al., *Negro as a Business Man*, 65. According to Arnett Lindsay, "unfair banking practices along with the general discrimination heaped upon Negroes . . . necessitated the organization of banking institutions of their own."

11. In Harris's complete list of all black-owned banks from 1888 to 1932, no New York banks are listed, as compared to six in Chicago, six in Philadelphia, and four in Washington, DC. Harris, *Negro as Capitalist*, app. 2.

12. Christopher Robert Reed, "A Reinterpretation of Black Strategies for Change at the Chicago World's Fair, 1933–34," *Illinois Historical Journal* 81(1) (Spring 1988): 5.

13. Nicholas A. Lash, "Asymmetries in US Banking: The Role of Black-Owned Banks," in *Global Divergence in Trade, Money and Policy*, eds. Volbert Alexander and Hans-Helmut Kotz (Cheltenham, UK: Edward Elger, 2006), 95.

14. Rick Kogan and June Skinner Sawyers, "Jesse Binga: Banker and Realtor," in *Chicago Portraits*, ed. June Sawyers (Chicago: Northwestern University Press, 2012), 39. Binga studied law for two years with one of the first black graduates of the University of Michigan Law School, Thomas R. Crisup. "Michigan Black Lawyers 'Firsts,'" *Michigan Bar Journal* (May 2015): 20, http://www.michbar.org/file/barjournal/article/documents/pdf4article2622.pdf.

15. Christopher Robert Reed, *Knock at the Door of Opportunity: Black Migration to Chicago, 1900–1919* (Carbondale: Southern Illinois University Press, 2014), 174.

16. Ibid.

17. "Chicago's Only Banker," *Chicago Defender*, December 23, 1911. As noted by a contemporary historian, Binga's bank "marked the first attempt of Negroes to do a strictly commercial banking business in a Northern city." Harmon et al., *Negro as a Business Man*, 77–78.

18. In Chicago, one black home was bombed every twenty days between 1917 and 1921, a total of fifty-eight homes in three years. St. Clair Drake and Horace

Cayton, *Black Metropolis: A Study of Negro Life in a Northern City* (Chicago: University of Chicago Press, 1945), 178–179; Allan H. Spear, *Black Chicago: The Making of a Negro Ghetto, 1890–1920* (Chicago: University of Chicago Press, 1967), 177–178.

19. Katz, *Negro in Chicago*, 131.
20. "I am an American citizen, a Christian and a property owner. No man can make of me a traitor or a coward. No power on earth can change my faith in God. I will defend my home and personal liberty to the extent of my life." "Chicago's Only Banker," *Chicago Defender*, December 23, 1911.
21. Carl R. Osthaus, "The Rise and Fall of Jesse Binga," *Journal of Negro History* 58(1) (January 1973): 43. "Banks or banking associations may be organized under the provisions of this Act in all cities, towns, and villages with a minimum capital stock . . . in all cities and towns of fifty thousand inhabitants or more, of two hundred thousand dollars." 16a Ill. Comp. Stat. 683 (1913).
22. Christopher Robert Reed, *The Depression Comes to the South Side: Protest and Politics in the Black Metropolis, 1930–1933* (Bloomington: Indiana University Press, 2011), 18–19.
23. Charles W. Calomiris, "Runs on Banks and the Lessons of the Great Depression," *Regulation* 22(1) (1999), http://object.cato.org/sites/cato.org/files/serials/files/regulation/1999/4/deplesson.pdf.
24. Reed, *Depression Comes to the South Side*.
25. Lash, "Asymmetries in US Banking," 95. See Charles Gerena, "Opening the Vault: Black-Owned Banks Have a Long History of Providing Financial Services to Underserved Communities, but How Important Are They in Today's Market?," *St. Louis Federal Reserve Review*, Spring 2007, 48.
26. Illinois Banking Commission, *Bank Resources and Liabilities, 1929–1930*.
27. John A. Carroll, "The Great American Bubble," *Real America Magazine*, April 1935, 16–20. The author was a former president of the Chicago and Cook County Bankers Association. In addition, when Binga asked Mr. Brown, first vice president of First National Bank of Chicago for assistance, Brown derided Binga, saying, "Why you are no banker." Hurt and confused, Binga believed Brown blocked every effort he afterward made to save the bank. Harris, *Negro as Capitalist*, 162.
28. Calomiris, "Runs on Banks and the Lessons of the Great Depression"; Elmus Wicker, *The Banking Panics of the Great Depression* (Cambridge: Cambridge University Press, 2000), 86. Reed, *Depression Comes to the South Side*, 18–19.
29. W. E. B. Du Bois, "Binga," *The Crisis*, December 1930, 425.
30. Reed, *Depression Comes to the South Side*, 19.
31. Dempsey Travis, *An Autobiography of Black Chicago* (Evanston, IL: Agate, 2013), 45.
32. Ibid., 51.
33. Robert Lynn Fuller, *"Phantom of Fear": The Banking Panic of 1933* (Jefferson, NC: McFarland and Co., 2012), 63–64; Jason Breslow, "Were Bankers Jailed in Past Financial Crises?," *Frontline*, January 22, 2013, http://www.pbs.org/wgbh/frontline/article/were-bankers-jailed-in-past-financial-crises/.
34. Patricia Carter Sluby, *The Entrepreneurial Spirit of African American Inventors* (Santa Barbara, CA: Praeger, 2011), 59–60.
35. Ibid.
36. Harmon et al., *Negro as a Business Man*, 79. The advantage of affiliation was the power to rediscount (exchange a negotiable debt instrument for a second time to increase market liquidity), the right to hold Federal Reserve notes paying 6 percent interest, access to minimal liquidity protection, and of course, the prestige that accompanied membership.
37. Earl Louis Brown, "Negro Banks in the United States" (M.A. thesis, Boston University, 1930), 49.

38. Harris, *Negro as Capitalist*, 145, 162–163.

39. Irma Watkins-Owens, *Blood Relations: Caribbean Immigrants and the Harlem Community, 1900–1930* (Bloomington: Indiana University Press, 1996), 133.

40. "Historic Census Browser," University of Virginia Library, http://mapserver.lib.virginia.edu/.

41. *New York Age*, April 13, 1916, 2.

42. *Sun and New York Herald*, May 23, 1920, 84.

43. Watkins-Owens, *Blood Relations*, 133. *New York Tribune*, January 27, 1920, 23.

44. *New York Age*, October 5, 1916, 1.

45. By December 1928, seven New York banks (the Dunbar National Bank, the Chelsea Exchange Bank, the Corn Exchange Bank, the Empire City Savings Bank, the Chatham and Phoenix National Bank and Trust, the Chase National Bank, and the Colonial Bank) were all listed as banks with savings departments "conveniently located" for blacks in New York, though none were lending to blacks at the time. *New York Age*, December 15, 1928, 2.

46. Ibid.

47. Watkins-Owens, *Blood Relations*, 133.

48. Arnett G. Lindsay, "The Negro in Banking," *Journal of Negro History* 14(2) (April 1929): 198.

49. Minimum capital requirements were roughly the same for banks in New York and Illinois. N.Y. Banking Law § 60(3) (Consol. 1909); 16a Ill. Comp. Stat. 683 (1913). The state's discretion was more robust in New York than in Illinois and Massachusetts—in New York, the bank superintendent could deny a banking charter for any reason if he was not satisfied with the character of bank managers. N.Y. Banking Law § 8 (Consol. 1909). N.Y. Banking Law § 63 (Consol. 1909). "The Auditor may, in his discretion, withhold the issuing of the said certificate authorizing the commencement of business when he is not satisfied as to the personal character and standing of the officers or directors elected or appointed, in accordance with sections three and four of this Act; or when he has reason to believe that this bank is organized for any purpose other than that contemplated by this Act." 16a Ill. Comp. Stat. 677 (1913); Mass. Gen. Laws 168 § 8 (1921).

50. *New York Age*, February 17, 1923, 1.

51. Watkins-Owens, *Blood Relations*, 133. The newspaper reported that "A short-order restaurant now occupies the quarters which were intended for the bank, and the rest of the building is used for offices and furnished room accommodations." *New York Age*, February 17, 1923, 2.

52. Watkins-Owens, *Blood Relations*, 133.

53. *New York Age*, April 13, 1916, 2.

54. Ibid.

55. Ibid.

56. *New York Age*, October 6, 1923, 1.

57. *New York Age*, January 26, 1924, 1.

58. *New York Age*, October 6, 1923, 1. These accounts required a $200 initial deposit. Of the bank's special interest or savings department, African Americans made up 85 to 90 percent of the bank's clientele.

59. Ibid.

60. *New York Age*, July 10, 1920, 1.

61. Ibid., 1.

62. Brown, "Negro Banks," 28.

63. Ibid.

64. Arthur I. Blaustein, *Star Spangled Hustle* (Doubleday, 1972), 72.

65. George Bernard Shaw, *Man and Superman*, quoted in ibid., 76.

66. Brown, "Negro Banks," 25–26, 28.

67. "Report of Opening of the Bank," *Time*, September 24, 1928.

68. Ibid.

69. The bank's balance sheet statements from 1928 to 1933 suggest it maintained stability through the Great Depression because it invested heavily in safe government securities. Office of the Comptroller of the Currency, *Individual Statements of Condition of National Banks at the Close of Business 1932, 1933* (Washington, DC: U.S. Government Printing Office, 1933).

70. "The Cooperative a Very Present Help in Time of Trouble," *Dunbar News*, March 9, 1932.

71. Lindsay, "Negro in Banking," 200.

72. *New York Age*, September 22, 1928, 1.

73. Ibid.

74. "Business & Finance: Harlem Bank," *Time*, September 24, 1928.

75. *New York Age*, September 24, 1932, 1. Announcing the opening of the bank, William R. Conklin, the agent for the bank's organizers, stated that the bank "would fill a longfelt want" of blacks in Harlem. *New York Age*, August 18, 1928, 2.

76. *New York Age*, July 15, 1933, 4. "Business & Finance: Harlem Bank," *Time*, September 24, 1928.

77. "Work, Waste, Wealth: Dunbar Bank," *The Crisis*, August 1933, 186.

78. *New York Age*, September 22, 1928, 1; April 6, 1929, 1. In 1929, Fred. R. Moore, editor of the *New York Age*, and Dr. Robert Russ Moton, principal of the Tuskegee Institute, both accepted invitations to serve as members of the bank's board of directors.

79. Watkins-Owens, *Blood Relations*, 133–136.

80. *New York Age*, July 15, 1933, 4; July 8, 1933, 1. On July 10, 1933, the Dunbar National Bank opened a new branch for the residents of Harlem. The additional quarters were located at 135th Street and Seventh Avenue, in "the quarters previously occupied by the Mercantile Bank and Trust Company."

81. "Dunbar Apartments," *We Shall Overcome: Historic Places of the Civil Rights Movement*, http://www.nps.gov/nr/travel/civilrights/ny2.htm.

82. Aberjhani and Sandra West, *Encyclopedia of the Harlem Renaissance* (New York: Checkmark Books, 2003), 265. Willard B. Gatewood, *Aristocrats of Color: The Black Elite, 1880–1920* (Fayetteville: University of Arkansas Press, 1990), 341.

83. Aberjhani and West, *Encyclopedia of the Harlem Renaissance*, 265. "Dunbar Bank Closes," *Afro-American*, April 30, 1938, https://news.google.com/newspapers?nid=2211&dat=19380430&id=yQQnAAAAIBAJ&sjid=SAMGAAAAIBAJ&pg=6066,1912328&hl=en.

84. The first black nationalist was Martin Delaney a pre–Civil War abolitionist who urged blacks to return to Africa instead of trying to make it work in the United States.

85. Marcus Garvey, "The Negro's Greatest Enemy," September 1923, cited in "Chapter in Autobiography," *The Marcus Garvey and Universal Negro Improvement Association Papers*, ed. Robert A. Hill, vol. 1 (Berkeley: University of California Press, 1983), 5.

86. Camilo Jose Vergara, *Harlem: The Unmaking of a Ghetto* (Chicago: University of Chicago Press, 2014), 292.

87. Manning Marable, *Malcolm X: A Life of Reinvention* (New York: Penguin Books, 2011), chap. 1. "Marcus Garvey Timeline," *American Experience*, http://www.pbs.org/wgbh/amex/garvey/timeline/timeline2.html.

88. David Van Leeuwen, "Marcus Garvey and the Universal Negro Improvement Association," http://nationalhumanitiescenter.org/tserve/twenty/tkeyinfo/garvey.htm.

89. Marcus Garvey, *Life and Lessons: A Centennial Companion to the Marcus Garvey and Universal Negro Improvement Association Papers*, eds. Robert Abraham Hill and Barbara Blair (Berkeley: University of California Press, 1988), xxvii.

90. Manning Marable, *How Capitalism Underdeveloped Black America* (Chicago: Haymarket Books, 2015), 131. Marcus Garvey, "West Indies in the Mirror of Truth," *Champion Magazine*, January 1917.

91. Marable, *Malcolm X.*

92. Richard R. Wright Jr., "The Financial Condition of Our People," Address before the Philadelphia Preachers' meeting, *Christian Recorder*, May 19, 1921.

93. Alexa Benson Henderson, "Richard Wright and the National Negro Banking Association: Early Organizing Efforts among Black Bankers, 1924–1942," *Pennsylvania Magazine of History and Biography* 117(1/2) (January–April 1993): 54, 59. *St. Louis Argus*, September 30, 1932, Tuskegee Institute News Clipping File. http://www.nationalbankers.org/history.htm. The organization changed its name to the National Bankers Association (NBA) in 1948.

94. Kevin F. Modesto, " 'Won't Be Weighted Down': Richard R. Wright, Jr.'s Contributions to Social Work and Social Welfare," *Journal of Sociology & Social Welfare* 31(2) (June 2004), http://scholarworks.wmich.edu/cgi/viewcontent.cgi?article=2984&context=jssw.

95. *St. Louis Argus*, September 30, 1932, Tuskegee Institute News Clipping File.

96. "History," National Bankers Association, http://www.nationalbankers.org/history.htm.

97. *Pittsburgh Courier*, September 24, 1927.

98. "Richard R. Wright and the National Negro Bankers Association: Early Organizing Efforts among Black Bankers, 1924–1942," *Pennsylvania Magazine of History & Biography*, CXVII(1-2) (January / April 1993), https://journals.psu.edu/pmhb/article/viewFile/44835/44556.

99. *Pittsburgh Courier*, September 24, 1927.

100. Brown, "Negro Banks," 30.

101. Some 9,000 banks failed during the Great Depression. David C. Wheelock, "Regulation, Market Structure, and the Bank Failures of the Great Depression," *St. Louis Federal Reserve Review*, March / April 1998, 27.

102. "Richard R. Wright and the National Negro Bankers Association," 63.

103. *Norfolk Journal and Guide*, July 23, 1927.

104. "Richard R. Wright and the National Negro Bankers Association," 65–66.

105. For a history of Coolidge and Thrift Week, see Sheldon Garon, *Beyond Our Means: Why America Spends While the World Saves* (Princeton, NJ: Princeton University Press, 2013).

106. Robert E. Weems, *Business in Black and White: American Presidents and Black Entrepreneurs in the Twentieth Century* (New York: New York University Press, 2009), chap. 1.

107. NNBL Minutes, 1932. "The attitude taken by Mr. Spaulding when he came to the rescue of the Citizens Trust Company was that of maintaining confidence throughout the entire Negro commercial and insurance field." Brown, "Negro Banks," 39.

108. It also became the first African American–owned bank to be FDIC-insured after the Great Depression. Willard C. Lewis, "Citizens Trust Bank," *New Georgia Encyclopedia*, August 26, 2013, http://www.georgiaencyclopedia.org/articles/business-economy/citizens-trust-bank. Harmon et al., *Negro as a Businessman*, 74–75. Brown, "Negro Banks," 38.

109. Harris, *Negro as Capitalist*, 61. "Richard R. Wright and the National Negro Bankers Association." Juliet E. K. Walker, *The History of Black Business* (Chapel Hill: University of North Carolina Press, 2009), 13. In the 1992 reprint of Harris's *The Negro as Capitalist*, the editors say eight survived.

110. Jesse Binga remarked, "Why, there is a house which I once offered $22,000 for and could not get it. Today it could not be sold for $6,000." Harris, *Negro as Capitalist*, 168–169. A 2013 study from the London School of Economics on

the causes of bank failures in Chicago during the Great Depression found that "banks which failed the earliest in the 1930s had invested more in non-liquid assets (in particular, mortgages) in the 1920s." Natacha Posten-Vinay, "What Caused Chicago Bank Failures in the Great Depression? A Look at the 1920s," London School of Economics, Department of Economic History, June 2013.

111. "Richard R. Wright and the National Negro Bankers Association," 72.

112. Harmon et al., *Negro as a Business Man*, 72.

113. Harris, *Negro as Capitalist*, 54; Brown, "Negro Banks"; Carter G. Woodson, *The Mis-Education of the Negro* (Washington, DC: Associated Publishers, 1933), 40. Illinois Banking Commissioner Balance Sheets 1922–1932. In his review of the balance sheets of the largest black-owned banks from 1903 to 1930, Harris shows that the average capital investment to total deposit ratios for black banks were higher than industry norms for the same period. Harris, *Negro as Capitalist*, 57–58, 156, 163–164, 144–145.

114. Harris, *Negro as Capitalist*, 54; Brown, "Negro Banks."

115. Other banks, too, had poor customers, but they were able to diversify their deposits and loans such that the accounts of the poor did not dominate their balance sheets.

116. Capital is a measure of the owners' or total shareholders' equity or ownership interest in the bank. Capital is a measurement used to indicate the proportion by which a bank's assets (mainly loans out to borrowers) exceed a bank's liabilities (mainly deposits). In short: Assets – Liabilities = Capital. "The ratio of capital investment to total deposits . . . averaged 32.9 per cent from 1903 to 1930. In state banks the norm should have be about 18 per cent. In brief, the banks under consideration should have had a large deposit business. This weakness was paralleled." Harris, *Negro as Capitalist*, 59.

117. Ibid., 58–59.

118. Total cash / demand deposits ratio for black banks averaged 41.4 percent for the years 1910–1930, compared with the industry norm of 35 percent. Harris, *Negro as Capitalist*, 57–59.

119. Higher leverage means higher risk, but also higher profits. Capital acts as a buffer against loss to depositors and other counterparties because the higher the equity / capital, the more losses are borne by bank owners and shareholders before being passed on to depositors. Anat Admati, *The Bankers' New Clothes: What's Wrong with Banking and What to Do about It* (Princeton, NJ: Princeton University Press, 2014).

120. Robert L. Boyd, "Black Business Transformation, Black Well-Being, and Public Policy," *Population Research and Policy Review* 9(2) (1990): 117–132, 119. https://www.jstor.org/stable/40229887?seq=1#page_scan_tab_contents. Harris, *Negro as Capitalist*, 172. Before 1930, blacks were still excluded from the trading houses where securities were exchanged, so they held few securities. Black banks did hold some U.S. treasury notes, and the Binga and Douglass banks held a few private bonds in large white enterprises and a few black-owned businesses. Harris, *Negro as Capitalist*, 146, 159. For a detailed list of securities held by the Douglass and Binga banks at the time of receivership, see Harris, *Negro as Capitalist*, 146–147 and 159–160, respectively.

121. "Negroes pay about two per cent more for money than white business men on ordinary loans, about fourteen per cent for first mortgage loans, and much more for second mortgages." J. H. Harmon Jr., "The Negro as a Local Business Man," *Journal of Negro History* 14(2) (April 1929): 153. As explained by a contemporary account, white banks did not like to lend to black borrowers primarily due to "the liquidity of the loans as indicated by the marketability of the property which secures them." Harris, *Negro as Capitalist*, 56.

122. Kenneth A. Snowden, "Mortgage Banking in the United States, 1870–1940," Research Institute for Housing America, Research Paper No. 13-02 (November 2013), 54, 58. Joseph Morton, *Urban Mortgage Lending: Comparative Markets and Experience* (Princeton, NJ: Princeton University Press, 1956), 149–155.

123. From 1900 to 1920, there was chronic mob violence in which whites attacked blacks and ransacked or burned their homes. Massey and Denton, *American Apartheid*, 34. By the 1920s, segregation was enforced through banks, realtors, and neighborhood "improvement associations," whose main purpose was to organize collective action to keep out black homeowners and expel those who dared cross the color line.

124. A 1919 Chicago study described the boundary making around black neighborhoods as "a kind of guerrilla warfare." Blacks were under constant threat from "rampaging bands of whites [who] roamed the streets for days, attacking blacks at will." Beryl Satter, *Family Properties: Race, Real Estate, and the Exploitation of Black Urban America* (New York: Henry Holt, 2010), 39; Massey and Denton, *American Apartheid*, 30.

125. According to one black realtor, "The appearance of the first blacks in an all-white block triggered a response that caused the whites to treat them as invading enemy aliens." Travis, *Autobiography of Black Chicago*, 32. The Chicago Real Estate Board (CREB), the professional association of Chicago real estate brokers, convened a meeting in 1917 to organize a response to the "invasion of white residence districts by negroes." In 1924, the National Association of Real Estate Boards agreed not to sell to blacks outside of designated black areas. Rose Helper, *Racial Policies and Practices of Real Estate Brokers* (Minneapolis: University of Minnesota Press, 1969), 172–182; Arnold R. Hirsch, *Making the Second Ghetto: Race and Housing in Chicago, 1940–1960* (Chicago: University of Chicago Press 1988), 31–33.

126. "Whites do not want to buy [properties occupied by Negroes] and Negroes cannot afford to." Harris, *Negro as Capitalist*, 169. E. Franklin Frazier, *Black Bourgeoisie* (New York: Simon & Schuster, 1957).

127. Kevin Boyle, *Arc of Justice: A Saga of Race, Civil Rights, and Murder in the Jazz Age* (New York: Henry Holt, 2004), 69, 247; Marable, *Malcolm X*.

128. "Because there is a white fear of being inundated with lower-class black 'hordes,' it becomes necessary to prevent the entry of middle-class blacks." Raymond Franklin, *Shadows of Race and Class*, cited in Melvin L. Oliver and Thomas M. Shapiro, *Black Wealth/White Wealth: A New Perspective on Racial Inequality* (New York: Routledge, 1997), 40–41.

129. Homer Hoyt, *One Hundred Years of Land Values in Chicago: The Relationship of the Growth of Chicago to the Rise in Its Land Values, 1830–1933* (Chicago: University of Chicago Press, 1933), https://archive.org/details/onehundredyears o00hoytrich.

130. W. Edward Orser, *Blockbusting in Baltimore: The Edmondson Village Story* (Lexington: University Press of Kentucky, 1997), x–xi, 4–7.

131. "The Truth about the North," in *Black Protest and the Great Migration*, ed. Eric Arnesen (Bedford / St. Martin's, 2002), 68.

132. Richard Rothstein, "From Ferguson to Baltimore: The Fruits of Government-Sponsored Segregation," Economic Policy Institute, April 29, 2015, http://www.epi .org/blog/from-ferguson-to-baltimore-the-fruits-of-government-sponsored -segregation/.

133. If a bank has to meet demands for deposit withdrawals that exceed what that they hold in reserves, they can either borrow from another bank to meet the needs or sell their assets to a bank or individual, often in a "fire sale." Fernando Duarte and Thomas M. Eisenbach, "Fire-Sale Spillovers and Systemic Risk,"

Federal Reserve Bank of New York Staff Reports, October 2013, revised February 2015, 1.

134. Harris, *Negro as Capitalist*, 163.

135. Ibid.

136. Harmon et al., *Negro as a Business Man*, 72. Lindsay blamed this problem on the lack of large black businesses, stating, "Commercial banks need the support of profitably operated business enterprises. And it must be admitted that up to this time a sufficiently large number of well-established businesses among Negroes are not found in many of the cities. Therefore, we do not find many Negro banks actually making money in this field."

137. Modern banking is much more complex than this simple money multiplier reflects. Paul Sheard, "Repeat after Me: Banks Cannot and Do Not 'Lend Out' Reserves," Standard & Poor's Rating Services, August 13, 2013, https://www.globalcreditportal.com/ratingsdirect/renderArticle.do?articleId=1177975&Sct ArtId=176005&from=CM&nsl_code=LIME&sourceObjectId=8163576&source RevId=1&fee_ind=N&exp_date=20230814-23:17:33.

138. Michael McLeay et al., "Money Creation in the Modern Economy," *Bank of England Quarterly Bulletin* (2014 Q1): 3, http://www.bankofengland.co.uk/publications/Documents/quarterlybulletin/2014/qb14q1prereleasemoney creation.pdf.

139. Abram Harris noted that "the white bank is the final resting place of the funds lent by the Negro bank." Harris, *Negro as Capitalist*, 167.

140. Ibid., chap. 7.

141. Massey and Denton, *American Apartheid*, 126–140.

142. Economist Robert Gordon explains that blacks had lower life expectancy and often died of diseases because Jim Crow laws did not allow for sewage and water treatment in black areas. Infant mortality rates for blacks were double that for whites. Robert Gordon, *The Rise and Fall of American Growth: The U.S. Standard of Living since the Civil War* (Princeton, NJ: Princeton University Press, 2016), chaps. 7 and 16.

143. W. E. B. Du Bois, "A Negro Nation within a Nation," in *African American Political Thought, 1890–1930*, ed. Cary D. Wintz (New York: Taylor & Francis, 1996), 159–160.

144. Gunnar Myrdal, *An American Dilemma: The Negro Problem and Modern Democracy* (New York: Harper & Bros., 2007), 205.

145. Du Bois, "Negro Nation within a Nation," 162.

146. Ibid.

147. Ibid., 165.

148. Du Bois, "As the Crow Flies," *Amsterdam News*, October 10, 1942.

149. Earl Ofari, *The Myth of Black Capitalism* (New York: Monthly Review Press, 1970); Harris, *Negro as Capitalist*; Frazier, *Black Bourgeoisie*.

150. Harris, *Negro as Capitalist*, 175.

151. Ibid.

152. Woodson, *Mis-Education of the Negro*, 46. Other black leaders were similarly "appalled by Harris' opposition to black enterprise, although few addressed the substance of his criticism." "Richard R. Wright and the National Negro Bankers Association," 76.

153. Woodson, *Mis-Education of the Negro*, 33.

154. Ibid., 83.

155. Black banker Lindsay Harmon explained that "the Negro merchant must face a racial handicap in having most whites refusing to patronize him because of his color while failing at the same time to get the trade of his own people who may be a little jealous of his progress or high position or who cannot overcome

thinking that the white merchant can give him the most for the least money." Harmon et al., *Negro as a Business Man*, 40.

156. Woodson, *Mis-Education of the Negro*, 110.

157. Quoted in Weems, *Business in Black and White*, 22. The Commerce Department calculated the "Purchasing Power of Negroes" in 1935 to be $2 billion dollars.

158. Woodson admonished blacks to "begin immediately to pool their earnings and organize industries to participate in supplying social and economic demands." Woodson, *Mis-Education of the Negro*, 108.

159. W. E. B. Du Bois, *The Souls of Black Folk* (New York: Dover, 1994), 128.

Chapter 4 The New Deal for White America

1. Historian Ira Katznelson explains that "the wide array of significant and far-reaching public policies that were shaped and administered during the New Deal and the Fair Deal era of the 1930s and 1940s were crafted and administered in a deeply discriminatory fashion." Ira Katznelson, *When Affirmative Action Was White* (New York: Norton, 2005), 17, 51. See also Ira Katznelson, *Fear Itself: The New Deal and the Origins of Our Time* (New York: Liveright Publishing, 2013).

2. Katznelson, *When Affirmative Action Was White*, 17–20. Manning Marable, *Malcolm X: A Life of Reinvention* (New York: Viking Press, 2011), 168. Mike Royko, *Boss: Richard J. Daley of Chicago* (New York: Penguin, 1988), chap. 7.

3. Katznelson, *Fear Itself*; Katznelson, *When Affirmative Action Was White*, 8–9; Robert Caro, *Master of the Senate* (New York: Random House, 2009), 215.

4. Katznelson, *When Affirmative Action Was White*, 60.

5. Caro, *Master of the Senate*, 93.

6. Katznelson, *When Affirmative Action Was White*, 48.

7. Ibid., 37.

8. "Fully 65 percent of African Americans fell outside the reach of the new program; between 70 and 80 percent in different parts of the South." Ibid., 43.

9. Paul Frymer, *Black and Blue: African Americans, the Labor Movement, and the Decline of the Democratic Party* (Princeton, NJ: Princeton University Press, 2011), 112; Dempsey Travis, *An Autobiography of Black Chicago* (Evanston, IL: Agate, 2014), 36.

10. Katznelson, *Fear Itself*.

11. Charles Calomiris and Stephen Haber, *Fragile by Design: The Political Origins of Banking Crises and Scarce Credit* (Princeton, NJ: Princeton University Press, 2014) explains that southern populists created a system that was economically inefficient, but was geared toward offering credit to the South as well as maintaining small banking.

12. Louis Hyman, *Debtor Nation: The History of America in Red Ink* (Princeton, NJ: Princeton University Press, 2011), 51.

13. Gail Radford, *Modern Housing in America: Policy Struggles in the New Deal Era* (Chicago: University of Chicago Press, 2008), chap. 4. Ickes complained "that most of the projects that came before [the PWA] were conceived more for the speculative benefit of their promoters than for the advantage of the people who need modern housing at a low price." Hyman, *Debtor Nation*, 51–52.

14. Hyman, *Debtor Nation*, 52–53.

15. Robert Caro, *The Power Broker: Robert Moses and the Fall of New York* (New York: Vintage, 2012), chap. 27.

16. Kenneth T. Jackson, *Crabgrass Frontier: The Suburbanization of the United States* (New York: Oxford University Press, 1985), 198, 202.

17. W. E. B. Du Bois, *The Souls of Black Folk* (New York: Dover, 1994), 3.

18. New home construction doubled from 1936 to 1941. In 1936, the FHA had lent a half billion dollars in guaranteed mortgages. By 1939, they had already issued $4 billion in mortgages and home improvement loans. Housing starts were 332,000 in 1936 and 619,000 in 1941. Melvin L. Oliver and Thomas M. Shapiro, *Black Wealth/White Wealth: A New Perspective on Racial Inequality* (New York: Routledge, 2006), 17. Jackson, *Crabgrass Frontier*, 205.

19. The federal guarantee revolutionized mortgages because the fund insured 90 percent of individual home mortgages. According to Julian Zimmerman, FHA commissioner in the 1950s, when the scheme was first proposed, "it was such an innovation that many considered it radical and unworkable." According to Zimmerman, "it was the last hope of private enterprise. The alternative was socialization of the housing industry." FHA, *The FHA Story in Summary, 1934–1959* (Washington, DC: U.S. Government Printing Office, 1959), 4; cited in Hyman, *Debtor Nation*, 53.

20. According to Louis Hyman, the FHA program "completely reversed . . . the conventional justification for government intrusions." FHA money was "not the dole" and "not taxpayer money." Hyman, *Debtor Nation*, 55.

21. Ibid., 71; this family income of $2,500 per year in 1938 was equivalent to a yearly income of $42,753.35 in 2017. *Bureau of Labor Statistics, Consumer Price Index Inflation Calculator*, https://www.bls.gov/data/inflation_calculator.htm.

22. First, prior to their passage, a borrower would need a down payment of anywhere from 40 to 70 percent of the home price to purchase a home. After these loans, a down payment of 10 percent was enough because the government would now essentially insure up to 90 percent of the collateral. Second, by extending the repayment period to thirty years and insisting that all loans be fully amortized, they reduced monthly payments and dramatically reduced defaults. Third, they created uniform housing standards that all new houses had to meet, which favored new, homogeneous homes. And fourth, by eliminating high default risks, the programs brought mortgage interest down from 15 percent to 2–3 percent, making it possible for families of moderate means to become homeowners. Jackson, *Crabgrass Frontier*, 204–205. Hyman, *Debtor Nation*, 56–57.

23. Oliver and Shapiro, *Black Wealth/White Wealth*, 17.

24. Dalton Conley, *Being Black, Living in the Red: Race, Wealth, and Social Policy in America* (Berkeley: University of California Press, 2010), 37; citing Douglas Massey and Nancy Denton, *American Apartheid: Segregation and Making of the Underclass* (Cambridge, MA: Harvard University Press, 1993), 54.

25. Conley, *Being Black*, 37.

26. Oliver and Shapiro, *Black Wealth/White Wealth*, 18; Jackson, *Crabgrass Frontier*, 208; FHA, *Underwriting Manual* (Washington, DC: U.S. Government Printing Office, 1936), part 2, para. 233. http://epress.trincoll.edu/ontheline2015/wp-content/uploads/sites/16/2015/03/1936FHA-Underwriting.pdf.

27. Beryl Satter, *Family Properties: Race, Real Estate and the Exploitation of Black Urban America* (New York: Henry Holt, 2010), 43; citing Arnold R. Hirsch, "Choosing Segregation: Federal Housing Policy between Shelley and Brown," in *From Tenements to the Taylor Homes: In Search of an Urban Housing Policy in Twentieth-Century America*, ed. John F. Bauman, Roger Biles, and Kristin M. Szylvia (University Park: Pennsylvania State University Press, 2000), 211–212. *Shelley v. Kraemer*, 334 U.S. 1 (1948).

28. Jackson, *Crabgrass Frontier*, 209. Though the FHA generally refused mortgages for blacks in white neighborhoods, it was sometimes willing to approve of loans in all-black neighborhoods. The catch? The neighborhood could not be "blighted," and most black neighborhoods were deemed blighted due to their aging homes and overcrowded living quarters, so they were excluded anyway.

29. As Beryl Satter explains, "it is not surprising then, that the late 1940s saw an upsurge of violence against the black families that moved into white neighborhoods." Satter, *Family Properties*, 45.

30. David L. Kirp, John P. Dwyer, and Larry A. Rosenthal, *Our Town: Race, Housing, and the Soul of Suburbia* (New Brunswick, NJ: Rutgers University Press, 1995); Conley, *Being Black*, 37. For example, the FHA lent sixty times more mortgages to the white Nassau County, New York, suburbs than to Bronx County from 1934 to 1960. Massey and Denton, *American Apartheid*, 54.

31. Paterson and Camden, New Jersey, were two such cities.

32. Oliver and Shapiro, *Black Wealth / White Wealth*, 18.

33. Charles Abrams, *Forbidden Neighbors* (New York: Harper, 1955), 229.

34. "The Second Great Migration," in *In Motion: The African-American Migration Experience*, comp. and ed., Howard Dodson and Sylviane A. Diouf (Washington, DC: National Geographic, 2004). By the end of the migration, 80 percent of blacks resided in cities. Population density in central Harlem in 1970 was 103,000 people per square mile, according to the New York Department of City Planning. New York University Furman Center, *State of New York City's Housing and Neighborhoods in 2014* (New York: New York University School of Law & Wagner School of Public Service, 2014), https://wagner.nyu.edu/files/faculty/publications/NYUFurmanCenter_SOC2014_HighRes.pdf.

35. Mandi Issacs Jackson, "Harlem's Rent Strike and Rat War: Representation, Housing Access and Tenant Resistance in New York, 1958–1964," *American Studies* 47(1) (2006): 53–79.

36. Marable, *Malcolm X*, 108.

37. Black migrants were derided as "backwards rural people" who could not possibly be expected to maneuver through the complexity of home ownership. As expressed by one real estate speculator, "How are you going to educate dumb animals?" Satter, *Family Properties*, 75; citing Favil Berns interview, June 10, 2001, 48.

38. Travis, *Autobiography of Black Chicago*, 157–159.

39. See Satter, *Family Properties*.

40. Travis, *Autobiography of Black Chicago*, 128–129.

41. According to Satter, the contract sellers "used the home as 'bait' to defraud the Negro out of a substantial sum of money and then push the [buyer] out into the street [in order to] defraud another party." Satter, *Family Properties*, 5.

42. Ibid., 242–244, 248–249.

43. Ibid., 6. Travis, *Autobiography of Black Chicago*, 157.

44. Satter, *Family Properties*, 137, citing John W. Baird interview, February 13, 2004; *Baird and Warner, Inc., 1855–1980: Celebrating 125 Years in Real Estate* (Chicago: Baird and Warner, 1980).

45. Du Bois, *Souls of Black Folk*, 8.

46. Hyman, *Debtor Nation*, 141–144. And the difference was not between suburban living and city living. Whites paid lower interest in both areas and blacks paid higher interest in both.

47. In sum, the main barrier to black mortgages in the 1950s, according to a representative of the National Association of Home Builders, was "the lack of adequate financing" caused by "deep-rooted prejudice." White insurance companies had provided much of the initial investment funds for the FHA markets, but black insurance companies did not have adequate capital. By 1945, the thirty-five members of the National Negro Insurance Association (NNIA) had only $1.5 million in capital—they held a total of 424 mortgages. The Mechanics and Farmers affiliate North Carolina Mutual Life Insurance Company accounted for 55 percent of these funds. In contrast, the top twelve white insurance companies alone held $633 million in mortgages. Hyman, *Debtor Nation*, 142.

48. White families had an average of $2,428 and blacks held $122. Ibid., 138.

49. Ibid., 139.

50. E. Franklin Frazier, *Black Bourgeoisie* (New York: Simon & Schuster, 1997), 25.

51. Ibid. For Urban League critique, see James Foree, "League Gets Alarming Data on Credit Victims," *Daily Defender*, September 16, 1959, A7.

52. "Black suburbanites did not borrow more extravagantly in absolute numbers, but relative to their incomes, they carried nearly double the debt burden of white households." The black middle class was five times as likely to borrow as whites, and 81 percent of black households bought using credit, compared to 40 percent of whites. Hyman, *Debtor Nation*, 140.

53. Ibid., 32.

54. Ibid., chaps. 1–2. Hyman explained that in the postwar credit economy, the "lines of race would definitively cross lines of class." Alan Greenspan, "Remarks at the Economic Development Conference of the Greenlining Institute, San Francisco, CaliforniaOctober 11, 1997," https://www.federalreserve.gov/boarddocs/speeches/1997/19971011.htm.

55. Hyman, *Debtor Nation*, chaps. 1–2.

56. According to historian Louis Hyman, "the modern credit system of the twentieth century was built by white men for white men, leaving other Americans to borrow in older, more expensive and dangerous ways." The credit system did not just build wealth for whites, it "constrained the credit options for poor, urban African Americans [in ways that] would have been inconceivable for the rest of America." Ibid., 7.

57. Travis, *Autobiography of Black Chicago*, 136–137.

58. Ibid., 158.

59. "Hearings before the United States Commission on Civil Rights: Housing" (Washington, DC: U.S. Government Printing Office, 1959), 738–739. A survey found that "not even a token number" of mortgages were lent to blacks by 141 commercial banks and 229 life insurance companies in the country.

60. Travis, *Autobiography of Black Chicago*, 158.

61. Ibid., 128–129, 136, 157, 159.

62. Ibid., 137.

63. Edward Irons, "Black Banking—Problems and Prospects," *Journal of Finance* 26(2) (May 1971): 424.

64. Travis, *Autobiography of Black Chicago*, 160.

65. Ibid., 163.

66. Ibid., 155, 175.

67. Ibid., 143. This caused a division, with a splinter group still called the Negro Chamber of Commerce.

68. Ibid., 169.

69. Carver Federal Savings Bank, "Why Carver," https://www.carverbank.com/about-carver.

70. David L. Mason, *From Buildings and Loans to Bail-Outs: A History of the American Savings and Loan Industry, 1831–1995* (Cambridge: Cambridge University Press, 2004), 169.

71. Douglas Martin, "M. Moran Weston, 91, Priest and Banker of Harlem, Dies," *New York Times*, May 22, 2002, http://www.nytimes.com/2002/05/22/nyregion/m-moran-weston-91-priest-and-banker-of-harlem-dies.html.

72. "Harlem's Banker-Priest: Father Weston Heads New York's St. Philip's Episcopal Church and Oldest Black Savings Firm," *Ebony*, March 1969, 93.

73. Emile Milne, "Thirty Years Financing the Family: Carver Federal Savings Still Strengthens the Black Family with Home Mortgages, but Caught Up in a Changing Urban Scene, Now Competes Vigorously for the General Market," *Black Enterprise*, July 1979, 188. See also Dennis Hevesi, "William R. Hudges, 100,

Who Led Black-Owned Banks, Dies," *New York Times*, September 5, 2007, http://www.nytimes.com/2007/09/05/nyregion/05hudgins.html?_r=0. From its inception, Carver was backed by "the cream of Harlem's black businessmen, as well as clergymen like the Rev. M. Moran Weston."

74. Martin, "M. Moran Weston"; Charlayne Hunter, "Church in Harlem Plays Vital Role in Community," *New York Times*, December 6, 1970, http://www.nytimes .com/1970/12/06/archives/church-in-harlem-plays-vital-role-in-community .html.

75. Martin, "M. Moran Weston."

76. Marable, *Malcolm X*, 108.

77. Leslie Eaton, "A Shaky Pillar in Harlem; Black-Owned Carver Bank Seeks Solid Financial Base," *New York Times*, July 11, 1999, http://www.nytimes.com/1999 /07/11/nyregion/a-shaky-pillar-in-harlem-black-owned-carver-bank-seeks -solid-financial-base.html.

78. Milne, "Thirty Years Financing the Family."

79. Eaton, "Shaky Pillar in Harlem."

80. Gaston's bank merged with Citizens Trust in Atlanta in 2003. Cliff Hocker, "Citizen's Trust to Acquire CfS Bancshares," *Black Enterprise*, September 1, 2002, http://www.blackenterprise.com/mag/citizens-trust-to-acquire-cfs-bancshares/; http://www.bloomberg.com/research/stocks/private/snapshot.asp?privcapId =2254253.

81. Carol Jenkins and Elizabeth Gardner Hines, *Black Titan: A. G. Gaston and the Making of a Black American Millionaire* (New York: Ballantine, 2005), 164.

82. Martin Luther King Jr., "We Are Still Walking," December 1956, New York, The Martin Luther King, Jr. Papers Project, https://swap.stanford.edu/20141218225454 /http://mlk-kpp01.stanford.edu/primarydocuments/Vol3/Dec-1956 _WeAreStillWalking.pdf.

83. "Advice for Living," *Ebony*, March 1958. This was a monthly advice column in *Ebony* magazine. King would respond to letters sent by readers asking for advice on a wide range of issues. For more information on the column, see http://kingencyclopedia.stanford.edu/encyclopedia/encyclopedia/enc _advice_for_living_1957_1958/; http://kingencyclopedia.stanford.edu/encyclo pedia/documentsentry/advice_for_living6/index.html.

84. "'Why direct action? Why sit ins, marches and so forth? Isn't negotiation a better path?' You are quite right in calling for negotiation." Martin Luther King Jr., "Letter from Birmingham Jail," https://web.cn.edu/kwheeler/documents/Letter _Birmingham_Jail.pdf.

85. Jenkins and Hines, *Black Titan*, 234.

86. Andrew Young, *An Easy Burden: The Civil Rights Movement and the Transformation of America* (New York: HarperCollins, 1996) 229–230; cited in Jenkins and Hines, *Black Titan*, 202–205.

87. Jenkins and Hines, *Black Titan*, 218.

88. In his highly acclaimed dissertation, \ Frazier studied the black family during and after slavery and explained the ways harsh social conditions had changed family structure, including the creation of matriarchal families. Published as E. Franklin Frazier, *The Negro Family in the United States* (Chicago: University of Chicago Press, 1939).

89. Frazier, *Black Bourgeoisie*, 25.

90. Ibid., 25–26. Though the appeal was rooted in "racial pride," Frazier believed it was leading the "black bourgeoisie" toward an inferiority complex. Frazier saw the Garvey movement and the Harlem Renaissance as a missed opportunity, a "Renaissance that failed." To Frazier, the writers of the Renaissance were "shaking off the psychology of limitation and implied inferiority" and looking toward racial emancipation outside the expectations of white middle-class values. This,

Frazier claimed, was the cause of black racial inferiority. Poets like Countee Cullen and Langston Hughes made "no apology for the free, unconventional life of the Negro masses." Ibid., 123–124.

91. Ibid., 165.

92. Ibid., 173. He chastised whites who encouraged the belief that "wealth through business will solve their problems" but never took any black businessmen into their "white business groups which own and control the life of the American economy."

93. Ibid., 236.

94. Notable among them was the Tri-State Bank, formed in Memphis in 1946 by a group of black leaders including Richard R. Wright III, the grandson of his namesake and NNBL founder. The bank played a prominent role in the civil rights struggle when Dr. King urged blacks in Memphis to deposit their money there and many did. The first black-owned bank west of the Mississippi River was the Douglass State Bank in Kansas City, formed in 1947. The Broadway Federal Bank was formed on its heels later that year in Los Angeles, California, in order to offer mortgages to black veterans who were being routinely denied loans from white banks. Joseph A. Pierce, *Negro Business and Business Education: Their Present and Prospective Development* (New York: Plenum Press, 1995), 100. U.S. Department of Commerce, *Savings and Loan Associations Owned and Operated by Negroes* (Washington, DC: U.S. Government Printing Office, 1951).

95. Fewer than nine of these black-owned banks were formed between 1934 and 1960, and five of those were formed in 1959.

96. Credit Union National Association, "Long Run Trends (1939–Present)," https://www.cuna.org/Research-And-Strategy/Credit-Union-Data-And-Statistics/Long-Run-Trends-(1939—Present)/.

97. FDIC, "Commercial Bank Reports," https://www5.fdic.gov/hsob/HSOBRpt.asp.

98. Mehrsa Baradaran, *How the Other Half Banks: Exclusion, Exploitation, and the Threat to Democracy* (Cambridge, MA: Harvard University Press, 2015), chap. 3.

99. John R. Walter, "The 3-6-3 Rule: An Urban Myth?," *Federal Reserve Bank of Richmond Economic Quarterly* 92(1) (Winter 2006): 51.

100. Calomiris and Haber, *Fragile by Design*, 16, 191.

101. The McFadden Act of 1927 prohibited branching across state lines. "The National Bank Act," Senate Report No. 473, 69th Congress, 1st Session, 6, http://www.federalreservehistory.org/Media/Material/Event/11-128; 12 U.S.C. § 264 (transferred to 12 U.S.C. §1811). The FDIC was created by the Glass-Steagall Act and made permanent by the Banking Act of 1935. Federal Reserve Bank of New York, "Banking Act of 1933," Circular No. 1248, http://www.federalreservehistory.org/Media/Material/Event/25-203.

102. Abram Harris, *The Negro as Capitalist: A Study of Banking and Business among American Negroes* (New York: Haskell House, 1970), 177.

103. Public Law 73-66, 73rd Congress, H.R. 5661, 3, June 16, 1933, https://fraser.stlouisfed.org/scribd/?title_id=991&filepath=/files/docs/historical/congressional/1933_bankingact_publiclaw66.pdf&start_page=1.

104. Scholars measure the extent of segregation using a racial "isolation index," which shows the extent to which a given race lives within neighborhoods populated predominantly by people of that race. In Chicago, for example, the isolation index for blacks rose from 10 percent in 1910 to 90 percent in 1940. The highest isolation index was 44 percent for Italians in Boston, but most other immigrant groups lived in fairly integrated neighborhoods among whites and other immigrants. Stanley Lieberson, "An Asymmetrical Approach to Segregation," in *Ethnic Segregation in Cities*, ed. Ceri Peach, Vaughn Robinson, and Susan Smith (London: Croom Helm, 1981), 61–82. Satter, *Family Properties*, 30; Massey and Denton, *American Apartheid*, 29–31.

105. "A. P. Giannini," *Who Made America,* Public Broadcasting System, https://www.pbs.org/wgbh/theymadeamerica/whomade/giannini_hi.html.

106. Office of the Comptroller of the Currency, "The Humble Beginnings of a Large Bank," http://www.occ.gov/about/what-we-do/history/giannini-bank-article-html-version.html.

107. Hyman, *Debtor Nation,* 94–95.

108. "For Italian Americans highly segregated in slum neighborhoods and routinely called 'wops,' 'dagoes,' and 'guineas' before the war, the 1940s brought brand-new money for college and homes." Nell Irvin Painter, *The History of White People* (New York: Norton, 2010), 365.

109. Ibid., 371. Caro, *Master of the Senate,* 693. Sarah Turner and John Bound, "Closing the Gap or Widening the Divide: The Effects of the GI Bill and World War II on the Educational Outcomes of Black Americans," *Journal of Economic History* 63(1) (March 2003): 145–178.

110. Painter, *History of White People,* 366. Between 1944 and 1956, the GI Bill resulted in $14.5 billion in education subsidies for half of the returning veterans, some 7.8 billion people. That was just a fraction of the $120 billion the VA and FHA spent on housing from 1934 to 1964, all of which was open to Jews, Italians, and other recent immigrants.

111. Ibid., 371.

112. Ibid., 362.

113. Modern research by Thomas Piketty, Robert Gordon, and others shows that the era from the New Deal until 1970 was an exceptional era of prosperity and wealth equality in American history. This boom was a temporary boost to middle-class wealth and standards of living. Thomas Piketty, *Capital in the Twenty-First Century* (Cambridge, MA: Harvard University Press, 2014); Robert J. Gordon, *The Rise and Fall of American Growth: The U.S. Standard of Living since the Civil War* (Princeton, NJ: Princeton University Press, 2016), 14.

114. National Archives, *Executive Order 8802: Prohibition of Discrimination in the Defense Industry,* June 25, 1941, https://www.ourdocuments.gov/doc.php?flash=false&doc=72.

115. Travis, *Autobiography of Black Chicago,* 94.

116. John David Skrentny, *The Minority Rights Revolution* (Cambridge, MA: Harvard University Press, 2004), 148.

117. Stephen Robertson, "Toward a Spatial Narrative of the 1935 Harlem Riot: Mapping and Storytelling after the Geospatial Turn," paper delivered at the New Approaches, Opportunities and Epistemological Implications of Mapping History Digitally: An International Workshop and Conference, German Historical Institute, October 20, 2016. Stephen Robertson, "Mapping a Riot: Harlem, 1935," National Council on Public History Conference, Working Group on Interpreting the History of Race Riots and Racialized Mass Violence in the Context of "Black Lives Matter," Baltimore, March 19, 2016.

118. King, Randolph, and Adam Clayton Powell were active in both national and local movements.

119. Harris, *Negro as Capitalist,* 177.

120. Thomas Bauman, *The Pekin: The Rise and Fall of Chicago's First Black-Owned Theater* (Urbana: University of Illinois Press, 2014), 24.

121. Frazier, *Black Bourgeoisie,* 56. Pierce, *Negro Business and Business Education,* 69. Indeed, although these businesses served only black customers, the total volume of sales meant that blacks were spending an average of two dollars a year on these stores. To further illustrate the problem, in 1938 there were about 2,600 black businesses in Chicago alone. There were 2,800 white businesses in Chicago that received nine-tenths of their business from blacks.

122. Harris, *Negro as Capitalist,* 177–180.

123. Albon Holsey, Speech to the National Association of Teachers in Colored Schools, Jackson, Mississippi, July 1929.

124. Cheryl Greenberg, *"Or Does It Explode?," Black Harlem in the Great Depression* (Oxford: Oxford University Press, 1997), 135.

125. *Green v. Samuelson,* 168 Md. 421 (Md. Ct. App.).

126. Ibid. This case was followed by a 1938 decision in which the Supreme Court held that blacks were allowed to picket businesses that employed an all-white staff under principles of labor law. *New Negro All. v. Sanitary Grocery Co.,* 303 U.S. 552 (1938).

127. "If Negro Quarters for Negroes—Negro Dollars for Negroes, Too," *New York Daily Mirror,* 1935.

128. William H. Chafe, *The Achievement of American Liberalism: The New Deal and Its Legacies* (New York: Columbia University Press, 2013), 191.

129. Quoted in Richard M. Dalfiume, "The 'Forgotten Years' of the Negro Revolution," *Journal of American History* 55(1) (June 1968): 90.

130. Hubert H. Humphrey, Address to the 1948 Democratic National Convention Address, July 14, 1948, Philadelphia, http://www.americanrhetoric.com/speeches/huberthumphey1948dnc.html.

131. Douglas Blackmon, *Slavery by Another Name: The Re-Enslavement of Black Americans from the Civil War to World War II* (New York: Random House, 2008), 382.

132. Raymond H. Geselbracht, *The Civil Rights Legacy of Harry S. Truman,* vol. 2 (Kirksville, MO: Truman State University Press, 2007), 57, 78.

133. C. Vann Woodward, *The Strange Career of Jim Crow* (New York: Oxford University Press, 2002), 132.

134. Ibram X. Kendi, "Racial Progress Is Real. But So Is Racist Progress," *New York Times,* January 21, 2017, https://www.nytimes.com/2017/01/21/opinion/sunday/racial-progress-is-real-but-so-is-racist-progress.html?ref=opinion; citing Mary L. Dudziak, *Cold War Civil Rights: Race and the Image of American Democracy* (Princeton, NJ: Princeton University Press, 2011), 47–53 268.

135. Quoted in Robert E. Weems and Louis A. Randolph, *Business in Black and White: American Presidents and Black Entrepreneurs in the Twentieth Century* (New York: New York University Press, 2009), 61.

136. Roy Wilkins, *Talking It Over with Roy Wilkins: Selected Speeches and Writings* (Norwalk, CT: M&B Publishing, 1977), 64. Weems believes that the division's termination likely had to do with racial discrimination in the Eisenhower administration. Kenneth O'Reilly claims that Eisenhower was "habitually uncomfortable in black company." Kenneth O'Reilly, *Nixon's Piano: Presidents and Racial Politics from Washington to Clinton* (New York: Free Press, 1995), 165. Weems and Randolph, *Business in Black and White,* 39 (this cited page relates to the footnoted sentence's statement on the closing of the Department of Negro Affairs).

Chapter 5 Civil Rights Dreams, Economic Nightmares

1. Wil Haywood, *Showdown: Thurgood Marshall and the Supreme Court Nomination That Changed America* (New York: Knopf, 2015), 5.

2. Robert A. Caro, *Master of the Senate* (New York: Random House, 2002), 159. The term was first used by Doris Kearns Goodwin.

3. Robert A. Caro, *The Passage of Power* (New York: Random House, 2012), 488.

4. Ibid., 490.

5. Curtis Hessler, "The Civil Rights Act of 1963: Brass Tacks," *Harvard Crimson,* April 1964, http://www.thecrimson.com/article/1964/4/21/the-civil-rights-act-of-1963/.

6. See generally, Taylor Branch, *At Canaan's Edge: America in the King Years, 1965–68* (New York: Simon & Schuster, 2006).

7. Beryl Satter, *Family Properties: Race, Real Estate and the Exploitation of Black Urban America* (New York: Henry Holt, 2010), 173; James R. Ralph Jr., *Northern Protest: Martin Luther King Jr., Chicago, and the Civil Rights Movement* (Cambridge, MA: Harvard University Press, 1993), 42, 59.

8. "The year 1965," according to Lee Rainwater and William Yancey, "may be known in history as the time when the civil rights movement discovered, in this sense of becoming explicitly aware, that abolishing legal racism would not produce Negro equality." Lee Rainwater and William L. Yancey, *The Moynihan Report and Controversy* (Cambridge, MA: MIT Press, 1967), 11.

9. Bayard Rustin, "Funding Full Citizenship," *Council Journal* 6(3) (December 1967).

10. Whitney M. Young, *Beyond Racism: Building an Open Society* (New York: McGraw-Hill, 1969), 90–94, 116–118, 153.

11. Rick Perlstein, *Nixonland: The Rise of a President and the Fracturing of America* (New York: Scribner, 2008), 137.

12. Jesse Curtis, "Awakening the Nation: Mississippi Senator John C. Stennis, the White Countermovement, and the Rise of Colorblind Conservatism, 1947–1964" (Ph.D. dissertation, Kent State University, 2015), 147.

13. William Brink and Louis Harris, *Black and White: A Study of U.S. Racial Attitudes Today* (New York: Simon & Schuster, 1967), 100, 120.

14. Martin Luther King Jr., "I Have a Dream," Speech, Lincoln Memorial, Washington, DC, August 28, 1963.

15. Martin Luther King Jr., *The Autobiography of Martin Luther King, Jr.*, ed. Clayborne Carson (New York: Warner Books, 1998), 70.

16. Ibid., 295.

17. Ibid., 10.

18. It would require "white Americans [to] recognize that justice for black people cannot be achieved without radical changes in the structure of our society. The comfortable, entrenched, the privileged cannot continue to tremble at the prospect of change of the status quo." Martin Luther King Jr., *Where Do We Go from Here: Chaos or Community* (Boston: Beacon Press, 1967).

19. Clayborne Carson and Peter Holloran, eds., *A Knock at Midnight: Inspiration from the Great Sermons of Reverend Martin Luther King, Jr.* (New York: IPM / Warner, 1998), 61.

20. Historians Frances Fox Piven and Richard Cloward explained, "Blacks became more indignant over their condition—not only as oppressed racial minority in a white society but as poor people in an affluent one." Frances Fox Piven and Richard Cloward, *Poor People's Movements: Why They Succeed, How They Fail* (New York: Pantheon, 1977), 269.

21. William Julius Wilson, *The Truly Disadvantaged: The Inner City, the Underclass, and Public* Policy (Chicago: University of Chicago Press, 2012), chap. 7.

22. Ibid. at 27; U.S. Bureau of the Census, "Characteristics of the Population Below the Poverty Level, 1983," 5, https://www.census.gov/content/dam/Census /library/publications/1985/demo/p60-147.pdf.

23. The Federal Reserve studied the racial wealth gap in 1967 and concluded that "the evidence appears overwhelming that the net wealth position of black families is substantially poorer than that of white families of similar characteristics." Richard Sterner, *The Negro's Share: A Study of Income, Consumption, Housing, and Public Assistance* (New York: Harper & Brothers, 1943), 93. For whites and blacks earning more than $20,000 a year in 1967, whites had a net wealth of $100,009 and blacks had $30,195. At the bottom, for incomes less than $2,499 a year, whites had $10,681 and blacks had $2,148. Henry S. Terrell, "Wealth Accumulation of Black and White Families: The Empirical Evidence," *Journal of Finance* 26 (1971): 377.

24. The reason for the large wealth gap had nothing to do with black savings patterns. In fact, "the bulk of consumption studies show[ed] that blacks saved more at any given level of income." Terrell concluded that "these rather stark findings on wealth accumulation suggest that economic equality for black families will not be achieved when the current annual income gap between black and white families is eliminated because a considerable wealth gap will remain as a legacy of past economic deprivation." Ibid.

25. Robert A. Caro, *The Power Broker: Robert Moses and the Fall of New York* (New York: Vintage, 2012).

26. Economist Frank Davis observed that the "condition of economic stagnation and decay in the black ghettos of America is not self-correcting within the price system. Rather, the pull of economic forces sets up a permanent condition of inequality between a low-income labor-intensive black economy and the rest of the economy." Frank G. Davis, *The Economics of Black Community Development: An Analysis and Program for Autonomous Growth and Development* (Chicago: Markham Publishing, 1972), 79.

27. Kenneth B. Clark, *Dark Ghetto: Dilemmas of Social Power* (New York: Harper & Row, 1965), 11.

28. According to Harvard's President Emeritus James B. Conant, the economic situation in the ghetto was "social dynamite." Kennedy's Secretary of Labor Arthur J. Goldberg said that the conditions pressing on black Americans, including the lack of jobs, was "potentially the most dangerous social condition in America." Paul C. Tullier, "School Dropouts Build Explosive Unemployment in Ranks of Youth," *Kansas City Times,* May 3, 1963, 38.

29. In other Los Angeles neighborhoods, there were 5,900 residents per square mile. In Watts, there were 16,400 per square mile. "Report of the President's Task Force on the Los Angeles Riots, August 11–15, 1965" (Revised Master), 6, folder "Califano Los Angeles Riots, Ramsey Clark Report," Box 47, Office Files of Joseph A. Califano, Lyndon Baines Johnson Presidential Library.

30. David J. Garrow, *Bearing the Cross: Martin Luther King, Jr. and the Southern Christian Leadership Conference* (New York: Quill, 1999), 439.

31. Ibid.

32. King, *Autobiography,* 291, 302–307, 326–329.

33. Ibid., 328–329.

34. John David Skrentny, *The Ironies of Affirmative Action: Politics, Culture, and Justice in America* (Chicago: University of Chicago Press, 1996), 71.

35. Governor Brown called the rioters "terrorists" and promised to deal with them "forcefully." Elizabeth Hinton, *From the War on Poverty to the War on Crime: The Making of Mass Incarceration in America* (Cambridge, MA: Harvard University Press), 71.

36. Skrentny, *Ironies of Affirmative Action,* 73.

37. Gerald Horne, *Fire This Time: The Watts Uprising and the 1960s* (Charlottesville, VA: Da Capo, 1997), 36.

38. U.S. Congress, Senate, Committee on Banking and Currency, Subcommittee on Financial Institutions, "Consumer Credit and the Poor," 90th Congress, 2nd Session, April 19, 1968, 1; Louis Hyman, *Debtor Nation: The History of America in Red Ink* (Princeton, NJ: Princeton University Press, 2013), 194.

39. Murray Seeger, "Washington Ghetto Smoldering Ruins Block after Block," *Los Angeles Times,* April 7, 1968, 18.

40. U.S. Senate, Hearing before the Subcommittee on Financial Institutions of the Committee on Banking and Currency, 90th Congress, 2nd Session, "Federal Trade Commission Report on Credit Practices," April 19, 1968, 18, 22.

41. Sauter Van Gordon, "Flames Erase Long Stretch of Chicago's Madison Street," *Washington Post,* April 7, 1968, A7.

42. Hyman, *Debtor Nation,* 180.

43. David Caplovitz, *The Poor Pay More: Consumer Practices of Low-Income Families* (New York: Free Press, 1967), chap. 4. The most common purchases were appliances and furniture, and because families living in unstable housing in the ghettos moved more often, they bought more furniture.

44. Andrew Brimmer, "Small Business and Economic Development in the Negro Community," in *Black Business Enterprise: Historical and Contemporary Perspectives,* ed. Ronald W. Bailey (New York: Basic Books, 1971), 165–168.

45. Caplovitz, *Poor Pay More,* xvii.

46. Even among inner city borrowers, blacks paid more for credit than did whites. Ibid., 16–17, 81, 88, 90–91, 96–97, 107–109, 110–112, 119, 125.

47. Federal Trade Commission, *Economic Report on Installment Credit and Retail Sales Practices of District of Columbia Retailers* (Washington, DC: U.S. Government Printing Office, 1968).

48. "Federal Trade Commission Report on Credit Practices," 74–82, 101–106. "Consumer Credit and the Poor," 9–10.

49. Ibid., 3–4.

50. Caplovitz, *Poor Pay More,* chap. 4.

51. Ibid., chap. 5.

52. Ibid., 25, 100.

53. Ibid., 21.

54. "Consumer Credit and the Poor," 7.

55. Caplovitz, *Poor Pay More,* 157.

56. FTC, *Economic Report,* 24–33. Eleven low-income market retailers obtained 2,690 judgments in 1966 resulting in 1,568 garnishments and 306 repossessions. General market retailers reported only seventy judgments for the same year. The low-income retailers had one suit for every $2,599 of their net sales. The general market retailers averaged one suit for every $232,299 of sales.

57. Caplovitz, *Poor Pay More,* conclusion. Caplovitz himself had misunderstood this dynamic, and when he offered reflections in the 1967 reprint of *The Poor Pay More,* he conceded that it was a mistake to see the ghetto credit merchants as "nefarious exploiters of the poor" and believed that a more thorough analysis could reveal more about the "economic constraints that operate on these men." "Consumer Credit and the Poor."

58. Hyman, *Debtor Nation,* 193.

59. Adam Bernstein, "William Proxmire, Ex-Senator, Dies," *Washington Post,* December 16, 2005.

60. U.S. Senate, "William Proxmire: A Featured Biography," http://www.senate.gov /artandhistory/history/common/generic/Featured_Bio_ProxmireWilliam .htm.

61. "Consumer Credit and the Poor," 6–7.

62. Ibid., 80–85. U.S. Congress, Senate, Committee on Banking and Currency, Subcommittee on Financial Institutions, "Financial Institutions and the Urban Crisis," 90th Congress, 2nd Session, September–October 1969, 151, 324–327. U.S. Senator Proxmire Reports to You from Washington, 1964–1977," http://content .wisconsinhistory.org/cdm/compoundobject/collection/proxmire/id/4972 /show/4793/rec/6.

63. "Financial Institutions and the Urban Crisis."

64. Michael Zweig, "Black Capitalism and the Ownership of Property in Harlem," Stony Brook Working Papers, August 1970. A study of Harlem found that more than 85 percent of the businesses and properties in Harlem were owned by outsiders or nonresidents of Harlem.

65. "Financial Institutions and the Urban Crisis," 428.

66. Ibid., 9, 13.

67. Ibid., 89–91.
68. Ibid., 94–95. In 1967, SBA Director Howard J. Samuels created Project OWN as the government's minority business aid program. The program was intended to funnel loans to black and white enterprises in ghetto areas. Though Johnson had supported the program, his heart was not in it, and it seemed that he was only using minority enterprise as a crisis management tool to deal with unrest. Largely a political ploy, the program was not robust—by the end of 1968, only 5.7 percent of SBA money went to minority businesses. Robert E. Weems and Louis A. Randolph, *Business in Black and White: American Presidents and Black Entrepreneurs in the Twentieth Century* (New York: New York University Press, 2009), chap. 4.
69. "Financial Institutions and the Urban Crisis," 236.
70. He even wrote a book devoted to small business. William Proxmire, *Can Small Business Survive?* (Chicago: H. Regnery, 1964).
71. "U.S. Senator Proxmire Reports to You from Washington."
72. "Financial Institutions and the Urban Crisis," 74. "Consumer Credit and the Poor," 30–38.
73. "Financial Institutions and the Urban Crisis," 74–82, 101–106. "Consumer Credit and the Poor," 5–6, 34–36.
74. "Financial Institutions and the Urban Crisis," 134.
75. Hyman, *Debtor Nation*, 204.
76. "Consumer Credit and the Poor," 9–10.
77. Caplovitz, *Poor Pay More*, 183–184.
78. Ibid., 192.
79. Ibid., 95.
80. Hinton, *From the War on Poverty to the War on Crime*, 50, 77.
81. House Committee, Economic Opportunity Act of 1964, 305.
82. Tyson, who was father of Neil deGrasse Tyson, suggested that the government deposit funds into black banks instead. Cyril deGrasse Tyson, *2 Years before the Riot! Newark, New Jersey, and the United Community Corporation, 1964–1966* (New York: Jay Street, 2000), 256, 490–491.
83. Jacob S. Hacker and Paul Pierson, *American Amnesia: How the War on Government Led Us to Forget What Made America Prosper* (New York: Simon & Schuster, 2016), 251. According to economists Alberto Alesina, Edward Glaeser, and Bruce Sacerdote, the main reason the United States did not adopt New Deal era or European-style welfare programs was that the programs were seen to benefit black people. Alberto Alesina, Edward Glaeser, Bruce Sacerdote, "Why Doesn't the United States Have a European-Style Welfare State?," *Brookings Papers on Economic Activity* 2 (2001): 3.
84. Martin Luther King Jr., "Beyond Vietnam—A Time to Break Silence," Speech at Riverside Church Meeting, New York, April 4, 1967, http://www.americanrhetoric.com/speeches/mlkatimetobreaksilence.htm. In Clayborne Carson et al., eds., *Eyes on the Prize Civil Rights Reader: Documents, Speeches, and Firsthand Accounts from the Black Freedom Struggle* (New York: Penguin, 1987), 201–204. The total OEO budget was $1.7 billion in 1968 and $1.9 billion in 1969—an all-time high. By 1974, it was $328 million. Robert H. Hayeman, ed., *A Decade of Federal Antipoverty Programs: Achievements, Failures, and Lessons* (New York: Academic Press, 1977), 41. The cost of the Vietnam war by the end of the Johnson administration was over $100 billion. http://www.english.illinois.edu/maps/vietnam/domestic.htm.
85. Lyndon B. Johnson, "To Fulfill These Rights," Commencement Address at Howard University, June 4, 1965. In *Public Papers of the Presidents of the United States: Lyndon B. Johnson, 1965*, vol. 1 (Washington, DC: U.S. Government Printing Office, 1965), 635–640.
86. Johnson, "To Fulfill These Rights."

87. Taylor Branch, *At Canaan's Edge: America in the King Years, 1965–68* (New York: Simon & Schuster, 2006).

88. Skrentny, *Ironies of Affirmative Action,* 105.

89. Julian E. Zelizer, "Fifty Years Ago, the Government Said Black Lives Matter: The Radical Conclusions of the 1968 Kerner Report," *Boston Review,* May 2016, http://bostonreview.net/us/julian-e-zelizer-kerner-report.

90. Nicholas Pileggi, A. Long, Smoldery Summer, *New York Magazine,* June 21, 1982; National Advisory Commission on Civil Disorders, The Kerner Report (Princeton, NJ: Princeton University Press, 1968).

91. The report was a follow up to his book with coauthor Nathan Glazer, *Beyond the Melting Pot: The Negroes, Puerto Ricans, Jews, Italians, and Irish of New York City* (Cambridge, MA: MIT Press, 1963).

92. He had said at a conference in 1965 that the problem of black poverty "is practically the property of the federal government." Hinton, *From the War on Poverty to the War on Crime,* 59.

93. Daniel P. Moynihan, "The Negro Family: The Case for National Action," U.S. Department of Labor, Office of Policy Planning and Research, 1965, https://www.dol.gov/oasam/programs/history/webid-moynihan.htm.

94. Ibid.

95. U.S. Congress, House Budget Committee Majority Staff, *The War on Poverty: 50 Year Later,* A House Budget Committee Report, March 3, 2014, http://budget.house.gov/uploadedfiles/war_on_poverty.pdf.

96. Katharine Beckett, *Making Crime Pay: Law and Order in Contemporary American Politics* (New York: Oxford University Press, 1997), 32.

97. "The Wages of Hatred," *Wall Street Journal,* July 18, 1966. For more on the backlash, see Rick Perlstein, *Nixonland: The Rise of a President and the Fracturing of America* (New York: Simon & Schuster, 2010), 121; Michelle Alexander, *The New Jim Crow: Mass Incarceration in the Age of Colorblindness* (New York: New Press, 2011), 42.

98. These rioters were described as having been "bred" from "broken homes, illegitimacy, and other social ills," all of which have "warped the mind" of black youth, a problem that was terminal. Hinton, *From the War on Poverty to the War on Crime,* 4, 75.

99. Ibid., introduction.

100. Ibram X. Kendi, "Racial Progress Is Real. But So Is Racist Progress," *New York Times,* January 21, 2017. Gerard DeGroot, *Selling Ronald Reagan: The Emergency of a President* (New York: I. B. Tauris, 2015), chap. 6; Alexander, *New Jim Crow,* 44.

101. According to Michelle Alexander, those trying to reassert racial separation and hierarchy after Jim Crow ended found that "they could install a new racial caste system without violating the law or the new limits of acceptable political discourse, by demanding 'law and order' rather than 'segregation forever.'" Alexander, *New Jim Crow,* 40.

102. Wallace said that "the same Supreme Court that ordered integration and encouraged civil rights legislation" was now "bending over backwards to help criminals." Ibid., 42. Senator Strom Thurmond suggested that any capitulation to integration demands would cause "a wave of terror, crime and juvenile delinquency." Eddie S. Glaude, *Democracy in Black: How Race Still Enslaves the American Soul* (New York: Crown, 2016), 77.

103. DeGroot, *Selling Ronald Reagan,* 162.

104. Zelizer, "Fifty Years Ago."

105. The National Advisory Commission on Civil Disorders, The Kerner Report (New York: Pantheon Books, 1988), 1.

106. Skrentny, *Ironies of Affirmative Action,* 99.

107. Branch, *At Canaan's Edge,* 560.

108. Wil Haygood, *Showdown: Thurgood Marshall and the Supreme Court Nomination That Changed America* (New York: Alfred A. Knopf, 2015).

109. King, "Beyond Vietnam."

110. Michael E. Dyson, *I May Not Get There with You: The True Martin Luther King, Jr.* (New York: Free Press, 2000), 93.

111. King, *Autobiography*, 350.

112. This way, "we would place the problems of the poor at the seat of government of the wealthiest nation in the history of mankind." Ibid., 350–351.

113. Gerald McKnight, *The Last Crusade: Martin Luther King, Jr., the FBI, and the Poor People's Campaign* (Boulder, CO: Westview, 1998), 20–22. King, *Autobiography*, 353.

114. King, *Autobiography*, 309.

115. By 1967, SCLC was running Operation Breadbasket in twelve cities, and King reported that the operation resulted in 800 new jobs for black workers and $7 million in annual income for families. Ibid., 276.

116. Peniel E. Joseph, *Stokely: A Life* (New York: BasicCivitas Books, 2014), 104.

117. Perlstein, *Nixonland*, 123–124.

118. Ibid. at 96.

119. Rebecca Carroll, ed., *Uncle Tom or New Negro? African Americans Reflect on Booker T. Washington and Up from Slavery 100 Years Later* (New York: Broadway Books, 2006), 3.

120. Stokely Carmichael, "What We Want," *New York Review of Books*, September 22, 1966, 5–6, 8. Skrentny, *Ironies of Affirmative Action*, 74.

121. James Baldwin, *The Fire Next Time* (New York: Vintage International, 1963), 21.

122. Peniel Joseph explains that Carmichael was Malcolm's philosophical heir, having listened to his pivotal debate with Bayard Rustin at Howard while he was a student. Joseph, *Stokely*, 53.

123. Manning Marable, *Malcolm X: A Life of Reinvention* (New York: Viking, 2011), 7. "Malcolm not only spoke their language, he had lived their experiences—in foster homes, in prisons, in employment lines. Malcolm was loved because he could present himself as one of them." Ibid., 480.

124. Ibid., 187.

125. Manning Marable and Leith Mullings, eds., *Let Nobody Turn Us Around: Voices of Resistance, Reform, and Renewal: An African American Anthology* (Lanham, MD: Rowman and Littlefield, 2000), 435.

126. Malcolm X, *Malcolm X Speaks: Selected Speeches and Statements*, ed. George Breitman (New York: Grove Press, 1965), 39.

127. Ibid.

128. Newton, Cleaver, and Seale had all been engaged in racketeering and had served prison sentences. Cleaver infamously admitted to rape. Peniel E. Joseph, *Waiting 'Til the Midnight Hour: A Narrative History of Black Power in America* (New York: Owl Books, 2006).

129. Joshua Bloom and Waldo E. Martin Jr., *Black against Empire: The History and Politics of the Black Panther Party* (Oakland: University of California Press, 2013), 390.

130. Ibid., 70–72.

Chapter 6 The Decoy of Black Capitalism

1. His personal beliefs on civil rights, according to his biographer, were "shallow, intellectual, and abstract rather than intense, emotional, and engaged." Dean J. Kotlowski, *Nixon's Civil Rights: Politics, Principle, and Policy* (Cambridge, MA: Harvard University Press, 2002), 11.

2. Rick Perlstein, *Nixonland: The Rise of a President and the Fracturing of America* (New York: Scribner, 2008), chap. 23.

3. Kotlowski, *Nixon's Civil Rights*, 106.

4. Beryl Satter, *Family Properties: Race, Real Estate and the Exploitation of Black Urban America* (New York: Henry Holt, 2010), 259.

5. Nixon for President Committee, "Bridges to Human Dignity: An Address by Richard M. Nixon on the CBS Radio Network," April 25, 1968. Folder: Nixon, Richard M., 1968 (1), Box 14, Special Name Series, DDEPPP.

6. For a review of government programs to promote black business, see Robert E. Weems, *Business in Black and White: American Presidents and Black Entrepreneurs in the Twentieth Century* (New York: New York University Press, 2009).

7. Richard Nixon, "Address to the Republican National Convention," Miami, FL, August 8, 1968, American Presidency Project, http://www.presidency.ucsb.edu/ws/?pid=25968.

8. Interview with Roy Ennis, *U.S. News & World Report*, November 25, 1968, 60.

9. Rick Perlstein, *The Invisible Bridge: The Fall of Nixon and the Rise of Reagan* (New York: Simon & Schuster, 2014); Richard Nixon, "Annual Address to the Congress on the State of the Union," Washington, DC, January 22, 1970, American Presidency Project, http://www.presidency.ucsb.edu/ws/index.php?pid=2921.

10. Kotlowski, *Nixon's Civil Rights*, 173.

11. John A. Farrell, "Nixon's Vietnam Treachery," *New York Times*, December 31, 2016, citing Haldeman's notations of a promise made by Nixon to southern Republicans. http://mobile.nytimes.com/2016/12/31/opinion/sunday/nixons-vietnam-treachery.html?smid=fb-nytimes&smtyp=cur&referer=http%3A%2F%2Fm.facebook.com.

12. Earl Caldwell, "N.A.A.C.P. Softens Anti-Nixon Stand," *New York Times*, July 6, 1971, http://query.nytimes.com/mem/archive-free/pdf?res=9801E4DF1E3FE63ABC4E53DFB166838A669EDE.

13. The National Association of Real Estate Boards (NAREB) vigorously fought provisions in both the 1964 and 1966 Civil Rights Acts that would have penalized segregation. Satter, *Family Properties*, 194, 212; Taylor Branch, *At Canaan's Edge: America in the King Years 1965–68* (New York: Simon & Schuster, 2007), 517.

14. Michal R. Belknap, *Federal Law and Southern Order: Racial Violence and Constitutional Conflict in the Post-Brown South* (Athens: University of Georgia Press, 1987), 219.

15. As George Metcalf said of the FHA, "what Congress did was hatch a beautiful bird without wings to fly." Nikole Hannah-Jones, "Living Apart: How the Government Betrayed a Landmark Civil Rights Law," *ProPublica*, June 25, 2015, https://www.propublica.org/article/living-apart-how-the-government-betrayed-a-landmark-civil-rights-law; Douglas S. Massey and Nancy S. Denton, *American Apartheid: Segregation and the Making of the Underclass* (Cambridge, MA: Harvard University Press, 1998), 196.

16. Kotlowski, *Nixon's Civil Rights*, 50.

17. Edward J. Blum and Paul Harvey, "How (George) Romney Championed Civil Rights and Challenged His Church," *Atlantic*, August 13, 2012, http://www.theatlantic.com/national/archive/2012/08/how-george-romney-championed-civil-rights-and-challenged-his-church/261073/.

18. Russell Baker, "Observer: The Son of Pragmatism," *New York Times*, December 17, 1968, http://query.nytimes.com/mem/archive/pdf?res=9B03EED71730E034BC4F52DFB4678383679EDE.

19. Arthur I. Blaustein and Geoffrey P. Faux, *Star Spangled Hustle* (Garden City, NY: Doubleday, 1972), 130.

20. Nikole Hannah-Jones, "Living Apart: How the Government Betrayed a Landmark Civil Rights," *ProPublica*, June 25, 2015, https://www.propublica.org/article/living-apart-how-the-government-betrayed-a-landmark-civil-rights-law.

21. Charles M. Lamb, *Housing Segregation in Suburban America since 1960: Presidential and Judicial Politics* (New York: Cambridge University Press, 2005), 137.

22. Kotlowski, *Nixon's Civil Rights*, 55; "Balanced Communities" and "Position Paper on Open Communities (II)," n.d., Box 10, Richard C. Van Duesen Subject Files, Record Group 207, General Records of the Department of Housing and Urban Development, National Archives, College Park, MD.

23. Romney had said that to "solve problems of the 'real city,' only metropolitan-wide solutions will do." Florence Wagman Roisman, "Affirmatively Furthering Fair Housing in Regional Housing Markets: The Baltimore Public Housing Desegregation Litigation," *Wake Forest Law Review* 42 (2007): 333, 387.

24. Christopher Bonastia, *Knocking on the Door: The Federal Government's Attempt to Desegregate the Suburbs* (Princeton, NJ: Princeton University Press, 2006), 106.

25. Lamb, *Housing Segregation*, 82–85.

26. Hannah-Jones, "Living Apart."

27. Kotlowski, *Nixon's Civil Rights*, 56.

28. Ibid.

29. Hannah-Jones, "Living Apart."

30. Kotlowski, *Nixon's Civil Rights*, 61

31. Lamb, *Housing Segregation*, 129.

32. Hannah-Jones, "Living Apart."

33. "We will not seek to impose economic integration upon existing local jurisdictions; at the same time, we will not countenance any use of economic measures as a subterfuge for racial discrimination." Richard Nixon, "Statement about Federal Policies Relative to Equal Housing Opportunity," June 11, 1971, American Presidency Project, http://www.presidency.ucsb.edu/ws/?pid=3042.

34. *James v. Valtierra*, Brief for Appellants James et al., 402 U.S. 137 (1971), 17–18.

35. Dempsey Travis, *An Autobiography of Black Chicago* (Evanston, IL: Agate, 2013), 156.

36. "What We Want," *New York Review of Books*, September 22, 1966, 5–6, 8.

37. "Black Power Idea Long in Planning: S.N.C.C. Dissidents Wrote Document Last Winter," *New York Times*, August 5, 1966.

38. A 1968 survey by the Ford Foundation found that "94 percent" of blacks surveyed in fifteen major cities said they wanted more black banks and stores in their communities. Over 70 percent believed that the black community should strive to shop at black stores whenever possible. Weems, *Business in Black and White*, 102.

39. F. Nailor Fitzhugh, vice-president, Pepsi-Cola, Inc., personal interview, New York City, July 18, 1968.

40. Thomas A. Johnson, "M'Kissick Holds End of Violence Is Up to Whites," *New York Times*, July 22, 1967; A. Phillip Randolph Institute, *A "Freedom Budget" for All Americans: Budgeting Our Resources, 1966–1975 to Achieve "Freedom from Want"* (New York: Author, 1966).

41. "Words of the Week," *Jet*, June 13, 1968, 30.

42. Robert E. Weems and Lewis A. Randolph, "The National Response to Richard Nixon's Black Capitalism Initiative: The Success of Domestic Détente," *Journal of Black Studies* 32(1) (2001): 70.

43. James Forman, "Total Control as the Only Solution for the Economic Needs of Black People," Speech presented at the National Black Economic Development Conference, Detroit, MI, 1969, 7, http://www.episcopalarchives.org/Afro-Anglican_history/exhibit/pdf/blackmanifesto.pdf.

44. William L. Henderson and Larry C. Lebedur, "Programs for the Economic Development of the American Negro Community: The Moderate Approach," *American Journal of Economics and Sociology* 30(1) (January 1971): 27–45.

45. Richard F. America Jr., "What Do You People Want?," in *Black Business Enterprise: Historical and Contemporary Perspectives*, ed. Ronald W. Bailey (New York: Basic Books, 1971), 136, 140.

46. Dunbar McLaurin and Cyril Tyson, "The GHEDIPLAN for Economic Development," in *Black Economic Development*, ed. William Haddad and G. Douglas Pugh (Englewood Cliffs, NJ: Prentice-Hall, 1969), 126–131.

47. H. Naylor Fitzhugh, ed., *Problems and Opportunities Confronting Negroes in the Field of Business* (Washington, DC: U.S. Department of Commerce, 1962), 74–75.

48. Andrew Young and Edward Irons, dean of Howard's Business School, had also suggested their own versions of a domestic Marshall Plan before McLaurin's. McLaurin would soon become vice president of one of the country's largest black banks, Industrial Bank in Washington, DC. Laura Warren Hill and Julia Rabig, eds., *The Business of Black Power: Community Development, Capitalism, and Corporate Responsibility in Postwar America*. (Rochester, NY: University of Rochester Press, 2012), 24.

49. The Presidential Nominating Conventions, *Congressional Quarterly Service*, July 30 1968, 62.

50. Roy Innis, "Separatist Economics: A New Social Contract" in Haddad and Pugh, *Black Economic Development*, 50–59.

51. S. 3876, H.R. 18715, 90th Congress, 2nd Session, 1968.

52. Section 201, § 1921; Robert J. Desiderio and Raymond G. Sanchez, "The Community Development Corporation," *Boston College Law Review* 10 (1969): 217, 247.

53. Senate, Committee on Banking and Currency, Subcommittee on Financial Institutions, "Financial Institutions and the Urban Crisis," 90th Cong., 2d sess. (1968), 27.

54. Weems, *Business in Black and White*, 115–123. The meeting with McKissick and Innis was kept a secret by the administration, and Nixon made sure never to be seen in public with the black radicals. Innis later shunned the president, but McKissick stayed loyal, and historian Robert Weems suspects that he aligned himself with the president to reap a personal benefit. After he switched from black militant to black Republican, he received $17 million to start "Soul City," an independent black community in North Carolina.

55. Blaustein and Faux, *Star Spangled Hustle*, 56–58.

56. Kenneth B. Clark, *Dark Ghetto* (New York: Harper & Row, 1967), 189.

57. For a description of the dialogue surrounding the bill's passage, see John McClaughry, "Black Ownership and National Politics," in *Black Economic Development*, ed. Haddad and Pugh.

58. Weems and Randolph, "National Response," 73.

59. Blaustein and Faux, *Star Spangled Hustle*, 58.

60. Weems, *Business in Black and White*, 90–95, 107–109.

61. Memorandum, Howard J. Samuels to Matthew Nimetz, September 27, 1968. Quoted in Ibid., 105, n. 57.

62. Dan T. Carter, *The Politics of Rage: George Wallace, the Origins of the New Conservatism, and the Transformation of American Politics* (Baton Rouge: Louisiana State University Press, 2000); Ian Haney-Lopez, *Dog Whistle Politics: How Coded Racial Appeals Have Wrecked the Middle Class* (New York: Oxford University Press, 2014).

63. Campaign ad, "The Wrong Road," https://www.c-span.org/video/?153104-1 /presidential-campaign-commercials-1968.

64. Nixon campaign ad, "Black Capitalism." Described in Joe McGinnis, *The Selling of the President 1968* (New York: Simon & Schuster, 1969).

65. Both commercials are in the Nixon archives, https://ws.onehub.com/folders /nwsx31jv (start at 55:43).

66. Nixon Presidential Library files, Q&A with students, transcript, File 8, ARRA 24, at the University of Oregon, 1968 (on file with author).

67. Draft speech, "Human Dignity," First Draft, April 6, 1968, labeled RN's Copy, File 8, ARRA 24, Nixon Library (on file with author).

68. Nixon, "Address to the Republican National Convention."

69. John Herbers, "New Drive Planned for Negro Self-Aid," *New York Times,* December 13, 1968, http://query.nytimes.com/mem/archive/pdf?res=9503E6D91730E034BC4B52DFB4678383679EDE.

70. "Nixon Urges 'Black Ownership' to Help Solve Racial Problems," *New York Times,* April 26, 1968, http://query.nytimes.com/mem/archive/pdf?res=9C05E5D91E39E134BC4E51DFB2668383679EDE.

71. Earl Ofari, *The Myth of Black Capitalism* (New York: Monthly Review Press, 1970), 3.

72. Kotlowski, *Nixon's Civil Rights,* 133.

73. Monroe W. Karwin, "Best Laid Plans . . ." *Wall Street Journal,* December 24, 1970, 1. The *Wall Street Journal* reported that much of the appeal of Nixon's voluntary action program "rested in his view that it could serve as a substitute for costly Federal aid programs. Black Capitalism held the same allure."

74. Max Ways, "The Deeper Shame of the Cities," *Fortune,* January 1968.

75. "Black Capitalism," *Chicago Defender,* May 27, 1968; Tom Wicker, "In the Nation: A Coalition for What?," *New York Times,* May 19, 1968, http://query.nytimes.com/mem/archive/pdf?res=9F01E7DE1330EE3BBC4152DFB3668383679EDE.

76. Dean Kotlowski, "Black Power Nixon Style: The Nixon Administration and Minority Business Enterprise," *Business History Review* 72 (1998): 418. Gerald S. Strober and Deborah H. Strober, *Nixon: An Oral History of His Presidency* (New York: HarperCollins, 1994), 110.

77. William F. Buckley Jr., "On Black Capitalism," *National Review,* March 25, 1969. When the AFL-CIO denounced black capitalism as apartheid, William Buckley offered a forceful rejoinder in the *National Review:* "What makes apartheid objectionable is not that it is anti-democratic, but that it is compulsory." He then flipped the criticism on its head, "The call for special efforts to help the black people especially develop may be anti-democratic in the sense that it *imposes special burdens on the white community,* but it is surely democratic in the conventional context in that it helps those who need help the most."

78. Kotlowski, *Nixon's Civil Rights,* 135–136.

79. "The Black Capitalism program was more alive in the typewriters of the press than in the minds of the President and his chief aides." Blaustein and Faux, *Star Spangled Hustle,* 128.

80. Ibid., 131; Kotlowski, *Nixon's Civil Rights,* 138; Weems, *Business in Black and White,* 145.

81. Kotlowski, *Nixon's Civil Rights,* 137.

82. The board included the chairmen of General Motors, Sears, Woolworth, Continental Illinois National Bank, Levi Strauss, Marriott, Johnson and Sons, Bank of America, State Farm, Quaker Oats, and other CEOs or top management from Fortune 500 firms. The black members of the council were Berkley Burrell, director of the NBL; Joseph Goodloe, president of North Carolina Mutual Insurance Company; and John H. Johnson, president of Johnson Publishing.

83. Blaustein and Faux, *Star Spangled Hustle,* 143–146.

84. Theodore Cross, *Black Capitalism: Strategy for Business in the Ghetto* (New York: Atheneum, 1969).

85. Theodore L. Cross, "A White Paper on Black Capitalism," in *Black Economic Development,* ed. Haddad and Pugh, 34, n. 1.

86. Ibid., 24–25.

87. Ibid., 25–26.

88. Ibid., 27.

89. Blaustein and Faux, *Star Spangled Hustle*, 149–150, 154.

90. Ibid., *Star Spangled Hustle*, 155–157.

91. Weems, *Business in Black and White*, 180–181; Blaustein and Faux, *Star Spangled Hustle*, 166.

92. *Chicago Tribune*, December 7, 1969, section 4, 11, http://archives.chicagotribune .com/1969/12/07/page/67/article/mesbic-multiplies-money-for-minorities#text.

93. The newspaper reported that the fate of the OMBE was riding on the success of this program. Ibid.

94. Richard Rosenbloom and John Shank, "Let's Write Off MESBICS," *Harvard Business Review* (September–October 1970): 94; James K. Brown, "Arcata Investment Company: The Prototype MESBIC," *Conference Board Record* (April 1970): 58.

95. The GAO study of the MESBIC program found that only 19 percent of investors in the program had made equity investments and over 65 percent had made loans. "Interagency Report on the Federal Minority Business Development Programs," Executive Office of the President, Office of Management and Budget, Department of Commerce, Small Business Administration, March 1976, 40–42.

96. "Black Capitalism: The Crowning Blow," *Newsweek*, October 4, 1971.

97. Kotlowski, *Nixon's Civil Rights*, 141. Moynihan called the program "the most powerful engine of the Federal establishment to help promote minority enterprise."

98. Blaustein and Faux, *Star Spangled Hustle*, 202–203.

99. Kotlowski, *Nixon's Civil Rights*, 147–148.

100. "Financial Institutions and the Urban Crisis," 359.

101. The Post Office savings bank had been phased out in 1966; the deposits were still in flux until they were formally discontinued in 1971. So the postal deposits were small accounts from the low-income and small cash amounts collected from the Post Office's money order sales. Mehrsa Baradaran, *How the Other Half Banks: Exclusion, Exploitation, and the Threat to Democracy* (Cambridge, MA: Harvard University Press, 2015), chap. 7.

102. Blaustein and Faux, *Star Spangled Hustle*, 203–205.

103. John David Skrentny, *The Ironies of Affirmative Action: Politics, Culture, and Justice in America* (Chicago: University of Chicago Press, 1996), 121–125, 142.

104. Kotlowski, *Nixon's Civil Rights*, 106.

105. Moynihan had urged Nixon to "dissolve black urban lower classes" by turning "militant" blacks into "judges, professors, congressmen, cops." Ibid., 97–98.

106. Skrentny, *Ironies*, 121–125.

107. U.S. Congress, House, Select Committee on Small Business, Subcommittee Chairman's Report, "Tax Exempt: Foundations and Charitable Trusts," 90th Congress 2nd Session, March 26, 1968, 2.

108. Karwin, "Best Laid Plans."

109. Michael Brower and Doyle Little, "White Help for Black Business," *Harvard Business Review*, May 1970.

110. Blaustein and Faux, *Star-Spangled Hustle*, 222, citing Department of Commerce, Office of Minority Enterprise, "MESBIC Report—Summer of 1971," 2 (unpublished document).

111. "Nixon's 'Black Capitalism' Plan Has Fallen Far Short of Goals," *San Bernardino Sun*, June 27, 1970, 3.

112. Whitney M. Young Jr., "It's Good Business for Business to Solve Social Problems," *New York Times*, January 11, 1970, http://www.nytimes.com/1970/01/11 /archives/point-of-view-its-good-business-for-business-to-solve-social.html.

113. Whitney M. Young Jr., *Beyond Racism: Building an Open Society* (New York: McGraw-Hill, 1969), 151, 163–164.

114. Whitney M. Young Jr., "The Ghetto Investment," *New York Times*, March 14, 1971, http://www.nytimes.com/1971/03/13/archives/the-ghetto-investment.html.

115. In fact, during the years 1968 and 1969, "brutal state repression helped legitimate the Panthers in the eyes of many supporters and fostered increased mobilization." Joshua Bloom and Waldo E. Martin Jr., *Black against Empire: The History and Politics of the Black Panther Party* (Oakland: University of California Press, 2013), 369.

116. Ross K. Baker, "The Transformation of the Panthers," *Washington Post*, February 13, 1971, B1–B2.

117. Peniel E. Joseph, *Waiting 'til the Midnight Hour: A Narrative History of Black Power in America* (New York: Macmillan, 2007), 287.

118. Robert Staples, *Introduction to Black Sociology* (New York: McGraw-Hill, 1976), 98.

119. Henderson and Lebedur, "Moderate Approach," 194.

120. Federal Bureau of Investigation File, Roy Wilkins, Open Letter to Stokely Carmichael and Other Comments re: Subject's Resignation from BPP, https://vault.fbi .gov/Roy%20Wilkins/Roy%20Wilkins%20Part%2015%20of%2017.

121. Weems and Randolph, "National Response," 66; Stephen E. Ambrose, *Nixon*, vol. 2: *The Triumph of a Politician, 1962–1972* (New York: Simon & Schuster, 1989), 125–126.

122. Jesse L. Jackson, "Breadbasket Leader Rejects Black Capitalism," *Muhammad Speaks*, February 21, 1969; Weems, *Business in Black and White*, 155–156; Thomas H. Landless and Richard M. Quinn, *Jesse Jackson and the Politics of Race* (Ottawa, IL: Jameson, 1985), 49.

123. Kotlowski, *Nixon's Civil Rights*, 151.

124. Weems and Randolph, "National Response," 80–81

125. Henderson and Lebedur, "Moderate Approach," 170–171, 175.

126. Weems, *Business in Black and White*, 136–138. Weems explains that the Nation of Islam asked the administration for federal government contracts after they endorsed the program.

127. Cited in Warren and Rabig, *Business of Black Power*, 28.

128. Kotlowski, *Nixon's Civil Rights*, 150–151.

129. U.S. Department of Labor, Bureau of Labor Statistics Report, "Blacks in the 1970's: Did They Scale the Job Ladder?," June 1982, https://stats.bls.gov/opub/mlr /1982/06/art5full.pdf.

130. Kotlowski, *Nixon's Civil Rights*, 261; Kenneth Bancroft Clark and John Hope Franklin, *The Nineteen Eighties: Prologue and Prospect* (Washington, DC: Joint Center for Political Studies, 1981), 19.

131. For a review of black capitalism critics from the political left, see Weems, *Business in Black and White*, 145–155; Bernard H. Booms and James E. Ward Jr., "The Cons of Black Capitalism: Will This Policy Cure Urban Ills?," *Business Horizons* 12(5) (1969): 21; Earl Ofari, *The Myth of Black Capitalism* (New York: Monthly Review Press, 1970); Hill and Rabig, *Business of Black Power*, 31–33.

132. Robert L. Allen, *Black Awakening in Capitalist America* (Trenton, NJ: Africa World Press, 1990), 95, 191.

133. Adam Fairclough, *To Redeem the Soul of America: The Southern Christian Leadership Conference and Martin Luther King Jr.* (Athens: University of Georgia Press, 2001), 393.

134. Manning Marable, *How Capitalism Underdeveloped Black America* (Chicago: Haymarket Books, 2015), xxxvi (originally published 1983). Earl Ofari derides the black elite yet shows unfamiliarity with the actual state of black business when he talks about their exploitation. Ofari, *Myth of Black Capitalism*, 10. For analysis of Ofari's misreading of the census numbers, see Weems, *Business in Black and White*, 154.

135. Almost 60 percent of these businesses were in the South (with 30 percent being owned by women). Blaustein and Faux, *Star Spangled Hustle*, 61, 80.
136. In 1968, the top twenty-one black banks held total assets of $207 million compared to over $400 billion for white banks, i.e., 2,000 times greater. Ibid., 81.
137. As one critic recounts, these were "beauty parlors, short-order operations, and one- or two-man retail outlets which really promised very little in terms of growth." Robert Imbriano, "OMBE: The Sound of One Hand Clapping," *Black Enterprise* 8 (June 1978): 87–93, 188–190.
138. Kotlowski, *Nixon's Civil Rights*, 129.
139. Daniel Mitchell, *The Numbers and the Ghetto: An Opportunity for Change* (Cambridge, MA: Center for Community Economic Development, 1970).
140. Blaustein and Faux, *Star Spangled Hustle*, 86–87.
141. Ibid., 86.
142. Ibid., 101–102.
143. James Rowe, "Bank Policies Assailed as Lax on Ghetto Aid," *The Washington Post*, A2, July 12, 1971.
144. Blaustein and Faux, *Star Spangled Hustle*, 101.
145. Thieblot's study shows that "it took longer for bankers to break the all-white tradition of their industry than was required by various others, and we know that the proportion of employment which is Negro is less than the average in most other industries." Armand J. Thieblot, *The Negro in the Banking Industry* (Philadelphia: Wharton School of Finance and Commerce, 1970), 64–65.
146. Ibid., 106.
147. Ibid., 48.
148. Ibid., 64.
149. Ibid., 65.
150. Ibid., 50.
151. Ibid., 106–110.
152. Ibid., 114. "Stevenson Raps Banks over Bias," *New Pittsburgh Courier*, June 24, 1967.
153. Nicholas A. Lash, "Asymmetries in US Banking: The Role of Black-Owned Banks," in *Global Divergence in Trade, Money and Policy*, ed. Volbert Alexander and Hans-Helmut Kotz (Cheltenham, UK: Edward Elger, 2006), 91–110. Fifty-six of the top one hundred black-owned businesses emerged between 1969 and 1976. Kotlowski, *Nixon's Civil Rights*, 150.
154. Fred C. Allvine, "Black Business Development," *Journal of Marketing* 34 (1970): 2. In 1969, they numbered fewer than 30 of a total 13,762 commercial banks.
155. Courtney N. Blackman, "An Eclectic Approach to the Problem of Black Economic Development," *Review of Black Political Economy* 2(1) (Fall 1971): 3–27.
156. Mona Sarfaty, "Soul Business—Roxbury's Unity Bank," *Harvard Crimson*, October 28, 1968, http://www.thecrimson.com/article/1968/10/28/soul-business-roxburys-unity-bank-pblbast-spring/.
157. Jackie Robinson, *I Never Had It Made* (New York: Putnam, 1972), 184.
158. Ibid., 207.
159. Ibid., 189.
160. Ibid., 186.
161. Janet Spencer, "A Black Bank in Harlem Finds the Road Rocky," *New York Times*, January 6, 1974, http://www.nytimes.com/1974/01/06/archives/a-black-bank-in-harlem-finds-the-road-rocky-a-black-bank-in-harlem.html; see also Edward Cowan, "Negroes Forming Bank in Harlem," *New York Times*, June 30, 1963, http://query.nytimes.com/mem/archive/pdf?res=9E00E4D91430E036A05753C3A9609C946291D6CF.
162. Robinson, *Never Had It Made*, 192–193.
163. Ibid., 195–197.

164. Spencer, "Black Bank in Harlem"; Cowan, "Negroes Forming Bank in Harlem."

165. An article in the *Harvard Crimson* explained that the bank was conceived in 1968 by John T. Hayden, a black graduate of the Harvard Business School, after he wrote a term paper about "the economic needs of the ghetto community." He contacted Donald E. Sneed, who was active in civil rights boycotts and owned a real estate company in Roxbury. The Unity Bank Association consisted of eighty-eight organizers who were active community leaders. Sarfaty, "Soul Business."

166. Rana Foroohar, *Makers and Takers: The Rise and the Fall of American Business* (New York: Crown, 2016), 48, 49.

167. Andrew Brimmer, "Trouble with Black Capitalism," *Nation's Business*, May 1969, 79.

168. Kotlowski, *Nixon's Civil Rights*, 139.

169. Weems and Randolph, "National Response," 76; Brimmer, "Trouble with Black Capitalism," 57, 78–79; Andrew Brimmer, "Economic Integration and the Progress of the Negro Community," *Ebony* 25 (August 1970): 118–121.

170. Weems and Randolph, *National Response*.

171. Andrew F. Brimmer, "The Black Banks: An Assessment of Performance and Prospects," *Journal of Finance* 26(2) (May 1970): 400–402.

172. Ibid., 387.

173. Brimmer, "Black Banks," 383–386.

174. Gregory Price, "The Cost of Government Deposits for Black-Owned Commercial Banks," *Review of Black Political Economy* 23(1) (June 1994): 9–24; Gregory N. Price, "Minority Owned Banks: History and Trends," *Federal Reserve Bank of Cleveland Economic Commentary*, July 1, 1990.

175. Ronald A. Ratti, "Pledging Requirements and Bank Asset Portfolios," *Federal Reserve Bank of Kansas City Economic Review*, September–October 1979, https://www.kansascityfed.org/PUBLICAT/ECONREV/EconRevArchive/1979/3-4q79ratt.pdf.

176. "All studies of Black-owned banks have noted the large portion of funds kept in highly liquid assets, primarily U.S. government obligation." Timothy Bates and William Bradford, "An Analysis of the Portfolio Behavior of Black-Owned Commercial Banks," *Journal of Finance* 35 (1980): 755n4, citing a sample showing nonminority banks held 29.5 percent in highly liquid forms, compared to 46.5 percent of minority banks in the same model.

177. Lash, "Asymmetries in US Banking"; Irons, "Black Banking," 424; Bates and Bradford, "Analysis of Portfolio Behavior"; Edward C. Lawrence, "The Viability of Minority-Owned Banks," *Quarterly Review of Economics and Finance* 37(1) (1997): 1–21.

178. Lash, "Asymmetries in US Banking," 99; John T. Boorman, "The Prospect for Minority-Owned Commercial Banks: A Comparative Performance Analysis," *Journal of Bank Research* 4(2) (1974): 263–279.

179. Andrew Brimmer, "Recent Developments in Black Banking: 1970–1971," *Review of Black Political Economy* 3(1) (1972): 58–73.

180. Brimmer, "Black Banks," 390; Lawrence, "Viability of Minority-Owned Banks," 1–21.

181. Brimmer, "Black Banks," 390.

182. Brimmer concluded that the buying of so much in government securities by black banks was part of "the normal quest for diversification" and demonstrated "an effort on the part of the banks to minimize the exceptionally high risk of lending in the ghetto." Ibid., 299.

183. Irons, "Black Banking."

184. "The ghetto is dependent on one basic export," according to Tabb, "its unskilled labor power." William K. Tabb, *The Political Economy of the Black Ghetto* (New York: W. W. Norton, 1970), 22.

185. Economist Lester Thurow explains that in the event the dominant group did trade due to social or economic pressure, they did so as "a discriminating monopolist." Lester C. Thurow, *Poverty and Discrimination* (Washington, DC: Brookings Institution, 1969), 117.

186. Kotlowski, *Nixon's Civil Rights*, 156.

187. Cross, "White Paper on Black Capitalism."

188. Adam Smith, *The Wealth of Nations* (Cambridge, MA: Hackett Publishing Co., 1993), 132.

189. George Simmel, *The Philosophy of Money* (London: Routledge, 2004), 447.

190. Karl Marx, *Selected Writings: The Communist Manifesto* (Oxford: Oxford University Press, 1977), 247.

191. Jacob Hacker and Paul Pierson, *American Amnesia: How the War on Government Led Us to Forget What Made America Prosper* (New York: Simon & Schuster, 2016).

192. Perlstein, *Nixonland,* chap. 23. David J. Garrow, "The FBI and Martin Luther King," *Atlantic,* August 2002.

193. Martin Luther King Jr., *The Autobiography of Martin Luther King, Jr.,* ed. Clayborne Carson (New York: Warner, 1998), 351.

194. Taylor Branch, *Parting the Waters: America in the King Years, 1954–63* (New York: Simon & Schuster, 1988), 563.

195. Peniel E. Joseph, *Stokely: A Life* (New York: Civitas, 2014), 209.

196. Henderson and Lebedur, "Moderate Approach," 198.

197. Harold Cruse, quoted in *Booker T. Washington and His Critics: Black Leadership in Crisis,* ed. Edwin M. Epstein and David R. Hampton (Encino, CA: Dickenson, 1971), 236.

198. Ibid. Interview with Daniel Watts, New York City, July 18, 1968.

199. Letter from Alan Greenspan to candidate Nixon, Nixon Presidential Library files, Subject: The Urban Riots of the 1960s, September 26, 1967.

200. Milton Friedman, *Capitalism and Freedom* (Chicago: Chicago University Press, 1962), 109–115.

201. The only exception was when black collective action increased the cost of discrimination by staging large-scale boycotts, but that was hardly what Friedman was referring to.

202. Justin Fox recounts the rise and eventual fall of rational and efficient market theories and the Chicago school's embrace of them. Justin Fox, *The Myth of the Rational Markets: A History of Risk, Reward, and Delusion on Wall Street* (New York: Harper, 2009).

203. See generally, E. J. Dionne Jr., *Why the Right Went Wrong: Conservatism—From Goldwater to Trump and Beyond* (New York: Simon & Schuster, 2016). Dionne makes the case that the modern Republican Party is essentially the party of Goldwater.

204. "Goldwater's conservatism operated in the South less like a genuine political ideology and more like Wallace's soft porn racism: as a set of codes that voters readily understood as defending white supremacy. Goldwater didn't win the South as a small-government libertarian, but as a racist." Ian Hanley López, *Dog Whistle Politics: How Coded Racial Appeals Have Reinvented Racism and Wrecked the Middle Class* (Oxford: Oxford University Press, 2014), 17–22.

205. The John Birch Society was an example of the early alliance between segregationists like Wallace with libertarianism. Another link was John Olin, who began to funnel money toward libertarian organizations, including his own Olin Foundation and the Federalist Society, after witnessing the 1969 takeover of the Cornell campus by a black power group during alumni weekend. Olin also funded Charles Murray's research, which produced several tracts on racial inferiority, including *The Bell Curve.* Jane Mayer, *Dark Money: The Hidden History of the Billionaires Behind the Radical Right* (New York: Penguin, 2016), 94–111, 167–196.

206. "Lee Atwater's Infamous 1981 Interview on the Southern Strategy," Video, *Nation*, https://www.youtube.com/watch?v=X_8E3ENrKrQ.

207. James Kwak, Introduction, *Economism: Bad Economics and the Rise of Inequality* (New York: Pantheon Books, 2017).

208. Ronald Reagan, "Address to the Nation on United States–Soviet Relations," September 29, 2014, The American Presidency Project, http://www.presidency.ucsb.edu/ws/?pid=40457.

209. "Security from domestic violence, no less than from foreign aggression, is the most elementary and fundamental purpose of any government, and a government that cannot fulfill that purpose is one that cannot long command the loyalty of its citizens." Barry Goldwater, "Speech Accepting 1964 Republican Presidential Nomination," July 16, 2014, http://www.washingtonpost.com/wp-srv/politics/daily/may98/goldwaterspeech.htm.

210. Joseph, *Stokely*, 225.

211. "Goldwater . . . aggressively exploited the riots and fears of black crime, laying the foundation for the 'get tough on crime' movement." Michelle Alexander, *The New Jim Crow: Mass Incarceration in the Age of Colorblindness* (New York: The New Press, 2010), 42. See also, Lopez, *Dog Whistle Politics*, 19.

212. Sabrina Jones and Marc Mauer, *Race to Incarcerate: A Graphic Retelling* (New York: The New Press, 2013), 29.

Chapter 7 The Free Market Confronts Black Poverty

1. Rick Perlstein, *The Invisible Bridge: The Fall of Nixon and the Rise of Reagan* (New York: Simon & Schuster, 2014), 628, 695.

2. "There is a limit to what can be accomplished by laws and regulations, and I seriously question whether anything additional is needed in that line." Ronald Reagan, "Remarks on Signing the Bill Making the Birthday of Martin Luther King, Jr., a National Holiday," November 2, 1983, http://www.presidency.ucsb.edu/ws/?pid=40708.

3. Ronald Reagan, "Opening Speech of the 1966 Gubernatorial Campaign," reported in *The Courier-Journal*, January 5, 1966, A12.

4. See Ronald Reagan, *A Time for Choosing: The Speeches of Ronald Reagan* (Chicago: Regnery Gateway, 1983), 47.

5. Josh Levin, "The Welfare Queen," *Slate*, December 19, 2013, http://www.slate.com/articles/news_and_politics/history/2013/12/linda_taylor_welfare_queen_ronald_reagan_made_her_a_notorious_american_villain.html. "As of 1986, white households received 90.5 percent of all non-means-tested transfers and 63.4 percent of means-tested payments, while black households receive only 8.2 percent of non-means-tested payments but 2.3 percent of means tested payments. These differences are especially pronounced for black women who h[ead] families by themselves: just 3 percent receive a non-means-tested benef[it." Mi]chael K. Brown, *Race, Money, and the American Welfare State* (Ithaca[: Cor]nell University Press, 1999), 11.

6. Jeremy Mayer, *Running on Race: Racial Politics in Presidential C[ampaigns, 1960–]2000* (New York: Random House, 2002), 71.

7. Michelle Alexander claims that "the drug war from the o[utset had little to do with] public concern about drugs and much to do with [racial politics."] Michelle Alexander, *The New Jim Crow: Mass In[carceration in the Age of Color]blindness* (New York: The New Press, 2010), 4[9].

8. Newt Gingrich admits that the war on cri[me targeted black people] and punished them much more hars[hly than white people for the same crime. See] ment. Ava DuVernay and Spence[r Averick, *13th*, documentary film,] 2016.

9. David M. Kennedy, *Don't Shoot: One Man, a Street Fellowship, and the End of Violence in Inner-City America* (New York: Bloomsbury, 2011), 10.

10. Alexander, *New Jim Crow,* 52.

11. Adam Walinsky, "Crack as Scapegoat," *New York Times,* September 16, 1986, http://www.nytimes.com/1986/09/16/opinion/crack-as-a-scapegoat.html.

12. Jill Leovy, *Ghettoside: A True Story of Murder in America* (New York: Spiegel and Gran, 2015).

13. Ibid., 8.

14. James Baldwin, *The Fire Next Time* (New York: Vintage International 1963), 21.

15. Richard L. Berke, "In 1992, Willie Horton Is Democrats' Weapon," *New York Times,* August 25, 1992, http://www.nytimes.com/1992/08/25/us/the-1992-campaign-political-week-in-1992-willie-horton-is-democrats-weapon.html.

16. Fox Butterfield, "Study Finds Big Increase in Black Men as Inmates since 1980," *New York Times,* August 28, 2002, http://www.nytimes.com/2002/08/28/us/study-finds-big-increase-in-black-men-as-inmates-since-1980.html.

17. Alexander, *New Jim Crow,* 180.

18. "Excerpts from Clinton's Speech to Black Ministers," *New York Times,* November 14, 1993, http://www.nytimes.com/1993/11/14/us/excerpts-from-clinton-s-speech-to-black-ministers.html?pagewanted=all.

19. Ford handwritten comment, "Q&A for American Newspaper Reception," April 13, 1976, Box 24, Presidential Handwriting File, GRFL; *Washington Post,* April 11, 1976, C7. In the 1980s, 90 percent of whites surveyed in a few suburban cities still agreed with this statement: "White people have a right to keep blacks out of their neighborhoods." Douglas S. Massey and Nancy A. Denton, *American Apartheid: Segregation and the Making of the Underclass* (Cambridge, MA: Harvard University Press, 1998), 110.

20. Massey and Denton, *American Apartheid,* 207, 213; Nikole Hannah-Jones, "Living Apart: How the Government Betrayed a Landmark Civil Rights Law," *ProPublica,* June 25, 2015, https://www.propublica.org/article/living-apart-how-the-government-betrayed-a-landmark-civil-rights-law.

21. The ghetto isolation index was 91 percent in Chicago, the same as it was before the Great Depression. Public housing, according to historian Arnold Hirsh, created a [sec]ond ghetto" that was "solidly institutionalized and frozen in concrete." [Hi]rsch, *Making the Second Ghetto: Race and Housing in Chicago* [Univer]sity of Chicago Press, 1998).

[Livin]g *Black, Living in the Red: Race, Wealth, and Social Policy in* [Uni]versity of California Press, 1999), 38–39. Peter Mieszkowski [Ec]onomic Explanation for Housing Segregation," *New* [No]vember–December 1979, 35. Massey and Denton,

[finan]cial assets owned by white middle-income [$35–]50,000) in 1984, similar black households [Thomas M. Shapiro, *Black Wealth/White* [Equali]ty (New York: Routledge, 2006), 25.

[i]n *Black and White: American* [Cen]tury (New York: New York

Policy (Cambridge, also strengthened

enforcement of voting rights and job discrimination cases by the Department of Justice and the Equal Employment Opportunity Commission.

30. Presidential Statement, September 12, 1977, Martha Mitchell Files, MBE 5/77–3/78 Folder, Box 14, Carter Library.

31. Weems and Randolph, *Business in Black and White*, 193.

32. Jimmy Carter, "Minority Bank Deposit Program Memorandum for the Heads of Departments and Agencies," April 8, 1977, http://www.presidency.ucsb.edu/ws/index.php?pid=7327&st=minority&st1=bank. Nathaniel Sheppard Jr., "Minority Bankers Are Chagrined as Deposits by U.S. Show Drops," *New York Times*, November 24, 1977, http://www.nytimes.com/1977/11/24/archives/minority-bankers-are-chagrined-as-deposits-by-us-show-drops.html?_r=0.

33. "Minority Fronts," *60 Minutes*, 2(14), Sunday, December 17, 1978, 14, Burrelles Luce Transcripts, Livingston, NJ.

34. James H. Lowry and Associates, *A New Strategy for Minority Business Development*, undated report, Louis Martin Files, Box 71, Carter Library.

35. In 1977, there were only 113 black firms that employed more than a hundred workers. There were another 1,060 black owned corporations that had more than twenty employees. This was 0.46 percent, less than one-half of 1 percent of all blacks engaged in private enterprise. As for black executives, there fewer less than two hundred individuals who were employed by large enterprises or managed them themselves. Manning Marable, *How Capitalism Underdeveloped Black America* (Chicago: Haymarket Books, 2015), 146–149.

36. Most of President Carter's efforts to help blacks were done through executive and agency actions, according to Carter biographer, Burton Kaufman, "and their greatest impact was on mid- and upper-income minorities, not the poor." Burton I. Kaufman, *The Presidency of James Earl Carter, Jr.* (Lawrence: University Press of Kansas, 1993), 110.

37. Republican Party Platform of 1988. "An American Vision: For Our Children and Our Future," August 16, 1988, http://www.presidency.ucsb.edu/ws/index.php?pid=25846&st=minority&st1=bank. F. McCoy, "A Decade in Review: The B. E. Board of Economics Takes a Hard Look at Forces over the Past 10 Years to Continue to Impact on the Economic Development of Black America," *Black Enterprise*, June 1992, 208–214.

38. Ronald Reagan, "Remarks at a White House Briefing for Minority Business Owners," July 15, 1987, http://www.presidency.ucsb.edu/ws/index.php?pid=34548&st=minority&st1=bank.

39. Ronald Reagan, "Remarks in Denver, Colorado, at the Annual Convention of the National Association for the Advancement of Colored People," June 29, 1982, http://www.reagan.utexas.edu/archives/speeches/1981/62981a.htm.

40. Republican Party Platform of 1988, http://www.presidency.ucsb.edu/ws/?pid=25846. "Each year the U.S. Department of Commerce's Minority Business Development Agency and the U.S. Small Business Administration's (SBA) Office of Government Contracting and Business Development collaborate to hold regional conferences and activities. The recognition also aims to promote the growth of minority-owned businesses as well as encourage equal access to federal contracts, capital, management, and technical assistance." Jessie Carney Smith, ed., *Encyclopedia of African American Business*, vol. 2 (Westport, CT: Greenwood Press, 2006), 536.

41. Weems and Randolph, *Business in Black and White*, 219.

42. Ibid.

43. Republican Party Platform of 1988.

44. Republican Party Platform of 1984, http://www.presidency.ucsb.edu/ws/?pid=25845.

45. Public Papers of the Presidents of the United States, *The Administration of Jimmy Carter* (Washington, DC: U.S. Government Printing Office, 1980), 74, https://books.google.com/books?id=T3mqobvfZecC&pg=PA77&lpg=PA77&dq=carter+women%27s+business+initiative&source=bl&ots=dxdEBnNLnt&sig=L-f3SVOb9k-P-9EpYu_nPi5OaxY&hl=en&sa=X&ved=0ahUKEwjr86HChqXRAhXo6IMKHcr4Dd0Q6AEIODAF#v=onepage&q=carter%20women's%20business%20initiative&f=false.

46. Women's Business Ownership Act of 1988, Pub. L. 100-533, 100 Cong. Rec. H 5050, House, October 25, 1988, https://www.congress.gov/bill/100th-congress/house-bill/5050.

47. The only race-based preferences that could be justified were those in cases of proven discrimination by a particular institution. The remedy had to address that institution's particular discrimination and no more. For example, if a given police department could prove that it had discriminated against black officers, it could devise a program to hire more black officers. However, a department could not decide to hire more black officers in order to respond to a general history of injustice in criminal enforcement.

48. Wil Haywood, *Showdown: Thurgood Marshall and the Supreme Court Nomination That Changed America* (New York: Knopf, 2015), 5.

49. *Regents of the University of California v. Bakke*, 438 US 265, 395–396 (1978).

50. *City of Richmond v. J. A. Croson Co.*, 488 U.S. 469, 505–506 (1989).

51. Jason Sokol, "Which Martin Luther King Are We Celebrating Today?," *New York Times*, January 16, 2017, https://www.nytimes.com/2017/01/16/opinion/which-martin-luther-king-are-we-celebrating-today.html?mwrsm=Facebook.

52. Martin Luther King Jr., *Where Do We Go from Here: Chaos or Community?* (Boston: Beacon Press, 1968).

53. Specifically, it requires banking regulators to (1) preserve the number of minority depository institutions; (2) preserve the minority character in cases of merger or acquisition; (3) provide technical assistance to prevent insolvency of institutions not now insolvent; (4) promote and encourage the creation of new minority deposit institutions; and (5) provide training, technical assistance, and education programs. FIRREA, 12 U.S.C. 308 (2013).

54. Richard Nixon, Executive Order 11458, "Prescribing Arrangements for Developing and Coordinating a National Program for Minority Business Enterprise," March 5, 1969, http://www.presidency.ucsb.edu/ws/?pid=60475.

55. Jonathan J. Bean, *Big Government and Affirmative Action* (Lexington: University Press of Kentucky, 2001), 71.

56. Subsection (1)(A) holds that if a bank is privately owned, the 51 percent ownership applies to individuals and (1)(B) holds that it applies to 51 percent majority stock ownership. FIRREA, 12 U.S.C. 308(b)(1)(A)–(B) (2013).

57. FIRREA, 12 U.S.C. 308(b)(1)(C) (2013).

58. General Accounting Office, Report to Congress, "Minority Banks, Regulators Need to Better Assess Effectiveness of Support Efforts," GAO-07-6, October, 04 2006, http://www.gao.gov/products/GAO-07-6.

59. Kathryn J. Edin and H. Luke Shaefer, *$2 A Day: Living on Almost Nothing in America* (New York: Houghton Mifflin Harcourt, 2016), 17.

60. "Text of President Clinton's Announcement on Welfare Legislation," *New York Times*, August 1, 1996, http://www.nytimes.com/1996/08/01/us/text-of-president-clinton-s-announcement-on-welfare-legislation.html.

61. Initiatives included Empowerment Zones, Enterprise Communities, expansion of the Low-Income Housing Tax Credit, and the Community Development Financial Institution Fund. "Background on the Clinton-Gore Administration's Community Development Record," November 4, 1999, https://clinton4.nara.gov/WH/New/New_Markets_Nov/factsheets/comdevl.html.

62. Cited in Dr. Julia S. Rubin and Gregory M. Stankiewicz, "Evaluating the Impact of Federal Community Economic Development Policies on Targeted Populations: The Case of the New Markets Initiatives of 2000," Paper presented at the annual meeting of the Board of Governors of the Federal Reserve Board, Chicago, IL, July 2003.

63. "We must stop trying to cure the inner city's problems by perpetually increasing social investment and hoping for economic activity to follow. Instead, an economic model must begin with the premise that inner city businesses should be profitable and positioned to compete on a regional, national, and even international scale." M. E. Porter, "The Competitive Advantage of the Inner City," *Harvard Business Review* 73(3) (May–June 1995): 55–71.

64. The Ninety-First American Assembly, *Community Capitalism: Rediscovering the Markets of America's Urban Neighborhoods* (New York: Columbia University Press, 1997), 3.

65. According to Clinton administration official Gene Sperling, the legislation was meant to create "incentives that would encourage the private sector to find profits and create opportunities." Ibid.

66. Tammy Draut, David Callahan, and Corinna Hawkes, "Crossing Divides: New Common Ground on Poverty and Economic Security," *Demos*, September 1, 2002, 3.

67. S. Shepard, "Investment Proposed for Impoverished Areas," *Atlanta Journal and Constitution*, January 16, 1999, 6A. Alice O'Connor, "Swimming against the Tide: A Brief History of Federal Policy in Poor Communities," in *Urban Problems and Community Development*, ed. Ronald F. Ferguson and William T. Dickens (Washington DC: Brookings Institution, 1999), 44–45.

68. Bill Clinton, Proclamation 6713, 108 Stat. 5617, August 9, 1994, http://www.gpo.gov/fdsys/pkg/STATUTE-108/pdf/STATUTE-108-Pg5617.pdf.

69. Bill Clinton, "Remarks by the President on New Markets Initiative," May 11, 1999, https://clinton4.nara.gov/WH/New/html/19990511.html.

70. Riegle Community Development and Regulatory Improvement Act of 1994, Pub. L. 103-325, 108 Stat. 2160 (codified as amended in scattered sections of 12 U.S.C.) (1994).

71. James Post and Fiona Wilson, "Too Good to Fail," *Stanford Social Innovation Review*, Fall 2011, http://www.ssireview.org/articles/entry/too_good_to_fail.

72. Lois J. D. Wacquant and William Julius Wilson, "Poverty, Joblessness, and the Social Transformation of the Inner City," *Welfare Policy for the 1990s*, ed. Phoebe H. Cottingham and David T. Ellwood (Cambridge, MA: Harvard University Press, 1989), 92.

73. David Moberg, "The Left Bank," *Chicago Reader*, 1994, http://www.chicagoreader.com/chicago/the-left-bank/Content?oid=884620.

74. Robert A. Solomon, "The Fall (and Rise?) of Community Banking: The Continued Importance of Local Institutions," *Irvine Law Review* 2 (2012): 955, http://papers.ssrn.com/sol3/papers.cfm?abstract_id=2201901.

75. Post and Wilson, "Too Good to Fail."

76. Katharine Esty, "Lessons from Muhammad Yunus and the Grameen Bank: Leading Long-Term Organizational Change Successfully," *OD Practitioner* 43 (2011), http://c.ymcdn.com/sites/www.odnetwork.org/resource/resmgr/364.pdf.

77. Post and Wilson, "Too Good to Fail."

78. Mehrsa Baradaran, *How the Other Half Banks: Exclusion, Exploitation, and the Threat to Democracy* (Cambridge, MA: Harvard University Press, 2015), 164.

79. Richard Douthwaite, *Short Circuit: Strengthening Local Economies for Security in an Unstable World* (Foxhole, UK: Green Books, 1996), 153; see also Sharon Stangenes, "South Shore Bank Thrust into Spotlight," *Chicago Tribune*, November

15, 1992, 7, discussing Bill Clinton's advocacy of South Shore Bank during his 1992 presidential campaign.

80. Jann S. Wenner, "The Rolling Stone Interview: Bill Clinton," September 17, 1992, http://www.jannswenner.com/archives/bill_clinton.aspx.

81. "[The CDFI Fund of $382 million proposed by Clinton is] significantly less ambitious than Mr. Clinton's campaign proposal to use $850 million of federal money to establish 100 community development banks around the country modeled after Chicago's successful South Shore Bank." "Banking on the Inner City," *Washington Post,* July 19, 1993.

82. 12 U.S.C. §§ 4701(b), 4702(5)(A)(i)–(iii) (2006).

83. Community Development Banking and Financial Institutions Act of 1993, 140 Cong. Rec. S 3132, Senate, March 17, 1994.

84. House Subcommittees on Policy Research and Insurance and on Economic Stabilization, *Traditional and Non-Traditional Lenders' Role in Economic Development* (Washington DC: Government Printing Office, 1992), 21.

85. Ibid., 1.

86. Ibid., 4–5 (emphasis added).

87. Lawrence H. Summers, U.S. Secretary of Treasury, "Building Emerging Markets in America's Inner Cities," Remarks to the National Council for Urban Economic Development, March 2, 1998, http://www.treasury.gov/press-center/press -releases/Pages/rr2262.aspx.

88. "Surviving the Recession: How Microlenders Are Coping with Changing Demand, Risk and Funding," *Field Trendlines Series* 1 (July 2010), http://www .fieldus.org/publications/TrendlinesMicrofinance.pdf; Robert Barba, "Deal Shows ShoreBank Was Savvy to the End," *American Banker,* August 24, 2010, 1; Lehn Benjamin et al., "Community Development Financial Institutions: Current Issues and Future Prospects," *Journal of Urban Affairs* 26 (2004): 189.

89. Cited in D. Pappas, "A New Approach to a Familiar Problem: The New Market Tax Credit," *Journal of Affordable Housing and Community Development Law* 10(4) (2001): 323.

90. New Markets Tax Credit Coalition, "New Markets Tax Credit Fact Sheet," http:// nmtccoalition.org/fact-sheet. The legislation gave Treasury the power to administer and interpret the tax credits, but left the venture capital portion in the jurisdiction of the SBA, which caused confusing fragmentation. The significance of this allocation of responsibility was also part of the message. Treasury and SBA were more business-friendly than HUD, whose mission, ostensibly, was more community-oriented.

91. Federal Reserve Bank of Minneapolis, "Mass CDFI Recertification Push Winnows List, Ensures Compliance," http://www.minneapolisfed.org/publications _papers/pub_display.cfm?id=5289.

92. "By our estimates, less than 2% of the $450 billion in NMTCs issued over the past [12] years has gone to minority banks," said Doyle Mitchell, CEO of Industrial Bank of Washington, DC, and immediate past Chairman of the NBA. Carolyn M. Brown, "Black Banks Shut Out of New Federal Tax Credit Program," *Black Enterprise,* July 15, 2015, http://www.blackenterprise.com/small-business/minority -banks-shut-out-of-new-federal-tax-credit-program/2.

93. According to one scholar, the result of the grants has been to "take profits out of the slum when the real objective should have been to build profits into it." T. L. Cross, *Black Capitalism: Strategy for Business in the Ghetto* (New York: Atheneum, 1969), 16.

94. "Civil Rights Chief Faults CRA as Toothless Legislation," *American Banker,* May 21, 1992, https://www.americanbanker.com/news/civil-rights-chief -faults-cra-as-toothless-legislation ("regulators are not enforcing the law aggressively").

95. Warren L. Dennis, *The Community Re-Investment Act of 1977: Its Legislative History and Its Impact on Applications for Changes in Structure Made by Depository Institutions to the Four Federal Financial Supervisory Agencies* (Lafayette, IN: Credit Research Center, Krannert Graduate School of Management, Purdue University, 1978).

96. FDIC, "Community Reinvestment Act (CRA) Performance Ratings," http://www2 .fdic.gov/crapes/crafaq_v4.asp.

97. Richard Scott Carnell, Jonathan R. Macey, and Geoffrey P. Miller, *The Law of Financial Institutions*, 5th ed. (New York: Aspen, 2013), 385; Charles W. Calomiris, Charles M. Kahn, and Stanley D. Longhofer, "Housing-Finance Intervention and Private Incentives: Helping Minorities and the Poor," *Journal of Money, Credit, and Banking* 26(3) (August 1994): 654–656.

98. Financial Services Modernization Act of 1999, 145 Cong. Rec. S 4736, Senate, May 5, 1999, https://www.congress.gov/congressional-record/1999/05/05 /senate-section/article/S4736–2.

99. Jeffrey Marshall, "Lenders Cry Foul over Fair Lending Prosecutions," *American Banker*, October 1, 1994, http://www.americanbanker.com/issues/159_115 /-47003–1.html.

100. Banking law scholars Jonathan Macey and Geoffrey Miller claimed that the bill "promotes the concentration of assets in geographically non-diversified locations, encourages banks to make unprofitable and risky investment and product line decisions, and penalizes banks that seek to reduce costs by consolidating services or closing or relocating branches." Jonathan R. Macey and Geoffrey P. Miller, "The Community Reinvestment Act: An Economic Analysis," Yale Law School Faculty Scholarship Series, 1993, 295.

101. House Subcommittee on Oversight and Investigations or the Committee on Financial Services, *Preserving and Expanding Minority Banks*, 110th Cong. 465 (Washington DC: U.S. Government Printing Office, 2007), https://www.gpo .gov/fdsys/pkg/CHRG-110hhrg39916/html/CHRG-110hhrg39916.htm.

102. OneUnited Bank, Carver Bank, and Broadway Bank have all had noncompliance ratings. See Federal Financial Institutions Examination Council, "CRA Rating Search," https://www.ffiec.gov/craratings/default.aspx.

103. See Carnell et al., *Law of Financial Institutions*, 328; Michael S. Barr, "Banking the Poor," *Yale Journal on Regulation* 21 (2004): 121, 603. "CRA's broad standards and 'enforcement' mechanisms . . . have long been derided by both proponents and detractors of CRA. Community advocates urge stricter rules and harsher consequences of failure. Bankers lament the lack of clear rules or safe harbors and the intrusive role of the public." Calomiris et al., "Housing-Finance Intervention and Private Incentives," 634, 673 (stating that "the vagueness of the CRA has led to arbitrary enforcement").

104. See generally Richard Sanders and Stuart Taylor, *Mismatch: How Affirmative Action Hurts Students It's Intended to Help and Why Universities Won't Admit It* (New York: Basic Books, 2012).

105. Louis Hyman, *Debtor Nation: The History of America in Red Ink* (Princeton, NJ: Princeton University Press, 2011), 232.

106. These CDOs had "very high and imperfectly understood embedded leverage, creating positions in the trading books of banks which were hugely vulnerable to shifts in confidence and liquidity." Financial Services Authority, "The Turner Review: A Regulatory Response to the Global Banking Crisis," March 2009, http://www.fsa.gov.uk/pubs/other/turner_review.pdf.

107. This is due to the yield-spread premium that a lender pays out to the loan originator. The premium is tied to the rate or terms of the mortgage; thus, the higher the rate the more money a broker is able to earn. For further discussion, see Lynnley Browning, "New Fed Rule for Mortgage Brokers," *New York Times*,

February 17, 2011, http://www.nytimes.com/2011/02/20/realestate/20mort .html?_r=0 .

108. David Schmuddle, "Responding to the Subprime Mess: The New Regulatory Landscape," *Fordham Journal of Corporate and Financial Law* 14 (2009): 727–729. Baradaran, *How the Other Half Banks*, chaps. 2 and 4; 12 U.S.C. § 226 (1980); 12 U.S.C. § 226 (1982).

109. Massey and Denton, *American Apartheid*, 108.

110. Commercial banks rejected equally qualified black applicants twice as often as whites nationwide, and in some cities, the rate was three times more than whites. The *Boston Globe* reported in October 1991 that "It can no longer be doubted that banks are discriminating against blacks." In 1989, reporters from the *Atlanta Journal-Constitution* used the Freedom of Information Act to acquire over 10 million loan applications to S&Ls between 1983 and 1988 and found that even when they controlled for income and neighborhood, blacks were significantly disadvantaged in the loan process. In fact, high-income blacks were rejected more often than low income whites in thirty-five metropolitan areas. Oliver and Shapiro, *Black Wealth/White Wealth*, 20.

111. HUD, "Unequal Burden: Income and Racial Disparities in Subprime Lending," https://archives.hud.gov/reports/subprime/subprime.cfm.

112. Oliver and Shapiro, *Black Wealth/White Wealth*, 20. One reason for the discrimination in lending could have been established relationships with banks and bankers. For example, "11.8 percent of white [loan] applicants have had previous business with the bank to which they applied, in contrast to only 2.4 percent of their African American counterparts." Conley, *Being Black*, 41; Massey and Denton, *American Apartheid*, 108–109.

113. See generally Jacob S. Rugh and Douglas S. Massey, "Racial Segregation and the American Foreclosure Crisis," *American Sociological Review* 75(5) (2010), http:// journals.sagepub.com/doi/pdf/10.1177/0003122410380868.

114. A 1983 study found that "almost two-thirds of all poor blacks bought their household appliances either exclusively or primarily on credit, often on terms that exceed market credit rates by over 100 percent." Marable, *How Capitalism Underdeveloped Black America*, 162.

115. Hyman, *Debtor Nation*, 243.

116. According to Louis Hyman, "the gap between what was loaned and what was repaid increased seven times, to $35 billion a year." Ibid., 219.

117. Rob Wells, "Bank Mired in Loan Bias Scandal," *Register-Guard*, December 27, 1992, D1.

118. See Baradaran, *How the Other Half Banks*, chaps. 1–3.

119. Charles Duhigg, "The Future of Superbanks," *Frontline*, June 16, 2009, http://www .pbs.org/wgbh/pages/frontline/breakingthebank/themes/future.html.

120. Black banks were failing over the course of several decades, from a total of forty-eight in 1980, to thirty-four in 1990, to thirty in 2004. Nicholas A. Lash, "Black-Owned Banks: A Survey of Issues," *Journal of Developmental Entrepreneurship* 10 (2005): 191. Fifty-nine new black banks were started between 1963 and 1990, twenty-two of them after 1980. E. C. Lawrence, "The Viability of Minority-Owned Banks," *Quarterly Review of Economics and Finance* 37 (1997): 1–21.

121. Volbert Alexander and Hans-Helmut Kotz, *Global Divergence in Trade, Money and Policy* (Cheltenham, UK: Edward Elger, 2006) 97.

122. Between 1985 and 2013, 85 percent of community banks holding less than $100 million in assets failed or were consolidated by larger banks. FDIC Quarterly Report, "Community Banks Remain Resilient among Industry Consolidation" 8(2) (2014): 36, https://www.fdic.gov/bank/analytical/quarterly/2014_vol8_2/article.pdf.

123. When the bank failed in 1990, it had $101.9 million in assets, 22,000 depositors, ninety-seven employees, and two Brooklyn branches. Andrew L. Yarrow,

"Freedom Bank's Failure Hits Harlem Like a Death in the Family," *New York Times*, November 12, 1990, http://www.nytimes.com/1990/11/12/nyregion/freedom -bank-s-failure-hits-harlem-like-a-death-in-the-family.html.

124. Today, the cap is $250,000. FDIC, "Deposit Insurance at a Glance," https://www .fdic.gov/deposit/deposits/brochures/deposit_insurance_at_a_glance-english .html.

125. Andrew F. Brimmer, "The Dilemma of Black Banking: Lending Risks vs. Community Service," *Review of Black Political Economy* 20 (1992): 18.

126. Anthony D. Taibi, "Race Consciousness, Communitarianism, and Banking Regulation," *University of Illinois Law Review* 1992 (1992): 1103.

127. Yarrow, "Freedom Bank's Failure Hits Harlem Like a Death in the Family."

128. Taibi, "Race Consciousness," 1103.

129. The FDIC did decide that two other black-owned banks, Unity Bank in Boston and Detroit's Bank of the Commonwealth, were essential to the community. Alexander and Kotz, *Global Divergence in Trade*, 191.

130. Murray Kempton, "Freedom National Bank Was Killed by Greed, Not Racism," *Atlanta Journal-Constitution*, December 21, 1990.

131. Yarrow, "Freedom Bank's Failure Hits Harlem Like a Death in the Family."

132. Studies showed that their problems were completely unrelated to poor management. See Timothy Bates and William Bradford, "An Analysis of Portfolio Behavior of Black Owned Banks," *Journal of Finance* 35 (1980): 753–768, https://www.jstor.org/stable/2327496?seq=1#page_scan_tab_contents.

133. John T, Boorman and Myron L. Kwast, "The Start-Up Experience of Minority-Owned Commercial Banks: A Comparative Analysis," *Journal of Finance* 29 (1974): 1123–1141, https://www.jstor.org/stable/2978388?seq=1#page_scan_tab _contents.

134. Bates and Bradford, "Analysis of Portfolio Behavior of Black Owned Banks," 753.

135. FIRREA, 12 U.S.C. 1821(e) (2013).

136. Bates and Bradford, "Analysis of Portfolio Behavior of Black Owned Banks," 760–762.

137. Alexander and Kotz, *Global Divergence in Trade*, 192. See generally Gregory Price, "The Cost of Government Deposits for Black-Owned Commercial Banks," *Review of Black Political Economy* 23 (1994).

138. Harriet T. Taggart and Kevin W. Smith, "Redlining: An Assessment of the Evidence of Disinvestment in Metropolitan Boston," *Urban Affairs Quarterly* 17 (1981): 91–92. Bankers responded to Taggart and Smith's findings by stating that "capital export" was not a result of intentionally discriminatory policies, but rather the result of lower demand for residential loans in inner-city areas.

139. Kenneth T. Jackson, *Crabgrass Frontier: The Suburbanization of the United States* (Oxford: Oxford University Press, 1985), 217.

140. Brimmer, "Dilemma of Black Banking," 14.

141. The greatest wealth gap between blacks and whites existed in 1989, when whites had seventeen times the wealth of black households. Rakesh Kochhar and Richard Fry, "Wealth Inequality Has Widened along Racial, Ethnic Lines since End of Great Recession," Pew Research Center, December 12, 2014, http://www .pewresearch.org/fact-tank/2014/12/12/racial-wealth-gaps-great-recession/.

Chapter 8 The Color of Money Matters

1. David Jackson, "Ten Years Ago: Obama Makes National Debut," *USA Today*, July 27, 2014.

2. Sarah Pulliam Bailey, "A Startling Number of Americans Still Believe President Obama Is a Muslim," *Washington Post*, September 14, 2015.

3. "We find that while economic dissatisfaction was part of the story, racism and sexism were much more important and can explain about two-thirds of the education gap among whites in the 2016 presidential vote." Brian F. Schaffner, Matthew MacWilliams, and Tatishe Nteta, "Explaining White Polarization in the 2016 Vote for President: The Sobering Role of Racism and Sexism," Paper presented at the Conference on the U.S. Elections of 2016: Domestic and International Aspects, January 8–9, 2017, Interdisciplinary Center Herzliya, Herzliya, Israel, 2–3, http://people.umass.edu/schaffne/schaffner_et_al_IDC_conference.pdf; "Since 1988, we've never seen such a clear correspondence between vote choice and racial perceptions." Thomas Wood, "Racism Motivated Trump Voters More than Authoritarianism," *Washington Post*, April 17, 2017, https://www.washingtonpost.com/news/monkey-cage/wp/2017/04/17/racism-motivated-trump-voters-more-than-authoritarianism-or-income-inequality/?utm_term=.d1d5050f98d3.

4. Thomas B. Edsall, "The Not-So-Silent White Majority," *New York Times*, November 17, 2016, quoting Mary D. Edsall and Thomas Byrne Edsall, *Chain Reaction: The Impact of Race, Rights, and Taxes on American Politics* (New York: W. W. Norton, 1992), 182.

5. Robert P. Jones, Daniel Cox, Betsy Cooper, and Rachel Lienesch "Anxiety, Nostalgia and Mistrust," Public Religion Research Institute, 5, http://www.prri.org/wp-content/uploads/2015/11/PRRI-AVS-2015-Web.pdf; Michael L. Norton and Samuel R. Sommers, "Whites See Racism as a Zero-Sum Game That They Are Now Losing," *Perspectives on Psychological Science* 6(3) (2011): 215–218, http://www.people.hbs.edu/mnorton/norton%20sommers.pdf.

6. Ben Fountain, "American Crossroads: Reagan, Trump and the Devil Down South," *The Guardian*, March 5, 2016.

7. The White House, "Remarks by President Trump in African American History Month Listening Session," February 1, 2016, https://www.whitehouse.gov/the-press-office/2017/02/01/remarks-president-trump-african-american-history-month-listening-session.

8. Tim Hains, "Trump Proposes 'New Deal for Black America' in Charlotte," *RealClear Politics*, October 26, 2016.

9. Donald J. Trump, "Donald J. Trump's New Deal for Black America," October 31, 2016, https://www.donaldjtrump.com/press-releases/donald-j.-trump-announces-a-plan-for-urban-renewal.

10. David Leonhardt, "In Climbing Income Ladder, Location Matters," *New York Times*, July 22, 2013.

11. Jeff Chang, *We Gon' Be Alright: Notes on Race and Resegregation* (New York: Macmillan, 2016), introduction and chap. 3.

12. Median household income was $37,000, which was $10,000 less than the rest of the state. Malcolm Gay, "White Flight and White Power in St. Louis," *Time*, August 13, 2014.

13. Stephen Gandel, "The Economic Imbalance Fueling Ferguson's Unrest," *Fortune*, August 16, 2014.

14. "Video: Protester Justifies the Looting in Ferguson," Fox 2, August 11, 2014, http://fox2now.com/2014/08/11/video-protester-justifies-the-looting-in-ferguson/.

15. Raj Chetty and Nathaniel Hendren, "The Impacts of Neighborhoods on Intergenerational Mobility," NBER Working Paper No. w23001, May 2015, http://www.equality-of-opportunity.org/images/nbhds_exec_summary.pdf.

16. "How Racism Doomed Baltimore," Editorial, *New York Times*, May 9, 2015; Michael Powell, "Bank Accused of Pushing Mortgage Deals on Blacks," *New York Times*, June 6, 2009.

17. Scott Dance, "Riots Erupt across West Baltimore, Downtown," *Baltimore Sun*, April 27, 2015.

18. Eddie S. Glaude Jr., *Democracy in Black: How Race Still Enslaves the American Soul* (New York: Crown, 2016), introduction; Chuck Collins, Dedrick Asante-Muhammed, Josh Hoxie, and Emanuel Nieves, "The Ever-Growing Gap: Failing to Address the Status Quo Will Drive the Racial Wealth Divide for Centuries to Come," Institute for Policy Students, 2016, 3, http://www.ips-dc.org/wp-content/uploads/2016/08/The-Ever-Growing-Gap-CFED_IPS-Final-2.pdf; Heather Beth Johnson, *The American Dream and the Power of Wealth* (London: Routledge, 2006), 9.

19. Crystal Wright, "Barack Obama Has Done Zero for Black People," *The Telegraph*, August 3, 2015.

20. Pew Research Center, "1. Demographic Trends and Economic Well-Being," June 26, 2016, http://www.pewsocialtrends.org/2016/06/27/1-demographic-trends-and-economic-well-being/#fn-21776–13; Collins et al., "Ever-Growing Gap," 3; Board of Governors of the Federal Reserve System, *Financial Accounts of the United States: Third Quarter 2016*, Federal Reserve Statistical Release, December 2016, https://www.federalreserve.gov/releases/z1/current/z1.pdf.

21. The average net worth of white families with a college education in the United States is around $360,000. For blacks in the same position, it is $32,000. Without a college degree, whites have a net worth of $80,000 and blacks, $9,000. William R. Emmons and Bryan J. Noeth, "Why Didn't Higher Education Protect Hispanic and Black Wealth?," Federal Reserve Bank of St. Louis, August 2015, 1, https://www.stlouisfed.org/~/media/Publications/In-the-Balance/Images/Issue_12/ITB_August_2015.pdf; Amy Traub and Catherine Ruetschlin, "The Racial Wealth Gap: Why Policy Matters," *Demos*, 2016, http://www.demos.org/publication/racial-wealth-gap-why-policy-matters; Rakesh Kochhar and Richard Fry, "Wealth Inequality Has Widened along Racial, Ethnic Lines since End of Great Recession," Pew Research Center, December 2014, http://www.pewresearch.org/fact-tank/2014/12/12/racial-wealth-gaps-great-recession/; Rakesh Kochhar, Richard Fry, and Paul Taylor, "Wealth Gaps Rise to Record Highs Between Whites, Blacks, Hispanics," Pew Research Center, September 26, 2011, http://www.pewsocialtrends.org/2011/07/26/wealth-gaps-rise-to-record-highs-between-whites-blacks-hispanics/.

22. Collins et al., "Ever-Growing Gap."

23. The wealth gap is best described as a "sedimentation of racial inequality," according to Oliver and Shapiro. Melvin Oliver and Thomas Shapiro, *Black Wealth/White Wealth: A New Perspective on Racial Inequality* (New York: Routledge, 1997), 5. William Julies Wilson called it "the accumulation of disadvantages . . . passed from generation to generation." William Julies Wilson, *The Truly Disadvantaged: The Inner City, the Underclass, and Public Policy* (Chicago: University of Chicago Press, 2012), 126.

24. Dalton Conley, *Being Black, Living in the Red: Race, Wealth, and Social Policy in America* (Berkeley: University of California Press 2010), 115.

25. James Surowiecki, "The Widening Racial Wealth Divide," *New Yorker*, October 10, 2016.

26. "Barack Obama, "'83's Keynote Speech at the 2004 Democratic National Convention, July 27, 2004, Boston," *Columbia College Today*, January 2005, http://www.college.columbia.edu/cct_archive/jan05/cover_speech.php.

27. Melvin Oliver and Thomas Shapiro have explained that the disparity in basic wealth explains more than any other racial disparity because "the command over resources that wealth entails is more encompassing than is income or education, and closer in meaning and theoretical significance to our traditional notions of economic well-being and access to life chances." Oliver and Shapiro, *Black Wealth/White Wealth*, 2.

28. Lawrence D. Bobo and Ryan A. Smith, "From Jim Crow Racism to Laissez-Faire Reaction: The Transformation of Racial Attitude," in *Beyond Pluralism: The*

Conception of Groups and Group Identities in America, ed. Wendy F. Katkin, Ned Landsman, and Andrea Tyree (Champaign: University of Illinois Press, 1998).

29. Charles Murray, *Losing Ground: American Social Policy, 1950–1980* (New York: Basic books, 2008).

30. Conley, *Being Black,* 90: Kathryn J. Edin, and Luke Shaefer, *$2.00 a Day: Living on Almost Nothing in America* (New York: Houghton Mifflin Harcourt, 2015).

31. Census Bureau, *Black-Owned Firms: 2002,* August 2006, http://www2.census.gov /econ/sbo/02/sb0200csblk.pdf.

32. Conley, *Being Black,* 59, 73; Thomas Shapiro, Tatjana Meschede, and Sam Osoro, "The Roots of the Widening Racial Wealth Gap: Explaining the Black-White Economic Divide," Institute on Assets and Social Policy, Research and Policy Brief, February 2013, http://iasp.brandeis.edu/pdfs/Author/shapiro-thomas -m/racialwealthgapbrief.pdf.

33. Yet voluminous research clearly demonstrates that welfare did not cause black poverty. Conley, *Being Black,* 116; Edin and Shaefer, *$2.00 a Day,* 14–18; Martin Gilens, "How the Poor Became Black," in *Race and the Politics of Welfare Reform,* ed. Sanford F. Schram, Joe Soss, and Richard C. Fording (Ann Arbor: University of Michigan Press, 2003); Steve Chapman, "Whites Have a Role in the Plight of Black Families," *Chicago Tribune,* February 25, 2015, http://www.chicagotribune.com /news/opinion/chapman/ct-whites-blacks-families-moynihan-report-perspec -0226-jm-20150225-column.html; Jill Quadagno, *The Color of Welfare: How Racism Undermined the War on Poverty* (Oxford: Oxford University Press, 1996).

34. Ronald Angel and Marta Tienda, "Determinants of Extended Household Structure: Cultural Pattern or Economic Need?," *American Journal of Sociology* 87 (1982): 1360–1383.

35. Daniel Schneider, "Wealth and the Marital Divide," *American Journal of Sociology* 117 (2011): 648–656; Michael Sherraden, ed., *Inclusion in the American Dream: Assets, Poverty, and Public Policy* (Oxford: Oxford University Press, 2005), 376; Oliver and Shapiro, *Black Wealth/White Wealth,* 126–127.

36. Jeanne Brooks-Gunn and Greg J. Duncan, "The Effects of Poverty on Children," *Future of Children* 7 (Summer / Fall 1997): 55–71.

37. The experiment, designed by Stanford researcher Walter Mischel, presents children with the option of eating a marshmallow right away or waiting fifteen minutes to get two marshmallows. Mischel followed these children for decades and found that those who exhibited delayed gratification and waited for the two marshmallows were more successful than those who ate the one marshmallow right away. They made more money, had gotten better grades, and were less likely to be in prison. The experiment has been used by schools and motivational speakers for years to demonstrate the important lesson that self-control is the most important trait for success. American Psychological Association, "Delaying Gratification," https://www.apa.org/helpcenter/willpower-gratification.pdf.

38. Roberto A. Ferdman, "The Big Problem with One of the Most Popular Assumptions about the Poor," *Washington Post,* June 8, 2016.

39. Children's Defense Fund, "Child Poverty in America 2015: National Analysis," http://www.childrensdefense.org/library/data/child-poverty-in-america-2015 .pdf; Edin and Shaefer, *$2.00 a Day.*

40. Sendhil Mullainathan and Eldar Shafir, *Scarcity: The New Science of Having Less and How It Defines Our Lives* (London: Picador, 2014).

41. Glaude, *Democracy in Black,* 24.

42. U.S. Department of the Treasury, *Freedmen's Bank Forum,* video, September 23, 2016, http://www.yorkcast.com/treasury/events/2016/09/23/freedmansbank /(pertinent dialogue starts at 19 minutes).

43. Joseph G. Altonji and Ulrich Doraszelski, "The Role of Permanent Income and Demographics in Black / White Differences in Wealth," National Bureau of Eco-

nomic Research Working Paper 8473, September 2001, http://www.nber.org /papers/w8473.pdf; Sharmila Choudhury, "Racial and Ethnic Differences in Wealth and Asset Choices," *Social Security Bulletin* 64 (2001), https://www.ssa .gov/policy/docs/ssb/v64n4/v64n4p1.html. Other researchers support this finding showing "no difference in the savings rates of blacks and whites." W. Hrung, "The Permanent Income Hypothesis and Black/White Savings Differentials," Department of Economics, University of California at Berkeley, 1997.

44. U.S. Census Bureau, "Quarterly Residential Vacancies and Homeownership, Fourth Quarter 2016," http://www.census.gov/housing/hvs/files/currenthvs press.pdf.

45. James Surowiecki, "The Widening Racial Wealth Divide," *New Yorker*, October 10, 2016; Michael J. Graetz, "The Truth about Tax Reform," *Faculty Scholarship Series* 1625 (1988), http://digitalcommons.law.yale.edu/fss_papers/1625; Amos Kiewe and Davis W. Houck, *A Shining City on a Hill: Ronald Reagan's Economic Rhetoric, 1951–1989* (New York: Praeger, 1991).

46. According to a *ProPublica* study, since George Romney left HUD, there have been only two occasions on which the agency has decided to enforce the Fair Housing Act—the main remaining bulwark against segregation. Nikole Hannah-Jones, "Living Apart: How the Government Betrayed a Landmark Civil Rights Law," *ProPublica*, June 25, 2015.

47. Ibid.

48. Nikole Hannah-Jones, "Choosing a School for My Daughter in a Segregated City," *New York Times*, June 9, 2016.

49. Jason M. Breslow, Evan Wexler, and Robert Collins, "The Return of School Segregation in Eight Charts," *Frontline*, July 15, 2014.

50. John Eligon and Robert Gebeloff, "Affluent and Black, and Still Trapped by Segregation," *New York Times*, August 20, 2016.

51. Ta-Nehisi Coates, "The Case for Reparations," *Atlantic*, June 2014.

52. The few times HUD has used its FHA powers, which is the only legislative bulwark against racial segregation, have been to enforce disability accommodations. Hannah-Jones, "Living Apart."

53. Jonathan Mahler and Steve Eder, "'No Vacancies' for Blacks: How Donald Trump Got His Start, and Was First Accused of Bias," *New York Times*, August 27, 2016.

54. Tina Nguyen, "What Ben Carson's History Reveals about His Potential Plans for HUD," *Vanity Fair*, December 6, 2016.

55. Rachel Weiner, "Mitt Romney at Private Fundraiser: I Might Eliminate HUD," *Washington Post*, April 16, 2012.

56. Jessica Attie of the Foreclosure Prevention Project at South Brooklyn Legal Services, quoted on British Broadcasting Company, *Newspod*, September 19, 2007. Kochhar et al., "Wealth Gaps."

57. Zoë Carpenter, "Five Years after Dodd-Frank, 'It's Still a Financial System That Needs Reform,'" *Nation*, July 23, 2015, https://www.thenation.com/article/five -years-after-dodd-frank-its-still-a-financial-system-that-needs-reform/.

58. Debbie Gruenstein Bocian, Wei Li, and Keith S. Ernst, "Foreclosures by Race and Ethnicity: The Demographics of a Crisis," Center for Responsible Lending, June 18, 2010, 8, http://www.responsiblelending.org/mortgage-lending/research -analysis/foreclosures-by-race-and-ethnicity.pdf.

59. Glaude, *Democracy in Black*, 18.

60. David Min, "Faulty Conclusions Built on Shoddy Foundations," Center for American Progress, February 2011, http://papers.ssrn.com/sol3/papers.cfm ?abstract_id=2103379.

61. Charles W. Calomiris and Stephen H. Haber, *Fragile by Design: The Political Origins of Banking Crises and Scarce Credit* (Princeton, NJ: Princeton University Press, 2014.); Mike Konczal, "No, Marco Rubio, Government Did Not Cause the

Housing Crisis," *Washington Post,* February 13, 2013: Elizabeth Laderman and Carolina Reid, "CRA Lending during the Subprime Meltdown," Federal Reserve Bank of San Francisco, February 2009, 115, http://www.frbsf.org/community -development/files/cra_lending_during_subprime_meltdown.pdf.

62. Kenneth J. Cooper, "Loans to Minorities Did Not Cause Housing Crisis, Study Finds," *New America Media,* February 9, 2011, http://newamericamedia.org /2011/02/loans-to-minorities-did-not-cause-housing-crisis-study-finds.php.

63. Lawrence Kudlow and Stephen Moore, "Are the Clintons the Real Housing Crash Villains?," *CNBC,* May 28, 2016.

64. Cooper, "Loans to Minorities Did Not Cause Housing Crisis."

65. Christopher S. Parker and Matt A. Barreto, *Change They Can't Believe In: The Tea Party and Reactionary Politics in America* (Princeton, NJ: Princeton University Press, 2014), 1–3.

66. Timothy Geithner, *Stress Test: Reflections on a Financial Crisis* (New York; Crown, 2014), 391–392. See also Senator Robert Menendez, "Fed Chairman Bernanke Confirms to Menendez that Community Reinvestment Act Is Not to Blame for Foreclosure Crisis," Press Release, December 2, 2008, http://www.menendez .senate.gov/newsroom/press/fed-chairman-bernanke-confirms-to-menendez -that-community-reinvestment-act-is-not-to-blame-for-foreclosure-crisis; David Min, "Why Wallison Is Wrong about the Genesis of the U.S. Housing Crisis," Center for American Progress, July 12, 2011, https://www.americanprogress.org /issues/economy/reports/2011/07/12/10011/why-wallison-is-wrong-about -the-genesis-of-the-u-s-housing-crisis/; Ben Bernanke, *The Courage to Act: A Memoir of a Crisis and Its Aftermath* (New York: W. W. Norton, 2015).

67. Neil Bhutta and Glenn B. Canner, "Did the CRA Cause the Mortgage Meltdown?," Federal Reserve Bank of Minneapolis, *Community Dividend,* March 1, 2009, https://www.minneapolisfed.org/publications_papers/pub_display.cfm?id =4136&. See also Governor Randall S. Kroszner, "Speech at the Confronting Concentrated Poverty Forum," Federal Reserve, Washington, DC, December 3, 2008, www.federalreserve.gov/newsevents/speech/kroszner20081203a.htm.

68. "More than 84 percent of the subprime mortgages in 2006 were issued by private lending institutions." Moreover, the GSEs had been fully privatized in 1968. Any decision they made to make more loans was a decision their shareholders believed would lead to more profits. The GSEs' market share of mortgages decreased from 50 percent to 30 percent from 2002 to 2005, while private, non-GSE mortgage buyers increased market share from 10 to 40 percent during those years. Konczal, "No, Marco Rubio."

69. For accounts on the myth of the "welfare queen" and how they are similar to "subprime borrowers" myths, see Anita Hill, *Reimagining Equality: Stories of Gender, Race, and Finding Home* (Boston: Beacon Press, 2011), chap. 3.

70. Peter J. Wallison, "The True Origins of This Financial Crisis," *American Spectator,* February 6, 2009, http://spectator.org/42211_true-origins-financial-crisis.

71. Jason Szep, "Activists Challenge Lenders in Mortgage Crisis," *Reuters,* March 19, 2007.

72. Hanwen Fan, Qiao Yu, and Xun Wu, "Global Saving Glut, Monetary Policy, and Housing Bubble: Further Evidence," Brookings Institution, July 10, 2015, https://www.brookings.edu/research/global-saving-glut-monetary-policy -and-housing-bubble-further-evidence/; Financial Services Authority, *The Turner Review: A Regulatory Response to the Global Banking Crisis* (London: Financial Services Authority, 2009), http://www.fsa.gov.uk/pubs/other/turner _review.pdf.

73. See Simon Johnson and James Kwak, *13 Bankers: The Wall Street Takeover and the Next Financial Meltdown* (New York: Pantheon, 2010), 129, citing JPMorgan Chase marketing flyer.

74. Rick Brooks and Ruth Simon, "Subprime Debacle Traps Even Very Credit-Worthy," *Wall Street Journal*, December 3, 2007.

75. Yield spread premiums (YSP) are the money paid to mortgage brokers for giving borrowers a higher interest rate on a loan. "Increased broker profits lead to worse loan performance suggesting that brokers earned high profits on loans that turned out to be riskier ex post." Antje Berndt, Burton Hollifield, and Patrik Sandas, "The Role of Mortgage Brokers in the Subprime Crisis," Carnegie Mellon University, *Research Showcase*, March 15, 2010, http://repository.cmu.edu/cgi/viewcontent.cgi?article=1561&context=tepper.

76. William Julius Wilson, *More than Just Race: Being Black and Poor in the Inner City* (New York: W. W. Norton, 2010), 7.

77. Powell, "Bank Accused of Pushing Mortgage Deals." "African-American and Latino borrowers were about 30% more likely to receive the highest-cost subprime loans relative to white subprime borrowers with similar risk profiles and that subprime loans in communities of color were more likely to carry prepayment penalties than subprime loans in majority communities." Bocian et al., "Foreclosures by Race and Ethnicity," 6.

78. Tami Luhby, "Housing Crisis Hits Blacks Hardest," *CNN*, October 19, 2010.

79. Eric S. Belsky and Nela Richardson, "Understanding the Boom and Bust in Nonprime Mortgage Lending," Joint Center for Housing Studies, Harvard University, September 2010, http://www.jchs.harvard.edu/sites/jchs.harvard.edu/files/ubb10–1.pdf, 186; Debbie Gruenstein Bocian, Keith S. Ernst, and Wei Li, "Race, Ethnicity and Subprime Home Loan Pricing," *Journal of Economics and Business* 60 (2008): 110.

80. Beryl Satter, *Family Properties: Race, Real Estate and the Exploitation of Black Urban America* (New York: Henry Holt, 2010), 374.

81. Jeff Kelly Lowenstein, "Judge Orders Compensation for Elderly Black Victims of Reverse Mortgage Scam," *Chicago Reporter*, January 28, 2016, http://chicagoreporter.com/judge-orders-compensation-for-elderly-black-victims-of-reverse-mortgage-scam/.

82. Jacob S. Rugh and Douglas S. Massey, "Racial Segregation and the American Foreclosure Crisis," *American Sociological Review* 75 (2010): 629–651.

83. Charlie Savage, "Wells Fargo Will Settle Mortgage Bias Charges," *New York Times*, July 12, 2012. Department of Justice, Press Release, "Justice Department Reaches Settlement with Wells Fargo Resulting in More than $175 Million in Relief for Homeowners to Resolve Fair Lending Claims," July 12, 2012, http://www.justice.gov/opa/pr/justice-department-reaches-settlement-wells-fargo-resulting-more-175-million-relief. *United States v. Countrywide Financial Corporation; Countrywide Home Loans, Inc.; Countrywide Bank*, Complaint, Case No. CV 11 10540-PSG (AJWN), http://www.justice.gov/crt/about/hce/documents/countrywidecomp.pdf.

84. Department of Justice, "Justice Department Reaches Settlement."

85. Powell, "Bank Accused of Pushing Mortgage Deals."

86. U.S. Attorney's Office, Central District of California, "Justice Department Reaches $335 Million Settlement to Resolve Allegations of Lending Discrimination by Countrywide Financial Corporation," Department of Justice, June 22, 2015, https://www.justice.gov/usao-cdca/dojcountrywide-settlement-information.

87. Richard H. Thaler and Cass R. Sunstein, *Nudge: Improving Decisions about Health, Wealth, and Happiness* (New Haven, CT: Yale University Press, 2008), 134.

88. Russell D. Kashian, Ran Tao, and Claudia Perez-Valdez, "Banking the Unbanked: Bank Deserts in the United States," 1, http://swfa2015.uno.edu/F_Banking/paper_90.pdf.

89. Susan Burhouse, Karyen Chu, Ryan Goodstein, Joyce Northwood, Yazmin Osaki, and Dhruv Shar, "2013 FDIC National Survey of Unbanked and Underbanked

Households," *FDIC*, October 2014, https://www.fdic.gov/householdsurvey
/2013report.pdf.

90. KPMG, "Serving the Underserved Market, 2011," 1, http://www.kpmg.com/US
/en/IssuesAndInsights/ArticlesPublications/Documents/serving-underserved
-market.pdf.

91. Frank Bass and Dakin Campbell, "Bank Branches Disappear from Poor Neighborhoods Like Longwood, Bronx," *Bloomberg*, May 9, 2013.

92. John Caskey, *Fringe Banking: Check-Cashing Outlets, Pawnshops, and the Poor*
(New York: Russell Sage Foundation, 1996).

93. Peter Eavis, "Race Strongly Influences Mortgage Lending in St. Louis, Study
Finds," *New York Times*, July 19, 2016.

94. Alexandra Stevenson and Matthew Goldstein, "Wall Street Veterans Bet on Low-
Income Home Buyers," *New York Times*, April 17, 2016.

95. "The Racist Roots of a Way to Sell Homes," Editorial, *New York Times*, April 29,
2016.

96. Pew Charitable Trusts, "Payday Lending in America," July 2012, http://www
.pewtrusts.org/~/media/legacy/uploadedfiles/pcs_assets/2012/pewpayday
lendingreportpdf.pdf.

97. Paul Kiel and Annie Waldman, "The Color of Debt: How Collection Suits Squeeze
Blacks Neighborhoods," *ProPublica*, October 8, 2015. Breno Braga, "Local Conditions and Debt in Collections," Urban Institute Working Paper, June 2016.

98. Kiel and Waldman, "Color of Debt."

99. Ibid.

100. Judith Scott-Clayton and Jing Li, "Report: Black-White Disparity in Student Loan
Debt More than Triples after Graduation," Brookings Institution, October 20,
2016, https://www.brookings.edu/research/black-white-disparity-in-student
-loan-debt-more-than-triples-after-graduation/, citing both 93/97 and 08/12
editions of the following: U.S. Department of Education: National Center for Education Statistics, *Baccalaureate and Beyond: A First Look at the Employment
Experiences and Lives of College Graduates, 4 Years On* (Washington: U.S. Department of Education, 1999, 2014), https://nces.ed.gov/surveys/b&b/.

101. Ibid.

102. Jake Halpern, *Bad Paper: Chasing Debt from Wall Street to the Underworld* (New
York: Farrar, Straus and Giroux, 2014).

103. Francis Robles and Shaila Dewan, "Skip Child Support. Go to Jail. Lose Job. Repeat." *New York Times*, April 19, 2015, https://www.nytimes.com/2015/04/20/us
/skip-child-support-go-to-jail-lose-job-repeat.html?_r=0.

104. Sophia Kerby, "The Top 10 Most Startling Facts about People of Color and Criminal Justice in the United States," Center for American Progress, March 13, 2012,
https://www.americanprogress.org/issues/race/news/2012/03/13/11351/the
-top-10-most-startling-facts-about-people-of-color-and-criminal-justice-in
-the-united-states/; Glaude, *Democracy in Black*, 24.

105. Glaude, *Democracy in Black*, 23; Stephen Lam, "The State of Black America in a
Word: 'Crisis,'" *MSNBC*, March 19, 2015.

106. Sara R. Collins, "How the Affordable Care Act of 2010 Will Help Low- and
Moderate-Income Families," Commonwealth Fund, July 13, 2010, http://www
.commonwealthfund.org/publications/blog/how-the-affordable-care-act-of
-2010.

107. Barack Obama, "Proclamation 8400—Minority Enterprise Development Week,
2009," August 20, 2009, https://www.gpo.gov/fdsys/pkg/DCPD-200900657/pdf
/DCPD-200900657.pdf.

108. Barack Obama, "Remarks in Washington, DC: 'Changing the Odds for Urban
America,'" American Presidency Project, July 18, 2007, http://www.presidency
.ucsb.edu/ws/?pid=77007.

109. Byron Tau, "Obama: 'I'm Not the President of Black America,'" *Politico*, August 7, 2012.
110. U.S. Department of Energy, "Minority Banks," http://energy.gov/diversity /working-us/minority-banks; National Science Foundation, "Chapter III— Financial Requirements and Payments," January 2008, http://www.nsf.gov /pubs/policydocs/pappguide/nsf08_1/aag_3.jsp.
111. Bureau of Fiscal Service, "Minority Bank Deposit Program (MBDP)," https://www .fiscal.treasury.gov/fsservices/gov/rvnColl/mnrtyBankDep/rvnColl_mbdp _resources.htm); Office of the Comptroller of the Currency, "U.S. Treasury Department's Minority Bank Deposit Program," Winter 2006–2007, http://www.occ .gov/static/community-affairs/community-developments-newsletter/Winter06 /cd/minoritybankdeposit.html.
112. Federal Deposit Insurance Corporation, "Policy Statement Regarding Minority Depository Institutions," https://www.fdic.gov/regulations/resources/minority /sop5-only.pdf.
113. Robert E. Weems, *Business in Black and White: American Presidents and Black Entrepreneurs in the Twentieth Century* (New York: New York University Press, 2009), 222, citing MBDA Basics, http://www.mbda.gov.
114. Federal Deposit Insurance Corporation, "Policy Statement Regarding Minority Depository Institutions," https://www.fdic.gov/regulations/resources/minority /sop5-only.pdf.
115. House of Representatives Subcommittee on Oversight and Investigations of the Committee on Financial Services, "Preserving and Expanding Minority Banks," October 30, 2007, https://www.gpo.gov/fdsys/pkg/CHRG-110hhrg39916/html /CHRG-110hhrg39916.htm.
116. Ibid.
117. "Written Testimony of Robert Patrick Cooper, Chairman Elect National Bankers Association before the Subcommittee on Government Oversight and Investigations of the Committee on Financial Services of the U.S. House of Representatives," Committee on Financial Services, October 30, 2007, 6, http://archives .financialservices.house.gov/hearing110/htcooper103007.pdf.
118. GAO Report, "Minority Banks, Regulators' Assessments of the Effectiveness of Their Support Efforts Have Been Limited," October 30, 2007, 4, http://www.gao .gov/products/GAO-08-233T.
119. "Written Testimony of Robert Patrick Cooper," 2.
120. House of Representatives, "Preserving and Expanding Minority Banks," 9.
121. Ibid., 26.
122. Ibid., 33.
123. Nicholas A. Lash, "Asymmetries in US Banking: The Role of Black-Owned Banks," in *Global Divergence in Trade, Money and Policy,* ed. Volbert Alexander and Hans-Helmut Kotz (Cheltenham, UK: Edward Elgar, 2006), 99–100.
124. "Written Testimony of Robert Patrick Cooper," 2. NBA President Cooper said black banks were "requesting specific, prompt, forceful action at the legislative, regulatory, policy, and procedural level to change the environment in which minority banks operate."
125. House of Representatives, "Preserving and Expanding Minority Banks," 20.
126. Ibid., 37.
127. U.S. House of Representatives, Committee on Financial Services-Subcommittee on Government Oversight and Investigations, "Testimony of Kim D. Saunders on Behalf of Mechanics and Farmers Bank," October 30, 2007, 10, https://www .mfbonline.com/downloads/Saunders_House_testimony_10-30-07.pdf.
128. House of Representatives, "Preserving and Expanding Minority Banks," 36.
129. Ibid.
130. Public Law 111–203, 124 Stat. 1556.

131. National Bankers Association, "Remarks by Thomas J. Curry, Comptroller of the Currency," October 3, 2013, 2, https://www.occ.gov/news-issuances/speeches /2013/pub-speech-2013–155.pdf.

132. Kristin Broughton, "Black-Owned Banks Must Revisit Their Business Models, M&F Chief Says," *American Banker* 180(89) (June 2015).

133. Ibid.; Russell D. Kashian, Richard McGregory, and Derrek Grunfelder Mc-Crank, "Whom Do Black-Owned Banks Serve?," Federal Reserve Bank of Boston, *Communities in Banking* (Summer 2014); Patrice Gaines, "What Happened to the Black Banks?," *Ebony*, June 15, 2016, http://www.ebony.com /career-finance/black-banks-pt-1#axzz4BgQFnrIF; FDIC, "Minority Depository Institutions: Structure, Performance, and Social Impact," *FDIC Quarterly* 8 (2014).

134. Tim Fernholz, "Too Small to Save," *American Prospect*, January / February 2011, http://prospect.org/article/too-small-save-0; Becky Yerak, "ShoreBank's Financial Hole Deepens," *Chicago Tribune*, August 2, 2010.

135. David Greising, "Recession Played a Part, but ShoreBank Wounded Itself, Too," *New York Times*, May 22, 2010, A25A.

136. See Nick Carey, "Regulators Close Well-Connected ShoreBank," *Reuters*, August 20, 2010.

137. John D. McKinnon and Elizabeth Williamson, "GOP Lawmakers Probe Chicago Bank Bailout," *Wall Street Journal*, May 10, 2010.

138. Jeremy Hobson, "Big Banks to ShoreBank's Rescue," *American Public Media*, May 18, 2010.

139. Glenn Beck, "'Glenn Beck': ShoreBank's Tangled Web," *Fox News*, May 21, 2010.

140. "ShoreBank Fails; Will Be Reincarnated as Urban Partnership Bank," *Crain's Detroit Business*, August 22, 2010.

141. Federal Deposit Insurance Corporation, "Supplemental Fact Sheet for ShoreBank Failure," https://www.fdic.gov/news/news/press/2010/pr10193a.pdf.

142. Aaron Elstein, "Saving Carver Federal, New York's Last Black Bank," *Crain's New York*, March 22, 2015.

143. "At December 31, 2013, the Bank had $10.5 million in subprime loans, or 2.7% of its total loan portfolio, of which $844 thousand are non-performing loans." Carver Bancorp, Form 10-Q, *Edgar*, February 13, 2014, 46.

144. Elstein, "Saving Carver Federal."

145. Ibid.

146. Beth Healy, "Minority Banks Face Steep Odds," *Boston Globe*, March 11, 2012. Elstein, "Saving Carver Federal."

147. Carver's management, its board of directors, and CEO, are black, but its owners, CFO, and other top officials are not. Bloomberg, "Company Overview of Carver Federal Savings Bank," http://www.bloomberg.com/research/stocks/private /people.asp?privcapId=4437282.

148. Aaron Elstein, "Shareholders OK Carver's Rescue by Wall St. Banks," *Crain's New York*, October 25, 2011.

149. "Its earnings were a scant $491,000 over the nine-month stretch ended Dec. 31." Elstein, "Saving Carver Federal."

150. Ibid.

151. OneUnited Bank, "Company Profile," https://www.oneunited.com/about-us /company-profile.

152. Paul Kiel, "Bank That Got Bailout Help from Barney Frank Is Struggling," *ProPublica*, July 30, 2009. The $12 million was conditioned on the bank being able to raise $20 million from its shareholders, which it did. Damian Paletta and David Enrich, "Political Interference Seen in Bank Bailout Decisions," *Wall Street Journal*, Eastern Edition, January 22, 2009, A1.

153. Wendell Cochran, "Bank in Maxine Waters Case Was Weakest to Get TARP Help," *NBC News*, August 9, 2010; Rosalind S. Helderman, "California Rep. Waters Cleared of Ethics Charges," *Washington Post*, September 21, 2012.

154. Michelle Malkin, "Maxine Waters: Swamp Queen," *National Review*, April 27, 2011.

155. Beth Healy, "OneUnited Gets 'Needs to Improve' on Community Lending," *Boston Globe*, November 6, 2014.

156. Mark A. Kellner, "Historic Black Church Faces Foreclosure from Minority-Owned Bank," *Washington Times*, March 18, 2012.

157. Ibid.

158. Beth Healy, "Church Members Rally against Foreclosure," *Boston Globe*, March 3, 2012.

159. Kellner, "Historic Black Church Faces Foreclosure."

160. The dispute went to litigation, where a bankruptcy court ruled in favor of the bank. Yawu Miller, "Bankruptcy Court Rules against Charles St. AME," *Bay State Banner*, November 9, 2016, http://baystatebanner.com/news/2016/nov/09/court-rules-against-charles-st.

161. Beth Healy, "Harvard Professor Offers Help in Church-Bank Fight," *Boston Globe*, March 6, 2012.

162. Beth Healy, "Minority Banks Are Struggling, Even with Bailouts," *Boston Globe*, March 11, 2012.

163. Broadway Federal Bank, "About Broadway," http://www.broadwayfederalbank.com/history.htm. Broadway Financial Corporation, Broadway Federal Bank Corp. Form 10-K, April 14, 2011, http://www.sec.gov/Archives/edgar/data/1001171/000119312512392728/d409680d10ka.htm.

164. Author interview with Jim Sills, 2015.

165. Lisa Allen, "Broadway Financial Completes Recapitalization," *Deal Pipeline*, September 4, 2013. E. Scott Reckard, "African American Churches Protest Foreclosures by Black-Run Bank," *Los Angeles Times*, November 03, 2012.

166. When Carver bank foreclosed on a mortgage to the Redeemed Christian Church of God, the church claimed that the bank was acting unlawfully, and Carver had to initiate a lawsuit to collect on the loan. The church countersued the bank, painting the foreclosure as unjust, unconscionable, and in bad faith. The court sided with the bank, stating, "[Carver bank] may be ungenerous, but generosity is a voluntary attribute and cannot be enforced even by a chancellor. . . . Here there is no penalty, no forfeiture, nothing except a covenant fair on its face to which both parties willingly consented. It is neither oppressive nor unconscionable. . . . Rejection of [the bank's] legal right [to foreclose on the property] could rest only on compassion for [the church's] negligence. Such a tender emotion must be exerted, if at all, by the parties rather than by the court." But Carver was in no position to extend such a tender emotion—being itself watched by regulators and on the brink of failure. *Carver Fed. Sav. Bank v Redeemed Christian Church of God, Intl. Chapel, HHH Parish, Long Is., NY, Inc.*, 2012 NY Slip Op 50921 (N.Y.S.C.) (2012).

167. Pamela Foohey, "Lender Discrimination, Black Churches, and Bankruptcy," *Houston Law Review* 50 (2016): 1–55.

168. Rory Van Loo, "A Tale of Two Debtors," *Albany Law Review* 72(231) (2009), https://papers.ssrn.com/sol3/papers.cfm?abstract_id=2353716; Jean Braucher, Dov Cohen, and Robert M. Lawless, "Race, Attorney Influence, and Bankruptcy Chapter Choice," Arizona Legal Studies Discussion Paper No. 12–02 (2012); Foohey, "Lender Discrimination."

169. Larry Muhammad, "The Black Press: Past and Present," *Nieman Reports*, September 15, 2003.

170. The study attributed the "striking" trend of bank decline to the fact that "deep poverty figures were substantially larger for communities served by BOBs." Kashian et al., "Whom Do Black-Owned Banks Serve?"

171. Trymaine Lee, "Black-Owned Banks Struggle to Stay Out of the Red," *Huffington Post,* May 11, 2015.

172. "I believe the need for black-owned and black-run banks is greater now than it was before the recession." Grant explained that those customers who are turned down by mainstream banks "come to black banks as a last resort." Jeanne Lee, "Black-Owned Banks Fight to Bounce Back," *Nerdwallet,* February 19, 2016, https://www.nerdwallet.com/blog/banking/black-owned-banks-fight-to-bounce -back.

173. Kevin Wack, "What Can Be Done to Save Black-Owned Banks?," *American Banker,* August 30, 2016.

174. Greg Whitt, "An Emotional Killer Mike Preaches Economic Empowerment in the Face of Police Brutality," *Uproxx,* July 8, 2016.

175. Teri Williams, "Why #BankBlack Is Working," *American Banker,* January 17, 2017.

176. Carimah Townes, "Black Lives Matter Launches Site to Support Black Businesses across the Country," *ThinkProgress,* December 20, 2016, https://thinkprogress .org/blm-businesses-to-support-3cd33537a2e0#.yf96ces7z.

177. John Reosti, "Deposits Surge at Black-Owned Banks after Celeb Appeals," *American Banker,* July 20, 2016; "Black Money Matters: The Newest Movement," *Community Voice,* August 8, 2016, http://www.communityvoiceks.com/black-money -matters-the-newest-movement/article_cd822174–5d75–11e6-b98a-43b31 df4eac4.html.

178. Reosti, "Deposits Surge."

Epilogue

1. Ben Johnson, "Great Horse Manure Crisis of 1894," *Historic UK,* http://www .historic-uk.com/HistoryUK/HistoryofBritain/Great-Horse-Manure-Crisis-of -1894/; Dedrick Asante-Muhammad, Chuck Collins, Josh Hoxie, and Emanuel Nieves, "The Ever-Growing Gap," Corporation for Enterprise Development, August 2016, 11, http://cfed.org/policy/federal/The_Ever_Growing_Gap-CFED _IPS-Final.pdf.

2. Richard Wilkinson and Kate Pickett, *The Spirit Level* (London: Bloomsbury Press, 2011); Richard Wilkinson, "How Economic Inequality Harms Societies," TED Talk, July, 2011, https://www.ted.com/talks/richard_wilkinson; Christin Pazzanese, "The Costs of Inequality," *Harvard Gazette,* February 8, 2016, http:// news.harvard.edu/gazette/story/2016/02/the-costs-of-inequality-increasingly -its-the-rich-and-the-rest/; G. Sitaraman, *The Crisis of the Middle-Class Constitution: Why Economic Inequality Threatens Our Republic* (New York: Alfred A. Knopf, 2017).

3. Richard H. McAdams, "The Economic Costs of Inequality," *Chicago Unbound,* November 2007, 28.

4. Paul Krugman, "Why We're in a New Gilded Age," *New York Review of Books,* May 8, 2014; Joseph Stiglitz, "Inequality and Economic Growth," *Political Quarterly* 86 (2015), doi: 10.1111/1467–923X.12237; Paul Krugman, "Is Vast Inequality Necessary?," *New York Times,* January 15, 2016.

5. Robert Gordon, *The Rise and Fall of American Growth: The U.S. Standard of Living since the Civil War* (Princeton, NJ: Princeton University Press, 2016); Thomas Piketty, *Capital in the Twenty-First Century* (Cambridge, MA: Harvard University Press, 2014); McAdams, *Economic Costs of Inequality,* 22; Sitaraman, *Crisis of the Middle Class Constitution.*

6. Hacker and Pierson explain that historically, economic growth has accompanied a mixed economy format—government and private markets working together toward a common goal of economic growth—and that inequality and deregulation of markets are both a drag on growth. Jacob Hacker and Paul Pierson, *American Amnesia: How the War on Government Led Us to Forget What Made America Prosper* (New York: Simon & Schuster, 2016).

7. The results were not so stark for the young. Among white millennials, 40 percent favored reparations and 11 percent were unsure. Polls taken by Pew and Gallup find that 61 percent of Americans believe that more changes are needed to achieve racial equality. Only 28 percent of whites believe that the government should play a major role in achieving that change, compared to 64 percent of blacks. However, 46 percent of whites supported the government playing a minor role. Jesse J. Holland, "Poll: Millennials More Open to Idea of Slavery Reparations," *Associated Press*, May 11, 2016, http://bigstory.ap.org/article/b183a0228 31d4748963fc8807c204b08/poll-millennials-more-open-idea-slavery -reparations; Gallup, "Race Relations," http://www.gallup.com/poll/1687/race -relations.aspx; Renee Stepler, "5 Key Takeaways about Views of Race and Inequality in America," Pew Research Center, June 27, 2016, http://www .pewresearch.org/fact-tank/2016/06/27/key-takeaways-race-and-inequality/.

8. Historically, reparations have been framed as compensation for slavery, such as the Reconstruction-era land grants or a direct money transfer, as was demanded by black militants during the 1960s. Confederate veteran Walter R. Vaughan demanded reparations for slavery during Reconstruction, James Forman asked for $500 million, the NAACP endorsed reparations in 1993, and prominent Harvard Professor Charles Ogletree has made legal arguments in their support in the last decade. Ta-Nehisi Coates, "The Case for Reparations," *Atlantic*, June 2014.

9. Rachel L. Swarns, "272 Slaves Were Sold to Save Georgetown. What Does It Owe Their Descendants?," *New York Times*, April 16, 2016.

10. Kathryn Vasel, "Georgetown to Offer Slave Descendants Preferential Admission Status," *CNN*, September 1, 2016.

11. Douglas Blackmon, *Slavery by Another Name: The Re-Enslavement of Black Americans from the Civil War to World War II* (New York: Random House, 2008), 392.

12. Al Brophy, *Reparations: Pro & Con* (Oxford: Oxford University Press 2006), 179.

13. Frank Newport, "In U.S., 87% Approve of Black-White Marriage, vs. 4% in 1958," *Gallup*, July 25, 2013.

14. Siddhartha Mukherjee, *The Gene: An Intimate History* (New York: Simon & Schuster, 2016), 341–350. For a full discussion of racial superiority myths, see Karen E. Fields and Barbara J. Fields, *Racecraft: The Soul of Inequality in American Life* (London: Verso, 2012); Ibram X. Kendi, *Stamped from the Beginning: The Definitive History of Racist Ideas in America* (New York: Nation Books, 2016).

15. Frederick Douglass, *Narrative of the Life of Frederick Douglass* (Mineola, NY: Dover, 1995) (originally published 1845), chap. 2.

16. C. Vann Woodward, *The Strange Career of Jim Crow* (New York: Oxford University Press, 2002).

17. James Baldwin, *The Fire Next Time* (New York: Vintage International, 1963), 83.

18. Ibid. at 94.

19. Melinda D. Anderson, "The Promise of Integrated Schools, *Atlantic*, February 16, 2016, https://www.theatlantic.com/education/archive/2016/02/promise-of -integrated-schools/462681/.

20. W. E. B. Du Bois, "Is Man Free?," *Scientific Monthly* 66 (May 1948): 432–433.

ACKNOWLEDGMENTS

Thank you, Jared Bybee, for helping me think and making it possible for me to write; Cyra, for being so loving and supportive; Lucia, for assuring me that no one will read it; Ramona, for tolerating such a boring book. Thank you, Baba and Madar, for your love, support, and encouragement. And thank you, Shima, Hediyeh, and Darius, for being such great examples of hard work. Thank you, Rebecca Smylie, for your brilliant editing, your words of encouragement, and your invaluable friendship.

Thank you, Joyce Seltzer, for believing in this project and helping me shape it and share it, and thank you to Harvard University Press. Thank you to Dean Bo Rutledge for your flexibility, support, and encouragement. Of the many colleagues who spent time reading early versions of this book, making invaluable comments, or otherwise pointing me in the right research direction, I especially thank Kent Barnett, Andrea Dennis, Al Brophy, Andrew Kahrl, Bill Nelson, Daria Roithmayr, Judge Glock, Christy Chapin, Dylan Penningroth, Beryl Satter, Nathan Connolly, Usha Rodrigues, Lori Ringhand, Logan Sawyer, Beth Burch, Dan Coenen, Sarah Gordon, Morgan Ricks, Yesha Yadav, Greg Roseboro, Gregory Kornbluh, and Brian Distelberg. Thank you, Glen Nelson, for your invaluable guidance in framing the narrative.

T. J. Striepe expertly selected and sorted all of the books and articles that went into making this volume. My enthusiastic and hardworking research assistants never cease to amaze me with their thorough research, organizational skills, and tireless efforts to find the right answers. Thank you, Chris Neill, Greg Donaldson, Amble Johnson, Jessie Kimball, Max Wallace, Patrick Shuler, Kelsie Willett, Bradley Daniel Dumbacher, Kaden Canfield, Shreya Desai, Brittni Lucas, Chase Graham, Anna Stangle, Marcol Harvey, Chris Stokes, Olga Gambini, Michelle Tang, Ryan Sullivan, Andrew Smith, Carlos Alexander, Ryan Swindall, Bobby Seifter, Mary Honeychurch, Brittany Sumpter, Charles McGee, Harold Bacon, A. J. Trommello, Maria Rivera-Diaz, Keith Hall, Matthew Courteau, Hamed Roodposhti, and Gilbert Oladeinbo. Thank you to my administrative assistant, Nikko Terry, for your invaluable help, and to Heidi Murphy and Lona Panter for your publicity support.

Thank you to the many black bankers who spoke to me on the telephone or in person about their experiences, whether confidentially or on the record. I am especially grateful to the archivists at the Nixon Presidential Library, the Richmond City Library, the Freedmen's Bank Archives, the Wisconsin Historical Society Library, the Durham Historical Museum, and the U.S. Treasury archives. Finally, thank you to the University of Georgia for a research allotment so generous that I could travel to these locations and buy books—more books than I ever thought would be necessary to complete this project.

INDEX

Additional Praise for
Training the Best Dog Ever

Best Training and Behavior Book

—DOG WRITERS ASSOCIATION OF AMERICA

The first-ever Canine Life and Social Skills Award

—ASSOCIATION OF PET DOG TRAINERS

"I love this book!
I get every training book that's out there. This is better than good,
it's the best one I've seen in a very long time."

—STEVE DALE, "STEVE DALE'S PET WORLD,"
TRIBUNE MEDIA SERVICES

"Safe and humane . . .
A sturdy foundation for a happy, well-adjusted dog."

—DR. E. KATHRYN MEYER, VMD, PAST PRESIDENT,
AMERICAN VETERINARY SOCIETY OF ANIMAL BEHAVIOR

Editor's Pick:
"A comprehensive, easy-to-follow guide
to the power of positive reinforcement training."

—*THE BARK*

"This is the perfect program for families seeking extensive,
detailed, and positive training advice."

—LT. JOEL WALTON, CERTIFIED PET DOG TRAINER,
AUTHOR OF *POSITIVE PUPPY TRAINING WORKS*

Training the
Best Dog Ever

A 5-Week Program
Using the Power of

Positive Reinforcement

by Dawn Sylvia-Stasiewicz
and Larry Kay

WORKMAN PUBLISHING · NEW YORK

Copyright © 2010, 2012 by Dawn Sylvia-Stasiewicz

Library of Congress Cataloging-in-Publication Data is available.

ISBN 978-0-7611-6885-0

Originally published as *The Love That Dog Training Program,* now revised and updated.

Design by Ariana Abud
Original interior photography by Evan Sklar
Additional photography credits on page 287.

Workman books are available at special discounts when purchased in bulk for premiums and sales promotions as well as for fund-raising or educational use. Special editions or book excerpts can also be created to specification. For details, contact the Special Sales Director at the address below or send an email to specialmarkets@workman.com.

WORKMAN PUBLISHING COMPANY, INC.
225 Varick Street
New York, NY 10014-4381
workman.com

WORKMAN is a registered trademark of Workman Publishing Co., Inc.

Printed in the United States of America
First printing August 2012
10 9 8 7 6 5 4

For my children,
Courtlandt, Blaise, and Paige.
My love and respect for you is at the essence
of all that I am and all that I have done.
The greatest gift I have been given
is being your mother.
—DAWN SYLVIA-STASIEWICZ

For my parents, Rima and Saul Kay,
and my dog, Higgins. The lovingkindness
that is at the core of this book's lessons
I learned from you.
—LARRY KAY

Contents

The Next Steps

Appendices

Foreword to the New Edition

My coauthor, the late Dawn Sylvia-Stasiewicz, was a gifted dog trainer who knew that it wasn't just the dog that needed training, but the human. I'll never forget watching her work in one of her classes with a particularly unruly Labrador Retriever that wouldn't keep still, let alone follow cues for *sit, down,* or *off.* That dog's owner looked like he was about to quit the class. But Dawn matter-of-factly lured the Lab to the center of the classroom, praised him joyfully, and then lured him to sit. She praised the dog again and rewarded him with a morsel of a treat, given only after she had confirmed that the Lab had a gentle mouth. Then Dawn led the Lab across the room, pausing every couple of steps for another *sit*—with more praise and an occasional reward. Voilà! Magic, it seemed—especially when the Lab's appreciative owner replicated (sort of) what Dawn had just demonstrated. Dawn praised the owner for the tiny improvement. And each week in Dawn's class, that Lab and his owner improved slowly but surely—as did the bond between them.

Interviewing Dawn for hundreds of hours in preparing this book gave me a front row seat in a master dog training class. It also gave me a front row seat in Dawn's life. I heard about opera singer Helga Meyer Bullock (Sandra Bullock's mother) discovering that her Briard had been "groomed" by Dawn's young children, who pinned up the champion show dog's long coat with kiddie barrettes. I heard tales of Senator Ted Kennedy sitting on the kitchen floor and cooing to his beloved dogs. I even heard the story of when Vicki Kennedy introduced Dawn to the pup that America now knows as Bo Obama, and subsequently to the First Family. Dawn may have worked with some big names, but at the heart of those stories is the blessed bond that *all* people can develop with our well-loved dogs.

Beyond bringing her message to countless students through in-person teaching, Dawn's mission was to use her platform to help the movement of positive reinforcement dog training gain traction in the wider world. That's why Dawn would be thrilled that our book has been awarded the first Canine Life and Social Skills Award by the Association of Pet Dog Trainers (APDT) to honor its contribution to positive reinforcement dog training. Dr. Ian Dunbar, the founder of APDT, was one of Dawn's earliest mentors as she discovered the superiority of positive reinforcement training over outdated methods that emphasize dominance, suppression, and aversion. That the Dog Writers Association of America awarded this book its Maxwell Medallion for Best Training and Behavior Book is additional testament to the growing enthusiasm for positive reinforcement methods, and to the quality of Dawn's particular program.

For proof that positive reinforcement training works, look no further than Dawn's most famous four-legged client, Bo Obama. Photos of Bo's early days at the White House show him pulling on his leash. Some people concluded that Bo wasn't being properly trained, or that the president and his family weren't controlling him adequately. I wanted to answer those critics, but Dawn chose to remain above the fray. "Be patient, stay positive," she counseled me, like a true trainer. Dawn was right. Recent sightings show the president leading Bo around a pet store and cueing him to sit and lie down during an interview with kid reporters. The First Lady and Bo are often seen together with White House guests. Bo is growing up to be a wonderful family dog. "Be patient, stay positive." Yes, Dawn was right.

Anyone who spends five weeks training a dog knows that a flawless dog (or owner) is impossible. But I believe, just as Dawn did, that building a aggression—is a surefire way to raising the *best dog ever.* By following the five-week training program in this book, your dog—and you—will master the skills and develop the behaviors for a happy life together.

Here's wishing you and your dog a lifelong bond with lots of love, learning, and laughs.

Positively woof,
Larry Kay
March 2012

Foreword to the Third Printing

Thank you to professional dog trainers, reviewers, good humans, and especially Workman Publishing for supporting our book. *Training the Best Dog Ever* continues to be state-of-the-art for positive dog training. Nowadays, the positive reinforcement dog training "movement" is mainstream, taught by more professional dog trainers than ever before, integrated with families and all kinds of specialized training programs (including K-9 police dog training), and popularized on TV and the web.

And speaking of the web, please enjoy the short videos that my Positively Woof crew films with shelter dogs every week. You'll see how positive training gets shelter dogs ready to be adopted. More than 75 percent of all movie dogs were shelter dogs, according to the American Humane Association, which monitors the safety and well-being of animal actors. Imagine what happens when we train shelter dogs like movie dogs. I'm sure you'll be inspired by the results.

Thank you for training your dog positively!

Celebrate our bond,
Larry
April 2016

P.S. Join our more than 2,000,000 Facebook fans. Your visits help us raise funds for shelter dogs. Thanks!

›› facebook.com/positivelywoof

›› positivelywoof.com

›› on YouTube: Positively Woof

Introduction: The Call

I was in the kitchen with Maude, my African Grey parrot, when the phone rang. It was Vicki Kennedy, Senator Ted Kennedy's wife, calling.

"Dawn," she said to me, "I have a dog that I'd like you to evaluate. It's another Portuguese Water Dog and he'll be flying into Dulles in a few days. Do you have the time for this?"

I was a little surprised to hear that Vicki had her eye on another dog. The Kennedys had three dogs already—all Porties, as this adorable black-and-white curly breed is called by those of us who love them. I'd helped the Kennedys choose their dogs from Art and Martha Stern, breeders in Texas I worked with, and had trained all three at my country home in Hume, Virginia. Senator Kennedy

Senator Edward M. Kennedy and his wife, Vicki, as they return from sailing off the coast of Hyannisport, Massachusetts, with their dogs Splash and Sunny.

and Vicki had recently taken home their third Portie, a puppy named Captain Courageous, or Cappy for short. It didn't seem likely that they'd already be looking to add another member to their family.

"He's not for us," Vicki said. "We're not sure yet where the puppy will go—we just want to see if you think he'd be good for a family with children." I agreed to evaluate the dog, but as we were about to hang up, Vicki stopped me.

"Oh, and Dawn," she said. "Keep this between us for a few days, okay?"

I drove from my home in the country to the Dulles Hilton a few days later, where I was scheduled to meet one of Senator Kennedy's assistants and a dog named Charlie. I still knew very little about Charlie except that he was about five months old and was a littermate of Cappy's. He had been with a family who had returned him to Art and Martha because the family's older Portie and he didn't get along. Martha was looking for a family to "rehome" him with.

After picking Charlie up, I drove him to my ex-husband's dental office, where I had an appointment scheduled to fix a chipped tooth. I carried Charlie's crate into a private room in the back of the office and closed the door. He'd been so quiet in the car—I couldn't wait to let him out. As soon as I opened the crate door, Charlie poked his head out. Most dogs need time to adjust after a flight and traveling in a crate, and tend to emerge very hesitant and unsure of their surroundings. Not Charlie. He was as happy as a clam and calm as a cucumber. I attached the leash I had brought for him and took him out to go potty. Back inside, I walked him around the office. He happily stopped to be petted by the staff members. I was worried that the noises of the machines would frighten him, but while I had my tooth fixed, Charlie lay quietly beside me on the floor, enjoying the new chew toy I'd bought for him.

I fell in love with Charlie immediately. I often have a number of guest dogs boarding with me, and, as a dog trainer and dog person, I come to love all of them. But I fell hard for Charlie. He was a handsome puppy of excellent breeding and a quick learner. He got along with the other dogs in my training classes (about twelve at a time), with my own dogs, with the neighbor's dogs, and even with my two parrots. Maude, who herself has a particular fondness for dogs, seemed to intrigue him most. He'd sniff around her cage, and Maude loved it. She'd climb down from her perch and put her beak through the wire door near his nose. "Gimme a kiss, arrh . . . That's nice!" she'd squawk, then throw him some kibble. Charlie would catch the treat and roll on the floor, hoping for more.

A few weeks later, Vicki called to check on Charlie.

"He's amazing," I told her. "I think he's perfectly suited for a family and to be around children. I love him so much, I'm considering keeping him myself if the people you have in mind don't want him!"

That's when she broke the news: The family considering Charlie wasn't just any family. It was the First Family.

While some people might have collapsed with fear, I wasn't worried at all. I looked at this job like any other job: I simply needed to prepare Charlie—or Bo, as he would eventually be known—for the home he was going to.

I became a professional dog trainer out of a profound, abiding love of dogs. Throughout my childhood and teen years, I'd had a great fondness for my own family's pets and for dogs in general, and I always dreamed of one day having a houseful of children and animals. In 1982, I married a man I loved deeply, who was thirteen years my senior. He was a dentist with a growing practice near D.C. We agreed that I would stay home, raise our children, and help manage his dental practice, which we moved to the first floor of our home.

Four years after we married, we had a beautiful daughter we named Courtlandt. Fourteen months after that, we had Blaise, our son. And then, wouldn't you know it, nine months later I was pregnant again, this time with our second daughter, Paige. Having three very young children so close in age was crazy at times. Between the years 1986 and 1993 I was either pregnant or nursing (and always changing diapers). Despite the crazy scheduling, I was in heaven and had achieved what I always wanted: a house full of kids and pets. We had as many as five dogs at one time, including Boston Terriers, a Pomeranian, a Portuguese Water Dog, Border Collies, a Flat-Coated Retriever, an Irish Water Spaniel, a Giant Schnauzer, and an Ibizan Hound. Plus: two ferrets, several pet rats, a few rabbits, numerous hamsters, four Siamese cats, one snake, and two very talkative parrots—Jules, a Yellow-naped Amazon, and Maude, our African Grey. It was hard just keeping their names straight at times and I often look back and wonder how I managed. At one point, I was nursing Paige while Jazz, my Boston Terrier, nursed her puppies. I was one of those women others called Superwoman. Every morning I would get up, feed the children, feed the dogs, feed the birds, feed the cats, get the strollers, collect the leashes (taking extra care not to put the dogs in the strollers and the leashes on the children), head out for a walk around our neighborhood or take the kids to school, return and settle the dogs in their crates, and go to work at my husband's dental office downstairs. I was in constant motion, morning to evening. It was a hectic, frantic, wonderful life. Though my focus was on my family, I was involved in dog shows and began a side business training and boarding dogs, mainly to earn money for dog-show entry fees and conferences.

Then, one morning in 1995, I found myself sitting at my kitchen table, stunned, as my husband told me that he didn't want to be married any longer. At the time, our children were five, six, and seven years old. Now, without the financial security I had come to depend on, I needed to make some real money, and fast. The thought of getting a job and leaving my children every morning was unfathomable. I turned to dog training full-time, in between my children's school and sports schedules.

I knew from working with my own dogs that the talent I had when it came to training was special, and I had already gained a small reputation as a trainer who could teach owners how to raise dogs to be joyful, obedient, and devoted members of the family—especially families with children. That gave me some confidence as I started to spread the word about my business, and I put the deposit down on a small studio for my classes. It was such a scary but exciting time for me. Superwoman was also a business owner! I named my training program Positive Puppy Care, and later changed it to Merit Puppy Training. I continued to build up a reputation, and my list of clients grew. I moved out of our Washington home and into a house in the country: a wonderful place to live, and a perfect spot to train and board dogs.

I think involving children in the training process is a terrific idea. It's an experience that teaches them so many things—not only about dogs but about themselves. I certainly involved my own children, and they loved it. I held classes while they were in school in the morning, and then I'd pick them up and bring them to the next round of classes. In the evenings, my ex-husband would take them for dinner while I held more classes. I continued to expand my business, preparing dogs to compete in the show ring and, at the other end of the spectrum, teaching pet owners how to get their puppies learning at a very early age. Before long, my training services began to catch the attention of some of D.C.'s more powerful families. To be honest, I rarely paid attention to any of that. My main concern when it came to working with a family was that they were committed to training their dog and to providing a safe, happy home for their pet. In fact, I worked with Vicki and Senator Kennedy for months before I realized who they were. It was only after I received a check from them, and noticed the Edward Moore Kennedy printed on the top, that I realized that the Vicki Kennedy I had been speaking to on the phone about potty training and feeding schedules was the wife of *that* Ted Kennedy.

So, yes, it had been a long road to the White House, but it was one I felt ready to take.

Dawn Sylvia-Stasiewicz
March 2010

The
Basics

Chapter One

My Approach to Training

As the mother of three children and an animal trainer for more than twenty years, I have come to understand that the lessons learned in motherhood are applicable to dog training. This book shares my dog training system, which is based on the positive reinforcement approach. Unlike traditional, dominance-based dog training that was considered in vogue until recently, positive reinforcement training holds at its core that dogs learn good behavior by being rewarded for doing well, and that punishment doesn't have to come in the form of a reprimand or, worse, physical force. In positive reinforcement training, our job is to love and respect our dogs and to reward and punish them the way we would our children. In positive reinforcement, the bottom line is that a dog is a living, breathing creation of God that desires love and security. A dog also feels pain, just as we do, and it is our job to minimize that pain.

In my professional judgment, positive reinforcement is the best dog training system, whether you are in a family with many children or a single adult. Right now, far too many dogs are still being subjected to more traditional, punishing training techniques, including the use of choke collars and physical force. Those aversive punishment techniques focus on the "bad" things a dog does, leaving a dog to try to figure out, through trial and error, what he must do in order *not* to be punished. As you will read, I used to practice those traditional training methods—until I had my moment of epiphany: Positive reinforcement is better all around.

I know that positive reinforcement works. I also know that if you stay committed to the principles of this approach, you will, by the end of this book's five-week fundamentals course, have a happy, spirited dog. If your dog has already been trained using traditional punishment techniques, and you're hoping to retrain her with this system, I applaud you, and I assure you that it's possible. I've seen it work countless times. Positive reinforcement training has even saved so-called "death row dogs"—dogs some people thought impossible to rehabilitate—from euthanasia.

I will guide you through each step of my program the same way I guide my students. We will start with an orientation, which will help you prepare yourself, your home, and your family for life with a dog. Next is the five-week fundamentals course, which will help you master the basics, from potty training to *sit, stay,* and *come here.* You and your dog will then graduate to tricks training, which is designed to keep your dog engaged and curious, as well as adding some elements for fun. Finally, you will discover how to make sure your dog does well in the world at large, so that you're comfortable sharing your family's canine experience with visitors, in your neighborhood dog park, and on the road.

Why Train?

First and foremost, you train your dog because you want to control his behavior. I also believe there's another, equally important reason: Training, especially positive reinforcement training, is one of the best ways to bond with a dog. A well-trained dog that is truly connected to his owner will feel happy and safe, and have more success in our human world. *Not* training a dog is like *not* teaching a child to read: It's wrong. The sad fate of an untrained dog—an animal unable to cope with the world—is usually a highly restricted life.

How will training make him feel happy and safe? Your dog is learning from you all the time, whether you're taking the time to train him or not. Dogs don't understand right and wrong as we do, but they're always trying to figure out, through trial and error, what is safe and what is dangerous, and what feels good and what doesn't. Since your dog is looking to you for those answers, it is best to direct his learning from the first day he enters your life. If you guide your dog to do what you want and reward him when he does it, he is more likely to do it again. In fact, as you'll see, your dog will try to figure out what he did to get rewarded.

When you involve your children in training, you are teaching them about safety, responsibility, caring, and what it takes to be a best friend.

A dog that feels safe will usually be a safer dog. According to the Centers for Disease Control and Prevention, 4.5 million Americans are bitten by dogs every year, more than 2 million of them children. Nearly 400,000 of those children require medical attention. The vast majority of people who are bitten by dogs are bitten by one they know—either their family's dog or a friend's. A well-trained dog is far less likely to bite than an untrained or poorly trained dog.

I also believe that dog training makes all of us better humans; it can certainly help us instill good values in our children. When you involve your children in training, as I hope you will, not only are you helping your dog to enjoy children, you are teaching your children about safety, responsibility, caring, and what it takes to be a best friend.

Finally, as I said above, training is one of the best ways to bond with our dogs. If you've been the owner of a pet with which you've felt exceptionally bonded, you know that this type of relationship brings countless rewards. I loved witnessing the extraordinarily close relationship Senator Kennedy had with his dogs, especially Splash. Their relationship was legendary on Capitol Hill. Whenever I boarded the three Kennedy dogs in my home, and I took them back to the family, the Senator would interrupt whatever he was doing or whomever he was meeting with to greet the dogs and me. This lion of a man turned into a boy when he got down on the floor and played with his dogs. One evening, when the Senator came to my house to pick up Splash on his way home from the airport, the two of them were so noisy with glee that my daughter Paige rushed downstairs to see what all the commotion was. When I introduced her to Senator Kennedy, she was speechless that this man frolicking on the floor of her home was the same man she had seen so many times on television—so speechless that she quickly but politely excused herself and went back upstairs to finish her homework.

I had another client named Nat, whose yellow Labrador Retriever, Zack, often boarded with me. They were so closely bonded that Zack knew when Nat was coming to pick him up. Zack would start pacing and hanging around the foyer, sometimes even picking up his doggy backpack and carrying it to the door. Without fail, about five minutes later, the doorbell would ring and there would be Nat. I began to test Zack, seeing if I could throw him off track. I would put his backpack out early, as if I knew that it was time for him to leave, but Zack never bought it. I would ask Nat to vary his evening arrival time, but that didn't work, either. Zack always knew. I don't know how Zack was able to do this, but I do know that to have such a powerful human-dog relationship is an extraordinary life experience.

Why Commit to Positive Reinforcement Dog Training?

The idea that dogs can—and should—be trained through positive reinforcement, rather than aversive punishment, was first *formally* developed by Ian Dunbar, a veterinarian with a doctorate in animal behavior. As he says, punishment does not have to be nasty, scary, or painful. Therefore, if it doesn't have to be, then it shouldn't be. For dogs, withholding a reward is punishment enough and is, in fact, more effective than physical punishment.

Let me use a real-life story to illustrate how dogs are trained using positive reinforcement, compared to traditional, aversive techniques. I once had a client named Peter, who came to my class at the Boys and Girls Club in Georgetown, distraught that his Australian Shepherd, Wallaby, wouldn't stop jumping. No matter how much Peter reprimanded Wallaby, the dog just loved to jump. Because Peter had been taught to use aversive punishment techniques, he would try to stop Wallaby from jumping by kneeing him in the chest when he jumped. It wasn't working. Wallaby kept jumping. He didn't understand that jumping was bad—he is, after all, a dog, and some dogs naturally love to jump. To Wallaby, Peter's kneeing felt like random bullying.

Rather than have Peter punish Wallaby for doing something bad, I wanted to help him learn to reward Wallaby for doing something good. I worked with them, using a positive reinforcement protocol that I've found extremely effective in getting dogs to stop jumping. First, I had Peter greet Wallaby *only* when Wallaby was sitting. If Wallaby jumped, Peter ignored him. Peter just kept quiet, turned his back, and refused to pay Wallaby any attention. But when Wallaby sat, he found something amazing happened: He got a treat. And not just any treat, but his favorite treat, a stuffed Kong (a nearly indestructible rubber chew toy with a hollow center that can be stuffed with all kinds of treats). When Wallaby jumped, there was no treat (nor were there any more knees to his chest). In time, Wallaby figured out that there was a clear pattern here: If he jumped, he got no treat. But if he sat? Well, jackpot! It took about five weeks of class time, plus Peter's patient practicing of this technique at home, but by the end of the exercise, Wallaby no longer jumped.

A few weeks later, Peter returned to class, upset that Wallaby had started jumping again. I asked Peter if he was consistently using the Kong technique we had practiced. Peter hesitated. "Well . . . sometimes." Aha! As you'll see, inconsistent training is the most common cause of good behaviors falling apart. I worked with Peter on another technique: I had him *encourage* Wallaby to jump. That's right: We rewarded Wallaby for doing this "bad behavior" that he was already really good at. I had Peter ask Wallaby to jump at random times when Wallaby was least expecting it, even in the middle of class when we were working on something else. Over and over, Wallaby was rewarded with lavish praise and treats, just for jumping when asked to. If he jumped when Peter didn't ask, he got no reward. Instead, Peter turned his back.

Then a funny thing happened. Wallaby began to anticipate when Peter was about to ask him to jump and would wait for Peter's cue, knowing that he would be rewarded. Before long, Wallaby knew that he was rewarded for jumping only when Peter cued him by saying, "Wallaby, Kangaroo!" As Peter succeeded in controlling his dog's jumping, he also taught Wallaby impulse control and turned this previously bad behavior into a fun trick they both *enjoyed*!

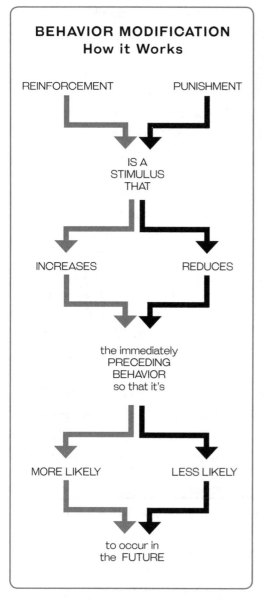

BEHAVIOR MODIFICATION
How it Works

REINFORCEMENT   PUNISHMENT

IS A
STIMULUS
THAT

INCREASES   REDUCES

the immediately
PRECEDING
BEHAVIOR
so that it's

MORE LIKELY   LESS LIKELY

to occur in
the FUTURE

Peter's story helps illustrate that a punishment doesn't always have to be a physical reprimand like kneeing your dog in the chest, which could easily have taught Wallaby not to approach Peter at all. A punishment can also be a withheld reward, as long as it reduces the immediately preceding behavior so that it's less likely to occur in the future. In other words: Peter did punish Wallaby. How? If Wallaby jumped when Peter didn't ask for a jump, Peter didn't give Wallaby praise or a treat, but instead turned away and ignored him. Not giving a reward becomes the punishment. We call this a negative punishment, meaning Wallaby's punishment is that he did *not* get any *reward* that he valued (Peter's attention or a treat). Negative punishment is similar to grounding an older child, giving a young child a time-out, or revoking the much desired television time in the evening. It is *taking away* a privilege.

A positive punishment would have been Peter's physically reprimanding Wallaby with, say, a knee to the chest when Wallaby tried to jump. With a child, positive punishment might be being yelled at or getting a spanking. If all a parent did was spank a child when he didn't behave, then the child's only reward would be *not* getting *spanked*—which is called negative reinforcement. (Child Protective Services would have other names for it.)

This concept of negative vs. positive isn't about bad vs. good. Negative means taking away; positive means giving. So, positive reinforcement means giving a reinforcement or reward. Negative punishment means not giving that reward. Positive reinforcement dog training is reward-oriented, which is

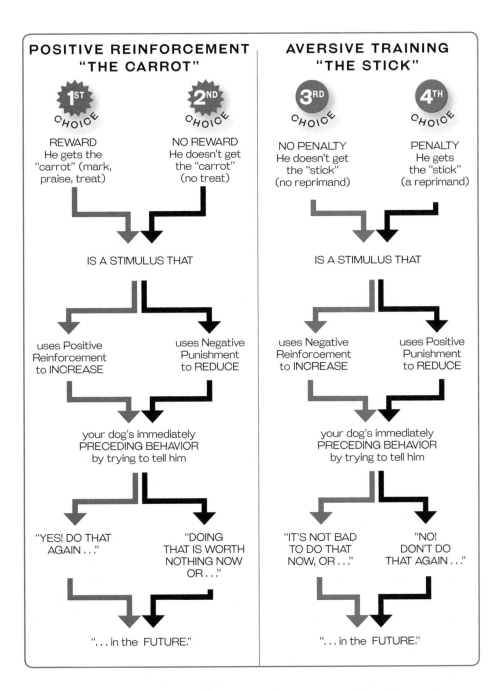

POSITIVE REINFORCEMENT "THE CARROT"

1ST CHOICE
REWARD
He gets the "carrot" (mark, praise, treat)

2ND CHOICE
NO REWARD
He doesn't get the "carrot" (no treat)

IS A STIMULUS THAT

uses Positive Reinforcement to INCREASE

uses Negative Punishment to REDUCE

your dog's immediately PRECEDING BEHAVIOR by trying to tell him

"YES! DO THAT AGAIN . . ."

"DOING THAT IS WORTH NOTHING NOW OR . . ."

". . . in the FUTURE."

AVERSIVE TRAINING "THE STICK"

3RD CHOICE
NO PENALTY
He doesn't get the "stick" (no reprimand)

4TH CHOICE
PENALTY
He gets the "stick" (a reprimand)

IS A STIMULUS THAT

uses Negative Reinforcement to INCREASE

uses Positive Punishment to REDUCE

your dog's immediately PRECEDING BEHAVIOR by trying to tell him

"IT'S NOT BAD TO DO THAT NOW, OR . . ."

"NO! DON'T DO THAT AGAIN . . ."

". . . in the FUTURE."

why we use both positive reinforcement (giving rewards) and negative punishment (taking away rewards). Traditional dog training is punishment oriented. It emphasizes positive punishment (giving a physical correction such as a sharp rebuke or a yank on a choke chain) and negative reinforcement (taking away the punishment, such as not yanking the choke chain).

This distinction between negative and positive can be a little tricky to understand, so let's go back to Peter and Wallaby. Peter used the positive reinforcement model to change Wallaby's behavior by effectively saying, "I like your jumping; do that some more." The reward reinforced Wallaby's positive behavior. Peter punished Wallaby using negative punishment: no praise or treats if Wallaby jumped when Peter didn't ask him to, which meant, "You can jump all day, but I'm ignoring you. Doing that is worth nothing."

Let's imagine that Peter continued to use the traditional, aversive training model. If Wallaby jumped on Peter, then Peter would be obligated to give the dog a positive punishment, a physical or verbal reprimand. This positive punishment would be designed to tell Wallaby, "Don't jump." When Wallaby didn't jump, Peter would do nothing, which would be a negative reward: Wallaby wouldn't get the punishment. In other words, Peter would be trying to tell Wallaby, "It's not bad to not jump." The negative reward would be an attempt to *reinforce* Wallaby's positive behavior (not jumping).

In my professional opinion, there's a flaw in that logic. Wallaby is never told specifically that he did the right thing—that *not* jumping is what Peter wants. Wallaby has to figure out what to do by process of elimination, but he is never told when he gets it right. Even a rat searching a maze finally gets a reward when he finds the cheese. A dog that has been trained only through the aversive punishment model has to figure it all out on his own. That requires abstract thinking, something that dogs' brains aren't wired to do.

Moreover, when an animal is given "the stick" too many times, he either rebels or gives up and loses his spirit. Traditional trainers look forward to the moment in training when the dog gives up. They believe that the animal's weakened state of surrender is the moment when they can then build up desired behaviors. While that approach might be effective for extreme cases involving severe dog behavior problems under the care of a very skilled and experienced trainer, it is a dangerous weapon in the hands of the average dog owner, and even more dangerous in the hands of a child.

In fact, the American Veterinary Society of Animal Behavior (AVSAB) is very concerned about the idea of families using dominance-based, aversive punishment methods. In a recent position statement, the AVSAB gives nine reasons why aversive punishment can be ineffective and possibly dangerous, especially in the hands of an unskilled nonprofessional. They warn that it can trigger or even "cause aggressive behavior." They also caution that such training can suppress aggressive behaviors while making the dog more fearful, which makes that dog more likely to attack without warning.

WHAT ABOUT BEING LEADER OF THE PACK?

Many traditional dog trainers who use aversive punishment techniques claim that we positive reinforcement folks don't understand dog pack psychology. They say that dogs desire a strong leader to dominate them and tell them what to do. Traditional trainers say that if the dog doesn't recognize you as the alpha dog, the leader of the pack, the dog will feel the need to become the leader and will end up being in charge of you.

It is true that dogs like to know who the leader is. But I believe that traditional dog trainers get themselves into trouble by concluding that the only kind of leadership that a dog respects is a bully boss who will yank him around by a choke chain; who will flip him on his back and sit on him, in what we trainers call the alpha roll position; who will give a dog only aversive correction.

Good leaders don't have to act like bullies to command respect—not in the human world or in the dog pack. Pet dogs don't need to be bullied to become your loyal follower. Pet dogs love to follow leaders who provide food, shelter, and safety: leaders they see as benevolent and fair. Good pack leaders provide social experiences and lots of fun.

"STOP THE VIOLENCE"

I am concerned about what happens to people when they harm an animal or—in the case of our children—see an animal get harmed, even if it's in the spirit of so-called training. If you'll allow me to get on my soapbox for a moment, I also believe that positive dog training strengthens our families and communities. This is one way in which we can stop the cycle of violence. Unfortunately, it's far too common that a youngster who first learns to commit violence against animals graduates to committing violence against people.

The American Humane Association has launched a major initiative called The Link to study the connection between animal cruelty and human violence. The organization that issues the "No Animals Were Harmed" disclaimer for movies and TV shows, American Humane reports that violent criminals were significantly more likely than nonviolent offenders to have "committed childhood acts of cruelty toward pets" and that abuse against animals occurs in an overwhelming majority of households where there is documented child abuse and neglect.

If your child (or her friend) abuses or harms a pet, it's best to discuss it with her (or the friend's parent) immediately. If she has seen an animal being hurt, reassure her that you will do everything you can to help that animal. Praise her for being compassionate. Ask if she has ever hurt an animal; if she has, thank her for telling you, then together gently pet your dog (unless the dog is fearful). Remind your child that it is never okay to hurt an animal, and praise her once more for being a good kid who cares.

Retraining a Traditionally Trained Dog

My dog Ebony and I are proof that traditionally trained dogs and pet owners can be retrained to work in a more positive way, focusing on reinforcing good behaviors rather than on what the dog has done wrong. When I first started working with my dogs, I learned to train in the "old school" aversive style that I now preach against. At the time, it was difficult to find an alternative because, well, there wasn't any. That was the way things were done, and it never occurred to me to question it until Ebony taught me otherwise.

Ebony was my first Portuguese Water Dog. I got her in the late 1980s with every intention of training her as a show dog. I soon found out, however, that she was dysplastic in one hip and carried the gene for progressive retinal atrophy. It would have been unethical to show her, earn a championship title, and then breed her. And so I didn't.

Instead, I took Ebony to the obedience ring, in which your dog is judged on how well she can obey cues and commands and follow your lead. To prepare her for the competitions, I trained with her on my own and with many other trainers, privately and in classes. Despite the hours we put in, Ebony didn't score well at the competitions. I kept trying, going to many competitions run by the American Kennel Club. Ebony progressed, but I could tell that something was off for her. She didn't like the choke chain and she lagged unhappily, with her tail tucked during practice and at obedience matches. She wasn't having any fun.

In 1991, I decided to stop tormenting poor Ebony; instead of entering competitions, we just went to watch. My kids were all very young, but I just loaded them, a diaper bag, the dogs, and their supplies into the car and off we'd go. When we got there, the kids would play, and I would watch the shows, taking notes. Afterward, I'd try to talk to the best trainers and pick their brains about how they got their dogs to perform so well. I was particularly taken by one superb trainer, Joan Woodard. Her dogs, a Golden Retriever and an Airedale Terrier, performed beautifully. What surprised me the most was that they were not wearing choke collars. I'd never seen that before. I tracked Joan down after one match.

Good leaders don't have to act like bullies to command respect—not in the human world or in the dog pack.

"I saw you in the ring," I said to her. "Your dogs worked beautifully and you're not even using choke collars."

Joan smiled and pointed to Ebony's choke collar. "Too bad," she said. "But thank you for admiring my dogs' work." And then she walked away.

I understand now that she probably didn't want to waste time on another one of us choke folk, but I wouldn't give up. I kept after Joan, show after show, until I finally wore her down. She explained that there was a bit of a movement happening in dog training circles, and agreed to introduce me to a small, close-knit group of trainers who were doing things a different way.

The next week, I drove with Ebony to a class that Joan held in positive reinforcement techniques. I felt as if I were entering an underground fringe group, and in many ways I was. This type of training was such a departure from what I had been accustomed to—to what I had been training others to do, as well—that I was amazed by how remarkably obedient, highly focused, and, most of all, happy the dogs in this room were. There were no choke collars, no physical corrections. Instead, there were treats and toys—lots of them. Even that was a difference. In traditional punishment-oriented training classes, treats are not allowed because, the thinking goes, they spoil dogs and make owners "soft."

The more I attended Joan's positive reinforcement classes, the more I got it. I began using this method with my own dogs, who took to it right away. Ebony, in particular, seemed like a completely different dog: She was spirited and joyful. *And she loved training.* She even loved her leash. Prior to this, she'd sulk and become dispirited when I put it on her, probably because she knew that before long, I'd be tugging at her neck and reprimanding her harshly. But after I began to train her with the methods of positive reinforcement, she would perk up when she saw me get the leash.

I never looked back.

Around that time, Dr. Ian Dunbar founded the Association of Pet Dog Trainers (APDT), a membership organization dedicated to promoting positive reinforcement training. I went to my first APDT conference in 1994, where I became even more inspired by many of the most dedicated dog trainers from around the country. I took along my (excuse the pun) dog-eared copy of Dr. Dunbar's 1979 landmark book, *Dog Behavior,* for him to autograph. Since that time, Dr. Dunbar has encouraged my work in positive reinforcement dog training, and we continue to exchange ideas, especially about dog training for families with children. I remain grateful to Dr. Dunbar and to Joan Woodard, my first positive reinforcement trainer, for helping me cross over.

I also remain eternally grateful to my dog Ebony, who passed away in 1995 at the young age of not yet seven years, having lasted only six months after being diagnosed with kidney failure. Ebony patiently showed me what a fast learner and happy dog she could be if I just rewarded her for all the good behaviors she offered me.

REHABILITATING PROBLEM DOGS

There are some instances in which a dog is too fearful or damaged to be rehabilitated, but if a dog *can* be rehabilitated, I firmly believe that positive reinforcement is the way to go.

Consider the most extreme case of animal abuse to garner public attention in recent history: Michael Vick's dogs. Who could have believed it? The quarterback for the Atlanta Falcons, convicted of running a dogfighting ring? Among the 47 dogs taken into custody, 22 were evaluated as beyond rehabilitation under the supervision of a guardian/special master appointed by the U.S. District Court for the Eastern District of Virginia. With the support of many experts, including some national humane organizations, these 22 "toughest case" pit bulls were slated for euthanasia.

While those dogs were on death row, Best Friends Animal Society petitioned the court to be allowed to reevaluate them, and was then granted court permission to rehabilitate the dogs under continued supervision of the federal court's special master. Best Friends practices only positive reinforcement methods at its Kanab, Utah, sanctuary. When the 22 Vicktory

Dogs, as these pit bulls have become known, arrived at Best Friends' Dogtown Sanctuary, they were either frighteningly aggressive or completely shut down. Dogtown Manager John Garcia told us in interviews for this book that through positive reinforcement training, the Vicktory Dogs learned to trust people and came to believe that the world was a safe place, filled with benevolent people who would not harm them. Ann Allums was one of the trainers responsible for the Vicktory Dogs' rehabilitation. As she explains, had they used aversive training techniques, not only would these dogs have failed to be rehabilitated, they would likely have gotten worse, as typically happens to dogs with unchecked behavior problems. Today, some of the Vicktory Dogs have already earned their Canine Good Citizenship certificate (which we'll discuss in Appendix 1) and have been placed in private homes.

The Essentials: Patience and Practice

Before you embark on this training program—from preparation, to the fundamentals course, and on to more advanced tricks training—I first want to applaud you for making the commitment to train your dog using positive reinforcement. And then I want to remind you that it won't always be easy. This program—and, indeed, any training program—will require a lot from your dog, and it will also require some things from you: mainly, consistent, patient practice. I want you to begin to keep in mind that every interaction with your dog is a training opportunity, starting, as I have said, with the moment he first walks into your home. I want you to know that the hard work happens between our classes, when I'll ask you to practice what you've learned, with constancy and consistency. I want you to do your home-work assignments. I want you to understand that training includes making time for exercise, brushing, petting, and play.

This consistent, patient practice is what will make the difference between having a dog that is highly trained and spirited and one that is frustrated and unsure. Patient practice will teach your dog that his good behavior is appreciated and desired and will be rewarded. Patient practice will remind your dog, again and again, that he is a good dog who deserves the loving care that you give him. Patient practice will create an essential bond.

I believe that consistent, patient practice will also do wonders for you. The more you practice, the more confident you'll become. The same goes for children. I encourage you to involve your children in this program and the tasks and homework assignments. Successful dog training experiences can help teach children to take responsibility and to make and keep a commitment. If they become frustrated by the amount of time or consistent work that dog training requires, or with their dog's inability to master something quickly, we have an opportunity to show them that hard work pays off. So many times, I have seen children and families transformed through dog training. It is an opportunity to learn about ourselves, to become more understanding and accepting, and to laugh at our mistakes and challenges.

Believe me, if you commit to training your dog now and to following the lessons in this book, your work will pay off. Before long you will begin to reap the countless wonderful, life-enriching rewards of having a well-behaved, well-socialized best friend.

Now, let's get started.

Chapter Two

Preparing for Dog Training

I hope that you're reading this before you've brought your dog home, because the first question to consider in dog training is also the one I believe to be the most fundamental: Why are you getting a dog? If you've already found the new love of your life, you still ought to ask yourself that all-important question.

The "right" reason to get a dog is that you want a companion *and* are at a point in your life where you know that you have the time and lifestyle not only to care for your dog but to care for him well. You are fully aware of the commitment a dog requires, and are prepared and equipped to honor that commitment. You're emotionally ready to give part of yourself to raising this animal that is completely dependent on you for his survival and well-being. Your finances are reasonably in order. Remember, desperately *wanting* a dog doesn't always mean that the time is right for *getting* a dog. If you're at an emotionally low moment in your life and are thinking of getting a dog to help you deal with depression or loneliness, I want you to really think about this decision before you take on the added responsibility. It's natural to want everyone to love your dog, but you should not get a dog in order to get approval or fulfillment from others.

If you are thinking of getting a dog for your child, while you yourself feel unsure about committing to a pet, I'd advise against doing it, because you must assume that you are going to be that dog's chief caretaker, despite your child's promises to the contrary. If you are thinking of getting your current dog a companion, be careful of falling into what dog trainers call second dog syndrome, in which you end up exerting less energy and spending less one-on-one time with the new dog than he needs, causing him to bond with your existing pet rather than with you. Second dog syndrome interferes with the bond you need to build with your new dog in order to train him successfully.

If, after giving these questions a lot of consideration, you determine that you are ready, congratulations are in order. The decision to bring a dog into your home and your family is, I believe, one of the most exciting, rewarding, and enriching decisions you can make.

Choosing the Right Dog for You

As any family with a dog will tell you, choosing the right pet for your family can be complicated. There are so many factors to consider. Would you prefer to rehome an older dog that is already trained? Are allergies an issue? If so, do you need to look for a breed that doesn't shed? Are you open to the joys (and mysteries!) of having a mixed-breed dog? What kind of dog will fit into your lifestyle, whether that means taking vigorous hikes every weekend or staying pretty close to home? Do you travel often? If so, would you find it easier to travel with a smaller dog that you can carry in the cabin of the airplane with you? What about big dogs? Most big dogs require a lot of space and eat more than smaller dogs, so is space or the cost of food an issue for you right now?

Once you figure out what kind of dog is best for your family, you need to decide whether your preference is to adopt a dog from a shelter or rescue organization or to purchase one from a breeder.

Adopting from a Shelter

f you are open to the idea of adopting your family's new best friend from an animal shelter, I'd like to thank you. According to the Humane Society of the United States, on average, between 15,000 and 20,000 dogs and cats are taken in at animal shelters every day across America. These adorable, lovable animals are just waiting for their new homes, and they are desperate to start a new chapter in their lives.

Seeing dozens if not hundreds of adorable puppies and dogs at one time can make the head spin, so plan your shelter visits carefully. While you want to have an emotional connection to the pet you take home, you also want to make sure that you engage your rational brain in the process. Try to learn as much as you can about the history of the dog you are considering, and try to figure out if the dog is, or can easily become, well socialized with people and other dogs. For a rescued puppy, ask if she arrived with littermates, and find out what you can about those littermates. Was the dog found as a stray or given up by an owner? If she was given up, ask why. Occasionally (and unfortunately) dogs are given up simply because they have outgrown their cuteness (or because post-holiday doubts have set in). Ask if the dog has been potty and crate trained. What is the dog like with other dogs? Does she growl? Does she guard food or toys? Can you take a toy (or a shoe) from her

Different breeds have their charms—but all dogs are not good choices for all people.

mouth? How is she with children? Has she ever bitten someone? What is she like when she is touched and picked up?

There are no questions you can't ask. Remember this key fact: You are making a commitment to this dog for the duration of her life. Some reputable rescue organizations work with an animal behaviorist, a behavior specialist, or an experienced professional dog trainer to evaluate each dog that has been given up for rehoming or found abandoned; however, many shelters and rescue organizations are woefully underfunded. Their dedicated staff struggle to meet the demands of caring for the skyrocketing number of abandoned animals, and are unable to provide behavior evaluations for each one. In that case, if possible, enlist the help of an experienced, professional dog trainer to go with you to evaluate the dog once you have made your choice. Even if you need to pay for the trainer's time, it will be money well spent.

Learn as much as you can about the history of the dog you are considering.

Working with a Breeder

If you choose to go the purebred route, the first thing to understand is the big difference between good breeders and bad ones. Some unscrupulous people set up factory farms to breed puppies as a cash crop. Many pet stores that sell puppies have purchased them from these puppy mills, so it is best to deal directly with the breeder. Educate yourself so that you do not accidentally support this cruel and unethical business. Check references: You may be unknowingly encountering a puppy mill if a breeder does not allow you to see his facility, has several breeds or litters for sale at the same time, offers to ship you a dog without interviewing you in person, won't talk at length with you on the phone, or won't offer the names and numbers of owners who have purchased puppies from him in the past. Although some puppy mills are regulated, they are all inhumane and should really be avoided altogether.

You will need to do some research to locate good-quality breeders. If you are researching particular breeds, get to know people at local breed clubs, American Kennel Club (AKC) conformation dog shows, and dog obedience trials. Talk to veterinarians; perhaps they will be willing to offer the names of clients for you to interview as part of your research. The AKC offers extensive programs that support quality breeding, including breeder education, registration, kennel standards, and inspections. The AKC's Canine Health

Foundation (akcchf.org) offers a comprehensive list of breed-specific concerns and makes available a vast online research library.

What the breeder charges may seem like a lot of money, but it is a small investment compared to what you'll pay to maintain your dog over his lifetime, and it is money well spent when you consider what a breeder provides you with: information about pedigree, detailed vet records, and a disclosure of all health issues. Most will microchip each puppy with an identification chip injected safely under the skin. Good breeders will tell you what and when to feed your dog; they'll inform you about any food allergies. Good breeders know how each puppy is developing. When you visit a good-quality breeder, everything about the dogs will appear to be happy and healthy: The puppies will be playful, well socialized, interested in visitors, and they'll be living in a clean and properly heated area. Also, a good breeder will not allow you to take the puppy until it is at least seven weeks old. This is important because puppies tend to be far better socialized and developed when they have those full seven weeks with their mother and littermates.

Good breeders will also expect as much of you as you do of them. They will interview you extensively: about your knowledge of and experience with dogs, the suitability and safety of your home, as well as your commitment to training and to the puppy's general welfare. They will likely match you with the puppy they believe has the right temperament for your family and fits your level of experience with dogs. They may ask for references from your veterinarian or others. Usually, they will want your whole family to visit their puppies, sometimes more than once, and some may also offer to let you meet the dam (mother) before she gives birth so she can be comfortable with you.

Good breeders will match you with your puppy.

And there's more: You will be asked to sign a contract that requires you to return the dog to them if you decide you cannot keep him at any point, though most breeders offer a refund only if the dog is returned within the first year. Since you and your dog will become a living part of their reputation, your breeder will want to stay in touch with you regarding your puppy's development, as well as his health and behavior.

Once you locate the breeder you want to work with, be willing to wait. Good breeders do not always have puppies for sale. They specialize in one or two breeds and typically whelp the litter in their own home. This takes time, but in the long run, it will be worth the wait.

Your Training Goals and Plan

As I sit down to write today, Boz, a two-year-old Border Collie, is curled up at my feet. Last spring, I lost Saxon, my beloved Giant Schnauzer, to cancer. As anyone who has lost a pet knows, it's a devastating and heart-breaking experience, and I may never get over the loss of Saxon. But about eight months after he died, I found myself wanting a new dog for myself, as well as for my Ibizan Hound, Brieo. We both could use the additional companionship, especially because Brieo is a "low dog," meaning that he prefers to follow rather than lead. But, given that I was still mourning Saxon, I wasn't quite ready to make a lifelong commitment to a new dog. And I know how unwise it would have been to have gotten a second dog just as a companion for Brieo.

After much thought, I decided that I would become a foster mom to Boz, meaning that I've taken him into my home temporarily until he finds his forever home. Boz was given up by a family that could not keep him anymore due to personal reasons. Now I am giving him everything I would be giving a dog I was taking in permanently. Boz has his own crate, bed, bowls, and all the rest of his supplies, as well as a lot of affection and one-on-one time with me. Becoming a foster parent for a dog can be challenging—and it's not for everyone. But if you have experience with owning dogs, and are on the fence about adopting again, fostering may be the perfect option for both you and the dog.

Successful training starts with a good plan.

Even though Boz will be with me only until we can find him a good, permanent home, I began training him from the moment I agreed to take him in. The same should go for you: Once you have chosen your dog, it's time to prepare *immediately*. While many dog trainers believe that there should be bonding time without training when a family first gets a dog, I urge you to begin training your dog immediately. When you use the positive reinforcement approach, training time *is* bonding time. It's showing your dog that he is being taken care of and being rewarded for doing well. If you don't train your dog early on, you are inviting future behavioral problems. An untrained dog will almost always learn how to get what he wants by doing the wrong thing, such as by jumping or barking, and then become confused and anxious when you try to untrain and retrain him later. A dog is happiest when he learns from the very first day in his new home that training is a natural and routine part of life. Simply be prepared to be consistent, firm, and fair.

Successful training starts with a good plan, and a good plan starts with clear goals. I actually post my goals and plan on my fridge as a constant reminder to focus on my long-term objectives. As countless students have also told me (and I've found), working toward dog training goals—and consistently meeting those goals over time—has given them (and me) more confidence about achieving goals in other aspects of life.

What Are Your Dog Training Goals?

Most elite athletes will tell you that if they can envision themselves shooting a free throw or hitting a home run, they are a big step closer to accomplishing that goal. That's why I want to guide you in a short exercise about your dog's future . . . and *yours.* Imagine that your dog is fully trained. What is her behavior like at home? Do you enjoy each other's company? What is it like when you have other people visit your home? How do you play together and how does she play with other dogs? What is it like to take her on walks? What is it like when you take her with you for recreation or on visits to friends' homes?

Now you're ready for the next step: setting training goals that will ensure that you end up with the dog that behaves the way you envision. As you and your dog begin to meet your goals, you will see how much progress you're making, and how much closer you are getting each day to having the relationship that you imagined.

It takes five weeks to lock in a new habit, which is one of the reasons that I recommend a five-week training program: It works best for your dog *and* for you. (Your dog isn't the only one who has to learn new habits!) So, choose goals that you imagine will keep you inspired for five weeks . . . and beyond.

Imagine a dog that is spirited, socialized, and well trained.

Checklist: Setting Goals

H ere is a checklist to help you set your goals. Try picking only your top ten, so that you can get an idea of what is most important to you. The list doesn't need to be perfect or final; it's just a tool to help you get focused and specific.

AT HOME

☐ My dog is impeccably **house-trained.** My dog knows where to go potty and goes potty on cue. When she needs to go outside, she gives me the signal that I taught her.

☐ **The crate** is my dog's home. She enjoys her crate, goes to it when asked, and keeps calm inside it.

☐ My dog **settles down** when I ask her. Although I love it when my dog is enthusiastic, she doesn't jump up unless she's invited.

☐ **Mealtimes** are enjoyable and calm. My dog sits to receive her food and does not guard it from people or other animals. She doesn't bother me when I am eating.

☐ **Grooming** my dog is a pleasant experience. She enjoys being handled while I brush her. She accepts bath time with ease and enjoys being handled and massaged.

☐ My dog obeys the **furniture rules** and **chews only** what is allowed.

☐ Although my dog likes being with me, she **isn't so needy** that she shadows me everywhere. When I leave the house, my dog relaxes. When I return, she is happy and mellow.

TRAINING

☐ My dog and I **love to train** for a quick minute when the opportunity arises. We also love doing our training homework daily and bond more closely while we train.

☐ **Sitting** calmly is my dog's way of saying please. He sits when asked and has learned the situations in which I usually ask him to sit.

☐ **"Down"** and **"stay"** are mastered. When I cue the command, my dog does it without hesitation.

☐ My dog **loves hearing his name** and is attentive when I say it.

☐ **"Come here"** is mastered. When I recall my dog, he comes to me right away.

☐ **Playtime** is fun for my dog and me. When others are invited to play, they are safe and so is my dog. When I ask him to give back a toy or let go of it, he does so right away.

☐ **Tricks** are now a fun part of our ongoing training. As my dog masters each trick, we are joyful and proud together. I love to show off his tricks to other people.

SOCIALIZATION

☐ When the **doorbell** rings, my dog is interested, but sits until cued to **greet a visitor.**

☐ **Walking** with my dog is joyful and relaxing. She loves walking on a leash by my side, and she responds when I ask her to finish sniffing and resume walking.

☐ When we **meet other dogs,** mine is well behaved regardless of what they do.

☐ When we encounter **strange noises or surprises,** my dog is mildly interested but doesn't freeze or try to fight or flee.

☐ When we go to the **groomer** or the **veterinarian,** my dog and these professionals are happy to see each other.

☐ When my dog is allowed to join me **inside a place of business,** she has impeccable behavior. I feel like I can take my dog anywhere.

☐ **Car rides** are peaceful with my dog. She loves to go in the car with me.

Proper socialization helps a dog feel safe and comfortable, even in new situations.

If you were able to narrow the list down to your top ten, good job; that will help you and your dog be successful together. Trust that whatever priorities you pick are going to be the right priorities, and don't worry about the others for now. Don't get stuck on trying to be perfect; in this book, perfect means "perfect for you." If you follow the training program, and are disciplined about doing your homework, you'll go far. After all, if you make no choices, you will end up neglecting your dog's social and emotional needs. So make your choices and feel good about them. Post your list of goals on the fridge or somewhere you can see it. Be inspired by it.

From Goals to Plan:
The Daily Routine

Keeping to a schedule tells your new dog, regardless of his age, that you, his benevolent leader, are in charge. It helps him learn the household rules and understand that he must "work" for his food and his privileges. Dogs respect and want that kind of safe certainty. In time, both you and your dog will find the daily schedule and routine . . . well, routine.

It's important to get your dog started on his routine as soon as you bring him home—each point on the daily routine represents an opportunity to train him—which means that you should begin preparing for a new schedule of your own weeks before you visit your shelter or breeder to choose your dog. While your dog's routine will ultimately depend on his needs and yours, every day must include time for feeding, potty, walking, and play.

Here's a sample routine for you to look over. But don't worry about it too much now: We'll cover every step in the course of our five-week training program, with detailed instructions.

Morning Routine

❯ **wake up.** Greet the dog at her crate, ask for a sit before opening the crate, direct your dog out of the crate, and ask for another sit.

❯ **potty.** From the crate, go outside (with a sit at the door) to do a potty on cue. Give your dog a treat when she obeys you. A sit at the door, then back inside for breakfast.

❯ **breakfast.** A sit as you prepare to give your dog her breakfast.

❯ **puppy potty.** If you have a puppy, go outside again to potty, using the potty-training protocol we'll discuss later (see page 50). Always give your puppy a treat when she goes potty.

❯ **brush and comb.** Handle your dog all over as you brush and comb her coat.

❯ **walk.** Use the walk training program (see page 75).

❯ **puppy potty.** Each time you crate and uncrate your puppy, take her outside to potty.

❯ **crate time is nap time.** Your dog learns to love her crate as you give her time in it when you go to work, go out on errands on which your dog cannot accompany you, or need time to do things around the house. As she becomes comfortable with these scheduled naps in her crate, the possibility of separation anxiety lessens.

Afternoon Routine

❯ **greet.** Each time you let your new dog out of the crate, continue the crate training protocol . . .

❯ **potty.** . . . and the potty-training protocol.

❯ **train.** Take time for your formal daily 10-minute homework practice. (Each week's suggested agenda is detailed in your five-week Fundamentals Training Program.)

❯ **puppy potty.** You know the drill.

❯ **socialization.** Depending on your dog's readiness, you may choose to go on a brief car ride or on a walk. You might visit a neighbor or neighboring dogs in a place where you can do socialization exercises. If you have children, this might be the right time to socialize your dog with your kids. (Socialization activities are spelled out throughout the book.)

❯ **relax at home.** Brushing, petting, or engaging in other quiet activities that bond you and your dog.

❯ **puppy potty.** Should be familiar to you . . . and becoming more familiar for your pup.

❯ **crate time is nap time.** The purpose, again, is to help your dog love his crate and not associate crate time with exile or punishment.

Evening Routine

❯ **greet.** Sometimes the afternoon crate time might be brief.

❯ **potty.** Notice how you're building your dog's association of getting out of the crate with going potty—all while practicing the *sit* cues on the way.

❯ **suppertime.** Similar routine to breakfast.

❯ **puppy potty.** It's that time again.

❯ **walk.** Can be a socialization walk or a special time for you and your dog. It's your call.

❯ **puppy potty.** You're another day closer to having a potty-trained dog.

❯ **family time.** Rotate a variety of activities, keeping your focus on your dog for 10 minutes. This may be a good time to involve your kids in assisting you with her training. It's important that the dog be socialized to your whole family. Remember that you must always supervise when kids are involved.

❯ **potty.** Build up your dog's understanding that potty time comes before good-night time.

Good Night

❯ **crate.** Into the crate for rest. If you've exercised enough today, your dog is more likely to sleep better, and so are you. I like to express my daily gratitude and blessing to my dog.

Middle of the Night

❯ **puppy potty.** Your middle-of-the-night puppy potty routine will come to an end. I promise.

Your Dog's Schedule and Training Logs

highly recommend that you record your dog's schedule, as well as her progress in meeting your training goals, in a notebook or logbook. It will allow you to chart your dog's progress, identify her strengths and natural body rhythms, and spot patterns and problem areas early. For example, you will potty train your dog more quickly and accurately if you know when your dog does her business, when she no longer needs certain puppy potty trips, and how she tells you that she needs to go out. Tracking small improvements will give you confidence and patience. As your dog gets older and her natural patterns change, you start a new log to help you identify new patterns and routines.

Adapt the daily training routines on the previous pages to your own lifestyle. Perhaps another person helps with afternoon dog walks, or you use doggy day care (particularly if you have a puppy that needs to go pee every three hours). In any case, it will help everyone caring for your dog do a better job; no one will be confused about what they are supposed to do. With my family, I write out weekly assignments that need to be checked off.

You can find a training log for each week in Appendix 3 (page 255). You can also download free printouts at positivelywoof.com. Each week's training log helps you focus on the new skills to learn, and there is space to record your dog's progress in developing skills and socialization. I recommend that you log everything, including sleeping and napping, waking up in the middle of the night, peeing and pooping, potty accidents, walking, playing, eating treats as well as meals, and even drinking water. If you know what time your dog ate or drank water, it becomes fairly easy to predict when she will need to go potty again. Write down your mistakes as well as your successes. Whether you have a puppy or an older, rehomed dog, you should ideally log everything for the full five weeks of the training program.

Preparing Your Home and Family

t's best to prepare your house, yard, and car before your new dog comes home. But even if you already have your dog, you can use this opportunity to correct any setup and safety issues in your home. Now is also the time to have a discussion with all family members about the new house rules. If you have regular visitors, such as a babysitter or housekeeper, prepare them as well.

Checklist: Around the House

P reparing for your dog's arrival involves not only buying supplies such as a leash and toys, but also taking measures to make your home safe for your new pet. You should also establish the extent to which any children in your household are allowed to interact with the dog, plus what rooms or areas will be no-dog zones (including parts of your yard or garden). Look over these checklists to make sure you'll be ready when your dog arrives—or to update your home for the dog you already have.

EQUIPMENT AND SUPPLIES

Your dog's basic equipment and supplies can be purchased inexpensively and resourcefully, or you can spend more outfitting your dog than you did buying her from a top-line breeder. How much you spend I'll leave up to you, but here's your shopping list.

☐ **Flat buckle collar.** When her collar is complete with dog tags, it's your dog's uniform. I recommend a flat buckle collar in either leather or webbed fiber. (You may need to start with a lightweight kitty collar, just to get your dog used to the feel of the collar while she's around your home, and use a heavier collar on walks.)

Flat buckle collar and leash

☐ **Dog tags.** One tag should display your name, the dog's name, and your phone numbers. Local laws may also require you to display

a dog license tag that includes current vaccination data. If you have a second residence, such as a weekend house or a beach house, you should have an extra set of tags with local phone numbers made.

☐ **Training collars (optional).** I am against the use of choke collars and prong collars, as they can be misused and can hurt a dog unnecessarily. I support the careful use of some head-collar training devices (the ones that look somewhat like horse halters), such as the Gentle Leader, as long as you follow the manufacturer's instructions, as improper use can hurt your dog. I'll tell you more about using the Gentle Leader in Chapter Eleven, Behavior Problems (page 194).

Gentle Leader training collar

☐ **Martingale collar, also called a Greyhound collar (optional).** If you have a dog with a narrow head, such as a Greyhound, you may want to use this collar, but only when taking the dog on a walk, because the collar may get caught on something. It has an extra loop that tightens around the dog's neck if he pulls, but will not choke the dog if you fit it properly.

Martingale or Greyhound collar

☐ **Harness (optional).** Many owners find that they can walk their dog with more control when his leash is attached to a harness instead of a collar. I prefer harnesses where the leash attaches at the dog's chest, rather than on his back. Many breeds treat the top-of-the-back attachment as an invitation to pull, while the chest attachment causes the dog to turn toward you when he pulls. Make sure that the harness fits snugly and check your dog for chafing.

Body harness

☐ **Leash.** I recommend a six-foot leash (instead of a four-footer) so that your dog can get a little extra freedom, especially during exercises when you tether him to your belt. If you're thinking about using a retractable leash, such as a Flexi, wait until your dog has completed the five-week fundamentals program, has developed excellent recall, and can walk politely at a loose heel.

☐ **Crate.** See the crate training section (page 53) to help you choose what's right for your dog and your decor.

Use the x-pen as a playpen . . .

☐ **X-pen.** If your budget will allow it, get a collapsible exercise pen, often called an x-pen, as your dog's movable playpen area. This lightweight, portable pen can be used to keep a dog in or out of an area. Set it up as a contained ring or divide a room like the Berlin

. . . or as a room divider.

Wall . . . to be taken down when your dog matures. You will find other uses for your x-pen while you go through this training program. To keep my dogs from moving ours, I tie dumbbell weights with bungee straps to the bottom of the pen.

□ **Baby gates.** These movable gates help you close off rooms or keep your dog confined to a particular room.

□ **Bedding.** Since your new dog may chew his bed, choose an inexpensive option at first—towels and cheap blankets.

□ **Food bowl and water bowl.** Although I'm a fan of bowls that fit into a raised housing, you may want to go as simple and lightweight as possible at first, especially as you're mastering the hand-feeding protocol (detailed in the next chapter). Once hand-feeding has been mastered, you can switch to a more deluxe setup, including a metal or ceramic bowl that is easy to sterilize.

□ **Food and treats.** See the feeding section in the next chapter (page 46) for guidance in making diet choices. Remember to set aside a portion of your dog's daily diet for training treats.

□ **Toys for play.** Allowing a dog to "own" only a couple of toys that he can play with whenever he wants to will help create opportunities for training. Don't allow him to destroy or shred toys; blocked intestines can require surgery. Always supervise toy play.

□ **Toys for chewing.**

Fill a Kong with treats for constructive chewing.

Chewing is a dog's natural impulse. So, rather than tempting your dog to chew things she shouldn't, direct her chewing behavior positively by regularly giving her toys that are made to be chewed. My favorite chew toy is the Kong, because younger dogs love them and yet they are practically indestructible. A Kong can be stuffed with treats or dog food to slow down a dog that eats too fast; you can give it to her while she is in her crate or as a reward.

Have a few stuffed Kongs handy as special rewards.

□ **Toys for training.** These are special toys that I "lend" to my dog as a reward during training sessions; after some brief moments of play, he has to give them back to me in exchange for a cookie, a training technique that I will teach you later (see page 117). They can be delicate rubber squeaky toys or special plush toys, and are always returned to me for safekeeping.

I also use tug toys and retrieving toys as training rewards. And then I always have a very special toy in reserve to trade with my dog when he has taken contraband, such as a shoe, or to stop unwanted chase behavior. For contraband trades, I recommend a plush toy that has lots of squeaky and crinkly features, and that can't easily be shredded. Avoid toys that would get chewed up if left with your dog for more than a minute.

☐ **Special training equipment and supplies.** As you go through the program in this book, I will discuss a number of special supplies, including a 50-foot leash for recall training (a rope tied securely to the end of your dog's leash can suffice), a clicker for trick training, and a treat pouch that clips to your belt.

Treat pouch

☐ **Coat grooming.** Your basic list includes a brush that is right for your breed, plus a comb, coat rake, and shedding blade. If you bathe your dog yourself, use a dog shampoo and coat conditioner.

☐ **Nail care.** Options include a nail clipper and emery board, or an electric nail grooming tool. I personally like the PediPaws. Also get some styptic powder or cornstarch to stop bleeding in case you accidentally cut too close.

☐ **Oral hygiene.** Use only toothpaste that has been formulated for dogs, plus a soft-bristled toothbrush. Dental treats can help when they're used as an addition to toothbrushing, but not as a substitute. Bad dental hygiene can lead to infection, which, when it travels through the bloodstream, can cause heart disease and more. Brushing your dog's teeth regularly is as important to his well-being as good dental hygiene is to yours.

☐ **Poop bags/waste disposal system.** If your dog uses a potty area in your yard, have a pickup tool or scoop and disposal container nearby. If he does his business on walks, make sure to pick it up with poop bags. I recommend biodegradable pickup bags; they're available at most pet stores as well as online.

☐ **First-aid kit.** You can buy a ready-made kit or assemble your own. At minimum, the kit should have a tick remover, cleaning solution such as hydrogen peroxide, antiseptic cream, gauze wraps, first-aid adhesive tape, scissors, and sterile eyewash. Some excellent first-aid kits, available at pet stores, contain upwards of 60 items.

Keep your dog healthy by being prepared for emergencies.

DOGPROOFING AND SETUP

You may find it hard to believe, but having dogs in my home actually helps me be a better housekeeper. I am always looking for ways to keep the dogs out of trouble in my house and yard. Here is a dogproofing checklist to make you a better housekeeper, too.

☐ **Shoes.** Most dogs can't resist the temptation of the smell of your feet on leather or canvas. If you wear your shoes in the house, put them away in a closet and remember to keep the door closed. If you don't wear shoes in your house, put all shoes by the door in an area that your dog can't get to. If necessary, put an x-pen around the shoes.

☐ **Toys.** Fuzzy shapes and easy-to-chew toys are too often a doggy delicacy. Put them away. Keep toy closets, toy boxes, and cabinets closed.

☐ **Homework, bills, important papers.** "My dog ate my homework" may convince your child's teacher, but bill collectors tend not to accept that excuse. Recently, when I wasn't paying attention, Boz chewed some pages out of a dog training log. Yes, even the experts make mistakes; with some dogs it takes only a moment's distraction.

☐ **Clothes.** Don't hang clothes so low that they can be dragged away, and keep them off the floor, especially once they've been worn and have your delightful smell on them.

☐ **Kitchen.** Counter surfing (when a dog jumps up to see what goodies are on the counters) is a favorite dog sport. Keep your counters clean of any traces of food, your cabinet doors shut, and objects that are dangerous or breakable well out of surfing reach. Also make sure that cleaning supplies (including sponges and gloves) are well beyond your dog's reach. In fact, it's wise to prepare your kitchen as though you were childproofing it: All potentially poisonous products should be stowed away, behind cabinet doors secured with childproof locks.

☐ **Garbage pails and wastebaskets.** Keep them out of reach, and empty them often.

☐ **Bathroom.** Keep toilet lids down, especially if there are chemicals in the water. Beware of toilet paper getting unspooled or even chewed right off the roll. Soap bars look like dog treats, so keep them out of surfing range. It's a lot to control, which is why it is usually easiest just to keep bathroom doors shut at all times.

☐ **Shut doors.** In fact, you may want to keep most doors shut when you can't supervise your dog. Especially make sure you shut any doors that open to the outdoors.

☐ **Towels.** Keep towels near the door so that you can wipe your dog's feet and coat. I suggest that you practice wiping your dog's feet and coat before he gets caught in his first rainstorm, so that he's comfortable when you need to dry him off quickly. Most dogs are more comfortable with your wiping their front paws first and then their hind paws.

❐ **Toxics.** While most toxic substances are in the kitchen and bathroom, make sure that no stray sprays, cleaners, or alcohol are misplaced or stored within your dog's surfing reach.

❐ **Bitter apple spray.** Most dogs don't like the taste of bitter apple spray. It works best when sprayed in advance to help teach the dog to keep out of a wastebasket, off a counter, or from chewing furniture. Another option is a hotsauce-and-perfume mix. Test any sprays to make sure that they don't stain.

❐ **Electrical cords.** Tack them to baseboards; keep them out of sight. If you can't supervise a dog in a room where he can reach electrical cords, consider taking the dog out of that room. Dogs can be electrocuted or strangled by electrical cords.

❐ **Curtain cords.** If your curtains have dangling cords, install cleats high up and tie off the cords.

❐ **Plants.** Make sure that your houseplants are out of reach. If you're not sure if a plant is toxic, the ASPCA website (aspca.org) has a good list of plants that are toxic to dogs and other pets.

❐ **Crate safety.** Make sure that your dog's crate is in a comfortable spot that is not too hot or too cold.

❐ **Baby gates.** Use baby gates to block off rooms, especially if doors can't be closed. Some people don't like hiking over baby gates, but I have done it for years and don't mind. Some baby gates include swinging doors if hiking and hurdling are a problem for you.

FURNITURE RULES

Is your dog allowed on the couch or comfy chairs? Some trainers believe that allowing dogs on furniture undermines your authority, but I don't agree. I think it's an issue of personal preference and that whatever decision you make, you can keep your authority intact.

Of course, most dog owners have a furniture story to tell. My rule is no dogs on the couch, which my dogs obey when I'm at home . . . but sometimes disobey when I'm out. One evening I came inside the house quietly and saw Jock, Merit, and Saxon scatter off the furniture like cockroaches. One of the pillows had been shredded. Even though Saxon had pillow fuzz all over his beard, I couldn't do anything about it, since I didn't catch him in the act. For a while after that, I put the x-pen panels on the couch and furniture, and kept the remaining pillows out of reach. In the end, when it comes to setting furniture rules, it's important to stay consistent, and not to tempt your dog by leaving him alone in the room while you're still training.

YARD SETUP

When your dog first comes home, you will always have to supervise him outside. Here are some precautions you should take to make your yard safer for your dog.

☐ **Fencing.** If your neighborhood allows fencing, make sure that there are no gaps in yours, including open gates and areas hidden by bushes. Swimming pools should be fenced or, at minimum, have a pool cover that the dog cannot squeeze under. Fence off or remove any other temptations, and seal off access to areas underneath the house, porches, and decks.

☐ **Electric fencing (optional).** Some people like so-called invisible fencing: electronic sensors that are placed or buried around the perimeter of the yard that trigger an electronic shock collar when the dog wanders near. I'm not a big fan of electric fences—if the dog endures the shock while chasing, say, a squirrel past the perimeter, he is less likely to return because he quickly learns that he will have to endure more shocks. I say that when your dog is outside in an unfenced yard, so are you. If you use an electric fence or shock collar, test it weekly to ensure that it's operating correctly—and at the correct voltage for your dog.

☐ **Mulch and plants.** Mulch and many plants can be toxic or impact your dog's bowels. Consider putting garden fencing around plant beds if you treasure their appearance.

Remove all poisonous plants. Refer to the ASPCA website (aspca.org) for a list and photos of well over 350 plants that are toxic to dogs.

☐ **Septic tank.** Make sure that the cover can't be pried open.

☐ **Grill.** Keep it covered.

☐ **Bird feeders.** Any bird feeders must be out of the dog's jumping reach, or moved where the dog isn't allowed to go.

☐ **Potty area.** If you don't want your dog doing his business everywhere he wants on your property (and who does?), establish his potty area from day one. If you have a yard, the ideal potty area will be located near the house for quick access, as well as within reach of a garden hose. It should be at least 10 feet by 10 feet, and about 3 inches deep, and layered with a bed of absorbent sand, covered with pea gravel or small river rock. Be prepared to clean the potty area often.

☐ **Patio.** If you live in an apartment and have a patio, you can build or purchase a children's sandbox to use as a potty area, complete with artificial turf (that must be cleaned), actual sod, or high-tech grids. Have your poop equipment nearby, whether you use biodegradable bags, a garden trowel, or a long-handled scoop.

☐ **Common areas.** If you live in a building or housing development with a common dog run, make sure to follow all the rules for cleanup.

CAR SETUP

An image that practically defines family life is a car trip—complete with a dog. We'll get to that idyllic journey with the family dog in Chapter Twelve. Right now, let's set up your car for everyday trips: going to the vet, to a friend's home, on errands, or to the park.

☐ **Backseat riding.** Your dog should ride in the backseat, ideally inside a carrier crate or strapped in with a dog seat belt harness.

☐ **Seat cover.** You can protect the seat with a blanket or purchase seat covers.

☐ **Ramp or steps.** Some dogs need help getting into cars, so be prepared to lift yours or use a ramp or steps.

☐ **Ventilation.** Make sure your dog gets proper ventilation, either by air-conditioning or a fan, or with windows that are open just enough to get some breeze.

☐ **Head in the car.** Although another iconic image is that of a dog sticking his head out a car window, it's dangerous to let your dog do that. Countless injuries occur from flying debris.

SAFETY RULES IN A HOME WITH KIDS

My kids have grown up around a whole menagerie of pets, especially dogs. Although I have allowed them to have their own gerbils, snakes, and cats, all our family dogs have been *my* dogs. I let my kids help with dog care, but I believe that dogs require too much hands-on effort to entrust their primary care to children. Over the life of a dog, your kids will go through many life changes, starting and stopping new fads and relationships more quickly than it takes to complete this training program—even if they promise with completely honest intentions that "this time is different."

When your dog or puppy first arrives at her new home, she may be frightened. But whether your family is adopting a shy dog, a carefree puppy, or a confident dog, explain to your children that everyone's habits and schedules will change. And if your dog has been in your home for some time, you can teach an old family new tricks. As every parent knows, children don't always have reliable impulse control, especially with all the excitement that comes with getting a new dog. Rule number one for you: You must supervise kids when they play with the dog. Rule number one for kids: They must ask to play with the dog. Ultimately, your job is to set the example; your kids will imitate what you do. It will be helpful to discuss the following rules with your children before the dog comes home. Remember that more than two million children have been bitten by dogs in the past year.

Your children will eventually learn impulse control, but right now you are training them as much as your dog. I supervised my kids around dogs until they were 11 or 12, but I'll leave it to you to determine when you feel that your child is skilled enough and mature enough to be left alone with the dog.

☐ **Ask permission.** You must ask me to play with the dog. I am the dog's supervisor.

☐ **Keep calm.** For the next few weeks, there will be no running or making loud noises in the house.

☐ **Get help.** If there is a problem with the dog and I'm not in the room, you must come get me immediately.

☐ **Keep the dog enclosed.** All doors to the outside must stay closed when the dog is not in her crate. Never let the dog out of the house unsupervised. If baby gates and x-pens are up to keep the dog out of (or inside) certain areas of the home, those barriers must not be moved without my help.

☐ **Stay seated.** You must sit on the floor while handling the puppy.

☐ **No physical punishment.** Never hit the dog when she makes a mistake. You could hurt her and she could hurt you back.

☐ **Let the dog sleep.** When the dog is sleeping, don't touch her. You could scare her and she might bite you. If you must wake the dog, ask me to do it.

☐ **No feeding.** You're not allowed to feed the dog or touch the dog while she is eating unless it is part of a training exercise I'm supervising.

☐ **Stay out of the crate.** Never climb inside the dog's crate unless it is part of a socialization program that a grown-up is supervising.

Establishing ground rules will keep both your dog and your children safe.

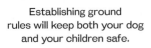

OTHER PETS IN YOUR HOME

When my daughter Paige was 12 and old enough to be entrusted with a cat, she did her research, saved her money, and bought a Siamese kitten that she named Isles. At this time, my Giant Schnauzer, Saxon, was seven years old, and had grown accustomed to being the king of the house. I knew that it was going to take a lot of time and patience before I could expect Saxon and Isles to coexist peacefully. Here's how I handled their introduction.

☐ **Baby gates.** Initially, they were kept apart with baby gates, and although they could see each other, no interactions were allowed.

☐ **Sitting and meeting.** Three months later, I formally introduced them. Every day, Paige and I would put Isles in my lap and give him a treat. When Saxon sat perfectly, we'd also give him a treat. If Isles got nervous or if Saxon started to get excited, that would be the end of the session.

☐ **Lie down.** Saxon graduated to "lie downs" and "settles" next to Isles and me.

☐ **Supervised interaction.** Over the course of an intensive week of supervision, Saxon and Isles could be around each other while I watched.

☐ **Unsupervised Interaction.** Eventually they could be together without supervision. In fact, Isles grew to like dogs, started to play with Saxon, and a great relationship developed between them.

My experience is that with patience and positive reinforcement training, most dogs will coexist safely with other pets. It just takes time. Right now, I keep Boz mostly separate from Brieo and from the other dogs that are boarding with me. Boz works well when he's with me one-on-one, but when he's with other dogs, he gets overexcited and tries to herd them (this is natural behavior for a Border Collie). Before I decide to introduce Boz to the other dogs here, I want to get him used to Brieo. I started by feeding him upstairs and tethering him on a leash at all times—a training technique I recommend using when a dog first comes home, which we will discuss in the next chapter. I'm experimenting with different activities, erring on the side of caution always, such as feeding the dogs in the same room, separated by a chair.

Once you bring your dog home, it may take weeks, or perhaps even months, to get him comfortable with your other pets, and vice versa. With the right supervision and step-by-step progress, however, the transition should go smoothly. Just remember: When introducing pets to each other, be extremely patient. To repeat myself: Always err on the side of caution.

Your Dog's Health

Your dog's vet and groomer will both play significant roles in her health over what I hope will be many, many years. My advice is that you interview a vet before you get your dog. Does the vet seem to have a good bedside manner and make a thorough examination? Is the facility clean? Does the staff seem friendly and helpful? Do the costs seem reasonable for your area? Does the vet offer emergency services or have a relationship with an emergency pet hospital that is close by? Talk to other pet owners who have used the vet's services. And, of course, you'll probably want to find a vet who is reasonably close to home in case something comes up that needs attention right away.

You will also want to have supplies at home in case any emergencies arise. As mentioned earlier, home emergency preparedness includes having a well-stocked first-aid kit. You will also want to create an information sheet that lists veterinarian and emergency pet-hospital contacts and driving instructions, alternate contacts in case you are not reachable, feeding and medication instructions, crating protocol, directions about the use of treats, calming instructions, and details of any health problems. The information sheet is important for a pet sitter or for friends who are helping you, or in case something happens to you (God forbid) and you're unable to care for your dog. (See page 230 for a detailed checklist for your dog's caregiver.) It's a good idea to keep the list posted on the fridge or some other visible place.

Familiarize yourself—and anyone who cares for your dog—with the contents of her first aid kit.

If you decide to use a professional groomer, the groomer may encourage you to bring your dog by for a quick visit just to get some treats and praise before the first grooming session. When you see well-groomed dogs, ask their owners about their groomers. Find a groomer in your price range who has good rapport with your dog, who follows instructions, and who will take the time to look at sample pictures of other dogs with you. Some groomers will allow you to stay during the session to make your dog more comfortable.

It's taken a lot of preparation—and a lot of time and work—just to get organized to bring your dog home. But everything you've done was an important and necessary step to ensure that you are going to take great care of your new pet. And here's the good news: You're ready.

Now go get your dog . . .

The Fundamentals Program

Chapter Three

Feeding, Potty Training, and Crating

We begin your five-week Fundamentals Training Program (see page 63) this week, but first I'd like to discuss three essentials: feeding, potty training, and crating. Having protocols in place for these everyday routines will establish your authority and give your dog the security that comes from having a sense of routine. You should begin these protocols *at the same time* you begin to train your dog in the fundamentals: the minute she comes home.

If you have a puppy, think of her as a blank slate. Nature has programmed this little dog to know that her survival means adapting to her environment. She'll immediately begin searching for rewards, and learning by trial and error what is safe and what is dangerous.

You are this creature's most important influence, and the earlier you begin to shape her behavior, to teach her those lessons, the safer and more secure she'll feel and the happier you'll both be.

For an older dog that has been rehomed, like Boz, immediate training is an ideal way to short-circuit bad behaviors and replace them with new healthy behaviors. To borrow a concept from neurolinguistic programming psychology: Training a rehomed, older dog represents a "pattern interrupt," allowing the previous patterns of bad habits to be replaced by new patterns and good habits.

Checklist: First Steps

Here is a checklist of what you should have completed so far, and what you'll begin this week:

COMPLETED ACTIVITIES

☐ Made a top 10 checklist of your training priorities.

☐ Purchased your dog's equipment and supplies.

☐ Dogproofed and set up your home, yard, and car.

☐ Discussed rules with your kids.

☐ Found a veterinarian.

THIS WEEK'S ACTIVITIES

☐ Start your dog's training log (page 256) and establish a routine to follow every day this week (page 26).

☐ Begin leash tethering (next page).

☐ Begin hand-feeding protocol (page 47).

☐ Play the Name Game while hand-feeding and handling your dog (page 48).

☐ Begin potty training (page 50).

☐ Begin crate training (page 53).

☐ Begin bite inhibition, handling, and gentling, assuming that there are no outstanding behavior issues (page 59).

☐ "Ouch" exercises: explore dog's mouth, count teeth and toes (page 59).

☐ Play Pass the Puppy (page 60).

☐ Play Peekaboo (see page 60).

☐ Begin Week One of Fundamentals Training Program (Chapter Four).

Daisy

Commands

Wait
Out!
Leave it!
That's enough
Go! Go! Go!
Go lie down
In your crate!
In the car!
Let's go!
Gentle

Hand signals:

sit   up
down
wait
come
twirl   follow point

Tricks

sit
down
sit pretty
Bang!
back up
twirl
tunnel
up!
Fetch my slipper!
✷ Flip the hula hoop
come

crawl
speak
(toys) Put it in!
stay
off

Find your happy place.

- Say your prayers
- Push the carriage (Still working)
- weave
- Find my keys
- Get me a kleenex + throw it away
- Fetch my slippers (both)

Tethering

One way to begin to bond immediately with your dog is through leash tethering. I use a mountain-climbing carabiner (usually available at hardware or camping stores) that clips to the leash and to my belt, so I can easily attach and detach the leash. You can also hook the leash through your belt. Some puppies don't like being tethered, so start tethering for brief periods—maybe only five seconds in the beginning. Give your dog a

A carabiner easily attaches to and detaches from a belt loop.

treat for exhibiting calm behavior when tethered, and slowly build up time. (For now, simply hand her the treat—using the same hand each time. You will learn more about the correct ways to give treats at the beginning of the Fundamentals Training Program.) Through tethering, your dog will learn to read your body language and literally feel more connected to you. Eventually you can graduate to walking on leash everywhere, before progressing to free roaming in certain areas (while still tethering in other areas, such as when you're doing the dishes and want your dog to settle down next to you). If your dog chews the leash, prevent that by spraying it with bitter apple or soaking it in unsweetened mouthwash such as Listerine.

If your dog jumps on you while tethered, back up a step and tether her to a doorknob or a sturdy table leg. If she jumps up as you approach her, walk away for a moment before stepping toward her again. With some patient practice, your dog will begin to understand that she is not supposed to jump on you, and you can try tethering her to your belt again.

When your dog is tethered to you, have your other family members or friends approach her to give a treat and then walk away. The goal is to have a calm dog that always follows your body language, which will lead her to turn, follow, or stop when you want her to. Right now, Boz is always on a leash, dragging it while I supervise him, or tethered to my belt so I have both hands free. When Boz is ready, we will take the next step: I will hold his leash in my hands. But first I need to let him learn about me—and understand that I'm in control.

Eventually your dog will learn to read your body language.

Feeding

G iving your dog too much food isn't a sign of love. My goal is to help you raise a well-fed dog that isn't fat; in fact, I prefer to keep a dog a little on the lean side. I do this by watching the amount of food I give her and by making sure she gets plenty of exercise. Weight can go on easily, but shedding extra pounds can take a dog many months. It's especially important to watch your dog's weight if she's of a breed that is prone to hip or joint problems.

A dog's metabolism slows down as she ages, so the amount of food you feed her will depend on her age. Because of their tiny stomachs, puppies must be fed three or four small meals a day. When most dogs are six months old, you can reduce the number of feedings to two, and from there, get your vet's advice on adjusting your growing dog's diet. Most adult dogs (I take the view that a dog is fully grown at age three) can be fed once or twice per day; my preference is twice for most dogs. I recommend changing the amount a dog eats depending on the time of year and your dog's activity level; more in summer, less in winter; more if she is active, less if she is sedentary. The amount of food a dog requires also depends on breed. Again, ask your veterinarian for advice on precise feeding amounts for your dog; instructions printed on dog food bags are not breed-specific. Your vet can also help you decide if your dog would be best served by a protein-rich diet.

The quality of commercial dog food has improved greatly in recent years. Some owners prefer to make their own dog food, or to use prepackaged raw ingredients that can be cooked and, in some cases, fed raw. (In fact, there is a raw dog food diet with the delightfully undelectable name BARF, which stands for Biologically Appropriate Raw Food.) Whatever nutritional program you and your vet decide to follow, be sure to keep track of your dog's progress. One reminder: Whenever you adjust your dog's feeding regimen, taper off the old as you slowly change to the new.

A note on vitamins and supplements: Some veterinarians and pet owners choose to add vitamin supplements (many of which are chewable)

Be sure to allow for training treats when planning your dog's diet. They have calories, too.

to the dog's daily diet. I think there's merit to supplements, but you should never use them without discussing them—and the proper dosage—with your vet. Supplements come in five categories:

◆ **VITAMINS**, especially A, various Bs, C, and E

◆ **PROBIOTICS** such as acidophilus and psyllium, which aid digestion and help skin and coat

◆ **OILS** for the skin and coat, such as flaxseed oil, olive oil, and fish oil

◆ **GLUCOSAMINE** and **CHONDROITIN**, which help maintain healthy cartilage, for joint support

◆ **ANTIOXIDANTS**, which can also be added to the dog's diet by simply mixing fresh sweet potatoes and fresh green vegetables such as broccoli, peas, and spinach into his food

FEEDING MORE THAN ONE DOG AT A TIME

If you already have other dogs in your home, start by feeding your new dog separately, as I have done with Boz and Brieo. Once you have completed the first week of hand-feeding and can easily pick up your dog's bowl while he is eating, you can graduate to having your dogs eat in the same room with a chair or x-pen wall between them, or on opposite sides of the room while you supervise. This setup helps avoid both fights over food and situations where a faster eater takes away the slower one's food. (For more on what to do in a dogfight, see page 217.) If you don't have other dogs at home, you may consider feeding your dog at the home of a friend who has a well-trained dog that has already had positive social interaction with your dog. Having a variety of hand-feeding experiences will lessen your dog's territoriality and food-guarding behavior.

HAND-FEEDING PROTOCOL

Before you start formally training your new dog, it's best that you feed her all meals by hand. Hand-feeding establishes you as the source of your dog's food, sending her the message that it's *your* food that you are, in your benevolence, giving to her. This wires her brain to see you as the friendly, higher-ranking person in her life who is also the source of her rewards, emotional comfort, food, water, and play. Hand-feeding also promotes safety; your dog becomes far less likely to guard her food. Food guarding can become a serious safety issue. While it may be a natural survival instinct in dogs, a pet dog that guards her food can be dangerous and unpredictable. This simple hand-feeding protocol is vital; it helps your dog mellow out when people are around her food while she is eating.

To begin, measure out your dog's food and put some of her meal in her bowl. Sitting in a chair (or on the floor if it's a puppy or small dog), scoop some food into your hand, and let your dog (who should be on a tether or leash) eat right out of your hand. Hand-feed the whole meal to her, and do it for every meal for a whole week. If you have a puppy, you will hand-feed small meals to her throughout the day. Don't wear rubber gloves and don't be squeamish. Have fun with it; hand-feeding is no messier than kindergarten finger paints. Just wash your hands before you start, and make sure you've rinsed off any soap or hand sanitizer.

While hand-feeding your dog, say her name in a loving way. This is called the Name Game, and I want you to do it whenever you hand-feed. As the week progresses and you and your dog get more comfortable with hand-feeding, touch her collar and pet her gently on the side of her body as you say her name. You're getting your dog used to being handled so that she will be better prepared for grooming and other times when you or the vet need to check her body or administer medications. If your dog stops eating when you touch her, stop petting her and keep offering her food. Alternate hands. When she gets comfortable with your touching her collar and petting her, try petting and touching a little bit between scoops. Then put another small portion of her premeasured meal in her bowl and hand-feed that until the bowl is empty. Let her see you refill her bowl and resume hand-feeding. Refill the bowl and hand-feed again and again, until her meal is complete. Pretty soon you will transition to feeding your dog from a bowl that you hold in your lap.

After she eats each small portion that you have scooped from the bowl, you want her to look at you before she gets more food; this will help your dog bond to you and respect you as her food source. If this process progresses well, begin, toward the end of the week, to alternate between hand-feeding small amounts and letting her eat out of her bowl directly (while you supervise her). When your dog seems comfortable (when she lets you touch her body and collar as well as her food and bowl without guarding her food or ducking away from you), use one hand to pick up her bowl before she has finished eating while you hand-feed her a scoop with your other hand. Get her used to being fed from different bowls and containers: metal, plastic, ceramic. You also want to begin hand-feeding her in various rooms of your home as you allow her access to these rooms. You can also hand-feed her in the yard and in the car. This will get your dog comfortable with your touching her and her food at any time and in any place. This concept—getting your dog used to performing activities in a variety of locations—is called generalizing. Generalizing is a fundamental concept that we will revisit throughout this training program, and it will be applied to every lesson you teach your dog.

Once you have completed your week of hand-feeding (including handling the dog and playing the Name Game), you can teach this practice to your children and spouse. Teaching everyone in your family the hand-feeding protocol will promote safety, family bonding, and generalized experience. A safety note for kids: Kids love to hold puppies, but they must be taught how to do this correctly. Sometimes a puppy will wriggle out of a child's arms and fall. Or sometimes a child will want to hold a puppy until the moment she actually touches it, and then back away or let go. When a child drops a puppy, it can hurt the puppy and harm both the child's and puppy's confidence. Therefore I never let a child stand while she holds a puppy.

Hand-feeding is a good opportunity for your child and dog to become comfortable with each other. Have the child sit on your lap or on a chair next to you, and do the hand-feeding protocol beginning with step one. I started involving my own children in hand-feeding when they were as young as four months and able to sit up and balance in my lap. Before that, I used a lifelike baby doll to acclimate my dogs to having a small child hand-feed them. If you have young children, for safety's sake, please use your own judgment and consider involving a professional trainer to supervise hand-feeding. I prefer a chair to the floor, because the dog's mouth is at the height of the hand rather than level with the child's face. If you have a young or small puppy that has been exercised and is now calm, relaxed, and not mouthing (which means the puppy is not still using her mouth to explore you and initiate play as she did with her littermates), then it's okay to have your relaxed child on the floor during hand-feeding.

As you and your child have success with these initial steps, start feeding in other rooms as you did when you were hand-feeding by yourself. When your child and dog seem comfortable with each other, graduate to having your child pause for a minute, then remove and refill your dog's bowl while she's eating (in exchange for food in the other hand).

After your children master hand-feeding, recruit a few friends and run them through parts of the protocol, too. Getting your dog used to having people around her food bowl will prevent future problems. It's much easier than repairing them later.

As you'll see later in the book, hand-feeding will be used whenever you teach your dog skills and new tricks. I often return to hand-feeding to keep my dog fine-tuned, or if he seems to be regressing in behavior or gets stuck on learning a particular cue or skill.

Potty Training

The myth that dogs house-train themselves is just that—a myth. They won't. We need to teach our dogs *our* rules, which may strike them as completely arbitrary. As far as they're concerned, they should be "allowed" to go potty whenever they need to, and wherever they may be at that moment.

All of my dogs have been terrific at going potty when told to. My Border Collie, Jock, would pee for me in exchange for praise and kisses, a cookie, or a single ball toss. He would pee 10 times in a row if I asked him to! My potty-training motto is "Fun things don't begin until after we go potty."

Please allow me to give you some house-training don'ts. (And by the way, I prefer the terms *house-training* or *potty training,* which make us think of our goal, rather than *housebreaking,* which makes us think of failure and punishment.) These are common house-training mistakes—and at one time, some of them were even considered the "right way" to house-train.

Punishing potty errors after they've happened is perhaps the most common training mistake; it only aggravates the problem. Going potty is a natural behavior. When we punish this behavior—or any other unwanted behavior—after it has happened, to the dog it seems that she is being punished for what she is doing now (like coming to you when you called her name or sitting in front of you and wagging her tail), not the mess she made a minute ago. If our timing is off, there is virtually no chance that our dog will understand what is making us so angry. It used to be thought that swatting a dog with a rolled-up newspaper and rubbing her nose in her mistake would get the message across, but I assure you with complete certainty that it will not. Rubbing a dog's nose in her pee or poop is counterproductive and mean-spirited—and it can give her a bacterial infection. The only way to deal with a potty error is to catch the dog in the act and scoop her up and take her, or lead her, quickly outside to the potty area. Until your dog is house-trained, do not allow her to have free access to the entire house, and supervise her always, perhaps by keeping her tethered to you or by using baby gates, x-pens, and closed doors.

Let's take another moment to consider how a dog's mistake might be handled in aversive training. Assume you come home to find dog poop on your rug. At this moment, the dog is resting quietly on her mat and she hears you call her name. She comes to you right on cue, but instead of getting praised for that, she gets yelled at. Now the dog has to figure out why you are yelling at her while pointing to cold poop on the rug, and then why she's being swatted with a newspaper. That's too complicated, as well as unclear, uninspiring, and mean. Positive reinforcement house-training is better all around.

When it comes to potty training, you must commit to patience.

So, what's the right way to potty train your dog? First, it's important to understand that it will likely take several months to potty train your dog completely. Commit to patience; mistakes will happen. Learn to laugh at them, if you can.

Your schedule and training log will be the main tools you use in potty training. By having your dog visit the potty area many times each day, and by logging when she does her business, you will become better able to predict when she will next need to go out. Make a note in your dog's training log when she pees and poops—I use a simple "#1" mark for pee and "#2" for poop—and in time you will shape her habits like a champion. Whenever a mistake is made, I consider that *my* mistake. As in all areas of dog training, we learn at least as much from our failures as from our successes, so I log the mistake, hoping to pick up on my pup's pooping and peeing pattern. Success requires your own constant attention, predictive abilities (made much easier with your training log), and timely rewards for your dog's good business practices.

After you take your dog to what will become her designated potty spot, say the word you want to associate with going potty in an upbeat way, such as "Boz, go peeps, go poops," or simply "go potty." As she does her business, praise her along the lines of "good pee" or "good poo" or "good potty" in a calm tone so that you don't distract her, and then give her a treat immediately afterward. Your puppy will learn to associate the potty area with the rewards you will give her for each success, and she will begin to look forward to being rewarded for doing her business in "her" area. Other trainers like to use the cue "do your business," paired with the reward praise "good business." Some people get creative when naming the potty cue; one colleague named the dog's potty cue after an ex-spouse. (He eventually grew tired of having to explain this joke and needed to teach his dog a new cue.) Whatever you name the cue, say it the same way every time, and realize that your dog may learn the verbal cue long after having learned the physical potty ritual.

If you live in a city building where your dog doesn't have her own potty area, you'll need to adapt this protocol. Surely there is an outside public "restroom," even if it's a hydrant (if that is customary and acceptable where you live) that your dog can be taken to. Just keep taking your dog to an acceptable spot and reward her for her success. If she starts doing her business on the way, quickly scoop her up and take her, or lead her, to the correct spot for her to finish.

Some of my clients prefer to paper train their dog indoors, using newspaper or pee pads. I'm not a big fan of this approach, because it's a two-step learning process. In paper training, first the puppy needs to learn to do her business on the paper or pad. Then she needs to unlearn that behavior, and learn that she needs to go outside and do her business at an entirely different spot—and one that doesn't even slightly resemble the newspaper or pee pad she has grown accustomed to.

But I also understand that not everyone has the option of training his or her dog outdoors. For instance, it can be dangerous for puppies that have not had all their vaccinations to go outside on a dirty sidewalk or street. If your vet recommends that you keep your puppy inside until she's had all her shots, use paper or pee pad training. Then when your vet says it's okay to take the dog out, have your puppy do her business on the pee pad or newspaper outside. Cut down the size of the pee pad, smaller and smaller, until you have eliminated it.

If you live in a city apartment and have a very small dog, you may prefer to set up a permanent litter box in the bathroom. That will work if you keep the rest of the house-training protocol consistent. Your challenge will come when you take your dog outside for a walk; you will have to teach her to generalize her potty behavior to this foreign environment. If she starts to go, scoop her up as if she were making a mistake in the house, get her to the nearest acceptable spot right away, name the cue as she does her business, and praise her for the success. Be patient and regard any mistake as a learning experience. Remember to write it in the training log to help you learn.

If your dog has already been potty trained but has started peeing in the house again, or if you have a rehomed dog that is said to be potty trained already but has regressed, then patiently act as though this is the first time in this dog's life that she is learning potty training. If your dog has persistent potty problems, it's possible that she has an underlying medical problem. Check with your vet.

If your dog pees when she gets excited—we call this glee pee—such as when you come home or when a guest arrives, take note and try to anticipate and avoid the situation. As soon as you enter your home, calmly greet your dog and take her immediately outside. Puppies are prone to glee pee whenever anything new happens, including simply moving to another room. They have little bladders, so take your new dog outside often to potty. As young as seven weeks, puppies are ready to start learning to potty outside. (But remember to check with your veterinarian if your dog hasn't gotten all her shots.)

Crate Training

The crate is your dog's sanctuary, the place where he can get away from it all. It's where he sleeps at night and where he's confined at times during the day. The crate needs to be respected as your dog's safe haven, not his jail, and should be associated with reward, not punishment. Although most dogs naturally love a cozy den environment, the crate is obviously not found in nature, so most dogs need to be trained to love their crate.

Of all the good reasons to crate train your dog, the most significant is that crate-trained dogs tend to be better trained in general. Crating teaches a dog to settle down and have quiet time. It encourages him to chew only on acceptable things, because *you* provide him with those things while he's in the crate. A crate-trained dog tends to be better able to cope with anxiety and—if necessary—rehoming. When a dog travels, his crate offers security and comfort. Veterinarian staffers and groomers truly appreciate working with crate-trained dogs, and so will you. When I have guest dogs boarding in my home, I require that they accept some kind of confinement, preferably a crate, until I determine that they are sufficiently mature to be trusted with free access to my home. The Kennedys' dogs Splash and Sunny can be in my home without crates, but young Cappy (Bo Obama's littermate) needs to be crated. Even if you work at home, crate train your dog. Using a crate is similar to having a playpen for a toddler or a crib for a baby: It provides a safe area that allows you to take your eyes off your youngster for a moment. Never get your dog out of the habit of being crated.

Throughout the life of a crate-trained dog, he is likely to spend more hours inside his crate than in any other one place, so it's important to keep it comfortable and clean. Inside the crate is your dog's bed or mat, which should have a machine-washable cover. Many dogs like having a padded side or bolster to nestle up against.

Wire-cage crate

Some people mistake crate training for potty training, so to be clear: The crate is not your dog's bathroom. Good crate training does facilitate good potty training, but if you insist on having your puppy potty inside your home, do not use the dog's crate as his bathroom. Instead, set up an x-pen adjoining the crate for your puppy's potty.

Soft-style crate

There are many types of dog crates. When choosing your dog's crate, factors to consider are cost, durability, portability, and style. The wire-cage style can be covered with a blanket or fitted cloth cover as long as it gets adequate ventilation. Some crates are portable and made of lightweight fabrics and mesh, similar to camping tents. Crates can also be stylish, with finishes that include molded plastic, stamped metal, wicker, and furniture-grade wood.

Plastic crate

CRATE-TRAINING PROTOCOL

Your main goal in crate training is simply to help your dog love her crate. The majority of puppies accept the crate without complaint, associating it with the comfy coziness of naptime. But if your dog isn't immediately comfortable with going in her crate, don't force her. That would be unproductive. Instead, use the following exercises to train her to like it. And remember: It's best to do this training session before your dog's meal so that she will really want the treats that you will toss around (and eventually inside) her crate. Using treats that your dog enjoys, toss a few of them around the crate and leading toward the opening, and then take a step back. Don't toss any treats inside the crate just yet. If your dog looks at you and then at the crate where the treats are, say "good" and toss a couple more treats near the crate's opening. (Have a lot on hand.) When she finishes those treats and looks to you for more, try placing a few just inside the opening, and then step back again. Little by little, toss the treats a bit deeper inside the crate.

While you do these first trials, stay silent except to praise your dog for showing any interest in the crate: sniffing around it, moving toward it, daring to go inside it. Don't say "in your crate" or any other verbal cues. Don't bend down or step forward, as your dog may be uncertain and feel cornered, which could make her averse to the crate. If your dog is already averse to the crate as some rehomed dogs are, slow the progress down and do many trials tossing treats around the crate—you may need to feed her entire meals outside her crate at first. To start helping her trust going inside the open crate, leave the door open and put treats inside, but don't force her. Be content with feeding your dog just outside the crate near the door opening. Be sure to clamp the crate door open so that it can't accidentally swing and startle her when she goes near it.

Once your dog is comfortable going inside the crate, it's time to feed part of her meal in a bowl inside the crate. Since you will also be doing the hand-feeding protocol right now, use your judgment on how much she should be allowed to eat from a bowl without you touching her. If you have been hand-feeding your dog in different parts of your home and using different bowls (as I hope you have), it will likely be easier for her to trust that it's safe to go into the crate to eat. This slow, deliberate progress is called behavior shaping, which is a technique you will use to teach your dog many training cues. You can also start getting your dog comfortable with the idea of eating in her crate by stuffing a Kong with part of her meal and setting it inside.

Your dog's next step is to eat an entire meal there. Put a portion of her meal in a bowl inside the crate and back away, leaving the crate door open; later, you will teach your dog to accept being fed with it closed. Remain silent as she goes inside to eat. When she has eaten all her food and looks to you for a refill, praise her. Continue feeding the rest of her meal in small portions. If she does not eat, she may not be ready for this step, so proceed more slowly and make sure that she is hungry when you try again. Don't force her; just praise what she does right and write that note in the training log. My Brieo is so well conditioned that when he sees me touching his food bowl, or when he comes back in the house after going potty, he'll run into his crate, whether or not I happen to feed him in his crate for that meal.

The next step is to name the crate. Naming is another technique you will use to teach your dog cues. Select the name for the crate; I suggest the obvious: "crate," "bedtime," or "den." As you place a couple of treats in it and she goes inside, say "good crate." Notice that you're not teaching her to do something that she hasn't already done, but simply giving a name to something she has been doing. Repeat this about 10 times throughout the day (for a few days), and make it a fun game by tossing kibble in and around the crate. Your dog is learning that good things happen there.

The crate is your dog's sanctuary.

Now it's time to direct your dog to go in on cue. A *cue* is a word or action that gives the dog information about what you want her to do. Start with her outside the crate. Let her see you put a few treats inside and then close the door. Open the door and say "crate." When she goes inside, say "good crate" and close the door. While she is inside, offer a few treats through the crate and praise her. Wait a few seconds before you let her out. If she stays in the crate or she goes out and goes back inside, say "good crate." When she comes out, praise her, including the words *good crate,* and close the door. Repeat this step about six times throughout the day. If you've made the exercise fun, your dog may want you to do it even more, and that's great.

Next, hold a few treats in your hand for your dog to smell, but don't put them in the crate. Open the door, say "crate," and when she goes inside, give her the treats and praise her. Repeat this step about six times. If she doesn't figure it out or resists, back up to the previous step.

The next step is to introduce her to being inside the crate for a longer time with the door closed. Start by showing your dog that you're putting some of her meal in the bowl. Hold the bowl in your hand, open the door, say "crate," and when she goes inside, say "good crate" and put the bowl inside. You may want to put some of her food in a Kong (stuffed with a special treat, like peanut butter) and place the Kong in her food bowl. As she starts to eat, gently close the door and say "good crate" again. When she finishes eating that portion of her meal, wait a few seconds before you open the door, and praise her for staying in the crate quietly, so that she understands that she's safe. Say "good crate" as she comes out, then put more kibble in her bowl or a Kong. Let her see you fill her Kong or food bowl so that she knows you are the provider of all these wonderful things, and then put the container in the crate (or simply toss kibble inside). When she goes in again, close the door while she eats. After she has finished, wait a moment again, praise her, and let her out. It is important that each time you let her out of the crate, you act like it's no big deal: no excitement, no relief, just a calm greeting and praise.

Next, ask her to go into the crate, and when she's inside, close the door for a moment, and give her the treat through an opening as you praise her and name the crate. Then open the door to let her come out, praise her and name the crate again as she exits, and close the door once she's out. If she chooses to stay inside, that's great because it means that she is understanding the process: Good things happen inside the crate! Repeat this exercise six times, each time keeping her in the closed crate for one second longer. (You will eventually add other cues, like *sit, down, settle,* and *off,* to crate training. But wait until you're into the Fundamentals Training Program before adding any of that.)

Now comes the hard part: getting your dog used to being in her crate while she can see you doing something else in the room. With your dog inside the crate, and the door closed, start by letting her see you take a step away as you put a treat through the closed door. Then return, pause a few seconds, and tell her she is a good dog in a very low-key, calm tone of voice. Then repeat the process and drop a special treat (like a piece of hard cheese) into her crate. Get up and turn away from her. Return and pause a few seconds before letting her out. Next, repeat the process, but this time give her a special toy to chew on or a stuffed Kong while she is in the crate. Increase your number of steps each time. Add some business in the room that she can see you doing, even if you're just shuffling papers, opening a bag, sitting down and watching a little TV, or getting her food ready, as you add time with each repetition. Each time you let your dog out of the crate, remember to treat it as an ordinary, almost boring moment. The goal is to teach your dog that she gets something really great in the crate when you leave (not when you return).

Associate your dog's crate with rewards and positive experiences.

The final stage in crate training involves your leaving the room. Some dogs will accept this step without complaint right away, but others may take many weeks to get through this stage, so don't press your dog to progress faster than she is ready or you may add to her anxiety and set her back in her training. Start by leaving for literally one second, returning, and letting her out. Build up time on each repetition. While you do these final-stage exercises, give your dog a Kong stuffed with treats and/or peanut butter. On each subsequent repetition, leave the room for a second or two longer. The hope is that your dog will become so engrossed in the Kong that she will barely register that you're leaving. Walk into an adjacent room and go about some business that your dog can hear, occasionally reentering to just check in on her and praise her; then leave again. When she's comfortable with that, practice keeping her in the crate when you leave your home. At first, leave as quietly as you can. Stay outside for a few minutes, and make a little noise as you reenter (but don't make a big deal). Subsequently, you can build up to being gone longer and making a little more noise as you leave. Eventually, go out and run a short errand.

Some dogs will whine or bark in their crates when you disappear from their view. If this happens, do not reappear when she's making noise, as you do not want to teach her that whining brings a reward (your return). Instead, wait until she settles down and stops whining, and then reappear quietly. Make notes in your logbook about how much time elapsed before she *started* whining, so that the next time you do this exercise, you can be sure to return more quickly, before she has a chance to get going. If your dog barks or whines for a very long time, you may need to bring in a trainer or behaviorist to determine if it's the beginning of true separation anxiety, or simply part of your dog getting used to her new home. It's counterproductive to get your dog so worked up that she gets into a pattern of barking and whining. (For more on barking problems, see page 200.) If your dog shows anxiety when you return, or there are signs that she was anxious while you were away (her pillow is shredded, for example), you may want to ask another person your dog already likes to stay in the room while you do these sets of exercises, and then start removing that person, too.

I also recommend moving your dog's crate to different rooms. Many years ago, my Irish Water Spaniel, Aisley, loved the crate when it was upstairs in my bedroom, where I also have my office. But during Aisley's training, I moved her crate downstairs to the kitchen and she barked her head off. We took a few steps backward on her training, but I continued to move Aisley's crate around to different rooms, playing crate games (such as tossing kibble in and around her crate) as we went, and she adjusted beautifully.

Throughout this training program, I recommend returning to the crate exercises if your dog's behavior backslides at all. This is not a form of punishment. Rather, it is a way to get her refocused on success. After Saxon died, Brieo understandably backslid: He didn't eat well, paced and looked for Saxon, and chewed on himself and developed a rash. I rebuilt Brieo's comfort and confidence by going back to basic crating and hand-feeding protocols; that helped a lot.

Bite Inhibition, Handling, and Gentling

All puppies play-bite when they are with their mother and littermates; it's natural behavior in the canine world. Mouthing typically occurs as a prelude to play (seen in puppies who mouth in order to encourage another dog or human to play), during play, or sometimes when he is feeling pain or physical discomfort. When a puppy bites too hard, a yelp or return bite teaches him to play more gently. Although dogs use their mouths to play and explore, they also need to learn that hard biting is not okay—ever. That's why we use handling and gentling exercises to teach them bite inhibition (also called having a "soft mouth") from the very start. Some dogs catch on right away, while others can take more than a month to get it. Merit, my Flat-Coated Retriever, took 45 days to stop biting. Ouch.

Bite inhibition protocols are different for puppies and adult dogs. For example, when a foster dog that is more than six months old comes to me that has been labeled aggressive or mouthy, I observe her behavior, body language, and eating habits to help me determine how I will approach these issues safely. The average dog owner may want to use a professional trainer or behaviorist who uses positive reinforcement methods to assess mouthing and biting behaviors, and help develop protocols for that particular dog. (For more information on aggression, see page 207.)

Biting is a natural behavior in the canine world.

Start bite inhibition training by sitting down with your puppy and putting a finger or hand in her mouth. If she mouths on you, say "ouch!" Say it loud enough so that your puppy gets the message, but not so loud that it frightens her. Let your hand go limp; do not pull it out of your puppy's mouth. When her bite slackens, say "good dog." Another technique is to tether your dog to a doorknob while you touch her mouth; if she bites, say "ouch" and walk away from her for a moment. (Remember, her punishment is that you've taken away the reward of playing with you.) Keep at this "ouch" exercise, building up to massaging your puppy's gums and counting her teeth. When she starts to lick your hand, gently praise her. Don't punish her for biting you, don't clamp her mouth shut or force your fingers down her throat. In this case, you *want* your puppy to figure it out.

Your dog will need to have her teeth examined and brushed. Once she allows you to touch her mouth freely, wrap gauze around your finger and wipe her teeth. Once she allows you to do this, you can graduate to a toothbrush.

One time, Saxon wouldn't eat his food, so I examined his mouth and found a small twig stuck in a back molar, and I removed it. If Saxon hadn't learned to be comfortable with my hands in his mouth, it could have become serious.

It's equally important that your dog be comfortable with being handled on the rest of her entire body, not just her mouth. Begin to help your puppy become accustomed to this by cradling her on her back while you rub her tummy to calm her. When she is calm, count her toes, touch her eyes, her ears, and as much of her body as she will allow. I have my students play Pass the Puppy, to get the pup used to being handled by others, and Peekaboo, by covering the puppy's eyes gently for a moment to get her used to being vulnerable. Also pretend to clip her nails with the clipping tools before you actually start using them or having a groomer do it. Ultimately, you are preparing your dog to tolerate new situations.

If your dog isn't comfortable with a particular handling or gentling exercise, try to discover the point at which she begins to get uncomfortable. Stay within her comfort range for the time being; then, at your next training session, repeat the exercise, again within her comfort range and moving on to the next step only if all goes well. If you push your dog faster than she is ready, she may shut down or become frightened. So stay alert to the limits of her comfort zone— and make sure to take play breaks between exercises.

Having a "soft mouth" is important for not only safety, but also health and hygiene.

Handling Mistakes with The Jollies

You will make mistakes that scare your new dog. You will drop something that makes a loud noise, or perhaps even accidentally falls right on her. You will stumble over your dog. You will get caught in her leash. You will turn on the TV set without realizing that the volume is cranked all the way up. These loud noises and unexpected commotions frighten almost all dogs that are new to a home.

When you accidentally frighten your dog, it's best to laugh it off immediately and play a quick round of The Jollies. Basically, you want to act as if you're having fun, in effect saying, "That is so cool that I tripped over you and dropped the groceries and now there's a broken glass jar that we all get to stay away from. Wow!" This is not unlike responding to a child who's taken a tumble. Children and dogs look to us to see if they should be upset or not. Have fun while you move your dog to safety, and continue doing The Jollies while you clean up the mess and give her a treat or two. If she's hiding, just keep doing The Jollies. Don't try to pet her or lure her out, though you may leave a few treats for her to take when she is ready. You're trying to teach her that the world is filled with unexpected and startling events, but we don't have to fear them.

Chapter Four

Week One: Fundamentals Training Program

E very year, I train hundreds of dogs—from puppies as young as seven weeks to rehomed older dogs. Many clients come to me for general training, while others seek to correct specific behavioral problems, such as poor house-training, chewing, jumping, and concerns about dominance and possible aggression. Later, in Chapter Eleven, I will discuss some common behavior problems and ways to address them, but for the next five weeks, I want you to focus on your Fundamentals Training Program.

I want to emphasize once more that training—including the potty training, crate training, and handling and gentling exercises discussed in the previous chapter—begins the moment your new dog comes home. Instead of letting your dog learn by trial and error (mostly error), help him learn what you want from the very start.

Clients often ask me how old a dog should be before training starts. My own puppies start class at seven weeks of age. Anything younger than that is too early—puppies need to remain with their mother at least that long to maximize their natural socialization skills.

This program will help you and your dog master these 10 basic skills: 1) sit, 2) recall, 3) leash walking, 4) down, 5) stay, 6) standing pose, 7) settle, 8) release, 9) off and take it, and 10) boundary training. When you use a system of positive reinforcement training methods and techniques, you will see how easy it can be to motivate your dog to learn, and to train him to follow your cues.

By the end of this five-week program, I expect that you will begin to notice a wonderful change in your dog. I call this delightful change *spiriting,* or the process of unlocking your dog's personality. The words "inspiration" and "spirit" stem from the same root, and I believe that when you spirit your dog, you inspire his best personality traits. In my classes, I get a lot of pleasure from watching that relationship form over the time I work with my students. Sometimes it seems to happen all at once: An owner who has done the homework consistently but hasn't experienced much success with his dog will come to the last night of class with a suddenly spirited dog. I love it when a dog "gets it" and wants to train. Maybe you've seen such a dog in your neighborhood: a well-trained, confident dog that loves to socialize—his owner has taught him how to be successful in our human world.

This week, we will focus on three specific skills: sit, recall (your basic "come here"), and leash walking. Dogs learn better in short bursts of time rather than in a long training session, so I recommend that you spend no longer than five minutes practicing any one exercise. At the end of each exercise, take a break and allow your dog playtime before moving on to another.

Also remember to vary the location where you practice the exercises. As we discussed with the hand-feeding protocol, dogs' brains are not naturally wired to generalize cues. Your dog may think that he needs to obey a certain cue only when he's in your kitchen facing the window on a sunny day with that bag of treats on the kitchen counter. By making sure to practice the exercises in a variety of places, at different times of day, both indoors and outdoors, you will help your dog begin generalizing every cue to different locations.

That said, expect your dog to regress when you move to another location. For instance, even if he responded brilliantly to the *sit* cue in the living room, he may have no idea what you are asking him to do now that he's in the kitchen. Be patient as you start again from the beginning.

Throughout this training program, and with each new skill you'll learn, I want you to follow three basic ground rules:

›› GROUND RULE #1: HAVE FUN. You and your dog will be more motivated if you approach these lessons expecting to enjoy yourself. There should be an air of recreation to the proceedings—it's all part of building the important habit of playing together.

›› GROUND RULE #2: DO THE HOMEWORK. Spend at least 10 minutes each day doing the homework assignments. Even if your dog has already learned a skill, or if he seems like he'll never learn it, practice it again and again. Log your effort even when there is no apparent progress. And be patient!

›› GROUND RULE #3: YOU'RE ALWAYS TRAINING. Every interaction is a learning opportunity. That includes every walk, every meal, and every time you pet your dog. And one key thing to remember: Your dog will learn better with many short bursts of training activities than with one long session.

Mind Your As and Ps

For each skill that you and your dog learn, you will progress through four stages together. My colleague, Dr. Pamela Reid, who is vice president of the ASPCA's Animal Behavior Center and a certified animal behaviorist, calls these stages the "Four As of Learning."

›› STAGE 1: ACQUIRED. The *first* session in which your dog successfully completes a new task.

›› STAGE 2: AUTOMATIC. You and your dog can *fluently* do the skill at least 80 percent of the time.

›› STAGE 3: APPLICATION. The two of you have *generalized* the skill so that you can apply it in a variety of places, including some real-life situations outside of training.

❱ **STAGE 4: ALWAYS.** The two of you maintain the skill so that it's a natural part of *everyday* life together.

This approach gives you a quick way to evaluate how you and your dog are progressing with each skill, and it will guide you to your next step. Think of each stage as a building block.

As you train, you are building a strong, benevolent relationship with your dog. In fact, dog training is also your Relationship Training System. This system emphasizes "Three Ps":

❱ **POSITIVE.** A good relationship is positive and supportive. When you use positive reinforcement, dogs enjoy learning. Unlike aversive training, my program will show you how to focus on the positive with every step.

❱ **PLAY.** Dogs enjoy people who are fun. It is essential to integrate play into training. I will show you how to get your dog hooked on positive play.

❱ **PALS.** To a dog, being a best friend means receiving loving care, sharing valuable rewards, having fun, and being a member of your pack who is valued because he follows your rules. I will help shape your relationship into one where obedience is tied to being best pals rather than adversaries.

Okay, your orientation is complete. Let's get to work.

Lures and Rewards: How to Use Training Treats

Treats are a critical component in training, so it's important that you not overfeed your dog before a training session. Hunger motivates a dog to perform. Also remember when portioning your dog's meals that training treats—some of which can be high in calories and fat—count as part of her daily diet. You will probably find that your dog likes certain treats better than others, so experiment. Ideally, like good-quality dog food, treats should be rich in protein. Treats should be tasty and as small as possible (without cheating the dog) so the dog can swallow it quickly and not lose focus on you and the next training moment. Likewise, soft treats are better to use than crunchy ones; since they can be swallowed more quickly, your dog can refocus on you right away. Anything your dog enjoys can be used as a treat reward and for luring: pieces of hotdogs, cheese, carrots, or any number of commercially available dog treats.

You will use the treats as lures, or as a tool to direct your dog to follow your hand for each cue. Since you're also hand-feeding this week, luring will be easier; your dog will be accustomed to the idea that good things are at your fingertips. Once this act of following your hand comes naturally to her—which it will, in time—you will be able to phase out the use of lures for each cue or trick.

1 LURE Hold a training treat in your fingertips at your dog's nose level and let her smell it. Move your hand slowly near her face, and watch as her head follows your hand. Continue to move your hand and watch as she follows with her nose, keeping it close to the treat.

1.

2 PRAISE AND TREAT As you lure your dog, say her name, praise her, and touch her collar as she tries to eat the treat. As long as your dog stays interested in the lure—she tries to nibble at the treat and (let's hope) not too much of your fingertips—move your hand away from her very slowly so that she follows. If your dog starts to lose interest or gets distracted, bring the lure closer to her nose and do something different: Try moving to a slightly different spot or move your hand a little more slowly or quickly. Joyfully say her name and be so interesting and emotive that she can't ignore you. After a minute—or whenever you feel that she has had enough— reward her with verbal praise, pet her collar, and finally let her eat the lure.

2.

Repeat this basic luring exercise many times a day during Week One with activities like Follow the Lure, which you'll find detailed in Chapter Nine. Keep track of your dog's progress by making notes in your logbook.

Whenever you reward your dog by allowing her to eat the treat, I want you to also get into the habit of touching her, especially around her collar. Getting your dog comfortable about being touched around her collar is important for a number of reasons. It helps with safety, especially if you need to urgently control your dog, or if she gets lost and a stranger needs to read her tags. It will also make it easier for the veterinarian and groomer to handle her, which they'll most definitely appreciate. Frequently touching your dog's collar will also help when you're ready to recall her to you. If the only time you touch your dog's collar is to put her leash back on, she may come to think that touching her collar (and recalling, by association) means that "fun is over." If that's the case, she may think that she should prolong her fun by running away from you or starting a game of Keep-away rather than coming when you call.

> *Dogs learn more easily when you are consistent.*

Each time you teach your dog a new skill or cue, use the same hand. Dogs like consistency, and they learn better when the things they're being asked to do look the same every single time. Get into the habit of being as consistent as possible with every lesson. I prefer to use my left hand because that's how I was taught. I give treats with my left hand, and I always have my dogs walk on my left side. In many training programs the left side is considered the correct side—you'll see that in dog shows almost all dogs are on the handler's left side—but either side is okay, just as long as you make a choice and stick with it while your dog becomes fluent (learning stage #2) for each new skill. After that, you can experiment with using either hand to lure and signal your dog, which will help her generalize.

Although many trainers like to put the treats in a pouch that clips onto the belt, I find that dogs often become so focused on the treat pouch that they don't focus enough on you. When I first started training Ebony, I forgot to take the treat pouch to class one evening, and she simply refused to work! I stopped using the pouch altogether after that, and now put training treats in my pocket. If you walk your dog on your left side, you should put your training treats in your left pocket so they're easy to reach and dole out at any moment. Remember to clean out your pockets before you put those pants in the laundry or you'll get grease stains. If you're intent on using a treat pouch, I recommend clipping it to your belt in the middle of your back where your dog can't see it, rather than at your hip where she may be continually tempted and distracted.

The Dog That Doesn't Respond to Food as a Lure

Not all dogs initially value food as a reward. If you have such a dog, try experimenting with different kinds of treats, including fresh meats that require refrigeration. I sometimes use human food—such as small pieces of hot dog, cooked chicken, cheese, raw or cooked carrots—as treats, because that way I can put a treat in my own mouth so the dog will stay focused on my face and body language. Also be careful not to overtreat your dog. If you give your dog treats throughout the day, and not just in response to good behaviors in training, it's likely that she will very soon stop valuing the treat.

What do you do if your dog simply won't respond to treats as a reward? Work to find out what she does value, and give that to her. Some dogs like to be touched, or prefer a brief round of play with a special toy. Some like soothing verbal praise the best, although I find that to be quite rare, occurring mostly in dogs with anxiety problems or a history of neglect or abuse.

If your dog works for the reward of playing with a special toy, then you need to limit the amount of time she plays with that toy, or use it exclusively for training purposes. Look ahead to Off and Take It Trades (page 117), because you'll need to adapt those techniques to trading for another toy; otherwise, your dog may be reluctant to give up the toy when you need her to. This can lead you to play "chase the dog," which will undermine effective training. Sometimes you can create desire in your dog by "selling" her on how great a toy is. For example, offer to play short games of fetch and then put the toy away before she gets bored and stops playing with you; you stop the game while she is eager to continue. Be careful not to oversell a toy that she doesn't like; I'm pretty sure you'll discover that your dog is too smart to fall for that one very many times!

It's a trickier situation if your dog works primarily for affection, because you certainly don't want to withhold affection from your beloved dog. In brief, you need to give your dog a clear signal that tells her that training has now begun and that she will get affection from you when she does what you need her to do. Such signals include petting a special toy (or petting the ground near her) while you make happy sounds, and as soon as she focuses on you, lure her to sit. In time, she will recognize that consistent happy "ritual" as a fun time for her to earn your extra affection.

If none of these techniques works, consult a dog behavior specialist or experienced trainer to determine if there is some problem that needs to be addressed. (Remember: Always choose an experienced professional who uses positive reinforcement training.) Talk to your veterinarian to rule out any underlying medical issues that may be affecting your dog's behavior.

Luring to Sit

Since *sit* is the most fundamental dog training cue, let's begin with that. Your dog will learn many other basic behaviors—such as *come, stay, down,* and *standing pose*—from the sit position. You should think of *sit* as your dog's ready position. If this were military training, *sit* would be like standing at attention. If this were a ballet studio, *sit* would be first position. My dog Brieo, foster dog Boz, and all dogs that board with me are required to sit for *everything* from the moment they get up in the morning to the moment they go to sleep at night. They sit when I open or close doors, when I come home and greet them, at mealtime, when it's time to go on a walk, when they get in and out of the car, and before and after playtime and training. Having your dog sit for everything emphasizes that you are your dog's benevolent leader, and that he takes his direction from you. Your dog will also learn that sitting is how he says "please," for which he is often rewarded with a treat. I don't like to anthropomorphize dogs, but in this case it's instructive to put words in your dog's mouth. "When I sit, the food bowl appears and I get to eat," he might say, or "When I sit, the door opens and we go for a walk."

As you teach your dog to sit, use only the lure at this stage, and don't say anything at all, like "sit" or "sit, Brieo." This may be challenging at first, because language is, of course, the primary tool we humans use to communicate. But the natural canine orientation is not verbal, it's visual. Verbal cues will just sound like noise to your dog and will get in the way of his acquiring the lure concept. You will be tempted! But, for the time being, your focus is on getting your dog used to following the motion of the lure. Also, if you have a rehomed dog that already understands verbal cues, I want you to stop using them, and retrain him, starting by luring with your hand signals. This will encourage him to watch you. I want your dog's attention focused on you while he is acquiring each new skill. In later lessons, we will add the verbal cues (a process we call naming the behavior).

1 LURE HIM TO YOU To begin, hold a lure in your fingertips. Touch the treat to your dog's nose and let him sniff it, as in the basic luring exercise (page 66).

2 RAISE THE LURE Now raise the lure slowly, straight up above his head. When his head begins to tilt up, continue slowly raising the lure. As he continues to follow the lure, his head will tilt up and his rump will lower to the floor. It's simple physics. The moment his rump touches the floor, say "good" as you feed him the treat and pet his collar with your other hand. Give him five seconds of joyful verbal and physical praise. I typically say "What a good puppy, good Brieo, what a good dog." I want your dog focused on you and, ideally, staring at you. You're also teaching him to make eye contact with you, which will further strengthen your bond and keep him highly focused on you. If he seems distracted, increase your enthusiasm: You need to be the most interesting thing in the world to your dog.

1.

2.

Some dogs will get this cue right away. Not so for others. If your dog seems to have trouble figuring out what you're asking him to do and won't sit for you even after several training sessions, you want to dissect the whole action into smaller parts. We call this breaking down a cue, or rewarding for the smallest successes, even for simply lifting his head. If his nose goes up in the air, treat him. Little by little, get your dog to move his nose a half inch higher on each subsequent repetition. Once you get his nose pointing toward the sky, his rump will automatically start to lower. Treat him as his rump starts to move down. On the next rep, reward him when his rump is a half inch lower. Eventually he'll touch down.

Be patient. Assume that it will take 10 repetitions of this exercise before your dog connects putting his rump on the floor with getting a treat. To your dog, getting the treat the first time probably seems like an accident; the second time, it becomes a coincidence. Once he makes the connection—sitting and treat go together—it becomes a learned pattern.

Even if it takes your dog 15 to 25 reps to make the connection, believe me, the more repetitions and practice time you put into this exercise, the easier it will be each time you work with your dog. You are giving him a very important foundation in teaching him to follow your lure. If you or your dog is bored because it's too slow, or you're frustrated because he isn't getting it, take a break before the dog totally loses interest. Do another quick activity the dog enjoys, such as a brief game of Follow the Lure. Make notes in your training log, and try a different activity for a while. If you're going to train for more than two minutes at a time, add some variety with one of the homework games or activities in Chapter Nine after each two-minute training exercise. If training is not mixed with playtime experiences, you may undermine your dog's confidence level and enjoyment of training.

Timing and Voice Marking

Doing many repetitions will help train *you* to have good timing: delivering the positive feedback at exactly the right moment to mark the behavior you want your dog to do. For example, when you say "good" the moment your dog's rump touches the floor, you are letting her know she has completed the task you were asking her to do. You're using the word *good* as a marker; if your timing is off, your dog will accidentally learn the wrong lesson because you marked the wrong moment. For example, if you mark "good" too late, your dog may understand that it's good when she tilts her head or opens her mouth or wags her tail. You want her to associate "good" with her rump touching the floor. So, as you repeat each exercise, make sure that you mark your praise precisely—in this case, the moment your dog's rump touches the floor.

You can use other marker words besides *good*. Common markers include "thank you" and "yes!" Whatever marker word you teach your dog, use it consistently, including how you pronounce the word. Try to say it the exact same way each time: at the same volume, in the same tone, and with the same level of emotion. Learning to give your dog well-timed markers is essential to *your* training, so work the program by doing many sets of reps with the intention of learning to give well-timed feedback markers consistently.

Perhaps you've heard about trainers who use clickers to mark a dog's good behavior. Basically, you click instead of saying "good." It's simply easier to click precisely at the right moment. Personally, I love the clicker. But I prefer voice markers during the five-week fundamentals course, because it's very important that your dog focus on you as much as possible—and that means the sounds you make as well as your physical motions. Also, because you're trying to coordinate so many new gestures, I think that learning the clicker right now can get in the way. But if you can't wait to start working with a clicker, flip ahead to Chapter Ten (page 153), where I introduce clicker training, before you move ahead to the next exercises.

A note on saying your dog's name: Use your dog's name only in the course of praise and reward. Never say your dog's name when you're trying to correct her behavior, such as when you tell her to get off the couch, to stop mouthing your hand, or to drop some contraband. For example, while I often say "good Brieo!" I never say "no, Brieo, get down" or "drop that, Brieo!" You don't want to inadvertently train your dog to associate her name with punishment. That can delay bonding and slow the learning process; some dogs may stop responding to their names.

When you call your dog by name in a negative association, play a round or two of the Name Game (page 143) as soon as possible.

Luring to Recall, Part One

Recalling means that your dog comes to you when you signal him. Recalls are initially important for your dog's safety, but they eventually allow you to give your dog more freedom; a dog that develops excellent recall skills can be granted more liberties and has more opportunities to socialize. Since recall can be a challenging behavior for many dogs to master, I have found it most effective to break down the cue and teach the last part of the cue first. That's right, this week you will teach your dog only the *last* part of the cue: sitting when he gets to you.

You'll need a partner for this exercise; if you have children, this is a wonderful training exercise to include them in. Ask your partner to hold your dog's leash. Put a treat in your hand and take three steps back. Lure your dog by holding the treat toward him, and then bringing it toward your knee. Have your partner release the leash. As your dog arrives, lure him to sit, using the hand motion I described earlier (page 70). Once he sits, mark it (say "good"), praise him, and reward him with the treat.

If your dog comes to you but doesn't sit, praise him but don't treat him. Then back up another three steps and repeat the exercise: Lure him by drawing the treat from his nose to your knee. If your dog doesn't sit on the repeat try either, do it once more: Praise him (no treat), back up three steps, and try it again. If he is still not sitting on the third try, give him the treat and praise anyhow, to reward his good recall. This means your dog isn't quite ready to link the sit with the recall. That's okay. Just continue to teach him to sit using the luring exercises above, and practice the recall/sit again in your next session. You may choose to decrease the distance to help him gain confidence and understand that he is being rewarded for following your instructions. This is known as building a positive reinforcement history.

If your dog is consistently coming to you and sitting on cue, try backing up a few more steps each time. Remember to use the same hand to cue and treat your dog.

Eye-Contact Exercise

Now for the fun part: I'd like you to end this recall exercise by spending a few minutes training your dog to look at your eyes. Once you've got this simple and fun exercise down, do it several times a day, at random intervals. Eye contact is crucial for bonding and for focus, so start practicing this with very young puppies. Pretty soon they'll be watching your each and every move.

To begin, touch a treat to your dog's nose, and allow her to sniff it. As soon as her interest is established, bring the treat to your eyes, say "good," and silently count off two seconds. If she stays focused on the treat for two seconds, feed it to her. On the next rep, add one extra second. On each successful repetition, add an additional second.

Continue to silently count the seconds, and to say "good" in a happy, rewarding voice. Take a small step to the side before you begin the next rep so that your dog begins to generalize the behavior to slightly different locations.

If your dog turns her head or breaks eye contact, move to another position and try again for a second. Do not reward her if she breaks eye contact, or you might accidentally train her to look away from you. If your dog is a jumper, step on her leash so that she can't jump up while doing this exercise.

I find that some breeds naturally do this better than others. For example, in my experience, Jack Russell Terriers are generally more easily distracted than German Shepherds; but I've also seen the opposite. Remember: All dogs attain success at their own pace.

Leash Walking: "Be a Tree"— The First Steps Together

One of my favorite things in the world is taking my dogs for long walks, which I generally do twice a day. We'll often wander down one of the horse trails on my property. Not only are our walks great exercise for them and for me, but all the exciting sights and smells help keep the dogs curious and engaged.

I can tell you, though, that the walks would be no fun at all if Brieo and Boz pulled on their leashes. We've all seen it: the dog that appears to be dragging its owner down the street, from fire hydrant to lamppost to garbage bin. You want to train your dog to walk on a loose leash, fairly close to your side. The goal isn't the perfect *heel*—that's unrealistic for any but the most focused animal. Even in elite dog shows, those highly trained dogs stay perfectly focused on the handler for only the brief moments when the spotlight is on them. I tell you that so that you'll have more patience and confidence as you teach your dog to walk on a leash. If he's the rare exception that doesn't pull, this is your lucky day and my only advice to you is to count your blessings and buy a lottery ticket.

If you walk your dog on your left side, hold the leash handle in your right hand and grip the middle of the leash in your left, so that the leash crosses in front of your body. If you prefer to walk him on the right side, do the opposite. Even though I sometimes loop the handle over my wrist, be careful: You want to avoid injury if your dog pulls too hard. If you use a Martingale collar, a head halter, or a body harness (preferably one that clips to the leash at the dog's chest rather than his back), your position when you hold the leash is the same.

The point of this training session—which should last no longer than five minutes—is to get your dog used to walking on the leash the way you want him to. I recommend that you use a six-foot leash and come prepared with lots of treats.

1 FOCUS FIRST Before you take your first steps together, make sure that your dog is focused on you. Then hold a treat in your left hand and lure your dog in the direction you want to walk. If you have a small dog, get ready to bend down a lot. Start walking forward, allowing a lot of slack in the leash.

2 "BE A TREE" When your dog starts to pull, stop walking, hold the leash tight to your chest, and stand still and firm, like a tree.

1.

3 MARK AND REWARD The moment he looks at you, say "good" and lure him toward you with the treat as you take two steps backward. Praise him, touch his collar, and reward him with the treat. Your timing needs to be precise, so watch for that moment when he looks at you, even if for only an instant at first, because that's when his attention is returning to you.

If your dog doesn't look at you, break down the lesson and reward his tiny improvements. If he continues to lean forward against the leash without trying to take a step, look for the moment when he slackens the leash and praise that. If

2.

he still doesn't give you attention, make a slight sound to attract him. If that doesn't work, silently "reel yourself in" to your dog (don't pull him toward you, but go hand-over-hand up the leash as if you were pulling yourself up a rope), and then lure him to start walking in the opposite direction. If he looks at you as you reel yourself in, praise, stop reeling, and lure. Remember that this isn't a walk for distance or heeling; it's a five-minute walking exercise to teach you how to hold a leash and to manage pulling. Be patient.

As you practice this exercise throughout the week, try to change it up to keep your dog interested and to generalize the behavior. Change directions as you walk. If you prefer to do this indoors, walk around objects, like chairs or tables. Try increasing the speed at which you walk, and practice making abrupt turns—not to trick your dog into making mistakes, but to see if you can use your lures and a fun voice to keep him completely focused on you.

In later weeks, we'll add distractions, such as another dog or an interesting human, but don't intentionally add them just yet. I want your dog to experience as much success as possible. If you are practicing this exercise outdoors and you encounter a person who wants to greet your dog, stop walking, step on the leash, and clutch the handle to your chest, to keep your dog still. If he is able to sit, request a *sit,* mark it, and praise and reward him. If he doesn't sit yet, manage the situation by stepping on the leash so he can't jump up while you meet the person. Stepping on the leash allows your dog to sit, stand (pose), or lie down, but he can't jump. Say a brief hello and calmly let the person know that you need to focus on training.

For now, it's best to try to anticipate and avoid distractions as often as possible.

Socialization Exercises

F ar too many dogs are surrendered to shelters or rescue organizations because they are not well socialized. This is far more often the fault of the owner than it is a reflection on the dog. As owners, it is our responsibility to take the time to socialize our dogs—with people, as well as with other animals—from the very beginning. That's why you should spend at least one session this week (as well as throughout the five-week program) training in the presence

It is our responsibility to socialize our dogs.

of other people, and, if your dog is fully vaccinated, with other dogs. If you know people with dogs, set up an indoor or outdoor playdate or playgroup. If not, ask your vet or groomer for names of people with well-behaved dogs. As your dog first socializes with other dogs, you may want to consider choosing dogs about the same size as yours, especially with teacup-size puppies.

Here's an exercise I like to do when I train with another person and his dog. Begin by allowing just two minutes off-leash (within a fenced area if outdoors) free playtime. Then recall your respective dogs. Because your dog is still learning the *recall* cue, you may need to physically interrupt her play-time by approaching her and luring her with the hand signal we practiced: treat to her nose, then to your knee. Spend at least 10 seconds praising your dog, and take a few moments to practice the *sit* cue. Treat her, and then release her for another round of play. It is important that you interrupt the play for three reasons: 1) to help build successful recall, 2) to teach your dog that recall does not mean the end of playtime, and 3) to remind your dog that she needs to keep you as her primary focus. Do this play-and-recall exercise for four rounds. This exercise can be used on dogs of all ages, although young puppies usually learn it more quickly than older untrained dogs. If your dog doesn't recall well from these play rounds, you may need to rely a bit on your training partner's ability to lure (or at least distract) the other dog, and then step between the dogs to lure yours.

If at the end of those four rounds your dogs seem to want to continue to play, try another activity, such as training your respective dogs near each other. But don't force the playdate to go any longer than is comfortable, and try to end on a positive note, ideally with both dogs (and both owners) want-ing to play again next time.

A few tips on being around other dogs: During these brief, off-leash play periods, observe whether your puppy hides or exhibits any aggression. If she needs to get away from the other dog, don't pick her up or you will teach her to want to jump up when she feels uncomfortable or feels a desire to be rescued, which could make her more fearful. Instead, let her move between your legs if she feels more comfortable there, and then have the other owner redirect his dog's attention (ideally, by luring and then having the dog sit to regain focus). I urge caution on taking your dog to a dog park at this stage, and I talk more about dog parks in Chapter Twelve. If you have a rehomed dog, you will probably want to socialize her for briefer periods as you dis-cover her comfort zone and behavior triggers and issues.

Okay, class dismissed. Remember to make your homework fun.

Orientation to Homework

In Chapter Nine, I have detailed 26 activities and games designed to help you and your dog have fun while you master the lessons in each chapter. I strongly suggest that you spend at least 10 minutes a day doing a few of these activities and games. The games are also good to shift to when your dog doesn't succeed at behavior you're trying to teach.

Why is doing your homework so important? In training your dog, you are engaging in a process called conditioning—you are modifying your dog's natural behavior to do what you want. Simply put, conditioning means learning through association. The more repetitions you do, followed by a reward, the more he expects that the next repetition will earn him the same reward. Eventually, he will become fully conditioned: He will perfect each cue (perform each behavior) without a treat or other reward. But that's only going to happen if *you* put in the time and effort.

As I've stated, dogs learn better with many brief lessons than with one long one, and you can turn 60 seconds into a mini-lesson. Having many short lessons throughout the day will help keep your dog in an always-learning attitude.

As you begin doing homework this week, I want you to focus on the fun of it. Celebrate the successes, laugh at the failures. Your dog loves fun and will be more confident when he's having a good time with you. Establish a pattern of having fun in your first week and it will carry with you throughout this course. In my classes, I often refer to homework as "funwork," especially when kids are in attendance. When a kid hears me say the word "homework," I can see his enthusiasm deflate quicker than a leaky balloon, and then fill right back up when I say that it's actually funwork. I'd like you to bring that attitude to homework this week.

Recommended Games and Activities

Add variety and fun to the training experience by playing these games (see details in Chapter Nine):

» Name Game

» Eye-Contact Exercise

» Follow the Lure

» Pass the Puppy and Peekaboo emphasize bite inhibition, handling, and gentling (assuming that there are no outstanding behavior issues)

» "Ouch" exercises: explore dog's mouth, count teeth and toes

Chapter Five

Week Two: Training in Everyday Life

For this week, and each subsequent week, we are going to build on the skills that your dog learned the previous week. If your dog can't keep pace with any of the lessons, that's okay. This isn't about getting a grade or comparing your dog with other dogs. It's about helping him have a great life with you. Proceed at the pace that works best for your dog and you.

If this means that you have to spend a lot of time this week reviewing last week's exercises, do that. In my classes, I always have dogs that can't do certain cues during the week I teach them. I remind those owners to continue to

help their dogs be successful, not to push them too hard, and to stay committed to the exercises—their dogs *will* get it. Trust me on that.

If you and your dog are ready to progress on to new skills this week,
then we will begin to integrate his training experiences into daily life. For
example, the tethering exercise will prepare him for anticipating your body
language during walks. We will also continue to work on the *recall* cue, and
begin to teach the *down* position.

Tethering

L et's begin with a quick and simple tethering exercise that you can practice for about 5 to 10 minutes every day—you'll find it a nice break
between more difficult exercises. Begin by tethering your dog to your belt
(see page 45), and be sure to have a few treats ready. Start moving around,
adding a few distractions along the way. If you're training inside your home,
walk calmly around tables and chairs, go into various rooms, sit and watch
television, talk on the phone, browse the Internet, or update your Facebook
page with your dog's photo. While tethered, do a few simple acts like filling
your dog's water bowl, touching the outside of his crate as you walk around
it, reaching into his crate and touching his sleeping mat (straighten it up or
fluff his bed). If you're training outside, tether yourself to your dog and move
around a small area in a somewhat random pattern: Take out a few objects
(like a brush, toy, and towel), set one on the ground and move away from it,
set down another object, and another, then pick them up in a different order
and put them away. As you do this exercise, notice every time your dog looks
at you, mark it by saying "good," touch his collar, pet him for a moment, and
reward him with one treat.

When you move, don't try to trick your dog with abrupt turns. In fact,
try to give him hints as to your next move by shuffling your feet as you turn,
bending down a little, swinging your arms around smoothly, or clapping
lightly. The more success your dog has (and the more he's rewarded), the
more likely that he will want to continue doing that behavior. Eventually this
bonding exercise will become habit to your dog: He will focus on you during
walks and while off leash at home or outside.

I want to remind you of some general reasons to practice tethering that
we introduced in Chapter Three. When you tether your dog to your belt
loop, you are literally keeping him close to you, helping him learn your body

cues as you turn, change speeds, pause, and start again. Tethered to you, he learns, with practice, to pay close attention to you and walk at your pace. And vice versa—*you* will learn to anticipate *his* body language: how he starts to drift away from you and explore something, or tries to go toward a room or object that's off-limits. If he misbehaves in some manner—say, he begins to venture toward something off-limits (perhaps that special couch) or to go potty inside—you will be so close that you can immediately direct him to stop pulling, drop contraband, or move away from an off-limits area or object.

Sit: Your Dog's Real-Life Rewards System

I want you to begin to ask your dog to sit for everything, including her meals. Because you're still hand-feeding this week, ask her to sit before every scoop of food you offer. Once she sits, it's okay if she stands up to eat, as long as she doesn't jump on you or at your hand. Once she's finished each portion, ask her to sit before feeding her again. Remember to practice this exercise in different places, including in her crate if crate training has progressed to that level.

Asking your dog to sit for everything (and not just during a training exercise) is what I call a real-life rewards system—a way to teach your dog the relevance of what *sit* actually means throughout the day. Your dog will understand that when she sits she gets a reward: to play with the toy that you are showing her, or to eat the food in the bowl that you are holding, or to go through the door that you are ready to open for her. She also will understand that when she does not sit, she gets a punishment: She doesn't get to hold the toy, eat the food, or walk

Asking your dog to sit for everything is her real-life rewards system.

through the door. As we began learning last week, the *sit* is your dog's ready position, and it should become her way of saying "please, may I?" In addition, you want to generalize the cue by training your dog in various locations and while out on walks.

Remember that we still haven't introduced the verbal cue for *sit*. My students are constantly forgetting this: They really have to concentrate on not using the verbal cue at this stage. The same will hold true for you: The more you practice your homework, the more natural it will become for you to use only the luring motion for *sit* at this stage. We'll introduce the verbal cue later.

Withdrawing Treats: Slot Machine and Jackpot Psychology

Once you have reached that 80 percent automatic threshold for *sit,* meaning that your dog sits on cue 8 out of 10 times, stop rewarding him with a treat at the end of every success. An interesting thing happens when you begin withdrawing treats that your dog has come to expect: He tries harder to get the treat, which keeps him interested in training.

Withdrawing some of the treats uses what I call "slot machine psychology." Ask yourself: Why do humans gamble? Because we know there's the possibility of a payoff but we enjoy the uncertainty of not knowing if or when it's going to come. The same thing holds true for your dog. Behaviorists have discovered that once a dog first acquires a skill (learning stage #1), the most effective way to reinforce that skill so that it becomes an "always" behavior (learning stage #4) is by using unpredictable and random rewards. It's just as psychologist Edward Thorndike posited about a hundred years ago in his trial-and-error theory of learning (now a cornerstone of modern behavioral psychology): Once they've been rewarded, dogs will try to figure out how to get that reward again. And *you* are the dog's slot machine.

An important component of this technique is a reward called jackpots—a virtual puppy bonanza. Instead of rewarding your dog with one treat, you give him 7 to 10, one at a time. (This will feel like a much bigger reward than if he eats them all in one gulp.) Be sure to say "good" with extra enthusiasm each time you dole out a treat in the jackpot. Awarding jackpots will increase your dog's curiosity, self-confidence, and enjoyment of training. Getting 10 treats is fun!

Let me illustrate how this works with an example. Imagine the first time your dog starts to sit even though your lure barely moved above his nose. This means he probably understands that your hand motion is asking him to sit. Now, *that* is worth a jackpot. Of course, his sitting may have been an accident, but that's okay. If he sits a bit quicker on the next trial after the first jackpot, I like to award another, smaller jackpot (a couple of extra treats rewarded one at a time). Here's what your dog may be thinking after two jackpots in a row: "That first jackpot may have been an accident, but, hey, maybe that second one was more than a coincidence; possibly there was a correlation between my sitting and that yummy food." Okay, your dog isn't thinking in that vocabulary, but psychologists like Thorndike, Ivan Pavlov, B. F. Skinner, and others have established that dogs like to figure out the cause of their successes and how to win repeat rewards.

Once they've been rewarded, dogs will try to figure out how to get that reward again. And you are the dog's slot machine.

It's not uncommon that a dog's success rate momentarily drops off after a jackpot; his own excitement may distract him and cause him to lose his focus. That's okay. The drop will most likely be temporary. If, however, the success rate drops below the 80 percent rate after a behavior has been learned, it may mean that your dog is bored or temporarily burned out, and needs to move on to another activity, such as a fun game of Peekaboo (page 60) or one of the other activities that your dog can already succeed at.

As your dog continues to master each cue, you will withdraw treats. When your dog achieves total mastery for a cue (which may take a number of weeks, so be patient), you will have withdrawn treat rewards altogether for that cue. We've introduced that mastery stage as learning stage #4: always. As you withdraw treats for one cue, it is important to begin another cue with treat rewards so that your dog stays interested in training. This technique builds his desire for lifelong learning.

Modifying the Sit Hand Signal: From Lure to Cue

Once your dog has moved to learning stage #2, automatic, for the *sit* cue and you have begun to introduce the slot machine techniques of withdrawing and jackpotting treats, it is time to modify the lure motion into a hand signal. Using a hand signal will allow you to gesture to your dog to sit when you stand a little farther away from her.

1 FOCUS FIRST The starting hand position is the same in both the luring movement and the modified cue: The hand is upturned and the fingertips hold a treat. Even though you've started to phase out treats, bring them back as you teach this (or any) new skill. Start by putting your hand into the starting hand position.

1.

2 HAND SIGNAL Next, raise your fingertips just above her nose, then slowly and deliberately straight up into the air. The moment her rump touches down, stop signaling, mark, praise, touch her collar, and treat her. If she succeeded in responding to this cue on this first attempt, that is worth a jackpot. The speed with which she responds to your modified cue becomes the new baseline for how high you raise your hand on the next rep.

2.

Sit Cue: Withdrawing Treats

Next comes a big learning step: Will your dog sit when you give the hand cue and are *not* holding a treat in your fingertips? Start this step by palming a treat in the hand that you use to give the visual hand signal, and palm another treat in your other hand. Try the hand signal cue as you had been doing previously, touching your fingertips lightly to your dog's nose, sliding the cue straight up above her nose, slowly and smoothly. The moment her rump touches down, mark it by saying "good," praise her, touch her collar, and finally, reward her with the treat in your cueing hand followed by the treat in your other hand. You may also put a few treats in your other hand to anticipate that first jackpot success. If she doesn't succeed, that's okay. Just turn around with her and try again. If she doesn't succeed on the next trial, go back to holding the treat in your fingertips for another few reps before trying this step again. It's okay to help your dog win this next jackpot by repeating the step she already knows a couple more times before returning to try this new step again.

Once your dog consistently succeeds at this step for about five trials, on the next rep, don't palm a treat in your cueing hand; instead palm a jackpot in your other hand. If she sits on your cue, mark it, offer praise, touch her collar, and finally, reward that jackpot. Continue for a few more reps like this, and then bring in the slot machine: Make the rewards unpredictable.

To prevent boredom, be sure to mix some playtime into the learning phase by working on other behaviors that she knows, or experiment by tossing a ball or toy, or simply pet her. These brief play breaks keep you and your dog in the spirit of learning. Also, remember to generalize to different locations; as your dog gets it, try locations that are slightly more distracting—how about a random *sit* during a walk? Little by little, she will recognize the starting hand-signal position and will watch your every move. As you continue rewarding her successes with treats, play breaks, games, and your affection, you are likely to discover that she gains confidence and starts to offer behaviors that you didn't even ask for, such as a paw shake or bringing a toy to you. When that happens, thank your dog with all the excitement of having just won the lottery yourself, and give her a jackpot.

Recall: Luring at a Distance and Adding the Verbal Cue

Last week, we learned the end of the important *recall* cue: that moment when your dog arrives in front of you. This week, we will acquire the whole cue by increasing the recall distance, still keeping a *sit* at the end. Start by practicing your dog's current baseline distance, whether it's three steps with a *sit* or one step without a *sit*. If he doesn't yet sit at the end of the recall, I want you and your dog to acquire that behavior before you add the distance. You may need to adapt the techniques in last week's *recall* exercise, such as starting with the *sit* exercise and then, once it has been acquired (learning stage #1), add a half step *recall* and acquire that. Add slight generalizations, such as moving a half step to the side. Then gradually increase the distance, even if it is only by inches at a time.

Once your dog has acquired the *recall* with the *sit* at a distance of three steps, you can practice this exercise with a partner. I recommend doing it indoors, ideally in a well-lit hallway with all doors closed. This will keep your dog from becoming too distracted, and help him stay focused on you more easily.

Your partner will hold the dog by the leash. Act very excited as you touch a treat to your dog's nose, tease him for a moment without giving him the treat, then turn and run four feet away. Stop and turn to face your dog. If he pulls on the leash, that means he is paying close attention to you! In that case, I recommend that your partner gently hold him in place bodily; you don't want the dog to pull harshly (which could hurt his neck) or learn a bad habit. Now you'll add a verbal cue. As you turn, happily say your dog's name and add, in an upbeat tone, "Come here!" At this point, your partner lets go of the leash.

Do all you can to attract your dog to come to you: Crouch (or even kneel on the floor for a puppy or small dog), pat your hands together (don't clap loudly if your dog startles easily), and lure him to come right in front of you (not to your side, but facing directly at your knees). As he arrives, cue the *sit*. When his rump touches down, praise him with extra excitement, touch his collar, and give him the treat. I call this exercise the Lassie Recall in honor of the TV show, because Timmy petted and praised Lassie each time she returned after having been lost.

If your dog is successful at this distance, add a little more distance on the next repetition; if not, shorten the distance a little. On subsequent reps, change it up: Sit, crouch, stand, switch ends of the hallway, or move to another spot entirely as you lure your dog to you.

If he isn't coming right to you when you call him, try these techniques:

» While your partner holds the leash, run back and forth between your dog and the spot, making playful sounds and movements. Each time you return to your dog, touch the treat gently to his nose so that he can smell it.

» Try running with your dog to the destination, then put him in a *sit* and treat him.

» Have your partner let go of the leash as you begin running away. This is called a *chase recall,* because the dog will try to catch up to you. *Chase recalls* are fun for most dogs; thus they increase the dog's desire to catch up to you and come when called.

A note on verbal cues: Since *come here* is the first verbal cue that your dog will learn in this training program, let's take a minute to consider the whole notion of verbal cues. If I were calling Brieo, I would say in my happy voice, "Brieo, come here!" The tone is not commanding; it is excited and playful. I prefer the cue words *come here* over a simple *come,* because the word *here* helps your voice to sound excited and happy, while the word *come* by itself can sound too commanding.

Try to say your dog's name only in a positive context, including at the start of any positive cue.

Add your dog's name to the beginning of any positive cue (including *recall* and *sit*), but remember not to add your dog's name when it is a negative or boundary cue (such as staying off the furniture). Also, be sure to say the cue only once. For example, don't say "Come here, Brieo, come here. Come," or "Sit-sit-sit-sit" even if your dog doesn't sit.

Repeating a cue can cause what behaviorists call learned irrelevance: When we repeat a cue (to sit, for example), our dog learns that the first time we say "sit" is irrelevant, and that he needs to wait until we say the word five times in a row and with a certain tone before he is supposed to sit. Don't accidentally teach your dog to think that the sounds coming out of your mouth are irrelevant. This is why it's very important to pay attention to your verbal cues, consistently offering them only once and always in the same tone of voice. If your dog doesn't get the cue, simply turn around and start over again with the lure. When he succeeds, remember to mark and reward.

Down: Luring Your Dog into a Down Position

If you ever need to control your dog in an urgent safety situation, such as avoiding an aggressive dog or a distraction that makes her either fearful or overly excited, you will be grateful that the *down* cue is part of her repertoire. *Down* is also a building-block cue when you get to *settle down* and relax, which you'll learn in Week Four.

Your dog is ready to learn *down* when she can *sit* fairly reliably. The cue takes advantage of her natural tendency to move her body to follow a lure, so it is an appropriate cue to learn after *sit*.

1 START AT SIT With your dog in the *sit* position, hold a lure in your fingertips with your palm turned down.

1.

2 LURE DOWN Slide the lure toward your dog's chest. Just before you touch her chest, lure straight down to the floor, staying close to her body.

2.

3 PRAISE, THEN TREAT LAST If she drops straight down, mark it (say "good"), praise her, touch her collar, reward her with the treat . . . and count your blessings, because your dog is already well on her way to mastering the *down.*

3.

Practice a handful of reps and begin to generalize by moving a step to the side and turning around and moving to a different spot. In subsequent homework sessions, generalize into different spaces. If your dog is a really fast learner for the *down,* begin to modify your lure motion into the actual hand signal cue by shortening the slide into her chest and then moving your palm downward slowly and smoothly to the floor. Remember to jackpot her and start to withdraw treat rewards using slot machine psychology as she becomes fluent for the cue. On subsequent reps and in future training sessions, generalize this behavior to various other places in your home and on walks.

Many dogs need help learning *down* because they tend to stand up out of the *sit* when the lure is offered. If your dog stands up, don't worry about it; she is trying to figure out what you want her to do. Let her work it through. Just take her back to *sit* and try again. The *down* will come with time, patience, and practice.

Another option for helping your dog learn *down* is to shape the cue by using a temporary breakdown learning step: Sit on the floor with your knees bent. Lure your dog to crawl under your legs. The only way she can get the lure is by dropping all the way down and crawling a step or two under your leg. This temporary breakdown step helps your dog become familiar with moving toward the *down* position. Some dogs are not naturally comfortable doing a *down* because the position may seem too vulnerable, or they may not understand what you're asking them to do. Once you have succeeded with this temporary breakdown shaping step, continue to work it over and over as you see her become more comfortable. By breaking it down, you make it easier for her to figure out what you want her to do, which decreases failure, which is always good.

Once she becomes comfortable doing the *down* this way, begin luring her under only one leg. As she succeeds with this step, you can withdraw this leg, too. When she begins to respond more quickly without having to crawl under your legs anymore, that tells you that she is getting it and trusts you to be in this vulnerable position. Remember to give your dog plenty of successful trials even if you have to proceed more slowly than you would like. Your patience will be rewarded.

Release: The Verbal Cue

You want to be able to tell your dog that she has done a good job and is now free to take a recess from training and be on her own for a while. That's where *release* comes in. Begin to teach the cue as you finish practicing each exercise and transition into a brief play period mixed with behaviors that your dog already knows well. Mixing the total freedom of the *release* with some practice cues will keep her focused and happy to do or try out just about anything you request. If you're not at the end of a training session, but sense that your dog needs a break, limit each *release* recess period to about a minute. If your dog has too much playtime, she may lose focus and forget about you. If you're training with a partner who also has a dog, release your dogs at the same time so that they can play together.

The simplest way to teach *release* is to drop your dog's leash—assuming that you're indoors or in a fenced area so that she can't run completely away—and say "release" or "go play" with a happy voice as you pat her side, then point her to the play area. Most dogs will naturally start to play or wander around until they find a play partner or a toy. Patting her and pointing let her know that it's okay to do something else now. She may not associate the verbal cue right away, but dropping the leash and patting her serve as her cue. Eventually she will also associate the verbal and physical cue that tells her it's playtime.

We'll learn more about the *release* next week. But for now, class dismissed. In other words, "Release!"

Homework

This week I want you to emphasize fundamentals that you've learned already, especially as you work with your new training partner and the partner's dog, which can be very distracting to a dog that is just learning. You'll also emphasize fundamentals in the troubleshooting exercises below. *Sit* will become an important fundamental building block as you now use real-life rewards—your dog should sit for *everything*.

❯ **SUPERVISED PLAY** Find a training partner.

❯ **TROUBLESHOOTING**

   ❯ **TETHERING** Treat your dog for focusing on you.

   ❯ **HAND-FEEDING** Have your dog sit to start hand-feeding.

   ❯ **BITE INHIBITION, HANDLING, GENTLING** Practice so that you're ready for next week.

   ❯ **CRATE TRAINING** Expand crate comfort with feeding and treats.

❯ SIT Luring for real-life rewards for everything: meals, crating, going out, walks, training.

❯ SIT Withdrawing treats and shaping the hand signal.

❯ RECALL Luring with added distance and verbal cue *come here.*

❯ DOWN Luring.

❯ RELEASE Verbal cue.

Recommended Games and Activities

In addition to repeating some or all the games your dog already knows, add these new games and activities (see details in Chapter Nine) to expand his interest in the fun surprises you bring.

❯ Which Hand?

❯ Supervised play with *recall* and *release*

❯ Come and Go with a partner: practice *sit* and *down*

Chapter Six

Week Three: Advancing to Verbal Cues

My hope is that you're seeing some progress: that your weekly training sessions, your playtime activities, and your daily repetitions of *sit, come here,* and *down* are beginning to pay off. However, it might also be the case that you or your dog is feeling completely lost. That is not uncommon in early stages of dog training; don't give up! Stick with this program and your reward will come. Time and time again, I have watched many student dogs "get it" for the first time in the final week. Review your training log and I am confident that you'll discover small improvements that you may have overlooked:

slightly faster reaction times, higher percentages of correct trials, or increased generalization. It's important that you acknowledge these small successes— they are your rewards for practicing the exercises consistently and patiently. If you're feeling overwhelmed, remember that you can always break down a behavior into smaller parts that you can string together into a full cue when you and your dog feel ready.

This week, we'll continue to build on what we've learned. We'll begin to combine *sits* with *recalls* and add the *release*. Your dog will learn to alternate between *sits* and *downs* by doing Puppy Pushups. We'll work to make walk- ing more controlled as you learn to change direction and walk side by side in an informal heeling formation. You will also learn two new cues this week: *cookie quick sits* and the *off and take it* trade.

This week you will also add verbal cues to hand signals. Even when add- ing the verbal cue, I want you to maintain the hand signal so that your dog continues to focus on you. We are just naming the cue, not replacing the hand signal. As a further clarification: Add the verbal cue only if your dog is already fluent in responding to your hand signal. If she can't do that, be patient and keep practicing before you add any verbal cue. I promise, she'll get it.

Troubleshooting: Leash Pulling

If your dog has already stopped leash pulling, that's great news (and very lucky for you). But my guess is that your dog's leash walking skills are still inconsistent and you're probably itching to go on a "real walk" without his pulling. I'll take a further guess that you've given in to his demand and have allowed him to pull every once in a while. I don't blame you. Going on a walk is one of the simple joys of owning a dog, and I know the frustration of having to spend the time focusing on training rather than on just enjoying a nice stroll.

However, you must continue to be steadfast, and follow the "be a tree" activity you learned in Week One (page 76). If he starts to pull, stop moving and wait for him to focus back on you. When he turns to look at you, mark it by saying "good" and lure him as you walk backward until he returns to you, then have him sit for his reward. Then you may start walking again; all walks start with a sit and a treat while your dog is learning. Right now, walk time is about teaching your dog that the only way he walks with you is if he's on a loose leash. Allowing him to pull you just rewards him for doing so.

As you become accustomed to your dog's walking behaviors, you should also try to anticipate when he is about to pull, so that you can lure him to turn and walk in a new direction with you. Your first hint that your dog is about to pull is that his focus has drifted away from you. The second hint comes when he starts to wander too far ahead of you or turns in a direction of *his* choosing. When you anticipate this and lure him in your own new direction, his focus will return to you, even if it's just for a few seconds. This exercise will help your dog become accustomed to keeping his focus on you, even in a highly distracting environment. Play a game with yourself: See how often you can anticipate and redirect your dog's focus before he actually starts to pull. When you get back home, write down those results in your training log and see which techniques work best for your dog: "being a tree," luring, or changing directions.

This week, to practice luring your dog to follow your lead, I want you to play the Follow the Lure game that you learned about in Week One (see Chapter Nine for details). Adapt the game for walk time by palming a treat in the hand on the side where you walk your dog. I walk dogs on the left side, so I palm the treat in my left hand. The other hand holds the leash handle. Move your dog-side hand, with the palmed treat, toward your dog's nose to get his attention. Allow him to sniff the treat before luring him to follow you in a new direction. Change directions often, luring him in circles and weaving between obstacles. Make it fun with *start-stop-sit-and-turn* routines. As you learn more behaviors and cues, mix those in, too.

It will probably take a few sessions to teach your dog to follow you and the treat instead of the great smells and distractions that you're competing against. If your dog is too distracted, try this exercise indoors or in an isolated spot outside. Over time, you will build up his focus on you.

Assume that for now your walks will be not much more than glorified pacing back and forth, wearing a groove in the concrete if necessary. Patiently build up to a 30-second walk without pulling, even if you have to start with a 3-second walk before turning into a tree. If you chart the progress in your training log, you'll be able to appreciate your patience even more.

You may also try to solve the leash-pulling problem by using certain types of training collars, such as the Gentle Leader head harness or a no-pull body harness (the leash attaches at the dog's chest). I am opposed to using choke chains or prong collars. (See Chapter Eleven, Behavior Problems, for insights into how to use training collars with positive reinforcement dog training.)

Supervised Play: Recall and Sit Combination with Release

This week I want you and your dog to become fluent with the *recall-sit* combination, because we're preparing to add more skills, such as *stay*, onto this foundation. You can practice this alone or during a socialization activity with another dog. Begin by allowing your dog to play for about a minute. Then recall her by saying her name and adding the verbal cue "come here." Using a lure, have her sit in front of you. Then touch her collar as you praise and handle her, and reward her with the treat.

Next, cue *release* (see page 91). If she understands and bounds off to play for another round, then she's getting that cue. If she continues to sit, the good news is that she's obviously getting used to remaining highly focused on you, and you'll need to guide her back to playing. As you learned last week, have your dog sit, say "good dog," pat her gently on the side, and point to the play area as you say "release" or "go play." Remember to be consistent because, as you already know, dogs don't generalize very well.

Repeat this *recall-sit-release* combination at least four times in each supervised play session. The *release* part of the combination is important because your dog needs to understand that being recalled doesn't mean that playtime is over. You want her to associate recalls with just one part of her play experience, as well as with things she values, like treats, praise, and your attention and affection.

Introduce the Sit Verbal Cue Paired with Hand Signal

It's time to pair the verbal cue to sit with the hand signal that you already know. As mentioned earlier, always maintain the hand signal when adding any verbal cue. It's crucial that your dog continues to focus on you. Typically, people who use choke chains are attempting to teach their dogs to rely on verbal cues and physical rebukes in order to get the dogs' attention and make them follow their commands. My opinion? If your dog is not yet fluent with your hand signal, then wait until he is.

To help him focus on this one word, do not say his name. For example, do not say, "Brieo, sit." Since you are back at learning stage #1 (acquiring a new skill), don't use the slot machine; treat him on every trial and generalize as you did previously. The moment his rump touches down, mark it with the praise "good sit."

After about six to eight repetitions like this, reintroduce the slot machine (remember, that means you'll slowly withdraw treats), but don't award any jackpots yet. Most dogs won't regress when the verbal cue is added; if yours does, it's likely that he's bored and you're not making it fun enough from his point of view. To keep your dog's interest, you can try

The signal for *sit* should be very clear—you'll be using it a lot!

various things: Move to a different location for each rep, spin around (most dogs love to spin), take his leash and run back and forth happily to get his spirit back up before the next rep, or simply do the reps more quickly. You may also move on to another exercise that he already knows and enjoys, and after a minute return to this one.

Remember to set your dog up for success when you pair any hand signal with its verbal cue. Once he responds with fluency to your hand signal and verbal cue together, reintroduce the slot machine to start withdrawing treats. It's okay if he tries harder to get his reward, but if he starts to lose focus and begins to fail trials, go back to a behavior that he already knows well and enjoys. Reward him for that and end the training session on a positive note, and go log it.

Puppy Pushups

Puppy Pushups are a quick sequence of *sit* and *down* and *sit,* followed by a one-treat reward. The purpose of the Puppy Pushup is to phase out food rewards while improving your dog's ability to keep her attention focused on you in all kinds of distracting environments. My colleague, Dr. Ian Dunbar, first taught me this technique a decade ago, and I have been using it in my classes ever since. I use this exercise whenever I want my dogs very focused on me: at the dog park, on the street, around people who are unfamiliar to them, or while waiting at the veterinarian's office. Success at

Puppy Pushups gives your dog a familiar ritual to get her focused on you in potentially uncomfortable settings.

Your dog is ready to do Puppy Pushups if she is already fluent with both *sit* and *down* hand signals. As she repeatedly performs *sit-down-sit,* she is learning to anticipate what cue you will give next and will respond more quickly. Have several treats ready in your hand so that you can reward her immediately. Once she has become fluent with Puppy Pushups in familiar settings (having succeeded on at least 10 reps in a row), start doing them in different, less familiar settings. You may need to reteach the Puppy Pushup sequence in each new setting. But even if your dog happens to learn this skill slowly, at some point she will suddenly get it, as if to say, "Oh! I know this one. We're in a different place, but what you want me to do is always the same." Once your dog learns more behaviors, add them to the Puppy Pushups sequence. At one time I would have my Border Collie Jock sit, pose (stand), down, roll over, shake paws, wave, back up, and do an *off* cue before I would give him his dinner. Jock loved it; dogs love earning their rewards.

Stay: Cookie Sit-Stays

A crucial cue, *stay* builds your dog's impulse control, teaching him to stay focused on you even in the face of distractions, which could be a life-saver. But to get there, you must be patient and your dog must have some maturity. The first step is to master the *cookie sit* (more on that in a second), because it teaches him to remain seated and always focused on you in the face of a distraction (a cookie).

1 PUPPY PUSHUPS AND SIT Start with your dog on his leash, sitting at the side on which you walk him, and do a set of Puppy Pushups (*sit-down-sit*) using *both* verbal and visual cues. Next, hold the leash an arm's length from where it clips to your dog's collar, and place that hand on your hip.

1.

2 TOSS TREAT Next, touch a treat gently to your dog's nose to get him focused on it, then toss it about three feet in front of him. If you have a smallish dog, toss it a bit nearer; if you have a big dog, a bit farther.

2.

3 HAND GLUED TO HIP As your dog jumps for the treat and tries to pull the leash, tense that arm tight against your hip (and use your body weight to keep steady) so that he will have only that arm's length of leash play. Don't yank the leash; just keep your hand glued to your hip.

3.

4 DOG REFOCUSES When your dog finally looks at you, mark it (say "good"). Then cue him to sit again, using both verbal and hand signals.

4.

5 TAKE IT! As soon as he sits, say "take it" and slacken the leash so that your dog can reach the treat. He dog will probably dash right for the treat. Mark and praise that, and do another trial.

5.

While teaching the *cookie sit-stay,* pay particular attention to your dog's focus on you. When your dog understands the importance of focus, he will sit more quickly and wait for you to send him. You'll notice his body language calm down as he realizes that he'll get the reward as soon as he sits. If he does not take the treat, step forward to help him take it successfully, then try another rep.

If your dog doesn't sit right away, don't give the *sit* cue again. Remember: Saying "sit-sit-sit-sit-sit" only teaches a dog not to pay attention until he hears the fifth cue. Instead, after a few seconds, watch for your dog to look at you and then request the *sit.* When that happens, mark it (say "good"), and send him to *take it.* (Make sure there's enough play in the leash for him to reach the treat without pulling.) After a few days of practice, your dog will probably be sitting quickly and consistently (for at least a full second before you cue *take it*). If not, just keep practicing at a pace that suits you and your dog. He'll get it in time.

Your dog's ability to stay on cue encourages good manners while socializing, and could be a lifesaver.

It's now time to add the *stay* hand signal and verbal cue (see the next section, the Conventional Stay Cue, for more details), wait three to five seconds before you send him to *take it,* and then mark and reward that. With the hand that is not gluing the leash to your hip, gently touch the treat to your dog's nose, and then toss it. Then cue your dog to *sit* (mark it "good"), and then gently put an open palm toward your dog's face and calmly say "stay." Count silently for three seconds, tell him quietly and calmly "good stay," wait another second, and then cue him to *take it,* using your hand signal to point him toward the treat along with the verbal cue.

If that succeeds, count silently for four seconds on the next trial. Add another second for each successful trial; subtract a second for each mistake. Find the amount of time that your dog can *stay* comfortably without failure, and increase the time slowly from there.

If your dog is highly motivated by toys, then once he has built up his *cookie sit-stay* to about 30 seconds, change to throwing a ball or a special squeaky toy instead of a treat. Also use the *cookie sit-stay* at mealtime to teach your dog to sit when it's time for him to be fed, which decreases jumping and teaches good manners.

The Conventional Stay Cue

I n addition to the *cookie sit-stay*, the conventional *stay* technique helps your dog acquire the hand signal for this important cue.

1 SIT AND FOCUS First, start with your dog sitting in front of you and show him an open palm (hand signal for *stay*). Touch a treat to his nose and then move it slowly to your eyes, to encourage him to keep looking at you.

1.

2 MARK, PRAISE, REWARD After a second, calmly mark "good" and reward him with the treat. While he is still sitting, take out another treat and repeat the exercise, adding time little by little.

2.

While teaching the conventional *stay*, add the verbal cue "stay" and use the hand signal of an open palm close to your dog's face (or alternatively, wave your hand in front of his eyes) before you give him the treat. Add an extra second on each successful rep until you reach 10 seconds, and then add 2 seconds for each successful trial until you reach 20 seconds, ultimately building up to 1 minute. Beyond 1 minute, add 10 seconds to each trial. Beyond 2 minutes, add 20 seconds to each trial until you reach 3 minutes. At the end of *sit* training (after you mark, praise, and reward the final successful *sit*), release your dog and reward him with lots of high-energy praise for sitting so still. Then switch to another training game (see Chapter Nine) that your dog enjoys and can do successfully.

If your dog starts to fail a trial by getting up out of the *sit*, resist the urge to force him back into the *stay*, especially if he fails just a few seconds shy of a longtime success. Instead, reduce the amount of time that he is in the *stay* position to a time frame in which he can be successful, and then practice reps in that time frame until he shows you that he is ready to stay longer.

To keep your dog interested in succeeding on those long stays, do a couple of short stays as warm-up trials, and again after the long trials. Be sure to jackpot your dog as he completes these longer trials. In your dog's training log, record the times—the failures as well as the successes—to help you know how long to have him stay on the next trial.

A *stay* is a great exercise to throw in randomly during evening hours to teach your dog not to beg at your dinner table and to relax while you watch TV or read this book. Prepare a stuffed Kong, request that he lie down, and give him the Kong when he follows through on your cue. After a few minutes of chewing, interrupt him by taking away the Kong. Cue him to *sit-stay* (for about 10 seconds if he can reliably already do at least that much time), and then mark and praise him and give him the Kong again. After another few minutes, take the Kong away again, cue him to *sit* and enjoy about 10 seconds of fun together, such as a good belly rub, or a quick round of Which Hand? (see Chapter Nine). Then praise him again and cue him to *sit*. As soon as he sits, give him the Kong again, and resume what you were doing. Each time you take away the Kong, do something a little different or change the sequence of cues to have him earn it back.

Off and Take It Trades: Phase 1

The *off* cue means "don't touch." It teaches your dog to stop a certain behavior, such as sticking her nose in the garbage, carrying your favorite shoe, crossing the threshold of a door that you just opened, or hoarding the Kong you gave her a couple of minutes ago. *Off* is a clear way to tell your dog that certain boundaries are not to be crossed without your permission.

When your dog is first learning *off,* the cue must be paired with the *take it* cue (except for boundary limits, which I'll discuss in the next chapter). The combination is based on the trade concept: that giving something up will get her something of equal or greater value in return. So, in this exercise, you'll be teaching your dog two cues: *off,* which means "don't touch," and *take it,* which gives her permission to come forward and take the item. Next week, we'll take this activity a step further to the trading stage. The trade will teach your dog not to run away and try to get you to chase her when she has stolen some contraband, by showing her that if she lets go of the illegal object, she'll be rewarded with a trade for something that she values just as much or even more.

1 SAY "TAKE IT" Begin with the *take it* part of the lesson. With your dog in front of you (I prefer that she stand, but sitting is okay), put about six treats in your closed hand. Shift one treat to your fingertips, steady your hand against your knee at your dog's nose level, and say "take it." Let her come forward and take the treat, as you mark it (say "good" or "good take it"). Do another rep right away by shifting another treat to your fingertips (your hand stays against your knee), and repeat the *take it* and marker steps. Then repeat again with a third treat.

1.

2 KEEP QUIET On the fourth repetition, begin teaching your dog the *off* command. Shift a fourth treat to your fingertips (keeping your hand against your knee), but this time close your hand around the treat and do not say "take it."

3 SAY "OFF!" Almost all dogs will attempt to get that treat before you say "take it." When your dog tries to take the treat, say "off" in a firm and deep voice. Imagine that you are a singer hitting a deep bass note when you say it. You want the *off* command to be sudden, forceful, and loud enough to be slightly shocking, so that it interrupts your dog's focus on the treat without scaring off her whiskers. Typically, the dog will back away and look curiously at you as if she is thinking, "What happened? Why didn't you give me the treat?" The moment she backs away, mark it by saying "good, take it" in your soothing, happy tone of voice and praise her while giving her the treat.

2.

3.

Once your dog has completed a couple of successful *off and take its,* add one additional second on the next rep before you say "take it." As she continues to succeed, increase the time between *off* and *take it* up to five seconds. If, on the other hand, your dog doesn't try to take it on the first try, then say "good" and cue her to *take it*—there is no sense in teaching her the *off* yet. You'll need to get some really great treats that your dog can't resist and entice her even more with extra rounds of *take its* as you lull her into the pattern before you teach the *off.*

To help your dog distinguish the *off* and *take it* verbal cues, mix the pattern: Sometimes use just the *take it,* other times add the *off.* Once your dog has acquired these basics and is progressing toward fluency, it is time to begin teaching her to generalize this valuable skill by doing *offs* and *take its* with toys and her food bowl.

Don't underestimate the importance of this exercise; it's a necessary step toward becoming a well-socialized dog. It helps prevent food guarding and resource guarding, the potentially dangerous behavior in which your dog may bite any hand that comes near her food or things she tries to "own," such as toys or food bowls. *Off* skills also provide you with an opportunity to reinforce your dog's bite inhibition skills. If she mouths your arm or hand, for example, you can say "off" and know she will eventually mouth more gently to the point of not mouthing at all. Throw in a startled "ouch" if your dog mouths you.

Catch Your Dog Doing Something That You Like

This is an exercise for *you,* not your dog: Your job is to reward good behavior that your dog offers on his own. When your dog does something that you like without being asked, joyfully mark it by saying "good sit" or "good down" or "good stay" or "good heel." Add praise and, on occasion, a treat or other reward such as a great ear or belly rub. Encourage his good manners now and you will get a spirited, curious dog that volunteers even more good manners in the future. It is simple psychology: What gets rewarded gets reinforced, what gets ignored disappears . . . Yes, it works on humans, too.

Your dog may start to offer *sit* or another behavior in hopes of getting a reward. This is his way of saying "please." Remember, the more often you catch him doing something that you like, the more likely he is to offer that behavior again. If he develops a habit of offering one particular behavior, continue to praise it, but offer treats randomly. Some breeds get bored easily and want to do something—anything—with you or they become demanding of your attention, so you need to recognize and encourage the good things that they do. Jot down these volunteered good behaviors in your training log and you will begin to observe your dog's patterns.

Walking Exercise: Informal Heeling

As you know, I don't think most dogs need to perform an extended, perfect heel; it's a fairly advanced skill that requires more concentration than most dogs can successfully muster at this level of training. Used in competition or when there is a significant distraction such as traffic, the formal heel requires full focus from both you and your dog. But you do want to start practicing *informal* heeling, an advanced form of walking by your side that will keep her closely focused on you while walking in typical real-life situations: around your neighborhood, town, city, and in stores and work environments.

Formal heel

Teach your dog the informal heel using your regular walking leash, held across your body. Your dog will learn to anticipate your walking changes by your changing body language, and you will learn to anticipate her changes, such as when it's time to sniff, go potty, or explore the world as a dog. The tethering exercises you've been doing at home will help a lot with this.

Start practicing the informal heel indoors, where there are few distractions. First, ask your dog to sit at your side. Say "ready" to cue her to look up at you, and mark and treat her when she does. Then walk forward four steps, marking and praising her if she follows and stays focused on you. Stop and immediately lure her to sit, then mark and reward her. Repeating this sequence (*walk-stop-sit, walk-stop-sit*) over and over will teach your dog to focus on you with a heads-up heeling gait as you walk together.

Informal heel

Next, practice this *walk-stop-sit* exercise while you're outside. Walk two or three quick steps, stop, and lure her to sit. Once your dog is focused enough to do the exercise fluently, start changing directions, adding *downs* and *cookie sit-stays,* doing a round of Puppy Pushups, or any other skill that your dog has already acquired. Do not teach new skills during heeling; keep your dog successful at this level by combining skills that she has already acquired.

If you're consistent in rewarding her for heeling, she will try to figure out how to get more treats and will learn that it happens when she walks at your side. When you reward your dog for staying close to you, she will, over time, be less likely to forge ahead of you to rush into the doggy park, chase the squirrels, greet another dog, or just pull on that leash for no apparent reason. Heeling also promotes good bonding.

A third way to walk your dog is with a loose leash, which is how you walked in the "be a tree" exercise (Week One). Loose leash walking can be used as a reward for good heeling. It allows your dog to sniff, roam a little, and be a dog.

Loose leash walking

Homework

Although your dog has learned a few new skills this week, you should still dedicate plenty of time to strengthening the foundation that you already have. These fundamentals are building blocks for the new skills. Almost every elite athlete and coach emphasizes practicing fundamentals over and over again. That is also true for dog training. If you spend all your training time learning new skills, your dog can easily forget what he already knows, what you have already put so much effort into teaching him. As you practice these new skills, make your fundamentals consistently excellent.

❯ **WALKING (FUNDAMENTALS)** "Be a Tree," play Follow the Lure.

❯ **WALKING (NEW SKILL)** Informal heeling with *walk-stop-sit-walk-stop-sit* exercise.

❷ **SIT (FUNDAMENTALS)** Luring and hand signal.

❷ **SIT (NEW SKILL)** Verbal cue combined with hand signal (don't give the verbal cue without also giving the hand signal).

❷ **PUPPY PUSHUPS (NEW SKILL)** Keeps dog's focus on you and sharpens cues.

❷ **COOKIE SIT-STAY (NEW SKILL)** Use *cookie-sit* fundamental as building block for new *sit-stay* skill.

❷ **SIT-STAY (NEW SKILL)** Build up *sit-stay* time with lots of rewards.

❷ **OFF AND TAKE IT TRADE, PHASE 1 (NEW SKILL)** Practice this completely new skill.

Training Games and Activities

So that practicing fundamentals doesn't become boring for your dog, make it fun. Rather than introduce a new game to your dog, see how you can adapt existing games to strengthen both her fundamentals and her new skills.

❷ Keep her focused on the lure with games like Follow the Lure (see page 144), and focused on you with the Eye-Contact Exercise (page 143).

❷ Play Come and Go (page 144) with the added requirement at each lap of doing a set of Puppy Pushups that starts and ends with a *sit*.

❷ Play Find Me, or Hide-and-Seek, (page 142) with some more difficult hiding places, using your partner to hold your dog. If she is able to remain sitting and staying while you leave the room without using a partner, try playing Find Me without a partner—as long as you hide quickly in easy-to-find hiding places. Remember that *staying* while you're out of sight may be too advanced for her maturity level and training history, so do your best to set your dog up for success.

Chapter Seven

Week Four: Completing the Foundation

This week marks the last week of the Fundamentals Training Program in which your dog will learn new skills (next week we'll review). With this solid training foundation, your dog will have good manners in the vast majority of typical real-life situations, and will be prepared to move into more advanced training and activities.

Before you begin this lesson, take a moment to remember that a well-trained, spirited dog is given plenty of opportunities for success and acknowledgment in everyday situations. Make it a habit to catch your dog offering behaviors that you like, and remember to mark each good behavior. Keep treats ready so that you can reward those spontaneous moments. (I keep airtight cups filled with treats around my home so they are always ready, placed high enough on shelves so that no dog can reach them.) Treating your dog for volunteered behaviors will add to his reinforcement history and encourage him to offer more good behaviors without being asked. Remember to praise your dog's improvements during socialization opportunities, such as when he reacts more calmly to other dogs and people.

Be mindful: Lead your dog with spirit.

Please keep your dog on the real-life rewards system, in which you consistently ask him to sit for everything he gets from you: food, water, toys, playtime, and walks. The more consistent you are with this approach, the more quickly your dog will come to understand that his good manners are more than a training exercise—good manners earn him things that he values. With the real-life rewards approach, you'll soon have a more self-confident dog that will offer and repeat desired behaviors because he knows that there is a reward in his future.

These first weeks of dog training are like building a house: The foundation is mostly invisible when you look at the finished product, but without that foundation the house won't stand. Regardless of how well you think you and your dog are doing, you both deserve to be acknowledged for all the hours you have put in. Keep in mind that your dog *is* making progress even if he doesn't always show it. If you review your training log, you'll appreciate the strong training foundation you have built.

In Chapter Four I shared with you some thoughts about "spiriting" the relationship with your dog. A spirited relationship is confident, trusting, consistently growing, and vibrant. This week, I want you to be mindful to lead your dog with spirit. In those moments when you feel that spirit's joyful warmth in your heart, please express it to your dog. If a blessing is something you already do in your life, bless your dog, your relationship with him, and yourself for being such a spirited dog owner who is making a difference in the life of one of God's marvelous creations. If blessing is not something you do, then take this opportunity to appreciate your dog's special gifts—every dog has them. Many people discover their own special gifts through good relationships with their loved dogs. My hope is that this mutual appreciation you and your dog have for each other will uplift both of you.

Recalls: Adding Distractions and More Distance

This week, we'll advance your dog's recall skill by adding distractions. Let's also generalize your dog's experience by practicing recalls in a variety of places, including outdoor locations (if you think that your dog is ready). You'll still need to work with a partner. When you practice outdoors, train only in fenced-in areas, or with your dog on a leash that is at least 20 feet long or is tied securely to a long rope. (You don't want your dog running away!) Choose a location free of other dogs, traffic, or people; the new smells will be distracting enough at first.

In this exercise, while your partner holds your dog's leash, joyfully tease her with a treat for a moment. Turn your back to them and run away. When you get about six to eight feet away, turn around quickly, get down on your knees, open your arms wide, and joyfully call out "come here!" (This is the Lassie Recall we learned in Week Two; see page 88.) If your partner observes that your dog remained focused on you as you ran away, he releases your dog. As she runs toward you, continue to act extremely excited. When she arrives, praise her and touch her all over, especially on the collar, as you reward her with the treat. On subsequent recalls, add a *sit* or *down* before your dog actually catches you; she will learn to control her impulses—and you'll be safer if an excited dog isn't jumping all over you or tugging at your clothing. As you build up the distance, keep in mind that the ability to do this exercise at *any* distance with new distractions is more important than doing it at a longer distance. When you practice at a new location with new distractions, decrease the distance. It will increase upon successful practice.

If, however, your partner observes that your dog looked away as you ran from her, you need to keep working to train her to stay focused on you. The first step: Your partner doesn't release her. Instead, he happily runs her to you for your reward and praise.

There are a number of reasons your dog may initially "fail" this exercise: You're not acting excited enough, she isn't focused in the moment (and may need a short play-training break that you know she'll succeed at and enjoy), or there are too many distractions in the environment. Try a less distracting location, such as a long hallway indoors. Or try using a favorite squeaky toy instead of a treat. If even that doesn't work, then continue the earlier recall exercises from Week Two, or try the Come and Go game described in Chapter Nine.

Once your dog becomes fluent with this recall exercise, it's time to add a game of Hide-and-Seek. While your partner holds the leash, run away and let your dog see you duck into a hiding spot, such as behind a couch or a partially closed door. Then *recall* her, using your typically upbeat, enthusiastic cue. When she finds you, jackpot and praise the heck out of her. After all, not only did she *recall* successfully, but she made an extra effort to find you. Dogs love surprises like this. Once yours succeeds in finding you in those easy hiding spots, you can add to the fun, and the challenge, by making your hiding places a little more difficult to find.

Stay: Adding Distractions and Distance

Another way to improve your dog's impulse control is to add distractions as you keep him in a *stay*. Start teaching this skill by having your dog *sit* and *stay* as you move a step away from him. Allow him to *stay* for a moment, and then return to him with praise and a treat. If your dog can't sit still for even one step, just lift your foot off the ground (as if you are about to take a step) and put it back down, and continue doing that until you can make that first step without his moving.

On the next trial, take a step in a different direction. Once your dog understands that your little movements aren't worth getting excited or anxious about, add a couple more steps, making an arc around your dog. As you move around, watch him carefully; most dogs have difficulty sitting still when they can't see their owners. Get to know your dog's body language; that will help you know instinctively if he is losing focus and about to move. For example, if he turns his head, that could be a sign that he is about to move his body. Before he moves, mark it ("good") and return to him. If he has moved, ignore it and realize that you need to break it down into smaller steps (and log it). Eventually, with practice and good timing, you will be able to circle all the way around your dog as he remains seated without turning around. Help him generalize this skill by practicing in a variety of places around your home, and then add outdoor locations with distractions when you feel that he is ready.

Down: Naming the Behavior

I'm hoping that last week's Puppy Pushups helped you modify both the *sit* and *down* hand signals. This week, please continue practicing Puppy Pushups as we add the verbal *down* cue to the hand signal.

To begin, pretend to hold a treat in the hand you use to cue your dog, and lure her into the *down* position. As soon as she begins to commit to going down, say "down," praise her, and reward her with a treat that you have hidden in your other hand. This technique teaches your dog two things at the same time: First, she begins to understand that the food doesn't need to be in the luring hand in order for her to get the treat. Second, she is beginning to learn that this behavior is named "down." Learning two things at the same time challenges your dog, building her confidence and positive reinforcement history.

When your dog performs the *down* as you give both hand signal and verbal cue, award a jackpot. The other option, and one of my favorites, is to do another series of Puppy Pushups. Instead of asking your dog to sit, as you did last week, bring her to the *down* position and back to the *sit* using both the visual and verbal cues. You will find that this quick rhythm of pushups helps teach her to work more behaviors for less food.

Standing Pose

It's important that your dog learns the *standing pose* (on all four legs) for a number of reasons, including grooming, veterinary checkups, wiping muddy feet, tick checks. (During dog shows, dogs are required to hold still for the judge's examination in the *standing pose,* which is also called a *stand* or *stack.*) Teaching your dog to *pose* also takes training up a notch, because having a third position in her repertoire (along with the *sit* and *down* positions) means she can't as easily guess which cue you will give her next. In the Puppy Pushup pattern you've been doing so far, your dog will eventually realize (or may have already) that *down* always follows *sit* and *sit* always follows *down.* That certainly might make her attention drift away from you. But by adding a third cue—the *standing pose*—to the Puppy Pushup rotation, your cueing sequence will become less predictable. She will no longer know for certain which cue will follow *sit, down,* or *pose.* She will need to stay focused on you to earn praise and treats.

I prefer the verbal cue "pose" because it sounds much different from the other verbal cues your dog is now learning, while the verbal cue "stand" sounds too similar to "sit" and "stay." But before you teach the verbal cue, start by luring your dog to *pose* from the *sit* position.

1 SHOW THE LURE At your dog's heel side, start with her sitting. Hold a treat in front of her nose and lure forward so that her natural movement is to stand up and sniff the treat.

1.

2 MOVE IT FORWARD Slowly move the lure forward so that your dog stands up all the way to sniff it. Don't let her eat the treat quite yet.

2.

3 WATCH HER POSTURE Once she's up on all fours and sniffing the treat, stop moving your luring hand and mark it (say "good"), praise her, and let her have the treat.

3.

As you repeat this exercise, your dog will perform each *pose* a little better and with a more relaxed posture than the last rep. As she does so, modify your motion into a hand signal by luring with an open palm (use your thumb to hold the treat in your palm). When she poses, mark it (say "good"), move the hand toward her, and reward her with the treat. She will learn that the open palm moving forward is her signal to pose, and will wait in anticipation of getting a treat as you move your hand toward her. With this technique, you can now increase your dog's ability to hold the *pose* by delaying your hand movement toward her as she waits for the treat. At first, delay giving her the treat by just one second, and then build up time on subsequent reps as she becomes successful. She doesn't need to hold the *pose* position for more than 30 seconds, which is just enough time to inspect her or go through a brief grooming ritual.

Once your dog has acquired a consistent lured *pose* with the new hand signal, retrain the whole cue while positioned on the other side of her. Once she becomes fluent with what you're asking her to do from both sides, it's time to add the verbal cue. Introduce the verbal cue—the word "pose"— once you have lured her all the way up and she is standing in front of your hand. At that point, mark the behavior, praise her, and give her the treat. Practice that sequence until she approaches fluency.

Your final step is to reteach the *pose* starting at the *down* position. My experience with most dogs is that once dogs become fluent at the *pose* starting from the *sit,* they tend to understand the same hand signal and verbal cue from the *down* fairly quickly.

Off and Take It Trades: Phase 2

This week I want you to begin conditioning your dog to give up items without resistance, by using the *off* cue. When you cue your dog *off,* remember to pair that cue with a valuable *take it:* Offer something of equal or greater value than what you're asking him to give up. This is not just a learning exercise but a real-life lesson. One time, my Flat-Coated Retriever, Merit, brought me a whole cooked chicken carcass that he had stolen off the kitchen counter after dinner. Most dogs would have gobbled it down right there. But not Merit. He was so well conditioned to bring contraband to me for *off and take it* trades that he proudly dropped the carcass right in my lap. I was afraid that Merit might have eaten some of the chicken bones, which are dangerous to dogs, but I shouldn't have worried. He brought the carcass fully intact and his mouth betrayed no sign of chicken bones or chicken breath. Immediately, I thanked and praised the heck out of him as he proudly wagged his tail and followed me back into the kitchen, where I prepared a great stuffed Kong for him. Had I trained the *off* without the *take it* trade, Merit would have had no incentive to bring me the chicken in the first place. Instead, he would have eaten it all, leaving no traces behind. There are two morals to this story: 1) teach your dog to trade *off* for *take it,* and 2) don't leave contraband on any table or countertop that your dog can jump to and surf.

By the way, it may seem as if I rewarded Merit for stealing the chicken carcass, but let's think it through. I rewarded Merit's *last* behavior, which was bringing me the contraband. If I were teaching him to steal an object from the countertop, I would need to have been in the kitchen to mark and reward the steal the moment he got that bird in his mouth.

You can also use the *off and take it* trade to eliminate some bad behaviors. Here's another example. I had a client dog—we'll call him Sneezy—that liked to chew tissues, especially used ones. Yuck. I showed Sneezy a tissue and told him "take it." Sneezy took it. The moment he started to chew on the tissue, I held a treat on his nose. Sneezy dropped the tissue and took the treat without any cues. Although Sneezy liked the tissues, he didn't like them as much as really good dog treats. Later, we worked an *off* into it by doing the *off and take it* trade. Sneezy not only stopped chewing tissues, he took tissues to his owner if he found them in a wastebasket.

To get ready to teach your dog the *off and take it* trade, gather one or two things that he values, such as a really good treat or a special toy. Start with *off* at his food bowl. The hand-feeding exercises have been teaching him not to guard his food; now it is time to take away his food bowl while he is eating. First, drop some really good food (such as small cuts of hard cheese) near his food bowl. As your dog moves away from the bowl to eat the cheese, pick up the bowl. When he finishes eating the cheese and looks up at you holding his bowl, say "good," then put it back down for him. Practice this a few times to make sure he is comfortable with your taking away his food bowl.

Next, offer your dog a handful of food; if he leaves his bowl to eat from your hand, mark it by saying "good" and praise him as he eats from your hand. When he finishes, drop some extra food in his bowl to show him that when your hand reaches toward the bowl, it means that you are giving something good, not taking away his food. Once you practice this enough to see that he is very comfortable with your hand reaching toward his bowl, try saying "off" while you hold a stuffed Kong for him to see. As he focuses on the Kong, cue "take it." As soon as he takes the Kong, pick up his bowl and let him see you put more food in it. Now cue *off* again and show him the bowl. As he drops the Kong and focuses on the bowl, cue "take it." Continue switching between his food bowl and the Kong for the rest of the meal, and allow him to finish the goodies from the Kong, too.

Practice *off and take it* trades often, because you are conditioning your dog to be comfortable with you and your hands around his food, toys, and bowls. It is easy for all animals (including humans) to slip back into impulsive behavior or to guard items they cherish.

You can also modify the *off and take it* trade so that when your dog gets hold of something you prize dearly—such as your new shoes—or a yucky tissue, he'll be willing to make the trade for something other than food, like a special toy or other object that can be chewed safely. I call this the *contraband* trade or the *substitution* trade.

1 CATCH HIM IN THE ACT When you spot your dog chewing on contraband, don't say anything right away. Just put the valuable trade object—for example, a stuffed Kong that's been in the fridge—behind your back and calmly approach your dog.

1.

2 GET EYE CONTACT While keeping the trade object behind your back, say "off" sharply, and only one time. When your dog releases the contraband, mark it (say "good"). When he refocuses on you, mark that, too.

2.

3 OFFER THE TRADE Let your dog sniff the trade object. Typically, he will drop the contraband, and you can put your foot on it as you make the trade. Praise him, touch his collar, and give him the object. Now that he's distracted, you're free to remove the contraband.

3.

Climbing Stairs with Confidence and Safety

It's normal for a puppy to be unsure or even fearful about climbing stairs. I advise teaching your puppy to climb up before climbing down: Looking upward is generally not as scary. The best way to teach a puppy to climb up is to start at the step just below the top, and lure her up. Praise her profusely, because this is literally a big step for her! After your puppy has mastered one step, place her on the second step from the top, then three steps from the top, then four, and so forth. Start close to the goal at first so your puppy can have success reaching the top right away. That will build up her confidence for increasing the distance to that goal.

Once your puppy has mastered going up three or four steps at a time, start teaching her to go downstairs. Attach some netting to keep a puppy or small dog from slipping between stair posts, if you're cautious like I am, and make sure you have lots of treats on hand. Begin at the step closest to the bottom, then increase one step at a time, as you did when you taught your puppy to go upstairs. If the stairs are open-backed (without risers), which can make some dogs fearful, then build your dog's confidence by teaching her first on stairs that are closed-backed (with risers).

Until you're sure that she has the confidence and coordination to climb stairs in both directions with your supervision, prevent an accident by blocking off all stairs with baby gates. And even once she has become more sure-footed, use baby gates to keep her off the stairs and from wandering into rooms unsupervised.

If you want your dog to have access to the stairs, she must learn not to bound up or down ahead of you. For safety and control, she must climb stairs safely at your side; otherwise, she may push or trip you. Both have happened to me. Ouch.

To teach safe stair behavior, try this exercise:

1 GET IN POSITION Attach your dog to a short leash so that she can't get ahead of you or lag behind (but make sure the leash isn't so short that it pulls her collar). Keep her on leash and position her between you and the wall. Before you take a first step, have her sit and focus on you.

1.

2 ONE STEP AT A TIME Use your leg to cross in front of her chest area, taking one slow step at a time to maintain her pace and block her from rushing ahead of you. On most staircases, this means that in one direction you will need to walk with her on the side opposite to what you have been teaching her. Take the stairs one step at a time, marking, praising, and rewarding for each step. If she tries to get ahead, immediately close the space with your leg (unless it's unsafe to do so). Pause after each step. To let your dog know that you'll now take the next step together, give her a hand signal such as patting your leg gently or pointing ahead.

2.

3 SIT AT THE END When you reach the bottom (or top) of the staircase, always request a *sit;* that will slow her down. Once she has good impulse control and can take the stairs by your side one step at a time, increase to two steps at a time, and so forth. Move slowly! Remember that your leg is keeping your dog from rushing ahead, so you need to move deliberately—and with good balance—in case she gets rambunctious. In time, add the verbal cue "slow" for each step as you continue stair training.

3.

When you're about to take the first step onto a staircase, I also recommend adding both visual and verbal cues if your dog already focuses well on you. To add these cues, begin by asking her to sit. Then say "stairs" and proceed as I've detailed above.

Until your dog becomes fluent with your stair-climbing protocol, cue her for *every* step, using the visual signal (patting your leg or pointing), and then adding the verbal cue "slow" when she is ready. As your dog masters this skill, you'll be able to withdraw the visual cue and verbal reminder for each step.

Boundary Training: Doors

For your dog's safety and the comfort of your visitors, it is essential that she obey your boundaries: no jumping on guests, no dashing through open doors or up stairs, no going into rooms or onto furniture that are off-limits, no paws on the kitchen floor just after you've cleaned it. The *off* cue is one tool in boundary training. Let's begin to use this cue to train your dog to sit and wait at the front door while you open it to go outside, or for visitors to come in. You should be very consistent with this: Whenever you open a door, your dog must wait for you to go through it before she follows you. It is important that you cross the threshold ahead of your dog so that you can prepare for and manage her for what is going on in the next room (or outdoors), such as another dog, a child, or something in the environment that might trigger her to jump or try to dash ahead of you.

You will start door training by teaching your dog to mind your directions at interior doors, and you'll graduate to exiting your own front door. Begin by having your dog sit at a doorway inside your home while on leash. After she sits, say "off" and then open the door slightly. If she moves out of the *sit,* immediately close the door and wait a second or two before trying again. Keep doing this exercise until she remains sitting as you open the door, even if it's just slightly ajar. When she does so, tell her "good" and open the door all the way so that you can lead her through the doorway, with the same signal you use to begin a walk: Perhaps it's a hand pointing the way or a pat-pat to your thigh as you take the first step.

Now that your dog has had her first taste of success, challenge her on subsequent trials by requiring her to wait for you to open the door a little wider before you mark "good," praise her, and open the door the rest of the way and lead her through. Remember to cue *off* before you start to open the door on each rep. The goal is to have your dog remain sitting in front of the open doorway after you have told her "off" and opened the door all the way, until you lead her through with you. If she hesitates to follow you, try luring her over the boundary by saying "come here."

Once your dog has become fluent with sitting on cue before you lead her through a variety of interior doors, it's time to allow her to remain standing until she follows you through those same doorways. Start by saying "off" the moment before you open the door a little bit. If she stands still, take one small step across the threshold, mark it (say "good"), open the door all the way, and allow her to follow you (by using your signal when you start walking). As soon as you've both gone through the doorway, cue her to *sit* (then mark, praise, and reward when she's successful). Deleting the *sit* before going through the door helps her understand that *off* always means "don't go there, don't touch it" in any generalized situation. Improve your dog's focus on you by using hand signals without verbal cues; when you are consistently her focus, add the verbal cue (I recommend "let's go") along with the hand signal.

Doorbells and Knocking

After your dog has mastered waiting at doorways, you have an additional skill to teach: how to respond to the doorbell and door knocking. While many dogs go a little nuts when the doorbell rings, you should condition yours to stay settled. It will take a patient partner to help you and your dog master doorbell training. Start with a closed door, and use the same kind of training technique that we learned with the *cookie sit-stay* (see page 100). In other words, with your dog sitting at your heel and your hand holding his shortened leash tight against your hip, have your partner ring the bell (or knock) and then stay silent. If your dog doesn't respond to the bell or if he looks at you, jackpot him. More likely, however, your dog will bark and rush to the door, so brace yourself and keep that hand glued to your hip as you wait for him to look at you. The moment he looks at you, mark it (say "good") and lure him backward and away from the door to follow you as you say "come here." Right now, don't even open the door, just continue to practice the *come here* routine each time you lure him away from the door after your partner rings the bell or knocks. Say "come here" only once; if that doesn't succeed, lure him to another cue such as a *down* or *sit*.

Another way to condition your dog to pay no attention to the doorbell sound is for you to show absolutely no reaction when you hear it. Your dog feeds off your reaction, so if you ignore the bell, he will learn to do the same. My dogs don't pay much attention to doorbells, door knocks, or phones ringing, especially since Maude (my African Grey Parrot) imitates all those sounds. If you don't have a trained parrot, you can ask your child or a friend to ring your doorbell while you watch television or read this book. When the bell rings, just keep doing whatever it is you're doing, without looking at the door or your dog. Your dog may go crazy for a while, but eventually he will figure out that reacting to the doorbell doesn't benefit him; he'll eventually settle down and quietly forget about it. Oh, and I almost forgot . . . it's okay to let your child back inside at the end of the session. She may have earned a treat of her own for her assistance!

Here's another exercise. Have your child or a friend ring the doorbell over and over again. Ignore the bell—as well as your dog's barking—until he settles down. When he finally quiets down, wait about three minutes and then casually answer the door to let your child or friend in. You and your human ally should have a calm conversation while walking around your home, ignoring your dog even if he gets excited again. If he tries to jump on either of you, turn away abruptly and keep your back to him as you continue moving away. When he settles down, calmly praise him in a low-key manner, then practice a few *sits* and *downs,* staying calm. Next, have your child or friend calmly cue him to do a *sit* and a *down.* Watch your dog's body language, and when he is calm, remain calm yourself and give him a stuffed Kong or a special toy that you have reserved for this occasion. While he chews or plays, resume conversation with your partner, remembering to keep your tone quiet. This training exercise is a very challenging waiting game and may take time (not to mention an ample supply of aspirin!).

Boundary Training: Furniture and Rooms

The easiest way to keep your dog out of rooms and off furniture is by using baby gates and x-pens to block those areas as off-limits. Little by little, you can experiment with removing the barriers for longer and longer stretches of time. But before you do that, be sure to reinforce your dog's enjoyment of her crate; make staying in the crate a habit. Then, at a moment when you can supervise her constantly, start experimenting with keeping boundaries without using physical barriers. The best way to do that is to keep your dog in a *settle,* which I'll teach you next.

The first step, though, is to take your dog out of her crate and to give her attention and rewards, such as a chew toy that will keep her occupied. If she wanders into off-limits areas, *recall* her right away. Lure her if necessary. Use the *off* cue only if you catch her taking her first step or two onto or into the off-limits space, or else you may not make it clear what exactly it is that you want her to stay off and out of.

Settle Down

A slightly different behavior from the *down* and *down-stay, settle down* or just *settle* tells your dog to rest in place; as a more relaxed version of *down-stay,* it can be maintained for longer durations. In the *settle,* your dog can be in any position as long as she lies quietly: on her side or back, sprawled out, or chewing on a toy. The *down-stay,* by contrast, requires a dog to stay down without moving. Once she has mastered *down,* use *settle* to give her a bit more freedom and relaxation while she's "confined" to the *down* posture. You may use *settle,* for example, if you are okay with your dog being in the same room with you for a prolonged wait while you are eating, watching TV, reading, or working. You can also use *settle* when you are out in the world with her, such as while standing in line at a store or sitting on a park bench. Some of my students have named the *settle* behavior "chill," which is fine as long as you are consistent.

1 START WITH DOWN To teach your dog to *settle,* start with her in the *down* posture. Have plenty of treats handy. While she stays down, hold an open palm slightly above her head, wait a few seconds, and then with your other hand silently reward her with six to eight treats, one at a time. I call this the vending machine technique, and it's important to keep vending the treats as you watch her posture.

1.

2 MARK AND TREAT As soon as you see her relax into the *settle,* mark that by saying calmly "good settle" (or "good chill"), and feed her the

2.

remainder of the treats. After the last one, count silently to five, show her that you have no more treats in your hand and, with a soft voice, *release* her briefly. Then repeat the *settle* behavior. It's important to keep that vending machine doling out the treats or your dog might get up. If she does, stop dispensing treats until she lies back down. Most dogs pick up the *settle* cue fairly quickly if they've already mastered the *down-stay.*

Another way to teach and reinforce the *settle* is by combining it with hand-feeding. Slowly hand-feed your dog her entire meal, putting a few pieces of kibble at a time (or the equivalent amount if you don't use kibble) between her front paws and close to her body while she stays down. Stop feeding when she doesn't relax. By the end of the meal, she will probably be lying comfortably, enjoying being fed like royalty.

Homework

When you do your homework this week and in all weeks to come, I want you to keep your good relationship with your dog in mind. The more your dog is focused on you, the more he will want to follow your cues and learn from you, especially as you reward him for good behavior and build up a wonderful reinforcement history together. Make it your mission this week to see what you can do to get your dog more focused on you, and make note of that in your training log. For example, practice the eye-contact exercise (see page 143), being especially mindful to show your happiness when he looks at you. When you're walking, notice his focus on you and how that might also be improving his informal heeling without pulling.

Even as you have your dog sit for everything—which is the cornerstone of the real-life rewards system—show your gratitude a little more when he does whatever you may request. Pay attention to his body language and reward all those great behaviors he offers naturally—and he will offer them a hundredfold.

As you're nearing the end of your dog's Fundamentals Training Program, you may think that your dog is getting it so well that he doesn't need to be rewarded; or that he isn't getting it fast enough, so he doesn't deserve rewards. Both those judgments are easy to lapse into at this stage, so keep your dog's success in mind. Make whatever level he has achieved seem like the pinnacle of success.

❯ **RECALLS** Add distractions by practicing at outdoor locations and with people around, especially kids, as well as adding distances from different directions.

❯ **STAY** Add distractions and distance as your dog is ready. Remember to take your time: Good *stays* come with a lot of patience, practice, and your dog's maturity.

❯ DOWN Add the verbal cue (name the behavior).

❯ STANDING POSE Lure, try to advance all the way to the hand signal without lure, and then to add the verbal cue.

❯ OFF AND TAKE IT TRADES Practicing the food bowl exercise also reduces food guarding.

❯ STAIRS TRAINING Assuming that your dog can already climb stairs, teach stair-climbing safety (your dog walks next to you on stairs, neither in front of you nor behind).

❯ DOOR TRAINING Start with interior doors before progressing to doors that lead outside.

❯ SETTLE Practice the vending machine technique, and *settle* while hand-feeding.

Training Games and Activities

Add some new wrinkles to the games and activities that your dog already knows. See Chapter Nine for details.

❯ Integrate Find Me with Come and Go by doing *recalls* back and forth between you and your partner in separate rooms.

❯ Add *pose* to Puppy Pushups. When your dog is able to *pose* from your hand signal or verbal cue, start with a predictable sequence: *sit-pose-down;* then mix it up with combinations like *pose-sit-pose* and *sit-down-pose*. Remember to make it fun and keep your dog interested as you try to improve her fluency without causing her to fail.

❯ Fetch/Retrieve. Introduce the game, but don't insist that your dog get it or like it yet. Just assess where she is with this right now and reward her for any success.

Chapter Eight

Week Five: Reviewing the Basic Skills

Y ou've done it. This is Week Five—the final
week—of the Fundamentals Training Program.
Congratulations!

In my classes, I spend this final week reviewing the 10
basic skills my clients and their dogs have begun to master.
Use this chapter the same way—as a
quick guide for assessing your dog's
progress. Then let it guide you to
the next level of training in the
following chapters. If your dog
has acquired each of the 10 skills
and does a few of them fluently,
you've made tremendous
progress. If not, don't worry;

just keep working. As I've mentioned, it's not reasonable to expect that every dog will be able to master every one of these skills in just one month. Some take a little more time, and others seem to get it all at once, after several weeks.

If we were in class together, I would ask that you spend some time showing us what your dog can do, and how well she performs the following activities. You might consider hosting a fun "Family Night" (or "Fun Night with Friends"), where your spouse and children (or friends) gather, and you and your dog show off the progress you've made. You both have worked very hard these past 5 weeks, and you certainly deserve to be acknowledged and celebrated for your effort.

The Quick Guide

The purpose of this quick guide is to help you assess your dog's current skill levels, see what's next for him to learn, and tune up any behaviors that may have become rusty. For example, at this point in the training he should be fluent in most (if not all) of the basic household manners protocols that you learned in the fundamentals program. At the very least, your dog should sit wherever and whenever you request him to do so. If his *sit* needs more work, remember to incorporate the behavior into the real-life rewards system: Have him sit for everything.

Keep up your enthusiasm, and always end on a positive note.

Whatever skill level you and your dog have reached during this training course, remember that sitting is *always* important, although it is usually the first behavior that a dog owner will take for granted. Sitting easily puts an end to most behavior problems: It is simply impossible for your dog to sit and jump on you at the same time.

One reminder before we get started with the review (and your dog's assessment): When doing any repetitive exercise, stay positive and have fun. Continue teaching a repetitive exercise only as many times as your dog stays interested. If he loses interest or fails too many times and gives up, switch to an exercise that he knows so that you end the training session on a positive note. Do your best to leave your dog wanting more and looking forward to the next session.

Skill 1: The Sit

⊙ LURING. Touch a treat to your dog's nose, then with the treat in your fingertips and your palm facing up, lure up above her nose. As she looks up, her rump touches down. Marker: "good." Do not use the verbal cue. Praise her, touch her collar, and then offer the treat last. See Week One, page 70.

⊙ YOUR DOG'S REAL-LIFE REWARDS SYSTEM. Lure your dog to sit for everything: before meals, walks, playtime, and socialization. For example, when it's time to take her for a walk, before you put the leash on her and go out the door, request that she sit. This teaches her that when she sits, good things can happen for her; it becomes your dog's way to say "please." See Week Two, page 83.

⊙ MODIFYING THE HAND SIGNAL FROM LURE TO CUE. As your dog achieves 80 percent success when luring, introduce the slot machine (slowly withdrawing treats) and reward jackpots for the best behaviors. Keep your eyes focused on her so that you don't miss a thing. See Week Two, page 85.

⊙ WITHDRAWING TREATS. Use the hand signal cue without treats. Hold the treat in the non-cueing hand. See Week Two, page 86.

⊙ ADDING THE VERBAL CUE. Once your dog is fluent with the visual cue (using only your hand signal), you may name that behavior using the verbal cue "sit." In this Fundamentals Training Program, always continue using the visual hand signal at the same time you say any verbal cue, because the repeated pairing helps your dog understand the link between the two. See Week Three, page 98.

⊙ GENERALIZED SITTING. Use the cue at random moments on walks, in crowds, and in situations and environments that are more distracting than your dog is used to. *New skill.*

⊙ EVERYDAY SITTING. Withdraw treats altogether in places that are familiar to your dog. Add new places, new distractions, and more distance so that she understands that although the setting and situation have changed, the behavior you're requesting is the same. Keep up the everyday habit of the real-life rewards system where your dog sits for everything. *New skill.*

Even the youngest puppy wants to please—you just have to keep her focus.

Skill 2: Recall

❯ **LURING, PART ONE.** Lure your dog to move toward you from a few steps away. Have a partner hold your dog by a leash as you lure by drawing the treat toward your knee, and then have your dog sit. Reward on the *sit*. If your dog doesn't sit, just reward on the *recall*. Once that skill has been acquired, add the *sit*. No verbal cue. See Week One, page 73.

❯ **LURING, PART TWO, WITH AN ADDED VERBAL CUE.** Continue the *recall* lure you learned in Part One, adding the verbal cue "[Dog's name], come here." Once your dog is fluent with this step, increase the distance one foot at a time (as long as the dog continues being successful), up to 10 feet. As you get farther away, make sure you are the most interesting thing in your dog's view, because he may not notice the treat. Be happy and animated as he runs to greet you. See Week Two, page 87.

❯ **RECALL-AND-SIT COMBINATION WITH RELEASE.** During supervised play, interrupt with a *recall* after about one minute. Use the recall cue that is currently most fluent for your dog: ideally, his name plus "come here," plus a hand signal (bring hands together and crouch). *Release* him back to another minute of play. This exercise works best when your dog has a human or dog partner to play with. See Week Three, page 98.

❯ **ADDING DISTANCE AND DISTRACTION.** Practice luring with a verbal cue and *recall-sit-release,* adding distance up to 10 yards. Add mild distractions, such as a toy held by a partner, or a partner walking in the other direction. Do the turn-and-run exercise described in Week Four, page 113.

❯ **GENERALIZED RECALLS.** Practice the cue outdoors, in a location with minimal distractions. Arrange supervised playdates in a backyard or park (inside a fenced area) to practice on a leash. Gradually increase the distance at which you recall your dog every minute or two, starting at a distance of a few feet and increasing only as your dog proves fluency. Adding distance requires careful supervision so that your dog doesn't run away. *New skill.*

❯ **RECALLS EVERY DAY AND EVERYWHERE.** It is important to incorporate recalls into your dog's daily routine to help keep him focused on you throughout the day. I don't recommend withdrawing treats altogether for quite some time—even many years—as *recall* cues are typically among the most difficult for dogs to maintain in generalized situations. It's best to be careful and safe. Don't expect your dog to have *recalls* mastered for every situation every day. *New skill.*

Skill 3: Leash Walking

❱ FIRST STEPS TOGETHER: "BE A TREE." Whenever your dog pulls on her leash, stand firm, draw your hands to your chest (as you hold the leash handle), and wait. When your dog looks back at you, mark "good" and recall her as you did in the "puppy come here" recall. If you lure her to sit in front of you, it blocks her ability to run around you. When she arrives, praise, treat, and walk in the opposite direction. Assume that these walks will not be for distance, but just back and forth. If your dog stays close to you without being asked, reward for that. See Week One, page 76.

❱ TETHERING. Tether your dog's leash handle to your belt as you walk around your home and go about your business. Reward your dog for staying close and focusing on you. See Week Two, page 82.

❱ TROUBLESHOOTING: LEASH PULLING. Continue doing the "be a tree" exercise. Play Follow the Lure to increase your dog's focus on you. Anticipate when she is about to pull ahead and, before she can pull, lure in another direction. For Follow the Lure, see page 144.

❱ WALKING EXERCISE: CHANGING DIRECTION. Intentionally change directions often as you walk, luring your dog, and helping her to follow your changes. Weave around obstacles. See Week Three, page 97.

❱ WALKING EXERCISE: INFORMAL HEELING. Have your dog generally walk at your side. Mark "good heel," praise and reward her randomly (slot machine technique) while continuing to walk. Practice quick starts and stops. Use tethering. Reminder: This is not a perfect heel, but one to keep your dog walking alongside you with moments to sniff, pee, and be a dog. See Week Three, page 107.

❱ INFORMAL HEELING: REAL-WORLD WALKS WITH DISTRACTIONS. When you are confident of your dog's ability to focus on you while facing mild distractions, go to a dog park or another place where there are increased distractions *and* a way to make a quick and safe exit if things don't go well. Do not force your dog to do something he isn't quite ready for. *New skill.*

Keeping your dog's focus will help you both navigate potentially dangerous distractions.

Skill 4: Down

◈ LURING. Start with your dog in a *sit* in front of you. Lure by holding a treat between your fingertips, palm facing down, and sliding the treat slowly toward your dog's chest. Keeping your dog's attention on the treat, draw your hand down. When your dog touches down, mark "good down," praise, and treat. Use hand signal only, no verbal cues. See Week Two, page 89.

◈ PUPPY PUSHUPS. Cue your dog with your hand signal to *sit,* then *down,* then *sit* again. Mark each response (say "good" after every *sit* or *down*), and lavish the praise and reward with the food treat only after the full rep (one rep = *sit, down, sit*). As she becomes fluent, add complexity starting with an extra *down* at the end and building toward an extra Puppy Pushup before you give the reward. When your dog learns more cues and dog tricks, include them in the Puppy Pushups routine. See Week Three, page 99.

◈ ADDING THE VERBAL CUE. Lure your dog into the *down* and add the verbal cue as she starts to respond. Remember that you are establishing a link between the hand signal and the verbal cue, so that your dog understands that this behavior also has a name. See Week Four, page 115.

◈ INCORPORATING THE VERBAL CUE WITH PUPPY PUSHUPS. When introducing all verbal cues the process is straightforward: After your dog understands your hand signal fluently, you are able to tag on a name. Once you have established the link between the visual and verbal cues, your dog will respond to both. Since your dog already knows how to do Puppy Pushups, tag on the verbal cues "sit" and "down" along with the visual hand signals. See Week Four, page 115.

◈ DOWN AND SIT AT A DISTANCE. Add distance one foot at a time, mixing random verbal and hand cues for *sit* and *down.* Initially, reward with treats at each small increase of distance (go to your dog and treat her for each success), and then begin to withdraw treats. Also combine this with longer *stay* exercises (see below). *New skill.*

Skill 5: Stay

◈ COOKIE SIT AND TAKE IT. This exercise prepares your dog to learn to stay by having him sit quickly and look to you for help instead of going after a cookie without your permission. Wrap about half of your dog's leash around your hand to shorten the tether enough that your other hand can comfortably reach his nose when he pulls forward during this exercise. With your dog sitting at your side and your hand that holds his leash "glued" to your hip, touch a treat to his nose (with your other hand) and let him sniff it. Next, toss the treat a few feet in front of him and stand still as he tries to get the treat (but cannot reach it because you're holding the leash short). When your dog looks back at you, mark it (say "good"), then cue him to sit with your hand signal, mark once more when he sits (say "good" again), and then immediately direct him to take the treat (point to it and say "take it") as you quickly unwrap the leash from your hand. See Week Three, page 100.

❯ **COOKIE SIT-STAYS.** Similar to *cookie sit,* but now add waiting time before releasing your dog to take the cookie. See Week Three, page 100.

❯ **STAY: THE CONVENTIONAL CUE.** As your dog sits in front of you, slide your outstretched palm gently toward his face as if stopping traffic, and say "stay." Keep your hand in position while you intermittently give treats for staying. Mark "good stay," praise, and reward him with another treat that you have in your other hand. The goal is to teach your dog that the longer he remains in the *sit-stay,* the more treats he will get. The better he stays, the fewer treats he will *need* because he now understands what he is being rewarded for. At first, keep the *stays* short and sweet, then build up his staying power slowly and successfully. As your dog builds up his *stay* power beyond 30 seconds, insert another cue to *stay* in the middle of that *stay* time (and reward for success) so he understands that longer *stays* get more rewards. See Week Three, page 103.

Skill 6: Standing Pose

❯ **LURING.** While your dog sits at your side, hold a treat in your fingertips and slowly lure her forward. As she moves to a standing pose to sniff the treat, mark it (say "good"), praise, and let her have the treat. As she gains success, practice this behavior starting with her sitting at your other side. Repeat the sequence to ultimate success as she learns to *pose* and remain steady while waiting for the treat to come to her. See Week Four, page 115.

❯ **THE VISUAL CUE.** Use the same setup as with the hand signal luring into a *pose,* but this time only pretend to hold a lure in your fingertips. When your dog follows your pretend lure, mark (say "good"), then praise and give her a treat with your other hand. See Week Four, page 116.

› ADDING VERBAL CUES. Once your dog is fluent with the *pose* cue starting on either side of you, add the verbal name "pose" once she is fully standing. See Week Four, page 117.

› POSE FROM DOWN POSITION. Once your dog is fluent with *posing* from the *sit* position on either side of you, and you have successfully named the verbal *pose* cue, start at the *down* position and use both the hand signal and verbal cue until she becomes fluent. See Week Four, page 117.

› CUE COMBINATIONS: ADDING POSE TO PUPPY PUSHUPS. Once your dog is fluent with the *sit-down-sit-down* Puppy Pushup combination, and she *poses* fluently from both a *sit* and a *down,* mix the three cues—*sit, down, pose*—and randomize the pattern. See Week Four, page 127.

Skill 7: Settle Down

› SETTLE DOWN. While he's in a *down* position, silently reward your dog as if you're a human vending machine with six to eight treats, one at a time. As he relaxes and settles, mark ("good settle"), feed the remaining treats (if any), then count to five silently and slowly, mark (say "good"), praise, reward, and *release* him. The reward for a well-performed *settle* is the happy release, lavish praise, and petting for a job well done, possibly leaving him eager to try it again. Don't end the *settle* behavior with another treat or he may link the last treat to your *release* cue and may subsequently think he should jump ahead of you and release himself before you do. See Week Four, page 125.

› SETTLE WITH REWARD. Once your dog has acquired the above *settle,* eliminate the human vending machine and give him a visual hand signal, such as an open hand over his head, as you verbally cue the word "settle." After about five to eight seconds, mark, praise, and reward, but do not release him. Jackpot initially to let him know that he is getting it. Once he gets it, increase the total time that you have him settle, with mark-praise-reward feedback every 8 to 10 seconds. Once he can settle fluently for 30 seconds, introduce the slot machine technique (withdraw treats randomly), with the ultimate goal of phasing out the treats completely, as you would with all successfully learned behaviors. For longer *settles,* you can reward with a stuffed Kong for a minute or two, and then take it away using the *off and take it* trade technique. Phase out the treats (withdraw them using the slot machine technique) once he has become fluent. See Week Four, page 125.

❯ **REAL-LIFE SETTLE.** When your dog is with you in a public place—while standing in line at the bank or at a friend's home—practice *settle*. Mark, praise, and reward (jackpot initially). *New skill.*

Skill 8: Release

❯ **RELEASE: VERBAL CUE.** During all supervised play periods, drop your dog's leash—assuming that you're indoors or in a fenced-off area so that he can't run completely away—and say "release" with a happy voice. See Week Two, page 91.

Skill 9: Off and Take It Trades

❯ **TAKE IT: COOKIE SIT-STAYS (REVIEW).** The *off and take it* trade builds on the *cookie sit-stay* behavior, so please review that skill so that your dog is fluent before you progress to the next stage. Remember to make it fun so that she will want to play this "game" some more. See the *cookie sit-stay* review in this chapter on page 135, and the detailed lesson in Week Three, page 100.

❯ **TAKE IT EXERCISE.** Put one treat in your fingertips at your dog's nose level, pivot just your hand—don't move your arm—and say "take it." Mark (say "good"), and repeat immediately. See below for the *off* part of this trade. See Week Three, page 105.

❯ **OFF AND TAKE IT TRADE, PHASE 1.** Do three *take it* exercises one after another, and then on the fourth do *not* say "take it." When your dog tries to take the treat, say "off" suddenly and loudly enough to be slightly shocking. Typically, the dog will back away and look up at you, trying to understand what you want. As soon as she moves even the slightest little bit away from your hand, mark (say "good") and give her the treat, praising her lavishly in the happiest tone of voice you can muster up. Once she seems to understand the "off" and "take it" directions, increase the delay between *off* and *take it*. See Week Three, page 104.

❯ **OFF AND TAKE IT TRADE, PHASE 2.** Pair the *off* cue with *take it* at your dog's food bowl to diminish food guarding. Use a stuffed Kong reward or other item that she values as much as or more than her food bowl. See Week Four, page 117.

Skill 10: Boundary Training

❱❱ **INTERIOR DOORS, PART ONE.** *Sit* and *stay* at doorway while on the leash. Mark your dog's good *stay,* praise, and reward. Open the door; if he starts to get up, close the door and re-cue him to *sit* and *stay.* Open the door again very slowly. If he stays for a moment, mark for the good *stay,* open the door and lead him through it. Require your dog to *sit-stay* a bit longer on each subsequent rep before opening the door all the way and leading your dog through. This phase is complete when you can open the door all the way without your dog moving. See Week Four, page 122.

❱❱ **INTERIOR DOORS, PART TWO.** Once the previous skill has been acquired, walk through the open doorway as your dog continues to *sit-stay.* After a moment, lure your dog to "come here" and then have him follow you through the door. Mark, praise him, and give him a treat. See Week Four, page 122.

❱❱ **FRONT DOOR.** At the closed front door, hold the leash as in *cookie sit-stay* (leash hand "glued" to your hip), have a partner ring or knock, and keep the leash glued to your hip as the dog barks and jumps. Remain silent until your dog focuses on you, then mark it and lure him as you *recall* with "come here." Tell your partner to ring again. When your dog stays and focuses on you, slowly open the door. Close the door again if he tries to jump on the visitor. If your dog remains sitting, then jackpot. See Week Four, page 123.

❱❱ **VISITOR.** Allow a visitor to enter; he shouldn't approach your dog if there is any hint that the dog may get excited, fearful, or protective. If the dog remains calm, the visitor may approach. See Week Four, page 124.

❱❱ **FURNITURE AND ROOMS.** Plan ahead and use baby gates and x-pens to keep areas off-limits. Use the *off* cue only when you catch your dog as he takes his first step or two onto or into the off-limits space. See Week Four, page 124.

❱❱ **CLIMBING STAIRS.** Use baby gates and x-pens to keep your dog off the stairs while he's uncrated. Use a short leash and keep him near you and against the wall as you walk stairs with him at your side, neither ahead of nor behind you. See Week Four, page 120.

Congratulations! You and your dog have done it. You have created a spirited bond. You are a team. It might be a good idea to bookmark this Quick Guide and take a few moments to flip back through the pages of the Fundamentals Training Program as you review each cue. You could probably turn to just about any page at random and recall a specific breakthrough, challenge, or story that makes you laugh . . . or just shake your head because what once seemed impossible is now becoming ordinary.

Visit positivelywoof.com to download a free certificate that you can fill out and display proudly. If your dog could high-five, this would be the time to do it. The good news is that the chapters ahead will actually teach him the High Five and other tricks, along with full-fledged canine good citizenship. As you'll see, continuing your training will strengthen your dog's bond with your family, keep him focused on figuring out how to earn more rewards, and give him less time to figure out how to be destructive. You've done the hardest work; now you will want to maintain your dog's good behaviors with consistent practice.

Take a bow!

Chapter Nine

Training Games and Activities

As I'm sure you learned the moment you brought your new dog home, these creatures *love* to play. The more we make learning fun for them (and for ourselves), the more our dogs want to learn.

At the end of each chapter of your Fundamentals Program, I have listed activities that may help with that week's lessons, and I also encourage you to experiment with any games you think may interest your dog and match her skill level. Some activities will start as favorites and then fade into the background as other games capture her interest even more.

Keep an open mind and try as many of them as you can. You'll come up with ideas for modifying them as your dog (and you) gets more skilled. You'll also invent your own games, especially if you involve your children in training. (Turn to page 149 if you're looking for ideas to involve kids in these games and activities.) Share your own games at our website (positivelywoof.com) and we'll post some of them with your name.

Whatever game or activity you choose, always remember to help your dog learn and clearly understand the rules of the game by marking her behavior and praising and rewarding her when she is successful.

The activities included here are designed to give your dog practice in four specific areas:

❯ Relationship development

❯ Skill training

❯ Behavior and safety

❯ Socialization opportunities

Relationship Development Activities

These simple games are intended to enforce the bond between you and your dog. The goal of each is to get your dog to focus his attention more intensely on you.

❯ **WHICH HAND?** This is a simple guessing game. Start by letting your dog see you put a treat in one hand. Close both hands and put them behind your back. Then bring them both out in front of your dog and say "which hand?" Open the hand that your dog first sniffs or touches; if it holds the treat, he gets to eat it while you gleefully praise him. If he guesses wrong, open the other hand for him to see it for a moment before you shut both hands. Then try another round. This game can be used to warm up a dog for training; once your dog understands the rules, use it if he starts to lose focus.

❯ **FIND ME.** This game is also known as Hide-and-Seek for Dogs. Your dog is ready to play this game once she can *sit-stay* for 60 seconds and can hold her *stay* for about 10 seconds when you leave the room. Start teaching the game by standing in plain sight in the next room while your dog holds her perfect *stay*. Then call her name and say "find me." When your dog finds you, mark that ("good find me"), praise her lavishly as you touch her collar, and reward her. Start the next round from the spot at which your dog just found you. Build up to harder-to-find hiding places and move to outdoor fenced-in locations.

Variation for beginners: If your dog can't yet *sit-stay* on her own for 60 seconds, you can use a training partner to keep her sitting while you hide. When you call out "find me," your partner releases your dog and (if necessary) lures her in your general direction.

❯ **THE NAME GAME.** Some games and activities can be simple, and this is one of them. The goal is to help your dog love hearing his name. Say your dog's name when you hand-feed him, when you quietly pet him, and at random moments during training. As your training comes to include exercises with greater distractions, test your dog's Name Game attention with random calls of his name when you're at home and in separate rooms, adding the cue "come here" once the dog knows his name.

❯ **EYE-CONTACT EXERCISE.** Ask for eye contact at random moments. For example, immediately after you have rewarded your dog for demonstrating a skill, touch another treat lure to her nose to establish her interest, then bring the treat to your eyes and, if her attention remains steady, mark, praise, and reward. If you have established an eye-contact verbal cue, such as "ready," "look," or "watch me," use it in these exercises. More advanced eye-contact exercises are to ask for eye contact using the verbal cue at random moments during a walk and when there are competing distractions.

❯ **CATCH YOUR DOG DOING SOMETHING YOU LIKE.** At least once every day, acknowledge a moment when your dog offers a good behavior without being asked. It can be eye contact, a smile, an offered *sit,* improved walking by your side, remaining attentive for a relatively long time, and so forth. I believe that the more you acknowledge your dog's volunteered efforts, the harder he will try to offer even more. For more on this, see Week Three, page 106.

Variation: Select a "bonus behavior of the day": Whenever your dog volunteers it, he gets an extra jackpot (excited praise and extra treats). This variation helps you become more focused on your dog; when you play this game, you will probably also notice other behaviors that he volunteers on his own.

Skill Training Games

Some of these skill training games are used to test behaviors and cues that your dog already understands; others will teach new skills and tricks. You can also try adapting them to practice a variety of cues simultaneously.

◆ COME AND GO. Your dog will need to have acquired some degree of *recall* to play this game, and you'll need a partner who is also armed with treats. Start by asking your dog to sit at your partner's side while you stand about 10 feet away. Have your partner crouch, point to you, and say "go!" An instant later you will crouch, open your arms, and say your dog's name as you recall her enthusiastically. For example, I would call my dog by saying "Brieo, come here!" When your dog comes to you, cue her to *sit* in front of you, mark ("good sit"), praise her, touch her collar, and give her a treat. Then tell her to *sit* at your side, crouch, and point to your partner and say "go!" It's now your partner's turn to crouch with open arms and *recall* her enthusiastically. Back and forth, take turns *recalling* your dog, cueing her to *sit* for a treat. In addition to reinforcing skills, Come and Go socializes her to take cues from a trusted partner.

Variations: 1) Increase the distance; 2) have your dog perform a different cue or behavior (one that she already knows) on each lap, such as a *down,* Puppy Pushup, or some other trick; 3) combine Come and Go with Find Me by recalling your dog to and from a different room than your partner is in; 4) play with more than one partner at a time and randomize which person your dog will go to next.

◆ FOLLOW THE LURE. This is a fun and easy game that builds your dog's positive reinforcement history. Touch a treat to his nose and slowly move it away so that he follows the treat. After about three seconds, praise him and, as you touch his collar, give him the treat. Take out another treat and do the exercise for four seconds, then five seconds, then six, and so forth. Lure him around you in a circle, through your legs, take a step or two forward, reverse directions. As he realizes how this game is played, start luring a bit faster. You are not aiming to trick him or to cause him to fail but rather to build up his skill at following your lures.

◆ FIND IT. Similar to the game Find Me, this game (also called Find the Treasure) teaches your dog to find an object. Your dog is ready to play this game once she can *sit-stay* for enough time for you to get out of the room, hide an object, and return (at least 10 seconds). Start with a toy that your dog is interested in, and let her sniff the toy. Then cue a *sit-stay* and hide the object in the next room; place it in plain sight on the first trial, and on subsequent trials build up to more difficult hiding spots, such as inside a cardboard box. As you progress with this game beyond the Fundamentals Training Program, add naming the object, which teaches your dog to distinguish certain objects.

❯ TETHERING. With your dog tethered to your belt, mark, praise, and reward him for focusing on you and for heeling, especially as you speed up, slow down, and make abrupt turns. You can also add other cues to these brief tethering exercises. (See page 75 for a more detailed introduction to this leash-walking exercise.)

❯ SUPERVISED PLAY WITH RECALL AND RELEASE. It's important that your dog have free play opportunities to bring variety to her training. You have been directing her lessons; she needs to have some time not to be directed. It is wonderful to witness two similar-size, well-socialized dogs square off in a play bow and wrestle (see page 180). If both dogs are able to share toys, you can introduce a tug toy (see Tug below) as a trading game.

To make supervised play also a learning opportunity, *recall* both dogs after a minute (or two minutes if both of them are playing particularly well), then mark, praise, and reward for the successful recall. As soon as your dog can sit, lure her to you and cue *sit,* mark, praise, and reward. Do not have your dog learn a cue during the *recall,* so if she recalls successfully but does not sit yet, praise her for the "come here." Make this *recall* brief and *release* her back to play, ideally at the same time as your partner releases his dog to begin another round of play.

❯ TUG. Playing tug with a rope toy or other tug toy can be tricky. On one hand, you want your dog to try to "own" the toy as he tries to tug it away from you; on the other hand, it is important for safety that your dog understand that this is a game that you control. To teach him to tug by your rules means that you need to teach it as a trading game, rather than a game about "owning" the object. As you've already learned, trading activities are an important step toward making sure your dog doesn't guard toys and food. Every trade needs to be for something he values at least as much as what he currently has. For many dogs, a reliable way to make the toy trade valuable is to offer a treat along with it.

The first time you give your dog the tug toy, have another toy and a good treat ready to help him trade away the tug toy immediately, using the *off and take it* trade protocols from Weeks Three and Four. Be prepared to cue *off* somewhat more forcefully than usual on the first couple of trials, and make sure that the trade is a valuable one from your dog's perspective.

Trade back to the tug toy right away, so that your dog learns that giving up the tug does not always mean that playtime is over. The more rigorous you are with controlling these early tug trades, the better your dog will become at *off and take it* trades.

❯ **RETRIEVE.** While some dogs simply don't enjoy retrieving, others are practically addicted to it. If your dog falls in the latter camp, you can use retrieving objects (a ball, a flying disc, or a toy that has been designed for retrieving) as lures.

Teaching a dog to retrieve starts with getting her excited about having the toy that has been reserved especially for this game. Most puppies will get excited about the special toy, while it is not uncommon to teach an older dog to fetch by using a special toy or ball that holds a treat that she will get to eat when she picks it up. Actually, you need two toys that you take out only for retrieving. Make sure your dog is excited about this toy before you toss it close enough that she will remain focused on it and will be able to focus back to you when you *recall* her. Try the verbal cue "fetch" as you toss the toy, although she will undoubtedly be more focused on the visual than on what you have to say.

The moment your dog picks up the prize, mark it ("good fetch"). After she enjoys her prize for a few moments, recall her with "come here" as you wave an identical toy to entice her. If your dog brings the first toy, you're in luck, so praise her profusely as you get her to drop it by showing her the other one and treating her when she does drop it. At the same time, toss the identical toy a few feet away and cue "fetch." If she returns without the first toy, then toss the second one the moment she reaches you and run to the first one. When she gets the second toy, *recall* her as you lure her toward you with the first one—sometimes a dog will carry one toy to the other one if they are fairly close together. Getting your dog to drop the retrieved first toy usually makes for a good *recall* skill as well as a good *off and take it* trade.

Training games are a great way to develop skills and strengthen your bond.

Another way to build your dog's interest in fetching is to keep her in *cookie sit-stay* (keep the leash "glued" to your hip after you toss the toy) for an extra moment until she focuses on you. This technique works best if your dog has already mastered the *cookie sit-stay* lesson. For more on retrieving, see Chapter Ten's detailed breakdown of dog tricks on page 168.

Behavior and Safety

You can turn basic behavior and safety training into games, which will make learning these very essential skills more fun and engaging.

❯ HAND-FEEDING (see Chapter Three for hand-feeding protocol). While you're practicing the hand-feeding protocol, you can also play some of the games described in this section. Play Find Me by feeding a portion of your dog's meal each time she finds you, and take her food bowl with you when you hide again. Play Come and Go with a partner from whom you have already conditioned your dog to accept hand-feeding. You can even play a rally game (see page 244) by feeding your dog a portion of her meal at each station.

❯ BITE INHIBITION, HANDLING, AND GENTLING (see Chapter Three and the Fundamentals Training Program Week One [Chapter Four] for more detail). Randomly, throughout the day, pet your puppy as a handling and gentling exercise; this may require rewards if he is uncomfortable with being touched. Play Pass the Puppy and Peekaboo, count his toes, handle his feet, pretend to clip his nails. Explore your dog's mouth, massage his gums, count his teeth—and remember to say "ouch" to help him learn his bite inhibition.

❯ CRATE TRAINING (see Chapter Three for additional detail). When you play Find It, include your dog's crate as a hiding place. Play games and do training exercises right around the crate. In general, make your dog's crate her sanctuary and also a familiar place that is not isolated from the rest of her real-life experience.

❯ LEASH WALKING (see walking exercises throughout the training program). Think of every walk as a training opportunity that is also a game: Pause to practice a couple of cues that your dog already knows, and then continue walking. Be sure to mark, praise, and reward his correct behaviors. Your dog's success during those random training moments during a walk will give him a sense of accomplishment along with variety and fun.

Socialization Opportunities

A well-socialized dog is one that gets along calmly and confidently with other dogs and other people without being fearful, aggressive, or too exuberant. The sooner you make socialization a regular part of your schedule, the sooner you both will be able to reap the rewards: more opportunities for fun, filled with new experiences and people.

❯ **VISITS.** Make a plan to visit public places as often as you feel that your dog is ready. Go to the vet just to say hi, and if you plan on using a groomer, do the same: just a friendly visit to say hi . . . and get a treat and some petting. Find stores and outdoor public places that a dog is allowed to visit.

❯ **WALK TRAINING: GREET YOUR NEIGHBOR.** It's likely you'll meet other people walking their dogs when you walk yours. As you approach another person with a dog—assuming that you feel comfortable and safe—call out hello as you stop and cue your dog to *sit* and *stay*. If the neighbor continues to advance, ask her in a friendly voice to pause because you and your dog are training right now. Generally, the neighbor will gladly comply. If both of you have time for a brief chat, speak to each other at a slight distance, then advance a few paces and pause again. Try to keep your dog in a *sit-stay,* regardless of what the other dog is doing; however, as always, it is best to avoid problems rather than try to cure them once they happen. As your dog learns greater impulse control, you will be able to greet some neighbors with a handshake while your respective dogs are sitting.

❯ **DOG PARK VISIT.** When you first go to a dog park, try to go at off-peak hours so you and your dog can acclimate, do some training, and get comfortable. Make sure to practice *recalling* and *releasing* your dog, so that she gets conditioned to *recalls* equaling a reward far more often than the end of playtime. Your ability to recall your dog reliably also means that in the event of a dog fight, you will be better able to get your dog out of the melee. In fact, with experience, you will notice certain combinations and body postures that are signs that a fight is about to erupt, and you can recall your dog in anticipation. (See page 216 for more on dog park visits.)

❯ **SUPERVISED FREE PLAY.** Try to organize playdates at the dog park during off-peak times. Use periodic recalls and encourage your play partner to do the same, before releasing your dog back to play. This will help your dog understand that a *recall* does not mean the end of playtime.

Kids and Dogs

Your goal is to help your dog enjoy kids, not merely tolerate them. If you don't have kids of your own (and assuming that your dog has been checked out by your vet or a qualified trainer and does not have a fear of or an aggression toward kids), I want you to beg, borrow, or steal someone else's . . . well, stealing may be going a bit far. Make sure to involve the child's parent to help you monitor safety while the child learns the proper way to interact with your dog. By the way, it is probably more comfortable and safer for a child to give your dog a treat from a flat palm than from closed fingertips.

Almost all the games described in this chapter can involve kids, depending on each child's maturity, self-control, confidence, and coordination. Don't force children to do something they're not ready to do, even if you have made special arrangements to have a child come and play with your dog. Some kids get freaked out if a dog licks their hand; they are content to merely pet a dog or watch from a distance—which is fine because just having a child around will provide a mild distraction for your dog. Many children love the games Which Hand?, Come and Go, and Find Me. To help build your dog's trust and comfort with children, involve them in hand-feeding if both the kid and dog are ready to do that. Supervise all interactions very carefully.

Kids will also invent some wonderful games. My kids have invented many that make me smile just thinking about them:

❯ CASH REGISTER. Fill a toy cash register with dog treats. When the dog sits, shakes paws, or does some other cue, the child pushes the cash register key and gets a treat for the dog. Sometimes the game includes dressing up the very patient dog in loose clothing and parading like at a fashion show.

❯ TEA PARTY. The child-size table is set for high tea, complete with plastic cups and folded napkins. The dog gets a setting at the table with his own tiny bowl and a bib napkin draped on his chest. Somehow, my children often wound up eating part of a dog biscuit, while my dog got the peanut butter sandwich. Although it's harmless, I don't recommend integrating this into your version of the game.

❯ FIRST COMMUNION. The kids adapted the Beg trick (see page 175) to pray together with the dog. One kid blesses everyone and doles out crackers and dog biscuits to the parishioners.

Dog Parties

The more elaborate kids' games and activities include dog parties. If you have guests at a dog party, make sure beforehand that your dog enjoys being around each of those guests. The same goes for guest dogs: Make sure that any dog that is invited already gets along with every other dog and person. Dog parties should be relatively brief and have structured quiet time. If the party is at a park, be careful about other possible guarding issues. Here are a few of my favorite kid-appropriate dog party ideas. For more dog party ideas, visit positivelywoof.com.

❯ WELCOME HOME PARTY. This quiet party happens at least a week or two after you first bring home your new best friend. Depending on how your dog is adjusting to having new people around, you may be able to have a couple of guests hand-feed or pet him. Your kids can take some "ownership" for the new family dog's enjoyment by giving tours of the dog's new setup, by making decorations, and by leading a quiet game.

❯ BIRTHDAY PARTY. Your dog has two birthday anniversaries: the day she was born and the day she came home with you. Show off the tricks and cues your dog can do. Play some of the games in this section. Loosely wrap a present with some smelly treats in newspaper for your dog to shred open.

❯ DOG TRAINING SCHOOL GRADUATION. Proudly show off your dog's new skills and tricks that you learned in this Fundamentals Training Program—and make it official by filling out a Best Dog Ever diploma, available to download free from our website positivelywoof.com. By now, your dog's socialization will be stronger, so you may want to have at least part of the celebration in public. If other dogs are involved, you may want to include a fun dog show where everyone shows off what his or her dog can do.

Download your diploma and display it with pride. Visit positivelywoof.com.

The
Next Steps

Chapter Ten

Clicker Training and Dog Tricks

After my canine students complete the five-week fundamentals course, I begin the next, more advanced phase of instruction with trick training. I like to combine teaching dog tricks with what is called clicker training, because the clicker can dramatically speed up learning tricks. And a dog who knows tricks is a challenged and spirited dog. The opposite—a bored, unengaged dog—is more likely to become destructive or dispirited or both. It's not so unlike how our children behave in school when they're bored, or when the work becomes much too easy for them.

When that happens—when, say, gifted children must sit through eight hours of lessons that they already understand and are not challenged by in any way—they may become restless, distracted, and frustrated. They may look for things to occupy their minds; often, those things include disruptive behaviors.

The same goes for our dogs. When they feel consistently challenged in positive ways, they are far less likely to get into trouble. The five-week fundamentals course required you to invest a lot of time with your dog: time during which you were focused almost exclusively on her, when you challenged her a lot, praised her often, and provided her with many treats. Now that we've completed that phase, it's unrealistic to think that your dog won't want the same level of attention and interaction. She will. Tricks are a great way to provide that positive attention, and clicker training makes learning tricks easier and more successful. Once you and your dog understand the basics of clicker training, it will probably take the two of you about one week to learn each trick if you practice for five minutes about five times each day. If you don't have that much time, then it may take a little longer. In all cases, maintain the real-life rewards system of having your dog sit before "earning" anything.

Tricks are also fun. Let us not forget that one of the reasons that we own dogs is because they bring our families joy. Countless times, I've had the pleasure of watching my students experience the amusement and pride that comes with showing off their dog's ability to shake hands, roll over, or fetch the newspaper. And it's equally fun for our dogs, who are hardwired to play.

"Click" Marks the Spot

In the Fundamentals Training Program, you learned to mark your dog's success at following your lures and cues by saying a marker word such as "good." As we embark on this next phase of training, I am going to introduce you to a different method of cueing and rewarding your dog called clicker training. In clicker training, we replace the marker word such as "good" with a *click* sound from a handheld clicker.

While clickers have evolved since having been introduced more than a hundred years ago as a children's "cricket" toy, they all make that distinctive click sound to mark the precise moment when your dog does what you have requested. The clicker fits in your palm. Dog training

Box-style clicker

clickers have evolved from a simple box style to more ergonomic button styles that feature a finger loop. Some are attached to a target pointer that guides your dog to shift his head, paw, or body to a specific posture or target.

The clicker has advantages over voice marking. For example, the clicker makes a clearer and more distinct noise than our voices, which can fluctuate in tone and volume. While your voice may be affected by the weather or the kind of day you're having, the clicker makes a consistent sound that your dog will come to associate with treats. And the precision of the clicker means you can mark the *exact* moment your dog has performed a particular behavior, such as lifting a paw to start a handshake. A clicker is like a single snapshot; your voice, on the other hand, is like a long-exposure photo. That ability to mark behavior precisely also means the clicker is a wonderful tool for acknowledging any behavior that your dog offers naturally. I'll show you how to use the clicker to "free shape" your dog's natural quirks into delightful tricks.

Button-style clicker

Target pointer with embedded clicker

Karen Pryor, the godmother of clicker training, was among those who first popularized the technique to train marine mammals. In the 1960s, Karen's husband, who was preparing to open Sea Life Park in Oahu, Hawaii, asked her to help train the park's dolphins. A mom raising young children, she had previously studied zoology and behavioral biology. The dolphin training that Karen and other trainers developed was so effective and efficient that the clicker technique eventually became common practice throughout marine mammal parks around the world. However, it took Karen many years to introduce clicker training techniques into the dog world, in part because old-school aversive training seemed to do the job well enough.

Today, the clicker plays an important role in training dogs using positive reinforcement. To understand why, imagine this simple example: When you taught your dog to sit, you first lured his nose up, causing his back legs to fold. When his rump touched down, you *marked* it by saying "good," then you praised him, and rewarded him with a treat. In clicker training, instead of saying "good" to mark a desired behavior, you click the clicker once to mark the precise moment your dog's rump touches the floor. After the click, you praise and treat as before.

Believe me, it works! But one word of caution: When you train using the clicker, limit the length of each training session to five minutes. As you learned in the fundamentals program, dogs learn better in short sessions several times each day than in one long session. If your dog seems to have interest and focus left over at the end of the session, that's great—it probably means he will be more interested when you begin the next session. It is also typical to finish a training session before you and your dog have fully shaped the new behavior into a new cue. When that is the case, start the next session by reviewing a few steps so that your dog builds up a habit of success and locks in the learning from the previous session.

And one more thing: The sound of the clicker may alarm or frighten some dogs. If that's the case, muffle the clicker by wrapping it with a couple of heavy socks. Peel off layers of socks as he seems more comfortable. If he still seems frightened, try adding more socks so that the click is barely audible. Help demystify the clicker for your timid dog by allowing him to sniff the clicker (but do not force him to do so), and let him watch you put the clicker in your hand and wrap it with socks.

Introducing the Clicker with Hand-Feeding

First, let's teach your dog the value of the click. Begin that lesson by once again hand-feeding all your dog's meals over the next four days. In general, I find that hand-feeding is a good exercise to reintroduce whenever my dogs (or other dogs that I am boarding and training) are learning a new, difficult skill, or when I sense that they are beginning to lose focus.

1 CLICK AND HAND-FEED Sit on a chair or, if it's easier, on the floor and have your dog sit in front of you. With her food bowl in your lap or at your side, hold the clicker where your dog can't focus on it. Be silent and keep other sounds to a minimum. As soon as you click, hand-feed a bite of food. When your dog finishes the bite of food, pause for a moment, make sure you have your dog's focus on you or

1.

on her food, and then click again. Let your dog see you reach immediately into the bowl for her next handful. Pause once more before clicking again. Repeat these steps about five times to help your dog begin to make the connection between the click and the food. Most dogs pick this up fairly fast and enjoy this new game.

2 PAUSE BEFORE FEEDING This time, pause a second longer for the click; continue to feed immediately after the click. On each of the next five handfuls, lengthen the intervening pause by one additional second. Then, on the next five handfuls, randomize the length of pauses between clicks from one to 10 seconds. Keep giving the food immediately after the click. Remember to stay silent.

2.

3 KEEP HER FOCUS Your dog's happy, animated body language will let you know she is getting the connection between the click and the food. Once she figures that out, try adding a slight delay after the click before giving her each handful of food. Watch your dog to see if she is looking at the food after the click; this means she understands that a treat will follow each sound of the clicker. It also means she is having fun learning what, to her, is another new game.

For subsequent meals, go through Step One more quickly, saving more of the meal for Steps Two and Three. Within a few days, your dog should be making a clear connection between the click and the food. Remember to hand-feed her at different locations to help her generalize the connection between the click and the treat.

The Paw Shake

et's practice clicking on a brand-new skill, rather than on one your dog has already learned, which will also bring us to our first trick: the Paw Shake. As a reminder: I recommend teaching any new trick in a quiet room where there are no distractions.

1 OFFER A TREAT First, with your dog sitting in front of you, let him see you place a treat in the palm of your hand and then close your hand around the treat. Hold that closed hand at the level of his chin, then move it up slightly. Watch closely: If your dog moves

his paw at all, then click immediately and treat. As his nose follows the treat going up, his body will try to stretch up to get it, meaning he may move his paws or even slightly lift one. It's okay if his head stretches up to try getting the treat, because his paw will move, too—even if ever so slightly—and that's the moment when you click and treat.

If he doesn't move his paw after five seconds, reset to a different spot (for example, turn around) and signal him to do a cue that he already knows, such as a *down*. When he performs the cue, click and open your hand for him to get the treat. You're helping him understand that the click is his marker for good behavior—and most important to him, a signal that he has earned a treat.

If he succeeds, do it again: Whenever he moves his paw, click and open your hand for him to eat the treat. If he fails, ignore it this time: no click, no treat, just start over, no harm done. He will come to understand the clicker game. He will also understand that he needs to figure out what he did that earned that last successful click and treat. He will try again, so be patient.

2 LURE UP Let's say he's now beginning to move his paw a little toward your hand. Mark the slight paw movement with a click and reward him with the treat every time. Within five minutes he will catch on that you're waiting and watching for him to move his paw.

When that moment happens, it will seem like a light in his brain has switched on—he's catching on. Now he'll move his paw a little more deliberately each time, so, little by little, slightly delay the click (and treat) until he moves his paw ever more deliberately. This may take a number of sessions, so be patient.

3 POLISH THE TRICK Now you will put your open, empty hand in his view. Since he is already moving his paw, challenge him by delaying the click (and treat) until he raises his paw slightly higher, coming closer and closer to touching your hand. When he finally touches your hand with his paw, click and treat him with a jackpot. The correct way to jackpot with the clicker is to click only once, give him the extra treats in your open palm, and verbally praise the heck out of him! Pay attention to petting him around his collar, which reminds him that touching his collar is a good thing.

3.

When your dog paws at your hand a few times in a row, it means that he is making the connection between the Paw Shake, the click, and the treat, so taper the jackpots back to a single treat. Teaching each trick becomes a game of waiting, watching, and clicking to mark the right behavior when it is offered. If he offers a different behavior, ignore it. You must stay focused on just a single behavior at a time when teaching a new trick.

Once your dog understands what you want and is touching your hand confidently, it is time to name that behavior. Most people like "shake," so let's add that word as your verbal cue, while you also continue to use the hand signal.

Now that the behavior is named and he understands what you want, you can raise the bar—perhaps clicking only when he touches your hand right away. If he's too slow, don't click. Just ignore it and request another shake. When you want more from your dog, it can cause a bit of frustration, but in a good way, because during a phase of mild frustration the dog will work harder to get to the next level you've set. He wants to hear the click and get the treat.

Once your dog becomes quick and completely fluent with the Paw Shake, it's time to raise the stakes again: Try giving the verbal cue without the hand gesture. (The first time he shakes successfully with only your verbal cue, that's worth a jackpot.) Next, interchange reps of verbal-only and visual-only cues, then pair verbal and visual cues together again, then separate and interchange them again. Continue to click and treat for each success. Once your dog achieves fluency with the verbal-only and visual-only cues, start withdrawing the treats slot-machine style.

Congratulations! Your dog has mastered his first dog trick, and you have successfully learned to shape a behavior.

TRAINING CONCEPT: SHAPING

As you taught your dog the Paw Shake, you were shaping his behavior—in other words, gradually conditioning him to do what you want. Many dogs offer a paw shake naturally, which often makes this a great early trick. Look for those behaviors that *your* dog does naturally, because those will be the easiest to shape and put on cue. Later in this chapter (page 171), I'll show you some free-shaping techniques that are designed to discover and encourage your dog's natural behaviors.

You can shape behaviors that your dog offers naturally into tricks and skills.

You've been shaping your dog's behavior throughout the Fundamentals Training Program. For example, think back to when you first taught your dog the *recall* cue. In the beginning, you rewarded him for a *recall* of just a step or two. Then you rewarded him for coming to you from many steps away. You eventually shaped his full *recall* across a room, eventually adding a *sit,* until you reached a fluent full *recall* in many different locations. Little by little, your dog's behavior was being shaped as he came to understand that he was to come to you whenever you recalled him, from whatever distance, regardless of the distractions.

There are two types of shaping techniques we'll discuss as you learn clicker training: directed shaping and free shaping. I recommend that you and your dog learn both techniques, as each one has advantages in specific situations to expand your dog's learning abilities.

Directed Shaping

You used directed shaping when you taught your dog the Paw Shake. You directed her when you held the lure slightly above her head so she would stretch up to try and get it. When she moved her paw, you clicked that behavior and gave her a treat. As you raised the criteria by delaying the click until she lifted her paw higher and higher, you continued to direct her behavior, shaping it to touch your hand. After she first touched your hand, you continued to use directed shaping to refine her movement and reduce her response time.

Hand Targeting

When you used directed shaping to teach your dog the Paw Shake, your hand became a target for your dog to touch. If you choose to enrich your dog training experience with dog tricks, you will want to teach your dog the generalized skill of target touching your hand with his nose. Once your dog has learned that your hand is a target, you will be able to direct him to touch it whenever and wherever you hold it out and say the word "target" or "touch."

An open palm is a good place to begin target training.

To transform your hand into a target, hold a treat in your fingertips or your open hand (use your thumb to hold the treat in place against your palm). When he fluently touches your hand target, it's time to name it ("touch" or "target") by using the visual hand target and verbal cue together. After a few days of fluency, try alternating verbal-only and visual-only cues, also using a few reps of verbal and visual cues together.

Some advanced trick trainers distinguish between requesting nose touches and paw touches by using a fist target for one and a palm target for the other, as well as distinct verbal cues for each.

Your dog can learn to treat almost anything as a target.

Once your dog has learned that your hand is the target that he is supposed to touch, it's time to start using it to teach a specific trick.

Targeting: Rollover

Let's use target touching to teach your dog to roll over. The Rollover is a fun trick to show off, and it also helps build your dog's trust that she's safe when you put her on her back. Not only will an audience appreciate that, but so will your vet and groomer. If your dog has hip problems, the Rollover may not be a healthy trick; instead, try luring her onto her side. Even if your dog has healthy hips and back, it's best to teach the Rollover on a somewhat soft surface such as a carpet or the lawn.

1 START IN A DOWN To teach the Rollover, start by cueing your dog to lie down. Then put a treat in your fingertips and lure from her nose across the back of her shoulder area, in the opposite direction from the way that her hips are tucked. Click and treat when her nose and head follow the lure just a little.

1.

2 LURE ACROSS Rep by rep, inch by inch, lure farther and farther across her shoulders. Click and treat each time she catches up to touch your slow-moving hand with her nose while she starts rolling onto her back.

2.

3 ONTO HER BACK When your dog gets to this halfway point (she's fully on her back), that's worth a jackpot. After the halfway point, keep luring her to flop over to her other side.

3.

4 FLOP AND ROLL UP Once she has flopped over, continue to lure her to that final upright *down* position. That earns her another jackpot. When she starts to gain coordination for the full motion, speed up her movement by luring a little faster, but not so fast that she can't keep up. Click and treat each success.

4.

To shape the lure into a rollover hand signal, shorten the sweeping motion of the lure. Start the luring motion with your palm facing up, and when your dog gets to the halfway point (she's up on her back), flip your luring hand over so that it's now palm down as you sweep down the other side of her body and your dog flops to follow. Continue clicking and treating as your dog masters this step. As she becomes fluent with your luring motion, add the verbal cue "roll over." Begin to experiment with giving only a verbal cue once she is fluent with the hand lure and the new verbal cue together. When your dog follows only the verbal cue, that's worth a jackpot.

Removing the Hand Target to Teach Wave, High Five, and Fist Bump

Let's return to the Paw Shake. Since you don't want your hand target to be part of the finished trick, the next step is to remove the target. Let's do that by teaching your dog to raise her paw in the air as if she were waving. This trick is a variation on the Paw Shake, as you'll teach her to wave using a similar movement, but you will want her to raise her paw higher and not touch the target.

First, you'll transform the Paw Shake into a High Five or Fist Bump by raising the target (your hand) higher and higher. With each success, remember to click and treat as you have done with previous tricks and behaviors. Make sure to generalize your dog's understanding by offering your hand a little to the left, to the right, higher, and lower. Typically, a dog picks up this "game" of touching your moving hand quite quickly. But anytime your dog doesn't get it, just back up to the step where she was last successful and restart by breaking down the next sequence. Rotate your hand so that your palm faces your dog and you have a High Five for her to touch. Close your hand and you'll teach her the Fist Bump. Now you have taught your dog three tricks in one: Paw Shake, High Five, and Fist Bump.

To shape the Paw Shake into the Wave, offer your dog the signal to shake by moving your hand in toward her. As she tries to touch your hand, move it a little higher. Click and treat on her upward motion before her paw actually touches your hand. On subsequent reps, raise your hand a little higher for your dog to earn the click and treat. As she becomes fluent with the upward motion, try shaping her movement to follow your hand in a pattern of up, down, then up again in a wave (and of course, click and treat for each success) until she becomes fluent with following that pattern. If she's not catching on, break it down: Just go up and down until she's fluent.

When your dog has become fluent with that step, it's time to wave from a short distance. On this next trial, as she follows up, down, up and is about to touch your hand, move your hand away as you click, then treat her. Even though she didn't touch your hand target, she did follow your hand gestures and was waving, which gets a click and a reward. Little by little, withdraw your hand a bit farther. Mix in some low Paw Shakes to create a guessing game—where will your hand appear next? Your dog will probably like this added challenge as long as she continues to win most of the time.

Add the verbal cue—at the same time you're giving the hand signal—when your dog achieves fluency. Typical verbal cues for the Wave are "wave" and "hi." Once she's fluent with that step, try alternating verbal-only and visual-only cues. If that doesn't come naturally for your dog, go back to the point where she was successful and try again (click and treat), reestablishing fluency before advancing to the next step. Eventually you'll be able to stand a few paces away, flash your dog a Wave hand signal or verbal cue, and have her Wave in return. Cute!

As your dog learns this trick, you will also remove the target (your hand). Removing the target and replacing it with a hand signal and/or verbal cue is an important finishing step in teaching dog tricks.

More Targeting Techniques: Target Object and Target Stick

If you and your dog enjoy learning more advanced tricks, you can continue to challenge her learning and precision by using a couple of training aids that professional trainers use: the target object and the target stick. A target is like a substitute for a lure: When your dog touches the target upon your cue, she knows that she will be clicked and rewarded. You have already used your hand as a target when you taught your dog Paw Shake and Rollover: When she touched your hand, she earned a click and treat. Now your dog will learn that she'll be clicked and rewarded when she touches a target object or special pointer.

Start with a disc target, such as a Frisbee or a yogurt container lid.

Let's start with the target object. A Frisbee (which is large and easy for the dog to see) makes a good starting disc target. As your dog becomes fluent with disc targeting, you can advance to smaller and smaller discs, such as soft plastic food container lids. You can also train your dog to go to a certain spot by using a cone target, such as a soccer cone, that she can see at a distance. Once your dog learns to touch the cone fluently, gradually increase its distance as you cue her to "touch" or "target."

The first step is to get your dog curious about the target. Toss it on the floor near her; if she looks at it, click and treat. Shape your dog's curiosity about the target object by clicking and rewarding as she moves closer to it. Reward your biggest jackpot when she touches the target for the first time with either her nose or her paw. (You'll see later that some cues require a nose touch, such as when she's learning to walk through a dog door flap; other tricks, such as ringing a bell to get you to open the door for her to go potty, work better with a paw touch.)

A cone is ideal for long-distance targeting.

Once your dog fully understands that she gets rewarded when she touches the target, have her sit before you, and then cue her by pointing to the target and also by naming the behavior (I recommend "touch" or simply "target"), then click and reward when she does. Make sure to use good timing: Click precisely at the moment she touches the target. After each successful trial, move the target a bit farther away or to the side. Once she becomes more fluent with touching the target, have her *sit-stay* until you say "touch" or "target" as you point to the disc. Your dog will probably understand the verbal cue right away if you hold her *sit-stay* until you see her focus shift to the target. Then cue her verbally as you point to the target. In subsequent reps, withdraw your pointing gesture and just use the verbal cue.

You will use a similar technique to train your dog to touch the pointer end of your target stick. A target stick is typically one to three feet long and can be a dowel, ruler, yardstick, or a telescoping pointer (see page 155) made especially for clicker training. It should have a soft rubber pointer or padded tip for safety; also, the padded tip helps your dog distinguish what she's supposed to touch. Although I'm going to teach you to use the target stick, I urge you to exercise caution with it, especially around children, for safety reasons. The average family is better off using an object or hand for targeting.

To start training your dog to touch the target stick, hold the stick an inch from the tip, then click and treat when she looks at it. Move the stick a little closer to your dog and begin shaping her behavior toward touching the tip with her nose. Once she's done this, repeat until she can do it again easily. As she gets better at touching the target stick, hold it farther down the shaft. Place it high, low, and on your shoe.

Once your dog gets the basic idea that she gets clicked and rewarded when she touches only the tip of the target stick, you can start moving it to shape her movement. Move the stick slowly between your legs, around your body, and so forth. As you move, you'll see that having your dog follow the pointer end will move her in a pattern, such as walking around you or spinning in circles. Once she's fluent, you can add the same verbal cue that you used with the disc target: "target" or "touch."

Let's start with a simple movement trick: the spin.

1 HEAD TURN Hold the target stick so that the end is a few inches off to the side of your dog's face. Movement starts with a head turn: When she moves her head to look at the target, click and treat. Reward even the slightest head movement at first.

2 FRONT PAWS MOVE Move the stick a little farther. When your dog's front paws move, that means she's beginning to follow the pointer. It's worth a jackpot!

3 BACK PAWS MOVE Continue moving the pointer, and jackpot again when her whole body moves. It's more challenging to direct a dog to move away from you than toward you, and any success should be rewarded.

4 SECOND HALF As you continue to move the pointer in a circle, click the first head turn, then the front paws, and finally the back paws.

4.

5 ONE COMPLETE SPIN Draw the pointer back around to the starting point and give your dog the jackpot, remembering to click and praise. Once your dog has mastered one complete spin, add a second spin and move the target stick faster to add speed. Begin withdrawing rewards to shape her movement to become smoother and swifter.

5.

Removing the Target to Teach Ring the Bell

The final step is to replace the target (disc, stick, or hand) with a hand signal and/or verbal cue. Let's practice this by teaching your dog to ring a bell to let you know that she needs to go outside to potty.

Hang a cowbell or other large bell on the door you use to let her outside, and place it low enough that she can sniff it or bat it with her paw. Start to shape her understanding of the bell's meaning by ringing it yourself the moment before you open the door to take her outside to potty. Bend down to ring it—you want her to see you. Repeat this step over the course of a week before teaching your dog to ring the bell, so that she can get used to the sound and begin to associate it with going outside. If she's timid about the bell, you might want to dampen the sound by wrapping the bell's clapper in cotton.

The dog does not have to be in any particular position; standing near the bell is sufficient. You can use any kind of target (object, stick, or hand) to attract her to touch the bell. If you use your hand, for example, put it in front of the bell and have her target touch your hand hard enough to ring the bell. It's okay to cheat a bit—that is, if she hits your hand too lightly, you can move it back into the bell.

Once your dog has reached fluency with ringing the bell, begin the process of opening the door and taking her outside on each rep. If you are training her at times when she doesn't need to go potty, be sure to take her outside and over to the potty spot on each rep anyhow, and then bring her right back inside to begin another rep. Do that all in one silent action without cueing her to go potty. Remember to use the door training skills that your dog learned in the Fundamentals Training Program: She doesn't get to bolt outside ahead of you. Rather, she must wait until you cue her to go outside. My experience is that over the course of a month or two, your dog will learn to ask you to go potty by ringing the bell on her own.

Although ringing the bell is a very useful trick, be aware that your dog may train you to come running by ringing the bell. My Flat-Coated Retriever, Merit, would ring that bell anytime he wanted to go out and be with the children in the yard or take a swim in the pool at midnight. Ringing the bell is no different than when a dog learns to bark at the door when he wants to go outside; it's not always about needing to use the outdoor potty. He trained us well, so we had to remove the bell for a while.

Fetch/Bring It Here

Retrieving (fetching) is useful in real life when you want your dog to go get his Kong or ball from nearby, if you drop your keys on the floor and you can't bend over to get them, or if you want him to pick up his toys and put them in his toy basket. (And who wouldn't want that?) Retrieving is also useful in helping redirect your dog's attention when you anticipate that he may be about to have a behavior problem; I'll talk more about that in Chapter Eleven. You may also want to review Chapter Nine's fundamentals about retrieving.

To train your dog to fetch, start with him on leash and teach him the last part first: Let him take a retrieving toy such as a Kong or knotted rope toy to hold in his mouth by saying "take it." As he opens his mouth, click and give him the toy, then reward him with lots of praise as he holds the toy proudly in his mouth. After a few seconds, say "off" and offer your open hands underneath the toy. When he drops the toy, click, praise, and reward. You're using the cookie trade (or toy trade or *off and take it* trade) and *bring it here* techniques that you learned in the fundamentals course. (To review those techniques, see page 137.) If he has trouble with the previous steps but already knows how to *take it,* you can help him by breaking down those trade behaviors.

Once your dog can take the retrieving toy into his mouth and hold it reliably when you say "take it," it's time to move to the next step: Get into the *cookie sit* position ("glue" your hand to your hip with half the length of your dog's leash wrapped around that hand; see page 100 to review). However, do not ask your dog to sit. You want him to *stand (pose)* as you move the toy in front of his nose (using the empty hand) and toss it about three feet in front of him (or as far as needed to get to it when he does). If he stays, wait a second and then direct him to the toy by saying "take it." Run with him to get it. The moment he puts his mouth on the toy, click and reward with verbal and physical praise, but don't give him a treat. Instead, hold the treat on his nose. As soon as he sniffs the treat, he will drop the toy into your open hand. Click again and reward him with the treat for dropping the toy. When he can reliably run with you the three feet to pick up the retrieving toy when you say "take it" and then give it to you when you say "off," it's time to add a little more distance: On the next rep, toss the toy a foot farther away and run the exercise the same as before.

When your dog becomes fluent at four feet, don't add any more distance; he is now ready to learn the next step: bringing the toy back to you. In the starting position, toss the toy four feet away, wait a second, then say "take it," run with him, and now allow him to reach the toy before you get there. As soon as he picks it up and turns to bring it back to you (as he did in previous reps), encourage him by saying "bring it here." Stay where you are as you encourage him to bring the toy to you and drop it in your open hand when you say "off." Don't expect your dog to carry the toy all the way to you just yet, so make sure to be close enough that he just needs to carry it a foot or two before dropping it into your open hand. This is the *basic retrieve.*

Once your dog becomes fluent in these basic retrieving skills, you may increase distance by adding one foot at a time. If necessary, attach him to a 20-foot leash or a long rope tied securely to the leash handle. Run the exercise exactly as before: Start with your dog standing at your side, toss the toy, wait a second, say "take it" and run with him on the leash to take it, and then run back to do the "off" (he drops the toy into your hand). This procedure helps shape his understanding of the long retrieving route. The maximum distance I recommend right now is 20 feet, and it will probably take you and your dog many months—maybe even a year—before he retrieves toys reliably at this great distance.

A few tips for teaching your dog to retrieve: Remember to jackpot the milestone moments. It is more effective and fun to make this a brief exercise at various times rather than something done at one long training session. Finally, your dog's maturity and impulse control strongly influence how much he can handle without failure. It's a lot more important for him to pick up and hold the toy when you say "take it," and drop it when you say "off," than to be able to respond at great distances.

SHAPING BY BACK CHAINING

When you teach your dog to fetch, you use a behavior training technique called *back chaining*. Break down the whole *retrieve* behavior into parts and then link each part of the trick together. You *back chain* them by starting with the last part and working your way in reverse order to the beginning. For example, we use back chaining in the song "The Twelve Days of Christmas." We sing the last part first ("a partridge in a pear tree"), and repeat it over and over as we build backward day by day to the first and final part ("twelve drummers drumming"). When I sing that song, I relax at "five golden rings" on each verse, knowing that I can easily remember the upcoming five back-chained parts. But sometimes I forget

A dog can learn a more complex behavior when you first break it down into parts and then shape them back into a behavior later.

how many geese are a-laying or pipers are piping. That's what it's like for your dog when she learns a complex cue, trick, or routine: She looks forward to the doggy equivalent of those five golden rings, confident from that point that she can take it back to the ever familiar end.

As you teach tricks to your dog, help her learn a complex behavior by breaking it down into parts, which you'll then back chain as you shape them back together in reverse order. One example of a trick that benefits from the back chaining technique is toy cleanup (see page 182), which combines a number of cues your dog has already learned: *take it, off,* and *bring it here.*

Free Shaping

Sometimes your dog will do something completely on his own, without your direction or prompting, that you want to reward. Rewarding his natural behaviors is called free shaping, and it improves your dog's problem-solving abilities, gets him interested in offering new behaviors (since those are the ones he gets rewarded for), and helps spirit his personality.

Did you ever play the children's game Hot and Cold? In one variation of the game, your friend would think of one object in the room and you would move around the room to figure out which object your friend was thinking of. When you were far away from the object your friend would say "cold." When you got closer to it your friend would say "warm." When you were right next to the object your friend would say "hot." Free shaping works the same way, but rather than using the words *cold, warm,* and *hot,* you will click and treat for any behavior that your dog offers that is "warm" (close to what you want), click and jackpot when he is "hot," and not click when he is "cold." There are no prompts, cues, or messages to tell your dog what you want or how to do it. Free shaping is purely a trial-and-error waiting game.

Let's say that you want to use free shaping to teach your dog to lie down on his brand-new mat. You may already be thinking that instead of free shaping, you could simply lure him onto the mat or you could place a target on the mat and direct him to touch the target, then cue him into a *down* or a *settle.* For this exercise, though, instead of using the other tools you already have in your toolbox, let's use free shaping to teach him to lie on the mat. The mat is next to where you are standing, and because your dog sees you with the clicker and the treats, he knows that it's time for fun, so he sits in front of you without being asked. You tell him "good sit," but don't click or treat. He waits patiently, but nothing happens. You wait, your dog waits.

If he doesn't realize that he is supposed to do anything other than just stay still, you can give him a hint by tossing a treat on the mat, then click and jackpot him as soon as he steps onto the mat. Then let him play with a toy before resuming the lesson, or end the session and go for a walk together, depending on his focus and eagerness to continue this game. (Time frames for free-shaping exercises will average 5 to 15 minutes, depending on your dog's experience and curiosity level. Always make sure to end the game on a happy note with his achieving success on the last trial, even if it's by giving an easy jackpot on his new mat.)

In any case, if your dog moves just a little bit, click and treat. He repeats the move and earns another click. He does it a third time, but this time there's no click—you're waiting for him to move toward the mat or even look at the mat. Your dog yawns—a sign that he's getting bored or anxious—and you click that. Now he's puzzled. He's not sure what he's getting clicked for, so he starts offering behaviors randomly. That is a key moment in free shaping. When he turns his head toward the mat, he gets clicked (and treated). He repeats that move, another click. He does it again, a third click. He does it a fourth time, but no click. He turns his head toward the mat again—this time more strongly to make sure you see him move—and this time you reward him with a click and a small jackpot. He repeats that strong move, another click (not a jackpot this time, just one treat). He does it again strongly, another click. And again, click. He moves strongly again, but this time there's no click. So he moves even more strongly and wins a click and a small jackpot.

Now your dog's moves toward the mat become more self-assured. After another minute of trial and error, he touches the mat for the first time and gets a jackpot (after the click, of course). So he touches the mat again with more certainty and gets another jackpot. He stands on the mat—another jackpot. So he continues standing on the mat, but nothing happens. He experiments with a couple of movements and dips his head toward the mat, a click. He dips his head again, another click. He touches the mat with his nose and wins a small jackpot. He repeats the nose touch—a click and one treat (but not a jackpot). He touches his nose to the mat more strongly—click and a couple of treats.

Finally, your dog lies down on the mat and wins a big jackpot, and lots of praise and petting. Then you cue him to sit next to the mat, and as he does so, right away you mark it verbally (say "good" but no click), and you wait. He waits, too. Then he turns and lies down on his mat, and you jackpot him again (and give more praise and petting). You repeat the sequence of having him sit next to the mat again, after which he lies down on the mat. You can now name the behavior ("on your mat" or whatever you choose) as he lies down. On subsequent reps, continue this pattern of saying the name as he initiates the *down*. On each rep, have him sit in a slightly different spot before he goes to the mat, and also reposition the mat slightly—this will help your dog generalize the behavior as you put it on verbal cue ("on your mat"). Once your dog is fluent with those steps, say the verbal cue ("on your mat") before he goes to the mat and jackpot him when he does.

Continue reinforcing the verbal cue, and once he becomes fluent, mix in some other cues that he already knows and move the mat around the room.

Congratulations! By depending on your dog to offer behavior, you have free shaped a new cue. You also helped him gain confidence in creative problem-solving as he figured out how to get the most clicks and treats.

Free Shaping and the 101 Box

Have you ever watched a young child play with a box? Some kids can be endlessly fascinated, enjoying the box even more than the toy that came inside it. Dogs can be encouraged to explore and play with a simple cardboard box, too. One way to better understand your dog is by observing her learning about something—in this case, a cardboard box—totally on her own. You can use free shaping exercises to discover your dog's natural behaviors. We call this game the 101 Box because there are at least 101 different ways to play with it.

Prepare for this exercise by trimming the flaps of a large box so that they are half their previous length. Lay the box on the floor near your dog, tipping it on its side carefully so you don't startle her. When she looks at it, click and treat. If she steps toward it, another click and treat. If your dog looks at the box again—or exhibits any behavior in relation to the box (sniffing, nosing, etc.)—click and treat. It's pretty simple: When you free shape with the 101 Box, click your dog for *any* new behavior she volunteers, praise and treat lavishly.

The play possibilities are endless with the 101 Box.

If your dog doesn't seem to be getting it, move away and toss a treat into the box to hint at how you want to shape her behavior. If she takes the treat or even moves toward it, click and treat with a jackpot, and end the session. Always make sure to end the 101 Box game on a happy note by running one last successful trial, then put the box away for now and give her a toy to play with or go out for a walk.

At some point in one of these sessions, your dog will get it: Anything she does with that silly box will earn her a click and a treat. You will probably see the moment when your dog gets it because she will suddenly offer a whole flurry of behaviors: pawing the box, stepping on it, bumping her nose against it, smelling it, flipping a flap, chewing on it, dragging it across the floor, climbing inside, putting her paws on top. When that happens, you'll be clicking and treating as fast as you can.

Once she gets it, start withdrawing treats for behaviors she's already shown. Instead, click and treat only for new behaviors she offers; this indicates that she is testing the box. If she has already moved the box slightly, then click and treat only when she moves it a little more. If she has already put her foot into the box, wait to click until she paws the bottom of the box. When shaping new behaviors, always look for opportunities to raise the bar. What's wonderful about the 101 Box is that there is no particular result that you're looking for; rather, you're simply looking for any new behaviors. Because you've changed the game and are now clicking and treating only for new behaviors, your dog may become a bit frustrated, but that will encourage her to experiment, be creative, and solve problems. Frustration in low doses is okay; it's part of the learning process we all go through.

Some dogs may be shy or scared of the box at first. If this is the case, don't force the situation. Just toss a treat in the box. Toss another treat, and another. If they are treats that your dog already values, she will know that they're in the box. If your dog looks at the treats, click and treat her, and then toss another. Toss a treat near the box. Leave the box on the floor as you shift to another exercise, such as luring her around you and through your legs—maybe she'll forget about her fear of the box as she goes near it. At the end of the exercise, if she hasn't eaten her jackpot of treats that have been accumulating in the box, pick them up and put them away as you put away the box. Try again another time and don't fret; some dogs take a long time to warm up to this strange, bountiful box.

Log all of those freely shaped behaviors—yes, you should still keep a training log—to give you insights into your dog's natural patterns. Does she first use her nose or her paw to explore the box? The next time you bring it out, does she repeat patterns or try something new? What does she do if you set down the box with the opening facing upward? You'll probably become as curious about your dog's natural behaviors as she is about the box. Having those insights into her behavior may help you identify other tricks, toys, and activities that she might enjoy. You may even enjoy making up your own original tricks based on some of your dog's unique behaviors with the 101 Box.

Any new behavior gets praise and a treat.

More Dog Tricks

N ow that you and your dog are familiar with clicker training and target touching, let's use that system to learn a few more basic tricks. You may discover that your dog really enjoys tricks training. I love it when my students make up their own tricks, often by observing what their dogs offer naturally and by free shaping. Study your training log. Be aware of how your dog progresses during these lessons so you can choose to focus your efforts on tricks that he is most likely to succeed at. Pick one trick to learn at a time; to keep your dog interested, always be prepared to switch to a game, activity, or other training exercise that he already knows. Once you and he master one trick, add another from the list. Students in my fundamentals classes can usually teach their dogs a new trick in about a week.

Sit Pretty (Beg)

W hile the Sit Pretty can be a good exercise for strengthening your dog's back and core muscles, don't use this trick with dogs that have back or hip problems, or dogs with long backs (such as Dachshunds and Basset Hounds), because it can put too much stress on the back.

1 LURE UP For this trick, I recommend using a treat lure, although a target stick can also be effective. Start with your dog in a *sit,* and begin *shaping* the Sit Pretty by holding a lure an inch above his head. As he lifts his head to the lure, click and allow him to eat the treat. Next, hold the lure an inch or so higher.

1.

2 BALANCE ASSIST On the next rep, hold the lure about three inches above his head. You are, of course, *shaping* your dog to crane his neck higher and higher to get the treat. Eventually, he will need to lift his paws to eat the lure. Watch his front paws closely; when he lifts a paw, that's a jackpot. Once he lifts a paw three times in a row, start raising the lure a bit higher still. Keep going up inch by inch, and when he lifts both paws for the first time, that's a big jackpot.

2.

3 PAWS UP Now try to get him to lift both paws consistently. When he does so, insert your forearm so he has a place to rest his paws for balance. Make that the new baseline for clicking and earning rewards. Eventually, try luring with an empty hand. When he lifts both paws and rests them on your forearm, that's worth a jackpot—click and treat him with your other hand. Continue the empty-handed luring until your dog seems to have gotten it and becomes fluent.

The next step is to name the trick. The most common verbal cues for this trick are "beg," "prayers," or "sit pretty." Or you can name it something totally silly like "Duck and Cover" and modify it by luring your dog's head downward so his nose and eyes are covered and under your arm. When you first add the verbal cue, say it at the same time you use your hand signal. After a few more reps, try a quick rhythm: On the first and second reps, use both the verbal cue and hand signal. Then, on the third rep, use only the verbal cue. If your dog Sits Pretty on just the verbal cue, that's worth a jackpot. Make sure to mark (say "good beg"), praise, and reward on every successful rep. Mix reps of verbal-only with verbal-plus-visual until your dog seems fluent with the trick on both the visual cue alone (your forearm crosses in front of your dog) and the verbal cue alone. The final step is to phase out treats by using slot machine techniques. Continue empty-handed luring until your dog is fluent.

To teach your dog to find his balance without your assistance, begin removing your arm for just a moment at first. Click, praise, and reward him for each increase in the amount of time that he can balance "sitting pretty" on his own.

The finished trick should look like this.

Cookie Nose

In this trick, your dog balances a dog treat on her nose. On cue, she lets the treat slide off her nose and catches it before it hits the floor. Some dogs will even flip the treat up in the air and catch it on its way down. The trick also teaches impulse control. A word of warning: Do not do this trick if your dog still has a food guarding problem; that might be flirting

with danger. Also, if you have a flat-faced dog, like a pug or bulldog, it w
probably be too difficult to balance a treat on her nose, so I suggest that you
skip this trick.

1 THE BALANCE Start by cueing your
dog to *sit-stay.* Hold a treat to her nose
in much the same way as you learned with
the *cookie sit-stay* in the Fundamentals
Training Program. (At first you may use
your hands to help your dog keep her head
still.) If she does not flinch, then click and
say "take it" as you bring the treat to her

1.

mouth by moving toward your dog to give her the treat rather than allowing
her to move forward to take it. This way, you are rewarding your dog for
staying still.

If your dog tries to get the treat before you tell her to take it, then say
"off." If she responds to your *off* signal, then after a moment say "take it,"
and allow her to take the treat from your fingertips (after you have moved
your hand with the treat toward her). If your dog doesn't respond to your
off right away, take away the treat and practice a different cue that she'll be
successful at before you try the Cookie Nose trick again.

When your dog is able to continue sitting still while you hold the treat
on her nose, hold the treat a moment longer before you say "take it." Little
by little, increase the amount of time before you say "take it." When she can
remain sitting still for 10 seconds while you hold the treat on her nose, it's
time to add the next step.

2 THE FLIP Balance the treat on her
nose. Let go of the treat, but do not
remove your hand until you're ready to say
"take it." Let her take the treat. Your dog
may tip her nose to slide the biscuit off;
some trainers *shape* the flip by placing a
hand under the dog's muzzle. On the next
rep, slowly move your hand an inch away
from your dog's nose before you say "take
it," and then two inches, and then three,
and so forth.

2.

Don't allow her to eat the
or if she misses the catch—
cus to the floor, where she
ther than on you and your
directional cues. As you'll see, not only does
this trick help your dog practice impulse control, it's also a real crowd pleaser—whether the
treat slides off her nose or flips into the air.

3.

Back Up

The *back up* is useful when your dog sits too close to the dinner table, or you're in a tight parking lot and you need to open your car door for her to jump up onto the backseat. The *back up* can also be useful during a heeling exercise: If she starts to move ahead of you, say "back up" and she will literally take a step back closer to you as you continue to walk forward.

Start with your dog standing in front of you and take one step toward her. If she backs up, click and treat. Take another step, and if she backs up again, give another click and treat. Continue backing up one step at a time, clicking and treating with each step. As you get closer to a wall or obstacle, lure your dog forward to restart the sequence, backing up one or two steps at a time until she is fluent and confident. Next, add the verbal cue ("back up") and simultaneous hand signal: Turn one hand palm down and gently flick your wrist toward your dog. Practice that one-step and two-step *back up* using verbal and visual cues together. Once that is fluent, add a third step, and then a fourth. Continue to use the *back up* in a variety of hallways and spaces around your home so she will generalize this behavior to other places.

Use the "chute" technique if your dog doesn't back up easily. Start teaching the *back up* in a hallway or along a wall or fence. Create a narrow chute by placing a row of chairs parallel to the wall. If your dog is smaller and might try to sneak out under the chairs, simply drape a sheet over them. Make the chute narrow enough that she can't turn around in it. First, stand one step into the chute and cue her to come forward to you—mark verbally (say "good"), but do not click or treat. Then walk toward your dog so that she backs up that one step out of the chute, and when she does so, click and treat. The reason you first cue your dog into the chute and then back her out of it, rather than start by trying to get her to back into the chute, is that it takes advantage of your dog's natural desire to get out of a confined area, rather than force her to go against her natural aversion to being backed up into a confined chute. Repeat a few times so she becomes fluent with backing up one step.

When your dog is fluent with that first step into the chute, you can add a verbal cue (say "back up") and simultaneous hand signal: Turn your hands palm down and gently flick your wrists toward your dog. Practice that one-step backup out of the chute using verbal and visual cues together. Once that skill is fluent, stand two steps into the chute and practice until that is fluent. These first steps may seem too easy for some dogs, but I'd like you to do them anyhow: This is an exercise that builds trust—your dog learns that she'll be safe when you're backing her up, that you're not putting her into a dangerous situation that she's unable to see.

This method makes backing up simple and rewarding for most dogs. If it's still too hard for yours, move on to a cue she already knows, and come back to this one another day (even if you're tempted to try to muscle her through it because you went to some effort to make the chute). For these first couple of steps, it's most important that your dog develop trust in you.

Once she is fluent and seems confident with these first two steps, then you can add another step. Start by standing three steps into the chute, cue her to come forward into the chute, mark it verbally when she reaches you, then immediately start to back her out, stepping toward her and using visual and verbal cues together. It will probably take a number of training sessions for your dog to feel comfortable backing up all the way out of the chute without turning around or looking behind her. Take it slowly. If she resists, change to another exercise that she's already successful at, such as doing a set of Puppy Pushups right there, and then lure her forward to you, until you're both out of the chute and ready for another activity. Return to the chute at another training session.

Move the chute to various places around your home so that your dog will generalize the *back up*. Eventually the chute will no longer be needed, so take it down one piece at a time, to help her gain fluency with each modification that you make, before taking down the next piece. Continue to use the *back up* in a variety of hallways and spaces. Eventually, she will generalize this behavior to all places without the chute.

Once your dog is fluent with the *back up,* you might have fun creating a dance step with her: back and forth, back and forth. You might even want to choreograph a dance routine: Keep your back to your dog as she follows you, then turn around and face her so that she backs up. (If dancing with your dog interests you, see the introduction to canine freestyle dancing on page 246.)

Bow

You've probably noticed your dog bowing to another dog as an invitation to play. You can train your dog to bow, which is a fun trick to cue at the end of a performance, especially if it's made directly from a Sit Pretty or a Wave. To begin shaping her Bow on cue, start with her standing. Lure her toward a down by pulling a treat from her chest to the floor, and click just as her front legs start to bend. (Click at the start of the leg bend to help your dog distinguish this from going all the way down as you have previously taught her.)

Once your dog has acquired the distinction between the full *down* and this front-leg bend, you can shape the bend down farther while her rump remains up in the air. It's okay to put your arm under her belly next to her back legs to keep her rump up, or you can use her leash as a sling under her belly to hold her back legs up while her front legs bend down. Jackpot her as she touches down the first time. Using the leash in this manner can be tricky; be sure that you know your dog well and that she is comfortable with the leash underneath her belly.

I generally find that it's best to introduce a modified hand signal before withdrawing the sling or arm assist. A distinctive hand signal is to slide an arm down in an arc toward the floor and continue the gentle arc up toward your dog. Once your dog bows fluently to your arcing arm signal, you should be able to completely withdraw the sling or arm assist from under her belly.

When she becomes fluent in bowing without the assist, add the verbal cue ("bow") at the end of each successful rep. After you have done about five successful reps that way, it's time to try a verbal-only cue without the hand signal. To begin, try a quick rhythm: First say the cue and immediately follow with the hand signal, repeat that on the next rep, and on the third rep say the cue as you start the hand signal and click (and stop your hand signal) as she bows. From that point, mix trials of verbal-visual, verbal-only, and visual-only cues.

Here's a polishing tip: To get a deeper Bow, glide your hand closer to your dog's chest before arcing up. As you arc up, ideally your dog will stay in the Bow position as she tilts only her head up to follow your arcing signal.

The play bow is an invitation to play.

Circle Me

In addition to being a fun trick, Circle Me is useful in getting your dog positioned at your heel to begin walking and for general behavior control. The trick also teaches your dog to pay attention to cues from both of your hands.

1 START THE LURE Let's teach Circle Me with a lure. Start with your dog sitting in front of you. Drop your leash if you are at home in a quiet environment that won't distract him, or tether the leash to your belt loop (giving him enough room to circle around you without pulling on it). You should be able to lure him around your right side fairly easily, especially if you've been playing Follow the Lure (see page 144).

1.

2 AROUND YOUR HIP Click and treat as he moves even with your right hip; that's his first jackpot. Next, continue to shape his movement so that he circles all the way behind you; that's his second jackpot.

2.

3 SHIFT THE LURE When he is behind your back, pass the treat from your right hand to your left hand, and continue to lure him toward your left hip; that's his third jackpot.

3a. | 3b.

4 LURE TO A SIT Finally, lure him to sit at your left side; that's your dog's fourth jackpot. Continue to practice this full circle until he is fluent with circling around you and sitting on your left.

4.

To polish the Circle Me, hold a few lures in your left hand and lure with your (empty) right hand. As your dog circles behind you, hold your left hand behind your back to lure him to *sit* at your left side for a jackpot. On subsequent reps, position the left hand closer and closer to the ending position at your left hip. Eventually, you will be able to hold a lure at your left hip while your empty right hand motions your dog to circle all the way around you. When he can circle you fluently, add the verbal cue "circle me." I recommend that you continue to use the hand signal even after you have named the cue for your dog.

Toy Cleanup

After your dog masters the retrieving skills she learned earlier in this chapter, you can teach her to clean up after herself. This complex trick combines retrieving skills with the *off and take it* cue. Try training your dog to enjoy cleaning up her toys by using back chaining (see page 170), and teach the last part of the trick first.

1 TAKE IT AND DROP IT Start by having your dog take the toy out of the box and immediately clicking and treating when she does so. Naturally she'll drop the toy to get the treat, which is fine while she begins to learn this part of the trick. Then have her drop the toy into the box by saying "off," then click and offer her another treat. On subsequent reps, have her hold the toy for a few more seconds before you click and treat, and have her drop the toy into the box again.

1.

The next step is to place the box with the toy a step or two away from your dog, and then signal her to take the toy (point to the toy and say "take it"), hold it, and drop it back into the box. Each step is worth a click and a reward.

When those parts of the trick seem fluent, try back chaining the rest of the trick: Have her pick up the toy again and drop it in the box. You will probably need patience, an upbeat attitude, and additional breakdown steps to keep your dog motivated.

If your dog merely looks at the toy at first, break down the behavior even further so that you can shape the *take it*. Start by clicking and treating when she merely looks at the toy, then wait to click until she gets closer to it, and then even closer, until she finally touches it for a jackpot. Next, she must pick up the toy for another jackpot.

2 PRACTICE RETRIEVING Using the Fetch/Retrieve techniques (page 168), teach your dog to bring the toy to you; that's another jackpot. I recommend sitting with the empty toy box in front of you. If you place your hands over the box, you may be able to get her to drop the toy in the box when you say "off." If she does, that's a jackpot.

If dropping the toy into the box seems to be difficult for your dog, I recommend teaching that part of the trick separately, and then back chain the rest of the trick onto it.

2.

3 ADD TOYS AND DISTANCE Once she has mastered picking up one toy and putting it in the box, add a second toy, and then a third. See how many objects you can actually get her to put in the box. I think you'll find that once she is fluently putting in three toys, she'll progress to a fourth and fifth fairly easily. When you're teaching this trick, make sure to put the toys and the box in slightly different spots on each rep to help your dog to generalize this behavior.

3.

To polish the Toy Cleanup, add a visual signal, like patting the box, and a verbal cue. I use "clean up" and point to a toy while I am near the box. Finally, move farther and farther away from the box as you cue your dog. How far you move away is determined by her success rate. If she is learning this behavior fairly well, you can move a short distance away from the box. Keep it simple, brief, and fun!

A Glance Back to the Beginning

At the end of my tricks training program, I enjoy asking my students to take turns talking briefly about the time they first brought their dogs home. Can you remember what your dog was like when you first saw her? What were you like? Do you still have the list of goals on your fridge? How have you progressed?

Now that you've learned the fundamentals and have continued to challenge your dog with new skills and tricks, it is a good time to revisit the goals you first set for yourself and your dog. What are you hoping for in the future? What additional skills or tricks would you like your dog to work toward? As I'm sure you're witnessing, the skills that your dog is mastering are not just helpful around the home, but they also make it possible for your dog to have a wider range of real-life experiences. How wonderful it is to be able to take your confident and spirited dog into public places.

As you move forward, keep your dog's training sharp by adding new skills, tricks, and socialization opportunities.

You've come so far—remember to keep celebrating the victories.

Chapter Eleven

Behavior Problems

Despite the number of hours you spend training, even the best-behaved dog may, at some time in his life, develop bad habits—from chewing or soiling the house to exhibiting aggression. Behavior problems are not a reason to panic or, worse, to give up on a dog. The truth of the matter is that most problems are not the fault of the dog, they are a result of human error. Even though we mean well, we sometimes make mistakes that cause our dogs to misbehave. For example, many dogs are relinquished to shelters and rescue organizations for being destructive or going potty in the home too many times. But both of these behaviors are preventable, and are often a result of our lack of attention to our dog's natural needs or our failure to set appropriate boundaries. When we're impatient with our dog's mistakes, we might aggravate his misbehavior by exiling him to the basement, garage, or laundry room, or simply by ceasing to spend the time required to train him, and he's left on his own, having to raise himself.

When a dog needs more attention, he'll do anything to get it, even if that something is bad. Dogs are social animals that want to belong to a pack, and they may rather be scolded than ignored, because to a dog, any attention (even if it's negative or punishing) is better than none at all. This can cause a destructive cycle. The more we scold him, the more he'll engage in the behavior that brings about a scolding. We promote this destructive cycle when we unwittingly reinforce our dog's bad behavior and encourage him to do it some more. Too many times, this cycle will reach a breaking point, where we decide the growing problem is just too much to handle, and end up giving up on the dog . . . and on ourselves. If you have done that, trust me, there's no reason to feel any shame about it. You will make mistakes. The key is to learn from them.

> *When a dog needs more attention, he'll do anything to get it.*

When a dog needs more attention, he'll do anything to get it. The first thing to understand is that a dog doesn't know that he is misbehaving. All he knows is that he's acting like he's supposed to: like a dog. Later, we'll discuss how to use specific tools to prevent and stop certain behaviors. But let me first outline a few common mistakes we all make with our dogs, all of which can, and should, be avoided.

One of the most common training errors we commit is to punish a dog *after* he's committed the offense—even if it's just minutes after, it makes things worse, not better. Say, for example, you come home to find your sofa pillow shredded, and your dog sleeping calmly on his mat, with pillow fuzz all over his beard. While you are, I imagine, understandably upset, he's just thrilled to see you and doesn't even remember the shredding. Therefore, if you scold him by yelling at him and rubbing his nose in the evidence, it's unlikely that he'll make the connection or remember the reprimand the next time he has an impulse to shred. Instead, he is more apt to learn that whenever you come home to find him lying calmly on his mat, he's going to get scolded. This conduct just confuses our beloved dogs and, I believe, weakens our bond with them. The best way to stop an unwanted behavior is to catch your dog in the act and redirect him to a different activity.

Dogs desire consistency, and they don't understand how to behave if we suddenly change the rules. For example, when we first get a puppy, it's common to let the little bundle of fur climb and jump all over us. After all, we're trying to bond with him, and, frankly, we love the feeling of being close to him. But when he eventually grows bigger and his climbing stops being a novelty, we change the rules: no more jumping, no more climbing, no more pawing, no more cute begging. If you change the rules on your dog, it's not fair to expect him to understand immediately either that things have changed or why he is being punished when he continues to follow the old rules. From the dog's perspective, your behavior seems arbitrary and mean. It's we who have been inconsistent, not the dog.

We also unintentionally cause or reinforce our dog's bad behavior by teaching him that what we say isn't important. As we discussed in Chapter Five (see page 89), behaviorists call this learned irrelevance. We need to remember to pay attention to our verbal cues, consistently offering them only once and in the same tone of voice. The same goes for visual cues: Offer a hand signal only once, and with precisely the same gesture as last time.

Learned irrelevance can also come about if we give too much praise. It's like eating too much candy. The first piece is delicious and we savor it, but the tenth piece . . . not so much. So it is with praising our dog: If we constantly praise or reward every little tiny thing he does, each instance of praise seems less valuable. Over time, our well-meaning attempts to provide positive reinforcement can start to backfire, as our dog learns that there is no special consequence to obeying a cue; whatever he does will be rewarded. And the same goes for punishment. If we reprimand or scold our dog too harshly or frequently, he will learn to tune it out or, worse, will give up and lose his spirit. Always be sure that what you say to him is important and has consequences.

Why Do Dogs' Behaviors Suddenly Change?

People often call, their voices steeped with worry, to ask me why their typically obedient and well-behaved dog has suddenly developed a bad habit. While there is never a simple or sure answer to this question, it's good to look first for some common triggers that can cause a dog to lose focus. Think of yourself: A sudden back spasm or chronic toothache distracts you in the middle of cooking, and you burn dinner. Hearing that certain song on the car radio triggers a memory of prom night all those years ago, you lose focus . . . and the highway turnoff. Some triggers we love, while others make us into absolute monsters. The same goes for dogs: Some triggers can suddenly turn our sweet dogs into hellhounds. We need to learn what our dog's triggers are, anticipate them, and replace the undesirable behaviors with desirable ones.

Health Triggers

My Irish Water Spaniel, Aisley, was the perfect puppy. She learned quickly and was well socialized. But when Aisley was nine months old she had a small seizure, after which she would snap at imaginary flies, get up in the middle of the night and twirl, and hide behind a chair as if she was trying to get away from the flies. Aisley also became increasingly aggressive toward other dogs and started displaying fearful behaviors toward strangers and my children. It was sudden and scary. A sudden behavior change for no apparent reason may mean your dog has a health issue that he can't communicate to you. His hip pain might make him snap at any dog that gets near his hindquarters. If he has a toothache, he may respond aggressively if you try to touch his face.

Therefore, my first word of advice to anyone whose dog suddenly develops a behavior change is to take him to a vet and determine whether there are underlying health issues. Also call the shelter or breeder where you got your dog, and discuss what you are experiencing.

Environmental Triggers

A dog's environment is constantly changing. Maybe your child's friend accidentally hurt her when your back was turned, and now when there's a sleepover, that child triggers your dog to hide or growl. Certain people or other animals trigger your dog's aggression or fearful behavior for what seems like no reason. Or the reason may seem obvious: Ever since the neighbor's tomcat bloodied your dog's nose, she barks and cowers behind you when any cat is around. The vacuum cleaner's monstrous rumble triggers her to start barking the moment she sees you take it out of the closet. That vacuum cleaner and other strange moving objects such as shopping carts, skateboards, and wheelchairs may trigger your dog's impulse to escape or try to run them down and tear them apart.

Tools to Address Behavior Problems

The saying goes that when the only tool you have is a hammer, everything looks like a nail. A good trainer's toolbox is chock-full of implements so that we can be sure to have at least one workable solution ready to use. It takes knowledge to know which tool to use in a given situation, and practice in how to use it well, so don't get frustrated if modifying your dog's bad behavior takes time and tests your patience. Just be consistent, firm, and loving—and, most of all, keep using positive reinforcement techniques—and I promise that you'll see a difference.

Redirecting

I have learned that when your dog is engaging in bad behavior, it's always more effective to refocus him—a training technique we refer to as *redirecting*—than it is to punish him.

Boz, the rescue Border Collie that I'm currently fostering and training, got very anxious and excited whenever he heard either a soda can being opened or the sound of my printer working. He'd start whimpering, growling, and rushing around until he found something to destroy, such as my appointment book or bedspread.

Once I recognized this pattern, I knew that the best way to stop it was to redirect him: Direct him to something else before I opened a can. I began by tossing Boz his favorite ball and cueing him to take it. Once he had the ball in his mouth, I'd pop the can, and before he could react, I'd tell him to bring me the ball (using the Retrieve trick that is detailed on page 168). I'd hold the can as if it were no big deal, request a *sit* from him, and ask him to drop the ball in my hand. Then I'd throw it for him to retrieve. I did this over and over again, several times a day for a while, and now when Boz sees me with a soda can in my hand, he automatically brings me his ball 80 percent of the time, knowing that he will be praised and rewarded. I have redirected Boz's barking and frantic behavior with a behavior that is far more rewarding for him: holding a ball in his mouth to bite on, retrieving, bringing it back to me, and starting the game over. I'm still working on him . . .

Redirecting is a useful technique for modifying many unwanted behaviors, and the key to it is good timing. For example, I need to make sure that Boz's ball is available *before* I get a soda can from the fridge. If it isn't visible and ready, and I wait until he is already barking at the can to find it, he will be very distracted and anxious, and it will be far more difficult to redirect him to get it. I need to time the redirection to occur before he begins barking.

1 REACT EARLY As soon as you see your dog go near contraband or an off-limits area (such as a garbage pail), get that special object. Over time you'll learn to anticipate your dog's moves and be ready more quickly. (The other recommended way to lessen this kind of unwanted behavior is to keep your home dogproofed.)

1.

2 REDIRECT HER ATTENTION Get your dog to focus on the high-value object and away from the unwanted behavior.

2.

3 REDIRECT HER ACTION Engage her fully with the rewarding activity and praise.

3.

Substitution Trades

Another useful technique is the *substitution* trade, or *contraband* trade. Dogs love making trades for something of equal or greater value. Remember my dog Merit's story? He stole the chicken carcass off the kitchen counter (where it should not have been left unattended), and brought it to me knowing that he would probably get an excellent trade, and he did: a stuffed Kong and tons of praise!

The key to making a substitution trade is to have the alternative ready at all times; you never know when you'll need it. I always have a stuffed Kong ready in the fridge or freezer. If your dog has a toy she particularly loves, make sure that it's in a place you can get to quickly. I recommend that you begin practicing substitution trades regularly along with the *off and take it* trades in the Fundamentals Training Program. See pages 104 and 117 for detailed instructions.

Counterconditioning, Desensitizing, and Habituation

When Boz sees me get a soda can, he's currently learning to redirect his own focus and get his ball. Since Boz's impulse is to behave destructively when he hears that soda can open, I am *counterconditioning* his reactions. Counterconditioning is the process of teaching a dog to do something that goes against his natural impulses. Merit dropped the chicken rather than give in to his impulse to eat it because I had counterconditioned him continually from eight weeks of age to know the value of making a substitution trade.

Desensitizing is a key component of counterconditionings, so much so that behaviorists often refer to them together with the acronym DSCC: desensitizing and counterconditioning.

In the Fundamentals Training Program, you learned to desensitize your dog to the sound of the doorbell by completely ignoring the sound when your partner rang it. You probably needed a whole lot of patience while your dog barked his brains out when the bell rang, but eventually he became accustomed to this sound—you had desensitized him to it. In other words, you taught him that the doorbell meant nothing at all, and reacting to it brought no reward. You modeled desensitized behavior for your dog by ignoring the doorbell yourself.

Sometimes, a dog needs to be counterconditioned gradually to deal with fears that may seem irrational to us. In my class there was once a Border Collie, Pip, that was fearful of the classroom's slippery linoleum floor. For Pip, touching the slick floor was like walking on ice, so she couldn't concentrate and couldn't learn. Pip was so fearful in the classroom that she wouldn't let me touch her. I suggested that Pip's owners bring a carpet to class. We rolled out the carpet every week for Pip to train on. She was comfortable on the carpet; she started to learn. Between classes, Pip's owners did homework with her on the carpet in different environments. Then they started generalizing with Pip, moving off the carpet and onto other nonslick surfaces. Back in the classroom, we reduced the size of Pip's carpet each week, but we always started training with her at exactly the same spot on the carpet. By week four, we were able to move the smaller carpet toward another area of the classroom. By the end of week five, Pip was training without the carpet, totally focused on her owners and the current lesson, not on the environment. She also allowed me to touch her body and her collar, hand her food, and cue her to sit. Pip became desensitized to the linoleum floor because we worked at a pace that made sense for her.

Also related to desensitization is the concept of *habituation*. An example of habituation is when next-door neighbors renovate their home. At first, the construction noise is distracting and we may find it challenging to focus, but after a while the noise fades into the background and we are no longer distracted. Sometimes we become so habituated that it actually seems too quiet when the sounds stop. The joke goes that the aristocrat from the big city couldn't sleep at his quiet country villa until he instructed his servants to carry garbage cans up to his bedroom and bang on them until he fell asleep. We can become habituated to the strangest things, and so can our dogs.

I habituated my Giant Schnauzer, Saxon, to the vacuum cleaner . . . very slowly. At first, I moved him out of the room whenever I turned on the vacuum cleaner (I have a lot of dog hair in my home). Then, I left the vacuum cleaner out in the living room in plain sight. Over time, Saxon came to see it as part of our decor—just another piece of furniture. Once he became habituated and stopped reacting to the vacuum's sound and movements, I took it one step further: I wanted to help him actually enjoy the vacuum cleaner. I dropped treats around it; I fed his meals around it; we trained next to it. Saxon made such a positive association with that machine that he followed it around as if it somehow fed him treats, and I had to tell him to move out of the way so I could vacuum the floors.

Solving Specific Behavior Problems

It's helpful to sort behavior problems into two main categories: *training problems* and *social problems*. While there is some overlap between the two, you will find that when you identify the category, it will be easier to select an effective remedy. In general, training problems are solved by using tools that refocus or diminish behaviors, such as desensitization and counterconditioning (DSCC) techniques, whereas social problems also require us to help our dog play well with others.

Training Problems

ach of the problems in this section comes about when a dog's training fundamentals have begun to break down. This happens. Even after you and your dog complete the Fundamentals Training Program, and your dog seems to be well trained, it's important to keep up the training—doing homework exercises or learning new tricks—or problems may arise. The good news is that most of these problems can be fixed by recommitting to the fundamentals and by using DSCC tools to diminish problem behaviors by replacing them with desirable ones.

LEASH PULLING

The best way to correct leash pulling is to have a zero tolerance policy. The more a dog is allowed to pull during walks, the more he will get into the habit of thinking he's in control of the walk, making it increasingly difficult for you to get back your control over his walking behavior. If your dog starts to pull, stop and do the "be a tree" exercise you learned in the Fundamentals Training Program (see page 76). Resume walking only after you have his full attention, and then lead him in a new direction. And if you're having pulling issues, it is better to go out for brief walks several times a day rather than a few long ones.

Review and incorporate the other leash walking exercises from the Fundamentals Training Program, including Follow the Lure and tethering. I also recommend doing some focusing exercises during the walks, such as a sudden stop followed by a quick cue to something, like a Puppy Pushup, with which your dog is already fluent. If you notice that some areas are too tempting or distracting, avoid those places until your dog has built up a history of success while on leash. After all, dogs see, smell, and hear things that we cannot, so be aware of this when leash walking. On some walks, try a give-and-take approach: Take control and keep your dog close to your heel for certain parts of the walk, then reward him with a looser leash to allow a round of sniffing and pee marking.

You may wish to consider a training collar (see next page), but don't use one as a substitute for proper on-leash walk training. If a dog pulls too hard, he could injure his neck and trachea, so be aware that any coughing or choking may require you to stop the walk immediately and get professional help. If you have a dog walker who takes him out for midday exercise while you are at work, keep in mind that many professional walkers take several dogs at a time, so leash pulling can escalate. If you can afford a private dog walker, you may wish to consider that option.

CORRECTIVE COLLARS AND PROPER HARNESSING

I support the careful use of a few specific training collars that are used only while walking a dog on leash (and always in addition to wearing a flat buckle collar that displays his dog tags). I recommend the Gentle Leader head halter, the No-Pull body harness, and the Martingale collar (also referred to as a Greyhound collar). Please keep in mind that the improper use of any training collar can hurt your dog, so follow the manufacturer's instructions and consider getting assistance from a knowledgeable trainer. For safety, take off any training collar when your dog plays with another dog or goes to the dog park.

As I've discussed earlier, I am against using choke chains and prong collars, which I find inhumane and ineffective. At best, these devices punish a dog for doing something wrong, without leading the dog toward the correct behavior. At worst, they can hurt a dog and suppress dangerous aggression. Suppressing a behavior can create a pressure-cooker effect: The aggressive impulse is still in the dog, and who the heck knows when the pressure will blow and the dog may become dangerous? If you've previously trained your dog this way, remember that it's never too late to cross over as I did; my dogs' retired choke chains now decorate the inside of my parrots' cages, attached to parrot toys.

The Gentle Leader head halter is an effective training tool for proper leash walking. The leash attaches to the halter under the dog's chin, so that when the dog pulls, he automatically turns back toward you. Be careful using a head halter; if the dog pulls too hard, he could flip around, twist his neck, and hurt himself.

Most dogs need to become accustomed to wearing a head halter before learning to walk while wearing one. Proceed very slowly; use lots of praise and treats. Start teaching your dog to like his head halter by giving him treats as you touch the halter to his head. Little by little, lure him to put his

Be sure to place the Gentle Leader training collar behind your dog's ear.

head inside the halter as you give him treats and jackpots, and take the halter away at the end of each rep. Before you snap the halter onto his face for the first time, loosen it all the way, and feed him treats while he focuses on you. Try some Puppy Pushups to take his mind off the halter. On subsequent reps, you'll see where you need to adjust the halter; make those adjustments when you take the device off his head. Once you get to the point that he allows you to buckle the halter, buckle it for only a moment at first while you treat him. On subsequent reps, add time and practice some training behaviors that he already knows. Before you try a walk, have him wear the head halter while he eats a few of his meals (supervised, of course). Continue to condition your dog to accept this strange device very slowly and for short periods of time.

When it's time to start walking, you may, as a safety precaution, attach a second leash to his regular flat buckle collar so that if he pulls too hard, you can give a little slack on the leash that's attached to the halter and keep him from hurting his neck. Ideally, when he pulls, he'll feel just enough pressure around his head to make him turn toward you. As he does, mark it, praise him, and lure or guide him to walk with you in the opposite direction.

Many people mistake a head halter for a muzzle and may think that your dog will bite. If people ask you why your dog is wearing a muzzle, I suggest that you take a moment to educate them in a friendly way that it's a training device and not a muzzle, and demonstrate how it works, which turns it into a socialization experience for your dog. Most people appreciate knowing this information, and you will help spread the word about positive reinforcement training.

Be aware that short-snouted dogs (technically known as brachyce-phalic)—such as Bulldogs, Boxers, Pugs, and Boston Terriers—can slip out of most types of head halters because they have flat muzzles. It's not impos-sible to use a head halter on a flat-faced dog, but you should take precaution by attaching a second leash to his flat-buckle collar so that your dog doesn't run loose if he slips out.

A body harness attaches at your dog's chest or back.

Certain body harnesses improve your dog's leash walking skills. I support the use of body harnesses that connect to the leash at the dog's chest (rather than above the dog's spine), as long as you follow the manufacturer's instructions. Similar to the head halter, a body harness that has a leash attachment at the chest will cause a pulling dog to turn back toward you.

The Martingale collar, or Greyhound collar, is a nonslip collar for dogs with narrow heads, like Greyhounds, Whippets, Ibizan Hounds, and other slender sighthounds (dogs that hunt by sight rather than by scent) on which a regular flat-buckle collar would slip off. The Martingale hangs fairly loose around the dog's neck until the dog pulls, which tightens the collar without strangling. While wearing a Martingale, he should also continue to wear the flat-buckle collar to which his tags are attached.

The Martingale collar is ideal for dogs with narrow heads.

Even if you use a training collar or harness, continue to develop your dog's excellent leash-walking skills through attention, treats, and positive reinforcement. Your goal is to have a well-behaved dog that walks nicely on a loose leash and is focused on you.

HOUSE SOILING

Sometimes a fully house-trained dog will start going potty inside the home. Before you address house soiling as a behavior problem, consult your veterinarian to rule out a possible health issue. If your dog develops a house-soiling problem, please remain committed to solving this manageable behavior problem with the spirit of learning and fun, and not with the threat of punishment. Unfortunately, house soiling is one of the most common reasons dogs are relinquished to shelters. Not necessary! All you need is patience and commitment. I have heard a long list of reasons my clients believe that their dogs have regressed when it comes to potty training: anxiety, not getting enough attention, new pets, new family members, a family member's stress, illness or departure, the urine smell in the carpeting from a previous dog or cat, a new cleaning product, new furniture, reupholstered furniture, rearranging the old furniture, or just a phase that the dog is maturing through. I respect all reasons; I look to all of them for possible clues to what may have triggered a dog's changed behavior. Whatever the cause, the first step (after a vet checkup) is to retrain your dog beginning from step one: Show her the potty spot, walk the same route to get there, reteach her potty signals and cues, and restart the same positive reinforcement potty-training methods you used when you first welcomed her into your family. Take her out to potty as if she were a puppy again. Go as often as possible: when you wake up, before you go to work, after meals, as soon as you come home, before and after any excitement, before going to sleep. Dogproof your home again, put up the x-pens and baby gates, close the doors, and make sure that everyone in the family is on board with this retraining plan.

Starting over also means reestablishing your dog's routine. That includes restarting crate training and the hand-feeding protocol. Reread this book's sections on potty training, crate training, and the hand-feeding protocol, and resume the assignments related to those lessons. As you start over, think back and make a list of changes in the environment to help you determine what may be causing your dog to regress. You may discover environmental changes; if so, you'll need to desensitize and countercondition your dog to adapt—on her own timetable. You may need to look at the rewards you are providing and determine whether you need to change them. Maybe you need to change *how* you give the rewards by making them seem as valuable and exciting as you did when your dog was a puppy.

Part of your detective work means being honest with what I believe to be the most important factor: your own consistency and behavior. Perhaps somewhere along the line you took it for granted that your dog was fully trained, and you therefore stopped praising and rewarding her too soon. Maybe you inadvertently encouraged your dog's house soiling by giving her too much negative attention or consoling pity when you first noticed an accident. If so, try to remain calm and matter-of-fact as you redirect your dog's focus, clean up the mess, and give her appropriate positive attention. You may need to give her more consistent interaction and supervision. You may need to modify your own schedule, provide more positive socialization opportunities, attend group training classes, or bring in caretakers to help you.

CHEWING

Along with house soiling, chewing is an extremely common (and preventable) reason that owners give up their dogs. Some dog owners will put up with chewing and not do anything about it for a while. Maybe they aren't sure of how to deal with it, or maybe they think that their dogs will stop on their own. Eventually, they become so frustrated over the destruction that they give up their dog. It pains me to see this happen because, in my experience, chewing happens when we do not give our dog enough valuable activity or attention. We end up punishing the dog for our mistake.

If your dog is a "chewer," your first question is this: "Is he bored?" Oftentimes a dog chews when there's nothing else for him to do. Is your dog getting enough exercise? Have you continued to put enough time into maintaining his training? In other words, is he getting enough positive interaction and stimulating challenge?

Chewing is a lot more tempting for dogs when their environment isn't dogproofed. Help your dog to be successful by gating off areas that are too tempting. Put away all contraband, use nonstaining bitter spray on tempting areas, and reread this book's section on dogproofing your home for more specifics. When your dog is out of his crate, supervise him. Make sure that you are continuing to help him love his crate, and that he doesn't view it as a place of exile. Chewing does not go away on its own; the problem requires your active participation in redirecting your dog's focus toward positive and engaging experiences. If you permit chewing (or other unwanted behaviors) to continue, you will be providing an unhealthy environment for your dog in which happy energy will diminish.

DIGGING

Most dogs like to dig; it's in their genes. Dogs can smell, hear, and sense creatures in the ground, so they will dig to find them. Digging engages all of a dog's senses: sight, hearing, touch, smell, and taste. If you don't want your flowers or plants dug up, you may have to fence them off. While that may not be the garden aesthetic you were hoping for, it might be better than a garden full of uprooted plants and potholes.

For persistent diggers, I recommend a compromise—what about allowing your dog to dig in certain areas? One of my favorite ways to make digging fun and acceptable is to buy or build a children's sandbox, fill it with sand, and hide a few newspaper-wrapped surprises in it. The dog gets to dig around for the packages, pull them up, tear them open, and eat the treat or play with the toy. To keep the sandbox in good shape, put a waterproof cover over it when it is not in use.

When you don't want your dog to dig, supervise her and redirect her behavior to a fun game before she gets too engrossed in the excavation. Get to know her behavior when she is about to dig (such as light pawing or jumping at the ground after she has sniffed the area) and redirect her to an activity that you can be actively involved in together.

JUMPING

In Chapter One, I told you about the Australian Shepherd, Wallaby, and his annoying jumping habit, which we turned into a fun trick. We thwarted his bad jumping by rewarding him only for good jumping (which happened when we asked him to jump).

Problem jumping usually happens because we have changed our dog's rules. We unintentionally encouraged him to jump by allowing him to jump on us as a puppy. We didn't set boundaries from day one, and now we are trying to change the rules. To him, our rule change seems arbitrary.

So what do you do if your dog suddenly starts jumping or, as is more common, you decide you no longer want him to jump? In order to be effective, you may need to change a few of your own behaviors, too. One solution to the jumping problem is to ignore it. For example, when you enter your home, help your dog relax by acting calm. As he jumps, ignore him while you go about your business for a few minutes. Once he quiets down, praise him for his calm behavior. Show him that jumping gets him nothing, whereas being calm earns him attention and praise.

Alternatively, as you enter, have a special chew toy in your hand and request your dog to sit. Your dog gets the toy only when he sits. Even though he wants to jump, he likely wants the toy even more. Over time, you will have successfully redirected your dog to sit whenever you enter your home. I keep extra chew toys and treats in my car in preparation for entering my house.

Another training technique is to ask a partner to hold your dog on a six-foot leash. Walk up to greet the dog. If he jumps, abruptly turn around and walk about six feet away from him, then count off 10 seconds and have your partner cue him to *sit*. Then try again. Repeat the procedure until your dog can sit still. When he succeeds, mark it, give him a treat from your pocket, and give him attention unless he starts to jump again. After a few failures, dogs tend to sit more quickly; if they see you turn abruptly, they may even sit right down. If your dog just stands quietly instead of sitting, reward this behavior. As you observe him starting to make the connection between getting your attention and his not jumping, decrease the amount of time that you stay turned away from him. Eventually you will decrease the time to one second, and after that the jumping will cease for a brief while. Continue to practice this to keep his jumping impulses under control.

If your dog jumps and tries to get your attention while you're trying to talk with someone, you have what I call an opportunistic jumper. The person you're talking with may give your dog mixed messages by rewarding him with affection when he jumps and then pushing him away. To manage opportunistic jumping, stand on your dog's leash while you continue to hold the leash handle, giving him just enough free tether to sit, stand, or lie down, but not enough to jump. You also need to teach others that your dog is not allowed to jump. If the person is willing, request that she stand still while you move back a couple steps and then cue your dog to *sit*. Then try to walk toward the person again. If your dog doesn't jump, mark and praise that; if he does, have your friend turn away while you stand on the leash as described above. This exercise helps a dog generalize his calm behavior.

ANKLE BITING

Many dogs—especially small dogs, young puppies, and herding dogs—love to chase moving objects such as our ankles, trouser bottoms, and fuzzy slippers. If your dog bites your ankles, stop moving and wait for her to let go (or at least pause), then *redirect* her to sit. Now that you have your dog's attention, mark it with some calm praise and redirect her again toward a new activity such as a game or a stuffed Kong. If you're concerned that it seems like you're rewarding your dog for ankle biting, redirect her to perform a brief series of exercises, like Puppy Pushups or Follow the Lure. Mark the behavior, praise her, and reward her. Whatever the redirected activity, make sure that you reward her, since her ankle biting may be her way of communicating that she needs to feel rewarded and noticed. Make sure to give your dog healthy attention.

You may also try deterring an ankle biter by spraying your ankles with bitter apple spray in advance. Make sure to test it for staining. Be aware that bitter apple spray doesn't change a dog's behavior overnight. You may need to do this for a whole month, while also practicing redirecting exercises.

BARKING

When your dog barks, you may be unintentionally rewarding him by your efforts to make him stop. Do you pet him and coo in a soothing voice that there's nothing to worry about? Or do you call out for him to stop it right now? Either way, you are teaching your dog that when he barks, he gets your attention.

Instead of trying to tell your dog what you *don't* want, you'll be more effective if you redirect your dog toward what you *do* want him to do. When he starts barking, redirect him to perform cues he's mastered, including Puppy Pushups and eye-contact exercises. Make sure that you're giving him this kind of attention at other times, so that you don't accidentally encourage him to bark in order to get your attention.

Many dogs bark when they are bored, excited, fearful, or experience a change in the environment like the sound of a car outside or a barking dog in your neighbor's yard. These distractions engage a dog, and they feel exciting or scary enough to cause him to respond. You can, therefore, reduce your dog's barking by regularly challenging and stimulating him with ongoing training exercises. As I'm sure you've noticed, dogs tend to bark less during training because they are focused on you and the task you have requested. They are so intent on figuring out how to earn that reward, they don't even remember to bark.

Some breeds are particularly vocal, prone to bark at every little thing they experience. If you have a yappy dog that barks to get attention, you may want to risk teaching him to bark and then *shush* on cue. The concept is similar to how we taught Wallaby, the jumping Australian Shepherd, to jump only on cue. Let's say your intensely vocal dog—we'll call him Placido— is barking right now. Walk up to Placido and

> Barking can be a sign that your dog is anxious or fearful.

quietly tell him "shush" as you put a treat on his nose. Hold it there for 10 seconds while you continue saying "shush" with your soothing voice. Then mark the behavior ("good shush") and let him eat his reward. After about 10 seconds of quiet, ask Placido to bark ("Placido, bark" or "Placido, sing"). If he barks, then mark it ("good bark") and hold another treat on his nose while saying "shush," and reward him as you did the first time. If Placido didn't bark when you asked, you can still put another treat on his nose, say "shush," and reward him after 10 seconds (if he remains quiet). If Placido starts barking during the *shush* cue, then withdraw the treat and redirect him to perform a few skills that he already knows fluently. Over time, you will have success with the *shush* cue, followed by redirection to a skills performance. Eventually, Placido will also learn to bark only on cue because that's the only time his solos are rewarded.

Barking can also be a sign that your dog is anxious or fearful, especially if he often barks—and also lunges—at other dogs, people, or inanimate objects. If this is the case, try to keep him calm and supported when he encounters things that spark his barking. For example, if, during a walk, you see a dog approaching that always triggers your dog to bark, try *redirecting* your dog's attention by requesting a *sit* as he maintains eye contact with you, and reward and praise him during his success. Once the dog has passed by, reward and praise your dog once more, and quickly move on. If, however, your dog has already started barking at the trigger dog before you can deal with the problem, your task is more challenging. In this case, try to lure your dog to a neutral spot as you *redirect* his focus to a treat, and then to you, as you cue him to *sit*. Do your best to keep his focus as the other dog passes. It's far easier to redirect your dog *before* he has been triggered, so sharpen your awareness and reaction time on walks.

Redirect a fearful dog's focus to something more positive.

During these walks, you can begin to move a little closer to the triggering distraction once your dog has become fluent with the exercise in which he sits and focuses on you. Watch his body language. Be content with just one single step closer to the trigger on each subsequent encounter as you set your dog up for long-term success, rather than risk a short-term experiment gone awry. Eventually, you will be able to have your dog sit as the trigger pauses, too, and perhaps the two can meet. If, on the other hand, the experiment does go awry and your dog goes crazy (or the other dog gets excited or starts barking and lunging), then immediately lure your dog away and try to ask the other handler nicely to move on. Make a mental note that you need to back up a few training steps so that your dog gets it right, and progress more slowly after that.

Eliminating problem behaviors is an important part of socialization.

I highly recommend using a training partner to practice well-socialized approaches, including the Greet Your Neighbor exercise and other socialization activities in Chapter Nine.

NOISE PHOBIAS

It's not unusual for a dog to be startled by a loud or sudden noise—the alarm clock, the garage door opening, the television being turned on—but some dogs go absolutely crazy with excitement or fear when they hear such noises. Most noise triggers can be handled by *desensitizing;* oftentimes, *counterconditioning* should follow. With Boz, I started to desensitize him by first redirecting his focus onto the ball as I opened the soda can. Subsequently, I counterconditioned him to get his ball when he saw me hold the unopened soda can.

To desensitize your dog to a noise trigger, begin to regularly introduce the sound at a low volume and from some distance away. Once your dog becomes more accustomed to the noise, and exhibits less anxiety around it, slowly begin to bring her closer to the source. You may also want to introduce a counterconditioning behavior, such as offering a toy that she already values, *just prior* to the noise being made. If she gets anxious, proceed more slowly, starting by taking a break from this exercise.

One interesting thing about sound sensitivity that I have learned over the years is that dogs that live with hair in their eyes tend to be more reactive to sound because they can't see enough of what is going on around them. Consider trimming the hair from your dog's eyes (if appropriate for her breed), so that he can see where the sounds are coming from. Clear vision will also enable your dog to focus on you with greater eye contact and attention.

EATING PROBLEMS

Overfeeding our dogs is not a sign of how much we love them. Dogs that carry extra weight are at greater risk for orthopedic problems, heart disease, stroke, and cancer. Sometimes we overfeed because we feel that we're not giving our dogs enough attention, but food is not a worthy substitute for that. If your dog has a weight problem, you should first check with your vet or a veterinary nutritionist to help you determine whether there is a health or diet issue at cause.

Managing your dog's everyday food environment is key to keeping him healthy. Keep food out of jumping and counter-surfing height. If you have kids, don't let them feed the dog from the dinner table or walk away and leave their plates, which can tempt a dog. Be aware of your dog's daily lifestyle, including calorie intake and exercise. If he begins to grow overweight training, keep in mind that training treats are part of his daily food portion, so account for the extra calories in his training treats. Many trainers believe that if your dog is fat, then *you* aren't getting enough exercise.

Eating too fast can be a cause of trouble, most severely resulting in gastric torsion (also called bloat): twisting of the stomach that causes severe bloating very quickly. Gastric torsion is often life-threatening and must be dealt with as a medical emergency. I believe in erring on the side of caution: Slow down a dog's eating rate, refrain from vigorous exercise an hour before and after feeding, and feed smaller meals more than once a day. Veterinarians continue to debate the causes of gastric torsion. Some believe that a little water should be added to processed kibble in order to release gases and slow down the bloat; the verdict is still out. Besides the risk of gastric torsion, if your dog eats too fast you may sympathetically offer him more food than is healthy for him.

To slow down a dog's food intake, put a large obstacle in the bowl, such as a big rock or large steel ball that cannot be swallowed. Wash the obstacle just as you wash your dog's bowl and make sure it's not made of lead or coated with sealer or paint. For my dogs and guest dogs that eat too fast, a Kong once again comes to the rescue: I put some of the meal into the Kong and then place it in the bowl along with the rest of the dog's food. In addition to helping a dog eat more slowly, the stuffed Kong also provides an engaging challenge as the dog figures out how to work the food out of the Kong.

Socialization Problems

I believe that a well-socialized puppy is a puppy that has been positively exposed to many dogs, kids, grown-ups, and environments that he may encounter again in his life. As long as we don't flood a dog with more than he is ready to handle, we can never oversocialize him. In my experience, many dog owners don't socialize their dogs comprehensively enough throughout their dogs' lives.

Ideally, learning proper social manners should begin before a puppy reaches four months of age. After four months, problems in socialization begin to grow, including an inability to understand other dogs' body language and behavioral feedback, like playing too rough and biting too hard, or a fear of people and other dogs that can trigger shyness or bullying. Dogs that have socialization problems tend to get fewer opportunities to socialize, and so their manners deteriorate even further. Unless socialization problems are corrected, a dog may eventually pose a serious safety risk.

My Ibizan Hound, Brieo, started life very well socialized. He accompanied me to my puppy training classes, where he had a seemingly endless supply of supervised play opportunities. However, as Brieo neared age two, he started to get pushy with some of the student puppies. I paid close attention to Brieo's "teenage period," and eventually realized that he was ready to socialize with more mature dogs. I decided to move him out of the puppy class and up to the next level; I saw an instant change. Now at age seven, Brieo has excellent social manners. He helps me babysit boarding guest dogs, entertaining them with excellent play skills, and loves playing with young puppies too.

For a dog that has developed serious socialization problems, positive reinforcement methods offer the best guarantee of lasting rehabilitation. In Chapter One I told you about the Vicktory Dogs, the 22 pit bulls that Best Friends Animal Society in Kanab, Utah, rescued from pro football player Michael Vick's illegal dog-fighting operation (see page 14). Although other experts determined that the dogs were beyond redemption and that the most humane act would be to euthanize them, Best Friends' Dogtown training manager, John Garcia, and certified pet dog trainer Ann Allums took in the dogs. Garcia and Allums rehabilitated these "death row dogs" using only positive reinforcement methods. Today, some of the Vicktory Dogs are fully rehabilitated, Canine Good Citizen–certified, and placed happily in new homes. (See Appendix 1 for information on the Canine Good Citizen certificate.)

Garcia and Allums treat each behavior problem as a puzzle that needs to be figured out. "We take it slow and treat every dog as an individual, just like humans," Garcia says. One particularly aggressive dog, Meryl, needed to learn that people could approach her in friendship rather than to get her to fight. Allums says that "within five minutes we found most of her triggers. It took one day to build basic trust with Meryl." She adds that if they had used punishment aversion methods, "Meryl would have lashed out and gotten worse."

Garcia and Allums's first step to building positive relationships was to get the Vicktory Dogs comfortable enough to hand-feed them, and then feed them in different locations to desensitize food aggression. The dogs began to think of their trainers as "great big goodie jars," says Garcia. Best Friends trainers reinforced the few things that each dog was doing right, introduced them slowly to other dogs and people to socialize them, and brought them into new situations (such as riding in a car) only when they were ready. Garcia and Allums have also given the dogs plenty of mental stimulation with stuffed Kongs and other interactive toys, cue training, and target training.

FOOD GUARDING AND RESOURCE GUARDING

If a dog guards his food or toys, that may be a warning that he could, at some point, become dangerous—and even vicious—without warning. It may happen, for example, that a dog used to guarding his food is peacefully gnawing on a favorite toy when a child arrives to pet him. The dog may suddenly become protective of his toy and lash out at the child.

When I train a dog that might be a food guarder, I watch his body language around the food bowl; if he drops his shoulder and head deeper into the bowl as I walk by, that's often a sign that he could be (or become) a guarder. In that case, I toss food around the bowl. Little by little I move closer, observing whether he's getting less sensitive to my presence.

If you fear that your dog has begun guarding his food, immediately resume the hand-feeding protocol discussed in Chapter Three. Remember to hand-feed your dog in different areas of your home and use different bowls, so that he doesn't perceive that he "owns" either his supper spot or bowl—all spots, bowls, and food belong to you and you are sharing them with your dog. When you feel it's time to transition away from hand-feeding, return to putting portions of the food in your dog's bowl so that he can clearly see that you are keeping the rest of it. Review the hand-feeding protocol to prepare your dog to accept food from other people and to be fed in the presence of other dogs and people.

If you are afraid to hand-feed your dog, you may want to bring in a professional to help you. One technique that I like to use with dogs that are too fearful or aggressive to be hand-fed is to have the dog watch me measure his total daily food ration and put it in a big bowl. I want him to understand that I am the giver of all good things, that I control the food bowl. Next, I let him see me put a handful into the dinner bowl and place the bowl on the floor—ideally, once he is sitting (if he is already fluent with that cue). After he eats that handful, it's very likely that he will look at me, at which point I say, "Good. You want some more?" Then I drop a few treats or kibble on the floor away from the bowl; as he goes for the treats I pick up the bowl, put more food in it, and set it down again. This is a quick and effective way to communicate that I'm in charge of the food. I may repeat that step until I'm confident that I can move closer to the bowl when he's eating. At that point I'll drop in a treat (such as a piece of cheese) while he's eating. We want the dog to understand that when hands reach into the food bowl we are giving more food and not taking it away, which helps relax anxiety and raises his confidence level to have us around him while he's eating. Once I'm confident that he's calm and accepts that I control the food, he's ready to begin hand-feeding.

As for other resources that could be guarded, such as a Kong treat, I don't ever let a dog chew uninterrupted for more than five minutes. That Kong belongs to me and is on loan to my dog in exchange for his polite behavior, starting with a *sit* to earn it. One sign that a dog may be a toy guarder is that he carries the toy away to a remote area of the home to chew it.

When taking a chew toy away from a dog, always make a trade for another treat or toy. That way he understands that you provide a variety of valuable resources. When I trade for a special toy such as a stuffed Kong, I often offer a nice piece of hamburger. Practice the *off and take it* trades and cookie trades that you learned earlier, and make frequent trades with your dog so that he experiences getting something back after he lets you take something else away. The more experience he has with trades, the more comfortable he will be chewing toys around you (and around other people as you include them safely in this training).

AGGRESSION TOWARD PEOPLE

If you have a dog that is aggressive toward people, you may want to use a qualified trainer or behaviorist to help identify her triggers and attempt to desensitize and redirect them.

When I evaluate an aggressive dog, I always involve a veterinarian to assess and diagnose any possible health or injury issue that may be causing the dog to behave in a way that most people would refer to as "aggressive." That word gets thrown around a lot when describing a dog's behavior and is often, in my experience, misused. Not all dogs that growl, guard, bite ankles, or bark a lot are aggressive. I'm very careful about using this word because too often, once that label is placed on the dog, it may seal her fate. There are few places that will rehome a dog that has been labeled aggressive.

A dog is typically called aggressive when she initiates dangerous behavior toward people—often arising from lack of human contact, incomplete socialization of the dog during the first four months, or the lingering effects of past trauma. In each of those cases, the dog doesn't know whom to trust and is not truly aggressive, but is acting out of fear.

The first step in dealing with aggression is to identify the dog's triggers. At the same time, the dog needs to trust someone. I approach this scenario with caution and in the most positive way possible. I read the dog's body language very carefully and make sure that she can read mine. I work patiently at a pace that is comfortable for that particular dog, always looking to increase her bonds to me.

In this exercise, you and your training partner will use food to help desensitize your dog. Make sure that she is hungry when you start this work. If you are able to put a leash on her safely, attach a long leash (6 to 12 feet) to your dog's collar, and rather than you or your partner holding it right away, let her drag it on the floor. Letting your dog drag the leash now will help her feel less trapped or frustrated later when you hold it, tether it to your belt loop, or step on the handle to stop her forward movement to a place that you don't want her to go. Anticipate the dog's moves by looking calmly for body language that says she is fearful or uncomfortable. A short list of such body signals includes hair standing on end, hunched shoulders, lowered head, cowering, hiding, and removing herself from the company of people or other dogs.

Begin by taking your dog to a calm environment. If the dog is comfortable with you but shows aggressive or fearful posture toward your partner, you have identified a trigger. As you and your partner chat pleasantly, have him toss a little kibble about halfway to your dog, and allow your dog to get it. Continue the calm chat with your partner as he tosses a little more kibble; the dog will get the kibble only when she feels comfortable and safe. There is no force and no timetable. The treats help your dog understand that no one will harm her, and furthermore that people are generally good. Carefully work the treats closer and closer to your partner.

As your dog becomes more comfortable with your partner, you will eventually be able to have him hand-feed her and work with her in training, games, and walks. In time, these kinds of introductions to more people will become more comfortable for your dog, which will help her confidence rise. It's difficult to put a time frame on how long it will take for your dog to progress to each level of success. That will depend on the severity of her problem and how committed you are to helping her. It may take three months of consistently rehearsing these exercises or it may take a full year.

If your dog has mild fear aggression around the veterinarian or groomer, take brief desensitization trips there just to go inside, give your dog a treat, and then leave. If they have a moment to greet her and give a treat, it will help.

AGGRESSION TOWARD DOGS

Some dogs can be delightful and gentle with people but behave shyly or aggressively toward other dogs. As in dealing with aggression or fearful behavior toward people, you may want a qualified professional to help identify and desensitize your dog's triggers. Try to learn your dog's history with other dogs and ask your vet to rule out health issues.

In this case, you will need patient canine partners to help desensitize and socialize your dog. My canine partner is Brieo. When I take on a new behavioral case or agree to foster a dog that has been labeled aggressive, I first evaluate the dog (which may take a week or two, including time for bonding). Nine times out of 10 I find that the dog would like to play with Brieo but doesn't know how. The so-called aggressive dog's attempts to play are harsh, mouthy, pushy, and overwhelming. The dog doesn't understand or acknowledge Brieo's body language—Brieo's way of conveying his boundaries.

For this assessment and desensitization training, I sometimes put a band muzzle on the problem dog. This prevents him from opening his mouth wide enough to bite hard, but allows him to drink, eat, pant, and play. If you use a muzzle, understand that it requires very close supervision and an extreme amount of knowledge and care. For example, never use a muzzle to prevent a dog from chewing furniture. Also,

Decrease aggression by first learning your dog's triggers.

never muzzle a dog if another dog might take advantage of the situation. Fortunately, Brieo is naturally good-natured, well-trained, and socialized so he won't take advantage.

One behavior that is often labeled aggressive is mounting. While mounting is undesirable and very annoying, it is not automatically "aggressive" per se. Mounting is a natural canine behavior and often occurs during acceptable play experiences. That said, when your dog tries to mount another dog, you should redirect your dog. Sometimes mounting can trigger a fight. Use your cue word "off" to stop your dog from mounting. Within a small group of well-socialized dogs, sometimes you and the other handler may use your combined judgment to allow the dog that is being mounted to turn around and growl or even snap at the mounting dog. For well-socialized dogs, that warning should be sufficient to communicate that that particular dog is off-limits. Watch the mounting dog's body language; if he squares up behind another dog and creeps forward, that's a sign that he's getting ready to mount and the perfect opportunity to cue "off." Both owners should redirect their dogs away from each other and practice some cues before resuming play.

An unacceptable aggressive behavior is fence fighting among neighbor dogs, as it can lead an otherwise sociable dog to behave aggressively. If they are not stopped and managed, both dogs may learn that fence fighting is acceptable, and it can become a bad habit that escalates to more aggressive lunging, digging to get under the fence, and even climbing over it, which can lead to a serious dog fight. The longer you allow fence fighting to continue unchecked, the worse it can get. If possible, talk to your neighbors to see if they are willing to find a safe way to try socializing and desensitizing the dogs to each other. Sometimes neighbors cooperate to make sure that when one dog is outside, the other dog is inside. It's worth a shot to talk things over calmly and try to come up with a plan that works for both of you.

Dog parks, while wonderful public spaces for off-leash socialization, can also become laboratories for aggression, fear, and improper play. In Chapter Twelve, I'll give you tips on making the dog park experience as successful as possible. That said, not all dogs are dog park material, and it is possible that your dog will not be able to enjoy that environment, especially once he matures or becomes less playful with other dogs as he ages and gets crotchety.

SEPARATION ANXIETY AND SHADOWING

Since dogs are pack animals, they typically desire to be part of a group. Therefore, for some dogs, being alone can lead to anxiety and fear. In my opinion, some common causes of separation anxiety are incomplete crate training, allowing your dog to shadow you all around your home, and never teaching her that being alone at times is healthy. If your dog has separation anxiety, immediately restart the crate training protocol that is detailed in Chapter Three. Successful crate training almost always *habituates* a dog to being alone, so that she enjoys the safety and comfort of her den. Here are a few crate training reminders:

❯ Slowly increase the time you keep your dog in the crate and the amount of time you leave her alone while she's in it.

❯ If your dog barks while she's in the crate, wait until she stops barking before you return to her, and don't make a big deal when you leave home or return.

❯ If you work at home (as I often do), do not let your dog shadow you around the house, to the bathroom, and so forth. Use the crate training protocol even when you are at home.

In general, if you're working with your dog to overcome separation anxiety or shadowing, slowly habituate your dog to her crate and leave her for short durations as you go from one room to another, then reappear before she gets anxious.

FEAR OF NEW SITUATIONS

If your dog has a pattern of fearful behavior in new situations, continue to socialize him, but do it slowly. Before you put him in new situations, reinforce his sense of well-being in those environments where he already seems comfortable, and don't force him into situations that make him uncomfortable. For example, if your dog is fearful when riding in the car, don't force him to go out with you whenever you'd like his company. Instead, introduce him to the car a step at a time, similar to the way you may have introduced him to his crate. Before getting him inside the car, take him around the parked car, feed and praise him, and then walk away with him. Another time, with the car door already open, let your dog sniff inside and eat a few treats, but don't try to lure him in just yet. You may then toss a few treats inside the car the next time; maybe he'll go in, but if not, don't force it.

The technique of forcing a dog to do something he doesn't want to do—which is, in essence, asking him to face his fears all at once—is called *flooding*. The thinking behind flooding is a belief that the sooner an irrational fear is exposed as "meaningless," that there is nothing that the dog needs to worry about, the sooner he will get over that fear. This technique is advocated by some trainers, but is one to which I am strongly opposed. In my professional judgment, forcing a dog to face fears you want to eliminate before he is ready would be like sticking me in a roomful of snakes and telling me that I just need to get over it.

I used to be terribly afraid of snakes. Even today, snakes are among my least favorite things to encounter in the wild. But some years ago, my family got a pet snake. It was not my idea. My son, Blaise, had just returned from visiting his cousin who had one. Blaise thought a snake would be the perfect pet for him. I needed to get comfortable with the whole idea . . . in my own time (preferably years). I began by reading about snakes and found that the more I learned about them, the more curious I became. So I watched videos about snakes, researched snakes on the Internet, located breeders who specialized in snakes, and talked to snake owners. I'm fortunate to live not too far from the National Zoo in Washington, D.C., which has a good collection of snakes. I planted myself safely behind the thick plate glass in the Reptile Discovery Center and stood there as long as I could, watching the tree snakes, water snakes, cobras, pythons, boa constrictors, and anacondas.

Reinforce your dog's sense of well-being whenever possible.

When it got to be too much for me—it didn't take long—I could get out of there quickly (and find refuge in the Gorilla Grove).

What I was doing—or at least trying to do—was to face my fears by desensitizing myself gradually. When the time came to bring home a baby ball python, I was ready and actually fairly comfortable with the idea. I even helped feed our snake and put her in the travel terrarium to transport her to the veterinarian for regular checkups.

Now, I know for a fact that if someone had said, "Dawn, your fear of snakes is irrational. Here, I'm going to lock you in a room with 10 nonpoisonous snakes and when you come out alive, you'll see how silly you're being," I would have either died of a heart attack or been imprisoned for murder.

We can't expect anything different from our dogs. It's far better—and, if you ask me, far more loving—to desensitize dogs than it is to flood them and risk causing them emotional stress or, worse, to become more fearful or aggressive. Some examples of flooding include forcing a dog to go to a dog park, dragging a dog into a swimming pool to teach him to swim, surrounding a dog with kids because he is afraid of them, or (as discussed earlier) forcing a dog to walk on a slippery floor that he fears.

If you're considering using a professional to help with your dog's behavior problems, stay away from anyone who wants to use flooding techniques. I feel that strongly about it.

HIDING

If your dog is hiding at home, that may mean she's not getting enough downtime away from people, especially playful children. Don't let your kids initiate contact with your dog when she is hiding. Be aware of potential family dynamics or behaviors, such as a family member unintentionally disturbing the dog while you have your back turned for a moment, or perhaps incomplete socialization with a family member who is away from home a lot. In the latter case, slowly introduce your dog to that family member and use food treats to help make positive associations. Also, make sure to check if your dog has any health issues or injuries; dogs often hide their weaknesses, maybe because they fear being hurt again or being cut off from the pack.

Final Thoughts on Behavior Problems

I know that we'd all like easy solutions to cure our dogs' behavior problems. But the fact is, there aren't any. The only real solution is consistent attention, commitment, and hard work. Over the 20 years that I have been training, I have seen an increase in the prescription of medicines that are supposed to cure certain canine behavioral issues such as anxiety. However, if the dog owner doesn't also change his or her own behavior along with the dog's environment and routine, the medicine won't be effective.

Some people use electronic training collars as if they were magic tools, but I always urge them to think again. These collars administer an adjustable penalty tingle/shock (ranging from mild to strong) via a handheld remote control. When used effectively, they can shape a dog's behavior similar to the way clicker training works. However, these collars must be used with great care, and I've worked with far too many dogs that have been repeatedly, and painfully, shocked by improperly used collars.

I was once adamantly against electronic fencing, which can give a dog a mild shock if he wanders beyond a perimeter barrier; however, I know there may be no other reasonable alternative in a neighborhood that prohibits the building of actual fences. If you must use electronic fencing, please use it only as a short-term confinement—maybe while you're gardening or cleaning your yard and want your dog with you. And it's certainly appropriate to use it during outdoor supervised play or training sessions. That said, I don't think it's right to put your dog outside for the day while you go to work or run errands, leaving him contained only by the electronic fence. Chasing a squirrel or deer may seem so exciting to a dog that he decides it's worth more than the electrical shock. But once he has crossed that boundary, he may not return for fear of being shocked again.

You probably know from your own life that bad habits are hard to break. Even when we have stopped a bad habit, it can return, were we to give up our continued effort. Our dogs' behavior problems can also flare up again, and when they do, we must recommit and address the problem, regardless of the time and effort it requires.

The alternative to correcting our dogs' behavior problems is to ignore them until they become so serious and destructive that we give up on the dogs. Correcting behavior problems by using positive reinforcement gives us the blessing of a rich life together with our beloved best friends. When we cherish our dogs as living, breathing creatures of God that see, hear, and feel pleasure and pain in ways similar to our own, we develop greater respect for other humans and for ourselves. How glorious to be inspired by a creature that shares so little of our language but so much of our heart.

Chapter Twelve

Your Dog in the World

og training never ends; it just gets easier. Socializing always needs a tune-up. If you keep your eyes open, you'll see that "teaching moments" happen every day, and even the most ordinary experiences are training opportunities. With a well-socialized dog and your spirited bond that seems to strengthen daily, a big world awaits.

Dog Parks

Your dog needs to be socialized off leash as well as on leash. Even dogs that like the comfort of knowing you're in control of the leash may experience frustration at the limitations the leash places on them. It's like a child in a toy store: The child wants to touch the toys. If the parent holds her back too much, she may act out. Your dog can respond similarly. Supervised off-leash time is important to keeping him from becoming frustrated, and it is a great technique to help spirit your dog.

Only attempt off-leash play if the area is fenced in.

For many dogs, an off-leash visit to a dog park can be the highlight of the day. Unfortunately, that visit can be fraught with challenges. The frequent occurrence of dog bites, dog fights, and poop on our shoes has given some dog parks a bad rap.

Dog park etiquette is essential. Translation? Use good manners and common sense. Here are some tips:

❯ Remove any harness, special collar, or clothing except for the flat-buckle collar that holds your dog's ID tags. He could get tangled in his or another dog's fashion statement. Obey leash laws; keep your dog on leash until you have entered the play area, and keep his leash with you.

❯ Dog parks are not for small children. Accidents can happen quickly, especially when exuberant dogs are happily chasing and wrestling.

❯ Scoop the poop. A poopy park is a health hazard, and not cleaning up after your dog is discourteous. Carry at least one bag at all times, or use the park's waste disposal tools.

❯ Volunteer to help keep your dog park clean and safe; consider

Playing with other dogs is an important part of socialization.

making a donation for cleanup tools, toys, even play structures and fence repair. Many parks have volunteer cleanup activities and etiquette presentations, with an increasing number of them sponsored by local pet shops and pet product makers. I support this good trend.

❯ Make sure your dog has good *recall:* Practice *recall* each and every time you visit the dog park. (Remind yourself of the technique by checking out the Recall Quick Guide in the Fundamentals Training Program on page 132.) Your dog needs to learn that your cue to *come here* usually does not signal the end of playtime, and that he'll often be able to return immediately to playing with his buddies. When I see owners chasing their dogs when it's time to leave the dog park, I know they must have inadvertently taught them that *come here* always means the end of playtime.

❯ Use *recalls* as segues to other training cues that your dog already excels at. This will strengthen his ability to follow your instructions consistently, even in the midst of distractions. Make these training moments extremely brief at first; your dog needs and wants free play without too many instructions.

❯ Never leave your dog alone or unsupervised at a dog park. Even when you're socializing with other owners, make sure that you know exactly what he is doing.

❯ Don't let him rush at a dog that is entering the play area. It may intimidate the dog that is about to join the playgroup.

❯ Know when your dog has had enough and leave the park on a happy note. Like children, dogs can get grouchy when they're tired or overheated.

❯ Be honest about your dog's socialization abilities. A dog park is not appropriate for dogs that are aggressive, unsocialized, or have a history of fighting, biting, or uncontrollable barking. If your dog has any of these issues, resolve them before your first trip to the dog park, and do not use the park as a way to desensitize your dog's behavioral shortcomings.

❯ Your dog may not get along with all other dogs, just as humans don't get along with all humans. Try to anticipate his or another dog's aggressive or uncomfortable body language, and remove your dog from the potentially dangerous situation before a fight starts.

❯ If a fight breaks out, take responsibility for controlling your dog and removing him from the fight right away. Do your best to keep a calm voice so that you don't add to the chaos. Many fights escalate into a melee or bully pack for no apparent reason. You just have to be prepared: The more you practice successful *recalls,* the greater the likelihood that your dog will recall to you when a fight breaks out.

❯ Fights can break out over guarding toys or food. Therefore, it's best not to show your treats. I am very careful and sneaky when I give my dog a quick treat for good behavior, such as a *recall.* If you take a toy, figure that you have donated it to the park; but don't take it at all if you're not sure your dog can and will share it with any other dog.

❯ Apologize quickly if your dog makes a mistake, even if you feel embarrassed, defensive, have an explanation, or want to blame another dog or human. Mistakes are inevitable; learn from them. But don't expect others to apologize to you, even if you apologize to them when it's clearly a no-fault situation.

❯ Avoid disciplining another dog. It's best to focus on removing your dog from the situation if a dog is overly aggressive with yours. If you need to request another owner to control her dog better, be polite and kind. For example, if you need to ask that someone's dog not terrorize yours when you're trying to enter the park, try also to say something nice about her lovely dog.

WHISTLE RECALL

The whistle is especially useful at a dog park or in a wilderness location where your dog is off leash. But make sure that your dog is fluent with the voice *recall* ("come here") before you attempt a *whistle recall.* If you can whistle with your mouth, make sure that you can make a consistent, loud sound. Otherwise, I highly recommend using a loud mechanical whistle for recall; an unbreakable metal whistle that can be heard over long distances if your dog happens to run off, get lost, and panic. My cowriter, Larry, often recalls his Golden Retriever, Higgins, with a metal whistle that he has kept on his key chain for more than nine years. For beginners, I recommend using a whistle that you can hear rather than an ultrasonic dog whistle that takes a bit of getting used to. (If you want to use an ultrasonic whistle, be sure to follow the directions so you blow it properly. Learn how to test and tune its screw adjustment, and don't blow too hard or you will overpower the tones.)

Start teaching the *whistle recall* by whistling while you stand next to your dog and treating him as if you were a vending machine, so that he associates the sound with the reward. Then build up *recalls* to a few paces, combining the whistle with the lure, the visual cue, and the verbal "come here"—we're using all the cues and not leaving anything to chance. Little by little, increase the distance and withdraw some of the cues.

Once you have built up to a *whistle recall* distance of about 10 yards, the next step is to use it during supervised play. The other dog may also come to you, but that's okay if it encourages your dog to *recall* successfully. At the beginning, use it at an off-peak time. Build success with that by being sure to reward your dog for coming when recalled, and then releasing him to play again so that he associates the *whistle recall* with a positive reward rather than the end of playtime.

When your dog has excellent *whistle recall,* generalized to all kinds of distracting settings, it's up to you to decide whether he is ready for a wilderness trial. Train your dog to *recall* with the whistle at short distances by playing Come and Go (see page 144) with your hiking partner, gradually increasing the distance between the two of you. Make sure to bring great treats to help motivate great *recalls.*

Road Trips

When my three kids were young, my family would spend one month every summer driving from Virginia to Palm Beach, Florida, to visit my mother. We'd go to the beach every day, visit play parks, and spend hours at the animal safari experience. I loved exposing my children to life in Florida, where I grew up. The van would be packed with us humans, plus three dogs—Jock, the Border Collie; Merit, the Flat-Coated Retriever; and Saxon, the Giant Schnauzer—and two parrots, Maude and Jules. We were a traveling circus.

At the halfway point, we usually stayed in the same motel—it was called South of the Border—because it welcomed our trained menagerie. We'd rent the honeymoon suite so the gang could enjoy the Jacuzzi bathtub together. The kids would hold treats underwater, and the dogs would dive to get them. If we went out to dinner or to the swimming pool, the pets stayed in the room. I turned on the TV set and air-conditioning to drown out hallway noise that might agitate them. Fortunately, the dogs and birds kept fairly quiet, even when I was training them by exiting the motel room and returning with rewards and praise for quiet *settles*. I built up longer and longer periods of being out of the room, until I was eventually able to go out to dinner without having to check on the pets midway through the meal. The dogs got a final walk before settling in for the night, and a first walk the next morning before we loaded ourselves back into the van.

In the van, during those rare moments when all was quiet, I would look in my rearview mirror to see sleeping kids still buckled in and slumped over sleeping dogs that were draped across their laps. Those long drives were punctuated by rest stops, where we unloaded all the animals, stretched our legs, aired the bird cages, and ate quick snacks in the shade.

In Florida, we spent most of our time at the beach. All my dogs loved to swim, but Jock couldn't stand the feel of the sand under his paws and would always turn and head back to the car. Before long, I realized that I couldn't make him love the beach the way I wanted him to, and I had to leave him behind with my mom.

I'm telling you my story in the hope that you'll be able to glean some tips for making car trips with your dog workable and enjoyable. A well-planned road trip with your dog can create memories that last a lifetime. Before you risk a road trip, make sure that she can handle long rides. Start by acclimating her to the car with short trips around town, to shopping centers, a friend's home, the dog park. Spend a Sunday afternoon taking your dog (and your family) out to a picnic area or to a lovely trail for a hike or nature walk.

Consider getting a specialized seat belt to keep your dog safe on long trips.

If your dog has a tendency to get carsick, make sure you have gotten her over it before attempting a long family trip in the car. (Take her on short rides on an empty stomach for starters.) There are remedies and medications that your veterinarian can recommend or prescribe for you. Make sure you test her reaction to the medication before you take off on your family adventure.

Check in advance whether dogs are allowed where you will be going. Locate places to stay and eat that allow dogs. Hotels are most likely to take your dog if she is crate trained.

Some cafés provide outside dining with limited space for well-trained dogs. In advance, find out where emergency vet services are. If it's hot where you're going, remember that your dog is wearing a fur coat, so make sure that she will have plenty of shade and opportunities to cool down and rest. If you plan on camping, nighttime can be an adventure. If the weather is cold, protect your dog from hypothermia by taking an extra blanket or sleeping bag for

A well-planned road trip with your dog can create memories that last a lifetime.

her. Perhaps she could use a sweater to sleep in, too. I recommend tethering her leash while you sleep, so that she isn't apt to go chasing off in pursuit of a midnight sound or smell. You can stake the tether to the ground next to you or even tie her leash to you, as long as you don't choke either of you or make it impossible for either of you to get comfortable.

When I take my dogs hiking, I almost always keep them on leash. I live in deer-hunting country and my Ibizan Hound Brieo looks, runs, and jumps like a deer, so I am extra cautious about letting him go off leash. The longer your dog is conditioned to accept being on the leash, the easier it is to take the leash off and get good *recalls.*

While all dogs are different, I've found that most are generally ready to start going off leash in controlled situations after age five, as long as you have already laid an excellent foundation of training skills that includes a reliable *recall* system. I don't want to put a damper on anyone's dream of having a dog that can be off leash most of the time, but sadly, even the best-trained dogs can make mistakes or be in the wrong place at the wrong time. My Border Collie, Jock, was excellent off leash wherever we went. In 2002, we were attending a Super Bowl party in the countryside and Jock was in heaven retrieving sticks for the guests. When I called him he would turn on a dime to come back to me as fast as he could. Unfortunately, he was hit by a car and died instantly when a driver swayed off the road at high speed and hit him. Jock was 9½ years old and he was within my sight, but the car was going too fast. He never had a chance, and the driver who hit him kept going. So I advise not letting your dog off leash for long periods, and make sure you know where he is at all times.

Checklist: **For Trips**

Nothing is more important for a happy trip than a well-packed bag of doggy supplies. What follows is a basic list of trip necessities; over time, you will learn to customize the list for your dog's particular needs. For example, if he is prone to sticking his nose where he shouldn't, you'll probably want to load up on extra Benadryl—though be sure to check with your vet about dosage first. Once, Jock stuck his nose into a hill of fire ants while we were at a rest stop in Florida. He was not a happy camper. Fortunately, I had an emergency kit in my van for the kids and the dogs and was able to clean Jock's nose, disinfect it, and then give him a Benadryl tablet to reduce the possibility of an allergic reaction. One more example: Sometimes the change in drinking water can make a dog sick or affect his appetite, so you may need to mix home water with the new water.

❐ Trip dog tag with destination phone number and address

❐ Rabies shot certificate or tag

❐ Local phone numbers: emergency vet, poison control, snakebite assistance

❐ Leash

❐ Poop pickup bags

❐ Flashlight with extra batteries

❐ Dog food

❐ Training treats

❐ Clean drinking water from home

❐ Food and water bowls

❐ Lightweight travel bowl for hiking

❐ Blankets/dog bed

❐ X-pen or crate

❐ First aid kit: includes tweezers, tick remover, snakebite kit, antibiotic cream, hydrogen peroxide, sterile gauze bandages, and tape

❐ Mylar space blanket for treating hypothermia

❐ Medicine if necessary (Remember, some medication needs to be refrigerated; if so, you must make accommodations for that.)

❐ Flea and tick prevention (including heartworm pills in many locales)

❐ Mosquito repellent (on coat, not rubbed into skin) and mosquito-repelling citronella candles

❐ Medicated ear and eye cleaners

❐ Grooming kit: comb, brush, blow-dryer (if needed), shampoo, creme rinse

❐ Dog towels

❐ Toys: Kong, balls, safe toys that can't be swallowed

Water Safety

Although some breeds love to swim, many dogs don't know how and need to be taught. For nearly 20 years I owned a home with a swimming pool, and I've also sailed with my dogs off the coast of Florida and in the Caribbean. So, I had to teach my dogs *and* my kids to swim. Some breeds are at a disadvantage in the water, such as those with long bodies or flat faces, including Dachshunds, Basset Hounds, Pugs, and Boston Terriers. Bulldogs have very short legs compared to their broad bodies and heavy heads, which makes it dangerous for most of them to swim at all.

Other breeds, such as Porties, Poodles, Labradors, and many water retrievers and spaniels, were originally bred for water work and generally take to water quickly. However, never assume that your dog will be a natural in the water, no matter what its breed. Tragically, I know of an owner who threw his water breed puppy into the Potomac River thinking that would "teach" it to swim by instinct, but the dog failed and drowned.

For many dogs, swimming in a pool that has a single exit can be a more fearful experience than swimming in a lake or at a calm beach that has a sloping, visible shore. In all cases, you may want to start out having your dog wear a life jacket; there are some excellent brands made specifically for dogs. If you're teaching her to swim in a pool or off a boat, you may want to invest in a water ramp for dogs.

In a pool, start teaching your dog to swim by luring her into the water with a treat, or picking her up and taking her into the water with you. Keep her very close to you at first while you determine how comfortable she is, and remain very near the steps, ladder, or ramp. Help her become familiar with this exit by helping her climb the stairs or ladder. Having another, swim-trained dog along to "demonstrate" swimming can give her confidence and encouragement. If your dog resists, do not force her, as that may increase fear. Help her in the beginning by keeping your hand under her tummy, toward her rear legs. This will help her stay balanced.

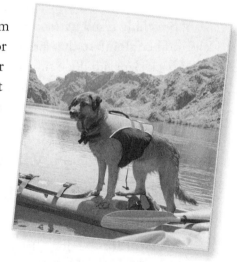

When using a life jacket, follow the manufacturer's instructions. Get your dog used to wearing it, make adjustments, and practice swimming in shallow water before going out in a boat.

In lakes, rivers, and beaches, be aware of strong currents that could over-power your dog or cause her to panic. Be aware of water temperature as well, as water that is too cold can cause dangerous hypothermia. If the shore or beach is hot, your dog's paws may blister, so use caution. If it is a hot day, remember that your dog is wearing a fur coat and could get heatstroke more easily than you, so keep her shaded and cool, and keep plenty of drinking water on hand. Most dogs swallow water as they swim, so use your judgment about letting her swim in stagnant or ocean water. After swimming, rinse her off and dry her, paying careful attention to her ears and eyes, which can easily become infected.

If your dog is confident around water, teach her to go in only with per-mission. Use boundary training techniques like the ones you learned in the fundamentals program (see the Quick Guide for boundary training on page 138), and *sit-stay,* which serves as your dog's request to you for permission to swim. Having a solid *recall* could save your dog's life, so practice that in and around the water. If your dog is willing, practice retrieving and swimming games and activities by modifying the retrieving techniques I shared with you in Chapters Nine and Ten.

Always supervise your dog around water. Be ready to guide her to safety, and potentially to rescue her if she gets into trouble. To be safest, you should learn basic lifesaving techniques. Consider taking a dog first-aid and CPR course, or at least viewing a related DVD or Internet video.

Breathing resuscitation on a dog is performed mouth-to-nose while seal-ing off her mouth so that air does not escape. Chest compression, Heimlich, and back slaps are done similarly to the ways they are on humans. Ask your vet for recommendations on these lifesaving subjects.

Veterinarian Visits and Your Dog's Health

Taking a dog to the vet is essential . . . but it is not always a happy moment for the dog. Try to take your dog for a health checkup if you are planning a family vacation, or if you will be leaving him behind with a caretaker for an extended time, in order to get a baseline reading of his health. Help him get used to vet visits by dropping in for quick, periodic "hello" visits (rather than for a medical reason), so that he can get used to going into the office and be less anxious when a medical visit or checkup is required.

Maintaining your dog's health can also affect training. Sight, hearing, orthopedic issues, general health, and energy level will change over time. For example, an older dog with arthritis or hip dysplasia may be unwilling to jump up into the car and may no longer sit easily. Bladder problems can lead to peeing in the house. Watch your dog's behavior; if it changes, you should take him to the vet for a checkup.

Your dog's nutritional needs will also change as he gets older. As I've mentioned, if your dog is getting fat, it usually means that *you* are not getting enough exercise. However, don't just dash off on a hike that your dog may not be ready for—the first thing to do is to visit your vet for a special "old dog checkup" before deciding if it is a matter of lack of exercise, a behavioral issue, or perhaps an underlying health problem. A common myth that mixed breeds and mutts are automatically healthier than purebreds is indeed a mutt myth.

Dental care is important because diseases of the mouth, teeth, or gums can infect the dog's bloodstream and quickly shut down his kidneys, which can be fatal. Use the handling and gentling exercises to inspect your dog's mouth, teeth, and gums. Regularly brush his teeth (see page 59), and give him dental treats now and then.

Grooming

Like children, dogs need to be bathed regularly, have their hair brushed often, and get their nails clipped. Some dogs also require special grooming to trim their hair, especially in warm weather. To prepare your dog for her first grooming experience, make sure she is comfortable with being handled. Next, run a soft brush or comb lightly over her as you praise and treat her. I hand-feed a dog her entire meal while I groom her for the first time. Pretend to clip her nails, too, before attempting it for the first time, so that she gets used to the look and sound of the clipper. She may never learn to like getting her nails clipped, but it's necessary, and with practice, she'll eventually come to at least tolerate it.

If you groom your dog yourself, keep her hair out of her eyes. While a dog is in training, I prefer to clip the dog's eye hair away, even if the breed standard calls for a shaggy face. If you are really set against clipping the hair around her eyes, at least use hair clips or make a ponytail if she tolerates it. Your dog must be able to see clearly while she trains.

Before you give your dog her first bath (or even turn on the water), hand-feed a meal to her in the bath area. The next day, get plenty of treats on hand, tap into all your patience, and put on some old clothes! While the dog is in the tub or shower, hand-feed some treats before you start to wash her. If you use a tub, take a facecloth, tie it in a knot, wedge a treat in it, and let your dog splash around with the homemade toy. With my Flat-Coated Retriever, I put my bathing suit on and got in the tub with him to help him enjoy being there. If the weather is warm, get a kiddie pool, fill it with water, and let the kids and your dog splash around together—while you supervise carefully. My kids were always feeding treats to the dogs when they were in the kiddie pool together.

If you decide to hire a professional groomer, the groomer may encourage you to bring your dog by for a quick visit just to get some treats and praise before the first grooming session. To find a groomer, begin by asking owners of well-groomed dogs who they use. Find a groomer in your price range who has good rapport with your dog, and who follows instructions and is willing to look at photos of cuts you admire. Some groomers will allow you to stay during the session to make your dog more comfortable. Every groomer I have worked with has allowed me to leave all my puppies for two- to three-hour short grooming sessions, before ever leaving them for the long all-day grooming process.

Hiring Caregivers

Of all pets, dogs need the most attention while their owners are away. Therefore, you may need to enlist someone to care for your dog while you go on a business trip or vacation or if you work long hours. See the caregiver's checklist on page 230.

Dog Walkers and Pet Sitters

Dog walkers come to your home, exercise your dog, and return him home safely. Some dog walkers will also give your dog his medication at precise times, feed meals, provide bathing and grooming services, and help with training.

Decide whether you need a professional dog walker who is licensed, bonded, and insured, or whether you will rely on a trusted neighbor or friend. National membership organizations, notably the National Association of Professional Pet Sitters and Pet Sitters International, host certification and continuing education programs, provide insurance and business services to members, and provide online listings for the public to find their members. There are also many online directories of local pet sitters, and some veterinarians' staff members provide pet-sitting services as a side business.

If you're thinking of hiring a professional dog sitter or dog walker, make sure to do a phone interview and check references, ideally for at least three candidates so that you can compare. Discuss business terms: cost, how much time she will spend with your dog and what she does, services included and optional services, list of references, licensing, bonding, and insurance. Keep in mind that additional services you want your dog to have, such as hand-feeding, may cost extra. Does the candidate walk more than one dog at a time? If so, ask how she manages that and what sizes the dogs are. Personally, I would not want my dog walked by a person who walks small and large dogs together. Although most pet sitters are not dog trainers, and you shouldn't have high expectations that your dog will be trained while in their care, ask if she uses positive reinforcement. Also ask what her experience is, if she belongs to professional organizations, what continuing education or training courses she is taking, and what her first-aid training is.

With sitters, if a candidate seems acceptable, references are positive, and her good professional status is confirmed, you will want to interview her in your home. Introduce her to your dog. Does she interact with him professionally, positively, and competently? When you demonstrate cues and protocols, does the candidate try them out effectively? A good candidate will also walk your dog with you during the interview, which will help you see how she works and how your dog responds to her.

Once you have made the selection, have a brief orientation session, ideally at your home. If the dog sitter will be staying overnight in your home, find out how many hours she will actually be there and how many hours your dog will be alone and without supervision or companionship, and discuss the morning and evening routines. Be clear about your house rules, including furniture rules, sleeping arrangements, dog toy rules, protocols for coming and going, safety rules, dogproofing requirements (for instance, is it okay to leave a purse unattended, or keep food on countertops?). If your dog has daily medications that he must have, show the sitter (or walker) how to give the dosage and make sure she understands how to do it. Decide what daily training, activities, and games will be done to keep up your dog's skills. Have her practice hand-feeding your dog to get established. Don't worry about seeming fussy or overprotective—a good pet sitter will appreciate your attention to detail.

After you return from your trip, evaluate the experience with the pet sitter. Some pet sitters have evaluation forms and leave notes for you as part of their service. Your dog may behave differently with the pet sitter than with you; find out what those differences are. Discuss any problem areas.

Doggy Day Care

The questions you would ask a pet sitter should also be asked of a doggy day care provider, including costs, service options and programs, staffing, experience, business practices, and insurance. Visit the facility; some are located in commercial districts and others are run by individuals who work from home. Does the facility look and smell clean, seem professionally organized, and have a comfortable temperature? What kind of attention, training, and socialization opportunities are provided? Does it have enough space and crated areas for dogs to be left alone when they need it? Are there separate spaces for puppies, smaller dogs, and older dogs? How long have the operators been in business? Are they willing to offer you the names of clients who are happy with their services? If dogs pee or poop in the common area, is it cleaned up right away? Some facilities have indoor and outdoor services and provide walks. If there is an outdoor part of the facility, make sure that the fence is secure, and that there are covered and shaded areas. Some facilities provide pickup and drop-off services, and even live webcams for you to check on your dog during the day. Remember to prepare your caregiver's checklist (see page 230) for your day care provider; most facilities also provide their own standardized intake form.

Boarding

If you plan to go away without your dog, you may wish to have a facility board her. Many dog day care facilities have overnight boarding options, as do some veterinarians. Some individuals (like me!) board a few guest dogs in their home, providing the dogs with a family atmosphere.

Interview these facility operators as you would a dog walker, pet sitter, or day care operator, and prepare your caregiver's checklist accordingly. In addition, you will want to discuss and evaluate their boarding policies. For example, although many boarding facilities provide their own food (it's simpler for their own logistics), I recommend that you arrange to provide your dog's regular food. In my boarding business, I provide bedding and toys to decrease damage and loss and to minimize guarding. Ask for a tour and check out where the dogs are kenneled or crated. Does the entire facility smell and look clean? Do the dogs seem happy, well-groomed, and healthy? If it's a home, does the home appear to be dogproofed and are countertops clear of temptations to counter surf? Ask how often the dogs receive direct attention and go outside to do their business and play.

Board-and-Train Programs

Some trainers who board also offer training programs. I have provided board-and-train programs for 20 years, and am proud of the work that I do, so I'll tell you how I do it to help you evaluate board-and-train providers. I started the program to help keep puppies out of kennels where they would otherwise have received inadequate training and socialization. In my program, a few dogs stay in my home for anywhere from two weeks to six months as though they're my own, and we work on a personalized training program. I have dog crates and x-pens all over my home; some dogs may be tethered to me or crated while I evaluate their behavior, social skills, and training. I do not leave dogs outside. My clients' dogs don't meet the other dogs until I am ready to introduce them, and I make those introductions one dog at a time, usually starting with my Ibizan Hound, Brieo. I also offer a program where dogs shuttle back and forth between the owner and me, so that I do the training and the owner keeps up the homework. If clients' dogs are sufficiently socialized and able to travel well, I take them to my group training classes.

No matter how excellent the board-and-train program, the owner must continue the dog's training or the learning will fall apart. Therefore, I accept only dogs of owners who I am confident will do so. Any trainers who promise that their intervention will permanently train or cure your dog aren't being realistic or accurate. Offering any form of a guarantee to a client is considered unethical and you should look elsewhere.

Checklist: For Caregivers

After you have carefully selected the people to whom you are entrusting your cherished, spirited best friend, you'll need to provide them with basic information about your dog's habits and requirements, as well as your contact information. Here is a master checklist for you to adapt to your specific needs.

☐ Vet contact

☐ Emergency vet/animal hospital contact

☐ Vaccination record and other health information

☐ Medicine instructions

☐ Your contact info and schedule

☐ Backup contact (friend, neighbor, family member)

☐ Location of supplies: medicine, first aid kit, food, treats, leash, poop bags, toys, training toys and supplies, grooming and bathing supplies

☐ Meals (when to feed, ingredients, bowl-washing instructions)

☐ Treat instructions (when to give treats, quantity allowed per day, when to use stuffed Kongs)

☐ Leashing instructions (harness; tighten the collar one notch for walk, loosen after walk)

☐ Walking instructions (which side your dog heels on, cues he knows during walks, routes to travel, cautions about any possible trouble spots)

☐ Socializing instructions (whether dog park visits are okay and, if so, the protocol)

☐ Behavior problems, quirks, habits

☐ Crate or bed instructions

☐ List of cues your dog knows with verbal and hand signals

☐ List of tricks, noting verbal and hand signals

☐ Short list of favorite training games and activities

☐ Training cues and/or tricks that your dog is currently learning

☐ Toys for regular use and special training toys

☐ Brushing protocol and location

☐ Bathing and grooming protocol

Everyone who cares for your dog should be briefed on his needs and routine.

Selecting Your Dog's Trainer

If, after you've completed our work together—or your dog is exhibiting behavior issues that seem beyond your control—you decide to hire a professional trainer, I applaud your commitment to your dog. In addition to good instruction and feedback, training lessons will provide another valuable socialization experience for your dog. When choosing a trainer, ask for recommendations from your veterinarian or from owners who have well-behaved dogs.

Naturally, I highly recommend that you choose a trainer who uses positive reinforcement rather than aversive punishment training. Unfortunately, there are a few trainers who say that they teach positive reinforcement but actually don't. You can look at the website of the Association of Pet Dog Trainers to try to locate a positive reinforcement trainer in your area.

In the end, I believe it's best that you visit a class before signing on to any training program. A good trainer will explain the lessons so that they are easy to understand, and interact well with people as well as the dogs. The dogs in the class will seem happy. After the class, talk to the students and get their opinions.

Don't be afraid to interview the trainer (in fact, a good trainer will appreciate that). Ask about his experience. Ask if he uses a positive reinforcement method and how he follows those principles. Ask about choke collars and training protocols. Ask if the trainer is flexible about using unorthodox hand signals, which I believe is a good sign that he will be able to help you adapt to your dog's learning pace and tastes. In short, keep asking questions until you're sure you've found a trainer who is right for you and your dog's particular needs.

On Friday, October 9, 2009, Bo Obama celebrated his first birthday with some special guests that included the Kennedy Porties: Splash, Sunny, and Bo's littermate, Cappy, who was also celebrating his first birthday. The one official photo that the White House released to commemorate that day showed Cappy, with his paws up on the table, quickly gobbling up his brother's doggy birthday cake. (As the First Lady later noted in an interview, Bo didn't seem to mind.)

Friday, October 9, 2009, was notable for another reason, too. That was the day President Obama received notice that he had been awarded the 2009 Nobel Peace Prize. In the White House Rose Garden that day, he began his comments to the media by saying that earlier that morning, Malia had said to him: "Daddy, you won the Nobel Peace Prize, and it is Bo's birthday." And, he continued, Sasha had then joined in: "Plus we have a three-day weekend coming up."

The President was clearly humbled by the Nobel committee's surprise announcement. He mused about his daughters' comments: "It's good to have kids to keep things in perspective." I later heard all about it on the news and I thought, "Yes, Mr. President, it's good to have the perspective that comes from having kids . . . and dogs."

Appendices

Appendix 1.
Canine Good Citizen (CGC) Certificate Test Prep Course

The Canine Good Citizen (CGC) Certificate, administered through the American Kennel Club (AKC), is the gold standard when it comes to evaluating a dog's socialization skills. These tests are managed by official AKC evaluators, many of whom offer CGC training classes. There are many benefits to having a CGC-certified dog, including admission to therapy-dog training and being welcomed at an increasing number of workplaces and rental homes.

The CGC exam is challenging. For each of the 10 test items, your dog needs to have reached learning stage #4: always able to perform fluently in many generalized situations (to review the four learning stages, see page 65). You may praise and encourage her throughout the test, but you can't use food treats or toys to lure, encourage, or reward her. A dog is automatically dismissed if she "growls, snaps, bites, attacks, or attempts to attack a person or another dog" or potties during the test.

This appendix is designed to prepare your dog to achieve the CGC level of obedience, even if you never plan to take the test. I believe it's helpful to assess your dog's obedience skills after you've completed the Fundamentals Training Program and to review them each year. But remember: If you and your dog fail, you are still a good dog owner; you just need to continue your training and, perhaps, allow your dog to mature further.

Test Item #1: Accept a Friendly Stranger

Your dog will pass this test if, when in public, you can greet people without his causing a disturbance, nosing in, or being fearful. Will he sit still at your heel and stay until cued while someone greets you? Can he accept not being the center of attention while you speak with someone else? In the presence of strangers, does your dog appear comfortable and not shy, fearful, anxious, or aggressive?

Practice by having your training partner hold a treat while approaching you and your dog. Hold your dog's leash with half of it wrapped around your hand, and keep that hand glued to your hip. Get ready to stand like a tree as you did when you taught your dog the *cookie sit-stay*. If he lunges in excitement, your partner should immediately back up a step and stand still. When your dog refocuses on you, mark that (with a click or a verbal "good") and *recall* him using both a verbal cue and hand signal, and have him *sit*. Now ask your partner to resume approaching you. If your dog lunges again, repeat the process. As your partner gets close enough to give him the treat, your dog may get up again, and if so, have your partner withdraw the treat immediately, back up a step, and give a silent hand signal for *sit*. Work with your partner in advance to get the timing right and to teach the hand signal. When your dog earns his first reward treat from your partner, make sure to mark and praise that moment . . . and reward a jackpot.

To help your dog gain fluency for this behavior, gradually increase the amount of time before you mark and reward his calm *sit*. Next, have a friendly conversation with your partner while your dog continues to sit. During these conversations, praise your dog, starting at about 10 seconds and increasing the interval between praises by a couple of seconds at a time.

Since the goal is for your dog to become fully automatic with this cue, practice with different partners and in different situations. After a minute or so of conversation, start walking together and stop again. Try it at home when a friend comes to your front door. Take your dog to a friend's home. Little by little, withdraw food treats. When your dog can consistently accept the approach of most friendly people, and can sit quietly as you and your friend converse, all without treats, then you are ready to pass this test.

Test Item #2: Sit Politely for Petting

This test requires that your dog sit calmly and without fear while a friendly stranger pets her. A dog that sits while being petted has confidence and generally does well in social interactions with people. But some dogs fear being petted, and this shows up as aggression or shyness, different sides of what behaviorists call the fight-or-flight-or-freeze response, all of which are fear-generated impulses. Your dog may have no problem passing this part of the test, because she knows the world as a gentle and loving place. However, many dogs have had harsh experiences early in life or are born innately fearful of even the friendliest person who approaches. If your dog has a serious fear problem, refer to Chapter Eleven on behavior issues, and consider working with a behavior specialist.

If your dog has no serious fear issues, she is ready to learn this skill. Maybe she's exuberant or mouthy, so sitting still while someone touches her can be very challenging. The protocol for teaching your dog to sit politely while being petted is similar to the protocol for Test Item #1: Have your partner approach her as long as the dog is calm. The moment she starts to get up out of her *sit* or starts to mouth or paw, your partner needs to back away.

Start by asking people you know to practice the handling and gentling exercises in Chapter Three (see page 59). Start acclimating your dog to being petted by people whom she already knows: trusted partners and members of your family. Consider setting up a hand-feeding protocol with each of them.

Give your dog plenty of food rewards and soothing praise while she is being petted. Little by little over a span of weeks, withdraw the food rewards (but continue the praise). Always be present and calm during these sessions. It may be helpful for you to direct the other person's touch so that your dog knows that you are right there making everything safe and enjoyable for her.

Of course, in the real world, good safety means using common sense and caution in allowing others, especially children, to pet your dog. Children can easily get overexcited and pet a dog inappropriately. Many children will run right at a dog and want to pet her or play. Make certain that the adult who is responsible for that child approves of the child's touching your dog, and know your dog well enough to be sure that she is okay with being touched by this child. Assuming that you're okay with the situation, instruct the child and the adult to pet your calm dog on the side, not on the head, which can spook her.

Test Item #3: Appearance and Grooming

Will your dog sit or stand calmly while being groomed? Can an expert, such as a vet, examine him all over? What happens when someone touches his paws, ears, nose, and collar, and looks in his mouth? Does he appear healthy (well-groomed, clean coat and ears, alert, proper weight)?

The first step to having someone else brush and examine your dog is being able to do that for him yourself. Chapter Three's handling and gentling exercises will help get ready for this test. Have various partners brush him gently while you give him treats and lots of calm praise and encouragement. They should examine your dog all over: Check his ears, eyes, nose, teeth, collar, feet, shoulders, hips, tail, back, belly region. Have him lie down, sit, and stand for various exams, and note any positions that are more challenging for him to tolerate being touched.

Test Item #4: Walk on a Loose Leash

Will your dog walk on a loose leash while doing each of the Fundamentals Training Program lessons? Does your dog pay attention to you while walking so that when you turn, stop, or speed up, she stays with you?

In this test, you will not be judged for a competition-style walking at heel. But your dog will be required to stay with you as you walk through a course set up with markers or perform a series of turns (left, right, U-turn), stops, and starts.

When you practice the Fundamentals walking exercises, check in with your dog at random moments to keep her focus on you. Incorporate those turns, stops, starts, and changes of pace. Withdraw the treat lures and emphasize giving her well-timed praise to mark her correct loose-leash walking.

Test Item #5: Walk Through a Crowd

Will your dog stay focused on you as you walk with him past other people, or does he get excited and tug on his leash to check them out? Can he walk through a crowd without showing signs of fight-or-flight-or-freeze fear or anxiety?

Start by walking in familiar places with people who are familiar to your dog. At first, have these people spread out and stand still as you walk through the "crowd." Next, have them bunch a little closer together, and after that have them move around a bit. Little by little, you'll build up your dog's tolerance for distractions. If treat lures help keep him focused on you, by all means use them while you train, and then phase them out later. Use your voice to keep him focused on you.

If you want to get really fancy with training for this test, weave through the crowd while keeping your dog focused on you, so that during the test a straight path through the crowd will seem simple.

Test Item #6: Sit, Down, and Stay at 20 Feet

When you leave your dog's side, does she have enough impulse control to continue to sit and stay where you left her? When you're 20 feet away from her, will she listen to you and perform some basic cues?

During the test, the evaluator will clip a 20-foot leash onto your dog's collar or harness. Get your dog comfortable with having her collar handled, and practice by having a partner clip a strange leash or a long lead onto your dog's collar. If you practice this cue in a park, make doubly sure that you have that long lead clipped on.

The Fundamentals Training Program covered this skill thoroughly, though you may not have built up the distance to 20 feet. Practice Puppy Pushups at longer distances, and if your dog responds to you beyond 20 feet, this item will probably seem easy on exam day.

Build her impulse control by putting her in a *sit* or a *down,* and then turn and walk away from her. If necessary, stop after just one step before turning to face and praise your dog. Go back to her to give more praise and a reward. In the next round, add another step before turning around. See if you can build up the distance beyond 20 feet, meanwhile phasing out the treats.

As you walk back to your dog, she must stay in place. Practice this part of the test item by stopping if she tries to move as you return. During the test, you may remind your dog to stay as often as you need to when you walk toward her. Still, I suggest that you build up her distance and duration when you practice, so that a single cue will work. Doing Puppy Pushups, giving praise, and pausing frequently will help keep her focused on what you're asking.

Test Item #7: Recall (Come When Called)

When you *recall* your dog from 10 feet away, does he come to you right away, even when there are mild distractions? During the exam, the evaluator will provide mild distractions, such as petting your dog when you recall him. Practice distractions, such as petting and supervised play with a partner's dog, so that yours understands that coming to you when called needs to be his top priority at any moment. Make sure to reward him for *recalls* during training with a high-value reward (and possibly a high-value activity such as being released back to supervised play), so that he learns the incentive for always coming to you when called. Review the recall section in the Fundamentals Quick Guide (see page 132).

Test Item #8: Reaction to Another Dog

When you greet someone who is also walking a dog, does your dog remain focused on you? Is your dog unable to control her impulse to run right up to the other dog, or will she stay at your side while you speak briefly with the other person? Will she cower from or be aggressive toward the other dog, or will she be able to show appropriate and mild interest?

In the test, you and your dog will approach another dog and handler, then stop when you're close enough to shake hands with the handler and engage in a brief conversation before moving on. During that exchange, your dog needs to stay at your side and show just a mild interest in the other dog, and stay focused on your cues to stop walking, stay, and start walking again.

To train for this, arrange with your training partner to walk your respective dogs toward each other on cue. How well socialized your dogs already are with each other will help you determine how close you can come to each other. The goal is to walk close enough to shake hands, but that will probably take many trials. If possible, train for this skill with many dogs (because yours will probably perform better with some dogs than with others), until she builds up skill, confidence, and impulse control.

Test Item #9: Reaction to Distractions

How will your dog react when a startling distraction happens? Will he panic and run away, become aggressive and bark or lunge, or just get startled for a moment and then express appropriately mild curiosity? How does he react not only to sudden or loud noises, but also to visual distractions?

A CGC-socialized dog behaves well around all kinds of distractions that happen within five feet of him. The evaluator will assess your dog's response to sudden loud noises, such as a door slamming or a metal folding chair being dropped on a hard floor. Your dog will be expected to react to these disturbances with nothing more than natural curiosity.

The more distractions your dog is exposed to, the better, as long as you don't make him more fearful. Be jolly when the noise happens (see The Jollies, page 60), and be prepared to move on to something else if it doesn't go well. It's helpful to desensitize your dog to these strange noises and visual distractions in short training increments and then move on to another exercise or game before returning for another brief distraction exercise. If he becomes fearful, move onto something else or go back to his last successful trial. Moving ahead too quickly may cause your dog to panic unnecessarily or go potty on the floor (which, unfortunately, means he automatically flunks the CGC test) and make him fearful about things he wasn't fearful about beforehand. Take all the time your dog needs to adjust; his long-term well-being is more important than earning the CGC certificate before he is ready.

For the noise distractions, introduce them at a distance and make sure that your dog can see the action as it is happening. At the start, drop the items only a few inches from the ground and at a farther distance. Over time, build up height to shoulder level and closer ranges.

To desensitize your dog to a visual distraction (such as a stroller, portable lawn sprinkler, or even a plant that sways in the breeze), start with the item on the ground and let your dog sniff it. To build a dog's confidence and comfort level, work with him as he stands near the object but do not introduce him to it. Instead, play with him near the object, or review some training that he already knows. If he shows curiosity on his own, praise and reward him. Much like the way you introduced your dog to his crate or the 101 Box (page 173), it's helpful to put treats around and even on the object and be very patient as your dog warms up on his own time schedule. Always be upbeat and jolly when you're introducing these objects, but don't push your dog faster than he's ready, because that would be flooding, which I am opposed to and discussed in Chapter Eleven. Instead of flooding, desensitize your dog to the object at a pace that makes him comfortable.

The next step is to introduce a bit of movement. Get down on his level and touch the object as you act jolly (and confidently move that stroller or touch the lawn sprinkler or swaying plant a little). Little by little, move closer.

Test Item #10: Supervised Separation

What happens when you leave your dog with someone else for a few minutes? Does she continue to be a well-mannered dog, or does she become fearful or agitated? A well-socialized dog is confident and comfortable enough to be away from you without barking or whining.

Train your dog to do this valuable social skill much as you trained her to *sit-stay* for longer and longer times, including when you left the room. Start this lesson with a training partner whom she already knows and likes. Let your partner play with, handle, brush, or train her as you move a little distance away. Keep coming back to praise and treat your dog, and then move a little farther or stay away for a little longer.

Build up your dog's comfort level so that she is at ease with your leaving the room for a moment, and then longer moments, building up her comfort beyond three minutes. Praise and treat when you return, but don't be too effusive. Many dogs perform better on this skill when you treat and praise as you leave, too, but when you leave the room, don't make a big deal about that either. Just be calm when you leave and when you return.

Appendix 2.
Specialized Training

When I was in my early twenties, I got bitten—quite hard, in fact—by the dog show bug. I'll never forget the first show I attended, at an arena in Fairfax, Virginia. I was floored. I loved being around people with so much knowledge about different breeds, and seeing how talented they and the dogs were. Where did these people come from, I wondered. What made them so devoted? How did they become so knowledgeable? And how did they get their dogs so well trained? I began to understand that there was far more to a champion dog than just good genes.

After I had children, I took them along to dog shows on the weekends and eventually my three children, Ebony (our Portie), and I were a common sight at dog shows around the Washington, D.C., area. It wasn't always easy traveling with this entourage. I remember at one show, one of my daughters started to complain, soon after we arrived, that she had to go potty. Our only option was a portable outhouse. So I parked and unloaded the stroller, and, since I had nobody to keep an eye on my kids or Ebony, the five of us pushed our way into the tiny plastic restroom. Inside, as efficiently and cleanly as possible, I was able to get Courtlandt and Blaise, my two older children, to do their business without falling down the hole while I put a fresh diaper on Paige—all while holding Ebony's leash. When I opened the door, we were met by a cheering crowd. "Portie in a Porta-Potty!" someone yelled. Yes, we were a colorful part of the local scene.

Another time, I took my kids to see one of our favorite dogs, Nina, compete in a conformation dog show. Nina was a beautiful Briard that I had trained and boarded often. Nina belonged to the late Helga Meyer Bullock, opera singer and mother of actress Sandra Bullock. My kids knew Nina well. They hand-fed her and loved brushing her lush coat and making a fuss over her. Once when Helga came to the house, she discovered her dog's long coat pinned up in my daughters' brightly colored barrettes. We all laughed as Nina strutted around the house with her show dog "look at me" attitude while sporting her unique coiffure. Anyway, at the dog show, my kids got so excited when Nina finally entered the ring that they couldn't help squealing in delight. Nina got distracted and looked toward the familiar squeals, broke her show dog strut, and lost that dog show. Oops.

While you may never want to show your dog at this level, there are many great activities and extraordinary experiences awaiting you and your best friend. Each of these activities requires specialized training. This appendix will give you ideas about activities and specialized training experiences that are available—many of which you can participate in through a local American Kennel Club affiliate. Some clubs invite all breeds, including mixed-breed dogs. Other AKC clubs specialize in a specific breed. To find out about local AKC club programs that sanction more than 22,000 dog events annually, check the AKC website (akc.org/clubs).

There are also many excellent non-AKC events. Check out the Association of Pet Dog Trainers' website (apdt.com), which lists many specialized training events for the public, especially APDT Rally competitions, which I'll tell you about later in this appendix. The APDT encourages all dogs to participate, including those with physical disabilities.

So, let's get started.

Therapy Dogs

In the 1960s, child psychologist Boris Levinson coined the term "pet therapy" after he accidentally discovered that his patients made significant progress when they interacted with his dog, Jingles. Now therapy dogs and their owners volunteer in hospitals, rehab centers, literacy programs, hospices, disaster relief, and trauma and therapeutic environments.

Although I have long believed in the value of using dogs to help people heal, I didn't truly understand the extent to which this is true until I myself became the recipient of therapy dog service. In April 2006, I was hospitalized after a serious car wreck. While driving along the peaceful, picturesque

Just touching a dog can lift the spirit.

northern Virginia country roads, I swerved to avoid a deer herd. My SUV rolled over, skidded off the road, and tumbled into a ditch. At least that's what I was told; I have little recollection. I remember floating in and out of consciousness as my Giant Schnauzer, Saxon, lay across my chest after having climbed from the safety pen, which had popped open. He nuzzled my neck and growled fiercely at anyone who tried to come near me. It was my good luck that a neighbor appeared. I have a vague recollection of her speaking very gently to Saxon, assuring him that he was a good dog and that the police, ambulance, firefighters, and MedEvac helicopter were all there to help me. He trusted her and allowed her to coax him away from protecting me so that they could help me. Bless this woman, who I believe to this day was my guardian angel.

A highly skilled team of doctors were able to save my life. But six weeks later, my recovery took a turn for the worse and I was MedEvac'ed to another hospital when my broken clavicle pierced an artery and I developed a potentially fatal blood clot. After a 12-hour emergency surgery, I began my real recovery.

My time in the hospital was incredibly challenging—not only physically, but psychologically. While I lay in the hospital bed, having to undergo a seemingly endless array of emergency procedures and assessments at all hours (while also battling tremendous pain), I became terrified of dying. I was more convinced each day, as I failed to make progress in healing, that I was getting closer to death. (I was so scared that I wouldn't allow my hospital door to be closed.) I was slowly losing my will to live.

And then it happened. It was an innocent moment, a small gesture that changed my life. A stranger walked into my room holding a little terrier and put him on my tummy. I could barely move, but was able to pet the dog with one arm. Simply by putting an arm around that small dog for that brief visit, I got away from thinking about my pain and fear, and I felt back in touch with life.

I became so committed to the training of therapy dogs that I made that part of my business. I work with the dog owner to make sure that the candidate is extremely well socialized and able to stay calm regardless of the setting. I expose the dog to a variety of potential distractions: visual, sound, movement, and smell. I take the dog around to many other people and dogs. I also do my best to make sure that dog owners are prepared to face the emotional challenges of therapeutic settings while handling their dogs.

One of my four-legged clients, a young German Shepherd named Ripley, I have trained to become a therapy dog at the Walter Reed National Military Medical Center. Ripley belongs to William Waybourn, whose Hank (also a German Shepherd) already does therapy work at Walter Reed. William came to me because he believes, as I do, that the only effective way to train a healthy, happy therapy dog is with positive reinforcement.

Despite all the attention therapy dogs receive when they are on the job, it's not always easy for either the dog or the owner. Since dogs must be bathed within 24 hours of the visit, William wakes up at 4 a.m. to bathe Hank so that he's clean and completely dry by the time they arrive at the hospital. At the end of a therapy dog's long shift of nonstop attention and the stress of meeting so many people while also encountering noisy equipment, busy hallways, and unusual smells, William finds that Hank needs to sleep for the rest of the day.

But that seems like a small price to pay to William, who views his therapy-dog experience as an extraordinary opportunity to serve. "The quality of people I meet under the most difficult circumstances is remarkable. No one wants to stay in the hospital; everyone wants to get home," he says. The therapy dog "gives them an opportunity to take the focus off the difficulties they're facing." I agree completely.

If you believe that you and your dog might be right as a therapy-dog team, I encourage you to look into volunteering with a local therapy-dog organization. Training and certification programs are provided by Pet Partners and by Therapy Dogs International.

Obedience Training

You and your dog may have finished the five-week fundamentals program, but there are still plenty of opportunities to bond and have fun together. Obedience competitions are a great way to keep your training sharp, add new cues, and meet other like-minded dog owners.

RALLY OBEDIENCE

Rally obedience (also known as Rally or Rally-O) is a sport in which your dog proceeds through an obstacle course performing a series of specific obedience tasks. The course typically consists of 10 to 20 signs that instruct the team what to do. These events are a fun and fulfilling activity for many dogs and their owners, and a wonderful way for your dog to socialize with other well-trained canines.

The two most popular sanctioning bodies for Rally in the United States are the AKC and the APDT. Both have three levels of competition: The AKC labels theirs Novice, Advanced, and Excellent; the APDT's levels are One, Two, and Three. Both the AKC and the APDT have a series of awards and titles that dogs can earn in Rally contests, and both organizations encourage junior competitors.

To earn the distinction of AKC Rally's Novice class, your dog must be able to successfully perform everything covered in our Fundamentals Training Program, such as *sit-stay, down-stay, recall,* and focusing on you. She must also be able to walk at your heel around a designated course, make turns, change speeds, start and stop abruptly, back up, weave, and spiral in front of judges. You are allowed to give hand signals, encourage your dog verbally, pat your leg, and clap your hands throughout the course, but no food lures or treats are allowed. APDT's Level One Rally covers skills similar to AKC Novice; the main difference is that in APDT Level One, you can keep your dog on leash.

To earn the more advanced Rally certificates, your dog performs complex turning and heeling patterns, including abrupt pivots and diagonal turns, turning in the opposite direction from you, following cues while moving (and at a distance from you), and going over jumps without hesitation. To earn the Excellent Class, at each station you may give only a hand signal and encourage your dog verbally.

AKC OBEDIENCE TRIALS

If you and your dog are ready to enjoy even greater challenges in obedience training, I invite you to consider the extraordinary world of obedience trials. How far can you go in AKC obedience trials? All the way to the National Obedience Invitational, where dogs vie for the National Obedience Championship (NOC). But to be invited to compete, your dog must first earn all three levels of Competitive Obedience Trials: Novice, Open, and Utility. The Novice trial is similar to the CGC test: The only additional tasks are perfect *recalls* at any moment and off-leash *heeling*. The Open Class includes off-leash *heeling* with many turns and changes of speed, jumps and hurdles, and drops to a *down* in the middle of a *recall*. The Utility Class has been jokingly dubbed "Futility" by many dog owners because the tasks that dogs are asked to perform are extremely challenging, and this certificate is very difficult to earn. For example, utility dogs are able to go into a pile of objects and find a specific object that has the handler's scent on it, follow directional cues to retrieve a specific glove, be cued to go away from the handler and then jump specific hurdles on the *recall*. If a dog can successfully perform these tasks, it's likely he will have accumulated enough points to earn an invitation to compete for the NOC.

CANINE FREESTYLE DANCING

Another way to practice obedience training is canine freestyle dancing, in which you choreograph a dance routine with your dog. You're the choreographer and your dog is your dance partner. For this training, your dog will, in essence, be performing a series of tricks that, when put together, look like a graceful dance routine. (You may find that it's easiest to teach some dance moves by using clicker training along with targeting devices, and then replacing the training aids with hand signals and verbal cues.)

Similar to human dancing competitions, canine freestyle routines are set to music. Beginners often start with a 30-second routine and build up to a 90-second routine. More advanced performers perform entire songs. Lately, some performers have taken to wearing costumes, including something for the dog. In addition to "couples dancing," some canine freestyle clubs and training programs have choreographed group dances that become that group's signature exhibition performance.

Any behavior that a dog does reliably can be adapted into a canine freestyle routine, including every skill you learned in the Fundamentals Training Program. Canine freestyle is a fun way to practice skills, teach new skills, invent moves, and chain together a routine. It helps dogs and their owners develop superior communication, response, and skills. There are a number of associations, websites, and local groups that have performance events.

There are also some helpful books, DVDs, and Web videos that will help you get started. If you're looking for some special inspiration on canine freestyle, I highly recommend you learn about Carolyn Scott and her Golden Retriever, Rookie, who are considered the Ginger Rogers and Fred Astaire of canine freestyle. Rookie and Carolyn had an extraordinary bond; when you see a video of them you'll notice immediately how completely focused they are on each other.

Canine freestyle helps develop superior communication, response, and skills.

Together, they introduced canine freestyle to countless people around the world. In addition to performing on television and at contests, they danced at nursing homes, schools, and churches. Rookie danced well into his teenage years, which I hope inspires us all to remember that old dogs can indeed learn new tricks. Sadly, Rookie crossed to the other side of the "Rainbow Bridge" in 2008. I like to imagine that heaven is even more joyful with Rookie performing with the angels.

High-Energy Canine Sports

M any dogs require activities that burn off a lot of energy. For these dogs, high-energy canine sports are a great option.

AGILITY COURSE

The dog agility obstacle course is an exciting competition to watch. Each team—which consists of your dog and you, or a handler—races through an obstacle course that includes a variety of jumps, weave poles, bridges, and tunnels. The teams race against the clock and lose points for mistakes, such as missing an obstacle and having to go back to try again, knocking over a hurdle crossbar, hesitating while sprinting through a tunnel or while racing up and over a tall A-frame, or jumping off too early after running across a suspended

Just like their human counterparts, canine athletes need to train hard to do well.

bridge or teeter-totter. Sometimes the mistakes can be human error, such as not being able to keep up with your dog, or using imprecise body position, which can cue your dog to go the wrong way. Agility training takes a lot of practice and is great exercise for you and your high-energy dog.

Agility has become so popular that there are now commercial sponsors and cash prizes for some of the higher-profile competitions, which include a featured invitational competition at the annual AKC Nationals. There are agility athletic organizations, such as the United States Dog Agility Association, that present regional, national, and international meets. In recent years, the AKC has taken a squad of 12 duos to the FCI Agility World Championships in Europe. The FCI, or Fédération Cynologique Internationale, is essentially the International Kennel Club or World Canine Organization.

FLYBALL RELAY RACES

Another great option for high-energy dogs are flyball relay races. In these events, a team of four dogs races in relay fashion. The first dog runs down a 51-foot course over four hurdles; pounces on a mechanical box that releases a tennis ball, which the dog catches in his mouth; then returns over the jumps. When the dog crosses the start/finish line after a successful run, the next dog is released. Two teams of four dogs face off in a side-by-side race, and the first team to finish is the winner. Dogs and handlers train and compete with the same high-caliber precision that elite human sprinters use in their relay races.

In the past year, more than 250 teams belonging to the North American Flyball Association (NAFA) have run the whole race in under 20 seconds (yes, that's four dogs in under 20 seconds total!), as measured by electronic timing systems. NAFA's website (flyball.org) displays a dizzying array of statistics, including a breed analysis of which dogs are fastest. Not surprisingly, Border Collies and Jack/Parson Russell Terriers dominate the list. Since flyball has become such a fast and precise canine sport, NAFA's rulebook takes longer to read than it would take most teams to complete a race. Visit NAFA's website for the most up-to-date listings of competitions and clubs, which bear names like Spring Loaded, Instant Replay, and Rocket Relay. At NAFA events you will likely find out about flyball training in your area, or you can learn how NAFA can help you start a club if there isn't one nearby.

DISC DOG

Not long after the Wham-O toy company first introduced the Frisbee flying disc across America in 1958, people realized that many dogs loved catching

Even small dogs can get big air!

them, too. As people became more skillful and creative at playing with flying discs, they included their dogs in their innovative play. Today, the disc dog world embraces a variety of competitions, including long-distance throws that champion dogs race more than 50 yards to catch in midair. Disc dog fanciers also have competitive canine freestyle choreographed routines that feature the dog's athletic jumps and fast-paced throws of several discs. There are disc dog clubs, competitions, and classes across America, as well as exhibitions and special shows. Dogs with a lot of energy and jumping ability excel at catching the flying disc.

Specialized Skill Training

M any breeds were originally bred to take on jobs: tracking, hunting, retrieving, water work, and herding. Today, those dogs' instincts and abilities are very much alive, and often need a high-energy outlet that doesn't involve ripping up your sofa or digging up your garden. I have participated in most of the training programs in this section with various dogs of mine. Together, we have traipsed the woods and fields, spent hours in the water, and worked while surrounded by a herd of sheep.

TRACKING

Dogs' ability to smell is far beyond our human sense. That's why they are able to find people trapped in rubble, sniff out contraband and dangers, provide forensic details at crime scenes, detect cancer, predict epileptic seizures, and tear open your child's backpack to eat that week-old jelly donut.

To earn the AKC's title of Champion Tracker (CT), a dog must be able to pass two very difficult tests. He must first earn a Tracking Dog Excellent (TDX) by following a scent over 1,000 yards that has been "aged" at least three hours before the dog starts, and includes at least five changes in direction and human cross tracks. He must also earn the Variable Surface Tracking (VST) distinction by tracking in a real-world situation, which may include rainy or snowy weather and an "aged" track over various surfaces rich with naturally fragrant vegetation, streams, sand, and smooth concrete. When a dog earns the TDX, VST, or CT, everyone celebrates; it's like being on a golf course when someone aces a hole-in-one.

The best way to learn about tracking is by going to a tracking event; they usually need volunteers to help prepare the courses on a Saturday, and tests are typically held on Sunday. The AKC website is a good place to start your own tracking of tracking events and training in your locale.

HUNTING SKILLS: LURE COURSING, GUNDOG, EARTHDOG

Hunting skill events include lure coursing, gundog hunting tests and field retrieving, and earthdog. *Lure coursing* involves chasing a lure over a field course that includes abrupt turns to simulate an animal's escape. Lure coursing has traditionally been limited to purebred sighthounds (dogs that hunt by sight rather than by scent), but it has recently been expanded to include all kinds of dogs. Typically, a field of two or more acres is set up with a lure course rig: A lure like a plastic shopping bag is tied to a very long and strong motorized fishing/trolling line that is looped around a maze of pulleys. A few dogs race at the same time to catch the lure. The sport is not recommended for dogs younger than one year old because of joint stress. The AKC and the American Sighthound Field Association (asfa.org) sanction many lure coursing events. Other groups have developed their own versions of this sport, including steeplechase lure courses that combine some of the types of jumps that are also found on agility courses.

Gundog hunting tests were developed to help hunters evaluate their dogs' abilities. The AKC sanctions hunting and retrieving events, with separate competitions for pointing breeds, retrievers, spaniels, and hounds—all of which have different special jobs on the hunt. Other popular organizations that sanction hunt dog events and tests include the United Kennel Club and North American Hunting Retriever Association. Hunting tests include quartering (racing ahead to locate the game and then going back and forth between game and hunter on cue), trailing prey, and sit-to-flush (sitting silently for a cue to chase birds into the air). In retrieving trials, a dog must find and retrieve a shot bird, often aided only by the general sound of a gunshot and a vague sense of where the bird has landed. Retrievers are judged on the ability to find the bird quickly, pick it up cleanly so that it is balanced in the dog's mouth, run back to the handler directly, and give the bird to the handler and judge for inspection to see that it has not been mauled by a "hard mouth." Skilled hunt dogs earn designations, starting with Junior Hunter (JH) and advancing to Senior Hunter (SH), and ultimately Master Hunter (MH); many are then invited to compete at the National Amateur Field Championships (NAFC).

Earthdog tests provide a structure for terriers, Dachshunds, and Miniature Schnauzers to show off their hunting instincts and develop the skills they were bred for long ago: rooting out ground animals that would otherwise vex farmers and hunters. Earthdogs courageously "go to ground" inside a tunnel and follow a scent to a den. Earthdog course builders design and dig a network of tunnels for canines to find their quarry. Some trainers like to use a section of wide PVC pipe to lure-train their dogs into the tunnel, and then add on more sections of pipe, including 3-way and 4-way fittings. Some tunnel mazes are permanent structures that are used by clubs for training and hosted tournaments. I think the tunnel builders have as much fun creating vast earthdog mazes as the dogs have navigating them. The AKC and American Working Terrier Association (AWTA) have established non-competitive tests for introducing earthdogs to quarrying and for evaluating higher skills up to the Master Earthdog designation.

WATER WORK AND DOCK DIVING

As we've discussed, all dogs need to be taught to swim, even if they are bred for the water. Some dogs, once they get in the water, would be content to play there all day. For them, there are water work and dock diving. In well-managed canine water programs, safety is always covered before a dog sets one paw in the water. Many programs require (and often provide) dog life jackets. Not surprisingly, the Portuguese Water Dog Club of America has an active water-dog program.

Water work includes rescue exercises, such as towing a person on a life ring, boat work, a variety of retrieving and delivery skills that include underwater retrieving, and even water scent work. Swimming competitions require the dogs to navigate around a set of buoy markers. Training programs include summer camps for you and your dog to vacation at together.

In *dock diving,* dogs take a running or standing broad jump off the end of the dock and into the water. Winners are the dogs that jump the farthest. If you have a water dog, you can probably guess that the main training technique is to lure the dog by throwing a toy in a nice arc so that your dog pops up off the end of the dock for greater distance, rather than leaping out flat. Toy lures are allowed during competition. Dogs compete in categories based on size, experience, and age. For safety, cover the dock with a nonslip carpet and make sure that the water is at least four feet deep and cleared of all branches and debris.

Isn't it funny, though, that many of those same dogs consider bath time a form of torture? (Note to self: Ask the AKC to sanction a bathing event.)

SHEEPHERDING

When I saw competitions in which one Border Collie would herd some 20 sheep around a course, I decided to try sheepherding. Although I had fun working at it twice a week for about three months, I was an utter failure, not because of my Border Collie, Jock, but because I didn't have any of what sheepherding handlers call "stock sense." Standing smack in the middle of a herd of livestock was overwhelming for me, especially when I couldn't see

Jock. If you're thinking of trying out sheepherding, the first question you should consider is how much stock sense *you* have. Before you introduce your dog to the sheep, try herding livestock yourself, without your dog. See what it's like to work the sheep, "reading" and anticipating their movements, so you'll know how to teach your dog—assuming *he* has stock sense. The most complete and current listing of upcoming sheepherding trials can be found at the United States Border Collie Handlers' Association (USBCHA) website (usbcha.com); the AKC has also developed a sanctioned sheepherding program. At these trials, you will witness extraordinary dogs and meet owners and prospective trainers.

AKC Conformation Show Dog Basics

The fact is that few dogs *conform* to the AKC's "breed standard" physical structure and appearance that is necessary to become successful in the show ring. The original focus of these AKC conformation dog shows was to give awards to the best dogs in order to improve the breeding stock. In addition to having superior genetics, a champion show dog is trained to *gait* properly (move a certain way that's deemed correct for the breed) and *stack* correctly (stand still and pose in that breed's correct posture while being inspected all over).

Just because a dog was born to champion show dog parents doesn't mean that she can be a show dog, too. Champions have a certain body structure, as well as a temperament that comes alive and sparkles in the ring with that *je ne sais quoi* "look at me" charisma. Show dogs trained with positive reinforcement can have a competitive edge because they often exude an easy confidence and distinctive personality that can make all the difference between the rare champions among the many competitors. Show dogs must love the traveling, and so must you enjoy devoting your weekends to these shows and the weekdays preparing for—and recovering from—them. To do well at dog shows, it must become a total way of life that is enjoyable for the human as well as for the dog.

If you're thinking about becoming a show dog "parent," start by visiting a few shows as a spectator. Talk to the fanciers—fans, breeders, owners, exhibitors, handlers, groomers, and vendors—at appropriate times, when it seems that they aren't busy preparing. Most shows have time set aside for this kind of interaction; after all, they're also social events. A few shows are *benched shows,* which means that there are structured hours when attendees are invited to look at the dogs up close and speak with their owners and handlers. At a benched show, dogs and people must be able to keep their poise and be sociable for many hours. When you're at a show, if you're anything like me, you'll be tempted to pet these beautiful animals, but don't touch them without getting permission. Buy a copy of the show program to orient yourself to the schedule and to help you take notes on dogs and people that you have met so that you can follow them at future shows. That will be your first step toward becoming a fancier yourself. Wear comfortable shoes; there is a lot of walking and standing around at dog shows. If you take the big leap into showing your dog, start at *match shows,* which are for practice and experience, and are usually more informal.

Nowadays, most champions are shown by professional, paid handlers who often specialize in presenting a certain breed. Less common is the show dog handler like Norm Randall, who is called an "all-rounder" because he can show a variety of breeds successfully. Before retiring, Norm showed 67 different breeds, including my Boston Terrier, Jasmine. Showing a small Boston Terrier is much different from showing a Giant Schnauzer, which is different from showing a Flat-Coated Retriever, and different still from showing an Ibizan Hound. Since pro handlers often earn bonus prize money if "their" dog wins, they tend to be very selective about the dogs (and the humans) they take on as clients. Although they generally own their own dogs, most of the best pros make their living showing the dogs of their clients. The reality is that most handlers also have day jobs, and must fit in their preparations and travel for dog shows around their work schedules. They devote their weekends to dog shows because they love dogs and being around the show ring, and are happy to help each other out.

Some AKC-recognized dog shows are restricted to specific breeds. Called *specialty shows,* they often feature separate competitions for amateur and professional handlers, and classify the dogs by sex, age, and previous competitive track record. There are more than 170 AKC-recognized breeds, each with its own AKC-sanctioned club, alphabetically from Affenpinscher to Yorkshire Terrier.

Each breed club helps maintain a consistent breed standard via dog shows and events, promotes responsible and healthy breeding practices, provides educational programs and materials—as well as opportunities to meet others who enjoy that breed.

Other shows, called *group shows,* focus on one of the seven dog groups: Sporting, Hound, Working, Terrier, Toy, Non-Sporting, and Herding.

The Sporting Group includes America's most popular dog, the Labrador Retriever. The Hound Group includes the Beagle, which was America's most popular dog during most of the 1950s and has become known across the world via the *Peanuts* comic strip's dog, Snoopy. The Working Group includes the Portuguese Water Dog, which has become more recognized since the Obama family brought Bo home. The Terrier Group includes the Cairn Terrier, which has been immortalized as the character Toto in the *Wizard of Oz* movie. The Toy Group includes the small Chihuahua, which sadly has recently become one of the most common dogs in America's animal shelters. The Non-Sporting Group is a diverse group that includes Dalmatians, which also, sadly, increases the rescue shelter population every time a *101 Dalmatians* movie comes out. Also in the Non-Sporting Group is my beloved Boston Terrier, which was originally a cross between the Bulldog and the now extinct White English Terrier, and is considered the first genuinely American breed, having been recognized by the AKC in 1891. The Herding Group includes Scotland's Rough Collie, which became popular in America when I was growing up watching *Lassie* on TV.

AMERICA'S MOST FAMOUS DOG SHOW: "THE WESTMINSTER"

If you have watched a dog show on television, you probably saw an "all-breed" competition such as New York's Westminster Kennel Club Dog Show. First held in 1877, seven years before the American Kennel Club was established, "The Westminster" is America's longest-running canine contest. From among the 2,500 invited dogs that have won prizes at other significant dog shows, Westminster judges select one grand prize–winning dog that is anointed Best in Show. Winners earn a place in history, but there is no prize money. Westminster dogs do increase in value as breeding stock and a few rare champions receive short-term commercial endorsement opportunities. Most competitors are involved in pursuit of honor and for their love of the breed.

The path to Westminster's Best in Show finals features two preliminary contests during the two-day competition: Best of Breed and Best of Group. In Best of Breed, one judge selects one dog from among a highly elite field of the same breed. The same judge also selects a Best of Opposite Sex for that breed and from one to five Awards of Merit, but only the one Best of Breed winner goes to the next round, Group Judging. My first show dog,

Jasmine, a Boston Terrier bitch, once qualified to show at The Westminster with her handler, Norm Randall, whose own Boston Terrier male was once a Westminster Best of Breed winner.

At the Westminster show's Group Judging round, each of the more than 170 Best of Breed winners is judged within one of the seven dog groups to determine the seven Best of Group winners. In each group, the one all-rounder judge awards four dogs a prize, but only each first-place winner advances to the finals, where one dog is judged Best in Show.

Since 1934, the Westminster show has also featured a Junior Showmanship competition that judges young handlers' skills, not the dogs' conformation. More than 100 handlers, ages 10 to 18, who have won 10 or more Junior Showmanship first place awards over the past year, are invited to compete. Eight finalists compete for the title Best Junior Handler. The skill and poise of these young people are inspirational.

Appendix 3.
Training Logs

On the following 10 pages are blank training logs for each of the five weeks in your dog's Fundamentals Training Program. Each week's log lists that week's lessons, and there is space for you to write detailed notes: For example, "Mabel is getting great at reading my body language when she's tethered to me," or, "Bailey loves his crate but is not ready for me to close the door." Even if you're tempted to ignore the many inevitable less-than-perfect training moments, I promise that you'll learn more when you write it *all* down. Besides, once you've completed the five-week program, I believe you'll find it instructive (and fun) to go back through your old logs. After all, part of the purpose of these training logs is to better understand patterns of how you and your dog learn together.

Write directly in this book, or download copies of these training logs at positivelywoof.com.

WEEK ONE

Use this log to chart your dog training progress. See Feeding, Potty Training, and Crating (Chapter Three, page 43) and the Fundamentals Program Week One (Chapter Four, page 63) for review.

	day 1	day 2
USING TREATS AS LURES Practice luring your dog with treats. *Page 66.*		
LURING TO SIT Touch treat to dog's nose, lure up (rump goes down), mark, praise, touch collar, treat last. *Page 70.*		
LURING TO RECALL, PART 1 Take 2 or 3 steps back, lure dog. Mark, praise, touch collar, treat last. **EXTRA:** If dog already sits, add a sit before the treat. Be animated and happy when you lure. *Page 73.*		
EYE-CONTACT EXERCISE Touch treat to dog's nose, then bring it to your eyes. Mark and reward for dog's eye contact. *Page 74.*		
WALKING: "BE A TREE" When dog pulls leash, stop and hold leash firmly to your body. When dog looks back at you, mark, lure, and start again. *Page 76.*		
LEASH TETHERING Tether your dog while moving around your home. *Page 45.*		
HAND-FEEDING Feed all meals by hand from dog's bowl. Your dog sees that you are the giver of food. *Page 47.*		
POTTY TRAINING Keep track of input (meals and treats) and output (potty time). Note accidents. *Page 50.*		
CRATE TRAINING Teach dog to love his crate. Many treats and meals in and around crate. *Page 53.*		
BITE INHIBITION, HANDLING, GENTLING "Ouch" exercise. Lots of gentle handling. Touch paws and all over body. *Page 59.*		
GAMES AND SOCIALIZATION ACTIVITIES *Page 79.*		

day 3	day 4	day 5	day 6	day 7	NOTES

WEEK TWO

See the Fundamentals Program Week Two
(Chapter Five, page 81) for review.

	day 1	day 2
TETHERING EXERCISE With your dog tethered to you, move randomly around your home or yard. Every time dog looks at you, mark, touch collar, and treat. *Page 82.*		
REAL-LIFE REWARDS SYSTEM Cue your dog to sit for everything, including all meals, at start of walks and training, before going into and exiting crate, and playing. *Page 83.*		
SIT: HAND SIGNAL, FROM LURE TO CUE Try to increase your dog's speedy response to your hand signal (visual cue) without causing failure. *Page 85.*		
SIT: WITHDRAW TREATS Put the treats in your other hand while cueing *sit*. Then withdraw treats slowly by using slot machine technique. *Page 86.*		
RECALL: INCREASE LURING DISTANCE, ADD VERBAL CUE Add *sit* at end of recall. Increase distance one step at a time. Add "[Dog's name], come here!" verbal/visual cue. *Page 87.*		
DOWN Start from *sit*. Slide treat toward dog's chest then lure straight down. When dog begins following *down,* mark, praise, touch collar, and then treat last. *Page 89.*		
RELEASE: VERBAL CUE After training, drop leash and say "release" or "go play." Pat dog and point to play area. *Page 91.*		
HAND-FEEDING AND CRATE TRAINING Hand-feed all meals in and around crate. Teach dog to love his crate. *Pages 47, 53.*		
POTTY TRAINING Keep track of input (meals and treats) and output (potty time). Note accidents. *Page 50.*		
BITE INHIBITION, HANDLING, GENTLING "Ouch" exercise. Lots of gentle handling. Touch paws and all over body. *Page 59.*		
GAMES AND SOCIALIZATION ACTIVITIES *Page 93.*		

day 3	day 4	day 5	day 6	day 7	NOTES

WEEK THREE

See the Fundamentals Program Week Three
(Chapter Six, page 95) for review.

	day 1	day 2
WALKING Add informal heeling with *walk-stop-sit-walk-stop-sit* exercise. Troubleshoot leash pulling with "be a tree," leash tethering, Follow the Lure. *Page 107.*		
SIT: ADD VERBAL CUE Combine the verbal cue with hand signal throughout this training program. Continue giving clear hand signals. *Page 98.*		
PUPPY PUSHUPS *Sit-down-sit.* Mark each *sit*, *down*, and *sit*. Praise, touch collar, and treat at end of each cycle. Sharpen dog's response to cues and focus on you. *Page 99.*		
COOKIE SIT-STAY "Glue" leash hand to hip, touch treat to dog's nose, and toss it beyond dog's reach. Cue *sit* (then mark). Then send to *take it*, mark, and praise. *Page 100.*		
SIT-STAY (ALTERNATIVE METHOD) Dog sits, touch treat to dog's nose, then hold between your eyes. Increase dog's focus on you. Increase time when successful. *Page 103.*		
OFF AND TAKE IT: PHASE 1 Hold six treats, shift one to fingers, say "take it." On fourth rep keep quiet: If dog tries to get it, say "off" sharply. As dog looks at you, say "take it." *Page 104.*		
RECALL AND SIT COMBO WITH RELEASE After each minute of supervised play, *recall* ("come here") and *sit* (mark, praise, touch collar, reward). *Release* to play again. *Page 98.*		
CATCH YOUR DOG DOING SOMETHING YOU LIKE Evaluate yourself. How well do you recognize and acknowledge your dog for offering behaviors without being asked? *Page 106.*		
POTTY TRAINING Keep track of input (meals and treats) and output (potty time). Note accidents. *Page 50.*		
BASELINE BEHAVIORS Hand-feeding; crate training; bite inhibition, handling, and gentling. *Pages 47, 53, 59.*		
GAMES AND SOCIALIZATION ACTIVITIES *Page 109.*		

day 3	day 4	day 5	day 6	day 7	NOTES

WEEK FOUR	day 1	day 2
See the Fundamentals Program Week Four (Chapter Seven, page 111) for review.		

RECALLS: ADD DISTRACTIONS AND DISTANCE Generalize to outdoor locations. With training partner's help, practice the Runaway and Lassie Recall exercise. *Page 113.*

STAY UNTIL RECALLED: ADD DISTANCE, DURATION, AND DISTRACTIONS Add steps and time gradually, generalize to new locations. Circle around dog as he sits and stays. *Page 114.*

DOWN: NAMING THE BEHAVIOR Practice Puppy Pushups (*sit-down-sit*), adding verbal cues to hand signals. *Page 115.*

STANDING POSE As dog sits at your side, lure forward so that he stands to follow treat. When fluent, add to Puppy Pushups sequence, and add verbal cue ("pose"). *Page 115.*

OFF AND TAKE IT TRADES: PHASE 2 Practice trades for items of equal or greater value. Trade special treats for portions of meal in food bowl. *Page 117.*

CLIMBING STAIRS Cue a *sit*. Step and block dog with your leg. Mark, praise, and reward each step. Sit and praise at the end. *Page 120.*

DOOR TRAINING Cue a *sit*, then say "off" before you open door and lead through with hand signal. Then mark, praise, reward. Later, add verbal cue "let's go." *Page 122.*

SETTLE DOWN From *down-stay* position, offer treats one by one (vending machine technique). When dog relaxes, say "good settle." Also, hand-feed in *settle* position. *Page 125.*

CATCH YOUR DOG DOING SOMETHING YOU LIKE Also, use Real-Life Rewards System. *Page 106.*

POTTY TRAINING Keep track of input (meals and treats) and output (potty time). Note accidents. *Page 50.*

BASELINE BEHAVIORS Hand-feeding; crate training; bite inhibition, handling, and gentling. *Pages 47, 53, 59.*

GAMES AND SOCIALIZATION ACTIVITIES *Page 127.*

day 3	day 4	day 5	day 6	day 7	NOTES

See the Fundamentals Program Week Five
(Chapter Eight, page 129) for review.

	day 1	day 2
SIT **1.** Lure with a treat to a *sit*. *Page 131.* **2.** Hand signal without a treat. *Page 131.* **3.** Sit in public at three random moments. *Page 131.*		
RECALL AND RELEASE **1.** Luring *recall*. *Page 132.* **2.** *Recall* with verbal cue. *Release*. *Pages 132, 137.* **3.** *Recall-sit* combination during play. *Page 132.*		
LEASH WALKING **1.** Tethering exercise. *Page 133.* **2.** Walking exercise: change direction. *Page 133.* **3.** Walking exercise: informal heeling. *Page 133.*		
DOWN **1.** Luring to a *down*. *Page 134.* **2.** Puppy Pushups. *Page 134.* **3.** *Down* and *sit* at a distance with verbal cues. *Page 134.*		
STAY **1.** *Cookie sit and take it*. *Page 134.* **2.** *Cookie sit-stay*. *Page 135.* **3**. Conventional *stay* cue for 30 seconds. *Page 135.*		
STANDING POSE **1.** Luring to a *stand* from *sit*. *Page 135.* **2.** Stand visual cue without treat. *Page 135.* **3.** Puppy Pushups: add *stand* verbal cue. *Page 136.*		
SETTLE DOWN **1.** Human vending machine. *Page 136.* **2.** *Settle* visual and verbal cue. *Page 136.* **3.** Real-life *settle* at three random moments. *Page 137.*		
OFF AND TAKE IT TRADES **1.** *Cookie sit-stay*. *Page 137.* **2.** Phase 1 trade. *Page 137.* **3.** Phase 2 trade (food bowl). *Page 137.*		
BOUNDARY TRAINING **1.** Interior doors. *Page 138.* **2.** Visitor. *Page 138.* **3.** Climbing stairs or steps on cue. *Page 138.*		
GAMES AND SOCIALIZATION ACTIVITIES *Page 141.*		

day 3	day 4	day 5	day 6	day 7	NOTES

Acknowledgments

raining the Best Dog Ever has been shepherded and groomed by a loyal team. To all, Larry and I offer our gratitude. As in dog training, all imperfections in this book are a result of our own shortcomings, not those who have "gone to ground" with us like tenacious terriers.

To President Obama and the First Lady, Malia and Sasha: Thank you for entrusting me with Bo and for doing so much training follow-up with him. Bo Obama's development into such a wonderful dog is to the credit of our First Family. You are showing the world that positive reinforcement dog training makes a difference for families.

To Senator Kennedy and Vicki, thank you for your warm relationship and the more than dozen years working with you, your staff, Splash, Sunny, Cappy, and his littermate the world now knows as Bo.

Highly skilled staffers coordinate the lives of very public people. So that I could enjoy the privilege of working with these wonderful dogs, thanks especially to Dana Lewis, Catherine McCormick-Lelyveld, and the First Lady's staff, and to all who have worked with the Kennedys, especially Delmy Contreras.

Thank you to Art and Martha Stern of Amigo Kennels for your relationship as ethical and loving breeders extending back to those wonderful years with my own Portuguese Water Dog, Ebony.

To Dr. Ian Dunbar, we offer our profound gratitude; thank you for inspiring generations of dog trainers and encouraging this book. Thanks to Karen Pryor, Dr. Pamela Reid, and Best Friends Animal Society staffers Ann Allums, John Garcia, John Polis, and Barbara Williamson, who contributed their loving understanding of dog behavior and the human-animal bond. Whatever recognition this book receives, we share with many great dog trainers and humane educators; may this book advance the growing platform for positive reinforcement training.

Thanks to all my dog training students, clients (two- and four-legged), and interns for giving me the gift of a career that has been a fun and soulful adventure for more than 20 years. Thanks to my dog training website angel, Kelli Lee, and special thanks to my co-instructor, Ludwig Smith, who often filled in while I was writing this book.

The making of any book is a unique story. *Training the Best Dog Ever*'s journey began with my coauthor, Larry Kay, who (if he ever takes a sabbatical from his writing career) would be a superb dog trainer and advocate for pets transforming the lives of kids and families. Thank you, Larry, for going beyond the call of duty to make this book into one that makes a difference.

Special thanks to our agent, Kristine Dahl, and the ICM team, particularly Colin Graham and Laura Neely. Thank you, Ellis Levine, for introducing us to Kristine. Like a fleet-footed sighthound, Kristine saw how to shape the proposal and find the ideal publisher.

And to that ideal publisher, Peter Workman: Larry and I feel blessed to have been brought into the Workman "family." Everyone in this elite pack takes on roles beyond their pay grade. Special thanks to all who shaped this book, particularly editors Susan Bolotin and Avery Finch and art director Ariana Abud. Photo maestro Anne Kerman and her team made the photo shoot in Workman's studio a howling (though always well behaved!) success. Special thanks to blue-ribbon editor Aimee Molloy, who trained our words to do tricks and guided two authors through the editorial agility course at full speed. While we feel remiss in not acknowledging everyone at Workman Publishing individually, please accept our thanks for consistently valuing our authors' input and making this project a true win-win partnership.

My personal gratitude goes to my extended family and friends for the power and trust in the way that you have loved me. Thank you to William Waybourn and Ripley, who added to my therapy dog experience by opening the doors to serving our wounded warriors with you at Walter Reed National Military Medical Center. My dogs have taught me more than I taught them, including perseverance, unconditional love, and that we don't need to choke our best friends with a chain to get them to do what we want.

Most of all, to Courtlandt, Blaise, and Paige: My love and respect for you is at the essence of my life. Even though I became a dog trainer to have a career while being a mom, above all that the greatest gift I have been given remains that of being your mother.

Larry Kay's Personal Thanks

The first time I saw Dawn in her classroom I understood what a talented trainer she was and how much she loved guiding people and dogs into beautifully bonded relationships. A piece of Dawn's legacy is that effective dog training is really human training. Thank you, Dawn, for making our collaboration a great adventure. Testing your system on my "golden oldie," Higgins, proves that we can indeed teach old dogs new tricks when the love bond is spirited.

Special thanks to my loyal colleagues for all things canine: Kate Luhr, Lauren Wygant, and everyone at the Association of Pet Dog Trainers. An especially loud howl to the pack at Positively Woof for launching our ARF (Advocacy, Readiness, Fun) platform with style, spirit, and spunk.

I am blessed with brilliant colleagues, true friends, and a family that is my bedrock. My scribe tribe has given great advice and support, especially animal philosopher Dr. Gary Steiner and authors Jan Burke, Steven Goldman, and Dr. Darryl Tippens. To Steve Basil, Jonn Howell, and the men of the ManKind Project's award-winning Valley Oaks iGroup: Thanks for your good humor and seeing the truth in me even when I am blinded by my own shadow. Thanks to my Hesby Oaks neighbors who allowed Higgins and me to practice Dawn's system with you and your dogs. To all my loving family in Los Angeles, Chicago, the Northwest, and Buenos Aires: You inspire the best in me, thanks for the lifelong belly rub.

Robert Benchley (grandfather of Dawn's client, the writer/performer Nat Benchley who is mentioned on page 6) is widely quoted as having said that "a dog teaches a boy fidelity, perseverance, and to turn around three times before lying down." Thanks, Higgins, for teaching this boy *many* essential life lessons; someday I'll master that lying-down technique of yours.

Higgins
December 25, 1996–June 23, 2012

Index

Photo Credits

PRINCIPAL PHOTOGRAPHY BY EVAN SKLAR

ADDITIONAL PHOTOGRAPHY CREDITS

Cover: gephoto/shutterstock.

Interior: p. xiii Associated Press, p. 19 GK Hart/Vikki Hart/Getty Images, p. 19 top right
Kadmy/fotolia, p. 37 Steve Shott/Getty Images, p. 39 brozova/fotolia, p. 46 GK Hart/Vikki
Hart/Getty Images, p. 216 top Associated Press, p. 216 bottom Ton Koene/age fotostock,
p. 220 Tracy Morgan/Getty Images, p. 223 James Forte/Getty Images, p. 242 Courtesy of
Canine Companions for Independence, p. 247 Gerard Brown/Getty Images, p. 248 GK
Hart/Vikki Hart/Getty Images, p. 268 Lisa Bevis.

Special thanks to Dawn Animal Agency and their wonderful canine models: Pat, Golden
Retriever; Sally, Portuguese Water Dog; Murphy, Chesapeake Bay Retriever; Luna, Mixed
Breed; Sam, American Staffordshire Terrier; Wilma, Boston Terrier.

About the Authors

Before becoming the dog trainer to President Obama's family, **Dawn Sylvia-Stasiewicz** trained each of Senator Ted Kennedy's Portuguese Water Dogs. Sylvia-Stasiewicz, who was a professional dog trainer in the Washington, D.C./Northern Virginia area for more than 20 years, ran popular Merit Puppy dog training classes, training and boarding animals for the Washington elite. She brought a mom's approach to training, basing her work on theories of positive reinforcement. She died unexpectedly in early 2011.

Larry Kay is a Los Angeles–based writer and filmmaker. He authored *Life's A Bark: What Dogs Teach Us About Life and Love,* created and produced the award-winning *Animal Wow* dog care and safety DVD for kids, was a contributing editor for *Dog Fancy* magazine, and was a pets reporter for AOL and the American Animal Hospital Association. His writing credits include documentaries and educational films for PBS, and interactive edutainment for Disney and The Muppets. Larry is inspired by shelter dogs and makes short films with them.

Visit Larry at:
positivelywoof.com
YouTube: Positively Woof
Facebook.com/positivelywoof

Positively WOOF
CELEBRATE OUR BOND